E-SERVICES ADOPTION: PROCESSES BY FIRMS IN DEVELOPING NATIONS

ADVANCES IN BUSINESS MARKETING & PURCHASING

Series Editor: Arch G. Woodside

Recent Volumes:

ADVANCES IN BUSINESS MARKETING & PURCHASING
VOLUME 23A

E-SERVICES ADOPTION: PROCESSES BY FIRMS IN DEVELOPING NATIONS

EDITED BY

MOHAMMED QUADDUS
Curtin University, Perth, Australia

ARCH G. WOODSIDE
*Department of Marketing,
Carroll School of Management,
Boston College, Boston, MA, USA*

United Kingdom — North America — Japan
India — Malaysia — China

Emerald Group Publishing Limited
Howard House, Wagon Lane, Bingley BD16 1WA, UK

First edition 2015

Copyright © 2015 Emerald Group Publishing Limited

Reprints and permissions service .
Contact: permissions@emeraldinsight.com

British Library Cataloguing in Publication Data
A catalogue record for this book is available from the British Library

ISBN: 978-1-78560-325-9
ISSN: 1069-0964 (Series)

ISOQAR certified
Management System,
awarded to Emerald
for adherence to
Environmental
standard
ISO 14001:2004.

Certificate Number 1985
ISO 14001

INVESTOR IN PEOPLE

CONTENTS

LIST OF CONTRIBUTORS

Md Shah Azam	Department of Marketing, University of Rajshahi, Rajshahi, Bangladesh
Mohammed Quaddus	Curtin University, Perth, Australia
Arief Rahman	Department of Accounting, Islamic University of Indonesia, Yogyakarta, Indonesia
Arch G. Woodside	Department of Marketing, Carroll School of Management, Boston College, Boston, MA, USA

E-SERVICES ADOPTION PROCESSES IN DEVELOPING NATIONS: INTRODUCTION TO ABM&P VOLUME 23A

Arch G. Woodside and Mohammed Quaddus

ABSTRACT

This chapter serves to recognize the uniqueness of the moment; the number of new users of e-services worldwide will double during 2015–2108 (moving from 2 billion users mostly living in the developed nations to an additional 2 billion users mostly living in developing nations). This radical embrace of new e-service technologies will substantially improve the quality of lives for most residents globally. A profound happening occurring now! The new technologies combine rapidly delivering of a multitude of services at extremely low cost to adopters now having extremely low incomes relative to residents living in developed nations. Adoption of e-service among residents in developing nations ends the debate as to whether or not marketing to the "bottom of the pyramid" is possible. The more relevant issues focus on describing and explaining e-service adoption processes in developing nations. How are these processes being implemented? What obstacles had to be overcome in achieving these

E-Services Adoption: Processes by Firms in Developing Nations
Advances in Business Marketing & Purchasing, Volume 23A, 1–5
Copyright © 2015 by Emerald Group Publishing Limited
ISSN: 1069-0964/doi:10.1108/S1069-096420150000023001

adoptions? How were these obstacles overcome? Read this volume for research providing useful answers to these questions.

Keywords: Adoption; e-services; developing nation; diffusion; innovation; Octopus

1. INTRODUCTION

During the three years 2015–2017, brand new internet and e-services adoptions will occur for more than 1.5 billion users. In developing countries, dramatic increases incomes, quality of life, and communications in general are now occurring. The following brief case appearing in the Economist (2010) gives credence to these dramatic developments. Buying a mobile phone was the wisest $20 Ranvir Singh ever spent. Mr. Singh, a farmer in the north Indian state of Uttar Pradesh, used to make appointments in person, in advance, to deliver fresh buffalo milk to his 40-odd neighbors. Now his customers just call when they want some. Mr. Singh's income has risen by 25%, to 7,000 rupees ($149) a month. And he hears rumors of an even more bountiful technology. He has heard that "something on mobile phones" can tell him the current market price of his wheat. Mr. Singh does not know that that "something" is the internet, because, like most Indians, he has never seen or used it. But the phone in his calloused hand hints at how hundreds of millions of people in emerging markets – perhaps even billions – will one day log on. Only 81 million Indians (7% of the population) regularly use the internet. But brutal price wars mean that 507 million own mobile phones. Calls cost as little as $0.006 per minute. Indian operators such as Bharti Airtel and Reliance Communications sign up 20 million new subscribers a month.

Most residents in the developing world will be mobile subscribers for the first time during 2015–2017. The current new embrace of the internet and e-services adoptions is relying on third and fourth mobile technologies. The greatest impact of this technology migration is now taking place in the developing world. Mobile broadband already accounts for over three-quarters of connections in the developed world and, by 2020, the figure will reach 92%. In contrast, less than a third of connections are currently on higher speed networks in the developing world. However, this is projected to nearly reach two-thirds of connections by 2020. In absolute terms, the number of mobile broadband connections in developing markets will increase by 3.1 billion over the period (The Mobile Economy, 2015).

This volume in the ABM&P series offers nitty-gritty details in describing and explaining the electronic services adoptions in developing nations. The volume includes first-person holistic reports on e-services adoption processes. The chapters describe the glitches adopters experience in such adoptions and how they overcome context and personal blockages in using these new services as well as how such adoptions dramatically increased the firm's operating efficiencies and financial performances. Thus, this volume responds to readers' need for knowledge on how e-services adoptions get done in developing nations – knowledge that includes details of problems experienced and successful solutions implemented.

The two main chapters in this volume include two in-depth case studies of four e-services adoptions (other two case studies are included in Volume 23B). Each connects in many instances to the extant literature on adoption of services. Each offers new theory to adoption and diffusion theoretical propositions. Each tests the relevancy and usefulness of these advances in theory. Each provides practical insights for executives seeking knowledge of what to do, when to do it in marketing new e-services in developing nations, as well as what not to do and how not to do it in such good contexts. As editors we extend our gratitude to the authors for sharing the fruits of their research in this volume of the series. The remainder of this chapter provides brief introduction to the two remaining chapters and stresses the process nuances and usefulness the reader will find in each.

2. DIFFUSION AND ADOPTION OF NEW INFORMATION AND COMMUNICATIONS TECHNOLOGIES BY SMALL AND MEDIUM ENTERPRISES

In the chapter "Diffusion of ICT and SMEs Performance," Md Shah Azam reports on a field study that focuses on adoption of new information and communications technologies by 11 decision-makers for small and medium-sized enterprise (SMEs). The recorded interviews were transcribed and analyzed using NVivo 10 to refine a new ICT adoption model. His final research model comprises of 30 first-order and five higher-order constructs which involve both reflective and formative measures. Partial least squares (PLS)-based structural equation modeling is employed to test the theoretical model with a cross-sectional data set of 282 SMEs in Bangladesh. Survey data were collected using a structured questionnaire issued to SMEs selected by applying a stratified random sampling technique. The structural equation modeling utilizes a two-step procedure of data analysis.

The analysis reveals that the adoption and diffusion of ICT by SMEs in Bangladesh were largely influenced by cognitive evaluation, facilitating condition, environmental pressure, and country readiness with owner innovativeness and culture indirectly affected through cognitive evaluation. Organizations were interested in implementing ICT for better organizational performance. Surprisingly, ICT use was not found to have any significant effect on overall organizational performance. However, the structural model depicted a unique interrelationship between ICT use, integration, degree of utilization, and organizational performance. The analysis revealed that ICT use, although not directly related to organizational performance, was indirectly related through integration and the degree of utilization. This finding supports the perspective that organizations may not attain better performance by new ICT adoption in their firm if adoption is not integrated with different functional areas and used properly.

3. TOWARD A CONCEPTUALIZATION OF DIGITAL DIVIDE AND ITS IMPACT ON E-GOVERNMENT SYSTEM SUCCESS

Unequal access and ICT usage, the digital divide, however is identifiable as one of the major obstacles to the implementation of e-government system. As digital divide inhibits citizen's acceptance to e-government, this divide should be overcome despite the lack of deep theoretical understanding on this issue. In Chapter 3, Arief Rahman investigates the digital divide and its direct impact on e-government system success of local governments in Indonesia as well as indirect impact through the mediation role of trust. In order to get a comprehensive understanding of digital divide, his study introduces a new type of digital divide, the innovativeness divide.

The research problems were approached by applying two-stage sequential mixed method research approach comprising both qualitative and quantitative studies. In the first phase, an initial research model was proposed based on a literature review. Semi-structured interview with 12 users of e-government systems was then conducted to explore and enhance this initial research model.

The study's findings confirm 13 hypotheses. All direct influences of the variables of digital divide on e-government system success receive support. The mediating effects of trust in e-government in the relationship between capability divide and e-government system success as well as in the relationship between innovativeness divide and e-government system success were supported, but was rejected in the relationship between access divide and e-government system success. The findings support the moderating effects of demographic variables of age, residential place, and education.

As the author says this research has both theoretical and practical contributions. It contributes to the developments of literature on digital divide and e-government by providing a more comprehensive framework, and to the implementation of e-government by local governments and the improvement of e-Government Readiness Index of Indonesia.

4. CONCLUSION

Useful nuances and readable roadmaps describing and explaining how e-services get done in developing nations are the major contributions of this volume. The chapters cover how e-service adoption processes include overcoming obstacles as strategies convert plans into implemented outcomes. Given that the number of users of e-services will double during 2015−2018 (increasing from 2 to 4 billion) and that most of this increase is coming from new users in developing nations, this volume is particularly timely. If you have questions and comments about the specific e-services adoption processes in the chapters, please contact the authors or editors directly.

REFERENCES

Economist. (2010). The next billion geeks. *The Economist*, September 10. Retrieved from www.economist.com/node/16944020. Accessed on June 12, 2015.

The Mobile Economy. (2015). Retrieved from www.gsmamobileeconomy.com. Accessed on June 12, 2015.

Wikipedia. (2015). Retrieved from https://en.wikipedia.org/wiki/Octopus_card

DIFFUSION OF ICT AND SME PERFORMANCE

Md Shah Azam

ABSTRACT

Information and communications technology (ICT) offers enormous opportunities for individuals, businesses and society. The application of ICT is equally important to economic and non-economic activities. Researchers have increasingly focused on the adoption and use of ICT by small and medium enterprises (SMEs) as the economic development of a country is largely dependent on them. Following the success of ICT utilisation in SMEs in developed countries, many developing countries are looking to utilise the potential of the technology to develop SMEs. Past studies have shown that the contribution of ICT to the performance of SMEs is not clear and certain. Thus, it is crucial to determine the effectiveness of ICT in generating firm performance since this has implications for SMEs' expenditure on the technology. This research examines the diffusion of ICT among SMEs with respect to the typical stages from innovation adoption to post-adoption, by analysing the actual usage of ICT and value creation. The mediating effects of integration and utilisation on SME performance are also studied. Grounded in the innovation diffusion literature, institutional theory and resource-based theory, this study has developed a comprehensive integrated research model focused

E-Services Adoption: Processes by Firms in Developing Nations
Advances in Business Marketing & Purchasing, Volume 23A, 7−290
Copyright © 2015 by Emerald Group Publishing Limited
ISSN: 1069-0964/doi:10.1108/S1069-096420150000023005

on the research objectives. Following a positivist research paradigm, this study employs a mixed-method research approach. A preliminary conceptual framework is developed through an extensive literature review and is refined by results from an in-depth field study. During the field study, a total of 11 SME owners or decision-makers were interviewed. The recorded interviews were transcribed and analysed using NVivo 10 to refine the model to develop the research hypotheses. The final research model is composed of 30 first-order and five higher-order constructs which involve both reflective and formative measures. Partial least squares-based structural equation modelling (PLS-SEM) is employed to test the theoretical model with a cross-sectional data set of 282 SMEs in Bangladesh. Survey data were collected using a structured questionnaire issued to SMEs selected by applying a stratified random sampling technique. The structural equation modelling utilises a two-step procedure of data analysis. Prior to estimating the structural model, the measurement model is examined for construct validity of the study variables (i.e. convergent and discriminant validity).

The estimates show cognitive evaluation as an important antecedent for expectation which is shaped primarily by the entrepreneurs' beliefs (perception) and also influenced by the owners' innovativeness and culture. Culture further influences expectation. The study finds that facilitating condition, environmental pressure and country readiness are important antecedents of expectation and ICT use. The results also reveal that integration and the degree of ICT utilisation significantly affect SMEs' performance. Surprisingly, the findings do not reveal any significant impact of ICT usage on performance which apparently suggests the possibility of the ICT productivity paradox. However, the analysis finally proves the non-existence of the paradox by demonstrating the mediating role of ICT integration and degree of utilisation explain the influence of information technology (IT) usage on firm performance which is consistent with the resource-based theory. The results suggest that the use of ICT can enhance SMEs' performance if the technology is integrated and properly utilised. SME owners or managers, interested stakeholders and policy makers may follow the study's outcomes and focus on ICT integration and degree of utilisation with a view to attaining superior organisational performance.

This study urges concerned business enterprises and government to look at the environmental and cultural factors with a view to achieving ICT usage success in terms of enhanced firm performance. In particular,

*improving organisational practices and procedures by eliminating the tra-
ditional power distance inside organisations and implementing necessary
rules and regulations are important actions for managing environmental
and cultural uncertainties. The application of a Bengali user interface
may help to ensure the productivity of ICT use by SMEs in Bangladesh.
Establishing a favourable national technology infrastructure and legal
environment may contribute positively to improving the overall situation.
This study also suggests some changes and modifications in the country's
existing policies and strategies. The government and policy makers
should undertake mass promotional programs to disseminate information
about the various uses of computers and their contribution in developing
better organisational performance. Organising specialised training programs for SME capacity building may succeed in attaining the motivation for SMEs to use ICT. Ensuring easy access to the technology by
providing loans, grants and subsidies is important. Various stakeholders,
partners and related organisations should come forward to support
government policies and priorities in order to ensure the productive use
of ICT among SMEs which finally will help to foster Bangladesh's
economic development.*

Keywords: Diffusion; ICT; SME; organisational performance; culture;
environmental pressures

1. INTRODUCTION

1.1. Overview

Information and communications technology (ICT) has become an integral
part of human life in the 21st century. The rapid expansion of ICT and its
application into various economic activities have opened new opportunities
for individuals, businesses and society. In particular, the introduction of
various ICT devices has increased productivity in business organisations
and has assisted them to manage intra- and inter-organisational affairs.
The technology also provides customers with the ability to conduct personal communications, business transactions and banking operations in a
more flexible and efficient manner.

Organisations are integrating ICT into business operations to enhance
productivity.[1] The wide-ranging applications of ICT, particularly
Internet-based digital technology, have reshaped the ways in which

communication occurs and have also made changes to the systems, procedures and processes of relevant services. Consequently, this affects the ways
in which customers, suppliers, regulatory bodies and other external parties
deal with business organisations.

The past decades have produced much research investigating the use of
information technology (IT) by both individuals and organisations (see
Agarwal & Prashad, 1997, 1998, 1999; Davis, 1993; Davis, Bagozzi, &
Warshaw, 1989; Kendall, Tung, Chua, Ng, & Tan, 2001; Mathieson, 1991;
Moore & Benbasat, 1991; Premkumar & Potter, 1995; Sathye & Beal, 2001;
Tan & Teo, 2000; Taylor & Todd, 1995b; Venkatesh, Brown, Maruping, &
Bala, 2008; Venkatesh & Davis, 2000; Venkatesh & Morris, 2000;
Venkatesh, Morris, Davis, & Davis, 2003). A primary focus of these
research studies is the identification of the factors that determine adoption
and diffusion of ICT.

Prior studies follow the notion that the use of ICT would enhance organisational performance. In the past few years, the growth in ICT usage has
increased tremendously across industries around the world. Business enterprises' investment in ICT has also increased dramatically which poses the
valid question about whether organisational spending on ICT results in
improved organisational performance. Zhu and Kraemer (2005) referred to
the wave of debate over the new 'IT value paradox' which was triggered by
Carr (2003) in the article 'IT Doesn't Matter'.

Prior studies reveal ambiguous results about the contribution of ICT to
business performance, such as having a negative effect (Warner, 1987);
zero effect (Venkatraman & Zaheer, 1990); a contingent positive effect
(Powell & Dent-Micallef, 1997; Tippins & Sohi, 2003; Wu, Yeniyurt,
Kim, & Cavusgil, 2006) and a direct positive effect (Bharadwaj, 2000;
Zhu & Kraemer, 2005). What is clear is that the contribution of ICT to
organisational performance is not straightforward and certain.

Organisational sustainability is largely dependent on the productive use
of ICT. Thus, answers to this renewed paradox will have important implications for the way businesses approach IT investment and management.
Zhu and Kraemer (2005) revealed that ICT use (e-commerce use) generates
organisational performance. By applying the notion of the resource-based
view, they reported that the integration of ICT with front-office functionalities and back-end databases can create unique ICT capabilities which
cannot be easily imitated and thus have the potential to create improved
business performance (Bharadwaj, 2000; Zhu & Kraemer, 2002). This
aspect of ICT use, named, 'ICT integration', has not been widely documented in the contemporary research literature and, hence, its effect on

business performance has not been clearly identified. Similarly, another aspect of ICT use may correlate with firm performance which is 'ICT utilisation', that is, whether the ICT is used properly and effectively.

This phenomenon of ICT use is particularly related to the developing country environment. Anandarajan, Igbaria, and Anakwe (2002) have stated that many information systems (IS) in the less developed countries are under-utilised and, thus, do not make a significant contribution to improving the performance of organisations that are using them (Forster & Cornford, 1992; Ordedra, Lawrie, Bennett, & Goodman, 1993). This statement is indicative of the fact that proper utilisation of ICT may result in improved firm performance; that is, utilisation can make a bridge between ICT use and firm performance. Integration may also act in the same way. Contemporary research initiatives have not produced adequate facts and figures about integration, utilisation and their effects, particularly the mediating effects, on firm performance which may be considered as the agenda for a new research study.

The perspective of the study, that is, the developed versus developing country perspective, has become another research motivation. The past few decades have witnessed an unprecedented increase in the trend of ICT usage to accomplish a wide range of functions at individual, organisational and society levels. The phenomenal usage growth has inspired organisations to become ICT-dependent in accomplishing various internal and external functions. The trend for organisations to become ICT-dependent is significantly higher in developed countries than for organisations from the developing world. Past studies have therefore mainly focused on the developed country context. Consequently, most of the theories in ICT have been formulated from the perspective of developed countries, particularly the American perspective (Zhu & Kraemer, 2005).

In reality, the theories formulated in the developed country environment may not be appropriate in addressing similar phenomena in developing countries as there remains a wide digital divide between the two types of countries. Utilising the advantages of high Internet penetration, developed countries have become ICT-dependent to accomplish various functions such as governance, business, education and utilities (for individuals and organisations) with this gradually trickling down to the developing world.

The success of various ICT applications in the developed world has a significant implication for technology adoption and usage behaviour in developing countries. Recent statistics have suggested significantly higher Internet usage growth (between 2000 and 2013) in the developing part of the world than in developed countries which has created the grounds for diverse use and utilisation of ICT in developing countries. The changing pattern of the world's ICT usage growth in recent years may attract researchers' attention towards developing and least developed countries (LDCs).[2]

Bangladesh is a member of the LDCs. The country is characterised by high population, low income and inadequate infrastructural supports such as inefficient technology, inadequate power supply, low teledensity, very low Internet penetration, absence of effective legal systems, and financial and banking mechanisms which are not supportive for facilitating communication and transactions via the Internet. Despite poor teledensity and Internet penetration, the government has planned to make Bangladesh a technology-dependent society by the 50th anniversary of the birth of the country in 2021 with this adopted in the national development plan, *Vision 2021*. The development of ICT and its utilisation in the country's economic development were included in the election manifesto and post-election agendas of the present government which have later attracted the attention of many researchers, policy makers, practitioners and the general public as a movement called *Digital Bangladesh*.

The growth indices, development initiatives and infrastructure of Bangladesh are identical with those of a typical developing country. The characteristics of the country and its move towards establishing an ICT-based society are the rationale behind undertaking this survey-based research on the diffusion of ICT and SME performance seeking reliable and valid research outcomes that are representative of developing countries.

1.2. Research Questions

The success of the use of ICT as a tool for increasing productivity in various sectors is the main driver for new adopters. The uniqueness of the technology viz., cost, convenience and efficiency (speed and accuracy) motivates users in their new and continued use of technology for personal and business use. The productivity implications of ICT have received the bulk of researchers' attention around the world in their studies of its adoption and diffusion phenomena. However, the majority of the previous ICT adoption-diffusion studies have investigated intention (e.g. Gefen & Straub, 2000; Kendall et al., 2001; Lal, 1999; Pavlov & Chai, 2002; Teo, Wei, & Benbasat, 2003) and actual usage behaviour (e.g. Anandarajan et al., 2002; Johnson & Hignite, 2000; Thatcher, Foster, & Zhu, 2006;

Venkatesh et al., 2008). Thus, the question about whether the adoption or use of technology induces improved organisational performance remains relatively under-researched, especially in the case of SMEs. This may be considered as a vital research gap which has therefore provided the motivation to link technology adoption-diffusion behaviour with organisational performance in studying the effects of ICT on SME performance.

The innovation adoption theories explain the adoption and diffusion phenomena mainly through intention (Ajzen, 1985; Davis, 1986; Fishbein & Ajzen, 1975; Rogers, 1983; Venkatesh et al., 2003). A criticism of the existing theories is that intention is a reflection of the adopter's internal schema of beliefs which may fail to adequately explain actual behaviour in a situation under incomplete volitional control. Intention, furthermore, may not be reflected in the decision if a time gap exists between intention and actual behaviour.

A recent technology adoption research study has examined the role of behavioural expectation in order to avoid the inabilities of the cognitive factor, behavioural intention. The new construct, behavioural expectation, is not a cognitive factor thus it is able to address the roles of various internal and external factors (Venkatesh et al., 2008). The measurement of behavioural expectation as well as its contribution to actual ICT usage behaviour from an organisational perspective has not been well examined.

The adoption and diffusion phenomena of technological innovation have been analysed by applying a number of theoretical models in the last few decades. The parsimony of the research model has been an important concern for researchers seeking accuracy in outcomes and ease of estimations.[3] To maintain parsimony in the analytical model, a number of external factors, such as various aspects of culture and environment, have remained outside of the study due to the scope of the research model previously employed to examine the diffusion of a technological innovation (viz., Ajzen, 1985; Davis, 1986; Fishbein & Ajzen, 1975; Rogers, 1983; Venkatesh et al., 2003, 2008). In some cases, although these external variables have attracted researchers' attention, the effects have not been comprehensively analysed.

Generally, the external variables have been considered either separately or a part of the context has been taken into consideration. For example, the effects of culture or environmental pressures have been examined separately to address the ICT adoption and usage behaviour in many past studies (see Teo et al., 2003 for environmental pressure and Erumban & Jong, 2006 for culture). Some other studies have analysed a part of culture or environment such as competitive pressure, in some cases normative pressure has been analysed (with other antecedent factors) to study the effects of environmental pressures on the diffusion of a technological innovation (see Zhu, Dong, Xu, & Kraemer, 2006; Zhu & Kraemer, 2005; Zhu, Kraemer, Xu, & Dedrick, 2004). Inclusion of an adequate number of variables on the other hand can improve model efficiency for reliable and valid research outcomes.[4]

In recent years, significant progress has been made in the process of statistical analysis. In particular, the introduction of PLS-SEM) (Chin, 2010) has offered robust estimates and an increased ability to handle a large number of latent variables in a single platform. It can also handle the compound or higher-order constructs by estimating higher-order hierarchical modelling (see Wetzels, Odekerken-Schröder, & van Oppen, 2009). The construction of a comprehensive research model with a range of variables, such as individual, organisational, cultural and environmental variables, and a robust analysis may offer a detailed and clear understanding about the organisational technology diffusion behaviour.

Contemporary researchers have applied additional variables with the existing innovation diffusion theoretical frameworks (see Venkatesh et al., 2003, 2008; Zhu & Kraemer, 2005; Zhu, Dong, et al., 2006; Zhu et al., 2004). For example, Venkatesh et al. (2003) included perceived performance expectancy, effort expectancy, social influence and facilitating condition as exogenous variables in the model. Facilitating condition is defined as the extent to which the organisation is able to use the technology. Employee skill and knowledge, compatibility and the organisational resource base constitute the facilitating condition. Past literature has supported the view that the higher the facilitating conditions, the higher the usage of a technological innovation in an organisation (Gupta, Dasgupta, & Gupta, 2008; Venkatesh et al., 2008).

ICT, particularly Internet-based digital technologies, functions over a public network. Thus, the technology infrastructure of a country, government telecommunication policy, and the availability and speed of the Internet may matter in organisational ICT usage behaviour. Like facilitating condition, country readiness may play a significant role in ICT diffusion behaviour. Recent studies have investigated country readiness a little. For example, government policy and the regulatory environment have been studied in some previous studies (see Zhu & Kraemer, 2005; Zhu, Kraemer, & Xu, 2006; Zhu et al., 2004). The effects of country readiness on organisational IT usage behaviour, although addressed conceptually (see Molla & Licker, 2005), have not been documented widely in the existing literature. Besides this, previous research studies have mostly favoured the view that organisations adopt technology that is useful and that provides them with some economic benefit while, although important, non-economic factors such as cultural and environmental factors have been overlooked (Thatcher et al., 2006).

The economic development of a country is largely dependent on SMEs in the present market-based global competitive environment. Although equally important in terms of economic significance, SMEs in developed countries have continued to contribute substantially to their country's growth process while those from developing countries have not fared well. The rapid expansion of IT and its application to almost every sphere of economic activity have initiated the process of encouraging SMEs to make the most cost-effective use of new technologies in production, marketing and networking (Mandal, 2007). Thus, how SMEs can be tapped into new opportunities and produce enhanced performance in economic development is considered to be a worthwhile research study.

Taking into consideration the notion of ICT's performance implications, recent high ICT usage growths in the developing world and SMEs' economic significance, this study has opted to examine how ICT affects economic development through improved organisational performance in the developing country context. Considering SMEs as a population, this study, thus, has attempted to answer the main research question: 'How does diffusion of ICT correlate with SME performance in Bangladesh'? The study has also raised the following primary questions:

RQ-1. What is the contribution of internal and external factors in behavioural expectation in the context of Bangladesh?

RQ-2. How does behavioural expectation correlate with ICT use by SMEs in Bangladesh?

RQ-3. What is the role of ICT use, integration and utilisation in determining SME performance?

1.3. Objectives

The main objective of this study is to formulate a theoretical framework for examining the contribution of the use and utilisation of ICT to SME performance. The specific objectives of the study are to:

RO-1. Explore the cognitive factors influencing ICT adoption by SMEs.

RO-2. Delineate the effects of culture and environmental pressure on the adoption and usage of ICT by SMEs.

RO-3. Measure the effects of facilitating condition and country readiness on ICT adoption and use by SMEs.

RO-4. Examine the role of behavioural expectation in explaining ICT usage by SMEs.

RO-5. Examine the contribution of ICT usage to SME performance.

RO-6. Examine the mediating effects of ICT integration and utilisation in explaining the contribution of ICT usage to SME performance.

1.4. Research Background

ICT, particularly the Internet, underpins almost every single activity under-taken in the modern world and affects everyone on the planet – even those who do not themselves have first-hand access to ICT (ITU, 2010). Good examples include food distribution, power networks, water supplies or mass transportation, all of which are controlled and managed today by ICT networks and applications.

According to the *World Telecommunication Report 2010*, released to review the mid-term status and achievement between the World Summit on the Information Society (WSIS) 2005 and the Millennium Development Goals (MDG) 2015, tremendous progress has been made over the past decade, with almost two billion people throughout the world now having access to the Internet.

Although significant progress has been evident in the world's Internet penetration, household Internet penetration levels vary substantially between countries and regions. At the end of 2008, one out of four house-holds in the world had access to the Internet but only one out of eight households in developing countries was connected, compared to three out of five in developed countries.

While by the end of 2008, 58.1% of households in Europe had Internet access, only 16.8% of households in Asia-Pacific countries were connected to the Internet. The Internet penetration of Asia-Pacific countries remains at a lower level in comparison to Europe, America, the Commonwealth of

Independent States (CIS) and the Arab States. The Internet penetration of Bangladesh is significantly lower (below 1%) than that of other Asia-Pacific countries, such as Japan, Malaysia, Korea, Singapore and Australia.

According to the World Bank (WB) (World Bank, 2010) the Internet penetration in various countries was estimated as 75.9% (USA), 76% (UK), 70.8% (Australia), 69.6% (Singapore) and 55.8% (Malaysia), while Bangladesh's Internet penetration was only 0.347% in 2008 (Azam, 2013). The Internet penetration of those countries was more recently calculated as 78.1% (USA), 83.6% (UK), 88.8% (Australia), 75.0% (Singapore), 60.7% (Malaysia) and 5.0% (Bangladesh) at 30 June 2012.[5] The statistics show an increasing trend in Internet penetration in all of the above countries; however, the volume of Internet penetration in Bangladesh is very small in comparison to the other countries. While many developed and developing countries have achieved significant advantages through the computerisation of government departments, business firms and educational institutions, the digital initiatives of Bangladesh still remain at risk due to the poor digital participation of the citizenry.

The Internet began operating commercially in Bangladesh in the mid-1990s. Bangladesh has a poor teledensity in comparison to other developed and developing countries around the world (ITU, 2013). Like many other developing countries, Bangladesh suffers from inadequate infrastructure, outdated telephone systems, limited access to telephones and computers, poor service quality with high prices, lack of qualified personnel and a low level of literacy and IT skills, as well as cultural and language barriers (Azam, 2007). The main obstacle to using the Internet in Bangladesh is its distribution. The Internet is still an urban privilege in Bangladesh as the facilities are more concentrated in urban areas, especially being Dhaka[6]-based. The population living outside urban areas is mostly deprived of gaining the benefit of the Internet although they have the potential.[7] The noticeable digital divide is observed in Bangladesh in the following areas (Rahman, 2003):

- Urban and rural populations
- Dhaka (the capital) and rest of the country
- Different educational streams
- Rich population and poor population
- Male and female
- Mainstream and tribal populations
- Government and private organisations.

Despite suffering from multidimensional problems in terms of Internet access, Bangladesh has the potential of achieving success in its use of the Internet in the education, development, business and other services sectors.

The Government of Bangladesh considers the ICT sector as the thrust sector in the fifth five-year plan of the People's Republic of Bangladesh. In order to enjoy high bandwidth at a lower usage cost, the country has been connected with the information super highway through submarine optic fibre networks with a 16-country consortium through the SEA-ME-WE-4 project.[8] The Government of Bangladesh inaugurated this connectivity on 21 May 2006 (Daily Star, 2006; Prothom Alo, 2006). The landing station has been established at Cox's Bazar, the southern city, near the Bay of Bengal.

Despite Bangladesh's poor Internet penetration, the present Government of Bangladesh has given the highest priority to ICT and has initiated diverse policies and programs to achieve the digital goal provisioned in the 2009 national election and post-election agenda. The country's yearly national budgets (in the last few years) have allocated a substantial amount of resources for ICT development thus reiterating the expansion of ICT networks to rural communities to achieve government, citizen and business interactions and exchanges through the Internet. The government has also initiated some modifications to the country's national ICT policy in 2009 which reiterate the necessity of establishing e-government, e-services and e-commerce environments in order to gain economic potential. In addition, the government has emphasised the formulation of appropriate policies and strategies to facilitate Internet-related communication, e-commerce operation and e-governance. In order to achieve the potential of ICT, the government is dedicated to utilising the Internet in the education and services sectors (Azam & Quaddus, 2009a, 2009b, 2009c). Although numerous policy initiatives have been adopted to utilise the potential of ICT in the economic development of the country, the success of digitisation or computerisation is still doubtful.

Bangladesh has initiated steps to possibly fight against the hurdles and hindrances of ICT adoption, such as, limited accessibility to the Internet, poor teledensity, poor electricity network. However, poor Internet penetration is still considered as the main issue in establishing an e-based transparent society along with other issues such as the limited affordability of computers and limited knowledge; inadequate legal and regulatory support; inefficient and traditional systems of banking operation; poor financial support and traditional payment mechanisms; lack of human resources; and high Internet usage cost as well as security concerns (Azam, 2005, 2006a,

2006b; Azam & Lubna, 2008a, 2008b; Azam & Quaddus, 2009a; Hossain, 2000; ITRC, 2000; Rahman, 2002).

Bangladesh is basically an agricultural-based country. Its recently developed industrial base, particularly the ready-made garments (RMG) industry, has emerged as the main vehicle for the country's economic development. The overall culture of the country is characterised by a high population, low incomes and quite a large number of unemployed people with labour cheap and available as a result. Like many other Asian states, Bangladesh's culture has also been characterised by high power distance, collectivism and low uncertainty avoidance (House, Hanges, Javidan, Dorfman, & Gupta, 2004). The power is concentrated at the top of Bangladeshi society.

The Internet usage statistics shown in the preceding section are inspiring Asian countries to utilise the potential of ICT in their economic development. The Internet penetration in Bangladesh likewise is also growing.

The rapidly increasing trend of ICT usage, particularly Internet use, in business provides a motivation for large organisations as well as for smaller organisations in developing countries to adopt this technology. This usage encompasses the management of organisational internal communication, external communication, shop floor management, inventory control and customer integration as well as online order processing and transactions to acquire increased and competitive organisational performance.

Small and medium-sized enterprises (SMEs) have played an important role in the development of all countries. SMEs in developed countries contribute substantially to those countries' growth processes. Although lagging behind, SMEs in developing countries are also contributing positively. The prospects and contribution of Bangladesh's SMEs in its economic development are enormous. SMEs account for about 45% of the manufacturing value-add in Bangladesh. They account for about 80% of industrial employment, about 90% of total industrial units and about 25% of the total labour force. Their total contribution to export earnings varies between 75% and 80% (Azam & Quaddus, 2009c, 2009d).

According to the Bangladesh Bureau of Statistics (BBS), SMEs provide about 44% of the country's employment. The 2003 Private Sector Survey estimated that about six million micro-, small- and medium-sized enterprises, defined as enterprises with fewer than 100 employees, contributed around 20–25% of gross domestic product (GDP) (The New Nation, 2008). The number of SMEs and their significant contribution to the national economy in terms of employment generation, GDP contribution and export earnings thus create a significant research opportunity exploring the adoption and diffusion of ICT.

1.5. Definition of Terms

Behavioural expectation: Refers to an individual's self-reported subjective probability of his or her performing a specified behaviour, based on his or her cognitive appraisal of volitional or non-volitional behavioural Antecedents. It is the immediate antecedent of actual behaviour which is stronger than intention and is able to include the effects of some contextual and other external factors (Venkatesh et al., 2008).

Cognitive evaluation: Refers to an individual's overall evaluation towards an innovation. The evaluation process involves functional as well as psychological consequences. These cognitive and affective evaluations form one's attitude, that is, negative or positive feelings about performing a behaviour: this has been widely researched in the consumer, marketing and IS research. This study modelled cognitive evaluation to address attitude which is reflected by salient beliefs and respective evaluations (Ajzen, 1985, 1991).

Country readiness: Refers to an individual's perceptions about the country's preparedness or resources base which may support one's (an individual or organisation) decision to use a technological innovation. Country readiness comprises technology infrastructure, financial infrastructure, legal infrastructure, and Government policy and supports.

Culture: Refers to the collective programming of the mind that distinguishes the members of one group or category of people from another (Hofstede, 2001).

Degree of utilisation: Refers to the degree through which the proper and actual use of technology is ensured.

Environmental pressure: Refers to the pressure arising from the institutional environment. For example, environmental pressure includes various encouragement, advice or pressures which a firm receives from its customers, suppliers, the regulatory authority and other stakeholders. Environmental pressure comprises normative, mimetic and coercive pressures.

Facilitating condition: Refers to an individual's perceptions of the availability of technological and/or organisational resources (i.e. knowledge, resources and opportunities) that can remove barriers to using a system (Venkatesh et al., 2003).

ICT: Refers to ICT which may range from a simple digital phone or computer operation to highly sophisticated computer-driven and Internet-driven automated equipment. In this study, ICT is used to refer to the computer and computer-driven Internet and networking technologies which include various levels of ICT applications such as: (i) basic computing (computer and Internet); (ii) computing with a homepage operation which entails product cataloguing systems; (iii) computing with a homepage operation which offers online order receiving and processing systems; (iv) computing with interactive homepage operations which involve online order processing with online transaction processing systems and (v) computing with complete internal and external digital communication (enterprise resource planning (ERP)).

ICT usage: Refers to an individual's self-reported subjective assessment about rate of usage of various ICT applications. This study applies terms '*ICT usage*' and '*ICT use*' interchangeably to indicate SMEs' ICT usage behaviour.

Organisational performance: Refers to the outcome of organisational processes in a given time. Profit growth, sales growth, market share, productivity growth and firm competitiveness are the dimensions of organisational performance.

SMEs: Refer to small and medium-sized enterprises. In this study, SMEs are defined according to the Industrial Policy 2010 of the People's Republic of Bangladesh as:

- A manufacturing firm with 100−250 employees or having fixed assets from 10 Crore (1 Crore = 10m) Bangladeshi Taka (BDT) to 30 Crore BDT (excluding the value of land and factory) is considered a medium enterprise while any firm with 25−99 employees or having fixed assets from 55 Lakh (1 Lakh = 10k) BDT to 10 Crore BDT (excluding the value of land and factory) is considered a small enterprise.
- Also, a firm in the services industry with 50−100 employees or having fixed assets from 1 Crore BDT to 15 Crore BDT (excluding the value of land and factory) is considered a medium enterprise while a firm with 10−49 employees or having fixed assets from 5 Lakh BDT to 1 Crore BDT (excluding the value of land and factory) is considered a small enterprise.

1.6. Research Significance

This research has been dedicated to the extensive study of the ICT diffusion process and its effects on SME performance. In its design, the study has extended beyond the traditional innovation diffusion theories and has combined this with the resource-based view to examine SME performance. The study has employed a mixed-method research approach to overcome the limitations of a mono-method application, that is, either a qualitative or quantitative method. In this research, the qualitative study has led to the presentation of a fine-tuned and contextualised comprehensive research model. A number of new constructs and measurement procedures have also been identified during the field study. The quantitative survey and analyses have validated the anticipated model. However, the significance of this research lies in its contribution to theory and its contribution to practice.

1.6.1. *Contribution to Theory*
To examine organisational performance, this study has reviewed several existing innovation diffusion theories and has combined them with the institutional theory and resource-based views. More specifically, the following theories have been reviewed: theory of reasoned action (TRA) (Fishbein & Ajzen, 1975); diffusion of innovation (DOI) theory (Rogers, 1983); theory of planned behaviour (TPB) (Ajzen, 1985); technology acceptance model (TAM) (Davis, 1986); unified theory of acceptance and use of technology (UTAUT) (Venkatesh et al., 2003); technology, organisation and environment (TOE) framework (Tornatzky & Fleischer, 1990); institutional theory (DiMaggio & Powell, 1983) and resource-based theory (Barney, 1991).

A comprehensive research model has been constructed by synpapering existing theories: the model focuses on the diffusion of ICT process and its impacts on organisational performance. As most of the previous innovation diffusion studies have focused on the developed country perspective, the primary research model has been fine-tuned and contextualised through a qualitative study. The rigour in the qualitative field study analysis has resulted in a comprehensive model which includes a range of variables from individual, organisational, socio-cultural and environmental levels. The qualitative research has also provided an extensive understanding about this field of research through the inclusion of some new variables and the examination of their relationship with other study variables. For example, the study has included integration and utilisation as new constructs and has anticipated their mediating roles in examining the effects of ICT usage on SME performance. The field study has also provided a valuable contribution by presenting the measurement procedures for the newly introduced variables. By adding some higher-order compound variables which cover a wide range of variables as each higher-order variable has two or more manifest variables, the framework has become a holistic research model.

The theoretical framework now offers an opportunity to examine the whole process of innovation diffusion and its effect on organisational performance in a comprehensive model which is an important theoretical contribution. The robustness of estimates, furthermore, suggests the suitability of the comprehensive model for analysing the diffusion of ICT by SMEs and its effects on organisational performance. This framework is potentially suitable for testing similar phenomena in the large organisation environment from both a developing and developed country perspective.

1.6.2. Contribution to Practice

This study provides a clear picture of how internal and external factors affect ICT usage by SMEs in a developing country and its consequent effects on organisational performance. In analysing the data collected from SMEs using different levels of ICT applications, it was revealed that SMEs with a positive cognitive evaluation towards ICT, and that had adequate technological resources and received positive pressures from their institutional environment were more likely to use ICT while the overall culture and country infrastructure were not complementary to the use of ICT.

The study has provided a unique contribution in addressing the ICT paradox in a developing country context. This study has found that ICT use does not increase the performance growth of SMEs straightaway. Organisations should acquire the integration and proper utilisation of the technology to achieve performance growth. This is consistent with the notion of the resource-based view of ICT which reiterates that combining ICT into different organisational functionalities (i.e. integration with front-end functionalities or back-end integration) can create IT capabilities that are rare, un-imitable, valuable and sustainable, thereby contributing to value generation. Managers, interested stakeholders and policy makers may follow the outcome of this study and focus on ICT integration and the degree of utilisation with the view of attaining superior firm performance.

This study has also explored the patterns of ICT usage by SMEs and forecasts the degree and magnitude of the effects of various individual, organisational and environmental factors on the adoption and usage of different levels of ICT applications. This study suggests some changes and modifications to Bangladesh's existing policies and strategies to promote ICT adoption and use by SMEs for economic development. Government policy and supports focusing on the integrated and proper use of technology could contribute positively to SME performance.

1.7. Organisation of the Chapter

The chapter is structured as eight sections followed by references and appendices. The first section has presented an introduction and overview of the study including the research background with an overview of the overall structure of the research. The section started with the grounding of the research questions and has drawn general and specific research objectives. The significance of the research has also been discussed.

The second section deals with the review of the literature. The literature review includes reviewing some important theories in the domain of innovation diffusion along with institutional theory and resource-based theory. The empirical studies are also reviewed to develop a conceptual framework for the study. A preliminary research model is proposed which provides the basis for the field study and for the quantitative data collection survey. The third section deals with research method. This section discusses the research methodology and design incorporated in the study. It first introduces the research paradigm of the study. An interpretive (qualitative) approach and a positivist (quantitative) approach are discussed. A mixed-method approach incorporating qualitative approach into a quantitative framework is adopted.

The fourth section deals with the field study and the development of the final research model. This section presents the detailed results of the qualitative data analyses. It presents a brief sample profile for the field study and a wide discussion of the factors and variables identified during the interviews. The section also illustrates the final model of the study by incorporating the field study results and the factors identified from the literature review. The fifth section deals with the hypotheses developed and the questionnaire construction. This section develops and describes the hypotheses for the study and also describes the instrument with its origins and sources. A brief description of the pre-testing of the survey instrument is also presented at the end of the section.

The sixth section deals with analysis of the quantitative data. This section presents the analyses of the quantitative data in detail. The rationale for sample size determination is firstly presented followed by the assessment of the non-response bias and outer model estimation. The outer model estimation deals with the assessment of the psychometric properties of the model which includes assessment of the reliability and validity of the measures. The composite reliability, content validity, construct validity and discriminant validity of the constructs and measures are discussed in detail. Finally, the results of the inner model estimates are presented. A summary of the entire analyses with the results of hypotheses testing is presented at the end of the section.

The seventh section discusses the findings of the PLS results in the light of the major research questions and the hypotheses proposed in this study. The theoretical and practical implications from these results are provided in this section. The final section (Section 8) presents the conclusion and future research directions. This section provides an overview of the study and presents its theoretical and practical contributions. The section also discusses the limitations and weaknesses of this study and concludes with a brief discussion of possible future research directions in the subject area of this study.

1.8. Summary

This section provides background information and an overview of the research approach documented in this chapter. The review of the literature pertaining to the research topic has shown where key aspects have not been explored, and thus has led to the research questions posed here. This section has formulated the research questions which provide the basis for determining the objectives of the study. The significance of the research and definitions of related terms have been discussed. Finally, the organisation of the chapter structure was outlined. The next section presents the literature review and outlines a primary research model.

2. LITERATURE REVIEW

2.1. Introduction

This section focuses on reviewing the literature, both the theories and empirical studies, to address the ICT diffusion process and firm performance from an SME perspective. Various theories relating to ICT adoption and organisational performance are critically reviewed to build a comprehensive model which finally employs individual, organisational, socio-cultural and environmental factors to look at SMEs' ICT usage behaviour and its consequential effects on firm performance. The following sections of the literature review serve a number of purposes. Section 2.2 describes the diffusion process while the theoretical frameworks that address ICT adoption-diffusion, institutional factors and firm performance are discussed in Section 2.3. Section 2.4 reviews empirical studies and Section 2.5 addresses the Antecedents of ICT use, while Section 2.6 discusses the Antecedents of firm performance. Finally, a testable research model (Fig. 1) is developed based on the discussion and literature review described in the sections below.

2.2. Diffusion Process

The adoption of a new product is a decision process that moves through different stages of time. Diffusion refers to the process by which an innovation is communicated through certain channels over time among the members of a social system. According to Rogers (1995), the decision process begins with knowledge about a new innovation and ends with implementation and confirmation that the innovation is being used. The process involves the five different phases, namely, knowledge, persuasion, decision, implementation and confirmation, through which the adoption and diffusion of an innovation occur.

A range of various characteristics, variables and factors affect the diffusion process in different phases (Rogers, 1983). For example, the socio-economic characteristics, personality traits and communication behaviour of the decision-making unit influence the knowledge stage while decision-makers' perceptions about the innovation affect the intention or decision to adopt an innovation. However, the implementation and continued use of the innovation are related to several other variables.

Researchers face two fundamental questions when studying the adoption and diffusion of an innovation. These questions are related to the differences between adoption and diffusion, and the patterns of adoption-diffusion of an innovation by an individual and organisation. The answers are not straightforward and vary as the process (discussed above) involves several stages of diffusion, namely knowledge, persuasion, decision, implementation and confirmation, through which the adoption and diffusion are projected into an integrated environment. However, according to the innovation diffusion research, the organisation first has to make a decision on the adoption of the innovation (e.g. new technology). Information about the innovation is collected. This information then leads to the formation of perceptions about the innovation (Xu & Quaddus, 2005). In a simplistic view, adoption may be defined as the mental state which accepts or rejects an innovation for use while the process by which an innovation becomes popular (implementation and confirmation) is called diffusion.

The second question is crucial for adoption researchers as there are big differences between the individual and the organisational adoption and diffusion processes. The individual adoption-diffusion process mainly relates to an individual's knowledge, personality, perceptions and motivation while the organisational adoption-diffusion process depends on the organisational rules and procedures and the people involved with the decision. Normally, a decision-making unit (in an organisation) comprises three or more people who are primarily guided by the company policy, rules, regulations and customs. Thus, the nature, complexity and the process of organisational adoption and diffusion appear differently to that of the process and nature of individual adoption and diffusion. This study explored the organisational adoption-diffusion process from the perspective of an SME which is similar to the individual adoption-diffusion process. In SMEs, the decision about ICT adoption is more likely to be made by the owner (Doukidis, Lybereas, & Galliers, 1996; Kendall et al., 2001; Matlay & Addis, 2003; Quaddus & Hofmeyer, 2007) with often little concern about the importance of ICT strategy and planning within their business (Beckett, 2003; Nejadirani, Behravesh, & Rasouli, 2011).

An innovation also passes through several stages in its life cycle which starts from the introduction stage and passes through growth, maturity and decline stages. People from different socio-cultural, economic and financial positions adopt an innovation in different stages. The risk-takers who come first and try an innovation promptly (during the introduction stage) are called innovators. Other types of adopters such as early adopters, early majority, late majority and laggards use an innovation during the growth, maturity and decline stages accordingly. Interestingly, while the laggards are the users of the innovation when an innovation reaches its decline stage, the innovators have already shifted to a new innovation which has just started its journey.

An innovation comes to the market to satisfy specific needs of individuals, groups or society. Thus, potential adopters use an innovation with the motivation of satisfying some specific needs. Similarly, SMEs use an innovation with the motivation of increasing organisational productivity to enhance organisational performance, such as profit increase, revenue increase or cost saving (Beard, Madden, & Azam, 2014; Madden, Azam, & Beard, 2013). Numerous past studies have investigated the adoption and diffusion of ICT based on the notion that ICT adoption, diffusion or use generates improved organisational performance. However, the question of whether the adoption and usage of the technology have succeeded in addressing the motivation or reasons for the adoption and usage is not well understood. This study thus has been motivated to look at the impact of the diffusion of ICT on organisational performance with particular attention given to the mediating effects of integration and utilisation. An integrated framework has then been developed by extending the scope of existing adoption-diffusion theories to address organisational performance. The following section discusses relevant theories of innovation, diffusion and organisational performance and outlines the theoretical framework for studying the ICT diffusion process and organisational performance.

2.3. Theoretical Framework

This research has investigated SMEs' ICT diffusion behaviour by extending the scope of existing diffusion theories through the link with firm performance. The theoretical grounding for the constructs under study was developed by combining the notions and principles of various theoretical frameworks applicable to the adoption and diffusion of ICT. The theories reviewed were the DOI theory (Rogers, 1983, 1995); TRA (Fishbein & Ajzen, 1975); TPB (Ajzen, 1985); TAM (Davis, 1986); TOE framework (Tornatzky & Fleischer, 1990); institutional theory (DiMaggio & Powell, 1983); UTAUT (Venkatesh et al., 2003) and resource-based theory (Barney, 1991).

2.3.1. DOI Theory (Rogers, 1983)[9]
The DOI theory (Rogers, 1983) explains the diffusion process of an innovation and highlights various factors that affect different phases of the

process. According to Rogers (1983), the diffusion process begins with the *knowledge* of the existence of the innovation and matures through *persuasion, decision, implementation* and *confirmation* stages. During the knowledge stage, the consumer is exposed to the innovation's existence and gains some understanding of how it functions. The persuasion stage refers to that period in which the consumer forms a favourable or unfavourable attitude towards the innovation. The persuasion stage is followed by a decision phase. If the decision is in favour of adoption, an implementation process starts. An innovation may be confirmed and incorporated into the culture of the user population, may undergo changes (re-invention) or may be rejected during the implementation phase.

The persuasion stage is considered to be the most important stage in terms of the relative importance of the five stages explained in the DOI theory since potential adopters gather information from various sources and attempt to determine the utility of the innovation during this stage (Rogers, 1995). Potential adopters' adoption intention or willingness is formed during the persuasion stage. Rogers (1995) highlighted five attributes of innovation as perceived by the individual or organisation – perceived innovation characteristics which determine adopter willingness or rate of adoption. These five innovation attributes are relative advantage, compatibility, complexity, trialability and observability. These innovation characteristics may explain 49–87% of the variance in the rate of adoption of the innovation (Rogers, 1995). The DOI theory (Rogers, 1983), although focused on the individual's innovation adoption process, is also effective in examining organisational innovation adoption (Attewell, 1992; Azam & Quaddus, 2009b; Brancheau & Wetherbe, 1990; Kendall et al., 2001; Tan & Teo, 2000).

Numerous past studies have shown the significant impacts of perceived innovation characteristics, as highlighted by Rogers (1983, 1995, 2003); on the rate of adoption of an innovation. Table 1 shows that the innovation characteristics highlighted by Rogers (1983, 1995, 2003) are supported by a number of empirical studies.

The impacts of *relative advantage, compatibility, complexity, trialability* and *observability* have been empirically proven in different countries around the world. Past studies have also revealed that Rogers' (1983, 1995, 2003) model is suitable for examining the adoption rate of a technological innovation from the organisational perspective, particularly the SME perspective.

Table 1. Empirical Evidence in Favour of Rogers' (1983) Model.

Attributes of Innovation	References
Relative advantage	Kuan and Chau (2001), Wymer and Regan (2005), Jeon, Han, and Lee (2006), Kendall et al. (2001), Tan and Teo (2000, 2004), Lim and Speece (2002), Sathye and Beal (2001), Holak and Lehman (1990), Azam and Quaddus (2009b), Scupola (2003b), Premkumar, Ramamurthy, and Nilakanta (1994)
Compatibility	Teo and Ranganathan (2004), Kendall et al. (2001), Jeon et al. (2006), Azam and Quaddus (2009b), Tan and Teo (2000), Hoppe, Newman, and Mugera (2001), Cooper and Zmund (1990)
Complexity	Jeon et al. (2006), Hoppe et al. (2001), Tan and Teo (2000), Lederer, Mirchadani, and Sims (1997), Cockburn and Wilson (1996), Azam and Quaddus (2009b)
Trialability	Kendall et al. (2001), Azam and Quaddus (2009b)
Observability	Azam (2007, 2009b)

2.3.2. TRA (Fishbein & Ajzen, 1975)

The TRA (Ajzen & Fishbein, 1980; Fishbein & Ajzen, 1975) is one of the well-researched theories for measuring behavioural intention: it explains the causes of behavioural intent and illustrates the structures of the relationships.

The TRA has two unique factors which are the attitude towards the behaviour (ATT) and subjective norms (SNs) that contribute to behavioural intention (BI) which finally explains the actual behaviour. The TRA is guided by the underlying basic assumption that humans are quite rational and make use of all available information, both personal and social, before they act (Crawley & Coe, 1990).

The TRA has been widely used in previous years to examine consumers' BI as well as to address the causes of actual consumer behaviour in various consumption-related issues (Bang, Ellinger, Hadjimarcou, & Traichal, 2000; Chang, 1998; Crawley, 1988; Crawley & Coe, 1990). The TRA has also been used in the IT field as the basis for testing several technologies and has spanned a variety of subject areas, for example, word processing (Davis et al., 1989); MS Windows (Karahanna, Straub, & Chervany, 1999); e-commerce (Vijayasarathy, 2004); Internet information management (Celuch, Taylor, & Goodwin, 2004) and e-banking (Shih & Fang, 2004, 2006). A particularly helpful aspect of TRA from an IS perspective is that attitude and SNs are theorised to mediate the effect of external variables on the intention to use new IT (Davis et al., 1989).

Many studies have shown the applicability of the TRA for studying individuals' BI and actual usage behaviour with regard to an innovation by revealing the significant effects of *attitude towards intention* (Chang, 1998; Davis et al., 1989; Lu, Yu, Liu, & Yao, 2003; Mathieson, 1991; Ramayah, Jamaludin, & Azam, 2007; Rhodes & Courneya, 2003; Taylor & Todd, 1995b) and SNs (Crawley & Coe, 1990; Ramayah et al., 2007; Taylor & Todd, 1995b; Venkatesh & Davis, 2000) on BI.

The TRA was subsequently reviewed and modified to comprehensively explain usage behaviour by adding more variables as antecedents of BI. For example, the TPB is an extension of the TRA which includes a new variable, *perceived behavioural control*, within the TRA framework.

2.3.3. TPB (Ajzen, 1985)

The TPB was proposed by Ajzen (1985, 1991) and, as explained in the previous section, is an extension of the TRA (Ajzen & Fishbein, 1980). The TPB was developed to address the original model's limitations in dealing with behaviours over which people have incomplete volitional control (Ajzen, 1985, 1991). Thus, it overcomes the problematic predictive validity of the TRA to explain the behaviour under study which is not under full volitional control. Ajzen (1985) made the extension by including one additional construct, *perceived behavioural control*, within the TRA framework to predict BI and behaviour. Perceived behavioural control refers to 'people's perception of [the] ease or difficulty of performing the behaviour of interest' (Ajzen, 1991). A number of external factors (such as environmental or organisational factors) can make a given behaviour easier or harder to perform.

The TPB holds that human action is guided by three kinds of considerations: beliefs about the likely outcomes of the behaviour and the evaluations of these outcomes (behavioural beliefs); beliefs about the normative expectations of others and motivation to comply with these expectations (normative beliefs) and beliefs about the presence of factors that may facilitate or hinder performance of the behaviour and the perceived power of these factors (control beliefs). The TPB also explains that certain factors or constructs, known as control beliefs, may facilitate and impede people's behaviour; thus, they can influence a person's adoption intention or their purchase of a product or service (Ajzen & Madden, 1986).

Many studies have shown the effectiveness and applicability of the TPB for examining individuals' behaviour towards an innovation by revealing the significant effects of *attitude towards intention* (Chang, 1998; Davis et al., 1989; George, 2002, 2004; Lu et al., 2003; Mathieson, 1991;

Ramayah, Ignatius, & Aafaqi, 2005; Ramayah et al., 2007; Ramayah, Jantan, Noor, Razak, & Ling, 2003; Ramayah, Noor, Nasurdin, & Sin, 2004; Rhodes & Courneya, 2003; Shih & Fang, 2004; Taylor & Todd, 1995a); SNs (Ramayah et al., 2003, 2004; Taylor & Todd, 1995b; Venkatesh & Davis, 2000); and *perceived behavioural control* (Cheung, Chang, & Lai, 2000; Jiang, Hus, Klien, & Lin, 2000; Jones, Sundaram, & Chin, 2002; Taylor & Todd, 1995a) on BI. Ajzen (1991) showed the direct link between perceived behavioural control and actual behaviour although it has an indirect effect on actual behaviour through significantly contributing to BI.

2.3.4. TAM (Davis, 1986)

The TAM was developed by Davis (1986) to explain IT usage behaviour. It is an adaptation of the TRA and states that BI to use a technology is directly determined by two key beliefs: *perceived usefulness* and *perceived ease of use*. Perceived usefulness assesses the extrinsic characteristics of IT, that is, task-oriented outcomes such as 'the prospective user's subjective probability that using a specific application will increase his or her job performance within an organisational context'. On the other hand, perceived ease of use examines the intrinsic characteristics of IT, that is, its ease of use (how easy it is to use), ease of learning, flexibility and clarity of the interface. Perceived ease of use is stated as 'the degree to which the prospective users expect the target system to be free of effort' (Davis et al., 1989).

The earlier version of the TAM included SNs with perceived ease of use and usefulness as antecedents of BI which was omitted from the later model. One key benefit of using the TAM to understand system usage behaviour is that it provides a framework for examining the influence of external factors on system usage (Hong, Thong, Wong, & Tam, 1999).

Various external variables such as computer self-efficacy, social influence, experience, voluntariness, diversity of technology, trust, culture and relevance have been added in the context of the TAM in different settings in previous initiatives to gain more insight into technology acceptance (Agarwal & Prashad, 1999; Davis et al., 1989; Hong et al., 1999; Shih, 2004; Taylor & Todd, 1995a; Venkatesh & Davis, 2000; Venkatesh & Morris, 2000; Wang, Wang, Lin, & Tang, 2003; Yoon, 2009).

The TAM (Davis, 1986) has been one of the most frequently used research models for examining systems' usage behaviour over the past two decades. Many previous studies have revealed that the fundamental components of TAM, perceived ease of use and perceived usefulness, were found to have strong significant effects on BI (e.g. Chau, 1997; Chau & Hu, 2002; Davis, 1989; Davis et al., 1989; Lu et al., 2003; Mathieson, 1991; Subramanian, 1994; Szajna, 1996; Taylor & Todd, 1995a; Venkatesh & Davis, 2000; Yoon, 2009).

2.3.5. TOE Framework (Tornatzky & Fleischer, 1990)

In addition to these individual adoption-diffusion theories, Tornatzky and Fleischer (1990) proposed a TOE framework to look at organisational aspects of technology diffusion. The TOE framework identifies the following three aspects of a firm's context that influence the process by which it adopts, implements and uses technological innovations:

(i) Technological context is concerned with existing technologies as well as new technologies relevant to the firm.
(ii) Organisational context addresses descriptive measures about the organisation such as scope, size and the amount of slack resources available internally.
(iii) Environmental context refers to the aspects of how a firm conducts its business, responds to its industry, customers and competitors, and deals with government.

This framework has received more attention and acceptance from diverse fields of study as it is consistent with the classical DOI theory (Rogers, 1983). Rogers emphasised technological characteristics, and both internal and external characteristics of the organisation, as drivers for technology diffusion.

Many previous studies have utilised the TOE framework to examine organisational technology usage behaviour and have analysed the effects of technological, organisational and environmental factors (e.g. Marques, Oliveira, Dias, & Martins, 2011; Oliveira & Martins, 2010; Zhu & Kraemer, 2005; Zhu, Kraemer, & Xu, 2003; Zhu, Kraemer, et al., 2006; Zhu et al., 2004).

2.3.6. Institutional Theory (DiMaggio & Powell, 1983)

The institutional theory posits that organisations face pressures to conform to these shared notions of appropriate forms of behaviours, since violating them may call into question the organisation's legitimacy and thus affect its ability to secure resources and social support (DiMaggio & Powell, 1983; Tolbert, 1985).

DiMaggio and Powell (1983) distinguished between three types of isomorphic pressures – normative, mimetic and coercive – and suggested that coercive and normative pressures normally operate through interconnected relationships while mimetic pressures act through structural equivalence.

Ajzen and Fishbein (1980) explored the role of SNs and studied how it affects individual behaviour. SNs, in other words, pressures from friends and family, play a vital role in the formation of the intention to use an innovation. When applied to organisations, a focal organisation can learn about an innovation and its associated benefits and costs from other user organisations to which it is directly or indirectly tied, and is likely to be persuaded to behave in a similar way (Burt, 1982). Many studies have considered normative pressure as an antecedent of organisational innovation adoption (Kuan & Chau, 2001; Teo et al., 2003).

Mimetic pressures are the influences of other structurally equivalent organisations that have initiated some innovations and have become successful. These pressures may cause an organisation to change over time to become more like the other organisations in its environment (DiMaggio & Powell, 1983). Many past studies have included mimetic pressures when looking at organisational ICT adoption behaviour (Premkumar & Ramamurthy, 1995; Teo et al., 2003).

Coercive pressures address various kinds of powers or influences, informal or formal, exercised by other organisations upon which an organisation is dependent. A dominant customer, supplier or parent organisation sometimes exercises their power or coercively influences the organisation to act in a certain way where the dependent organisation has no option other than to comply with the requirements. Coercive pressures are significant when studying ICT diffusion behaviour (Quaddus & Hofmeyer, 2007; Teo et al., 2003).

2.3.7. UTAUT (Venkatesh et al., 2003)

Venkatesh et al. (2003) proposed a new theoretical framework to explain user intentions and subsequent usage behaviour with regard to the use of IS. This theory applies a theoretical structure similar to the TRA or TAM. That is, the intention explains the actual usage of ICT while it (BI) receives various influences from the antecedent factors − performance expectancy, effort expectancy, social influence and facilitating condition. Gender, age, experience and voluntariness of use are anticipated as possible moderators of the four key constructs on usage intention and behaviour. Venkatesh et al. (2003) developed the theory through a review and consolidation of the constructs of eight models that earlier research had employed to explain IS usage behaviour, namely, the TRA, TAM, motivational model (MM), TPB, a combined technology acceptance model and theory of planned behaviour (C-TAM-TPB), model of PC utilisation (MPCU), DOI theory and social cognitive theory (SCT). Subsequent validation of UTAUT in a longitudinal study found that it accounted for 70% of the variance in usage intention.

Many past studies have shown the applicability of the UTAUT model for examining usage behaviour of a technological innovation in both developed and developing countries (e.g. Gupta et al., 2008; Venkatesh & Zhang, 2010).

2.3.8. Resource-Based View (RBV) (Barney, 1991)
The resourced-based theory, popularly known as the RBV of the firm (Barney, 1991), has been widely used to examine organisational competitive advantage. The theory has received attention from numerous researchers who have been willing to investigate firm performance. The RBV is a promising contemporary theory that combines strategic insights on competitive advantage and organisational insights on firm existence. According to Barney (1991), valuable, rare, imperfectly imitable and imperfectly substitutable resources could generate sustainable competitive advantage for the firm with the prerequisite of heterogeneity and imperfect mobility of resources among competing firms. Peteraf (1993) focused on heterogeneity, ex-post limits to competition, imperfect mobility and ex-ante limits to competition as the characteristics for strategic resources in the generation of sustainable competitive advantage for the firm.

Prior to the RBV framework (Barney, 1991; Peteraf, 1993), Porter (1985) indicated that competitive advantage and its constituents could measure the firm's success relative to its competitors. With the view to assess competitive advantage, numerous researchers have applied the RBV to investigate firms' performance (Bharadwaj, 2000; Powell & Dent-Micallef, 1997).

The RBV may also look at the performance impact of ICT taking into consideration that ICT resources and capabilities are intangible, unable to be imitated and unique. How IT resources and capabilities can generate firm performance or competitive advantage is the main focus of applying RBV within IS research. The traditional RBV of ICT is successfully applied to look at the impact of ICT on organisational performance (Bharadwaj, 2000; Powell & Dent-Micallef, 1997).

2.3.9. Review of the Existing Theories
The theoretical frameworks that address ICT diffusion can be categorised into three groups based on their focus, scope and structures. The DOI

theory (Rogers, 1983), TRA (Fishbein & Ajzen, 1975), TPB (Ajzen, 1985), TAM (Davis, 1986) and UTAUT (Venkatesh et al., 2003) all focus on the prospective users' BI to adopt an innovation. These theories primarily anticipate a positive link between users' perceptions about the innovation's characteristics and their BI. Adopters' perceptions about the innovation's characteristics are reflected in the perceived innovation characteristics in DOI theory (Rogers, 1983); attitude in TRA (Fishbein & Ajzen, 1975) and TPB (Ajzen, 1985); perceived usefulness and perceived ease of use in TAM (Davis, 1986); and perceived performance expectancy and perceived effort expectancy in the UTAUT (Venkatesh et al., 2003) model. Rogers (1983) stated that user intention is formed during the primary stage of the diffu- sion process, the persuasion stage, where perceived innovation characteris- tics play a vital role in explaining the intention. Innovation characteristics generally explain 49–87% of the variation in an innovation's adoption. Furthermore, Rogers (1983) indicated that the diffusion process starts from the knowledge stage, that is, when adopters are exposed to an innovation. Adopter demographics, risk-taking behaviour and innovativeness play a vital role in the early adoption of an innovation. Table 2 summarises the existing theoretical frameworks.

The TRA, TPB, TAM and UTAUT show a similar structural relation- ship among the various internal and external factors, BI and actual beha- viour, which is different from the DOI theory. All four of these theoretical frameworks anticipate that BI is the only antecedent of actual usage beha- viour. User perceptions about an innovation influence BI which ultimately explains actual usage behaviour. For example, the impact of attitude on actual behaviour is mediated through BI under the TRA and TPB frame- works. Likewise, the TAM and UTAUT model are designed to study the impacts of perceived ease of use and perceived usefulness (TAM) as well as performance expectancy and effort expectancy (UTAUT) on actual usage behaviour mediated through BI. In addition to the internal variables, var- ious external variables are used as antecedents of BI in the existing theories. For example, the TRA includes SNs – whether friends, family and peer groups like or dislike the performance of a certain behaviour – with attitude. The TPB includes SNs and perceived behavioural control – the ability to perform a certain behaviour. The UTAUT includes SNs and facilitating condition – the availability of the required technological and human resources to use a technological innovation – with perceived per- formance expectancy, effort expectancy and social influence.

The TOE framework (Tornatzky & Fleischer, 1990) anticipates a posi- tive link between external and internal variables and organisational

Table 2. Review of the Theoretical Frameworks.

Endogenous Variables	DOI	TRA	TPB	TAM	UTAUT	Exogenous Variables — Institutional Theory	Systems Use[a]	RBV	Proposed Theoretical Constructs
	Individual characteristics/innovativeness[b]	—	—	—	—	—	—	—	Owner/CEO characteristics
	Relative advantage	Attitude	Attitude	Perceived usefulness	Performance expectancy	—	—	—	Attitude
	Compatibility	—	—	—	—	—	—	—	
	Complexity	—	—	Perceived ease of use	Effort expectancy	—	—	—	
	Trialability	—	—	—	—	—	—	—	
	Observability	—	—	—	—	—	—	—	
Behavioural intention	—	Subjective norms	Subjective norms	—	Social influence	Normative pressure	—	—	
	—	—	Perceived behavioural control	—	Facilitating condition	—	—	—	Facilitating condition (organisational resources)
	—	—	—	—	—	Competitive pressure	—	—	Environmental pressure (industry environment)
	—	—	—	—	—	Coercive pressure	—	—	Country readiness (country infrastructure & resources)
	—	—	—	—	—	—	—	—	Culture (societal environment)

Table 2. *(Continued)*

Endogenous Variables	Exogenous Variables								Proposed Theoretical Constructs
	DOI	TRA	TPB	TAM	UTAUT	Institutional Theory	Systems Use[a]	RBV	
Behavioural expectation	–	–	–	–	–	–	Behavioural intention Facilitating condition	– – – –	Behavioural intention
Use	–	Intention	Intention	Intention	Intention	–	Behavioural intention Behavioural expectation Facilitating condition	– –	Behavioural expectation Facilitating condition
Performance	–	–	–	–	–	–	–	Use and utilisation of organisational resources	ICT use Degree of utilisation

[a] A theoretical framework employed to study system usage behaviour (Venkatesh et al., 2008).

[b] Personal demographics and innovativeness are the main influencers in the knowledge stage when adopters are exposed to an innovation. Early adopters intend to and adopt an innovation very promptly.

technology usage behaviour. This framework divides all external and internal antecedent factors into three different categories, namely:

(i) Technological context − the existing technologies as well as new technologies relevant to the firm
(ii) Organisational context − the descriptive measures about the organisation viz., size, and the amount of slack resources available internally
(iii) Environmental context − the aspects of how a firm conducts its business, responds to its industry, customers and competitors, and deals with government, and the process by which the organisation chooses, adopts, implements and uses a technological innovation.

By definition, the environmental context includes various aspects of environmental factors related to the adoption of an innovation. The concerns arising from the organisation's responses to its customers, competitors and regulatory authorities are environmental factors. Institutional theory (DiMaggio & Powell, 1983) posits that organisations face pressures to conform to the shared notions of appropriate forms of behaviour in an institutional environment. Firms working in an environment are influenced by their customers, suppliers, parent organisations and other similar firms. Institutional theory describes these influences by categorising three types of isomorphic pressures − coercive, mimetic and normative − and suggests that coercive and normative pressures normally operate through interconnected relationships while mimetic pressures act through structural equivalence. Institutional theory and the TOE framework explain the effects of environmental factors on the process by which an organisation adopts, uses and implements an innovation; however, they do not explain how these factors affect the formation of intention or entrepreneurs' perceptions while forming the intention to adopt an innovation. The TOE framework, although it considers the organisational and technological context in conjunction with environmental factors, is silent about any influence from perceived innovation characteristics.

Furthermore, how organisations deal with government policies, relevant legislation and relevant infrastructural supports is another aspect of environmental factors which is related to country readiness. The issues related to how an organisation conducts its business, responds to society and proceeds to choose or use an innovation are again different from the other two types of environmental issues, namely, environmental pressures and country readiness. These phenomena are environmental concerns that are more culture-specific.

The above-mentioned theories explain the influence of diverse factors on BI or actual behaviour (technology usage); however, none of them address any aspect of organisational performance. The notion that a satisfied user initiates repeat use and becomes a loyal user is a driver for the inclusion of organisational performance with technology diffusion research. Satisfied users also act as a reference for others who are willing to use the same innovation. Thus, the final outcome of an innovation adoption viz., enhanced organisational performance, has become an important concern in present IT research. The RBV (Barney, 1991) posits that resources which are valuable, rare, imperfectly imitable and imperfectly substitutable could generate sustainable competitive advantage. ICT usage is valuable and rare for the firm. However, combining the resources with organisational processes may make it imperfectly imitable and substitutable. Thus, the use and degree of utilisation of ICT in an SME play a vital role in enhanced firm performance.

The above-mentioned discussion spells out the fact that a single model doesn't comprehensively cover all relevant issues and also provides a platform to synpaper the theories (the TRA, TAM, TPB, DOI theory, UTAUT, TOE framework, institutional theory and RBV) and build a comprehensive theoretical framework to look at the innovation diffusion process of ICT in the SME sector and its resultant outcome in terms of organisational performance. The comprehensive theoretical framework combines relevant external and internal factors as antecedents of BI which influence ICT usage behaviour with a view to addressing the impact of ICT usage on organisational performance.

2.4. Review of Empirical Studies

This section highlights some important empirical findings which explore the research gaps in the existing literature and provides a logical grounding of various internal and external factors to be synpapered to develop an integrated theoretical framework for examining the diffusion of ICT and SME performance. When undertaking the critical review of the relevant literature, as shown in Table 3, the motivation for the research as well as the research direction were addressed.

The literature review revealed that studying the impacts of ICT usage on organisational performance is an important research issue which has not been widely documented.[10] Although the diffusion of ICT has been a much researched area of study in the past two decades, there remains a wide

Table 3. Review of Related Empirical Studies.

Author (Year Published)	Research Method	Independent Variables	Results	Comments
Zhu and Kraemer (2005) *Activity analysed:* E-business usage and value (post-adoption variation)	Quantitative survey Structural equation modelling (PLS) was employed with a data set of 624 retail industry firms across 10 countries. The integrated research model was grounded in the innovation diffusion literature and resource-based theory which featured technological, organisational and environmental factors used to examine e-business usage and value creation.	*E-business use:* Technology competence Org. size Org. international scope Org. financial commitment Competitive pressure Regulatory support *E-business value:* Front-end functionality Back-end integration E-business use	*E-business use:* Technology competence Org. size Org. financial commitment Competitive pressure Regulatory support *E-business value:* Front-end functionality Back-end integration *E-business use* The study reported significant differences in the firms' e-business use and value between developed and developing countries.	The study addressed e-business diffusion and value creation while other aspects of ICT applications, such as general purpose ICT, ERP, were overlooked. The study, although featuring technological, organisational and environmental factors, did not include cognitive evaluation, culture and country readiness in the model. The study investigated the phenomena from the developed country perspective.
Zhu et al. (2003) *Activity analysed:* Electronic business (EB) adoption	Quantitative survey Data source was ECaTT, a data set developed by Empirica, a research institute based in Bonn, Germany. The Logit model was used in a data set of 3,100 businesses and 7,500 consumers from eight European countries	Technology competence Firm scope Firm size Consumer readiness Lack of trading partner readiness Competitive pressure Industry dummies Country dummies	Technology competence Firm scope Firm size Consumer readiness Lack of trading partner readiness Competitive pressure Low EB intensity countries were similar to full sample while high EB intensity countries differed.	Only the adoption decision was examined which is not adequate for inferring the implementation process or its impact on firm performance. The study was based on a European countries' data set which poses the question as to whether the result would apply to developing or newly industrialised countries.

Table 3. (Continued)

Author (Year Published)	Research Method	Independent Variables	Results	Comments
Zhu et al. (2006) *Activity analysed:* Assimilation of Internet-based e-business (initiation, adoption and routinisation)	Quantitative survey Structural equation modelling (AMOS) was employed for the estimations with a data set of 1,857 firms in the retail industry across 10 countries. The model featured technological, organisational and environmental factors to examine the three stages of assimilation. The study also compared e-business assimilation between developed and developing countries to investigate whether there was any economic effect.	*E-business use:* Technology readiness Technology integration Firm size Global scope Managerial obstacles Competition intensity Regulatory environment	*Initiation:* Technology readiness Technology integration Managerial obstacles (-) Competition intensity Regulatory environment *Adoption:* Technology readiness Technology integration Firm size (-) Competition intensity *Routinisation:* Technology readiness Technology integration Firm size (-) Managerial obstacles (-) Competition intensity (-) Regulatory environment	The study focused on adoption and diffusion of e-business. From this study, it was not possible to predict if the diffusion of e-business had any positive impact on firm performance.
Molla and Licker (2005) *Activity analysed:* E-commerce adoption and institutionalisation (developing country perspective)	Quantitative survey Multiple discriminant function analysis was conducted with a data set collected in South Africa.	*Perceived org. e-readiness:* Awareness Resources Commitment Governance *Perceived external e-readiness:* Government e-readiness Market forces e-readiness Support industries e-readiness	Organisational factors, especially the human, business and technological resources, and awareness were more influential than environmental factors in the initial adoption of e-commerce. Environmental factors, together with commitment and the governance model that organisations installed, affected	The study focused on e-commerce adoption and institutionalisation while other applications of ICT were not included in the model. The study looked at the phenomena from the developing country perspective. However, it lacked the construction of a comprehensive model to analyse the phenomena. For example, cognitive

Study / Activity	Methodology	Variables	Findings	Notes
Hong and Zhu (2006) *Activity analysed:* E-commerce adoption *and* migration to e-commerce	Quantitative survey. The theoretical framework was developed grounded in technology diffusion theory. Multinomial logistic regression was used with a data set of 1,036 firms in a broad range of industries.	Technology integration Web spending Web functionalities Electronic data interchange (EDI) use Partner use Perceived obstacles *Control variables:* Firm size Industry type	*E-business adoption:* Technology integration Web spending Web functionalities Partner usage The adoption rate varied by firm size in the case of the overall sample and non-adopters versus adopters sub-sample while it had no effect on potential adopters versus adopters sub-sample. *Migration to E-business:* Web spending Web functionalities EDI (–) Partner usage (–) Perceived obstacle (–)	e-commerce institutionalisation. evaluation, institutional pressures, culture and country infrastructure were not included in the model. The study focused on e-commerce adoption and migration to e-commerce. The study was silent about the impact of e-commerce on firm performance. The study dealt with the phenomena from the developed country perspective.
Madden et al. (2013) *Dependent variable:* Small firms online market entry	Quantitative survey. Trivariate Probit model estimations were conducted with a data set of 1,001 small and medium-sized businesses in Australia.	The study included strategic reasons – efficiency, market expansion, introducing new goods, responding to customer requests, supplier requirements, anticipating competition – for entry into online business and the effect on market performance with various firm characteristics,	Firms that enter into the online market for market expansion are successful while firms that targeted cost reduction were disappointed. The study had no evidence that blended firms enjoyed any important advantage over their virtual competitors.	This study basically proved that ICT application (online market entry) in SMEs improved firms' market performance (market expansion and profit). This study included environmental pressures – such as customer requests, supplier requirements and anticipating competition; however, it did not explain

Table 3. (*Continued*)

Author (Year Published)	Research Method	Independent Variables	Results	Comments
		industry characteristics and web investment.		the effects of other technological, organisational and environmental factors on ICT use or subsequent firm performance.
Jehangir and Downe (2011) *Activity analysed:* Business performance	Quantitative survey. Linear regression was used with a data set of 243 Malaysian manufacturing firms.	*Business performance:* IT infrastructure IT human resources E-commerce capability	E-commerce capability: IT infrastructure IT human resources Business performance: E-commerce	IT infrastructure and IT human resources can create e-commerce capability which finally affects business performance.
Konings and Roodhooft (2002) *Activity analysed:* E-business effect on firm productivity and cost efficiency	Quantitative survey. The final sample included 836 firms. The survey was a postal survey in which survey instruments were sent to 5,718 firms.	IT infrastructure IT human resources E-commerce	Use of e-business was substantially higher among large firms than in small firms which however varied in different industries. Large firms engaged in e-business have higher total factor productivity than large firms that are not. E-business has no effect on factor productivity of small firms.	E-business contributed positively to the productivity, that is the performance of the firm.
Oliveira and Martins (2010) *Activity analysed:* E-business adoption by European firms	Quantitative survey. The final sample included 6,694 firms belonging to the EU27 members, excluding Malta and Bulgaria. Computer-aided telephone interview (CATI) technology was used with	The research model included: Technology readiness Firm size Expected benefits and barriers of e-business Improved products or services or internal processes Internet penetration Competitive pressure	Firms with high levels of TOE factors also had an enhanced level of e-business. High levels of competitive pressure led to high levels of e-business adoption. Industry-specific characteristics, not	The TOE framework, in general, is applicable to the study of European firms' e-business adoption. Competitive pressures and industry-specific characteristics are related to high levels of e-business adoption.

	the randomly selected samples. Factor analysis and cluster analysis were conducted for estimates.	Industry	country-specific characteristics, better explained e-business adoption.
Powell and Dent-Micallef (1997) *Activity analysed:* IT and firm performance	Empirical study Quantitative survey	Human resources Business resources Technology resources *Dependent variable* IT performance Overall performance Profitability Sales growth	The findings showed that IT alone did not produce sustainable performance advantages in the retail industry, but some firms gained advantages by using IT to leverage intangible, complementary human and business resources such as flexible culture, strategic planning—IT integration, and supplier relationships. The results also helped to explain why some firms outperform others using the same IT, and why successful IT users often fail to sustain IT-based competitive advantages. Human complementary resources accounted for significant overall performance variance – with the human resources set yielding a large positive coefficient for all performance measures. Technology resources did not account for any significant firm performance variance: they only influenced IT performance.
Gupta et al. (2008) *Activity analysed:* ICT adoption in a government organisation in a developing country	Quantitative survey Data were collected from 102 employees of a government organisation in India. PLS-based SEM was employed for data analysis.	*Intention* Performance expectancy Effort expectancy Social influence *Usage* Facilitating condition Behavioural intention	This framework can be used to look into the technology diffusion phenomena in other organisations (government or private) from a developing country perspective. An interesting outcome of this study was that the intention variable was not relevant in contexts where The study found that *performance expectancy, effort expectancy* and *social influence* were significantly associated with intention to use ICT while *facilitating condition* was found to have a significant positive effect on ICT-use behaviour.

Table 3. *(Continued)*

Author (Year Published)	Research Method	Independent Variables	Results	Comments
			The study did not find any significant relationship between behavioural intention and actual Internet usage. Intention to use is relevant in situations where the technology is new and the users have not used it which was not the case here.	the technology was already being used. The finding may suggest possible changes to the existing theoretical frameworks; thus, it should be re-examined in different contexts.
Venkatesh and Zhang (2010) *Activity analysed:* Use of IT at organisational level in USA and China	Quantitative survey A longitudinal survey was conducted of the employees in an organisation which operated in USA and China. In all, 300 employees were surveyed in each country from one business unit. PLS-based SEM was used as the analytical tool.	*Intention* Performance expectancy Effort expectancy Social influence *Usage* Facilitating condition Behavioural intention Gender, age, experience and voluntariness of use were included as moderators in various relationships.	*Intention* Performance expectancy Gender and age positively moderate the effects of performance expectancy, while the interaction of gender, age and experience negatively moderates effort expectancy (for both countries); however, the interaction of gender, age, voluntariness and experience on social influence has a negative effect in the United States. *Usage* Behavioural intention Interaction of age and experience positively affects facilitating condition in both countries.	The framework which included performance expectancy, effort expectancy, social influence, behavioural intention and facilitating condition, is worth working with in different countries. Although this framework provided an illustration of the factors influencing ICT usage behaviour in a developed as well as in a developing country, it did not indicate whether the use of technology could generate organisational performance. Importantly, the study indicated that PLS-based structural equation

| Venkatesh et al. (2008)
Activity analysed:
Use of new information systems | Quantitative survey
In all, 321 users of new information systems were surveyed in a longitudinal field study. | *Behavioural expectation*
Behavioural intention
Facilitating condition
Usage
Behavioural intention
Behavioural expectation
Facilitating condition
Gender, age and experience were used as moderators in various situations. | Behavioural intention and behavioural expectation played significant roles only in direct effects analysis while behavioural expectation emerged as the only significant factor in direct and interaction effects analysis for frequency and intensity of use; however, behavioural intention affected the duration of use. | modelling (SEM) was efficient in analysing the usage of IT.
Behavioural expectation emerged as a strong indicator for predicting the system usage behaviour addressing some of the key limitations of behavioural intention and facilitating condition and providing a better understanding of systems use.
Behavioural expectation could be included as a new construct to study IT usage behaviour. |
| Thong (1999)
Activity analysed:
Adoption of information systems (IS) in small businesses | Quantitative survey
Data analysis was carried out with a data set of 166 small businesses.
To collect data, a mail order survey was conducted with 1,200 small businesses in Singapore: while 294 responses were returned, only 166 were complete responses. | Decision-maker characteristics included innovativeness and IS knowledge.
IS characteristics included relative advantage, compatibility and complexity.
Organisational characteristics included business size, employees' IS knowledge and information intensity.
Environmental characteristics particularly included competition. | CEO innovativeness and IS knowledge, relative advantage and compatibility, complexity, business size and employees' IS knowledge were significantly related to the likelihood of IS adoption while business size, employees' IS knowledge and information intensity played a significant role in explaining the extent of IS adoption. | PLS-based structural equation modelling (SEM) was functional in the analysis of IS usage behaviour.
CEO innovativeness and knowledge, relative advantage/compatibility, business size and employees' knowledge (skilled human resources) emerged as key constructs for examining the likelihood of IS adoption by small firms.
Although CEO innovativeness and environmental pressures were not observed as significant in |

Table 3. (*Continued*)

Author (Year Published)	Research Method	Independent Variables	Results	Comments
				explaining the extent of information about IS, these factors should be looked into in different contexts.
Yap, Soh, and Raman (1992) *Activity analysed:* Success of computer-based information systems (CBIS) in small businesses	Quantitative survey Data analysis was carried out with a data set of 96 small businesses in Singapore.	Consultant effectiveness Vendor support CBIS experience Financial resources CEO support Level of user participation Number of administrative applications Presence of systems analyst	Consultant effectiveness Vendor support CBIS experience Financial resources CEO support Level of user participation	The study confirmed the significant effect of consultant effectiveness, vendor support, CBIS experience, financial resources, CEO support and level of user participation on CBIS success while administrative applications and the presence of a systems analyst had no significant effects.
Thong and Yap (1995) *Activity analysed:* IT adoption in small businesses	Quantitative survey Data analysis was carried out with a data set of 166 small businesses	Individual characteristics included CEO innovativeness, CEO attitude towards adoption of IT and CEO IT knowledge. Organisational characteristics included business size, competitiveness of environment and information intensity.	CEO characteristics Business size	With business size, CEO characteristics played a significant role in IT adoption by small businesses. Clearly, small businesses were more likely to adopt IT if CEOs were more innovative, had a positive attitude towards the adoption of IT, and had greater IT knowledge.
Kendall et al. (2001) *Activity analysed:*	Quantitative survey	Perceived innovation characteristics included	Relative advantage Compatibility	Relative advantage, compatibility and

E-commerce adoption by SMEs in Singapore	Data analysis was carried out with a data set of 58 SMEs in Singapore.	relative advantage, compatibility, complexity, trialability and observability	Trialability	trialability played significant roles in the adoption of e-commerce by Singaporean SMEs while complexity and observability were not found to have any significant effect.
Teo et al. (2003) *Activity analysed:* Adoption intention of financial electronic data interchange (EDI)	Quantitative survey Data analysis was carried out with a data set of 492 individuals from 222 non-adopting organisations in Singapore.	Coercive pressures Mimetic pressures Normative pressures	Coercive pressures Mimetic pressures Normative pressures	Adoption of interorganisational systems was largely influenced by the environmental pressures arising from institutional environments.
Dada (2006) *Activity analysed:* Group support systems (GSS) in two developing countries – Tanzania and South Africa	Case study The study modified the framework of Molla and Licker (2005) reflecting the notion of the UTAUT framework (Venkatesh et al., 2003).	*Initial adoption and institutionalisation:* Organisational factors (factors leading to usage behaviour from UTAUT framework) Environmental factors (e-readiness measure)	The study found that organisational factors were influential in the adoption and institutionalisation of GSS while country-level factors did not have any influence on the intention and likelihood of using GSS.	The results may be used as validation of UTAUT factors particularly perceived effort expectancy and performance expectancy, facilitating condition and subjective norms. The study, however, was important as it looked at the effects of country-level e-readiness, finally nullifying its effect which should be further looked into with a quantitative survey.
Marques et al. (2011) *Activity analysed:* Adoption of medical record system	Quantitative survey The study analysed the data set comprising 448 hospitals in Europe (data source: e-Business Watch	Technology (equipment and processes), organisation (size, location, managerial structure, human context (user involvement) and environmental context	Technology readiness, country wealth and education level were significantly associated with medical record systems adoption in European hospitals.	Country-level factors such as country wealth (GDP per inhabitant, % of households connected to the Internet, total spending on R&D as a % of GDP)

Table 3. (*Continued*)

Author (Year Published)	Research Method	Independent Variables	Results	Comments
	2006 decision-maker survey). The study added environmental aspects into the human, organisation and technology fit (HOT-fit) framework and built a new framework which it called the HOTE (human, organisation, technology and environment) framework.	(cultural environment of the country and regulatory influence) Three factors (country wealth, competition and technology readiness) were finally explored through principal component analysis.		emerged as antecedents for the adoption of a new information system. The study was conducted in the context of Europe; thus, it is not sure how this variable would behave in other countries particularly in developing countries.
Erumban and Jong (2006) *Activity analysed:* ICT adoption rate	Secondary sources of data were used. This study used data about cultural differences across countries based on Hofstede's dimensions. The proportion of ICT expenditure across 42 countries and per capita computers across 49 countries (from 1991 to 2001) were used to establish the ICT adoption rate. The study used ICT expenditure and per capita computer data for those countries for which the corresponding Hofstede indices were available.	Power distance Uncertainty avoidance Individualism Masculinity Long-term orientation Country dummy Education	*Without country dummy and education:* Uncertainty avoidance Individualism *With country dummy:* Power distance Uncertainty avoidance Masculinity Country dummy Education	The results of the study suggested that ICT adoption rate in a country was closely related to its national culture. The study revealed that power distance and uncertainty avoidance were the most important dimensions explaining ICT adoption rate in a country.

Study / Activity analysed	Methodology	Factors / Variables	Findings	Conclusions
Gibbs and Kraemer (2004) *Activity analysed:* Scope of usage of e-commerce	Quantitative survey Data collected from 2,139 establishments from three industries across 10 countries	External pressure Perceived benefits Government promotion Org. compatibility Legislation barriers Technology resources Financial resources Size Industry and country dummy *Organisational* IT sophistication; Top management support; Firm size	The study found significant effects of perceived benefits, external pressure, government policy, legislation barriers, technology resources, financial resources and all country dummies, except for Denmark, on the range of e-commerce usage.	The study confirmed the importance of strategic benefits, external pressure, technology and financial resources, and policy environment on the range of e-commerce use. US firms enjoyed significantly higher range of use than firms from other countries which also confirmed the significant country effects on the range of e-commerce use.
Thatcher et al. (2006) *Activity analysed:* Adoption of e-commerce systems in electronics and textile industries	The study adopted both qualitative and interpretive methodology. The four phases of the methodology were data collection, data reduction, data display and drawing conclusions.	*Industry* Importance of responsiveness; Importance of cost cutting; Multinational companies; Trend-setting companies *Government* Policies promoting B2B (business to business); Subsidies promoting B2B *Culture* Power distance; Uncertainty avoidance; Individualism versus collectivism; Masculinity versus femininity; Time orientation; High context versus low context	All factors under organisational, industry, government and culture were significantly associated with B2B adoption in the Taiwanese electronics industry. However, the effects varied with the adoption of B2B e-commerce in the textile industry. More specifically, IT sophistication, importance of responsiveness and government subsidy promoting ICT had positive effects: firm size and being a trend-setting company had no effects while all other factors were negatively associated.	This study confirmed that cultural dimensions were associated with the adoption of B2B e-commerce in both Taiwanese electronics and textile industries. Interestingly, the effects were positive in the electronics industry while the cultural dimensions were negatively related to B2B e-commerce adoption in the textile industry.

research gap between the perspectives of developed and developing countries on ICT diffusion behaviour. The applicability of existing diffusion theories to developing countries is also not clear. Contemporary researchers who wish to learn about the diffusion of an innovation from a holistic approach seek to analyse the important aspects of the ICT diffusion phenomena under an integrated and comprehensive model.

Previous studies have analysed various issues of the diffusion of an innovation by applying a wide range of theoretical frameworks. Most of them have investigated one aspect at a time of the contextual and environmental factors with the view of avoiding analytical complexity by creating a parsimonious research model. It is known that the inclusion of a large number of important and relevant variables improves the goodness of model fit and enhances the variation of the model explained. It is not unlikely that variables (endogenous or exogenous) have different effects in different contexts as well as with the number of different variables included in the model.

The literature review (see Table 3) and discussion in Sections 2.5 and 2.6 have built the foundation of an integrated and comprehensive research model. The primary model based on the literature review is presented in Fig. 1.

2.5. Antecedents of ICT Use

2.5.1. Cognitive Evaluation and Owner Innovativeness

Beliefs, evaluations, intention and actual behaviours are modelled in the TRA with SNs. Fishbein and Ajzen (1975) suggested that an overall affective evaluation, that is, one's beliefs (cognitive) towards performing a behaviour, and the respective evaluations (affective) heavily influence an individual's intention of performing the behaviour. The evaluation is made based on one's cognitive evaluation of the consequences of that behaviour (Ajzen & Fishbein, 1980; Sheppard, Hartwick, & Warshaw, 1988). The evaluation process involves functional consequences, that is, outcomes which are immediate, direct and tangible, as well as psychological consequences, that is, the consequences are internal, personal and abstract in nature. These cognitive and affective evaluations form one's attitude, that is, negative or positive feelings about performing a behaviour with this having been widely researched in the consumer, marketing and IS literature (Ajzen, 1985; Cho, 2004; Fishbein & Ajzen, 1975; Gehrt & Carter, 1992; Liao & Cheung, 2001; Mehta & Sivadas, 1995). Prior studies have shown the significant effect of attitude, that is, cognitive evaluation towards intention (Chang, 1998; Davis et al., 1989; George, 2002, 2004; Lu et al., 2003;

Mathieson, 1991; Ramayah et al., 2003, 2004, 2005, 2007; Rhodes & Courneya, 2003; Shih & Fang, 2004; Taylor & Todd, 1995a).

Personal characteristics play a significant role in individual decision-making or choice behaviour. Individuals affiliated with different demographic groups show different brand preferences. For example, variations in product preference and choice behaviour appear in educated versus non-educated, rich versus poor, urban versus rural and between individuals affiliated with different professional positions. Individuals are variously classified according to their receptivity and adoption of an innovation. Rogers (1995) categorised five different types of adopters according to the time of adoption as innovators, early adopters, early majority, late majority and laggards (Weber & Kauffman, 2011). Innovators are adopters who are innovative in nature and who are prepared to bear the risks associated with the early adoption of an innovation. The adoption of an innovation in a small firm is highly influenced by the personal characteristics and preferences of the owner or CEO with most small businesses being managed by the owner who also acts as the CEO (Solomon, 1986; Steinhoff & Burgess, 1986; Yap et al., 1992). Thus, innovative SME owners adopt innovation at the early stage. Prior studies have shown that the innovativeness of the CEO or owner of an SME significantly affects the adoption (Thong, 1999; Thong & Yap, 1995) and the implementation of IS (Thong, 1999).

2.5.2. BI and Behavioural Expectation

Intention is one of the strong predictors of the adoption of an innovation. From the earliest theories of adoption-diffusion, intention has been used to address the adoption of innovation. The TRA predicts intention as a function of attitude towards behaviour and SNs (Fishbein & Ajzen, 1975). The intention is measured through the function of five innovation characteristics, namely, relative advantage, perceived compatibility, perceived complexity, perceived trialability and perceived observability in the DOI model (Rogers, 1983). Perceived risk (Davila, Gupta, & Palmer, 2002; Lim & Speece, 2002; Tan & Teo, 2000) and adopters' characteristics (Rogers, 1983; Thong & Yap, 1995) are also correlated with intention. Again, perceived behavioural control has a direct correlation with BI (Ajzen, 1985). Intention has also been elaborately presented as the function of attitude towards behaviour and SNs while attitude towards behaviour is analysed as a function of perceived ease of use and perceived usefulness (Davis, 1986).

Despite significant improvements of the past innovation adoption theories from the TRA (Fishbein & Ajzen, 1975) to the TAM (Davis, 1986), some major drawbacks still prevail. Diversified uses of technology, from individual level to different trading situations, have involved some modifications of findings from previous studies in order to adequately address technology adoption-diffusion behaviour. Some new dimensional constructs have therefore been included within the existing theories as is evident in the literature. Venkatesh et al. (2003) proposed some modifications in the existing behavioural theory by having their UTAUT model address performance expectancy, effort expectancy and SNs as antecedents of BI to explain actual IT usage behaviour. Although intention, a reflection of the adopter's internal schema of beliefs, had great influence in earlier behavioural models, it cannot predict the situation when the adopter is not under full volitional control or the situation where a time gap exists between intention and actual behaviour (Venkatesh et al., 2008). However, a stronger predictor of actual behaviour may incorporate some other external (social and environmental) factors which need to be considered in the existing model. Venkatesh et al. (2008) further modified their UTAUT model (Venkatesh et al., 2003) and included behavioural expectation as a new construct which is a stronger predictor of behaviour than BI. Taking into consideration the scope and limitations of various previous theories, this study has included behavioural expectation as a possible predictor of actual ICT use.

2.5.3. Facilitating Condition and Country Readiness
The studies utilising the traditional RBV have proposed that if firms can combine IT-related resources to create a unique IT capability, this can result in superior firm performance (Bharadwaj, 2000; Ravichandran & Lertwongsatien, 2005). IT capability is addressed as the facilitating condition in ICT diffusion studies (Venkatesh et al., 2008). The facilitating condition is defined as individuals' perceptions of the availability of technological and/or organisational resources (i.e. knowledge, resources and opportunities) that can remove barriers to using a system (Venkatesh et al., 2003). Thus, network connectivity, Internet speed, computer hardware resources, software and skilled manpower produce favourable facilitating conditions which foster the use of ICT. This phenomenon is also evident in the previous classical behavioural theory as behavioural control in the TPB (Ajzen, 1985, 1991) and self-efficacy in SCT (Bandura, 1986).

The organisational ICT RBV and facilitating condition need to be stated differently as, although the organisation may have enough resources, this does not necessarily mean that these resources facilitate the achievement of better performance. The facilitating condition's effect on behavioural expectation and ICT use is not limited only to organisational resources.

The TOE framework (Tornatzky & Fleischer, 1990) includes environmental factors with technological and organisational factors for studying the adoption of ICT at firm level. Previous studies have considered various aspects of external environmental factors, such as institutional environmental concerns (Oliveira & Martins, 2010; Teo et al., 2003); country infrastructure and governance concern (Gibbs & Kraemer, 2004; Marques et al., 2011; Xu, Zhu, & Gibbs, 2004; Zhang, Cui, Huang, & Zhang, 2007; Zhu, Kraemer, et al., 2006) and cultural concerns (Burn, 1995; Erumban & Jong, 2006; Gefen & Straub, 1997; Straub, 1994; Thatcher et al., 2006).

The effects of country infrastructure, governance-related external factors and organisational facilitating conditions are alike. In reality, these aspects are related to country readiness (Marques et al., 2011) in the facilitation of ICT diffusion at individual, organisational and government level. The availability and geographical coverage of the Internet, speed and price of Internet service, ICT resources (hardware and software), regulatory framework, market conditions, delivery systems, government policy and support have direct effects on ICT adoption. The condition of the favourableness or unfavourableness of the infrastructural factors accelerates or inhibits ICT use at firm level. Thus, this phenomenon (country readiness) should be considered as a new aspect of the facilitating condition which is different to the facilitating condition (Venkatesh et al., 2008; Venkatesh & Zhang, 2010) explained in previous studies. This study thus considers both of these aspects which are logically added as separate predictors of behavioural expectation as the facilitating condition (firm-level resources) and country readiness (national level infrastructure and governance).

2.5.4. Culture and Environmental Pressure

Culture is a broad spectrum of behavioural study which has been defined differently in different studies in the literature. In the broadest sense, culture may be defined as the sum total of shared learned beliefs, values, norms and customs which guide individual or group behaviour in a society. Hofstede (2001) treated culture as the collective programming of the mind that distinguishes the members of one group or category of people from another. Although the effects of culture on leadership and organisational processes as well as on individual behaviour have been explored in many studies (House et al., 2004), its effects when studied in ICT adoption research are inconclusive.

The importance of culture in determining individual innovativeness relative to various personal and perceptual factors during adoption of an innovative or new product is a vital research issue. This aspect of cultural study is also neglected in consumer research. Parker and Sarvary (1996) suggest that culture has no significant impact on innovativeness at the individual level.

There is controversy about the role of culture in the use and adoption of IT. Some researchers favour the view that organisations adopt technology that is useful and provides them with some economic benefit with culture having no significant role. However, other researchers hold the alternative view that culture plays an important role in determining not only whether organisations in a particular country adopt a certain technology but it also impacts on the degree to which that technology is accepted and the ways in which it is used (Thatcher et al., 2006).

Although they are limited in number, some previous studies have reported a significant link between cultural dimensions and different facets of IT use (Bertolotti, 1984; Burn, 1995; Erez & Early, 1993; Gefen & Straub, 1997; Harris & Davison, 1999; Hill, Loch, Straub, & El-Sheshai, 1998; Ho, Raman, & Watson, 1989; Straub, 1994). Erumban and Jong (2006) found that the national culture and the ICT adoption rate of a country are closely related. They further reported that most of Hofstede's dimensions are important in influencing adoption with power distance and uncertainty avoidance dimensions seeming to be the most influential. Thatcher et al. (2006) supported this outcome in ICT adoption, particularly B2B e-commerce adoption, in the Taiwanese electronics industry context.

Organisations that operate within a cultural setting are believed to be influenced by the shared learned beliefs, values, norms and customs of the specific culture. Similar to national culture, organisational culture has been defined as the collective programming of the mind that distinguishes the members of one organisation from those of another.

In the 'Global Leadership and Organisational Behaviour Effectiveness' (GLOBE) study (House et al., 2004), culture has been examined in two ways: as the way of carrying out behaviour (practice) and the way through which behaviour should be carried out (values). House et al. (2004) used nine different cultural dimensions to study the effects of the national culture on the organisation and its leadership, namely, power distance, uncertainty avoidance, in-group collectivism, institutional collectivism, humane orientation, assertiveness, gender egalitarianism, future orientation and performance orientation. On the other hand, Hofstede (1984) used five dimensions to study culture, namely, power distance, individualism versus collectivism, masculinity versus femininity, uncertainty avoidance and long-term versus short-term orientation. Although House et al. (2004) have defined culture by further elaboration of Hofstede's (1984) concepts, both theoretical frameworks have been used in multidisciplinary fields of study when addressing culture.

After reviewing Hofstede's (1984) concepts and House et al.'s (2004) dimensions as well as the context of Bangladesh, the following dimensions have been included in the proposed research model: power distance (refers to the inequality of the distribution of power in a country); in-group collectivism (the degree to which individuals express pride, loyalty and cohesiveness in their organisations or families); uncertainty avoidance (the extent to which a society, organisation or group relies on social norms, rules and procedures to alleviate the unpredictability of future events) and gender egalitarianism (the degree to which a collective minimises gender inequality). The measurement items for national culture and organisational culture have been adapted from House et al. (2004).

In addition to country readiness and national culture, the usage of ICT at the firm level may be influenced by some other factors arising from the institutional environment (see Teo et al., 2003).

The impact of these aspects of environmental factors and their characteristics has been well addressed in institutional theory. This needs to be synpapered with the adoption-diffusion theories so as to reach the external variables reflected in Rogers' (1983) DOI theory and the subsequent TOE framework and other innovation diffusion frameworks.

Institutional theories have posited that organisations face pressures to conform to these shared notions of appropriate forms of behaviours, since violating them may call into question the organisation's legitimacy and thus affect its ability to secure resources and social support (DiMaggio & Powell, 1983; Tolbert, 1985).

DiMaggio and Powell (1983) distinguished between three types of isomorphic pressures – coercive, mimetic and normative – and suggested that coercive and normative pressures normally operate through interconnected relationships while mimetic pressures act through structural equivalence.

Ajzen and Fishbein (1980) explored the role of SNs and studied how they affect individual behaviour. SNs, in other words, pressures from friends and family play a vital role in the formation of intention to use an innovation. In organisational aspects, a focal organisation is able to learn about an innovation and its associated benefits and costs from other user organisations that are directly or indirectly tied to it, and is likely to be persuaded to behave similarly (Burt, 1982). Many studies have considered normative pressure as an antecedent of organisational innovation adoption phenomena (Kuan & Chau, 2001; Teo et al., 2003).

Mimetic pressures are the influences of other structurally equivalent organisations that have initiated some innovations and have become successful. This pressure may cause an organisation to change over time to become more like other organisations in its environment (DiMaggio & Powell, 1983). Many past studies have included mimetic pressures in exploring organisational ICT adoption behaviour (Premkumar & Ramamurthy, 1995; Teo et al., 2003).

Coercive pressures address various kinds of powers or influences, informal or formal, exercised by other organisations upon which an organisation is dependent. A dominant customer, supplier or parent organisation sometimes exercises their power or coercively influences the organisation to do a certain thing with the dependent organisation having no option other than to comply with the requirements. Coercive pressures are of great importance when studying the influences on ICT diffusion behaviour (Quaddus & Hofmeyer, 2007; Teo et al., 2003).

2.6. Antecedents of Organisational Performance

2.6.1. ICT Use, Integration and Degree of Utilisation

A large number of empirical studies have predicted IS usage behaviour by applying BI as the final dependent variable. The proposition 'positive intention leads to positive behaviour' has provided the rationale for such studies. Some studies have also examined actual usage as a dependent variable for predicting actual behaviour. Different indicators of systems use, such as duration of use, frequency of use and intensity of use, have been used to reach actual usage behaviour (Venkatesh et al., 2008). Organisational ICT use has also been examined in different stages of assimilation such as *initial adoption* (the firm's initial evaluation of an ICT-based operation at the pre-adoption stage); *adoption* (formal adoption of an ICT-based operation) and *routinisation* (full-scale deployment of ICT at the post-adoption stage in which the ICT-based operation becomes an integral part of the value-chain activities) (Fichman, 2000; Zhu, Kraemer, et al., 2006). Use of ICT has also been applied as the independent variable in examining the impact of ICT on organisational performance (Bharadwaj, 2000; Zhu, Dong, et al., 2006; Zhu & Kraemer, 2005). The results of such studies have revealed that greater ICT usage leads to greater impact on business performance.

Zhu and Kraemer (2005) explored beyond the dichotomous 'adoption versus non-adoption' phenomenon and examined the impact of actual ICT usage on organisational ICT value creation, that is, organisational performance. In analysing 624 firms across 10 countries in the retail industry, their study revealed that front-end capabilities and back-end integration of ICT had significant impact on organisational value creation while the impact of back-end integration appeared stronger than that of front-end functionalities. This outcome was consistent with the RBV as back-end integration may create ICT resources which are firm-specific and difficult to imitate thus providing enhanced firm performance. Integration thus becomes an important dimension of the post-adoption stages of ICT usage behaviour.

Anandarajan et al. (2002) reported that the mere adoption of IT by organisations does not necessarily confer benefits as these would only be achieved by its effective usage. The ICT adoption phenomena in developing countries as well as in less developed countries is assumed to be similar as other studies have shown that many IS in LDCs are under-utilised and hence do not make a significant contribution to improving the performance of the organisations that are using them (Forster & Cornford, 1992; Ordedra et al., 1993). In support of the previous studies, Song and Mueller-Falcke (2006) stated that SMEs are confronted with a number of challenges in adopting and using ICT with the result that they often underutilise the available technologies (see UNCTAD, 2006).

The above discussions reveal that the adoption and post-adoption stages of ICT usage comprise various strategic uses of ICT which start from the initial stage of ICT usage through to the highly integrated ICT-based environment. Proper utilisation of ICT is an important issue for the productive use of ICT in developing countries. The various uses of ICT may be categorised as *ICT usage* (Venkatesh et al., 2008) (depth of use which deals with frequency and intensity of ICT use); *integration* (Powell & Dent-Micallef, 1997) (breadth of ICT use which is related to the strategic use of the technology, that is, to what extent the technology is integrated with the organisational goals, plans and processes) and *utilisation* (how appropriately the ICT is utilised and how much of the facilities of the technology are used in different functional areas in the organisation, that is, frequency of use and its strategic applications), all of which have implications for organisational performance.

2.6.2. Organisational Performance

Defining and measuring business performance has been of interest to researchers for centuries (Pham & Jordan, 2007). Despite the controversy over the business value of computer investments, known as the 'productivity paradox', which still continues even in the face of successful evidence about pay-offs from IT (Brynjolfsson, 1993; Brynjolfsson & Hitt, 1996), numerous studies have found a positive link between IT use and organisational performance (Baldwin & Sabourin, 2001; Cragg, King, & Hussin, 2002; Dvir, Segev, & Shenhar, 1993; Gretton, Gali, & Parham, 2004; Pilat & Wyckoff, 2005). However, the measurement of firm performance is not straightforward. Past researchers have used different conceptualisations to measure business performance. Szymanski, Bharadwaj, and Varadarajan (1993) suggested studying business performance based on market share and profitability while Voss and Voss (2000) viewed performance as the outcome of the company business process.

Organisational performance, an important indicator of economic development, has been conceptualised in different ways in different studies. It can be measured objectively based on historical data (Bharadwaj, 2000; Sanders & Premus, 2005) or measured subjectively based on respondents' perceptions of organisational performance in relation to their expectations and goals, or in comparison with the company's competitors (Powell & Dent-Micallef, 1997; Ravichandran & Lertwongsatien, 2005).

In previous studies, various dimensions of organisational performance have been considered for linkages with ICT such as profit growth, market share, productivity growth, improved performance and the firm's competitiveness. In this study, organisational performance was measured using the subjective approach by evaluating the organisation's performance in different functional areas according to the plans and goals of the organisation that had been previously determined.

2.6.3. Mediation of Integration and Utilisation

Researchers and practitioners involved in studying ICT use and utilisation in the organisational context are interested in discovering the answer to the question of how and to what extent ICT usage is associated with organisational performance. The answer is equally important for the CEOs or owners of organisations that are currently using ICT or that intend to use ICT in different functional areas. The DOI theory contends that the impact of a new technology depends on the extent to which it is used in key value-chain activities. Previous studies have found different results when examining the impact of ICT usage on organisational performance, such as negative effect (Warner, 1987); no effect (Sager, 1988; Venkatraman & Zaheer, 1990); mixed effects (Powell & Dent-Micallef, 1997; Tippins & Sohi, 2003; Wu et al., 2006) and direct positive effects (Bharadwaj, 2000; Clemons & Row, 1991; Clemons & Weber, 1990; Feeny & Ives, 1990; Kettinger, Grover, Guha, & Segars, 1994; Li & Ye, 1999; Schwarzer, 1995). Zhu and Kraemer

(2005) suggested that merely examining the initial adoption might not reveal the variations in IT value, because IT creates business value in sequential stages. They again stated that despite its theoretical importance, usage has been under-studied in empirical research which was therefore their motivation for analysing the linkage between usage and performance impact. Zhu and Kraemer (2005) found a positive link between ICT use (e-commerce) and value creation which was consistent with empirical findings of the importance of usage in different contexts such as electronic data interchange (EDI) (Mukhopadhyay, Kekre, & Kalathur, 1995) and decision support systems (DSSs) (Devaraj & Kohli, 2003). Their findings also complied with the notion that 'without broad and deep use of e-business along the value chain, it would be impossible for e-business to generate any impact on firm performance in terms of sales, procurement, or internal operations' (Zhu & Kraemer, 2005, p. 70). Although not statistically examined, the above-mentioned notion and interpretation of study results – significant positive effects of ICT usage, front-end functionalities and ICT integration into back-office databases on firm performance – imply the mediating roles of ICT integration on firm performance.

Kim, Cavusgil, and Calantone (2006) revealed a mediation role of inter-firm systems integration to explain supply chain communication systems (SCCS) innovation on firm supply chain performance. This current study focuses on studying the effects of ICT innovation on firm performance; thus, it is logically anticipated that ICT integration may have a mediation role to explain the effects of ICT usage on organisational performance.

The degree of utilisation, that is, whether ICT is used properly and effectively is another aspect of ICT use which may also correlate with firm performance. Despite its practical importance for developing countries, this aspect of usage, that is, the appropriate usage of ICT, has been greatly under-studied. Anandarajan et al. (2002) stated that many IS in less developed countries are under-utilised and, thus, do not make a significant contribution to improving the performance of the organisations that have implemented them (Forster & Cornford, 1992; Ordedra et al., 1993). A conceptual linkage between ICT usage, degree of utilisation and organisational performance may be forecast from those statements which imply a mediating role for the degree of utilisation. There is a paucity of research studies that have looked at the inter-relationship of ICT usage, integration, degree of utilisation and organisational performance. This study has anticipated that ICT usage would impact on organisational performance with this impact mediated though integration and the degree of utilisation.

2.7. Preliminary Research Model

Based on the above literature review, a preliminary research model (Fig. 1) has been constructed to attain the research objectives. The model posits that the diffusion process of ICT starts with SMEs' intention to adopt the technology. The BI is largely influenced by the characteristics of the owner as Rogers (1983) stated that adoption of an innovation is a decision process in which an innovation passes through different states of adoption and is finally implemented or has its use confirmed. He further stated that the adoption starts from the knowledge stage where the adopter is first exposed to an innovation and passes through the persuasion, decision and confirmation stages. A variety of variables play different roles in various stages of an innovation adoption. Rogers (1983) affirmed that the personal characteristics of an adopter — such as demographics, income, risk-taking behaviour, innovativeness — largely influence the knowledge stage which is very important for early adopters.

'Cognitive evaluation' towards an innovation is an important factor which influences BI. The TRA (Fishbein & Ajzen, 1975) and the TPB (Ajzen, 1985) explain the influence of cognitive evaluation on BI.

Environmental pressures that have arisen from the institutional environment are believed to have a positive influence on BI. The TRA (Fishbein & Ajzen, 1975) and TPB (Ajzen, 1985) explain these influences as SNs with this also supported by a number of ensuing theoretical frameworks (such as UTAUT, Venkatesh et al., 2003). These theories focus on the individual adoption process thus the influence of family, friends and peer groups become significant. The organisational adoption behaviour is also

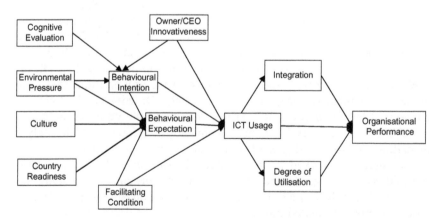

Fig. 1.   Primary Research Model Based on Literature Review.

influenced by similar variables which arise from the influence of close associates of the firms, partners and peer organisational groups. These phenomena have been addressed as environmental pressures (DiMaggio & Powell, 1983; Kuan & Chau, 2001; Teo et al., 2003) and have a significant effect on organisational adoption intention (Teo et al., 2003).

Venkatesh et al. (2008) explained BI as an important variable in the innovation diffusion process. They distinguished between intention and expectation stating that intention is a reflection of the adopter's internal schema of beliefs; thus, it cannot predict the situation which is not under the adopter's full volitional control. Furthermore, intention may also fail to adequately explain the situation where a time gap exists between intention and actual behaviour. Behavioural expectation is anticipated as a stronger predictor of actual behaviour (in comparison to intention) which may incorporate the influences of external variables arising from the socio-cultural environment. Venkatesh et al. (2008) also posited that behavioural expectation is highly influenced by BI, culture, country readiness and facilitating factors (or conditions).

As illustrated in Fig. 1, the preliminary model shows that behavioural expectation plays a significant role in predicting ICT use. The model incorporates two aspects of ICT usage behaviour. The depth of ICT usage, that is, the frequency or intensity of use, is indicated as ICT usage while the breadth of ICT use involves strategic uses of ICT. The breadth of ICT use is further categorised into two strategic variables, namely, integration which indicates the extent to which ICT is integrated into various functional areas, and utilisation which indicates how appropriately ICT is used in the organisation. Organisational performance is explained by the impact of ICT usage, integration and the degree of utilisation. The primary model also anticipates a mediating role for integration and utilisation to explain the impact of ICT usage on organisational performance.

2.8. Summary

This section has presented the literature review which addressed various aspects of the research. The conceptual grounding of the study has been postulated through reviews of relevant theories such as the DOI theory, TRA, TPB, TAM, UTAUT, institutional theory and the RBV. Relying on the structure developed by analysing existing theoretical frameworks, this section also reviewed relevant contemporary empirical studies. Finally, a preliminary research model was constructed (which was later fine-tuned and contextualised by a field study) to attain the research objectives.

3. RESEARCH METHODOLOGY

3.1. Introduction

This section presents the research design, research methods, and analytical tools and techniques employed to attain the objectives of the study. The study employed a mixed-method research approach which involved an exploratory qualitative field study followed by a comprehensive quantitative survey. The following sections discuss the entire research methodology employed in the study which includes the research paradigm, the qualitative field study design − process of transcription and qualitative interview analysis − and quantitative research design − survey instrument design, data collection, data screening, data validation and data analysis.

3.2. Research Paradigm

A paradigm is a set of assumptions or beliefs that provides a conceptual framework which, in turn, guides us in looking at and interpreting the world around us (Suppe, 1977; cited in Deshpande, 1983). Guba and Lincoln (1994) considered a paradigm to be a set of basic beliefs (or metaphysics) that deals with first principles through which the nature of the world, the individual's place in it, and the range of possible relationships to the world and its component parts are defined. In reality, a paradigm comprises the principles or philosophies which guide a person, a professional or a researcher in selecting challenging issues, developing models and theories, establishing criteria for methodology, instrument design and data collection, and also providing principles, procedures and methods appropriate for looking at similar phenomena (Filstead, 1979; cited in Deshpande, 1983). Based on the epistemological, ontological, procedural and methodological concerns, several paradigms or dichotomies have shaped research approaches in the fields of behavioural studies, business, IS and social sciences, such as positivism versus interpretivism, quantitative versus qualitative, induction versus deduction and exploratory versus confirmatory (Fitzgerald & Howcroft, 1998).

In general, two broad scientific paradigms, namely, the positivist and interpretivist research paradigms, have guided most research in business, behavioural studies, social sciences and IS (Hudson & Ozanne, 1988; Marsden & Littler, 1996). However, Myers and Klein (2011) emphasise critical research as an emerging stream in IS research and support Orlikowski and Baroudi's (1991) classification of research paradigm. Orlikowski and Baroudi (1991) suggest three research paradigms: positivist, interpretive and critical.[11] The recent IS literature is broadly guided by these philosophies.

The positivist research paradigm attempts to apply the methods and principles of the natural science model to explain behaviour or phenomena through causal relationships while the interpretivist approach attempts to interpret the inter-subjective meanings where a phenomenon is explained through multiple explanations or realities rather than by one causal relationship or one theory (Creswell, 2003; Denzin & Lincoln, 1994; Neuman, 2006). In critical research, a critical stance is taken towards taken-for-granted assumptions about organisations and IS, and where the aim is to critique to status quo 'through the exposure of what are believed to be deep-seated, structural contradictions within social systems' (Myers & Klein, 2011, p. 19).

Although a mixed-method approach was undertaken, especially during the field study based on which the initial research model was examined and fine-tuned, this study is primarily guided by the positivist research paradigm by administering extensive use of quantitative methods to objectively measure the variables and determine the causal relationships among the constructs under study.

3.3. Research Method

The positivist and interpretivist paradigms have been supported by numerous researchers in their separate explorations of reality. As the positivist paradigm depends on the methods and principles of natural science, it has no flexibility when it comes to interpreting phenomena from multiple realities which is, in fact, what the interpretivist research paradigm employs. In reality, the interpretation or analyses of various situations, events and phenomena in business, social sciences or behavioural sciences are not always straightforward when it comes to employing the principles of natural science in a single reality. On the other hand, the interpretivist paradigm has the flexibility to look at the event from multiple realities and can find the source of the problem while it does have a limitation regarding the generalisability of the results. Although both paradigms have their strengths and are successfully utilised in multidisciplinary fields of study, such as marketing, IS, organisational theory, social sciences and behavioural science, in fact, each method, either qualitative or quantitative, has its own limitations (Greene, Caracelli, & Graham, 1989). A single-method study could lead to inaccurate and inadequate results.

Thus, a combination of the two paradigms, the mixed-method approach, has been proposed as a third paradigm view based on pragmatism

(Tashakkori & Teddlie, 1998). A combination of qualitative and quantitative approaches within different phases of the research process is employed under this research paradigm. The mixed-method research approach is developed based on the notion that the combination of qualitative and quantitative methods would compensate for their mutual and overlapping weaknesses (Greene et al., 1989) as well as providing cohesive and coherent outcomes (Hohental, 2006).

Although purely qualitative researchers are not receptive to the idea of implementing a combination of two research-guiding philosophies in an integrated platform, a growing body of researchers are employing the mixed-method research approach in the field of IS and marketing.

In order to receive more insights from a mixed-method research approach, different types of research design are employed that may be classified as the triangulation design, the embedded design, the explanatory design and the exploratory design (Creswell, 2003). The triangulation design refers to the collection and comparison of the data from both qualitative and quantitative methods with the view to validate or expand the quantitative estimates using the qualitative data. The embedded design suggests the collection of both qualitative and quantitative data while either of the data types plays a supplementary role within the overall design. The explanatory design leads to the collection and analysis of quantitative data followed by the subsequent collection and analysis of qualitative data. Unlike the explanatory design, the exploratory design starts with qualitative data to explore a phenomenon and then estimates quantitative data.

In determining the appropriate mixed method for the current research, it was essential to again reflect upon the objectives. As discussed in Section 1 (see Section 1.3), the main aim of this research was to explore the internal and external factors that affect SMEs' intention and actual usage of ICT and its resultant outcome in terms of organisational performance. The study, in its design, required the synpaper of various theories of innovation diffusion and the creation of a link with the theories and conceptual frameworks from different fields, such as, resource-based theory, institutional theory and cultural study (Hofstede, 1984; House et al., 2004).

Based on previous theoretical frameworks and empirical studies, the initial model (see Fig. 1 in Section 2) was proposed. The model needed to be tested in terms of its applicability and validity to provide sufficient comprehensiveness to explain such behaviour. Thus, a field study through semi-structured interviews was employed. Finally, a survey was carried out to test the comprehensive model to ensure its generalisability and improve its explanatory power (the details of the process are in the next section). Based on the description of the process and the research objectives, a triangulation design was employed. This design allowed the data from both qualitative and quantitative methods to be compared and merged during the analysis to increase the reliability and validity of the research. Furthermore, triangulation has been acknowledged as the most common mixed-method approach (Creswell, 2003).

3.4. Research Process

This study investigated the factors that affect SMEs' intention to use and their actual usage of ICT and also examined how the different levels of ICT application can influence organisational performance. This study employed a mixed-method research approach which involved qualitative and quantitative methodologies. Moreover, the study executed different tasks in different phases to conclude the research: these are discussed in the following sections.

3.4.1. Step 1: Literature Review
The first phase of the study employed an extensive review of the literature related to the theories of innovation diffusion such as the TRA, TPB, DOI theory and the TAM. Since the study was related to SMEs, the theories related to organisational technology diffusion were also reviewed. Thus, the TOE framework and institutional theory have been reviewed. The RBV was reviewed within the proposed framework when looking at the contribution of organisational ICT usage to organisational performance. The study also examined the effects of culture and environmental pressures on the diffusion of ICT by SMEs in Bangladesh. Thus, contemporary cultural studies – such as Hofstede (1984) and House et al. (2004) (GLOBE study) – were reviewed. Most recent related studies, namely, Venkatesh et al. (2003, 2008), have been duly inspected to develop a conceptual framework for the study. The cross-evaluation of relevant theories has resulted in the discovery of some strong points in each theory which could contribute to conceptualising the key constructs of BI, actual usage of ICT and organisational performance. In addition to the theories and conceptual studies, a good number of contemporary empirical studies were also reviewed to augment the theoretical model in terms of its scope and meaning and to establish the inter-relationship between the constructs.

3.4.2. Step 2: Preliminary Research Model
The systematic and rigorous literature review, both of the theories and empirical studies, resulted in the development of a comprehensive model

for examining the effects of different variables and their interrelationships. A theoretically grounded, comprehensive initial research model was developed which gathered together the potential constructs within the domain of the study (see Fig. 1 in Section 2).

3.4.3. Step 3: Qualitative Field Study

The initial model developed through the literature review could be suitable for adequately explaining ICT diffusion by SMEs in Bangladesh, measuring organisational performance and exploring the appropriate antecedents of performance. The model was then evaluated for its consistency and suitability within the context and for its adequacy in explaining issues according to the study's objectives. Next, a field study was conducted by interviewing 11 owners or decision-makers of SMEs who were selected through a convenience sampling technique.

The objectives of the interview were to: (1) seek out and identify concepts and procedures that might not be reported or recognised in the literature review, and (2) evaluate the worthiness of the concepts identified in the literature review. Each of the interviews was recorded and later transcribed by the researcher with the view of transforming it into text. Each of the transcripts was analysed by NVivo 10.

3.4.4. Step 4: Model Refinement

The preliminary model was refined based on the exhaustive related literature review as well as the findings from the field study. Where necessary, the model was augmented with new items and/or constructs, or simplified at that stage through elimination of duplicate constructs and items. The primary model was refined, fine-tuned and finalised through this process.

3.4.5. Step 5: Hypotheses Construction

Basing on the refined model, a number of hypotheses were constructed at this stage with these hypotheses also supported by prior theories and relevant research. The resource-based theory (RBT) and institutional theory were used together with innovation diffusion theories to guide the development of the hypotheses.

3.4.6. Step 6: Questionnaire Design

Based on the hypotheses developed in the previous stage, a tentative questionnaire was designed. Each of the questions was used as a source of data and was adapted from previous relevant research with slight modifications to adjust to the context and to ensure clarity in expression for the interviewees. Some new measurements were also developed through the qualitative field study with these later supported by relevant literature. A total of 84 items and 16 constructs were included in the questionnaire to investigate the research problems. The questionnaire was validated through pre-testing and a pilot survey before conducting the countrywide main survey in Bangladesh.

3.4.7. Step 7: Pre-testing of the Questionnaire

As mentioned in the previous stage, the questionnaire was pre-tested to ensure that it was ready for wide circulation for the final data collection. ICT experts, owners of SMEs or their representatives, and some academics were invited to pre-test the questionnaire. The objective of pre-testing was to contextualise the instruments and also to ensure reliability of the questions. During the questionnaire pre-testing phase, different professionals and experts scrutinised the questionnaire from different perspectives and provided their feedback which enhanced the content validity of the questionnaire.

3.4.8. Step 8: Questionnaire Refinement

The questionnaire was modified in accordance with feedback received from the expert respondents during pre-testing. The tentative instruments were refined through a careful revision of the questionnaire. The changes, adjustments and modifications adopted during this stage resulted in the final questionnaire for the study.

3.4.9. Step 9: Data Collection

The main data collection process entailed distributing the final structured questionnaires to the owners or decision-makers of different SMEs in Bangladesh seeking their responses. In Bangladesh, SMEs are divided into two classes, namely, the manufacturing industry and the services industry. In considering the nature of businesses and their potential to contribute to the national economy, the manufacturing industry in Bangladesh and, particularly, the RMG industry was considered as the subject of this study due to its high potential in terms of its contribution to the GDP, employment generation and export earnings. A total of 300 SMEs were targeted for data collection: they were selected through a stratified random sampling from a list of companies developed by using the databases of Bangladesh Garment Manufacturers and Exporters Association (BGMEA), Leather and Footwear Manufacturers and Exporters Association of Bangladesh (LLMEB), databases of the Bangladesh Export Promotion

Bureau, SMEs Foundation of Bangladesh and the Yellow Pages. From a comprehensive list of SMEs, a sample was selected using the principle of stratified random sampling. The target subjects were either the owner of the firm or their representative.

A total of 282 responses were gathered proportionately from the RMG (225) and leather industries (57) which was considered adequate for PLS-based data analysis. Section 3.6.5 describes this step in detail.

3.4.10. Step 10: Data Analysis
A PLS-SEM (Barclay, Higgins, & Thompson, 1995; Chin, 2010) technique was employed to analyse the data collected through the comprehensive survey. A two-step procedure, involving assessment of the measurement model by examining its psychometric properties and estimation of the structural model, was followed for the quantitative data analysis.

3.4.11. Step 11: Result Interpretation and Report Writing
After successful completion of the entire data analysis (both qualitative and quantitative), the results were discussed and interpreted in accordance with the previously developed research questions and objectives. The write-up of the paper, however, was a continuous process which, in fact, began during the literature search: the final write-up started with the reporting of the results and their interpretations. The outcomes of different phases of the research presented in various sections were articulated and integrated during this stage. The process ended with a complete paper which includes the research questions, study objectives, literature review, research methodology, qualitative field study analysis and final model specification, hypotheses development, data analysis, results interpretation, conclusion and references.

3.5. Qualitative Field Study Method

This study has adopted a mixed-method research approach to attain its objectives. In accordance with the exploratory research design, this study has employed a qualitative field study followed by a quantitative survey. The study was dedicated to looking at the diffusion of ICT by SMEs in Bangladesh and the resultant outcome in terms of the organisational performance achieved through integration and proper utilisation of ICT. The study undertook an extensive literature review to develop the conceptual framework and primary model. Most of the literature reviewed for this study focused on developed countries' perspectives, and mainly the American perspective. As this was an initiative to look at the phenomena from a developing country perspective and, more clearly, from the Bangladesh perspective, the research instruments and the constructs may not have been well suited to this perspective. Thus, a qualitative field study was appropriate in order to contextualise the model and any modification or extension. To validate and enhance the factors and variables identified through the comprehensive literature review, the study, during this phase, explored the phenomenon of ICT usage by SMEs in Bangladesh and its effects on organisational performance by interviews with the owners of SMEs and other stakeholders. Researchers have argued that the goal of understanding a phenomenon from the point of view of participants and its particular social and institutional context was difficult to achieve when textual data were quantified (Kaplan & Maxwell, 1994). Therefore, it was believed that a 'pseudo case study' that involved a qualitative study of a small number of participants would meet the objectives of this phase of the study.

As such, a field study approach (Patton, 1999; Zikmund, 2000) was adopted as the research method for the qualitative phase. Qualitative methods permit the evaluator to study selected issues in depth and detail. Approaching fieldwork without being constrained by predetermined knowledge contributes to the depth, openness and detail of qualitative inquiry (Patton, 1999). The field study enabled the researcher to be involved in investigating the factors influencing diffusion of ICT and its effects on organisational performance in the participating SMEs.

3.5.1. Sample Selection

The study adopted the convenience sampling technique and selected 11 SMEs for qualitative interviews. This qualitative study began with the notion of an open-ended number of cases and stopped interviewing after the 11th case after taking into consideration informational redundancy and theoretical saturation (Denzin & Lincoln, 2005; Lincoln & Guba, 1985; Strauss & Corbin, 1998). The sample comprised 11 owners of different SMEs or their representatives who were selected by adopting a convenience sampling method. This is one of the most commonly used sampling methods in business research (Zikmund, 2000) as it relies on available subjects who are close at hand or easily accessible (Berg, 2004). The convenience or judgment sampling procedure is also effective for qualitative studies: appropriate and resourceful people who can easily be identified and included in the sample may provide a valuable contribution to the research.

As diffusion of ICT among SMEs and organisational performance were the focus, the study considered organisations that were using any kind of ICT in various functional areas such as in shop floor management, account management, inventory control, for qualitative interviews. The convenience sampling technique also allowed the researcher to include SMEs who were functioning at different user levels such as basic computing, e-commerce users and users of enterprise resource systems.

A wide range of SMEs operate in different sectors in Bangladesh. These sectors are broadly classified as the services industry and the manufacturing industry. SMEs play a substantial role in the economic development of a country. Despite the fact that the contribution of SMEs in economic development is similar, the definitions of SMEs are diverse in different country contexts. The Industrial Policy 2010 of the People's Republic of Bangladesh defines an SME as:

- A manufacturing firm having 100–250 employees or having fixed assets from 10 Crore BDT to 30 Crore BDT (excluding the value of land and factory) is considered a medium enterprise while any firm having 25–99 employees or having fixed assets from 55 Lakh BDT to 10 Crore BDT (excluding the value of land and factory) is considered a small enterprise.
- Also, a firm in the services industry having 50–100 employees or having fixed assets from 1 Crore BDT to 15 Crore BDT (excluding the value of land and factory) is considered a medium enterprise while a firm having 10–49 employees or having fixed assets from 5 Lakh BDT to 1 Crore BDT (excluding the value of land and factory) is considered a small enterprise.

Feasible organisations for the qualitative research were selected from the Yellow Pages directory. Personal connections and the nature of the organisation as well as the owner's availability and interest in participating in the interview were the criteria for sample selection.

3.5.2. Data Collection

The data collection and analysis method used in qualitative studies is different from that used in quantitative techniques (Lincoln & Guba, 1985). Interviews have been accepted as one of the major data collection techniques for qualitative studies (Maykut & Morehouse, 1994) and are therefore employed as a method of qualitative data collection in various fields of study. The main three different categories of interviews employed in data collection are: standardised (formal or structured); unstandardised (informal or non-directive) and semi-standardised (guided semi-structured or focused) interviews (Babbie, 2001; Merriam, 1998; Nieswiadomy, 2011). The overall objective of the study, the nature of the problem and the research perspective help in selecting the type of interview appropriate for the study. It was mentioned earlier that the purpose of this study was to explore and examine the antecedents of ICT adoption and usage by SMEs and their effects on organisational performance. Utilising the outcomes of previous research and theories, this study developed a primary model in order to inquire about the phenomena. Although much research has been conducted in this field in the past few years, these studies have mainly focused on developed country perspectives and, particularly, on the American perspective (Watson, Kelly, Galliers, & Brancheau, 1997; Zhu et al., 2004). The theories or the empirical evidence, although relevant, should be contextualised before their execution in addressing the phenomena from a developing country perspective.

This study, thus, has adopted a semi-structured interview for collecting relevant qualitative data to explore various variables and factors in order to refine the model to address SMEs' ICT diffusion and organisational performance from the Bangladesh perspective. By design, the semi-structured interview ensures that the list of themes, issues to be addressed and questions to be asked are identified and pre-defined by the researcher. Even though its nature is to have a significant understanding about the context and nature of the variables associated with the study and their interrelationships, the semi-structured interview ensures that information is captured from respondents' perspectives rather than being imposed by the researcher (Burns & Bush, 2000).

The semi-structured questions and probing guide were developed through the comprehensive literature review. The primary guiding semi-structured questions were also pre-tested by interviewing some SME owners so that any adjustments or modifications could be made thus ensuring that the guide was useful for the interviews and also confirming the data from respondents' perspectives. The semi-structured interview questions focused on the following areas of information that were needed from the field study:

- General perceptions, beliefs towards ICT and intended ICT use
- The main factors that influenced SMEs' intentions to use ICT
- The usage of different applications of ICT
- Conceptualisation of the national culture and its role in the diffusion of ICT by SMEs
- Conceptualisation and the role of environmental pressures in shaping SMEs' intentions to use ICT

- Conceptualisation and the role of country readiness in intention to use and usage of ICT by SMEs
- Conceptualisation and the factors associated with organisational performance
- The role of ICT use in organisational performance.

Before the interviews, the selected interviewees were personally contacted and an appointment was made for the interview. An outline of the interview along with a cover letter specifying several important perspectives of the research − such as the objective, scope and perspective of the study, process of the interview and the role of the interviewee − were also sent beforehand so interviewees would be comfortable with the formalities and able to express their opinions freely. The interviews were recorded in their entirety by a micro-audio recorder with permission duly given by interviewees. Applying the rules of transcription, the recorded interviews were transformed into text immediately after the interview, generally, on the following day.

3.5.3. Analyses of Qualitative Data

This study employed the content analysis technique to analyse the qualitative data (Siltaoja, 2006). Qualitative data analysis involves both inductive and deductive approaches to compare the qualitative data with the theoretical framework and also to develop a causal relationship between the constructs under study (Berg, 2001).

The themes, sub-themes and concepts explaining the variables and factors were explored by the inductive process. This process also explored the measurement scales of some variables or factors. The variables and factors explored by the induction process were further induced into a common framework. The ultimate objective of the field study was to prepare a comprehensive conceptual framework by comparing the induced framework with the initial research model developed from the literature review. This framework was therefore compared with the initial research framework.

In this study, NVivo (Version) 10 software was used to analyse the qualitative interviews. NVivo (registered under QSR International) is designed to facilitate common qualitative techniques for organising, analysing and sharing data. It can analyse unstructured or semi-structured data like interviews, surveys, field notes, web pages and journal articles from a range of sectors which includes social sciences, education, health care and business. The development of NVivo has provided greater convenience through using the programme and has also enhanced the capacity of the researcher to undertake interpretive analysis (Bazeley, 2007).

With the intention being to analyse the qualitative data by NVivo, the recorded interviews were transformed into interview transcripts. The NVivo 10 software first imported all interview transcripts and provided the opportunity for analysis by nodes, modelling and query support.

Through these analyses, the qualitative study's findings assisted in developing a comprehensive model with this then used as a basis for the construction of hypotheses. The outcome of the field interviews and the extensive literature review provided the rationale for the construction of hypotheses. The qualitative study finally refined the study model and developed hypotheses that formed the basis for the quantitative study, the main concern of this research.

3.6. Quantitative Study Method

Although the theoretical framework of the study was developed through an extensive literature review which was contextualised and fine-tuned through an in-depth field study, the design and execution of quantitative research was a vital part of this study as the study stood under the positivist research paradigm. The quantitative survey explored the degree and magnitude of Hypothesised relationships between the variables and constructs under study. Based on the theoretical framework discussed in the preceding section, a number of hypotheses were developed for possible rejection or acceptance which would help to infer the situation and policy implications (Anderson, 1973). As the study was seeking to empirically test some assumptions or hypotheses and the methods used in this phase were designed to be detached and independent of the specific situation under study, a quantitative method was considered most appropriate. The size and geographical dispersion of the sample units also provided the rationale for adopting a survey method and, in particular, a questionnaire-based survey.

3.6.1. Developing the Questionnaire
A questionnaire was the instrument used for data collection. Often, a questionnaire is called an interview form or schedule. Malhotra (2004) described a questionnaire as a formalised set of questions for obtaining information from respondents. A questionnaire is a very important research instrument for the researcher engaged in research based on quantitative primary data.

A researcher must prepare a questionnaire to collect primary data. The notion of translating the information needed into a question format is the principle behind the development of a questionnaire. Researchers should pay heed to carefully developing the questionnaire so that it is effective for collecting the needed information. The style, language and symbols used in the questions should match prospective respondents' status, culture and ability to make them (respondents) comfortable and motivated to respond. A well-developed questionnaire encourages respondents to provide accurate information which not only ensures accurate information but also minimises response errors.

The questionnaire was designed to collect SMEs' owners' or decision-makers' perceptions or evaluations of SMEs' intention to use or usage of ICT and how they were influenced by different factors and variables. The questionnaire also endeavoured to collect respondents' subjective assessments or evaluations about SMEs' performance and how performance was influenced by ICT utilisation and integration. The study adopted subjective or indirect measurements rather than direct or objective measures. As with many research debates, researchers have differences of opinion between applying subjective or objective measures. Some researchers believe that the responses to subjective measures are likely to be influenced by selection bias. In addition, it is also true that, in many cases, collection of quantitative data by observed measures is very hard and sometimes erroneous. For instance, small firms in developing countries are not formalised and they do not keep their business records formally. Sometimes, they hide some information due to reductions in tax and worry with regard to their competitors. In this situation, data from using objective measures would not be suitable or effective. Thus, although there was the possibility of selection bias, the use of subjective measures in this research was appropriate. The literature supported the general reliability of self-reported and subjective measures (Dess & Robinson, 1984). Nevertheless, care was taken to select measurement items that previous research had shown to be valid and reliable.

In general, the scaling technique is widely used to assess the variation in data collected by subjective measures. The scaling technique yields the highest level of information feasible in a given situation which permits the use of a great variety of statistical analyses. This study mainly used the Likert rating scale with the help of the semantic differential scale. The Likert rating scale has been widely used in psychology, sociology and business research as it is easy to construct and administer. A Likert scale provides the respondents with a complete picture of a phenomenon so they can easily indicate the degree of their agreement or disagreement with a variety of statements related to the phenomenon (Aaker, Kumar, & Day, 2004).

Respondents readily understand how to use the scale, making it suitable for mail or telephone surveys or personal interviews. The main disadvantage of the Likert scale is that it takes longer to complete than other itemised rating scales because respondents have to read each statement. The points on the rating scale could vary between two to any higher number, but most researchers prefer rating scales of between five and nine points (Cox, 1980; Reynolds & Neter, 1982). Although the literature shows that the correlation coefficient decreases with a reduction in the number of scale categories, affecting all statistical analyses based on the correlation coefficient (Givon & Shapira, 1984), the convenience and ease of execution of the questionnaire and its ability to encourage respondents to accurately assess their feelings during the survey should be considered equally. By including rating scales with too many points such as a 9-point rating scale, respondents may be confused in assessing their feelings between so many points. It may also create a situation in which the respondent evaluates his/her position deeply again and again when indicating his/her feelings. This may lead to a longer response time while, at the same time, spontaneous perceptions or responses may not be provided which would in the end cause a biased response. Thus, the rating scale should include a fair number of points that, on one hand, can produce scope for variations in perception while, on the other hand, being easily perceivable and executable by the respondent. In showing the researcher's understanding of this situation, this study has adopted a 5-point rating scale.

3.6.2. Questionnaire Translation

The study has endeavoured to investigate the diffusion of ICT and the effect of its usage on SMEs' performance by collecting primary data mainly from the owners of SMEs in Bangladesh. The native language of the study area is Bengali and a significant number of SME owners, particularly the owners of small industries in Bangladesh, are Bengali-dependent. Questionnaires in English were not suitable for data collection in this study context. The English version of the approved questionnaire was thus translated into Bengali before conducting the survey to achieve greater convenience and ease of operation. As the respondents easily understood the Bengali version of the questionnaire and could easily respond with the most appropriate answer, the questionnaire became very useful for data collection. Although the Bengali version of the questionnaire was easy to use and very useful for data collection, the translation of the questionnaire and creating equivalence between the Bengali version and the English version was not an easy task.

Four different procedures — namely, one-way translation (direct translation), back-translation (double translation), translation by committee and decentring — are used for translation of instruments. Among the above four alternatives, direct translation is the most frequently used translation procedure where a bilingual translator translates the questionnaire directly from a base language to the respondent's language. This procedure is considered as less expensive and less time-consuming than other translation procedures. It is important that the translator is fluent in both the languages and familiar with both the cultures otherwise direct translation of certain words and phrases may not project similar meanings and sentiments which may cause erroneous responses. However, back-translation is a two-way translation procedure which can overcome the errors of one-way (direct) translation procedure.

In back-translation, a researcher prepares material in one language and asks a bilingual translator to translate it into another (target) language. A second bilingual translator independently translates the material back into the original language. The researcher then has two original language forms to examine and even if he/she does not know the target language can make a sound judgment about the quality of the translation. However, several repeat translations and back-translations may be necessary to develop equivalent questionnaires, and this process can be expensive and time-consuming.

In the committee approach, a group of bilingual translators translate from the base language to the target language. The mistakes of one member can be caught by others on the committee. The weakness of this method is that committee members may not criticise one another and may even unify against the researcher. Werner and Campbell (1970) proposed decentring as a way to develop instruments that would be culturally appropriate when cross-cultural research is conducted. In the decentring process, the original language instrument is not considered final until the entire translation process is completed. Therefore, if a translator believes that a grammatical structure or word or tense must be changed to appropriately fit the cultural group under study, the original instrument should also be changed to reflect these linguistic and cultural characteristics. There is a constant comparison of the two instruments, and modifications are made to the first to account for limitations of the target language. Although the instrument may be more accurate culturally and linguistically, this may also be more costly in terms of time and resources, and the length of the instrument may be increased.

The literature describes back-translation as one of the most adequate translation procedures (Marin & Marin, 1991). The researcher has there-fore adopted the back-translation approach for translating the question-naire and ensuring equivalence of the two versions. To explain in more detail, the researcher first translated the original English questionnaire, which had been approved by the university's Human Research Ethics Committee, into Bengali. The first version of the Bengali questionnaire was thoroughly checked by a university academic in Australia. The refined ver-sion of the translated questionnaire was further reviewed by two university academics from Bangladesh who were involved in research in Australia. The final version of the Bengali questionnaire was again translated back into English. A third person, a researcher from Bangladesh, performed the back-translation of the questionnaire into English. The back-translated ver-sion of the questionnaire provided the opportunity to check whether the translated version of the items was projecting a similar meaning and approach as in the original version. Interestingly, although some words were found to be different, all items in both versions of the questionnaire were observed as being similar in meaning which finally ensured equiva-lence of the two versions of the questionnaire.

3.6.3. Pre-Testing of the Questionnaire and Pilot Test

The initial questionnaire was refined through pre-testing prior to adminis-tering the actual survey. Five people in Australia who had direct experience in running an SME in Bangladesh were invited to pre-test the question-naire. The objectives of pre-testing were to contextualise the instrument and to ensure reliability of the questions. During the questionnaire pre-testing phase, different respondents scrutinised the questionnaire from different perspectives and gave their feedback which finally enhanced the content validity of the questionnaire. In addition to respondents' feedback on the content of the questionnaire, the overall length of time taken and difficulties that arose during completion of the questionnaire were also inspected. A follow-up interview was conducted with each participant to identify any weaknesses in the instrument. Basing on the experience of the pre-testing and respondents' feedback on several points, the questionnaire was finalised after initiating the necessary corrections and modifications.

A pilot test was also undertaken administering a mini sample survey using the final version of the questionnaire. A total of 35 SMEs were selected through a convenience sampling technique and surveyed. The questionnaire was further refined through the pilot test. During the pilot test, numerous errors in the questionnaire were detected and a number of suggestions were received from respondents. As the questions had been generated to assess respondents' perceptions or evaluation of different statements by rating them on a Likert scale and, in some cases, on a semantic differential scale, respondents perceived that many of the questions were very close to each other in their meaning. In addition, many respondents faced trouble in differentiating their exact evaluation using the given five points. More specifically, respondents faced difficulties judging the intensity between '4' and '5' as well as between '1' and '2' on the 5-point rating scale. In addition to respondents' comments, these errors were also detected in the analysis of the data from the pilot study. As the respondents could not differentiate between their feelings in their evaluations, they mostly chose the extreme value. Thus the factor loading of the different items of some constructs tended to reach value '1'. To overcome this error, a statement about each point of the scale was given in the questionnaire which helped respondents to select the right point. The questionnaire was again revised to incorporate respondents' suggestions (which the researcher felt were logical) to ensure a valid and reliable questionnaire. The final version of the questionnaire was used to collect data from a national survey.

3.6.4. Sample Selection

Sample selection is one of the major tasks in a research project and, particularly, in survey research. Although this study was designed to draw the conceptual framework through the literature survey and to contextualise and fine-tune the framework through the findings from a qualitative field study, the main outcome was produced by analysing quantitative data (collected through a sample survey) to reject the null hypotheses and draw some policy implications. The results drawn from a survey are said to be representative if the sample contains characteristics that are similar to the population. The literature has suggested that the application of probability principles in sample selection may help to produce a representative subset of the population. The results of data collected from a representative subset of the population strengthen the confidence in anticipating any situation. Researchers select probability sampling by applying different strategies which include simple random sampling, proportionate stratified random sampling, disproportionate stratified random sampling and cluster sampling. Stratified sampling involves the extraction of proportionate representation of multiple groups of firms considered in the research (Reynolds,

Simintiras, & Diamantopoulos, 2003) where units within a group are similar and between groups that bear dissimilar characteristics. Each stratum includes the same characteristic of interest that facilitated the systematic random sampling procedure (Churchill, 1991; Malhotra, 2002). Contrary to random sampling, numerous researchers have adopted the convenience or judgment sampling technique. However, this study has adopted the disproportionate stratified random sampling technique for sample selection.

In addition to the sampling procedure, the size of the sample is also another important factor to ensure the representativeness of the sample as well as its suitability for executing the appropriate statistical tools. For example, in a qualitative field study, 4−8 cases are sufficient for analysis. However, the application of basic statistical tools in quantitative data analysis requires normal distribution. The rule of thumb suggests that more than 30 cases can justify the normality of data and may be used in any basic statistical analysis. However, requirements of sample size may vary in different types of statistical analysis and a variety of opinions was also observed in the literature even when applying the same tools (Hair, Anderson, Tatham, & Black, 1998; Tabachnick & Fidell, 1996). For example, the standard and sophisticated statistical analysis including structural equation modelling (SEM) recommends sampling of 200 as fair and 300 as good (Tabachnick & Fidell, 1996). Similar to that, Hair et al. (1998) recommended a sample size of 200 to test a model using SEM, because 200 is a 'critical sample size' (Hoelter, 1983) that can be used in any common estimation procedure for valid results.

Aaker et al. (2004) suggested an alternative approach which recommends using a comparable and similar extant study's sample size with a satisfactory level of reliability as a guide. A number of closely related innovation diffusion studies (Bayo-Morionesa & Lera-López, 2007; Twati & Gammack, 2006; Venkatesh et al., 2008) used a sample size ranging from 200 to 300. Based on the above-mentioned examples and notions from previous studies, this study has adopted a sample size close to 300 as SEM was the main tool being used for data analysis.

The SMEs in Bangladesh formed the population for this study while the owner of the firm or their designated representative engaged in the firm's decision-making were the study's subjects. There are approximately seven million micro-industries and SMEs in Bangladesh. Micro-industries were outside the scope of the study's objectives and therefore were excluded. According to Bangladesh's Industrial Policy 2010, the country's SMEs are categorised into two different industries − the manufacturing industry and the services industry. This study executed a multistage process to achieve a representative sample selection which started by categorising all industries in Bangladesh into the formal and informal sectors. Formal firms were considered for sample selection while informal firms were excluded. In a consecutive step, formal firms were categorised into large-scale enterprises and SMEs. In accordance with the objective of the study, large-scale firms were excluded and SMEs were considered for further treatment. Basing on their environment, SMEs were divided into two categories − rural firms and urban firms. Rural business firms were excluded from the sample frame as they lacked the infrastructure for ICT-dependent procedures in their rural environment while urban firms were given full attention. Urban firms were again classified into four distinct categories based on their location, namely, firms located in Khulna, Rajshahi, Chittagong and Dhaka.

Khulna, Rajshahi, Chittagong and Dhaka are four major cities in Bangladesh. Dhaka is the capital of the People's Republic of Bangladesh and 80% of Internet services are Dhaka-centric. One important locational benefit held by Dhaka is that almost every firm has its head office located there. Based on the number of organisations in their industry and their concentration and IT penetration, the firms located in Dhaka were considered for the study. Those firms were further divided into two groups based on the nature of the industry, whether it was the manufacturing industry or the services industry. Based on the export contribution and economic significance, the manufacturing industry was logically considered for sampling and the services industry was excluded. The manufacturing industry comprises various industrial units. Although each of these industrial units contributes positively to the national economy, their performance varies. Based on their contribution and its potential in the economic development of the country, some industries have been announced as the thrust sector for the economy. Owing to their contribution and economic potential, the RMG industry and leather and leather product industry have attracted the attention of the Government of Bangladesh, are considered as the thrust sector and receive preferential treatment and trade benefits.

In the manufacturing industry sector, the RMG industry is the leading industry contributing around 70–80% of export earnings and is therefore considered to be the goose that laid the golden egg in Bangladesh while the leather and leather product industry is an emerging industry. The study has logically considered both the leading industry and an emerging industry to build a sample frame. The proportion of the contribution of the RMG and leather industries in Bangladesh is roughly 80:20. The sample frame, thus, was generated by taking sample units from these two industries according to the proportion of their contribution. Understanding the nature of the study and the statistical tools to be used for analysis, this study decided to select a sample of 300 cases by incorporating 240 (80%) from the RMG industry and 60 (20%) from the leather industry. The sample units were selected on a random basis from a list of related industries. In accordance with the rough contribution of the two industries being 80:20, the sampling procedure was justified as proportionate stratified random sampling. Interestingly, if the number of firms engaged in the sectors had been considered, the selection of the sample may be fallen into disproportionate stratified random sampling as a very large number of firms are engaged in the RMG industry while the number of firms engaged in the leather industry is small.

Blalock (1960) suggested that the disproportionate stratified random sampling method is better than the proportionate stratified method in studies in which the differences in numbers among groups are large. Thus, the process and method adopted for selecting firms from the RMG and leather industries by the 80:20 ratio were still justified as disproportionate stratified random sampling. Churchill (1991) supported disproportionate stratified sampling as being a method by which to increase precision without increasing cost and to reduce the sample variation. This technique offers the opportunity to reduce sampling error to achieve an increased level of confidence by the representation of two different categories of pertinent sample characteristics that accurately reflect the population (Davis, 2000; Zikmund, 2000). A flow chart of the sample selection process has been provided in Appendix A.

3.6.5. Quantitative Data Collection

A list of companies was prepared from the BGMEA members' directory 2010–2011 which contained 2,917 firms and the Bangladesh Knitwear Manufacturers and Exporters Association (BKMEA) members' directory 2010–2011 which contained 1,987 firms. A list of firms engaged in leather and leather products manufacturing and exporting was developed from the Leather and Footwear Manufacturers and Exporters Association of Bangladesh (LLMEB) members' list 2010–2011 which contained 58 firms, a list from the Bangladesh exporters' category on the Export India web page which contained 28 firms, and names and addresses of another 45 firms were collected from the records of the Ministry of Trade and Commerce. With the aim of collecting responses from 300 firms (or a number close to that figure), a total of 1,320 questionnaires are sent out to respondents: 1,200 questionnaires to the RMG industry and 120 questionnaires to the leather industry.

Before sending the questionnaires, respondents were contacted by telephone. The reason for the telephone calls before sending the questionnaires was to take the opportunity to judge the category of the firms selected as primary sample units through screening questions and also to receive prior consent from respondents. Upon receiving respondents' consent, the survey instrument together with a covering letter explaining the purpose and instructions for the survey were sent directly to the person contacted which was believed to be an efficient way to receive a satisfactory response.

The first round of survey packages was sent out in the third week of September 2011. Surprisingly, no survey responses were received until November 2011 even after follow-up calls. Respondents were contacted through email and telephone calls. However, sending emails was deemed to be not effective in this context. The telephone follow-up, although calls reached the respondents, was not efficient for pursuing respondents to get them to complete and return the questionnaire. After realising the situation and having an extensive meeting with some experts including the supervisor of this research project, three educated surveyors were employed to follow-up and collect the completed questionnaires. Extensive training was provided to the surveyors to acquaint them with the research and survey. The surveyors also received training about remaining neutral during the follow-up process and the collection of responses. It was important to note that, at the preliminary stage, the researcher had planned to use an online survey procedure through Survey Monkey software in conjunction with a mail-out survey. A version of the questionnaire was also posted to the web for data collection. It was also surprising that the online data collection procedure was not successful. However, the final approach worked well, that is, using a combination of telephone follow-up and door-to-door physical visits resulted in a number of good responses. The first round of the study was conducted during the period from September 2011 to March 2012. A total of 150 completed responses were received during this period.

The second round of the study was conducted during the period from April 2012 to August 2012. During this phase, the researcher himself made repeated telephone calls to respondents. The surveyors also were more efficient in facilitating the procedure and were successful in boosting the number of responses. During the second phase, another package consisting of reminder letters, a copy of the questionnaire and a souvenir was once again sent to the contact persons. Thus, a more efficient result was achieved and a total of 132 responses were received during this phase.

Finally, 225 usable responses from the RMG industry and 57 useable responses from the leather industry were received. Finally, the data set containing 282 records was used for the entire data analysis of the study which included SEM. The final response rates were calculated as 22% from the RMG industry and 55% from the leather industry. As the size of the leather industry in Bangladesh is small, the researcher put in hard labour and paid extensive attention to collecting a suitable number of responses close to the targeted number of 60 which ensured a good response rate. However, administering a successful survey in a country like Bangladesh is a hard job as many of the popular modes for surveys are not suitable for Bangladesh. Previous research experience has admitted to receiving a lower rate of responses when surveying organisations in Bangladesh with a response rate of 17.5% considered as satisfactory (Saleh, 2006; Shamsuddoha, 2004). Thus, the response rate of 22% was valid for drawing inferences representative to the population. The sample size was also adequate for applying SEM.

3.6.6. Quantitative Data Analysis
This study employs SEM for quantitative data analysis. SEM, a second generation of the statistical analytical tool, incorporates a two-step procedure in data analyses which administers the assessment of the measurement model followed by undertaking the structural model estimation. The measurement model involves the assessment of the construct validity, convergent validity and discriminant validity of the reflective constructs. Convergent validity ensures that the items explaining a construct converge well through examining whether the items in each construct are highly correlated and reliable; while discriminant validity ensures that the reflective constructs are different from each other by estimating the average communalities, construct correlation and cross-loading matrix.

SEM was appropriate for analysing the data in accordance with the proposed conceptual framework. A growing number of researchers are adopting causal or SEM as it allows the analysis of complex networks of constructs, each construct typically measured by multiple variables. Covariance structure analysis, as implemented by LISREL, EQS or AMOS, is the well-known approach to causal modelling. However, PLS is a complementary approach with features that are well suited to the domain of technology research (Barclay et al., 1995).

Although a combination of software, including MS Excel (for data management); SPSS (for data manipulation and descriptive statistics); LIMDEP (for cross-correlation) and AMOS (for estimating some of the SEM components for cross-checking) was used for the treatment of the data, checking and rechecking of reliability and validity of the measurements, and facilitating data analyses in various stages of the research, the main part of the quantitative data analysis was performed by using PLS-Graph Version 3 software.

The decision by any researcher when selecting an appropriate analytical tool for reliable estimates is vital. Past research initiatives have employed both covariance-based structural equation modelling and correlation-based structural equation modelling to examine similar phenomena while these two different methods of SEM have some specialties and also some constraints. Chin (1995) reported that covariance-based SEM is superior on mathematical grounds while correlation-based SEM had superiority on practical grounds. The covariance-based structural equation modelling (CBSEM) software, such as AMOS, LISREL, considers reflective items when analysing both measurement and structural models while component-based structural equation modelling software, such as PLS-Graph, can handle both reflective and formative measures in estimating the measurement model and structural model.

The theoretical framework of the study involved a complex structure of hierarchical latent constructs comprised of both reflective and formative items. The nature of the study constructs and their measurement items thus justified the application of PLS-SEM (Barclay et al., 1995).

With the arguments as stated above, the PLS technique was considered to be the most appropriate data analysis tool for the quantitative study. This study attempted to use the PLS technique to establish the relationship between the different model constructs, thus testing the hypotheses. As such, the data collected in this study were analysed using the PLS technique utilising the PLS-Graph Version 3.0 computer software developed by Chin (2002) (www.plsgraph.com). In this regard, PLS path estimates were standardised regression coefficients, and the loadings of items on the constructs could be construed as factor loadings (Barclay et al., 1995). The PLS technique also produced R-squared (R^2) values for all endogenous constructs which could be interpreted in the same manner as R-squared (R^2) values produced by regression analyses (Igbaria, Guimaraes, & Davis, 1995).

3.6.7. PLS Procedures

In the preceding section, it was stated that SEM incorporates a two-step procedure in data analyses which administers the assessment of the measurement model followed by the structural model estimation. The measurement model involves the assessment of the construct validity, convergent validity and discriminant validity of the reflective constructs. This study, thus, followed the two-step sequential procedure by employing PLS-SEM (Barclay et al., 1995).

3.6.7.1. Step 1: Assessment of the Measurement Model. The measurement model dealt with the relationships between the observed variables and the constructs. Items which represented the observed variables measured the constructs. The analysis of the measurement model led to the calculations of loadings providing the researcher with an indication of the strength of the measures.

3.6.7.2. Step 2: Assessment of the Structural Model. The structural model dealt with the relationships between the constructs in a structured relational framework or path diagram. Through the analyses, the PLS technique presented a clear picture of the magnitude and degree of contribution of various constructs under a common and structured path diagram which helped the researcher to test the hypotheses according to the theoretical framework.

3.6.8. Assessment of Measurement Model
During the measurement model assessment phase, the relationships between indicators and their corresponding constructs were examined by assessing construct validity which consisted of convergent validity and discriminant validity. Individual item reliability and internal consistency were the measures for convergent validity which evaluated how closely the items in a single construct correlated with each other (Barclay et al., 1995; Santosa, Wei, & Chan, 2005). The discriminant validity of the study constructs was also assessed at this phase. Discriminant validity refers to the degree to which the study constructs differ from each other (Barclay et al., 1995). Adequate convergent and discriminant validity − item reliability, internal consistency and discriminant validity (Barclay et al., 1995; Hulland, 1999; Santosa et al., 2005) − build confidence and accuracy in the structural model estimation.

3.6.8.1. Convergent Validity. The assessment of convergent validity was a fundamental part of assessing the measurement model. The psychometric properties of the measurement model were assessed by evaluating the reliability, convergent validity and discriminant validity (Fornell & Larcker, 1981). The reliability of the constructs was assessed by considering composite reliability and Cronbach's alpha. Inter-item correlations were the strong measurement of convergent validity as it (convergent validity) assessed consistency across multiple operationalisations. The magnitude and significance of standard path loadings were considered to examine construct validity.

3.6.8.1.1. Item Reliability Item reliability assessed the loadings for each individual item. The loadings indicated the correlation of the items with their respective constructs. Therefore, maintaining low loading items would decrease the correlation between the items in the construct (Nunnally, 1994). Item reliability also measured the level of random error for each construct; the lower the item loading, the higher the level of random error. Therefore, this procedure could identify and eliminate the items in a particular construct that could increase the construct's level of random error (Fornell & Larcker, 1981).

High item loadings indicated the reliability of the measures of the latent variable; however, the previous literature supported some agreed level of item loadings as thresholds for fairly reliable measures (Hair et al., 1998; Igbaria et al., 1995). Igbaria et al. (1995) deemed 0.4 as an acceptable minimum loading. Hair et al. (1998) suggested that loadings above 0.3 were significant, above 0.4 were more significant and above 0.5 were very significant. Chin (1998a) believed that item loadings should be above 0.5. Carmines and Zeller (1979) maintained 0.7 as the reliability limit whilst Barclay et al. (1995) specified 0.707 as the minimum limit. However, Nunnally (1994) argued that in the case of strong theoretical support, further reviews of low loading items were warranted. This would be especially pertinent if the low loading items added to the explanatory power of the model.

Taking into account all the recommendations in the literature and to maximise the measurement model's ability to fulfil the requirements of convergent validity, 0.5 was determined as the minimum value.

3.6.8.1.2. Internal Consistency Internal consistency was measured through calculating composite reliability (Fornell & Larcker, 1981). Composite reliability is considered to be superior to traditional measures of consistency (such as Cronbach's alpha) because it is not influenced by the number of indicators (Hanlon, 2001). Eq. (1) is the formula for how internal consistency was calculated:

$$\alpha = \frac{\left(\sum \lambda_{yi}\right)^2}{\left(\sum \lambda_{yi}\right)^2 + \sum \lambda \mathrm{Var}(\varepsilon_i)} \tag{1}$$

where α = internal consistency, λ = component loading to an indicator, Y = construct, i = item, $\mathrm{Var}(\varepsilon_i) = 1 - \lambda_{yi}^2$.

Constructs with a coefficient value of 0.70 and above in the estimates of composite reliability were accepted as reliable for further analysis (as suggested by Barclay et al., 1995; Igbaria, Zinatelli, Cragg, & Cavaye, 1997).

3.6.8.1.3. Average Variance Extracted (AVE) Fornell and Larcker (1981) specified that average variance extracted (AVE) should be at least 0.5 for convergent validity to be satisfied. Thus AVE, although it is not a usual measure of convergent validity, was rationally computed for robustness of the statistical analysis. The AVE was calculated using Eq. (2):

$$AVE = \frac{\left(\sum \lambda_{yi}\right)^2}{\sum \lambda_{yi}^2 + \sum \lambda Var(\varepsilon_i)} \qquad (2)$$

where λ = component loading to an indicator, Y = construct, i = item, $Var(\varepsilon_i) = 1 - \lambda_{yi}^2$.

3.6.8.2. Discriminant Validity. The measurement model also involved evaluating the discriminant validity which was the extent to which different constructs diverged from one another. Discriminant validity, a proof of construct validity, is defined as the degree to which any given construct is different from any other (Barclay et al., 1995). The square root of the AVE and cross-loading matrix is a widely used measure for discriminant validity (Barclay et al., 1995; Igbaria et al., 1995). According to Igbaria et al. (1995), a model is assessed as having acceptable discriminant validity if the square root of the AVE of a construct is larger than its correlation with other constructs. On the other hand, the constructs may be considered as discriminant if the loading of items within a construct (shown in columns in a cross-loading matrix) are greater than the loading of any other item within the same column (Barclay et al., 1995). Both approaches for assessing discriminant validity were important in adequately proving discriminant validity at construct level as well as at item level.

3.6.8.2.1. Discriminant Validity at Construct Level Fornell and Larcker's (1981) suggestion involving estimating the AVE is often used as an effective criterion to prove discriminant validity among reflective constructs. According to this criterion, discriminant validity is assessed by comparing the square root of AVE with the inter-construct correlations. The

square root of AVE should be greater than the inter-construct correlations when the constructs are considered to have adequate discriminant
validity.

The inter-construct correlations are presented in the off-diagonals while
the square root of AVE is placed in the main diagonal in bold font on the
matrix. In order to prove discriminant validity among the reflective constructs, the off-diagonal elements (correlation of latent variables) must be
less than or equal to the bolded, diagonal elements (square root of AVE)
in the corresponding rows and columns (Barclay et al., 1995; Gefen,
Straub, & Boudreau, 2000; Igbaria et al., 1997).

3.6.8.2.2. Discriminant Validity at Item Level Barclay et al. (1995) suggested another way for assessing discriminant validity by using a cross-
loading matrix which considers loadings and cross-loadings of measures
to test discriminant validity at the item level. The cross-loading matrix
displays the constructs in the columns and the measurement items in the
rows which enables the researcher to check the item—construct correlation at any point. Thus, the correlation matrix provides an opportunity
to compare the construct—item correlation for discriminant validity. The
loading of items within a construct (shown in columns) should be greater
than the loading of any other item within the same column in order
to prove discriminant validity among the constructs (see Table 4 for
threshold values and assessment procedures for convergent and discriminant validity).

Table 4.   Threshold Values for Reliability and Validity.

Measurement	Assessment Procedure and Threshold Values
1. Convergent validity	
(a) Item reliability	Item loading ≥ 0.7
(b) Internal consistency	
i. Composite reliability	Calculated value ≥ 0.7
ii. Average variance extracted (AVE)	Calculated value ≥ 0.5
2. Discriminant validity	
(a) Construct level	$\sqrt{AVE} >$ correlation between the constructs
(b) Item level	Item loadings of construct $>$ all other cross-item loadings of the construct
3. Nomological validity	$R^2 \geq 0.10$

3.6.9. Structural Model Estimation and Nomological Validity
The structural model was estimated to examine the degree and magnitude of the relationships between endogenous and exogenous variables. More specifically, the structural model, using the PLS technique, estimated path coefficients, t-statistics, standard errors and R^2 to examine the Hypothesised relationships. The path coefficients indicated the strengths and direction of the relationships, and t-statistics and standard errors indicated the significance of the influence, while the R^2 value indicated the amount of variance explained. The variances associated with the endogenous variables determined the explanatory power of the proposed model. The nomological validity of the endogenous variables of the model was examined by the R^2 values (Santosa et al., 2005). As proposed by Falk and Miller (1992), this study used 0.10 as the cut-off value for nomological validity of the endogenous variables under the theoretical framework.

This study adopted a bootstrap resampling procedure to generate t-statistics and standard errors (Chin, 1998b; Gefen et al., 2000). The technique which bootstrapping employs for calculating the t-statistic is similar to the traditional t-test that is also used to interpret the significance of the paths between study constructs (Barclay et al., 1995). By utilising a confidence estimation procedure other than the normal approximation, the bootstrap procedure reproduced samples with replacements from the original sample set and continued to sample until it reached the specified number as required for the analysis. This study used 500 resamples for the bootstrap.

3.7. Summary

The methods employed and processes undertaken to attain the purpose of this study were the key focus of this section. As the study adopted a mixed-method research approach, the methods and procedures employed for executing the qualitative field study and quantitative survey were stated separately in different sections. The data collection process carried out through field interviews and the methods for analysing the interviews were described. The design and structure of the questionnaire, the tests of reliability and validity of the measures, and the methods of data analysis and hypotheses testing were also discussed in detail. The following section deals with the analysis of the field interviews and the fine-tuning or re-constructing of the research model.

4. FIELD STUDY ANALYSIS AND COMPREHENSIVE RESEARCH MODEL

4.1. Introduction

This section addresses the various stages of the qualitative research which was undertaken to provide a foundation for the comprehensive quantitative study. The field study was administered to compare the conceptual framework developed by the literature review with the context of the study. The main purpose of the qualitative research was to contextualise and fine-tune the research model. The field study also explored new constructs and their measurement items. The entire process of the qualitative research, from designing the field study questionnaire to the final outcomes, is reported in this section which concludes with a refined research model (Fig. 2) for this study.

4.2. Operation of the Field Study

4.2.1. Sample

Researchers have applied different principles to determine the sample size for qualitative data collection. Some researchers have agreed on an open-ended number of cases while other researchers have supported the idea of selecting a pre-defined range of cases. Eisenhardt (1989) and Perry (1998) favoured a restricted range of cases and suggested that 4–8 cases were appropriate for qualitative research while Sandelowski (1995) stressed that it was hardly possible to determine in advance the minimum number necessary to ensure an adequate sample size in qualitative research. The adequacy of the sample for credible research findings therefore becomes relative. Thus, the point of focus should be whether the sample strategy should be large or small to achieve the intended objectives of the investigation instead of judging a sample too small or too large. However, the sample size may be reasonably considered as adequate for analysis if either informational redundancy (Denzin & Lincoln, 2005; Lincoln & Guba, 1985) or theoretical saturation (Strauss & Corbin, 1998) is reached.

This study applied the notion of an open-ended number of cases and stopped interviewing after the 11th case taking into consideration informational redundancy and theoretical saturation. The sample comprised 11 owners of different SMEs or their representatives selected by adopting a convenience sampling method. Table 5 shows the demographic profiles of the interviewees who participated in the qualitative survey.

4.2.2. Demographic Profiles of Study Respondents

A convenience sampling method was used to select the sample respondents. The sample comprised owners or their representatives from eight small and three medium-sized organisations. The study also included five organisations from the manufacturing industry and six organisations from the services industry. Personal judgment was applied to ensure diversity among the sample units. The market competitive position of six firms was good; two firms possessed a very good market position while only one firm possessed an extremely good competitive position. On the other hand, one organisation declared that they were experiencing bad market conditions while one organisation explained that they had neither a good nor a bad market position.

Again, 10 organisations had experienced revenue increases in the last few years: among them, five organisations showed highly increased revenue and one organisation had secured substantially increased revenue in the last few years. The sample also included an organisation which had no change in its revenue in that period of time. It is important to note that all

Table 5. Sample Profile for Qualitative Research.

Firm ID	SME Type	Employees	Size	Market Position	Revenue
A	S	35	Small	Good	Increase
B	M	95	Small	Good	Increase
C	S	21	Small	Extremely good	High increase
D	S	47	Medium	Good	High increase
E	S	9	Small	Good	Increase
F	S	5	Small	Good	Substantial increase
G	M	21	Small	Good	High increase
H	S	92	Medium	Bad	Steady
I	M	35	Small	Neither good nor bad	Increase
J	M	35	Small	Very good	High increase
K	M	89	Medium	Very good	High increase

of the organisations included in the sample for the qualitative survey had experience of ICT use in their organisation.

4.2.3. Data Collection

The study employed direct and face-to-face interviews with the persons selected for the qualitative survey. The interviews were organised and recorded with the consent of the interviewee. The individuals participating in the field study were provided with a consent form which clearly outlined the purpose and ethical issues related to the study. It was also mentioned that his/her participation in the interview was completely voluntary and thus they could withdraw themselves from the study at any time. A semi-structured interview technique was used as the primary tool to collect data (the data collection procedure has been discussed in detail in Section 3). A complete English version of the semi-structured interview guide has been provided in Appendix B.

4.2.4. Data Analysis

The content analysis technique was employed to analyse the qualitative data (Siltaoja, 2006). During the qualitative data analysis, both inductive and deductive methods were utilised to compare the qualitative data with the theoretical framework and also to develop a causal relationship between the constructs under study (Berg, 2001).

The themes, sub-themes and concepts explaining variables and factors were explored by using the inductive process. The process also explored measurement scales of some variables or factors. The variables and factors explored by the induction process were further induced into a common framework. The ultimate objective of the field study was to prepare a comprehensive conceptual framework by comparing the induced framework with the initial research model which had been developed from the literature review. This common framework was then compared with the initial research framework presented in Section 2.

In the past, content analysis using Berg's (2001) guidelines was carried out through a completely manual process. In the manual process, the transcripts were read word by word, a process through which quite common phrases were identified. Similar patterns or relationships that existed were also marked and notes were taken of any section that was quite similar or common from one transcript to another. These phrases, similarities or patterns were analytically coded and finally categorised into various subsections known as factors and variables. The process for these analyses became easier and more sophisticated with the introduction of text analysis software, particularly NVivo.

NVivo provides some user-friendly tools which can be used to identify, record and analyse various themes, sub-themes and concepts, and the causal relationships among various concepts. It also provides options for inducing all of the concepts, variables or factors that were explored through the inductive process and provides options for model building. It becomes quite easy to explore categories and manage the themes, sub-themes and concepts using the free and tree nodes.

This study used Nvivo 10 to analyse the qualitative interviews. In order to analyse the interviews using NVivo, the recorded interviews were transformed into interview transcripts. NVivo first imported all of the interview transcripts. The researcher created numerous free nodes by labelling each segment of the data. Each 'free node' summarised and accounted for each concept in the data which provided the basis for developing various tree nodes comprising similar free nodes. The tree nodes were developed from the free nodes that had been developed in the immediate earlier stage. The tree nodes comprised a number of relevant free nodes with a similar concept which might become a construct. For example, 99 variables (free nodes) were explored while analysing the interviews for organisational performance. Further analysis was undertaken to combine similar variables into one which resulted in nine distinct variables. Later, those nine variables were grouped into three tree nodes named competitiveness, internal operation productivity and financial performance. These three distilled factors were again grouped into a distinct broader construct of interest which was called performance.

4.3. Findings (1st Stage: Inductive Analysis)

This section presents the findings from the field study analysis based on the first stage of content analysis. Factors and variables explored by the content analysis are firstly presented. Relationships among the study constructs and construction of the final combined model are presented in subsequent sections. A summary of the findings of the 1st stage inductive analysis comprising a high-level list of the factors and variables with subsequent frequencies is presented in Table 6.

Table 6. Factors and Items from Field Study.

Factors/Variables	Participants										
	A	B	C	D	E	F	G	H	I	J	K
Owner innovativeness											
Courageous		✓	✓	✓	✓	✓	✓	✓	✓	✓	✓
Knowledge of ICT		✓	✓	✓	✓	✓	✓	✓	✓	✓	✓
Receptive to new ideas	✓	✓	✓	✓	✓	✓	✓	✓	✓	✓	✓
Cognitive evaluation											
Usefulness											
Useful in the organisation			✓	✓				✓		✓	✓
Increases productivity		✓	✓	✓	✓	✓		✓	✓	✓	✓
Enables performing tasks more quickly								✓			
Helps increase chances of getting a raise	✓	✓	✓	✓					✓		
Ease of use											
The system is easy to use	✓	✓		✓		✓	✓				✓
Easy to become skilful using the system										✓	✓
We find the technology easy to use										✓	✓
Learning to operate the technology is easy for us			✓					✓	✓	✓	✓
Behavioural intention and expectation											
I don't find any differences between our intention to use ICT and what we are going to do in evaluating our ability or the facilities or constraints arising from the external environment	✓	✓	✓	✓		✓	✓	✓	✓	✓	✓
Environmental pressure											
Coercive pressure											
Conformity with parent corporation's practice			✓						✓		
Dominance of customer adopters					✓				✓		
Mimetic pressure											
Our major suppliers demand we use ICT					✓			✓			
Competitors use ICT			✓	✓			✓				
Competitors are benefited by using ICT			✓				✓	✓			

Normative pressure
  Customers use ICT
  Suppliers use ICT
  Stakeholders (important business partners) use ICT
  Regulatory bodies use ICT
Global pressure (time pressure)
  Pressure from globalisation
  Hard to sustain without ICT at present time
Facilitating condition
  Existing system and process compatibility
  Resources necessary to use the system
  Training and maintenance facility
Country readiness
  Technology infrastructure
  Internet service availability
  Speed and sophistication of Internet
  Hardware and accessories
  Uninterruptible power supply
  Human infrastructure
  Individual's knowledge of and skill in IT and Internet-based business
  Knowledge and skill in IT and Internet-based business at institutional level
  Institutional support for computer education (availability and affordability)
  Legal infrastructure
  Law relating to online communication
  Law relating to online consumer protection
  Financial infrastructure
  Online banking facility (adequate)
  Debit and credit card service

Table 6. (*Continued*)

Factors/Variables	Participants										
	A	B	C	D	E	F	G	H	I	J	K
Policy and subsidy											
Government tax and customs policy											✓
Government's motivational programme		✓						✓		✓	✓
Government grants			✓	✓	✓					✓	✓
Government subsidies			✓	✓	✓						✓
Culture											
In-group Collectivism											
Group members take pride in the individual accomplishments of their group managers	✓	✓	✓		✓		✓	✓		✓	✓
Group managers take pride in the individual accomplishments of their group members	✓		✓		✓		✓	✓		✓	✓
Managers encourage group loyalty even if individual goals suffer	✓				✓	✓	✓		✓		✓
Power distance											
Power is highly concentrated at the top of society	✓	✓			✓	✓	✓	✓		✓	✓
People blindly follow the leader	✓	✓	✓		✓	✓	✓	✓		✓	✓
Uncertainty avoidance											
Orderliness and consistencies are not apparent			✓		✓	✓	✓	✓	✓		✓
Lack of standard operational rules and procedures				✓	✓	✓	✓		✓		✓
Bengali values											
Face-to-face communication is vital in daily lives		✓			✓		✓	✓	✓	✓	✓
People respect and prefer to communicate through the Bengali language								✓		✓	✓
Strong and close social bonds		✓			✓	✓	✓	✓	✓	✓	✓
Ethical culture											
Bribery and corruption	✓				✓	✓					
Nepotism and politicisation	✓									✓	

ICT use
Basic computing and Internet
Have own homepage
Have interactive homepage which supports product cataloguing and order processing (online order receiving and processing)
Interactive homepage which supports online transactions and account management (e-business)
Online customer service and complete digitisation

Degree of utilisation
Diversified use of the same technology
Proper utilisation
Use full capacity

ICT integration
Entire organisation is under single system
External organisations are under integrated systems
Front-office functions are digitally integrated with back-office functions and databases
Extent of utilisation for external communication

Performance
Competitiveness (competitive performance)
Sales area has been widened
Interaction with customers has been increased
Competitive position has been improved
Internal operation productivity (internal performance)
The internal operation of the organisation has become transparent
Productivity of the employees has been improved
The internal operation of the organisation has become structured
Financial performance
Sales of the company have been increased
Profitability of the company has been increased
Overall performance is increased

4.3.1. Factors and Variables

4.3.1.1. Owner Innovativeness. The field study explored owner innovativeness as one of the important factors influencing ICT adoption by SMEs in Bangladesh. Six of the 11 respondents thought that the adoption of ICT was related to the risk-bearing ability of the owner of a firm. The respondents who noticed that the owners' or CEOs' risk-taking propensity or ability greatly impacted on ICT adoption by SMEs divulged the fact by saying; '*In my opinion, it is a big task [to implement ICT] and our owners have shown their courage by using such a high-cost and sophisticated software*' (Firm B), or '*... the owner of the company should be such a person who can take a high risk on his shoulder*' (Firm J), or '*[h]e loves to take high risks in various business situations*' (Firm C).

Seven respondents were also unanimous in recognising owners' or CEOs' innovativeness in the adoption and diffusion of ICT by SMEs in Bangladesh, saying that '*... our owners are knowledgeable and educated and once they felt the necessity of the technology in the organisation they decided to use it*' (Firm K), or '*[o]ur owner is highly educated and an innovative man*' (Firm C), or '*[t]hey [owner/CEO] have adequate knowledge on the use and utilitisation of ICT*' (Firm B).

Seven other respondents expressed their feelings differently in terms of supporting the influence of owners' or CEOs' innovativeness in the adoption or use of ICT by SMEs as: '*I can mention the special quality of the owner of this organisation which is that they can easily receive new things particularly newly innovated technology ... They [owners] should come forward and receive new ideas in relation to the use of ICT in the company*' (Firm B); '*[w]ithout innovativeness, nobody can run a venture. Our owner is an innovative person*' (Firm F); '*[o]ur owner has given utmost importance with computerisation. Innovative [receptive to new ideas] and risk-taking behaviour are the fundamental qualities of the owner*' (Firm I).

4.3.1.2. Cognitive evaluation. The field study indicated that respondents' cognitive evaluation of technology mattered in regard to the intentions towards ICT usage by SMEs in Bangladesh. Firm G admitted the influence by saying: '*[i]t (ICT) is entertaining. It is providing more scope for documentary evidence than telephone and other media. It is interactive, reasonable and easy ...*' and '*... customers send some documents which are easy to check, send or forward to the appropriate departments. It helps the employee to become confident ...*' Firm K and Firm E also felt similarly. For example, Firm K stated that:

[i]t [application of ICT] makes the operation easier. Suppose we have many departments. To run a business, I have to communicate with other departments and write a
letter to the head of another department: maybe he is situated on the 8th floor while I
am on the ground floor. If I have to send it physically to the department, it will take a
lot of time and effort. (Firm K)

As with Firms G, K and E, most respondents indicated their evaluation
of technology was driving them towards using it. The field study analysis
revealed that cognitive evaluation resulted from user perceptions of the
various benefits and barriers with regard to innovation. Various benefits
and utilities were assessed from the field study which were associated with
two perceptions – perceived usefulness and ease of use. The following subsections address users' perceptions about ICT through which a user or a
prospective user can develop cognitive evaluation, that is, favourableness
or unfavourableness towards the technology.

4.3.1.2.1. Perceived Usefulness The field study revealed that almost all
respondents felt that organisations' perceptions about the usefulness of the
technology influenced the adoption of ICT by SMEs in Bangladesh. For
example, Firm H stated: '*[w]e get information at the same time from every
corner of the country. If we don't use ICT, we cannot get information at the
same time from everywhere. In that case, some districts can get it earlier;
some districts may get it later which may create a disparity among different
units of the organisation. We receive information at the same time and very
promptly and timely [currently] through ICT*'.

Similarly, Firm D stated: '*[i]t saves time, reduces the cost and increases
efficiency as I can get access to the report from anywhere and can send my
response also from anywhere. So it provides better opportunity to overcome
the place and time barriers of the operations and business*'.

The usefulness of the technology was also explored in other firms' statements. Firm C indicated that ICT was a tool for organisational efficiency
and productivity while Firm I mentioned ICT's capability for creating
effective and efficient communication in a flexible manner. For example,
Firm I said: '*[c]ommunication through ICT reduces the time [prompt], it
produces evidence of communication. Cost reduction: place and time don't
matter with it*'.

4.3.1.2.2. Perceived Ease of Use As with perceived usefulness, the field
study also revealed that 'perceived ease of use' influenced the adoption and
use of ICT by SMEs in Bangladesh. Nine of the 11 respondents felt that
the ease of use of the technology mattered in their adoption intention
or usage of ICT with this explored from various statements. As Firm

A said: '*[n]ow I am quite comfortable and friendly with the diverse use of ICT.*' Firm H agreed with the notion and stated: '*[i]t [use of ICT] is interactive, reasonable and easy (to use) ... when a customer sends some documents which are easy to check, send or forward ...*' Firm F also supported this view by perceiving that international communication became easier through the use of ICT. Firm F stated: '*ICT mainly makes communication from our country with other countries easier*' (Firm F).

The analysis of the field interviews revealed that cognitive evaluation mattered in SMEs' adoption and usage of ICT. The field study again explored two constituents of cognitive evaluation which were perceived usefulness and perceived ease of use. By applying an interpretive research approach, the field study thus anticipated that, by its nature, the conceptualisation − cognitive evaluation − would be reflected through perceived ease of use and perceived usefulness of the technology.

4.3.1.3. Culture. The field study revealed that all respondents felt that culture influenced the adoption of ICT by SMEs in Bangladesh. For example, Firm B stated: '*[i]n terms of using ICT, a formal and disciplined work environment and capable and educated manpower are required ... however, it [importance of culture] has been stated in several counts in the previous discussion. To me, national culture is one of the strong constructs affecting individuals' or groups' ICT use behaviour*'.

Similarly, Firm F stated: '*[t]he cultural aspects are related to ICT adoption [intention or usage decision] by SMEs in various counts*'.

Firm J also felt the same and said: '*... as [we feel] the societal norms and practice deter [on many counts] automated and non-personal exchanges, we are facing trouble in getting upgraded and wide use of the technology*'.

The above-mentioned statements and quotes inferred that the national culture affected cognitive evaluation and intention to use ICT by SMEs in Bangladesh. The field study also explored various dimensions of culture that were related to SMEs' ICT usage intention.

The interpretive research revealed that 'power distance', 'in-group collectivism', 'uncertainty avoidance', 'ethical culture' and 'Bengali values' were dominant in the formation of the Bengali culture which may also have some relationship to ICT adoption by SMEs in Bangladesh.

4.3.1.3.1. Power Distance All respondents mentioned that huge power distance was evident in the social or managerial hierarchy which characterised Bangladeshi national culture. For example, Firm B stated: '*[i]n our* *country, the general people blindly follow their leaders although they do not accept them in their mind*'

Firm G expressed a similar assessment about the power distance dimension of national culture by saying: '*I don't expect that the people would obey and follow their leader without any question [but, in fact,] people cannot challenge their leader's or superior's decision and reflect their own opinion or decision*'.

Some interviewees reported that obeying the leader was a norm in the country's culture and, in reality, subordinates did not have any scope to question their leader. For example, Firm J stated: '*[t]hey [the common people] should not follow their leaders without question. In the present situation, in practice, there is no scope for the follower to question their leader*'.

4.3.1.3.2. In-Group Collectivism The field study also explored in-group collectivism as one of the strong cultural dimensions that influence ICT adoption by SMEs in Bangladesh. For example, Firm H said: '*I would feel pride with my affiliation to the organisation. In our organisation, workers take pride in the individual accomplishment of their managers and the managers also take pride in the individual accomplishment of their subordinates. I wish the organisation would be run collectively. I don't prefer the autocratic environment*'.

Past studies have suggested that the cultures of Asian countries are collective cultures while the cultures of Western countries are mostly individualistic (Hofstede, 2001; House et al., 2004). The view that the culture of Bangladesh was also considered to be collective was supported by many statements. For example, Firm G said: '*I like transparency in our organisation and for any problems that arise to be settled with discussion among all members concerned. The members of our organisation are not obliged to do everything but they do so as expected*'.

4.3.1.3.3. Uncertainty Avoidance One respondent (Firm F) considered uncertainty avoidance as a strong part of culture by saying: '*[o]ur organisation is not a disciplined or organised entity. The formal approach is not evident everywhere in the organisation. Maybe there exist some rules but those are for a few people. In our organisation, the needs of the organisation and what is the responsibility of the general workers are not clearly explained and recorded*'.

Similarly, Firm G said: '*like our country, orderliness and consistencies are not stressed in different functional areas in the organisation. Although many needs of the organisation are conveyed to the general workers by word of mouth, who is responsible for what and what the organisation expects from individuals are not clearly stated ... many inconsistencies are evident in various stages in society as in our organisation. If people do anything wrong, they may be forgiven as the requirements and their responsibilities are not clearly stated*.

4.3.1.3.4. Ethical Culture Ethical issues are crucial for the development of Bangladesh. Unethical approaches and misdeeds are becoming an integral part of day-to-day life and corporate culture in the country.[12] Politicians and bureaucrats are surrounded by nepotism, unfairness and corruption in their working environment. The field study explored the view that ethical culture was one of the strongest actors in the decision-making process of SMEs' ICT usage. For example, Firm A said: '*[i]n my personal experience, it is evident that inefficient workers or candidates are offered jobs in different areas in many organisations in Bangladesh. So they play bad roles to cover their inefficiencies ... The selection procedure should be transparent. In Bangladesh, the selection is full of nepotism*'.

Similarly, Firm J stated about politicisation and the bribery culture: '*[i]n our country, politicisation is quite common, and bribes have become a common phenomenon. I feel the individuals' qualifications and performance should be evaluated rather than their affiliation with politics, groups or economic strength*'.

Firm E emphasised the unethical issues of Bengali culture by saying: '*[i]n our country, we have championed in corruption several times around the world. Besides, corruption has become an integral part of our culture. We have achieved the championship in corruption for three consecutive years around the world*'.

4.3.1.3.5. Bengali Values The culture of Bangladesh is constituted with some values and norms called Bengali values that are different from the cultural dimensions stated by Hofstede (2001) and House et al. (2004). These values were explored in statements by Firms G, K and B. Firm G said: '*[i]n our country, people do exchange through [the language] Bengali. But ICT is not compatible with Bengali and there is no Bengali user interfaces for various ICT applications which is a vital problem for the mass use of technology*'.

Firm K emphasised people's preference for communicating in the Bengali language. For example, Firm K said: '*[w]e have pride in our language movement and independence. In honour of the language martyrs and their sacrifice in language movement and in respect of the Bengali language, the government of the country declared that all work and communication should be in Bengali which creates very easy communication among people with the same language'.*

Furthermore, the people of Bangladesh live in a society that maintains very close bonds among community members. This aspect of culture was explored in a statement from Firm B: *'face-to-face communication and personal social exchanges are vital in the day-to-day lives of the country's population'.*

4.3.1.4. Country Readiness. Every respondent expressed their concern about infrastructure and other country readiness indicators with regard to establishing an ICT-based working and market environment. For example, Firm D said: *'[t]o develop ICT and SMEs, the government has prime responsibilities. Nobody can use ICT without government approval as the government has some policy and rules. The infrastructure for ICT cannot be developed by individuals. The government should provide the developed infrastructure for using ICT such as the submarine fibre optic cable network, telephone systems, etc.'* The above-mentioned statement implied that country readiness was composed of various infrastructures. The field study revealed that country readiness comprised technology infrastructure, human infrastructure, legal infrastructure, financial infrastructure, policy and supports. The following subsections present respondents' assessments and predictions on different aspects of country readiness.

4.3.1.4.1. Technology Infrastructure Technology infrastructure was considered the most important aspect of country readiness which would enable an SME to implement ICT-based functionalities. Firm C indicated that Internet connectivity and Internet speed-related infrastructure were essential for developing an ICT-based business or society. Firm C addressed the issue as: *'[i]n our country, we are connected online through the submarine fibre optic cable network under the sea which connects our country to the east Asian countries and other countries around the world. Sometimes, this cable network is disrupted due to environmental uncertainty or man-made hostile activity and the whole operation stagnates'.* Firm C again mentioned the discriminatory Internet speed and sophistication of Internet services across the country by saying: *'although we are not facing any difficulties in Internet speed as we are directly linked with DSE [Dhaka Stock Exchange], we sometimes receive complaints from our customers who are not receiving adequate speed'.* The discriminatory Internet services were also proved by another statement from the same firm: *'[w]e have 24 hour Internet* *connectivity. We use Ravi Internet. Those who are using laptops, they use Grameen Internet. We don't have much problem with Internet speed'.*

Although power supply was not relevant to ICT operation particularly in developed countries, it was an important part of country readiness with regard to establishing an ICT-dependent working environment. This aspect of technology infrastructure was explored with the statement from Firm B: *'[w]e have a crisis with power supply in our country. Where it will go, we don't know. We also have our back-up plan. We will set up our own generator. We are also willing to establish a 1 (one) megawatt electricity generation plant'.*

Similarly, Firm F said: *'firstly, we feel that electricity should be available. Computer accessories should be available. What information we use, there should be a back-up facility. UPS [uninterruptible power supply] should be available. And the UPS back-up time should be enhanced'.*

4.3.1.4.2. Human Infrastructure Human infrastructure was considered to be another important part of country readiness in facilitating ICT in the workplace. An ICT-based operation requires knowledgeable and expert human resources for its operation and maintenance. Analysing statements from the various SMEs, the field study explored the view that human infrastructure was an important component of country readiness. For example, Firm C stated: *'[w]e face some difficulties and time lapses in getting adequate support according to our needs. If we get an educated and technologically competent employee at first [entry level], then we could save some effort and time which we spend in educating our new employees. Another important concern in terms of the use of ICT is the quality and skill of employees.'.*

Firm E expressed concern about employee skills at entry level by saying: *'[n]ew employees who come to work lack skills [ICT skills]'.*

On the other hand, Firm I highlighted the development aspects of human resources which are required for establishing an ICT-based working environment. Firm I stated: *'[I]n our time, there was no computer education at school and college level, now it is included at school and college. More comprehensive computer education should be given as part of a general education to provide fundamental computer skills'.*

4.3.1.4.3. Legal Infrastructure Legal infrastructure has implications for ICT-based operations. Communication and transactions via the Internet, in particular, require significant legislative supports. Organisations participating in online transactions and exchanges feel the necessity of having effective laws and practices to solve any dispute that occurs during an online transaction, communication or exchange. Firm K stated the importance of legal infrastructure: '*[w]e don't have adequate rules and regulations to solve any dispute of conflict arising from online communication, exchanges and transactions*'.

Firm I described the importance of legal support in regard to accepting digital signatures which was essential for any digital contract by saying: '*[t]o authenticate a digital contract, a digital signature should be accepted as valid in various contracts*'.

4.3.1.4.4. Financial Infrastructure ICT has provided enormous opportunities for individuals, businesses and society. In particular, the introduction of Internet-based business operations has become a revolution in managing businesses and transactions leading to changes in the ways in which these were traditionally carried out. These changes are also reflected in banking operations. Success in online business and transactions requires an efficient online banking mechanism. Developed countries are now almost online banking-dependent. Developing countries although lagging behind are also seeking to develop an efficient online banking mechanism. The field study explored the importance of financial infrastructure in the successful implementation of online business operations and transactions. For example, Firm K expressed their concern about online banking facilities by saying: '*[w]e don't have adequate rules and regulations ... Our banking mechanism for online transactions and operations is also not satisfactory*'.

Firm C mentioned the importance of online banking in regard to customer compatibility with the mechanism by saying: '*[n]ormally most of our customers are not habituated with online money transfers*'. Firm I raised a deep concern by saying: '*[i]n our country, we don't access bank accounts from home*'.

4.3.1.4.5. Policy and Supports Government policy and supports play a pivotal role in the implementation of ICT into different functional areas in a country. The field study explored the importance of government policy and supports in promoting ICT usage in Bangladesh and, in particular, for achieving organisational productivity and efficiency in the business sector. For example, Firm K stated: '*[a]t government level, they can reduce the tax and custom duties on ICT-related products. Once government has withdrawn all taxes and duties from ICT-related products, they can provide their other supports such as grants and subsidies to also encourage ICT usage at the organisational level and country level*'.

Firm C referred to the importance of government policy and supports. The present government's move towards establishing an ICT-based society is an example of policy and supports to launch an ICT-based business environment. The importance of policy and supports was also explored in this statement by Firm C: '*Besides this, the present government is very much encouraging ICT utilisation in the country and building a digital Bangladesh by 2021 so we hope that, within a few years, we will see some improvement at our national level and we will also receive some supports and grants from government in this regard*'.

4.3.1.4.6. Environmental Pressure The field study explored the view that environmental pressure has direct and significant influence on SMEs' adoption and usage of ICT. For example, Firm H said: '*[w]e have our own distribution system. We have some suppliers and other collaborators for ingredient supply. They are in a developed country and they have highly sophisticated ICT usage. On the other hand, those who are taking our product as middlemen are not IT-based*'.

Firm C mentioned the influence of environmental pressure on SMEs' adoption and usage of ICT focusing on the effects on competitors and suppliers: '*[w]e are encouraged to use better technology and upgrade our existing systems when we see that our competitors and suppliers are using better ICT. We also feel deterred from using and upgrading our technological standards when we see our customers do not have an adequate technological fit, and they are not receptive to or compatible with ICT and our systems*'.

From the above-mentioned statement, it can be easily assumed that environmental pressure has diverse effects. The field study explored different dimensionalities of environmental pressure, such as coercive pressure, mimetic pressure, normative pressure and global pressure which affect the adoption and diffusion of ICT by SMEs in Bangladesh.

4.3.1.4.7. Coercive Pressure Many SMEs in Bangladesh have adopted ICT-based operations or have ensured their online presence in conducting or supporting a business in response to pressures from the regulatory authority or dominant customers. For example, Firm I stated: '*[o]ur customers and suppliers do all their work online. We have to comply with them. Besides the amount that we claim for the service should be claimed online and the money is transferred online. Accessories and cloth from different countries: India, Sri Lanka, Indonesia, China, the UK. A very limited portion we collect from domestic sources. They are more competent online. They require everything ordered online and require payment online. They have high bandwidth online, they have no power interruption, they have high mobile online access, so they can access from anywhere at any time. They don't have bandwidth fluctuations*'.

Firm E also mentioned coercive pressure focusing on the demands of a powerful customer: '*our big customers encourage us to use sophisticated technology like them to make us compatible with their systems*'.

4.3.1.4.8. Mimetic Pressure Pressures from competitors influenced the adoption and diffusion of ICT by SMEs in Bangladesh. The study explored mimetic pressure as an important aspect of environmental pressure. For example, Firm B said that: '*[o]ur competitors are also using sophisticated technology. In fact, two of our competitors are using this software and they started [to do so] prior to our use. So, buyers can adequately know about their orders and their progress so he/she can understand the situation and the stage that it has reached, etc. at any time from their premises. They have given the customers these privileges and the opportunity to track their order so they are getting bigger advantages than us. Thus, they are achieving better performance and business than us. We are now at the initial stage. We have the intention to extend our technological support to the buyers' premises*'.

Firm G also stated: '*[i]n the competitive market, a business, like the garments trade, is impossible to run without ICT although it was possible in earlier days*'.

4.3.1.4.9. Normative Pressure The field study explored normative pressure as a dimension of environmental pressure which influenced the adoption and diffusion of ICT by SMEs in Bangladesh. For example, Firm B stated: '*[o]ur customers are high-profile ICT users. They have their own server and own homepage, as well as an automated customer and supplier service environment. They use specialised software. They have provided us with some scanners. During the procedure, we are connected with them*'.

Similarly, Firm J said: '*[o]ur all customers are also communicating with us through emails and online communication. Our customers are also suggesting that we use ICT communication*'.

Firm G indicated the importance of normative pressure with regard to accessing suppliers, competitors and customers by saying: '*[o]ur suppliers, customers, and competitors use the Internet, email and computer which is the same as what we use*'.

4.3.1.4.10. Global Pressure In addition to coercive, mimetic and normative pressures, some pressures have been affecting SMEs' ICT adoption and usage which differed from these existing three categories. These pressures, named as global pressure, were related to ongoing technological development and global market pressures. For example, Firm D stated: '*[i]n the age of globalisation, without adopting ICT, we cannot think of a business. At* *what stage would we be if we didn't use ICT or the Internet facility was closed? We would simply be paralysed/collapsed'.*

Firm K agreed with Firm D by saying: '*I can't work without ICT in the age of globalisation*'.

Firm K also said: '*[i]t [ICT usage] is the same as the technology usage behaviour of the individual. Say I am using a mobile phone. After some days, I find that a new phone has arrived on the market. Then I go for the new phone to get the new features, style and benefits or model. It is actually the effect of innovation. The old technology was obsolete and new technology emerges and we are all following these cycles. In other ways, I can tell that we are each affected by the hype of using technology*'.

Firm J mentioned the importance of global pressure in the adoption and diffusion of ICT by saying that: '*[i]f ICT is seized from our company, our company will collapse. We can't go one step without ICT. We are seriously ICT-dependent. We can't even sustain communication through letters, phone or fax. It is not possible to run without ICT. It is the demands of time and our surroundings*'.

4.3.1.5. Facilitating Condition. The field study explored the view that some resources and competencies were essential for using ICT-based technology or systems: these were computer hardware, software, skilled manpower and a compatible working environment. These were resource-based although essential for ICT-based operations, and their adequacy and diversity would accelerate or deter firms' ICT usage. For example, Firm I expressed this as: '*[g]ood quality computer, good bandwidth, computer literacy is required for ICT use*'.

Firm J mentioned the importance and effectiveness of a facilitating condition that focused on human resources by stating that: '*[w]e have skilled human resources and technology-competent employees. We have adequate hardware and software resources*'.

Similarly, Firm I said: '*We have Internet connectivity, computer hardware, skilled manpower, and other necessary resources [human resource and technology resources]*'.

Firm A commented about the procedure they followed which reflected the necessity of having skilled manpower in the adoption and diffusion of ICT by SMEs in Bangladesh. Firm A stated: '*[o]ur working operations are directed and controlled by different departments and their head or person-in-charge. We have an MIS (Management Information Systems) department. The head of MIS deals with and controls all ICT-related tasks. In fact, they are the custodian of ICT and its utilisation. We have that skilled manpower.*

We also have computer hardware and software resources. We have the connectivity'.

Many organisations mentioned the adequacy of resources which make them habituated to and almost dependent on ICT. For example, Firm I said: '*[i]t is not only a demand from our clients; it has become a part of our everyday work culture'*. Firm B supported this expression by saying: '*[n]ow I [as a leader of the organisation] am quite compatible and friendly with the diverse use of ICT'* while Firm I approached this differently as: '*[w]e have the problem that we are still depending on paper-based documentation'*.

The above-mentioned analyses indicated that the existing systems and working procedure may foster or deter technology usage by firms. This aspect referred to the facilitating condition of technology usage which was clearly reflected in the response of Firm J: '*[i]n each and every organisation, you will find some strengths and weaknesses; we have them also. But what I would like to state is that we have more strengths in our organisation in terms of using ICT. Our other organisational systems are ICT-compatible'*.

4.3.1.6. Intention or Expectation of ICT Use. The field study explored whether the respondents evaluated their move towards the adoption of ICT in two phases, namely, intention and expectation. They had their plan and most had the firm's willingness to move forward. Their plan was rational and did not fluctuate in considering different environmental factors or situations. For example, Firm C expressed the view that: '*[w]e can provide that support, as some of our competitors have already established this kind of set-up to support their customers. To make our organisation competitive, we will be able to establish the systems to integrate our customers and other stakeholders in the online environment'*.

Organisations rationally drew up their intention. The following statements also suggested that firms' intentions were not simply a plan:

> The supports and surrounding facilities screen the intention. We are not in any doubt about whether we could do this according to our intention. We will upgrade the existing technology. (Firm A)
>
> I think it is possible to implement our intention. (Firm C)

The above-mentioned analyses indicated that the intention of the organisations was well-founded and rational and was not easily changed by the effects of external or environmental factors. Thus, this intention should actually be called 'expectation'.

4.3.1.7. ICT Use. The field study explored the situation that, to some extent, all respondents were using ICT in their firms. The results from the field study analysis categorised all responding firms into six groups based on their level of ICT applications usage, namely, basic computing with Internet; static homepage; interactive homepage which supported product cataloguing; interactive homepage which supported online transactions, that is, e-commerce; and digitisation among different functional areas; and ERP. For example, Firm A said: '*Yes, we use ICT. We use Internet. To support our Internet operation, we use a computer, printer, scanner, etc. Besides this, we have installed a cc [closed circuit] camera for security purposes*'. Similarly Firm F said: '*Yes, we are using ICT. We are using the Internet, only the Internet. We have our own homepage*'.

Firm D mentioned the sophisticated operation of ICT in their organisation by saying: '*We also take orders through the Internet. We sell to some of our valued dealers and our branches. But the sales relate to any kinds of declarations and reports that we send through the Internet and also receive through the Internet. We collect dealers' requirements through mobile phone: although for those who have the Internet facility, we get their requirements through the Internet*'.

Firm G also mentioned e-commerce participation and said: '*[t]he customer places an order online in detail. We send this to the merchandise dept. and scrutinise it in that section then send it to the sample section. We select the price and then bid the price. Send the price to the customer once ... Most of the works are [Inter]net-based*' (Firm G).

The field study explored digitisation or automation as an application of ICT usage. More specifically, Firm B said: '*[b]esides, we have special software by which we analyse our production and other related works. Finally, I find that ICT is a very useful technology. Now I am quite compatible and friendly with the diverse uses of ICT. Our firm is also computerised*'.

4.3.1.8. ICT Integration. The field study explored organisational concerns about the integration of the variety of technological facilities used in an organisation. The field study supported the view that the integration of diversified technologies was dependent on the level of ICT usage by SMEs in Bangladesh. Integration was also seen to affect organisational performance. For example, Firm K said: '*[a]fter that [introduction of ICT use], the scope of ICT use has widened and strengthened. It seems that a new technology is just introduced in some department and gradually it will spread over the organisation and work under the common system*'.

Firm **B** mentioned integration with other firms within the industry by saying: *'[w]e have accumulated some of our closely related similar group of companies in very close contact for those who are working with us in the same network environment through our server. We are doing the above-mentioned works through ICT'*.

Similarly Firm **K** said: *'[i]f the external organisations are also integrated or communicated with entirely through ICT, the performance [organisational performance] will certainly be increased'*.

4.3.1.9. Degree of Utilisation. The field study explored the view that the degree of utilisation was an important factor explaining organisational performance, as was ICT integration. The factor degree of utilisation was also developed from the firm's usage of different levels of ICT applications. For example, Firm **B** said: *'[w]e can earn productivity and efficiency [organisational performance] through proper utilisation of ICT particularly through some software by which we can track, control and initiate alternative strategy ... those companies from whom we are getting benefits and gradually developing, they are actually developing due to the proper utilisation of the technology [ICT]. Some big companies from the world perspective are giving their employees Blackberries so, from anywhere around the world, they can mail and be connected with the network'*.

Similarly, Firm **H** said: *'[w]e are trying to develop the IT-literate competent employee day by day. We hope we shall be capable of the appropriate and comprehensive use of ICT'*. Some firms emphasised the importance of the appropriate use of technology for customer satisfaction as well as for organisational performance. For example, Firm **I** said: *'[i]f the ICT is not appropriate, we will not be able to satisfy the customer or target group'*. Firm **J** also said similarly: *'The performance depends on how well we will use ICT'*. Proper and appropriate use of ICT was considered crucial for organisational performance. By utilising ICT properly, organisations could attain improved organisational performance. However, ICT may cause decreased productivity or damaging output if not utilised properly. For example, Firm **K** stated: *'ICT enhances the employees' performance. ICT normally reduces the errors. But it depends on the person who operates the ICT. It depends on their skill. I have a doubt because if the ICT is not properly handled, it may produce bad and damaging output'*.

4.3.1.10. Organisational Performance. The field study explored the view that the use of different levels of ICT applications may foster the performance of the organisation. ICT integration and the degree of utilisation also had an effect on organisational performance. For example, Firm B said: '*[a]fter that [as we were not getting reasonable performance], I consulted with some external experts and learned that our existing technological set-up was good enough to do that job. We actually had a lack of operational knowledge about our set-up [which was not properly used] thus we were getting less productivity [organisational performance]*'.

The field study also explored different factors under the conceptualisation of organisational performance such as competitiveness, internal operation productivity and financial performance. For example, Firm D said: '*[i]t [use of ICT] also enhances the sales growth in respect to our competitors*'.

4.3.1.10.1. Competitiveness The field study explored competitiveness as a dimension of organisational performance. For example, Firm J said: '*[i]t [ICT use] enhances productivity. It enhances competitive position. It increases sales*'. Firm I also supported Firm J by saying: '*It is the tool which creates competitiveness*'.

Similarly, Firm H said: '*[t]he ICT helps to exchange information related to sales, marketing, HR, different policy strategy, market conditions, etc. which makes the company competitive ... To stay competitive, gaining the competitive advantage through IT [ICT] is essential*'.

4.3.1.10.2. Internal Operation Productivity The field study explored the view that ICT use influenced productivity in the internal operation of the organisation. Firm D said: '*[w]e work in this process [by using ICT] transparently and promptly and in the age of globalisation we are able to provide international standard products and related facilities and opportunities in our country promptly*'. Firm G supported the view that the use of ICT enhanced transparency and productivity in internal operations by saying: '*[s]o the organisations, those that are operating and starting operations in this field, are using the Internet and ICT which make them transparent to each other. [Inter]net connection is obvious. ... When we use ICT, we save time and are able to make the relationship transparent between all parties involved in the work*'.

4.3.1.10.3. Financial Performance Firms (B, C, D, E, G, I and K) expressed their views agreeing with the concept that ICT use facilitated organisational performance. For example, Firm G said: '*[i]t [ICT use] is entertaining. It [ICT use] provides more scope of documentary evidence than telephone and other media. It [ICT use] is interactive, reasonable and easy.*

It [ICT use] is not only saving time, but also providing some documentary evidence. It [ICT use] is easy to control, and to have a conversation with a customer through ICT is also easier. It [ICT use] reduces errors. It [ICT use] helps increase performance ... When we use efficient ICT, it enhances performance. It increases our company's service sales'.

Firm K also supported Firm G by saying: '*[i]t [ICT use] enhances the productivity of the company. The financial performance, that is, the sales, profitability and overall performance of the company are enhanced by the use of ICT*'

The field study explored nine different free nodes to address organisational performance (see Table 6). The interpretive analysis further categorised the nine free nodes into three sub-themes (first-order factors) of organisational performance. Further analyses included all of these three sub-themes (first-order factors) in a broader higher-order complex conceptualisation which is organisational performance. Thus, the field study explored organisational performance as a higher-order conceptualisation formed by three different aspects of organisational performance — competitiveness, internal operation productivity and financial performance — that were also measured by nine items.

4.3.2. Linkages among the Factors

The objective of the field study was to explore the variables and their measures. However, the development of the relationships between the factors is also considered to be an important task during a qualitative data analysis (Xu & Quaddus, 2005). Table 7 indicates the relationships between the factors that were explored in the qualitative analysis.

Table 7 is also an outcome of the analysis of field interviews presented in the previous section (Section 4.3.1). The table presents all of the explored factors and establishes a link (a causal link) between them. For example, the notion of CE → EXP represents the influence of cognitive evaluation on intention to adopt ICT by SMEs. It was observed that all firms except Firms E, G and H found that cognitive evaluation had a direct influence on their intention to adopt ICT at their own firm. The relationship between the two factors was explored and justified as Firm B said: '*... so I think mind set-up and attitude [cognitive evaluation] are largely related to ICT use. If I don't have a positive attitude, how can I accept [intention to adopt] the new thing? I wouldn't accept and use ICT ... I think they [similar SMEs] will change their attitude [cognitive evaluation] and would be interested to utilise ICT's potential in their organisation*'. Firm D expressed a similar

Table 7.   Causal Links Explored from the Qualitative Survey.

Construct	Participants										
	A	B	C	D	E	F	G	H	I	J	K
Cognitive evaluation											
CE & EXP	✓	✓	✓	✓		✓			✓	✓	✓
Owner innovativeness											
OI & CE		✓	✓	✓	✓	✓	✓	✓	✓	✓	✓
OI & EXP				✓	✓	✓	✓	✓			✓	✓
OI & USE	✓		✓	✓	✓	✓	✓	✓		✓	✓
Behavioural expectation											
EXP & USE	✓		✓	✓				✓	✓	✓	
Environmental pressure											
EP & EXP			✓				✓	✓	✓	✓	✓
EP & USE			✓		✓	✓	✓		✓		
Facilitating condition											
FC & EXP	✓		✓	✓					✓	✓	✓
FC & USE			✓			✓		✓	✓	✓	✓
Country readiness											
CR & EXP	✓			✓	✓				✓		✓
CR & USE						✓			✓		✓
Culture											
CUL & CE	✓			✓					✓	✓	✓
CUL & EXP	✓			✓					✓	✓	✓
ICT use											
USE & PERF	✓		✓	✓		✓				✓	✓
USE & INT	✓		✓	✓		✓				✓	✓
USE & UTL	✓		✓	✓		✓				✓	✓
Degree of utilisation											
UTL & PERF						✓			✓		✓
Integration											
INT & PERF						✓					✓
Performance											
USE → INT → PERF				✓			✓	✓			
USE → UTL → PERF				✓						✓	
USE → $\mid\frac{INT}{UTL}\rangle$PERF						✓					✓

CE = Cognitive evaluation, OI = Owner innovativeness, EXP = Expectation, EP = Environmental pressure, CUL = Culture, CR = Country readiness, FC = Facilitating condition, USE = Actual usage, INT = Integration, UTL = Utilisation, PERF = SME performance.

feeling indicating as follows that cognitive evaluation created a positive intention to adopt ICT:

> ... what types of work are being done in Bangladesh? If ICT is not used in that area, the nation will stay backward. So attitude plays a positive role in ICT-related decisions. It creates [a] strong intention to use ICT.

The relationships between constructs were developed from the direct statements. In some cases, it was not possible to find the relationship from a direct statement. In those cases, detailed data analysis was performed and interpretive research philosophy was applied to interpret the underlying relationship between the factors. For example, Firm C stated that: '[t]o operate ICT in an organisation, some resources are required. We should have competent employees who have adequate knowledge and capacity to understand and use ICT ... The monetary resources are required to buy the ICT resources, that is, the hardware, computer, printer, scanner, Internet connectivity, server, etc. and the software support which will manage the operation of ICT according to the company's needs in an integrated environment'.

From the above-mentioned statement, it was inferred that some resources were necessary for ICT use. The resources indicated the facilitating condition. The statement might also be used to develop the causal link between the facilitating condition and ICT use by the organisation. Although the statement was not directly expressing any distinct relationship, by analysis utilising the interpretive philosophy, a positive relationship may be indicated between the facilitating condition and ICT use.

4.3.3. Comparison between Field Study Findings and the Initial Model (2nd Stage: Deductive Model)

Most of the variables in the field study were supported by the literature which was discussed earlier in Section 4. This section discusses the factors which either evolved from the field study or were different from the existing literature.

The initial model developed through the literature review projected that ICT use, integration and degree of utilisation influenced SME performance. Similar to the literature review, the field study revealed that ICT usage in conjunction with integration and utilisation strongly affected SME performance. The field study also supported the mediating role of ICT integration and degree of utilisation to explain the influence of ICT usage on SMEs' performance.

The existing literature suggested that BI towards the adoption of an innovation leads to behavioural expectation which may be affected by many external factors like facilitating condition, country factors, culture, environment, etc. The primary model thus included two factors to indicate the firms' two different levels of willingness to adopt ICT. The field study, analysing the interviews, explored this situation which was different to what had been revealed in the existing literature. The field study justified one factor for addressing firms' willingness to adopt an innovation. The field study explored that the firm's intention was not only cognitive, it was rational with this screened through external factors and forces; that is, intention acted as expectation in the context of SMEs' ICT adoption behaviour in Bangladesh. Thus, BI has been screened out and only one factor, behavioural expectation, was justified for testing the Hypothesised relationship.

The field study also revealed two new constructs − *Bengali values* and *ethical culture* − for addressing national culture. The field study distilled the cultural dimensions explained in the existing literature (Hofstede, 1984; House et al., 2004) and discovered that three among the five cultural dimensions, *power distance, uncertainty avoidance* and *in-group collectivism*, may have some influence on ICT adoption or usage by SMEs in Bangladesh.

The field study explored various country-level factors that may have some influence on ICT adoption and usage by SMEs. The field study also revealed a new dimension of *environmental pressure*. The qualitative analysis explored the view that 'pressure from globalisation' was an important factor which may have some influence (in conjunction with coercive pressure, mimetic pressure and normative pressure) on the adoption of ICT by SMEs in Bangladesh.

The existing literature suggested that positive attitude led to positive intention which was formed through favourable or unfavourable perceptions about the innovation. Similar to the primary model, the field study explored this factor as a state of cognitive evaluation which was formed by SME owners' perceptions about the *usefulness* and *ease of use* of the innovation. The field study justified the formation of the constructs: *cognitive evaluation, culture, environmental pressure, country readiness* and *organisational performance* as a higher-order complex hierarchical conceptualisation.

4.3.4. Justification of the Findings in the Literature Review

With support from the literature, this section has provided the justification for the selected constructs and dimensions that were developed from the field study. It has emphasised that the factors and dimensions that were derived from the field study, on the basis of commonality and consistency, were also supported by the existing literature. Therefore, this justification has established the competency and adequacy of each construct and dimension in the existing literature. Table 8 presents the factors and the dimensions that have been finalised and the relevant support from the literature.

4.3.5. Justification of Combining BI and Expectation

BI plays a vital role as a strong and immediate antecedent in predicting actual behaviour. The past theories in behavioural studies have recognised the strong and important role of intention in predicting actual behaviour such as the TRA (Fishbein & Ajzen, 1975); TPB (Ajzen, 1985); TAM (Davis, 1986) and DOI theory (Rogers, 1983). The pattern and formation of these theoretical models have demonstrated the mediating role of

Table 8. Justification of the Field Study Variables by the Literature.

Constructs	Subconstructs	Reference
Cognitive evaluation	Ease of use	Venkatesh et al. (2003)
	Usefulness	Venkatesh et al. (2003)
Owner characteristics	Owner's innovativeness	Thong and Yap (1995), Thong (1999)
Environmental pressure	Coercive pressure	Quaddus and Hofmeyer (2007)
	Mimetic pressure	Teo et al. (2003)
	Normative pressure	Teo et al. (2003)
	Global pressure	Field study
Facilitating condition	–	Venkatesh et al. (2008)
Country readiness	Technology infrastructure	Field study
	Human infrastructure	Field study
	Legal infrastructure	Zhu and Kraemer (2005)
	Financial infrastructure	Zhu and Kraemer (2005)
	Government policy and supports	Roessner (1988), Goldsmith (1990)
Culture	Power distance	House et al. (2004), Hofstede (1984)
	Uncertainty avoidance	House et al. (2004), Hofstede (1984)
	In-group collectivism	House et al. (2004)
	Bengali values	Field study
	Ethical culture	Field study
Behavioural expectation	–	Venkatesh et al. (2008)
ICT use	–	Davis (1989), Venkatesh et al. (2008)
Integration	–	Zhu and Kraemer (2005)
Degree of utilisation	–	Field study
Performance	Competitiveness	Zhu and Kraemer (2005)
	Internal operation productivity	Zhu and Kraemer (2005)
	Financial performance	Zhu and Kraemer (2005)

intention which has been reflected in successive research initiatives around the world which have explored innovation diffusion in multidisciplinary fields of study such as in psychology, business, social sciences and IS research.

Taking into consideration the role of BI, many diffusion researchers have studied innovation diffusion behaviour involving intention as the final dependent variable (e.g. Gefen & Straub, 2000; Kendall et al., 2001; Lal, 1999; Pavlov & Chai, 2002). On the other hand, some researchers who have investigated actual usage behaviour (e.g. Venkatesh et al., 2008) have also included intention as an strong antecedent reflected by a number of cognitive, individual, social and environmental factors.

The innovation adoption theories have explained the adoption and diffusion phenomena mainly through intention (Ajzen, 1985; Davis, 1986; Fishbein & Ajzen, 1975; Rogers, 1983; Venkatesh et al., 2003). The existing theories have been criticised as intention is a reflection of the adopter's internal schema of beliefs which may fail to adequately explain actual behaviour in a situation in which the adopter is under incomplete volitional control. Intention, furthermore, may not be reflected in the decision if a time gap exists between intention and actual behaviour. A stronger antecedent, termed as behavioural expectation, was therefore proposed to explain technology adoption behaviour which was not a cognitive factor which would thus be able to address the roles of all external and internal antecedents (Venkatesh et al., 2008).

Warshaw and Davis (1985) explained BI as 'the degree to which a person has formulated conscious plans to perform or not perform some specified further behaviour'.

Warshaw and Davis (1984) explained behavioural expectation as 'an individual's self-reported subjective probability of his or her cognitive appraisal of volitional and non-volitional behavioural Antecedents'.

Venkatesh et al. (2008) argued that the role of intention logically involved a new construct, behavioural expectation, to address the reflections of numerous internal as well as external influences with the view to predicting actual behaviour. The limitations of intention in predicting actual usage behaviour were also reflected in subsequent research. Venkatesh et al. (2003) suggested that the conclusion of previously studied conceptualisations of systems use such as duration, frequency and intensity of use (these conceptualisations were used in many studies rooted back to Davis et al., 1989) was true only within an intentionality framework, where external factors were taken into account via facilitating conditions (FC), defined as 'the degree to which an individual believes that an organisational and technical infrastructure exists to support use of the systems' (Venkatesh et al., 2008, p. 484). To overcome the limitations of BI and the facilitating condition in predicting actual behaviour, a new construct, behavioural expectation, was proposed (Warshaw & Davis, 1984). Venkatesh et al. (2008) recognised the rationale and importance of behavioural expectation in explaining the limitations of BI and the strengths of behavioural expectation which was stronger than intention in predicting actual behaviour from a systems usage perspective in the organisational context. They proved it through a cross-sectional empirical study in a different time period.

The innovations and changes in models and theories have encouraged the investigation of existing issues in a developed and comprehensive setting of conceptualisations and underlying relationships among the study constructs. The chronological arguments and developments in IS research to address actual systems usage behaviour (e.g. Venkatesh et al., 2003, 2008; Warshaw & Davis, 1984, 1985) have suggested the inclusion of BI and behavioural expectation as predictors of actual behaviour.

Venkatesh et al. (2008) proved the strength of behavioural expectation and BI in an organisational setting by looking at the behaviour of newly innovated systems where the recipients or adopters had no experience during the first phase of the research. In supporting the outcome and recommending that the conclusion of the research was to introduce behavioural expectation as a new construct to predict actual behaviour, we doubted the applicability of behavioural expectation in a situation where the adopters had some experience with the innovations. In addition, would it perform similarly in a setting where adopters were carrying out rational behaviours?

Prior experience was found to be an important determinant of behaviour (Ajzen & Fishbein, 1980; Bagozzi, 1981; Fishbein & Ajzen, 1975; Triandis, 1979). Specifically, it has been suggested that knowledge gained from past behaviour will help to shape intention (Eagly & Chaiken, 1993; Fishbein & Ajzen, 1975). This is, in part, because experience makes knowledge more accessible in memory (Fazio & Zanna, 1978; Regan & Fazio, 1977) and also because past experience may make low probability events more salient, ensuring that they are accounted for in the formation of intentions (Ajzen & Fishbein, 1980). Thus, direct experience will result in a stronger, more stable BI–behaviour relationship (Ajzen & Fishbein, 1980). This stable BI was reflected in behavioural expectation as conceptualised by Warshaw and Davis (1984) and Venkatesh et al. (2008).

Where the adopters have proceeded with logical steps and realistically evaluated every situation, the BI was formed through the reflections of various realistic and possible benefits, the favourableness or unfavourableness of the innovations as well as the expected outcomes which were similar to the concept 'behavioural expectation'. Furthermore, respondents of this study were SME owners or their representatives who were responsible for organisational prospects and prosperity; thus, they behaved rationally in any decision involving the running of their businesses. They thought,

planned and had realistic intentions to stay competitive in the ongoing
changing globalised market environment. In this situation, we may conclude that the intention used in this study, in fact, indicates the rational
intention, that is, expectation. Thus the final model has combined intention
and expectation (these were proposed in the initial model separately) and
has used rational intention (expectation) as an immediate antecedent of
SMEs' technology usage behaviour.

4.3.6. The Comprehensive Research Model

As discussed earlier, a comparison was made between the initial model and
the findings of the field study. Justifications of the selected constructs and
dimensions were then made. As a result, this section proposes a comprehensive
model for the current research. Fig. 2 illustrates this comprehensive model.

The comprehensive model (cognitive evaluation, expectation, use and
organisational performance) states that cognitive evaluation and entrepreneurs' innovativeness are the primary antecedents of BI. The model argues
that in the situation of having prior experience, the outcome and

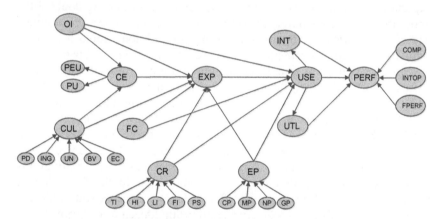

Fig. 2. The Comprehensive Research Model. *Notes:* CE = Cognitive evaluation,
OI = Owner innovativeness, EXP = Expectation, EP = Environmental pressure,
CUL = Culture, CR = Country readiness, FC = Facilitating condition, USE =
Actual usage, INT = Integration, UTL = Utilisation, PERF = SME performance.
(First-order constructs, PU = Perceived usefulness, PEU = Perceived ease of use,
PD = Power distance, ING = In-group collectivism, UN = Uncertainty avoidance,
BV = Bengali value, EC = Ethical culture, TI = Technology infrastructure, HI =
Human infrastructure, LI = Legal infrastructure, FI = Financial infrastructure, PS =
Government policy and supports, CP = Coercive pressure, MP = Mimetic pressure,
NP = Normative pressure, GP = Global pressure, COMP = Competitiveness,
    INTOP = Internal operation productivity, FPERF = Financial performance.

predictions are almost known to the adopters thus the intention becomes rational which is similar to expectation. Thus, the model uses expectation instead of intention to explain the actual technology usage behaviour. Expectation is again logically used in the model to adequately receive the influences of external forces – culture, environmental pressure and country readiness – along with the internal and organisational factors – cognitive evaluation, entrepreneurs' innovativeness and facilitating condition.

The model has extended one further step in comparison to the TRA, TPB, TAM, the DOI theory or other traditional innovation diffusion frameworks as it includes performance as the final outcome which is explained by the usage of the innovation. The model emphasises that straightforward use of the technology may not be fruitful for enhanced organisational performance. The usage of the innovation will generate organisational performance growth if it is properly utilised within an integrated framework. Thus two new constructs, ICT integration and utilisation, have been included as immediate antecedents of performance: they also act as mediators on the effects of ICT usage on organisational performance.

The model applies higher-order modelling to conceptualise cognitive evaluation, culture, environmental pressure, country readiness and organisational performance. That is, each of those constructs is conceptualised as a higher-order construct of two or more latent variables. The performance construct has been conceptualised as a higher-order construct of competitiveness, internal operation productivity and financial performance.

4.4. Summary

This section has presented the findings of the field study and has proposed a research model. Qualitative data were generated from 11 interviews conducted in Bangladesh to assess the experience, expertise and perceptions of SME owners or decision-makers on the adoption and diffusion of ICT at firm level. The main objective of this field study was to test the applicability of the proposed initial model based on the prior literature, and to explore the dimensionality of related constructs. Overall, the content analysis technique consisting of inductive and deductive phases was employed to analyse the data. Moreover, theoretical as well as lateral replication was used in the deductive phase. Factors and variables, as well as some measures, have been explored with these being further scrutinised in light of the relevant literature. Furthermore, relationships among factors have been established. Based on the analysis, a combined model (integrating all factors and variables from each interview) has been developed. Later, this model was compared with the initial model (derived from the literature review) to propose the comprehensive research model. The final model has demonstrated a wide and comprehensive process of ICT diffusion and its resultant outcome as organisational performance in the context of SMEs in Bangladesh. On the basis of the comprehensive model, several hypotheses have been constructed which are reported in Section 5. The following section (Section 6) reports the data analysis and findings of the quantitative survey.

5. HYPOTHESES AND QUESTIONNAIRE DEVELOPMENT

5.1. Introduction

This section presents the development of the hypotheses and quantitative research instruments based on the comprehensive research model (see Fig. 2). The model was primarily developed from a rigorous literature review process which was then contextualised and modified by the qualitative field study analysis. The hypotheses are presented in different subsections under Section 5.2. Following the presentation of the hypotheses, Section 5.3 discusses the development of the research instrument.

5.2. Hypotheses Development

5.2.1. Hypothesis Related to Cognitive Evaluation

The TRA (Fishbein & Ajzen, 1975) suggests that a structured model be used to examine the relationships between one's beliefs, evaluations, intention and actual behaviour. Fishbein and Ajzen (1975) suggested that an overall affective evaluation, that is, one's beliefs (cognitive) with regard to performing a behaviour and the respective evaluations (affective) heavily influence an individual's intention to perform the behaviour. The evaluation is made based on one's cognitive evaluation of the consequences of that behaviour (Ajzen & Fishbein, 1980; Sheppard et al., 1988). The evaluation process involves functional consequences, that is, the outcomes which are immediate, direct and tangible, as well as the psychological consequences, that is, the consequences which are internal, personal and abstract in nature. These cognitive and affective evaluations form one's attitude, that is, negative or positive feelings about performing a behaviour with this having been widely researched in the consumer, marketing and IS research (Ajzen, 1985; Fishbein & Ajzen, 1975; Gehrt & Carter, 1992; Mehta & Sivadas, 1995; Reynolds, 1974 (for catalogue shopping); Schlosser,

Shavitt, & Kanfer, 1999 (for Internet advertising); Liao & Cheung, 2001 (for e-shopping); Cho, 2004 (for intended online transactions). In this study, the affective and cognitive aspects were associated with SMEs' intention to use various applications of ICT. The owners' or managers' feelings about using ICT (favourable or unfavourable) are formed through their beliefs towards using ICT, which was termed as 'attitude' towards ICT in many previous research studies (Liao & Cheung, 2001; Mehta & Sivadas, 1995; Reynolds, 1974; Schlosser et al., 1999) as a higher conceptualisation of perceived ease of use and usefulness of the technology. The construct was measured by the owners' or managers' evaluation of the usefulness of the technology in their firms' current settings as well as the extent to which the technology was considered easy to use by their respective employees or operators. Thus, this evaluation, although similar to attitude, is termed 'cognitive evaluation'.

The outcome of the field study was supportive of previous studies with the 'cognitive evaluation' being positively related to the SMEs' intention to use ICT. All participants agreed upon the relationship between attitude and intention. The participants expressed the view that the owners' or managers' positive evaluations about the usefulness as well as ease of use of the technology led to the positive intention to use ICT. Unlike the formation of consumers' attitudes towards an innovation, the SMEs' owners had prior knowledge about the innovation and tried to make a rational decision by justifying the prospective gain and sacrifice in using the technology. To make the firm profitable, the owners or entrepreneurs avoided acting on impulse or making an emotional decision both of which are common in the consumer decision process. The intention of SMEs' owners or managers regarding ICT was not simply a dream or aspiration but rather a rational and justified intention which was at least screened through basic financial and managerial concerns. Thus, the intention was termed as an expectation which is a more expressed state of will than intention and can explain the effects of both internal and external factors (Venkatesh et al., 2008; Warshaw & Davis, 1984). The implication was that a positive 'cognitive evaluation' was an important indicator that would influence SMEs' expectation to use ICT. Based on the above discussions, the following hypothesis is proposed:

H1. Cognitive evaluation has direct and positive influence on SMEs' expectation to use ICT.

5.2.2. Hypotheses Related to Owner Innovativeness
The adoption of a new product is a diffusion process that moves through different stages over time. Moreover, diffusion is defined as the process by which an innovation is communicated through certain channels over time among the members of a social system (Kendall et al., 2001). According to

the DOI theory (Rogers, 1983, 1995, 2003), the diffusion process begins with knowledge of the existence of the innovation which is followed by persuasion, decision, implementation and confirmation stages. Rogers (1995) indicated that the decision-maker's characteristics, such as, socio-economic characteristics, personality variables and communication behaviours, play a vital role during the knowledge stage which also provides the basis for intention formation. Individuals' innovativeness has a significant influence on the formation of adoption intention of an innovation although it is formed during the persuasion stage.

The adoption of an innovation in a small firm is highly influenced by the personal characteristics and preferences of the owner or CEO of the organisation as most small businesses are managed by the owner who also acts as the CEO (Solomon, 1986; Steinhoff & Burgess, 1986; Yap et al., 1992). Interestingly, the SMEs have a flat organisational structure (Raymond & Magnenat-Thalmann, 1982; Steinhoff & Burgess, 1986). The CEO in an SME usually performs more than one function in running the business operations, makes most decisions, and has full control of organisational resources (Quaddus & Hofmeyer, 2007; Yap et al., 1992). Yap et al. (1992) explained how a CEO could play supportive roles in computer-based information systems (CBIS) in a small business by establishing the firm's appropriate CBIS goals, identifying critical business information needs, allocating sufficient financial resources to achieve CBIS goals and making decisions relating to CBIS implementation and control.

Rogers (1995) also categorised five different adopters according to the time of adoption as being innovators, early adopters, early majority, late majority and laggards (Weber & Kauffman, 2011). The innovators are the adopters who are innovative in nature and bear some risks associated with the early adoption of an innovation. The innovativeness of the CEO or owner of an SME has a significant effect on the adoption and implementation of IS (Thong, 1999; Thong & Yap, 1995). Therefore, based on the above discussion, it is hypothesised that:

H2a. Owner innovativeness has direct and significant effects on cognitive evaluation.

H2b. Owner innovativeness has direct and significant effects on SMEs' expectation to use ICT.

H2c. Owner innovativeness has direct and significant effects on SMEs' use of ICT.

5.2.3. Hypotheses Related to Environmental Pressure

The TOE framework (Tornatzky & Fleischer, 1990) posits the effects of some external or contextual variables such as organisational and environmental factors on the organisational aspects of technology diffusion.

The TOE framework identifies three aspects of a firm's context that influence the process by which it adopts, implements and uses technological innovations. The environmental context is an important context among them referring to the aspects of how a firm conducts its business, responds to its industry, customers and competitors, and deals with government. This framework has received more attention and acceptance from diverse fields of study as it is consistent with the classical DOI theory (Rogers, 1983). Rogers emphasised the technological characteristics, and both internal and external characteristics of the organisation, as drivers for technology diffusion.

The impact of environmental factors and their characteristics are well addressed in institutional theory which posits that organisations face pressure to conform to these shared notions of appropriate forms of behaviours, since violating them may call into question the organisation's legitimacy and thus affect its ability to secure resources and social support (DiMaggio & Powell, 1983; Tolbert, 1985).

DiMaggio and Powell (1983) distinguished between three types of isomorphic pressure – coercive, mimetic and normative – and suggested that coercive and normative pressure normally operate through interconnected relationships while mimetic pressure acts through structural equivalence.

Ajzen and Fishbein (1980) explored the role of SNs and studied how they affect individual behaviour. SNs, in other words, pressure from friends and family plays a vital role in the formation of intention to use an innovation. In the organisational aspect, a focal organisation is able to learn about an innovation and its associated benefits and costs from other user organisations with whom it is directly or indirectly tied, and is likely to be persuaded to behave similarly (Burt, 1982). Many studies consider normative pressure as an antecedent of organisational innovation adoption phenomena (Kuan & Chau, 2001; Teo et al., 2003).

Mimetic pressure is the influence of other structurally equivalent organisations that have initiated some innovations and have become successful. This pressure may cause an organisation to change over time to become more like other organisations in its environment (DiMaggio & Powell, 1983). Many past studies have included mimetic pressure when looking at organisational ICT adoption behaviour (Premkumar & Ramamurthy, 1995; Teo et al., 2003).

Coercive pressure addresses various kinds of power or influence, informal or formal, exercised by other organisations upon which an organisation is dependent. A dominant customer, supplier or parent organisation sometimes exercises their power or coercively influences the organisation to do a certain thing with the dependent organisation having no option other than to comply with the requirement. Coercive pressure has had great importance in previous studies on ICT diffusion behaviour (Quaddus & Hofmeyer, 2007; Teo et al., 2003). This study has applied a hybrid concept of environmental pressure combining all aspects of isomorphic pressure in a higher-order construct. Thus, the effect of environmental pressure in the ICT adoption/diffusion process at firm level is hypothesised as:

H3a. Environmental pressure has a significant influence on SMEs' expectation to use ICT.

H3b. Environmental pressure has a significant influence on SMEs' actual use of ICT.

5.2.4. Hypotheses Related to Facilitating Condition
Within the environmental context, the TOE framework (Tornatzky & Fleischer, 1990) also posits the influence of technological context and organisational context. The technological context is concerned with the existing technologies as well as new technologies relevant to the firm while the organisational context addresses descriptive measures of the organisation such as its scope, size and the amount of slack resources available internally. These factors are particularly important for IS' diffusion at organisational level as some resources such as technological resources and human resources are required for the operation of ICT. The presence of such resources may facilitate the adoption and use of the technology (Venkatesh et al., 2003).

The facilitating condition – the existence of technological or organisational support infrastructure – is grounded in the TPB (Ajzen, 1985). This construct is also included in other successive models such as the decomposed theory of planned behaviour (DTPB) (Taylor & Todd, 1995c), combined TAM and TPB (C-TAM-TPB) (Taylor & Todd, 1995a) and the MPCU (Thompson, Higgins, & Howell, 1991) which have looked at its effects on intention and actual usage of technological innovations. The construct *facilitating condition* (or PBC, perceived behavioural control) is included as an antecedent of intention (Ajzen, 1985; Taylor & Todd, 1995c; Thompson et al., 1991) and actual use (Ajzen, 1985; Tornatzky & Fleischer, 1990). Thus, based on the above-mentioned discussion, it is hypothesised that:

H4a. Facilitating condition has a significant influence on SMEs' expectation to use ICT.

H4b. Facilitating condition has a significant influence on SMEs' actual use of ICT.

5.2.5. Hypotheses Related to Country Readiness
Country readiness, an important external factor, has been discussed in various past studies that have examined the adequacy and access costs of basic information infrastructure (Kraemer & Dedrick, 1994; Shih, Dedrick, & Kraemer, 2005); government policy and legislation (Lee & Shim, 2007; Teo, Tan, & Buk, 1998); regulatory supports (Zhu & Kraemer, 2005; Zhu, Kraemer, et al., 2006); the rule of law, political openness and property rights protection (Caselli & Coleman, 2001; Oxley & Yeung, 2001; Shih et al., 2005); and education levels (Caselli & Coleman, 2001). Dewan and Kraemer (2000) reported that developed and developing countries differed in terms of the level of IT use and the factors shaping that use. In referring to Rogers (1983), Tornatzky and Fleischer (1990), and Caselli and Coleman (2001), Zhu and Kraemer (2005) mentioned that, at the general level, technology diffusion studies presented evidence of an unevenly occurring diffusion across countries with different environments which indicated that country-specific characteristics mattered when it came to technology diffusion. Likewise, a variety of economic, social and political factors, including income, education, technology policies, cultural norms and access to formal and informal communication networks impact on the extent of diffusion.

Iacovou, Benbasat, and Dexter (1995) and Kuan and Chau (2001) considered readiness primarily as the availability of resources (financial and technical) as well as strategic readiness. Country readiness has become an important factor to be investigated in the area of organisational technology diffusion studies as, even though an organisation has enough resources, this does not necessarily mean that they facilitate the situation towards better performance. Thus, the facilitating condition's effect on behavioural expectation and ICT use (Venkatesh et al., 2003, 2008) is not limited solely to organisational resources. Internet availability and facilities at national level, Internet speed, the cost of Internet access and ICT resources, regulatory framework, market conditions, delivery systems, and government policy and supports also have direct effects on ICT adoption producing a regulatory environment that accelerates or hinders ICT use at firm level.

The field study also supported the inclusion of country readiness as an antecedent of expectation and actual ICT usage behaviour. Participants in the field study indicated that country-level technology infrastructure, human infrastructure, legal infrastructure, financial infrastructure and government policy and supports were important concerns that created country readiness for rapid adoption and diffusion of ICT. The above-mentioned four dimensions of country readiness should not be considered in isolation from each other, but should be treated in a collective and mutually reinforcing manner. Hence, the country readiness construct represents an integrative measure of the level of readiness along these four dimensions. A second-order factor modelling approach can capture correlations among the four first-order factors and explain them using a higher-order construct that is an integrative latent representation of country readiness. Previous studies have noted that this operational approach represents a theoretically strong basis for capturing complex measures (Segars & Grover, 1998; Sethi & King, 1994; Stewart & Segars, 2002; Venkatraman, 1990; Zhu & Kraemer, 2002; Zhu et al., 2003). Country readiness is not quite evenly reflected in the four dimensions.

This factor is considered as a new aspect of the facilitating condition which is different from the facilitating condition (organisational-level resources and capabilities) explained in previous studies (Venkatesh et al., 2003, 2008) and is termed 'country readiness'. This study thus logically added country readiness as a separate predictor of behavioural expectation and actual use behaviour. Based on the above discussion, it is hypothesised that:

H5a. Country readiness has a significant influence on SMEs' expectation to use ICT.

H5b. Country readiness has a significant influence on SMEs' use of ICT.

5.2.6. Hypotheses Related to Culture

The existing theories have admitted the effects of various external environmental factors on the adoption and diffusion of an innovation in the organisational context (Rogers, 1995; Tornatzky & Fleischer, 1990). The theoretical frameworks developed by Hofstede (2001) and House et al. (2004) stressed the effects of culture on organisational leadership. Hofstede (2001) treated culture as the collective programming of the mind that distinguishes the members of one group or category of people from another and studied culture in five dimensions — power distance, collectivism, uncertainty avoidance, masculinity versus femininity and long-term versus short-term orientation.

House et al. (2004) addressed culture differently with nine dimensions — performance orientation, assertiveness, future orientation, humane orientation, institutional collectivism, in-group collectivism, gender egalitarianism, power distance and uncertainty avoidance. House et al. (2004) indicated that national culture has effects on leadership and organisational processes. Thus, the planning, execution and controlling aspects of an organisation are highly influenced by culture. By utilising Hofstede et al.'s (2001) and House et al.'s (2004) frameworks, many previous studies have examined the impact of culture on organisational technology adoption. Thatcher et al. (2006) reported that culture plays an important role in the adoption of a certain technology by organisations in a particular country and it also impacts on the degree to which the technology is accepted and the ways in which it is used. Past studies have also supported the link between cultural dimension and different facets of IT use (Bertolotti, 1984; Burn, 1995; Erez & Early, 1993; Gefen & Straub, 1997; Harris & Davison, 1999; Hill et al., 1998; Ho et al., 1989; Straub, 1994). Erumban and Jong (2006) found that the national culture and ICT adoption rate of a country are closely related. They further reported that most of Hofstede's dimensions were important in influencing adoption with power distance and uncertainty avoidance dimensions seeming to be the most influential.

This study has undertaken a qualitative research study to explore and justify the effects of various cultural dimensions in the diffusion of ICT among SMEs in Bangladesh. The analysis of the interview transcripts resulted in anticipation of the effects of five dimensions of culture, namely, power distance, uncertainty avoidance, in-group collectivism, ethical culture and Bengali values on the intention to use ICT.

The exploratory search also anticipated negative structural relationships between cultural dimensions and SMEs' intention to use ICT. Based on the above discussion, it is hypothesised that:

H6a. Culture has a significant influence on cognitive evaluation.

H6b. Culture has a significant influence on SMEs' expectation to use ICT.

5.2.7. Hypothesis Related to Expectation
The majority of the innovation diffusion theories included intention as a strong predictor of actual usage behaviour (Ajzen, 1985; Davis, 1986; Fishbein & Ajzen, 1975; Rogers, 1983; Venkatesh et al., 2003). As an immediate antecedent of actual innovation usage behaviour, BI can explain the effects of various internal or external factors in predicting actual behaviour. For example, intention is formed through the adopter's characteristics (Rogers, 1983; Thong & Yap, 1995); PBC (Ajzen, 1985); SNs (Fishbein & Ajzen, 1975); perceived ease of use and perceived usefulness

(Davis, 1986); and performance expectancy and effort expectancy (Venkatesh et al., 2003). Although intention, a reflection of the adopter's internal schema of beliefs, had a significant influence in earlier behavioural models, it cannot predict the situation which is not under full volitional control of the adopter or the situation where a time gap exists between intention and actual behaviour (Venkatesh et al., 2008). However, a stronger predictor of actual behaviour could incorporate some other external (social and environmental) dimensions which would need to be considered in the existing model. Venkatesh et al. (2008) further modified their UTAUT model (Venkatesh et al., 2003) and included behavioural expectation as a new construct which is a stronger predictor of behaviour than intention.

The field study did not find any differences between intention and expectation. Furthermore, it proved that the SME owner who intended to adopt a new technology did not simply dream about it nor was it unachievable. The intention was formed by justifying the feeling through taking into consideration several business and resource factors. For example, Firm A indicated that: '*[t]he supports and surrounding facilities screen the intention. We are not in any doubt whether we could do so according to our intention. We will upgrade the existing technology*'.

Based on the previous literature (Venkatesh et al., 2008) and the field study results, this study has hypothesised that behavioural expectation is a possible predictor of actual ICT use. Thus,

H7. Expectation has a significant influence on actual ICT usage.

5.2.8. Hypotheses Related to ICT Use

ICT use is included as the final dependent variable in most of the theoretical frameworks which involve IT innovation diffusion behaviour (Davis, 1986; Taylor & Todd, 1995a; Venkatesh et al., 2003, 2008). Past studies have employed ICT use as the final dependent variable based on the notion that ICT use would generate performance. Researchers have applied different aspects of IS use such as duration of use, frequency of use and intensity of use to measure the actual behaviour in relation to any IT usage (Venkatesh et al., 2008).

Some studies have employed different forms of IT usage such as ICT/system use (Anandarajan et al., 2002; Davis, 1986; Taylor & Todd, 1995a; Zhu, Dong, et al., 2006; Zhu & Kraemer, 2005); EDI integration (Iacovou et al., 1995); e-business initiation, adoption and routinisation

(Zhu, Kraemer, et al., 2006); and e-commerce migration (Hong & Zhu, 2006). Although the investigation of ICT use was found to be the focus of a number of ICT innovation diffusion studies in the past few years, ICT's impact on performance growth has become a vital issue in recent years. The literature has supported a direct and positive relationship between IT usage by SMEs and firm performance (Zhu, Dong, et al., 2006; Zhu & Kraemer, 2005).

Anandarajan et al. (2002) indicated a concern relating to the productivity paradox and stated that the mere adoption of IT by organisations does not necessarily confer on them the benefits that could only result from its effective usage. Past literature has enunciated that many IS in LDCs are under-utilised and thus do not make a significant contribution to improving the performance of the organisations that are using them (Forster & Cornford, 1992; Ordedra et al., 1993). In support of the previous studies, Song and Mueller-Falcke (2006) stated that SMEs are confronted with a number of challenges in adopting and using ICT and they often end up under-utilising the available technologies (see UNCTAD, 2006). IS usage implies the role that IS utilisation plays in generating organisational performance.

Zhu and Kraemer (2005) also indicated the positive and effective role of ICT integration on organisational performance. Thus, the motivation for organisational ICT adoption or usage is to integrate or properly utilise the technology for performance growth.

The field study supported the view that the integration of diversified technologies is dependent on the level of ICT usage by SMEs in Bangladesh. For example, Firm K stated: '*[a]fter that [introduction of ICT use], the scope of ICT use has widened and strengthened. It seems that a new technology is just introduced in some department and gradually it will spread over the organisation and work under a common system*'.

The field study further explored the view that the degree of ICT utilisation is also developed from the firm's usage of different levels of ICT applications. For example, Firm B stated: '*[we]e can earn productivity and efficiency (organisational performance) through proper utilisation of ICT particularly through some software by which we can track, control and initiate alternative strategy ... those companies [from whom] we are getting benefits and gradually developing, they are actually developing due to the proper utilisation of the technology (ICT). For example, in [the] international context, some big companies are giving their employees 'Blackberries' so they (employees) can mail and be connected with the network from anywhere around the world*'.

Based on the above discussion, it is hypothesised that:

H8a. ICT usage has a significant influence on integration.

H8b. ICT usage has a significant influence on utilisation.

H8c. ICT usage has a significant influence on performance.

5.2.9. Hypothesis Related to ICT Integration

The RBV (Barney, 1991) emphasises combining ICT resources to build unique IT capabilities which would generate organisational performance. The IT capabilities are dependent on how ICT is integrated and utilised among different functional areas. Recent studies have shown that ICT integration facilitates transactional efficiencies and expansion of existing channels. Zhu and Kraemer (2002, 2005) revealed that integration (of the front-end functionalities of e-business) helps firms to provide real-time product information to customers, offers customisation capability and facilitates self-service via online account management, thereby improving transactional efficiencies and expanding the existing channels: ICT integration (back-end integration) also enables information sharing within the firm and along the value chain.

The field study has justified the effects of ICT integration on organisational performance. For example, Firm B stated that: *'[w]e have accumulated some of our similar closely related group of companies into very close contact between those are working with us in the same network environment through our server. We are performing the above-mentioned work through ICT (as we have got good results)'.*

It (ICT integration) makes our communication and interaction with customers easy.'(Firm J). *Firm J also indicated the positive effect of ICT integration on organisational performance by saying,* '[w]e find the ICT is working better when we see that [ICT by integration] makes the communication with our supplier easy.

Based on past studies and the results of the field study, it is hypothesised that:

H9. ICT integration has a significant influence on performance.

5.2.10. Hypothesis Related to ICT Utilisation

As with ICT integration, appropriate utilisation of ICT can contribute to organisational ICT capabilities. Thus, according to the RBV, organisational performance also logically depends on the utilisation of ICT. Past studies have revealed that many IS in LDCs are under-utilised and hence do not make a significant contribution to improving the performance of the organisations that are using them (Forster & Cornford, 1992; Ordedra et al., 1993).

In analysing the field study interviews, it was anticipated that utilisation of ICT would influence organisational performance as the field study had explored whether ICT utilisation has a direct positive link with organisational performance. For example, Firm H stated that: '*[w]e are trying to develop the IT-literate competent employee day by day. We hope we shall be capable of appropriate and comprehensive use of ICT*'. Firm I expressed the importance of ICT utilisation on organisational performance in terms of ensuring customer satisfaction when it stated that: '*[i]f the ICT is not appropriate [appropriately utilised], we will not be able to satisfy the customer or target group*'. Firm J, agreeing with Firms H and I, also stated the importance of ICT utilisation by saying: '*[t]he performance is dependent on how well [how appropriate] we will use [utilise] ICT*'.

The field interview analysis revealed that most of the organisations, such as Firms H, I and J recognised the importance of ICT utilisation to secure improved organisational performance. However, Firm K expressed their strong concern about the erroneous process or bad organisational performance which may happen if ICT is not properly utilised. The importance of ICT utilisation on organisational performance is clearly reflected in the following statement:

> ICT enhances the employees' performance. ICT normally reduces the error. But it varies from person to person operating the ICT. It depends on their skill. I have a doubt if the ICT is not properly handled [properly utilised], it may produce bad and damaging output. (Firm K)

Based on the above discussion, it is thus hypothesised that:

H10. ICT utilisation has a significant influence on performance.

5.2.11. Hypothesis Related to the Mediation Effects of Integration and Utilisation

Numerous studies have found a positive link between IT use and organisational performance (Baldwin & Sabourin, 2001; Cragg et al. 2002; Dvir et al., 1993; Gretton et al., 2004; Pilat & Wyckoff, 2005). Although achieving enhanced organisational performance is the motivation for organisations using ICT, past studies have also revealed differing results such as research by Warner (1987) who found a negative effect; Venkatraman and Zaheer (1990) and Sager (1988) who found no effect; and Powell and Dent-Micallef (1997) and Tippins and Sohi (2003) who found mixed effects; while Bharadwaj (2000) and Zhu and Kraemer (2005) found direct positive effects. Previous sections (Sections 5.2.8, 5.2.9 and 5.2.10) have analysed ICT usage, integration and utilisation and have also hypothesised relationships between them. Hypotheses H_{8a}, H_{8b} and H_{8c} proposed that ICT usage would have positive effects on integration, utilisation and organisational performance. On the other hand, Hypotheses H_9 and H_{10} proposed that integration and utilisation would have positive effects on organisational performance. The above-mentioned relationships may imply that integration and utilisation have mediational effects which has not been widely investigated in previous studies.

Kim et al. (2006) revealed the mediation role of inter-firm systems integration in explaining the effects of SCCS innovation on firm supply chain performance. Although the mediation effects of integration have been empirically justified, there remains a paucity of empirical findings in support of the role of utilisation. This study thus looked at the inter-relationship of ICT usage, integration, degree of utilisation and organisational performance through the use of the field study analysis in which the mediation effect of utilisation was found. For example, Firm I indicated that: '*[i]f the ICT is not appropriate [appropriately utilised], we will not be able to satisfy the customer or target group*' and Firm J also stated the relationship by saying: '*[t]he performance is dependent on how well [how appropriate] we will use [utilise] ICT*'. The field study also justified the mediating roles of both integration and utilisation. For example, Firm K stated that: '*... if the technology is used [utilised] completely in different working areas in the entire organisation as well as if the external organisations are also integrated or communicated with entirely through ICT, the performance [organisational performance] will certainly be increased*'. Based on the above discussion, it is hypothesised that:

H11a. Integration plays a significant mediation role in explaining the effects of ICT usage on SME performance.

H11b. Utilisation plays a significant mediation role in explaining the effects of ICT usage on SME performance.

H11c. Integration and utilisation jointly play a significant mediation role in explaining the effects of ICT usage on SME performance.

5.3. *Questionnaire Development*

The previous section has discussed the various constructs under study and has anticipated possible relationships between them with the result that 10 sets of hypotheses (see Fig. 3) have been formulated. These hypotheses were tested by the survey data. The data were collected by a questionnaire survey in which the questionnaire contained a set of questions which specifically examined different hypotheses developed for this study. The following sections describe the questionnaire development.

5.3.1. *Overview of the Questionnaire*
This study collected data in two phases. The first phase was confined to collecting qualitative data by interviews which were conducted using a semi-structured questionnaire. The final phase involved data collection in order to test the hypotheses. An extensive survey was administered through a structured questionnaire which was designed to test the research hypotheses according to the comprehensive model as shown in Fig. 2.

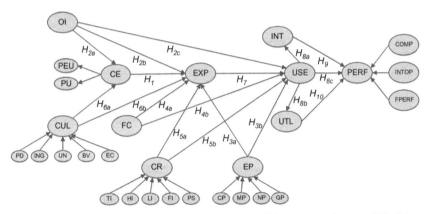

CE = Cognitive evaluation, OI = Owner innovativeness, EXP = Expectation, EP = Environmental pressure, CUL = Culture, CR = Country readiness, FC = Facilitating condition, USE = Actual usage, INT = Integration, UTL = Utilisation, PERF = SME performance.
(First-order constructs, PU = Perceived usefulness, PEU = Perceived ease of use, PD = Power distance, ING = In-group collectivism, UN = Uncertainty avoidance, BV = Bengali value, EC = Ethical culture, TI = Technology infrastructure, HI = Human infrastructure, LI = Legal infrastructure, FI = Financial infrastructure, PS =Government policy and supports, CP = Coercive pressure, MP = Mimetic pressure, NP= Normative pressure, GP = Global pressure, COMP = Competitiveness, INTOP = Internal operation productivity, FPERF = Financial performance)

Fig. 3. The Comprehensive Research Model and Hypotheses.

The questionnaire was developed from the existing relevant literature and field study. The questionnaire included a wide range of questions specific to the study hypotheses. A variety of forms, patterns and scales were used in different questions which included, where applicable, open-ended, closed-ended, dichotomous, numerical, categorical questions and questions with answers rated on a Likert-type scale. In order to assess respondents' perceptions, both semantic differential scales and Likert scales were used. The questionnaire was broadly divided into three main sections: questions related to respondents' demographic details; questions related to different factors of ICT use and questions related to organisational performance. The next section is divided into the following subsections: questions related to cognitive evaluation; owner innovativeness; expectation; environmental pressure; country readiness; culture; ICT use; integration and utilisation.

5.3.2. Measurement Instrument

This section discusses the development of the measurement instrument which includes the form of the instrument and its sources. The main sources of the instrument were the existing literature and the field study.

5.3.2.1. Cognitive Evaluation.

In accordance with the theoretical framework developed for this study (see Section 4), *cognitive evaluation* reflects the adopter's favourableness or unfavourableness towards an innovation with this view formed through various attitudinal beliefs and respective evaluations. Fishbein and Ajzen (1975) addressed various attitudinal beliefs and their evaluations as Antecedents of attitude towards an innovation. Many past studies have measured adopter favourableness or unfavourableness (attitude) towards an innovation by a few reflective items such as *'using the innovation is good/bad idea'*, *'the innovation makes work more interesting'*, *'working with the innovation is fun'* and *'I like/dislike working with the innovation'* (Davis et al., 1989; Venkatesh et al., 2003). In measuring the TPB constructs, Taylor and Todd (1995b) combined all belief items with the evaluative components using the expectancy-value approach suggested in the TPB (Ajzen, 1985, 1991, for example, $\sum_{i=1} b_i e_i$ for measuring the attitude, $\sum_{j=1} nb_j mc_j$ for the SN and $\sum_{k=1} cb_k pf_k$ for PBC). Shih and Fang (2004) followed this approach in predicting customers' intention to adopt Internet banking.

With reference to Ajzen (1991), Taylor and Todd (1995b) stated that the relationship between the belief structures and the Antecedents of intention (A [attitude], SN and PBC (or facilitating condition)) is particularly not well understood due to two factors. Firstly, the belief structures are combined into unidimensional constructs (i.e. $\sum_{i=1} b_i e_i$, $\sum_{j=1} nb_j mc_j$, $\sum_{k=1} cb_k pf_k$) in the theory. Such monolithic belief sets may not be consistently related to attitude, SN or PBC (Bagozzi, 1981, 1982; Miniard & Cohen, 1979, 1981, 1983; Shimp & Kavas, 1984). Secondly, the belief sets, especially those relating to attitude, are idiosyncratic to the empirical setting, making it difficult to operationalise the theory. In contrast to the TPB, the TAM (Davis et al., 1989) proposed a belief set, consisting of ease of use and usefulness that was consistent and generalisable across different settings. Based on the above discussion, Taylor and Todd (1995b) recommended a set of stable, decomposed belief structures for the TPB model.

The field study explored eight different items which measured SME owner favourableness or unfavourableness towards ICT. Interestingly, all eight measurement items belonged to two distinct factors. The past literature has recognised these two factors as *perceived usefulness* and *perceived ease of use* (Davis, 1986, 1989; Taylor & Todd, 1995b; Venkatesh et al., 2003). Guided by the field study and following the suggestion by Taylor and Todd (1995b), this study combined all eight reflective items to measure *cognitive evaluation*. Applying the principle of hierarchical modelling – molecular model (Chin & Gopal, 1995) – *perceived usefulness* and *perceived ease of use* were used as reflective first-order constructs of a hybrid conceptualisation called '*cognitive evaluation*'. The measurement items of the first-order constructs, although developed from the field study, were also supported by the existing literature. Items for the first-order manifest variables of the higher-order *cognitive evaluation* and their sources are stated in Table 9.

5.3.2.2. Owner Innovativeness and Facilitating Condition. Owner innovativeness was modelled as an antecedent of ICT adoption by SMEs. Thong and Yap (1995) adopted the *risk-taking ability* of the owner and the owner's 'ability to produce original ideas' to face the competitive environment as measurement items for owner innovativeness. The field study explored two items for measuring *owner innovativeness* which were similar to the measurement items adopted by Thong and Yap (1995) (see Table 10).

This study modelled *facilitating condition* as an antecedent factor of expectation as well as ICT usage. Past studies have adopted a few items related to the adopter's assessment of their firm's ability and resources, such as, assessing whether the adopter has the resources necessary to use the innovation, if the adopter has the knowledge necessary to use the innovation, if the innovation is incompatible with other systems, and if a specific person (or group) is available for assistance with any operational difficulties (Venkatesh et al., 2003; Venkatesh & Zhang, 2010).

Table 9. Cognitive Evaluation.

Items	Statement	Sources
Ease of use		
PEU1	My interaction with the technology would be clear and understandable	Field study, Venkatesh et al. (2003)
PEU2	It would be easy for me to become skilful at using the technology	Field study, Venkatesh et al. (2003)
PEU3	I would find the technology easy to use	Field study, Venkatesh et al. (2003)
PEU4	Learning to operate the technology is easy for me	Field study, Venkatesh et al. (2003)
Usefulness		
PU1	I would find ICT useful in my job	Field study, Venkatesh et al. (2003)
PU2	Using the technology enables me to accomplish tasks more quickly	Field study, Venkatesh et al. (2003)
PU3	Using the technology increases my productivity	Field study, Venkatesh et al. (2003)
PU4	If I use the technology, I will increase my chances of getting a raise	Field study, Venkatesh et al. (2003)

The field study explored the items relating to the existing systems or processes of the organisation (i.e. whether the systems or processes were compatible with ICT usage), the resources of the organisation (whether the organisation had the resources necessary to use the systems) and the skill of the employees (whether employees had the knowledge and skills necessary to use the systems). The measurement items for facilitating condition explored through the field study were similar to the measurement scales adopted by Venkatesh et al. (2003). Measurement items for owner innovativeness and facilitating condition along with their sources are presented in Table 10.

5.3.2.3. Environmental Pressure. This study modelled environmental pressure as an antecedent of behavioural expectation and usage of ICT by SMEs with a view to examining the effects of ICT on organisational performance. The institutional theory (DiMaggio & Powell, 1983) suggests that organisations face three dimensions of environmental pressure, namely, coercive pressure, mimetic pressure and normative pressure. Past studies have examined the effects of one particular dimension or the joint effects of these three dimensions to estimate the impacts of environmental pressure on organisational ICT adoption behaviour. For example, Teo et al. (2003) studied coercive pressures, mimetic pressures and normative pressures, Zhu et al. (2003) studied competitive pressures which are known as mimetic pressures, and Quaddus and Hofmeyer (2007) studied coercive pressures.

Table 10. Items for Owner Innovativeness and Facilitating Condition.

Items	Statement	Sources
Owner innovativeness		
OI1	He often risks doing things differently	Field study, Thong and Yap (1995)
OI2	He has original ideas	Field study, Thong and Yap (1995)
Facilitating condition		
FC1	The ICT system is compatible with other existing systems that we use	Field study, Venkatesh et al. (2008)
FC3	Our employees have the knowledge and skill necessary to use the system	Field study, Venkatesh et al. (2008)
FC4	We have the resources necessary to use the system	Field study, Venkatesh et al. (2008)

Past studies have employed various scale items to measure different dimensions of environmental pressure. For example, Teo et al. (2003) used seven subconstructs to measure the three dimensions of environmental pressure. Specifically, they adopted the subconstructs, extent of adoption among competitors and perceived success of competitor adopter for mimetic pressures; perceived dominance of suppliers, perceived dominance of adopter customers, conformity with parent corporation's practices for coercive pressures and extent of adoption among suppliers, extent of adoption among customers and participation in industry, business and trade associations for normative pressures. As they were also latent variables, these subconstructs were measured by multiple indicators (Teo et al., 2003). In contrast to predictive estimates, the dimensions of environmental pressure were directly measured by multiple items such as coercive pressure being measured by the adopter's assessment on whether the parent company liked the adopting firm's use of ICT, whether major customers demanded firms' ICT use and whether major suppliers demanded firms' ICT use (Quaddus & Hofmeyer, 2007); and competitive pressures were measured by the adopter's assessment about the degree affected by competitors in the local market and the degree affected by competitors in the national market (Zhu & Kraemer, 2005).

The field study explored 11 items which belonged to four distinct groups. Three of the four constructs, namely, coercive pressure, mimetic pressure and normative pressure (Teo et al., 2003), were similar to the dimensions adopted in previous studies. The field study explored a new dimension of environmental pressure named global pressure which had arisen from the ongoing initiatives of globalisation.

In accordance with the results of the field study analysis, coercive pressure was measured by the extent to which dominant customers and parent organisations forced SMEs to use the technology. Mimetic pressure was measured by items relating to the extent to which competitors used ICT and to those competitors who had largely benefited from their use of ICT. Normative pressure was measured by items relating to the extent of ICT use by customers, by suppliers, by important stakeholders or business partners and by regulatory bodies. The pressure relating to globalisation was measured through items which enquired about the extent to which the organisation used ICT to attain the business opportunities arising from globalisation, and about the extent to which the organisation believed that no business at present could be sustained without utilisation of ICT. All of the above-mentioned measurement items were supported by the existing literature except the items for global pressure which were explored from the field study.

Importantly, the final research model included overall environmental pressure as an antecedent of SMEs' expectation to use ICT. In accordance with the results of the field study, the effects of overall environmental pressure were measured by the four dimensions: coercive pressure, mimetic pressure, normative pressure and global pressure. These four dimensions were used as index of the higher-order conceptualisation. Past studies used composites of various dimensions to measure a compound variable; for example, Taylor and Todd (1995b) used a composite of *peer influences* and *superior influences* to measure *normative pressure*. Analysis of the field study findings, and particularly the interpretation of the free node and tree node structures, suggested the application of a molar model structure (Chin & Gopal, 1995) to measure overall environmental pressure as a second-order construct developed by these four constructs instead of through aggregation or averaging their effects. Table 11 presents contents and sources of all measurement items for the first-order latent variables of the higher-order environmental pressure.

5.3.2.4. Country Readiness. This study modelled country readiness as an antecedent of behavioural expectation and usage of ICT by SMEs. Past studies have addressed various environmental factors related to the preparedness of the country which may impact on fostering the usage of ICT by organisations, particularly SMEs. Important country readiness dimensions explored in the existing literature included national infrastructure (Huy & Filiatrault, 2006; Kurnia & Peng, 2010); regulatory environment (Zhu et al., 2003); government supports (Jeon et al., 2006); technology vendors supports (Doolin, McLeod, McQueen, & Watton, 2003) and technology readiness, country wealth and level of education (Marques et al., 2011).

Table 11. Items for Environmental Pressure.

Items	Statement	Sources
Coercive pressure		
CP1	My parent company likes us to use ICT	Field study, Quaddus and Hofmeyer (2007)
CP2	Our major customer demanded our ICT use	Field study, Quaddus and Hofmeyer (2007)
CP3	Our major suppliers demanded our ICT use	Field study, Quaddus and Hofmeyer (2007)
Mimetic pressure		
MP1	What is the extent of ICT adoption by your firm's competitors currently?	Field study, Teo et al. (2003)
MP2	My main competitors that have adopted ICT have benefited largely	Teo et al. (2003)
Normative pressure		
NP1	What is the extent of ICT adoption by your firms' customers currently?	Field study, Teo et al. (2003)
NP2	What is the extent of ICT adoption by your suppliers currently?	Field study, Teo et al. (2003)
NP3	What is the extent of ICT adoption by your important business partner currently?	Field study, Quaddus and Hofmeyer (2007)
NP4	What is the extent of ICT adoption by your regulatory bodies?	Field study
Global pressure		
GP1	I am encouraged to adopt ICT in accessing opportunities arising by globalisation	Field study
GP2	I feel this is the time when nobody can sustain [their business] without utilising ICT	Field study

The field study explored 16 items to measure the impact of country readiness. During the analysis, those 16 items were further grouped into five dimensions of country readiness, namely, technology infrastructure, human infrastructure, legal infrastructure, financial infrastructure and government policy and supports (see Table 12).

The availability and coverage of Internet services in Bangladesh, Internet speed, availability of necessary hardware and uninterrupted power supply were the items explored by the field study to measure technology infrastructure.

Items that measured human infrastructure related to the general people's level of education, knowledge of ICT, ICT skill and institutional supports for ICT training and education.

Table 12.   Items for Country Readiness.

Items	Statement	Sources
Technology infrastructure		
TI1	Availability and coverage of Internet service in the country	Field study
TI2	Speed and sophistication of Internet	Field study
TI3	Availability of necessary hardware and accessories	Field study
TI4	Uninterrupted power supply	Field study
Human infrastructure		
HI1	Level of education of the general people	Field study
HI2	General people's knowledge of ICT	Field study
HI3	Computing skill of the general people	Field study
HI4	Institutional support for computer education	Field study
Legal infrastructure		
LI1	Legal supports for digital communication and business through the Internet	Field study
LI2	Law relating to online consumer protection	Zhu and Kraemer (2005)
Financial infrastructure		
FI1	Online banking facility	Field study
FI2	Credit and debit card usage trend	Zhu and Kraemer (2005)
Government policy and supports		
GOV1	Government tax and customs policy	Field study, Zhu and Kraemer (2005)
GOV2	Government's motivational programme	Field study
GOV3	Government grants	Field study
GOV4	Government subsidies	Field study

The measurement items for legal infrastructure were legal protection for digital communication and online business, and online consumer protection.

Financial infrastructure was measured by items related to the extent to which online banking services are available and trend of debit or credit card use in the country.

Government policy and supports was one of the major constructs explored through the qualitative field study. The measurement items were government's tax and customs policy, motivational programme, government grants and supports.

By applying an interpretive research approach, a careful analysis of the field study, particularly the structures of theme, sub-themes and nodes, suggested that *technology infrastructure, human infrastructure, legal infrastructure, financial infrastructure,* and *government policy and supports* were subconstructs for measuring the construct of interest – *country readiness.* Past studies have used composites of various dimensions to measure a compound variable, for example, Taylor and Todd (1995b) used a composite of efficacy and facilitating condition – technology and facilitating condition – resources to measure PBC.

As with the formation of the construct environmental pressure, the field study suggested that country readiness be formed as a higher-order construct by applying the molar model structure (Chin & Gopal, 1995). Measurement items for all first-order constructs and their sources are shown in Table 12.

5.3.2.5. Culture. Culture has been variously defined in the past literature. Kroeber and Kluckhohn (1952) considered 160 different definitions of culture while attempting to develop an acceptable general definition of culture. The variations in conceptualisation of the term 'culture' have also been widened in the past 60 years.

Contemporary studies have followed Hofstede's (2001) framework to conceptualise national culture (Erumban & Jong, 2006). A more recent framework for cultural study developed by the GLOBE cultural study (House et al., 2004) has received numerous researchers' attention with this also having been developed based on Hofstede's (2001) framework. However, Hofstede's (2001) and House et al.'s (2004) frameworks have been the most recent developments in the study of culture.

In Hofstede's (2001) model, culture is conceptualised by five dimensions: power distance, collectivism, uncertainty avoidance, masculinity versus femininity and long-term versus short-term orientation while House et al. (2004) explained culture through nine dimensions: performance orientation, assertiveness, future orientation, humane orientation, institutional collectivism, in-group collectivism, gender egalitarianism, power distance and uncertainty avoidance.

Numerous past studies, investigating the effects of culture in the field of management, have considered a portion of Hofstede's (2001) or House et al.'s (2004) models as being relevant to their studies (Mustamil, 2010; Wahab, 2010).

This field study explored 14 items to measure the impact of culture. Through analysis, the field study grouped these 14 items into five dimensions of culture. Three of the five dimensions of culture that may affect the diffusion of IT among SMEs in Bangladesh and that were explored through the field study were related to the dimensions explained by Hofstede (2001) and House et al. (2004). The field study explored two new dimensions of culture which were Bengali values and ethical behaviour-related cultural issues. Although these aspects of culture were beyond the scope of Hofstede's (2001) and House et al.'s (2004) frameworks, it was considered that they may play an influential role in shaping SMEs' ICT diffusion behaviour. This study, thus, included five dimensions — power distance, collectivism, uncertainty avoidance, Bengali values and ethical culture — to measure the effects of culture.

As with environmental pressure and country readiness, culture was also measured as a higher-order construct by applying the molar model structure (Chin & Gopal, 1995). Items measuring the first-order cultural dimensions for culture and their sources are stated in Table 13.

5.3.2.6. Expectation and ICT Usage. This study modelled expectation and ICT usage as antecedents of ICT usage and organisational performance, respectively. Expectation was included in the research model to indicate the state of rational intention towards adoption of ICT. Past studies have applied a variety of measurement items for intention and expectation as well as for actual usage behaviour (Davis, 1989; Kendall et al., 2001; Venkatesh et al., 2003, 2008). For example, Davis (1989) applied three items to measure intention, namely; I plan to use the system in the next <n> month, I predict to use the system in the next <n> month and I am going to use the system in the next <n> month. On the other hand, Kendall et al. (2001) measured Singaporean SMEs' e-commerce adoption intention by assessing their intended state of various e-commerce applications. The intention was measured using a 6-point scale by categorising six different intended states of e-commerce applications; 1 = Current year, 2 = Intend to use within 1 year, 3 = Within 1−2 years, 4 = Within 2−5 years, 5 = Within 5−10 years and 6 = No intention. The order of these intended states was applied to assess various levels of e-commerce. The construct was estimated as a latent variable comprising multiple items, for example, willingness to have a homepage in the company, willingness to conduct sales through Internet, willingness to purchase the supplies through Internet, etc.

Venkatesh et al. (2008) differentiated the expectation from the intention and applied a relatively expressed state of intention for measuring expectation such as I will use the system in the next <n> month, I am likely to use the system in the next <n> month and I am going to use the system in the next <n> month. Interestingly, this current study did not find any differences between intention and expectation (see the field study analysis in Section 4). The field study analysis revealed that this state of willingness was different from the 'intention' that was used in past studies. More clearly, SMEs' intention to use any level of ICT was not only a cognitive

Table 13. Items for Culture.

Items	Statement	Sources
Power distance		
PD1	In this society, followers are expected to obey their leader without question/question their leader when in disagreement	House et al. (2004)
PD2	In this society, power is concentrated at the top/shared throughout the society	House et al. (2004)
PD3	I believe that followers should obey their leader without question/question their leader when in disagreement	House et al. (2004)
PD4	I believe that power should be concentrated at the top/shared throughout the society	House et al. (2004)
Uncertainty avoidance		
UN1	In this society, orderliness and consistency are stressed, even at the expense of experimentation and innovation	House et al. (2004)
UN2	In this society, social requirements and instructions are spelled out in detail so citizens know what they are expected to do	House et al. (2004)
UN3	In this society, orderliness and consistency should be stressed, even at the expense of experimentation and innovation	House et al. (2004)
UN4	In this society, social requirements and instructions should be spelled out in detail so citizens know what they are expected to do	House et al. (2004)
In-group collectivism		
INGR1	Group members take pride in the individual accomplishments of their group managers	House et al. (2004)
INGR2	Group managers take pride in the individual accomplishments of their group members	House et al. (2004)
INGR2	Managers encourage group loyalty even if individual goals suffer	House et al. (2004)
Bengali values		
BVAL1	Face-to-face communication is vital in our daily lives	Field study
BVAL2	In honour of the language movement, the Bengali language is available everywhere	Field study
BVAL3	Very close and tight social bond	Field study
Ethical culture		
ECUL1	Bribery/corruption are seen as common phenomena everywhere in the main institutions of society	Field study
ECUL2	Politicisation/nepotism are seen as common phenomena everywhere in the main institutions of society	Field study

wish or simply a plan or a dream, it was definite and rational. Based on the field study results, this study used 'expectation' as an logical immediate antecedent of actual usage behaviour: expectation was directly influenced by various individual, organisational and environmental factors.

Furthermore, the previous innovation diffusion studies have mostly focused on a particular technology or systems usage such as Internet, email, personal computers, e-commerce and EDI, ; thus assessment using items like I plan ..., I will ... or I predict ... may be logical grounds from which to measure potential users' intentions. This study has focused on the diffusion of ICT in general which has comprised a range of ICT applications. The field study explored various levels of ICT applications that were being currently used by different SMEs in Bangladesh. To overcome possible ambiguity in construct measurement, these ICT applications were categorised into five distinct levels of ICT operation: basic computing which includes computer and basic Internet operation such as email; homepage operation (static homepage); interactive homepage which supports product cataloguing and order processing (e-commerce); interactive homepage which supports online transactions and account management (e-business) and complete digital communication and exchanges within and outside the organisation (ERP). Applying the measurement approach adopted by Kendall et al. (2001), respondents' assessments about their expected use of those ICT applications were used as measures for expectation. Various states of expectation were assessed through a differential scale: 1 = current user; 2 = expect within 6 months; 3 = within 12 months; 4 = within 1–3 years and 5 = expectation is not specified.

As with intention, actual usage was measured variously in previous studies. Venkatesh et al. (2003) measured actual usage behaviour as the duration of use via system logs; Venkatesh et al. (2008) used observed scale items including duration of use, frequency of use and intensity of systems use to measure IS use; and Zhu and Kraemer (2005) measured e-business usage as a latent variable of multiple observed variables such as percentage of consumer sales conducted online, percentage of B2B sales conducted online and percentage of goods for resale ordered online. For assessing actual ICT usage, this study used a similar set of questions for *expectation.* While measuring actual ICT usage, respondents were asked about how often they used those five different levels of ICT applications. A semantic differential scale was used to collect details of respondents' actual ICT usage with '5' representing 'use quite often' and '1' denoting 'not used at all'. The measures for expectation and actual ICT usage and their sources are stated in Table 14.

5.3.2.7. Integration and Utilisation. This study modelled integration and utilisation as antecedents of organisational performance. Integration and utilisation were also predicted to be intervening variables between ICT

Table 14. Items for Expectation and ICT Usage.

Items	Statement	Sources
Expectation		
	Scale: 1 = current user; 2 = expect within 6 months; 3 = within 12 months; 4 = within 1–3 years, 5 = expectation is not specified.	
EXP1	ICT basic operation (computer, email, web surfing, etc.)	Field study
EXP2	Internet with own homepage (static homepage)	Field study
EXP3	Interactive homepage which supports product cataloguing and order processing	Field study
EXP4	Interactive homepage which supports online transactions and account management	Field study
EXP5	Complete digital/electronic communication and exchanges within and outside the organisation	Field study
ICT use		
	Scale: 5 = use quite often; 1 = not used at all.	
USAGE1	ICT basic operation (computer, email, web surfing, etc.)	Field study
USAGE2	Internet with own homepage (static homepage)	Field study
USAGE3	Interactive homepage which supports product cataloguing and order processing	Field study
USAGE4	Interactive homepage which supports online transactions and account management	Field study
USAGE5	Complete digital/electronic communication and exchanges within and outside the organisation	Field study

usage and organisational performance. Past studies used integration as a latent variable which was measured through multiple items, for example, to what extent company web applications are electronically integrated with back-office systems and databases and to what extent company databases are electronically integrated with suppliers and partners (Zhu & Kraemer, 2005).

Although a few studies stated the importance and consequences of ICT utilisation (particularly under-utilisation) in generating enhanced organisational performance from a developing country perspective, there was a paucity of empirical studies which quantified the variable, degree of utilisation, and measured its effects on organisational performance. The field study supported the importance of ICT integration in enhancing SMEs' performance and also reiterated the importance of the degree of utilisation of ICT in different functional areas such as production (or services), administration and accounts, as well as marketing and sales.

Combining the field study results with the relevant literature, integration was measured by the respondents' assessment of: (i) ICT is utilised in entire working areas in the organisation; (ii) all departments and functional areas of this organisation are integrated through a single ICT system; (iii) our website is well developed for front-end functionality which supports information, product catalogue, customer customisation and account management; (iv) our web applications are electronically integrated with back-office systems and databases and (v) company's databases are electronically integrated with suppliers and partners. The respondents' assessment was quantified using a 5-point Likert scale.

Due to the paucity of literature, measurement items for the degree of utilisation were explored from the field study. The degree of utilisation was measured by the respondents' assessment of the extent of appropriate utilisation of ICT into various functional areas such as production, administration and accounts, as well as marketing and sales. A differential scale was employed to measure utilisation with the measures being: 1 = ICT not at all utilised; 2 = utilised to conduct 20% of functions; 3 = utilised to conduct 20−50% of functions; 4 = utilised to conduct 50−80% of functions and 5 = utilised to conduct more than 80% of functions. Measurement items for integration and utilisation as well as their sources are given in Table 15.

5.3.2.8. *Performance*. This study has examined the diffusion of ICT by SMEs in Bangladesh: it has extended the scope of the traditional

Table 15. Items for Integration and Utilisation.

Items	Statement	Sources
Integration		
INT1	ICT is utilised in entire working areas in the organisation	Field study
INT2	All departments and functional areas of this organisation are integrated through a single ICT system	Field study
INT3	Our website is well developed for front-end functionality which supports information, product catalogue, customer customisation and account management	Field study, Zhu and Kraemer (2005)
INT4	Our web applications are electronically integrated with back-office systems and databases	Field study, Zhu and Kraemer (2005)
INT5	Company's databases are electronically integrated with suppliers and partners	Field study, Zhu and Kraemer (2005)
Utilisation		
UTL1	Utilisation of ICT in production and service-related functions	Field study
UTL2	Utilisation of ICT in admin and accounts-related functions	Field study
UTL3	Utilisation of ICT in sales and marketing-related functions	Field study

innovation diffusion model by including two stages of post-adoption phenomena relating to ICT, namely, ICT use and value creation in terms of organisational performance. Previous studies have measured organisational performance in various ways (Beard et al., 2014; Bharadwaj, 2000; Madden et al., 2013; Powell & Dent-Micallef, 1997; Zhu & Kraemer, 2005). The measurement items for organisational performance used in this study have been mainly adapted from prior studies such as those by Zhu and Kraemer (2005) and Powell and Dent-Micallef (1997). In addition to the items adapted from the existing literature, the field study also explored new items for measuring organisational performance. The results of the field study provided support for items previously used for organisational performance measurement and also suggested a second-order latent variable measurement structure.

The field study analysis revealed nine items for measuring organisational performance which were further categorised into three distinct groups, namely, competitiveness, internal operation productivity and financial performance. The overall organisational performance was measured as a higher-order conceptualisation comprising these three performance dimensions. Prior research has supported the measurement of organisational performance as a second-order construct (Rai, Patnayakuni, & Seth, 2006; Zhu & Kraemer, 2005; Zhu et al., 2003). This study employed higher-order modelling and measured organisational performance as a composite of first-order constructs: competitiveness, internal operation productivity and financial performance. All items for the first-order latent constructs of organisational performance and their sources are stated in Table 16.

5.4. Questionnaire Translation

It was stated in previous sections that the main objective of the study was to look at the diffusion of ICT and its resultant outcome as organisational performance in the Bangladeshi context. The owners of different SMEs were the subjects of the study: they were comfortable with and used to communication and exchanges in the Bengali language. Thus, the English version questionnaire was translated into Bengali before conducting the survey to achieve greater convenience and ease of operation. A complete English version of the survey questionnaire has been provided in Appendix C.

A back-translation method (Marin & Marin, 1991) was employed to create an accurate Bengali-version questionnaire and ensure equivalence of

Table 16. Items for Performance.

Items	Statement	Sources
Competitiveness		
COMP1	Interaction with customer has been increased	Field study, Zhu et al. (2004), Zhu and Kraemer (2005)
COMP2	Our sales area has been widened	Field study, Zhu et al. (2004)
COMP3	Competitive position has been improved	Field study
Internal operation productivity		
INTOP1	The internal process of the organisation became transparent	Field study
INTOP2	The internal process of the organisation became structured	Field study, Zhu et al. (2004)
INTOP3	Productivity of the employees has been improved	Field study, Zhu et al. (2004)
Financial performance		
PERF1	Overall performance is increased	Field study, Powell and Dent-Micallef (1997)
PERF2	Profitability of the company has been increased	Field study, Powell and Dent-Micallef (1997)
PERF3	Sales of the company have been increased	Field study, Zhu and Kraemer (2005), Powell and Dent-Micallef (1997)

the two versions (see Section 3). The back-translation process underwent a series of translations, check—recheck and modifications. The researcher first translated the original English questionnaire, which had been approved by the university's Human Research Ethics Committee, into Bengali. The first version of the Bengali questionnaire was thoroughly checked by a university academic in Australia who was a native Bangladeshi. This refined version of the translated questionnaire was further reviewed by two university academics from Bangladesh who were involved in research in Australia. The final version of the Bengali question-naire was again translated back into English. A third person, a researcher from Bangladesh, performed the back-translation of the questionnaire into English. This back-translated version of the questionnaire provided the opportunity to check whether the translated version of the items projected a similar meaning and approach to the original version. Interestingly, although some words were found to be different, all items in both versions of the questionnaire were observed to be similar in their meaning which finally ensured equivalence of the two versions of the questionnaire. A com-plete Bengali-translated version of the survey questionnaire has been provided in Appendix D.

5.4.1. Questionnaire Refinement and Pilot Test

The initial questionnaire was refined through pre-testing prior to administering the actual survey (as described in Section 3). The primary version of the questionnaire was distributed to five respondents in Australia who had direct experience in SMEs in Bangladesh. The feedback from these five respondents was used to modify the questions for the final survey. The questionnaire was translated into Bengali before being used to conduct the final survey.

Although the questionnaire had been refined and modified through pre-testing, a pilot test was also conducted by administering a mini sample survey with the final version of the questionnaire. A total of 35 SMEs were surveyed after being selected through a convenience sampling technique.

Some errors and mistakes related to different questions were detected and a few suggestions were received during the pilot test. The errors and mistakes were mainly associated with: (i) ambiguous meaning for some words; (ii) some questions being very close in their meaning creating confusion for respondents; (iii) difficulties experienced in indicating their appropriate evaluation on the Likert scale and (iv) the question's approach not being simple and easy.

Despite the errors, the data collected through the pilot survey were recorded and the study model was estimated. The analysis also indicated some loopholes in the questionnaire. For example, the factor analysis of the data collected through the pilot survey showed that the factor loadings of some constructs were '1'. The suggested reason for this was that when respondents were unable to differentiate the level of their evaluation in answering the questions, they mostly chose the extreme value. Thus, the factor loading of different items of some constructs tended to reach a value of '1'. Based on feedback from respondents during the pilot survey and errors detected through analysing the pilot survey data, the entire questionnaire was revised to ensure that it was a valid and reliable survey questionnaire. It is worth noting that the incorporation of all respondents' suggestions and the analysis results led to slight modification of the final version of the questionnaire by replacing some words and making changes in the expression of some questions which mostly involved simplification. The final version of the questionnaire was then used to collect data from a national survey.

5.5. Summary

This section has presented the construction of the hypotheses in accordance with the final research model developed in Section 4. To analyse the comprehensive research model (see Fig. 2), 18 hypotheses were developed to describe the relationships between the study variables (see Fig. 3). Furthermore, three hypotheses were developed to analyse the mediating roles of ICT integration and degree of utilisation to explain the influence of ICT usage on organisational performance. The development of the measurement scales and items was also presented. Next, the survey questionnaire was developed based on the existing literature and field study results. The back-translation method was employed to translate the instrument for the survey. Pre-testing and a pilot study were used to validate the questionnaire. The final questionnaire played the vital role in the data collection by a national survey which is discussed in Section 6.

6. DATA ANALYSIS

6.1. Introduction

This section presents the quantitative data analysis procedures and reports on the results. In particular, this section presents the procedure for and results from estimating the structural model using the PLS-SEM) by applying *PLS*-Graph Version 3, as well as reporting on the validation of the psychometric properties of the measurement model. Factor loadings, t-statistics and the composite reliability of the reflective constructs are presented as proof of convergent validity, while average communalities, the correlation matrix and cross-loading matrix are also provided as proof of discriminant validity among the reflective constructs. The relative importance of the formative items towards the formation of the related latent construct is also appraised. The assessment of the structural model commenced once the measurement model had been evaluated and adjusted. Estimates of path coefficients, t-statistics and R^2 values are presented to determine the degrees and magnitudes of the effects of exogenous variables and explanatory power of the model. This section concludes by describing the results of the hypotheses testing.

6.2. Overview of Survey and Data Examination

The study analysed 282 survey responses collected from different SMEs in Bangladesh. The response rate was calculated as 22% for the samples from the RMG industry and 55% for the leather and leather product industry. (PLS-SEM) was used as the key analytical tool for the estimates. The representativeness or generalisability of the research outcomes was largely dependent on the sample size. A reasonable number of observations could generate reliable results. The size of the sample was considered adequate for executing SEM for the estimates as it satisfied different sample size specifications as suggested by Hair et al. (1998), Gefen et al. (2000), Barclay et al. (1995) and Chin (1998a).[13]

The theoretical model of the study consisted of 25 first-order constructs and five higher-order constructs among which six constructs were endogenous. The sample size should be at least 60 (6 × 10 = 60) according to Gefen et al. (2000): in the model, the number of indicators within the most complex formative construct was six. Another recommendation was that it should be at least 50 (5 × 10 = 50) according to Barclay et al. (1995) and Chin (1998a) as the largest number of antecedent constructs leading to an endogenous construct as predictors in a regression was five. The study was finally run with 282 sample units for data analyses which could be considered sufficient for a robust PLS model.

6.2.1. Sample Profile

As the study utilised a disproportionate stratified probability sampling technique, different types of SMEs from the manufacturing industry sector were included in the sample which brought in logical grounds for generalising the inferred outcomes.

The study investigated the opinions and perceptions of the owner, owner-manager, manager (decision-maker) or delegated representative of SMEs located in or adjacent to the city of Dhaka. Dhaka was selected as the sampling area after taking into consideration the fact that a high concentration of industry was evident in or near Dhaka. Internet penetration was also high in Dhaka comprising approximately 80% of Bangladesh's total Internet users. The sample consisted of 79.2% from the RMG industry and 20.2% from the leather industry (see Table 17).

Of the firms surveyed, 96.1% had their own homepage, 32.3% had a product cataloguing-capable homepage, 17.7% have experience in e-commerce and 0.4% had an ERP system. The study included 18.1% of firms who enjoyed preferences as SMEs whereas only 7.1% had received any grants or subsidies for ICT.

Furthermore, the survey comprised 85.1% male and 14.9% female respondents (see Table 18). The sample also included respondents of

Table 17. Survey Firm Characteristics.

Description	F	%
Sector		
Ready-made garment industry	225	79.8
Leather industry	57	20.2
Size		
Small business	174	61.7
Medium business	108	38.3
Level of ICT use		
Homepage	271	96.1
Online cataloguing	91	32.3
E-commerce	50	17.7
ERP	1	0.4
SMEs' preferences and grants		
Received preferences as an SME	51	18.1
Received subsidies or ICT grants	20	7.1
Nature of customer		
Geographically diverse customers	234	83.0
Customers not geographically diverse	48	17.0
Internet connectivity		
Dial-up/DSL	29	10.3
Broadband (cable and mobile)	236	83.7
Mobile broadband	17	6.0
Operating offices or stores		
Single office or store	11	3.9
Two offices or stores	238	88.4
More than two offices or stores	33	11.7
ICT experience		
Started ICT before 2000	68	24.1
Started ICT since 2000	214	75.9

different ages, levels of education, levels of income and ICT experience which enhanced the representativeness of the sample data.

As shown in Table 18, 42.6% of respondents were aged below 34 years, 37.2% were 35–44 years and 20.2% were aged 45 years or above. In terms of education, 35.8% of respondents had Masters' degrees, 47.5% had bachelor degrees and 5.7% had higher secondary certificates: 11% had other academic qualifications.

The study also included 17% of respondents with monthly income below 20,000 BDT, 40.4% between 20,000 BDT and 30,000 BDT, 21.3% between 30,000 BDT and 50,000 BDT, 17.0% between 50,000 BDT and 100,000 BDT while 4.3% of respondents had monthly income over 100,000 BDT. Overall, 95.7% of respondents had prior ICT experience.

Table 18. Survey Respondent Characteristics.

Description	F	%
Gender		
Male	240	85.1
Female	42	14.9
Age		
Age 34 or below	120	42.6
Age 35–44 years	105	37.2
Age 45–60 years	54	19.1
Age Over 60 years	3	1.1
Education		
Master's degree	101	35.8
Bachelor degree	134	47.5
Higher secondary certificate	16	5.7
Others	31	11.0
ICT experience		
Have ICT experience	270	95.7
No ICT experience	12	2.3
Monthly income		
Below 20,000 BDT	48	17.0
20,000–30,000 BDT	114	40.4
30,000–50,000 BDT	60	21.3
50,000–100,000 BDT	48	17.0
Over 100,000 BDT	12	4.3

6.2.2. Data Examination

Prior to analysis, the data were first screened for outlier checking and missing values. Alreck and Settle (1995) recommended an extensive data clean-up process which involves the review of the data line by line to check for any errors due to missing or irrational data. In conjunction with reviewing the data line by line, this study adopted frequency tables and the Mahalanobis distance test for outlier checking. During screening, some missing values were found. As the number of missing cells was small in size considering the number of variables as well as the number of records, a different approach for missing value adjustment, involving a re-visit to the respondents, was employed in the belief that precaution was better than cure. However, there still remained some missing values even after re-visiting the respondents. Finally, an ML (maximum likelihood) algorithm was used for the imputation of the remaining missing values. The careful review and screening of the raw data resulted in 282 complete and usable data records for the final data analysis.

The theoretical model was composed of 25 first-order constructs which comprised 12 reflective and 13 formative constructs. The model also included five second-order constructs which comprised two reflective higher-order constructs and three formative higher-order complex conceptualisations. The theoretical model involved six endogenous latent variables to illustrate the structural relationships among the 25 first-order and five second-order latent constructs.

The model comprised 34 reflective items and 40 formative items which were composed of 25 first-order and six second-order conceptualisations. This was used to examine the effects of predictors for the endogenous latent variables of the study namely, cognitive evaluation, expectation of ICT usage, actual ICT usage, ICT integration, ICT utilisation and organisational performance. The number of constructs employed in the theoretical model indicated that the sample size of the study ($n = 282$) was adequate to proceed with PLS-SEM. The analysis also conformed to the minimum threshold requirement of allocating at least two indicators per construct for SEM (Kline, 2010; Rahim, Antonioni, & Psenicka, 2001).

6.2.3. Justification of Reflective and Formative Measures
The differentiation and appropriate use of formative and reflective constructs in estimates has been a recent advancement of SEM. IS researchers initially modelled mostly reflective constructs due to many reasons. These included the availability of software that was supportive for estimates of formative constructs (Chin, 1998a; Gefen et al., 2000); conceptual criteria for determining whether constructs should be specified as reflective or formative (Diamantopoulos & Winklhofer, 2001; Edwards & Bagozzi, 2000); lack of a consistent standard for assessing psychometric properties of measures (Bagozzi & Yi, 1998; Bollen, 1989); and lack of requisite knowledge for the subsequent estimates (Jarvis, MacKenzie, & Podsakoff, 2003). The introduction of PLS-SEM has provided the analytical tools suitable for modelling reflective and formative constructs. The development of software for component-based SEM has provided enormous opportunities for researchers who are involved in modelling reflective and formative constructs. However, it is difficult to anticipate the nature of an indicator, that is, whether it is reflective or formative.

Researchers have primarily judged the nature of a latent variable by applying the definitions of reflective and formative indicators as described below.

By nature, reflective items are highly correlated as they (reflective indicators) represent reflections, or manifestations, of a construct. Hence, variation in a construct leads to variation in its indicators (Bollen, 1989). For example, an individual change in the latent perceived usefulness construct results in corresponding changes in each manifest indicator of perceived usefulness. Thus, perceived usefulness has been identified as a reflective construct.

Formative indicators, on the other hand, are entirely opposite to the character of a reflective indicator. The formative items show direct causal relationships from the item to the latent variable, that is, the items cause the latent variable (Diamantopoulos & Winklhofer, 2001). In other words, the formative constructs are formed by their respective measurement items. Thus, the items are not correlated and measure different underlying dimensions of the latent variable (Chin, 1998b). For example, *country readiness* is measured by *technology infrastructure, human infrastructure, legal infrastructure, financial infrastructure*, and *government policy and supports*. The measurement indicators are not correlated and the variation in the latent construct does not lead to variation in its indicators. More clearly, an individual's favourable assessment about *country readiness* does not necessarily mean that all of its indicators are favourable for SMEs' ICT adoption. Thus, the country readiness construct has been identified as a formative construct.

Modelling reflective or formative constructs requires theoretical justification (Coltman, Devinney, Midgley, & Venaik, 2008; Diamantopoulos & Siguaw, 2006; Jarvis et al., 2003). However, it may be difficult to explore the theoretical interpretation of a construct, reflective versus formative. Jarvis et al. (2003) developed a set of conceptual criteria which are used as a guideline for justifying the nature of variables, reflective or formative, modelled to measure a phenomenon. More clearly, a variable is modelled as formative when the following decision rules hold; otherwise, it is reflective: the direction of causality is from indicators to constructs; the indicators need not be interchangeable; covariation among indicators is not necessary, and the nomological net of indicators can differ (Jarvis et al., 2003; Petter, Straub, & Rai, 2007; Rai et al., 2006).

The screening process, which applied the above conceptualisations and decision rules (see Appendix E for the decision rules in detail), resulted in the identification of 34 reflective items and 40 formative items for 12 reflective and 13 formative first-order constructs. Five second-order constructs comprising two reflective higher-order constructs and three formative higher-order complex conceptualisations were also justified.

6.2.4. Examination of Possible Biases

The distributions of the sample into various types of firms resulted in a balance between the different categories of SMEs which were of different type, size, scope of business and competitive position. A quarter of the respondents in the sample were from small enterprises and three quarters were from medium-sized enterprises. The survey instruments were supplied to different SMEs in Bangladesh anonymously selected using a stratified random sampling technique. Through the use of several follow-up calls and reminders by telephone and by sending surveyors as the researcher's representatives, the survey responses were received in two phases. In the first phase, a total of 150 responses were received. The researcher again initiated the push technique to receive more responses. At this stage, two trained surveyors were employed to contact respondents who had not yet sent the completed survey instruments. Repeated follow-up calls and SMS, and surveyors' personal contacts resulted in the receipt of 132 more responses. The study thus analysed the data set which comprised responses collected at two different points in time.

To ascertain the quality of the data, the study examined whether any systemic biases could exist due to there being two groups of respondents.

As the survey responses were received during two different time periods, a question could be asked about whether respondents who answered quickly may be in a more advantageous position in terms of their company's positioning or their status in using advanced ICT: knowing the situation better might thus motivate them to answer the questionnaire. On the other hand, late respondents may be affiliated with the group of firms that were running with a lower level of ICT use; thus, they could be less motivated to respond. However, it was not unlikely that the advanced group, in enjoying various facilities and the uniqueness of the technology, might overrate the benefits, utility and usage of ICT and other aspects of the study. To test this possible bias, the total sample was divided into two groups: Wave-1 (advanced group: firms responded quickly) and Wave-2 (general group: firms responded in the second time period).

The Mann-Whitney U test was used to compare the ranked means of some discrete variables between the two groups. A Kolmogorov-Smirnov (K-S) test was further used to examine if the sample distribution of Wave-1 group was equal to that of the Wave-2 group (Boes, Graybill, & Mood, 1974, reported in Zhu & Kraemer, 2005). As shown in Table 19, the p value of each variable was insignificant ($p > 0.10$). That is, all variables such as firm characteristics (sector, size, global business and SME preference); level of ICT use (homepage, online cataloguing and e-commerce); intention

Table 19. Test of Possible Biases.

Variable	Mean Rank		Mann-Whitney U Test			KS Test	
	Wave-1	Wave-2	Mann-Whitney	Z-stat	p value	Z score	p value
Firm characteristics							
Sector	142.14	140.77	9804.000	−0.202	0.840	0.081	1.000
Size	140.14	143.05	9696.000	−0.355	0.723	0.173	1.000
Global business	143.88	138.80	9543.000	−0.803	0.422	0.302	1.000
SME preference	140.44	142.70	9741.000	−0.349	0.727	0.135	1.000
Level of ICT use							
Homepage	142.30	140.59	9780.000	−0.524	0.601	0.102	1.000
Online cataloguing	143.00	139.80	9675.000	−0.407	0.684	0.190	1.000
E-commerce	140.00	143.20	9675.000	−0.498	0.619	0.190	1.000
Intention to use IT							
Online cataloguing	142.58	140.27	9738.000	−0.248	0.804	0.218	1.000
E-commerce	145.10	137.41	9360.000	−0.867	0.368	0.627	0.826
Subjective perception							
Perceived usefulness	137.29	146.29	9268.000	−0.973	0.331	0.691	0.727
Perceived ease of use	142.86	139.96	9696.500	−0.321	0.748	0.355	1.000
Personal characteristics							
Gender	141.18	141.86	9852.000	−0.114	0.909	0.041	1.000
Age	142.89	139.92	9691.000	−0.329	0.742	0.321	1.000
Education	136.40	149.34	8865.500	−1.647	0.100	0.716	0.684
Income	142.98	139.82	9678.000	−0.339	0.734	0.686	0.735

to use ICT (online cataloguing and e-commerce); subjective perception (perceived usefulness and perceived ease of use) and individual characteristics (gender, age, education and income) seemed to be equal between the groups. Thus, the study concluded that the category of respondents (Wave-1 or Wave-2) did not cause any survey bias.

6.3. Model Assessment

6.3.1. Assessment of the Measurement Model
The model consisted of 25 first-order constructs and five second-order constructs. Both first-order and second-order constructs contained reflective as well as formative items or indicators. Thus, the assessment of the measurement model involved several tasks that assessed the reliability and validity of the first-order reflective and formative constructs, and the higher-order reflective and formative constructs. The strength of the psychometric properties was assessed by examining the convergent validity and discriminant

validity of the reflective items and manifest indicators (for second-order reflective construct validation) while the formative constructs were validated by composite measurement as formative items do not measure the same underlying dimension. The indicators' weights, which measure the relative importance of the formative items in the formation of the constructs, were used to make composite latent variables. The same principle was applied in the validation of the higher-order formative constructs.

6.3.2. Convergent Validity

The assessment of convergent validity was a fundamental part of assessing the measurement model. The psychometric properties of the measurement model were assessed by evaluating the reliability, convergent validity and discriminant validity (Fornell & Larcker, 1981). The reliability of the constructs was assessed by considering composite reliability and Cronbach's alpha. The magnitude and significance of standard path loadings were considered to examine the construct validity.

6.3.2.1. Item Reliability.

Item reliability assessed the loadings for each individual item. Table 20 presents the detailed item loadings. The loadings indicate the correlation of the items with their respective constructs. Therefore, maintaining low loading items would decrease the correlation between the items in the construct (Nunnally, 1994). Item reliability also measured the level of random error for each construct; the lower the item loading, the higher the level of random error. Therefore, this procedure could identify and eliminate the items in a particular construct that could increase the construct's level of random error (Fornell & Larcker, 1981).

High item loadings indicated the reliability of the measures of the latent variable; moreover, the prior literature has supported some agreed levels of item loadings as thresholds for fairly reliable measures. Igbaria et al. (1995) deemed 0.4 as an acceptable minimum loading. Hair et al. (1998) suggested that loadings above 0.3 were significant, above 0.4 were more significant and above 0.5 were very significant. Chin (1998a) believed item loadings should be above 0.5. Carmines and Zeller (1979) maintained 0.7 as the reliability limit whilst Barclay et al. (1995) specified 0.707 as the minimum limit. However, Nunnally (1994) argued that, in the case of strong theoretical support, further reviews of the low loading items were warranted. This would be especially pertinent if the low loading items added to the explanatory power of the model.

Table 20. Psychometric Properties for First-Order Reflective Constructs.

Construct	Items	Loading	*t*-statistics	CR	AVE
Perceived usefulness	PU1	0.917	79.85	0.956	0.844
	PU2	0.938	11.91		
	PU3	0.940	29.24		
	PU4	0.878	55.52		
Perceived ease of use	PEU1	0.948	50.00	0.967	0.879
	PEU2	0.960	82.26		
	PEU3	0.963	9.22		
	PEU4	0.877	48.65		
Facilitating condition	FACICON1	0.769	30.92	0.875	0.701
	FACICON2	0.853	33.31		
	FACICON3	0.895	76.24		
Owner innovativeness	OWNER1	0.765	3.50	0.800	0.669
	OWNER2	0.674	1.99		
Power distance	PD1	0.963	89.29	0.964	0.930
	PD4	0.965	90.74		
In-group collectivism	INGROUP1	0.746	10.78	0.900	0.752
	INGROUP2	0.920	9.93		
	INGROUP3	0.924	6.53		
Uncertainty avoidance	UNAVOID1	0.980	63.54	0.974	0.951
	UNAVOID2	0.971	40.51		
Ethical culture	ECUL1	0.975	200.04	0.967	0.936
	ECUL2	0.960	130.29		
Integration	INTEGRA1	0.764	22.86	0.791	0.561
	INTEGRA2	0.639	13.68		
	INTEGRA3	0.832	35.89		
Internal operation productivity	INTOP1	0.898	75.44	0.898	0.746
	INTOP2	0.870	60.52		
	INTOP3	0.821	41.41		
Competitiveness	COMP1	0.732	11.63	0.731	0.478
	COMP2	0.757	13.44		
	COMP3	0.572	6.08		
Financial performance	FPERF1	0.771	30.24	0.847	0.650
	FPERF2	0.901	67.70		
	FPERF3	0.737	18.59		

Taking into account all the recommendations in the literature and to maximise the measurement model's ability to fulfil the requirements of convergent validity, the minimum value of 0.5 was determined. Hence, after the first PLS run, four items with loadings below 0.5 were discarded, these being INTEGRA4, INTEGRA5, PD2 and PD3. Although some of the constructs had a small number of manifest items, each of the constructs contained at least two indicators even after discarding the items with low loadings; thus, the final model conformed to the criterion suggested by Kline (2010) and Rahim et al. (2001) that there should be a minimum of two items in a construct.

The final run of the refined measurement model ensured high reliability of the measures as all reflective items were found to have satisfactory loadings. All of the items were found to have loadings above 0.707 while only one indicator had a loading of 0.572 which was acceptable as it satisfied the threshold suggested by Hair et al. (1998) and Igbaria et al. (1995).

6.3.2.2. Internal Consistency. Internal consistency is measured through calculating the composite reliability (CR) (Fornell & Larcker, 1981). CR is considered to be superior to the traditional measures of consistency (such as Cronbach's alpha) because it is not influenced by the number of indicators (Hanlon, 2001).

Constructs with a coefficient value of 0.70 or more in the estimates of CR were accepted as reliable for further analysis (as suggested by Barclay et al., 1995; Hair, Ringle, & Sarstedt, 2011; Igbaria et al., 1997). As shown in Table 20, all constructs met this criterion. The reflective construct *competitiveness* had the lowest internal consistency of 0.734 while *uncertainty avoidance* had the highest of 0.974. Most of the study constructs had an internal consistency of approximately 0.8 which was considered to be very satisfactory.

6.3.2.3. Average Variance Extracted. Fornell and Larcker (1981) specified that AVE should be at least 0.5 for convergent validity to be satisfied. Thus the AVE scores, although not a usual measure of convergent validity, were rationally computed for robustness of the statistical analysis.

As shown in Table 20, all of the reflective constructs satisfactorily met this criterion for convergent validity while a little deviation was seen in the AVE score for first-order reflective construct *competitiveness* which was also used as a manifest latent indicator for the higher-order variable *performance*. The variable *competitiveness* appeared with an AVE score of 0.478 which was not problematic as the score was very close to the cut-off value as suggested by Fornell and Larcker (1981). Thus, the AVE results indicated satisfactory convergent validity for all of the reflective constructs.

6.3.3. Discriminant Validity
The measurement model also involved the evaluation of the extent to which different constructs diverged from one another which is termed 'discriminant validity'. Discriminant validity, a proof of construct validity,

is defined as the degree to which any given construct is different from any other (Barclay et al., 1995). The square root of the AVE and the cross-loading matrix are widely used measures for discriminant validity (Barclay et al., 1995; Igbaria et al., 1995). According to Igbaria et al. (1995), the model is assessed as having acceptable discriminant validity if the square root of the AVE of a construct is larger than its correlation with other constructs (Hair et al., 2011). On the other hand, the constructs may be considered as discriminant if the loading of items within a construct (shown in the columns in a cross-loading matrix) are greater than the loading of any other item within the same column (Barclay et al., 1995). Both the approaches for assessing discriminant validity are important to adequately prove discriminant validity at construct level as well as at item level.

6.3.3.1. Discriminant Validity at Construct Level. The square root of the AVE and inter-construct correlations were compared to assess discriminant validity at construct level. According to Fornell and Larcker (1981), constructs are considered to have adequate discriminant validity if the square root of the AVE is greater than the inter-construct correlations.

Table 21 presents the square root of the AVE and the inter-construct correlations. The inter-construct correlations are presented in the off-diagonals while the values for the square root of the AVE are placed in the main diagonal in the matrix in bold font. In order to prove discriminant validity among the reflective constructs, the off-diagonal elements (correlations of latent variables) must be less than or equal to the bolded, diagonal elements ($\sqrt{AVE}$) in the corresponding rows and columns (Barclay et al., 1995; Gefen et al., 2000; Hair et al., 2011; Igbaria et al., 1997). The measurement model met the criterion for discriminant validity as the bolded diagonal values were seen to be greater than the off-diagonal correlation values in their corresponding rows and columns. Thus, the results proved adequate discriminant validity among the study constructs allowing the structural model estimation to proceed with no further item deletion from the model.

6.3.3.2. Discriminant Validity at Item Level. The study also assessed the discriminant validity at item level comparing the loadings and cross-loadings of the measures. The loading of items within a construct (shown in columns) should be greater than the loading of any other item in order to prove discriminant validity among the constructs (Barclay et al., 1995). Table 22 shows the loadings and cross-loadings of items and constructs in the cross-loading matrix. The cross-loading matrix displayed high

Table 21. Correlation Matrix for First-Order Reflective Constructs.

	FC	OI	INT	PU	PEU	INTOP	COMP	FPERF	PD	UA	ING	ECUL
FC	**0.835**											
OI	0.210	**0.818**										
INT	0.442	0.068	**0.749**									
PU	0.653	0.072	0.429	**0.919**								
PEU	0.649	0.222	0.414	0.533	**0.938**							
INTOP	0.557	0.051	0.521	0.638	0.337	**0.864**						
COMP	0.324	−0.033	0.531	0.197	0.131	0.302	**0.695**					
FPERF	0.389	0.033	0.586	0.500	0.321	0.730	0.314	**0.806**				
PD	−0.218	−0.144	−0.205	−0.130	−0.231	−0.155	−0.062	−0.145	**0.964**			
UA	0.023	0.110	−0.100	0.022	0.109	−0.022	−0.102	0.029	−0.277	**0.976**		
ING	−0.191	−0.180	−0.100	−0.175	−0.203	−0.136	−0.023	−0.211	0.448	−0.368	**0.867**	
ECUL	−0.299	−0.082	−0.261	−0.267	−0.243	−0.393	−0.114	−0.347	0.390	−0.376	0.357	**0.967**

FC = Facilitating condition, OI = Owner innovativeness, INT = Integration, PU = Perceived usefulness, PEU = Perceived ease of use, INTOP = Internal operation productivity, COMP = Competitiveness, FPERF = Financial performance, PD = Power distance, UA = Uncertainty avoidance, ING = In-group collectivism, ECUL = Ethical culture.

Table 22. Cross-Loading Matrix.

	PU	PEU	OI	FC	PD	ING	UA	ECUL	INT	INTOP	COMP	FPERF
PU1	**0.9179**	0.5182	0.0754	0.5828	-0.0767	-0.1167	0.0488	-0.2601	0.4686	0.6085	0.2474	0.5299
PU2	**0.9372**	0.4907	0.0539	0.6261	-0.0513	-0.1001	-0.0375	-0.2532	0.4338	0.6070	0.1920	0.4479
PU3	**0.9392**	0.4526	0.0981	0.5477	-0.0314	-0.0883	0.0017	-0.2137	0.3817	0.6203	0.1715	0.5262
PU4	**0.8787**	0.5017	0.0841	0.5549	-0.0622	-0.0997	0.0719	-0.2593	0.2777	0.5049	0.1213	0.3754
PEU1	0.4836	**0.9400**	0.1736	0.6457	-0.1848	-0.1710	0.1236	-0.2215	0.3537	0.3034	0.1219	0.2775
PEU2	0.5031	**0.9518**	0.1490	0.6269	-0.1920	-0.1942	0.0902	-0.2505	0.3905	0.3327	0.1496	0.3256
PEU3	0.5156	**0.9554**	0.1648	0.6275	-0.1637	-0.1889	0.0928	-0.2407	0.3593	0.3220	0.1495	0.2985
PEU4	0.4945	**0.8984**	0.2441	0.5226	-0.1414	-0.1420	0.1025	-0.1993	0.3343	0.3047	0.0928	0.3564
OWNER1	0.0406	0.2135	**0.7370**	0.2016	-0.1507	-0.1249	0.0647	-0.0625	0.0542	0.0215	-0.0407	-0.0173
OWNER2	0.0905	0.1416	**0.9072**	0.1496	-0.1069	-0.2190	0.1460	-0.0820	0.0651	0.0958	-0.0137	0.1223
FACICON1	0.7854	0.5153	0.1161	**0.7462**	-0.1557	-0.1627	-0.0007	-0.2819	0.4634	0.6478	0.3126	0.5109
FACICON2	0.4639	0.8794	0.1596	**0.6543**	-0.2131	-0.1769	0.0884	-0.2470	0.3362	0.3267	0.1156	0.2702
FACICON3	0.4545	0.8648	0.1838	**0.6671**	-0.2130	-0.1893	0.0895	-0.2697	0.3284	0.3423	0.1094	0.2834
PD1	-0.1187	-0.2211	-0.1325	-0.2121	**0.8434**	0.4126	-0.2643	0.3674	-0.1952	-0.1397	-0.0480	-0.1425
PD4	-0.1132	-0.2385	-0.1379	-0.2448	**0.8419**	0.4440	-0.2654	0.3943	-0.1675	-0.1517	-0.0013	-0.1152
INGROUP1	-0.0943	-0.1472	-0.1619	-0.1392	0.2669	**0.9135**	-0.3111	0.2711	-0.0255	-0.1098	0.0104	-0.1288
INGROUP2	-0.1207	-0.1900	-0.2295	-0.1260	0.3352	**0.8649**	-0.3804	0.3056	-0.0749	-0.0572	-0.0162	-0.1915
INGROUP3	-0.2109	-0.1847	-0.1537	-0.2011	0.3278	**0.6823**	-0.2901	0.3441	-0.1337	-0.1670	-0.0441	-0.2256
UNAVOID1	0.0439	0.1030	0.1269	0.0132	-0.2491	-0.3753	**0.9771**	-0.3560	-0.1153	-0.0214	-0.1171	0.0310
UNAVOID2	-0.0009	0.1117	0.1396	0.0352	-0.2470	-0.3740	**0.9740**	-0.3781	-0.0985	-0.0210	-0.0802	0.0480
ECUL1	-0.2880	-0.2463	-0.0582	-0.2953	0.2857	0.3013	-0.3636	**0.9768**	-0.2643	-0.3987	-0.1104	-0.3798
ECUL2	-0.2222	-0.2178	-0.1229	-0.2722	0.3117	0.3067	-0.3647	**0.9575**	-0.2369	-0.3581	-0.1191	-0.2951
INT1	0.3522	0.1620	-0.0275	0.2788	-0.0429	-0.0088	-0.1209	-0.1946	**0.7851**	0.4116	0.4646	0.4013
INT2	0.2805	0.5754	0.0879	0.4172	-0.0704	-0.0573	0.0470	-0.1663	**0.5810**	0.2714	0.2785	0.3336
INT3	0.3287	0.2592	0.1117	0.3026	-0.1562	-0.0500	-0.1214	-0.2223	**0.8483**	0.4652	0.4363	0.5557
INTOP1	0.5714	0.3221	0.0431	0.4592	-0.0664	-0.0821	0.0168	-0.3717	0.4683	**0.8980**	0.2193	0.7319
INTOP2	0.4566	0.1279	0.0588	0.3082	-0.0232	-0.0121	-0.0889	-0.3068	0.4974	**0.8697**	0.3045	0.6348
INTOP3	0.6343	0.4374	0.1106	0.6468	-0.1579	-0.1394	0.0176	-0.3417	0.3916	**0.8209**	0.2768	0.5378
COMP1	0.2482	0.1930	0.0510	0.3270	-0.0376	-0.0118	-0.0387	-0.0918	0.3215	0.2909	**0.7318**	0.2457

Table 22. (*Continued*)

	PU	PEU	OI	FC	PD	ING	UA	ECUL	INT	INTOP	COMP	FPERF
COMP2	0.0794	0.0780	-0.0843	0.1674	0.0201	-0.0095	-0.1027	-0.1266	0.5042	0.2222	**0.7563**	0.2816
COMP3	0.0414	-0.0922	-0.0398	0.1396	0.0415	0.0537	-0.0827	0.0347	0.2483	0.0426	**0.5725**	0.0491
FPERF1	0.5701	0.4592	0.0768	0.4449	-0.1568	-0.1869	0.1863	-0.3491	0.4263	0.6872	0.2103	**0.7711**
FPERF2	0.3992	0.2733	0.1120	0.2973	-0.1142	-0.2026	0.0621	-0.3469	0.5212	0.6306	0.2437	**0.9005**
FPERF3	0.2516	0.0614	-0.0028	0.1663	0.0704	-0.0004	-0.1821	-0.1405	0.4737	0.4528	0.3239	**0.7372**

PU = Perceived usefulness, PEU = Perceived ease of use, FC = Facilitating condition, OI = Owner innovativeness, PD = Power distance, ING = In-group collectivism, UA = Uncertainty avoidance, ECUL = Ethical culture, INT = Integration, INTOP = Internal operation productivity, COMP = Competitiveness, FPERF = Financial performance.

correlations between constructs and relevant measurement items. All reflective constructs of the model showed high correlation, with their respective measurement items being also significantly higher than the items in the same column measuring other constructs, the only exception being the correlation between *perceived ease of use* and *facilitating condition*. Items 2 and 3, measuring the *facilitating condition*, demonstrated a very high correlation with *perceived ease of use* ($r = 0.88$ and 0.86, respectively). This occurred because *facilitating condition* is measured through questions that are, in a sense, further proof of organisational technology competency making a system easy to use and fostering the adoption rate of digital technology. This measures whether the organisation has capable human resources who also have the skills to do the work in an automated environment, whether the organisation has adequate resources necessary to work in a digital environment and whether the existing systems are compatible with using digital technology. Thus, high correlation between some measurement items of *facilitating condition* and *perceived ease of use* was considered to be justified. This high correlation was not considered problematic as the correlations of *perceived ease of use* with its measurement items were observed as higher than those with high correlation ($r = 0.94, 0.95, 0.96$ and 0.90, respectively). Finally, it was concluded that the model now demonstrated both convergent and discriminant validity.

6.3.4. Indicator Weights for Formative Constructs

The theoretical model comprised both reflective and formative constructs. Among the 25 first-order and five second-order constructs of the model, 13 first-order constructs and four higher-order constructs were formative in nature. By definition, reflective items measure the same underlying dimensions and should be correlated, while formative indicators 'cause' the latent construct, also called the emergent construct, which is explained as a function of the formative measures. The SEM involved a two-step procedure which assessed the psychometric properties of the latent constructs by examining reliability using Cronbach's alpha or Fornell and Larcker's (1981) measure of CR; convergent validity by examining the loadings and *t*-statistics; and discriminant validity by examining the AVE and inter-construct correlations or loading and cross-loading matrix, before estimating the structural model. Although all of the tests for construct reliability and validity were considered as fundamental requirements for reflective constructs, these were not necessary requirements for formative constructs (Jarvis et al., 2003; Rai et al., 2006) as the items were not correlated and did not measure the same underlying dimension.

In estimating the measurement model, researchers have generally proceeded by evaluating the construct validity and reliability for reflective constructs; however, these two forms of validity should not be conducted in the same manner for formative measures, given the differences between reflective and formative measures. Construct validity is typically assessed by two aspects of validity: convergent validity which detects whether the measures for a construct are more correlated with one another than with measures of another construct, and discriminant validity which determines if the measures are isolated as distinct constructs (Petter et al., 2007). The methods of determining construct validity that focus on common variance, although applicable to reflective constructs, logically do not apply well to formative constructs as the correlations between indicators within a construct do not need to be higher than the correlations between indicators of different constructs (MacCallum & Browne, 1993) and there is no requirement that the measures of the construct be highly correlated (Rossiter, 2002). Unlike common factor analysis, where one examines the loadings, in principal component analysis for formative constructs, the weights must be examined.

Therefore, indicator weights, which provided information on the relative importance of the formative items towards the formation of the corresponding latent construct, were calculated. The weights for each of the 40 formative indicators are presented in Tables 23 and 24. The tables show

Table 23. Validity for First-Order Formative Constructs (Culture and Environment).

Construct	Items	Weight	*t*-statistics	Tolerance	VIF
Bengali values	BVAL1	−0.751	4.78**	0.961	1.04
	BVAL2	0.571	2.51**	0.980	1.02
	BVAL3	0.048	0.19	0.960	1.04
Coercive pressure	COERPRE1	−0.018	0.20	0.979	1.02
	COERPRE2	0.682	10.31**	0.844	1.19
	COERPRE3	0.512	7.19**	0.828	1.21
Mimetic pressure	COMPRE1	0.424	1.97*	0.995	1.01
	COMPRE2	0.877	7.68**	0.995	1.01
Normative pressure	NORMPRE1	0.559	7.09**	0.910	1.10
	NORMPRE2	0.583	7.09**	0.864	1.16
	NORMPRE3	0.228	2.16**	0.964	1.04
	NORMPRE4	0.110	0.99	0.979	1.02
Global pressure	GLOPRE1	0.063	0.40	0.971	1.03
	GLOPRE2	0.988	27.50**	0.971	1.03

**$p < 0.01$, *$p < 0.05$, VIF = variance inflation factor.

Table 24. Validity for First-Order Formative Constructs (Country Readiness and ICT Use).

Construct	Items	Weight	*t*-statistics	Tolerance	VIF
Technological infrastructure	TECH1	0.203	0.68	0.870	1.15
	TECH2	−0.386	1.21	0.721	1.39
	TECH3	0.828	3.94**	0.740	1.35
	TECH4	0.511	2.66**	0.969	1.03
Human infrastructure	HINFRA1	0.612	1.46	0.354	2.82
	HINFRA2	0.144	0.34	0.387	2.59
	HINFRA3	0.367	1.09	0.608	1.65
Legal infrastructure	LINFRA1	0.197	0.54	0.951	1.05
	LINFRA2	0.938	4.18**	0.951	1.05
Financial infrastructure	FINFRA1	0.897	2.81**	0.838	1.19
	FINFRA2	0.210	0.54	0.838	1.19
Government policy and supports	GOV1	0.808	3.26**	0.387	2.59
	GOV2	0.862	3.39**	0.384	2.61
	GOV3	−0.531	1.52	0.372	2.69
	GOV4	−0.688	2.15*	0.355	2.82
Expectation	EXP2	0.216	4.26**	0.951	1.05
	EXP3	0.237	3.78**	0.425	2.35
	EXP4	0.828	15.52**	0.452	2.21
	EXP5	−0.062	1.08	0.69	1.45
Usage	USAGE2	0.176	3.70**	0.981	1.02
	USAGE3	0.491	6.48**	0.542	1.85
	USAGE4	0.553	8.09**	0.543	1.84
	USAGE5	0.052	2.25*	0.983	1.02
Utilisation	UTL1	0.235	2.61*	0.919	1.09
	UTL2	0.863	11.12**	0.689	1.45
	UTL3	0.081	0.79	0.720	1.39

**$p < 0.01$, *$p < 0.05$, VIF = variance inflation factor.

that the weights for 26 formative items had significant *t*-values while this was not the case for 14 items.

As there were a number of formative indicators with insignificant weights, it was important to decide whether some indicators should be discarded in order to have formative constructs with indicators that would highly contribute to the emergent constructs. Diamantopoulos and Winklhofer (2001) suggested that if any of the item weightings for formative measures were non-significant, it may be appropriate to remove the non-significant indicators (one at a time) until all paths were significant and a good fit was obtained (this may be applicable in CBSEM. Zhu, Dong, et al. (2006) followed the guidelines of retaining measurement items with significant weights and above the cut-off value of 0.3 (Chin, 1998b).

Content validity is an issue that could have an adverse effect when adopting removal measures in formative constructs. Dropping the formative indicators that had non-significant weights could pose the question whether the construct was still measuring the entire domain and whether the content validity was preserved (Bollen & Lennox, 1991).

The works of Fornell, Lorange, and Roos (1990), Santosa et al. (2005) and Diamantopoulos and Winklhofer (2001) may be worth mentioning in support of retaining all the indicators of a formative construct regardless of their significance and the magnitude of their weight.

This study has developed 13 first-order formative constructs and four higher-order constructs in analysing all possible aspects of conceptualising the domain of the constructs. However, in its agreement with the proposition 'omitting an indicator is omitting a part of the construct', this study showed that it suspected that the meaning or definition of the constructs would be changed if any indicator was deleted. Thus, all the indicators of the formative constructs were logically retained for further analyses.

In addition to the indicator weights, the test of multicollinearity was conducted on the formative items. Unlike reflective indicators, where multicollinearity between construct items is desirable (illustrated by a high Cronbach's alpha or CR scores), excessive multicollinearity in formative constructs can destabilise the model.

The existence of very high correlations among measures may suggest that multiple indicators are tapping into the same aspect of the construct. Thus, low collinearity among items is vital in ensuring the stability of the estimates (Mathieson, Peacock, & Chin, 2001). Hence, this establishes that each indicator has its own distinct influence. In general, multicollinearity is examined by the variance inflation factor (VIF). Although a VIF value greater than 10 is acceptable, different threshold values for VIF are proposed as collinearity poses more problems in formative constructs. Kleinbaum, Kupper, Muller, and Nizam (1998) recommended that the threshold of VIF be 10 while Mathieson et al. (2001) and Hair et al. (2011) suggested 5 as the maximum threshold for detecting multicollinearity among indicators. However, Diamantopoulos and Siguaw (2006) stated that a VIF statistic greater than 3.3 was problematic for formative measures. The SPSS 19 statistical package was utilised to run the regression analysis with the PLS construct scores as the dependent variables and the items as independent variables (Andreev, Maoz, Heart, & Pliskin, 2009).

As shown in Tables 23 and 24, the results depicted that all the VIF scores were below 3.3 which was well below the recommended maximum threshold recommended by Kleinbaum et al. (1998), Mathieson et al.

(2001) and Hair et al. (2011). Therefore, all the formative items were logically retained.

6.4. Validation of the Higher-Order Model

The estimation of hierarchically structured latent variables is a very useful method under structural modelling which allows for more theoretical parsimony and reduces model complexity (Edwards, 2001; Law, Wong, & Mobley, 1998; MacKenzie, Podsakoff, & Jarvis, 2005). In the past, hierarchical modelling was mainly analysed within the framework of CBSEM and most of the cases focused on the second-order construct (Edwards, 2001; Edwards & Bagozzi, 2000; Jarvis et al., 2003; Law & Wong, 1999; MacKenzie et al., 2005; Petter et al., 2007). These researchers defined hierarchical constructs or multidimensional constructs as the constructs involving more than one construct. Although still limited in number, recent initiatives have explored a more advanced avenue in the analysis of hierarchically structured latent variables, both on the extent of hierarchy as well as in their underlying relationships.

Recent research has shown a third-order and fourth-order hierarchical latent variable model design with varied underlying relationships among the constructs, that is, formative or reflective, within a PLS-based path modelling framework (Akter, D'Ambra, & Ray, 2010, 2011; Wetzels et al., 2009). The higher-order construct may be defined as the latent variable which is created through the indicators and latent variables in a multiple hierarchy. For example, if a second-order latent variable consists of two underlying first-order latent variables, each with four manifest variables, the second-order manifest variables can be specified using all (eight) manifest variables of the underlying first-order latent variables (Chin & Gopal, 1995). Consequently, the manifest variables are used twice: for the first-order latent variable ('primary' loadings) and for the second-order latent variable ('secondary' loadings).

With this established, the outer model (measurement model) and the inner model (structural model) are thus specified accounting for the hierarchical component of the model and representing the loadings of the second-order latent variable on the first latent variables. Wetzels et al. (2009) extended this approach to address the higher-order hierarchical models.

Like first-order latent constructs, the second-order or higher-order constructs may also be composed of both reflective and formative indicators.

The formation of two different types of higher-order constructs, the reflective higher-order construct and the formative higher-order construct, may be explained by the following equations where Eqs. (3) and (4) explain first-order and second-order reflective constructs, while Eqs. (5) and (6) state the formation of first-order and second-order formative constructs, respectively:

$$y_i = \Lambda_y \cdot \eta_j + \varepsilon_i \qquad (3)$$

where y_i= manifest variables (e.g. items of perceived usefulness), Λ_y= loadings of first-order latent variable, η_j= first-order latent variable (e.g. perceived usefulness), ε_i= measurement error.

$$\eta_j = \Gamma \cdot \xi_k + \zeta_j \qquad (4)$$

where η_j= first-order factor (e.g. perceived usefulness), Γ= loadings of second-order latent variable, ξ_k= second-order latent variable (e.g. cognitive evaluation), ζ_j= error of first-order factors.

$$\eta = \gamma_1 x_1 + \gamma_2 x_2 + \ldots + \gamma_n x_n + \varepsilon \qquad (5)$$

where η = first-order latent variable, x_i = observed variables, γ_i = expected effect of x_i on η, ε = a disturbance term, with $\mathrm{COV}(x_i, \varepsilon) = 0$ and $E(\varepsilon) = 0$.

$$\Gamma = \varphi_1 \eta_1 + \varphi_2 \eta_2 + \ldots + \varphi_n \eta_n + \zeta \qquad (6)$$

where Γ = second-order latent variable, η_i = observed variables, φ_i= expected effect of η_i on Γ, ε = a disturbance term with $\mathrm{COV}(n_i, \zeta) = 0$ and $E(\zeta) = 0$.

This study has applied the above-mentioned functions to develop the hierarchical conceptualisations of the study constructs through a multistage process. The hierarchical conceptualisation can result in theoretical parsimony and ease of analysis. The analytical procedures for hierarchical reflective models and formative models are depicted in Tables 25 and 26.

6.4.1. Validation of Second-Order Reflective Construct: Cognitive Evaluation (Reflective–Reflective)

Cognitive evaluation was modelled as a second-order construct, capturing two beliefs towards technological innovation – perceived usefulness and perceived ease of use, as validated through the field study. Resulting from

Table 25. Description of Second-Order Reflective Constructs.

Description	Illustration
1 Construct the first-order latent variables such as LV11 and LV12 and relate them to their respective block of manifest variables (such as LV11: MV1-MV4; LV12:MV5-MV8) using Mode A (reflective) in their outer model. The loading represents the first-order loadings (see Eq. (3)).	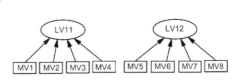
2 The second-order latent variable can now be constructed by relating to the block of the underlying first-order latent variables and their constructs, such as second-order construct LV21 by MV1-MV8, using Mode A (reflective) in their outer model (the indicators placed above the second-order construct represent the secondary loadings). The first-order latent variables (LV11 and LV12) are now related to the second-order variable LV21 as reflective dimensions. This inner model represents the second-order loadings (see Eq. (4)).	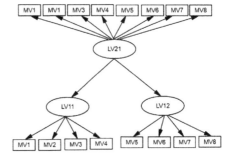

Researchers using PLS-SEM often refer to reflective measurement models (i.e. scales) as Mode A, and formative measurement models (i.e. indices) are labelled Mode B (e.g. Rigdon, Ringle, & Sarstedt, 2010).

the field study's strong support for capturing complex measures, this second-order approach viewed the two dimensions in a collective and mutually reinforcing manner. Accordingly, *cognitive evaluation* was operationalised to be an integrative measure of beliefs towards technological innovation (see Fig. 4).

The degree of explained variance of the second-order hierarchical cognitive construct was reflected in its first-order components, *perceived usefulness* (77.5%) and *perceived ease of use* (75.8%). As shown in Table 27, the path coefficients from second-order cognitive evaluation of the first-order constructs, *perceived usefulness* (0.880) and *perceived ease of use* (0.870), were greater than the suggested cut-off of 0.7 (Chin, 1998b; Zhu, Dong,

Table 26. Description of Second-Order Formative Constructs.

Description	Illustration
1 Construct the first-order latent variables (LV11 and LV12) and relate the manifest variables (LV11:MV1-MV4; LV12:MV5-MV8) to the formative constructs using Mode **B** (formative) in their outer model. The weight represents the first-order weights. Indicator weights are estimated to validate the formative constructs as well as calculate the composites (see Eq. (5)).	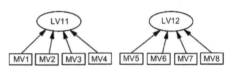
2 The second-order latent variable can now be constructed by relating the block of the underlying first-order latent variables (LV11 and LV12) to the second-order formative construct (**LV21**) using Mode **B** (formative) in their outer model. The first-order latent variables (LV11 and LV12) are now related to the second-order variable LV21 as formative dimensions and the weight of these paths represent the second-order weights (see Eq. (6)).	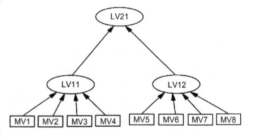

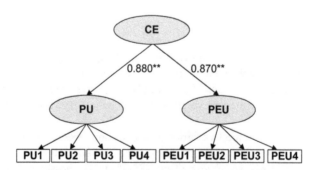

**p < 0.01, CE = Cognitive evaluation, PU = Perceived usefulness,
PEU = Perceived ease of use*

Fig. 4. Cognitive Evaluation.

et al., 2006) and were significant at $p < 0.01$. The CR (= 0.939) and AVE (= 0.66) of the second-order construct were also well above the cut-off values of 0.7 and 0.5, respectively (see Table 27) (Bagozzi & Yi, 1998; Gefen et al., 2000). Thus, the conceptualisation of *cognitive evaluation* as a higher-order, multidimensional construct seemed justified.

6.4.2. Validation of Second-Order Formative Constructs
The study involved four constructs as higher-order formative constructs, namely, *culture, environmental pressure, country readiness* and *organisational performance*. As with the first-order formative construct validation, the indicator weights and the test of multicollinearity were conducted to assess the validity of second-order formative constructs.

6.4.2.1. Culture (Mixed). *Culture* was modelled as a second-order composite variable of five first-order constructs — *power distance, in-group collectivism, uncertainty avoidance, Bengali values* and *ethical culture*. All first-order constructs were reflective except *Bengali values* which was a composite of three indicators (see Fig. 5). As shown in Table 28, the paths from *ethical culture* and *Bengali values* were significant while the other three paths were not found to be significant. Table 24 also showed that multicollinearity was non-existent among the five first-order constructs due to their very small VIF values (Diamantopoulos & Siguaw, 2006). As stated in Section 6.3.4, all formative indicators regardless of their magnitude and level of significance were retained to ensure the measurement of the entire domain and content validity (Bollen & Lennox, 1991) and thus the hierarchical conceptualisation of *culture* was justified for the structural model estimation.

Table 27. Second-Order Cognitive Evaluation Construct and Its Association with First-Order Components.

Construct	Component	Items	Loading	t-value	R^2	CR	AVE
Cognitive evaluation (second-order reflective)	Perceived usefulness	4	0.880**	72.57	0.775	0.939	0.66
	Perceived ease of use	4	0.870**	47.73	0.758		

**$p < 0.001$.

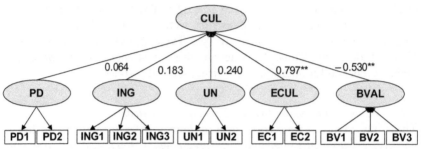

**p < 0.01, CUL = Culture, PD = Power distance, ING = In-group collectivism,
UN = Uncertainty avoidance, ECUL = Ethical culture, BVAL = Bengali values*

Fig. 5. Culture.

Table 28. Second-Order Culture Construct and Its Association with First-
Order Components.

Construct	Component	Items	Weight	*t*-value	Tolerance	VIF
Culture (second-order formative)	Power distance	2	0.064	0.37	0.840	1.191
	In-group collectivism	3	0.183	0.99	0.779	1.284
	Uncertainty avoidance	2	0.240	1.45	0.725	1.379
	Ethical culture	2	0.797**	6.18	0.788	1.270
	Bengali values	3	−0.530**	3.68	0.932	1.073

**p < 0.01$; VIF = variance inflation factor.

*6.4.2.2. Environmental Pressure (Formative–Formative). Environmental
pressure* was modelled as a second-order composite variable of four first-
order constructs – *coercive pressure, normative pressure, mimetic pressure*
and *global pressure*. All of the first-order constructs used as manifest indicators for the second-order formative construct, *environmental pressure*, were
also formative (see Fig. 6). As shown in Table 29, the paths from *coercive
pressure, mimetic pressure* and *global pressure* were significant while *normative pressure* did not produce any significant path weight. Multicollinearity
was non-existent among the four first-order constructs as the VIF value was
far below the conservative threshold level of 3.3 given by Diamantopoulos
and Siguaw (2006). Thus, the hierarchical conceptualisation of *environmental pressure* was justified for structural model estimation.

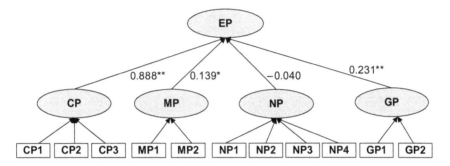

**p < 0.01, EP = Environmental pressure, CP = Coercive pressure, MP = Mimetic pressure,
NP = Normative pressure, GP = Global pressure*

Fig. 6. Environmental Pressure.

Table 29. Second-Order Environmental Pressure Construct and Its
Association with First-Order Components.

Construct	Component	Items	Weight	*t*-value	Tolerance	VIF
Environmental pressure (second-order formative)	Coercive pressure	3	0.888**	13.19	0.451	2.216
	Normative pressure	4	−0.040	0.48	0.475	2.107
	Mimetic pressure	2	0.139*	1.98	0.935	1.069
	Global pressure	2	0.231**	3.16	0.864	1.157

**p < 0.01, *p < 0.05; VIF = variance inflation factor.*

6.4.2.3. Country Readiness (Formative—Formative). Country readiness
was modelled as a second-order composite variable of five first-order
constructs — *technology infrastructure, human infrastructure, legal infrastructure, government policy and supports* and *financial infrastructure* (see
Fig. 7). All first-order constructs of the higher-order model were reflective.
Reliability and validity of the first-order reflective constructs were justified
in Section 6.3.2.1. As shown in Table 30, the paths from *technology infrastructure* ($\gamma = 0.543$, $t = 3.14$, $p < 0.01$) and *government policy and supports*
($\gamma = -0.624$, $t = 3.72$, $p < 0.01$) were significant while *human infrastructure*
($\gamma = 0.246$, $t = 1.10$, $p < 0.01$), *legal infrastructure* ($\gamma = 0.265$, $t = 1.62$, $p >
0.05$) and *financial infrastructure* ($\gamma = -0.061$, $t = 0.22$, $p < 0.01$) did not pro-
duce any significant effects. Multicollinearity was not existent among the

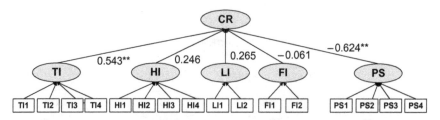

**p < 0.01, CR = Country readiness, TI = Technology infrastructure, HI = Human infrastructure, LI =Legal infrastructure, FI = Financial infrastructure, PS = Government policy and supports

Fig. 7. Country Readiness.

Table 30. Second-Order Country Readiness Construct and Its Association with First-Order Components.

Construct	Components	Items	Weight	*t*-value	Tolerance	VIF
Country readiness (second-order formative)	Technology infrastructure	5	0.543**	3.14	0.721	1.387
	Human infrastructure	4	0.246	1.10	0.569	1.757
	Legal infrastructure	2	0.265	1.62	0.884	1.132
	Government policy and supports	4	−0.624**	3.72	0.994	1.006
	Financial infrastructure	2	−0.061	0.22	0.566	1.768

**$p < 0.01$; VIF = variation inflation factor.

five first-order constructs as the VIF values were between 1.006 and 1.768 which was far below the conservative threshold level. Thus, the hierarchical conceptualisation of *environmental pressure* was justified for structural model estimation.

6.4.2.4. Organisational Performance (Reflective–Formative). The final dependent variable of the study, *organisational performance*, was also modelled as a second-order composite variable of three first-order reflective constructs, *competitiveness, internal operation productivity* and *financial performance* (see Fig. 8). As all first-order constructs were reflective, reliability, convergent validity and discriminant validity were duly justified before

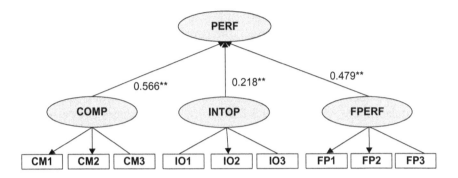

**p < 0.01, PERF = Performance, COMP = Competitiveness, INTOP = Internal operation productivity, FPERF = Financial performance

Fig. 8. Organisational Performance.

Table 31. Validity for Second-Order Performance Construct.

Construct	Components	Items	Weight	*t*-value	Tolerance	VIF
Performance (second-order formative)	Competitiveness	3	0.566**	7.33	0.888	1.126
	Internal operation productivity	3	0.218**	2.35	0.447	2.236
	Financial performance	3	0.479**	4.33	0.444	2.251

**$p < 0.01$; VIF = variation inflation factor.

estimating the composite variable (see Tables 21–23). As shown in Table 31, the paths from *internal operation productivity* ($\gamma = 0.218$, $t = 2.35$, $p < 0.05$), *competitiveness* ($\gamma = 0.566$, $t = 7.33$, $p < 0.01$) and *financial performance* ($\gamma = 0.479$, $t = 4.33$, $p < 0.01$) were significant. The largest VIF value of the constructs was 2.251 which confirmed that multicollinearity was non-existent. Thus, the hierarchical conceptualisation of *organisational performance* was valid for structural model estimation.

6.5. Structural Model

To assess nomological validity, a structural model was developed which comprised five exogenous and six endogenous latent variables. The

variances associated with the endogenous variables determined the explanatory power of the proposed model. The path coefficients and t-values were
calculated to address the effects of the constructs and their underlying relationships according to the proposed theoretical framework. The hypothesised relationships between the constructs could be calculated by two
methods, namely, 'bootstrap' or 'jackknife' (Gefen et al., 2000). 'Bootstrap'
is popularly used within the PLS framework as it produces both a t-value
and an R^2 value.

The technique which bootstrapping employs for calculating the t-statis-
tic is similar to the traditional t-test that is also used to interpret the significance of the paths between study constructs (Barclay et al., 1995).
Interpreted in a similar way in multiple regression analysis, the R^2 value is
also used to indicate the explanatory power of exogenous variables within
a model. In other words, this value estimates the variance associated with
endogenous constructs; thus, the proposed overall model could be evaluated. It is important to note that PLS had some advantages as it was ideal
for assessing the path loadings and structural relationships between the
study constructs which could handle both formative and reflective constructs (Chin & Newsted, 1999; Hanlon, 2001): it also did not require the
normal distribution of the data.

6.5.1. Nomological Validity

The nomological validity of the endogenous variables of the model was
examined by their R^2 values (Santosa et al., 2005). Falk and Miller (1992)
proposed that the minimum R^2 should be 0.10. As shown in Table 32, the
results of the SEM estimation employing a bootstrapping procedure indicated that all the R^2 values were above the minimum cut-off value proposed
by Falk and Miller (1992) which, in turn, ensured the nomological validity
of the model. The overall model explained 48.5% of the variance (R^2) of
organisational performance.

Table 32. Nomological Validity of the Endogenous Variables.

Endogenous Constructs	R^2
Cognitive evaluation	0.138
Expectation	0.585
Usage	0.765
Integration	0.416
Utilisation	0.239
Performance	0.485

The structural equation model estimation further explained that 13.8% of variance in *cognitive evaluation* was accounted for by *owner innovativeness* and *culture*. The estimation also indicated that 58.5% of variance in *expectation* was accounted for by *cognitive evaluation, owner innovativeness, culture, environmental pressure* and *country readiness. Expectation, owner innovativeness, environmental pressure* and *country readiness* also affected *actual usage* with an R^2 value of 0.765. The result indicated that 76.5% of *ICT usage* behaviour was accounted for by the exogenous variables, *expectation, owner innovativeness, environmental pressure* and *country readiness.* The model finally indicated 41.6% of variance in *integration* and 23.9% of variance in *utilisation* accounted for *actual usage.*

6.5.2. Tests of Hypotheses

As shown in Tables 32 and 33 (see also Fig. 9), the results depicted significant effects of *cognitive evaluation* on the *expectation* of ICT usage by SMEs ($\gamma = 0.155$, $t = 2.74$, $R^2 = 0.585$). Thus, Hypothesis H_1 was supported.

Table 33.   Results of the Structural Model.

	Loading	*t*-value
CE → EXP	0.155**	2.74
OI → CE	0.163*	2.20
OI → EXP	−0.067	0.97
OI → USE	−0.038	0.85
EP → EXP	0.405**	8.51
EP → USE	0.191**	3.25
FC → EXP	0.294**	5.13
FC → USE	0.070*	1.94
CR → EXP	−0.135**	2.83
CR → USE	−0.005	0.03
CUL → EXP	−0.048	0.71
CUL → CE	−0.333**	5.81
EXP → USE	0.697**	12.58
USE → INT	0.643**	19.59
USE → UTL	0.488**	12.49
INT → PERF	0.541**	8.01
UTL → PERF	0.180*	2.74
USE → PERF	0.079	1.09

**$p < 0.01$, *$p < 0.05$.
CE = Cognitive evaluation, OI = Owner innovativeness, EXP = Expectation, EP = Environmental pressure, FC = Facilitating condition, CR = Country readiness, CUL = Culture, USE = Actual usage, INT = Integration, UTL = Utilisation, PERF = SME performance.

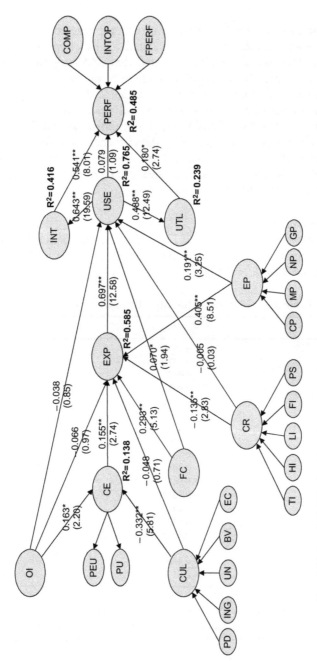

Fig. 9. The Comprehensive Model Estimates.

** p < 0.01, * p < 0.05, CE = Cognitive evaluation, OI = Owner innovativeness, EXP = Expectation, EP = Environmental pressure, CUL = Culture, CR = Country readiness, FC = Facilitating condition, USE = Actual usage, INT = Integration, UTL = Utilisation, PERF = SME performance.

Hypotheses H_{2a}, H_{2b} and H_{2c} were developed to assess the influence of *owner innovativeness* on *cognitive evaluation, expectation* and *ICT use,* respectively. The model estimation depicted a significant effect of *owner innovativeness* ($\gamma = 0.163$, $t = 2.21$) on *cognitive evaluation.*

Owner innovativeness was also hypothesised to have positive correlations with *expectation* and *ICT use.* The effects of *owner innovativeness* on *expectation* $\left(\gamma = -0.067, t = 0.97, R^2 = 0.585\right)$ and its effects on *ICT use* ($\gamma = -0.038$, $t = 0.85$, $R^2 = 0.765$) were not found to be significant. Thus, Hypothesis H_{2a} was accepted while Hypotheses H_{2b} and H_{2c} were rejected.

The hypothesised relationship between *environmental pressure* and *expectation* as well as *environmental pressure* and *actual ICT use* were postulated in Hypotheses H_{3a} and H_{3b}. *Environmental pressure* was found to have significant effects on *expectation* ($\gamma = 0.405$, $t = 8.51$, $R^2 = 0.585$) and *actual use* ($\gamma = 0.191$, $t = 3.25$, $R^2 = 0.765$). Thus, Hypotheses H_{3a} and H_{3b} were accepted.

The effects of *facilitating condition* on *expectation* and *actual use* were postulated in Hypotheses H_{4a} and H_{4b}, respectively. The SEM results presented a significant association between *facilitating condition* and *expectation* ($t = 5.13$, $R^2 = 0.585$) as well as between *facilitating condition* and *actual use* ($\gamma = 0.070$, $t = 1.94$, $R^2 = 0.765$). Thus, Hypotheses H_{4a} and H_{4b} were accepted.

As postulated in Hypothesis H_{5a}, the study results supported the association between *country readiness* and *expectation* ($\gamma = -0.134$, $t = 2.83$, $R^2 = 0.585$) while the results rejected the anticipated association between *country readiness* and *usage* ($\gamma = -0.005$, $t = 0.03$, $R^2 = 0.765$). Thus, Hypothesis H_{5a} was supported while Hypothesis H_{5b} was rejected.

The relationships between *culture* and two endogenous variables, *cognitive evaluation* and *expectation,* were postulated separately in Hypotheses H_{6a} and H_{6b}. The analysis depicted a significant association between *culture* and *cognitive evaluation* ($\gamma = -0.333$, $t = 5.81$, $R^2 = 0.138$) while it showed the opposite result to what was postulated in Hypothesis H_{6b} ($\gamma = -0.048$, $t = 0.71$, $R^2 = 0.585$). Thus, Hypothesis H_{6a} was accepted and Hypothesis H_{6a} was rejected.

The effects of *expectation* on *actual use* are postulated in Hypothesis H_7. The results depicted a strong and significant effect of *expectation* on *actual use* ($\gamma = 0.697$, $t = 12.58$, $R^2 = 0.765$). Thus, Hypothesis H_7 was accepted.

Hypotheses H_{8a}, H_{8b} and H_{8c}, respectively, postulated the effects of *ICT usage* on *ICT integration, ICT utilisation* and *SMEs' performance.* The model estimates showed a significant association between actual *ICT usage* and *ICT integration* ($\gamma = 0.623$, $t = 12.58$, $R^2 = 0.416$), they also showed significant effects on *ICT utilisation* ($\gamma = 0.488$, $t = 2.74$, $R^2 = 0.239$). The results indicated that actual *ICT usage* was not significantly associated with SMEs' *performance* ($\gamma = 0.079$, $t = 1.09$, $R^2 = 0.485$). Thus, Hypotheses H_{8a} and H_{8b} were accepted while Hypothesis H_{8c} was rejected.

As postulated in Hypothesis H_9, the study results showed that *ICT integration* had significant effects on SMEs' *performance* ($\gamma = 0.541$, $t = 8.01$, $R^2 = 0.485$). Thus, the relationship between *ICT integration* and SMEs' *performance* as postulated in Hypothesis H_9 was accepted.

Hypothesis H_{10} anticipated significant effects of *ICT utilisation* on SMEs' *performance*. The study results also indicated a significant association between *ICT utilisation* and SMEs' *performance* ($\gamma = 0.180$, $t = 2.74$, $R^2 = 0.485$). Thus, Hypothesis H_{10} was accepted. The results of the hypotheses tests are summarised in Table 34 and also illustrated in Fig. 9.

6.5.3. Test for Mediating Role of Integration and Utilisation

A system embraces the causes and effects among a number of variables that produce the final outcome through a process. Like predictors or independent variables, the process itself has some effects on the systems which,

Table 34. Results of Hypotheses Tests.

	Hypotheses	Comments
H_1	Cognitive evaluation has direct and positive influence on expectation	Accepted
H_{2a}	Owner innovativeness has direct and significant effects on cognitive evaluation	Accepted
H_{2b}	Owner innovativeness has direct and significant effects on expectation	Rejected
H_{2c}	Owner innovativeness has direct and significant effects on use of ICT	Rejected
H_{3a}	Environmental pressure has a significant influence on expectation	Accepted
H_{3b}	Environmental pressure has a significant influence on actual use	Accepted
H_{4a}	Facilitating condition has a significant influence on expectation	Accepted
H_{4b}	Facilitating condition has a significant influence on actual use	Accepted
H_{5a}	Country readiness has a significant influence on expectation	Accepted
H_{5b}	Country readiness has a significant influence on use of ICT	Rejected
H_{6a}	Culture has a significant influence on cognitive evaluation	Accepted
H_{6b}	Culture has a significant influence on expectation	Rejected
H_7	Expectation has a significant influence on actual usage	Accepted
H_{8a}	ICT usage has significant influence on integration	Accepted
H_{8b}	ICT usage has a significant influence on utilisation	Accepted
H_{8c}	ICT usage has a significant influence on performance	Rejected
H_9	ICT integration has a significant influence on performance	Accepted
H_{10}	ICT utilisation has a significant influence on performance	Accepted

in turn, is reflected in the outcome. Researchers try to understand the effects of the process on the possible outcome by mediation analysis. Mediation exists when a predictor affects a dependent variable indirectly through at least one intervening variable, or mediator. Fig. 10 illustrates mediation models with single and multiple intervening variables.

The concept of mediation analysis is not new, it can be traced back to the early genetics work of Wright (1921) followed by the stimulus response models of Woodworth (1928) in psychology. Although the study of mediation has a long history (Hyman, 1955; MacCorquodale & Meehl, 1948), it has become popular with the creation of basic measurement approaches for assuming the effect of mediation (Baron & Kenny, 1986; Judd & Kenny, 1981; Lindley & Walker, 1993). It has, furthermore, become easier with the application of SEM (Bollen, 1989).

In the basic measurement approach, Baron and Kenny (1986) and Judd and Kenny (1981) discussed four characteristics of mediation that are also used as the following steps for probing whenever there exists any mediating relationship in a recursive model:

Step 1: The initial variable has significant correlation with the outcome. If Y is considered as a criterion variable and X as the initial variable or predictor, the variations in levels of the initial variable, such as X, should significantly account for the variations in the criterion variable, such as Y.

$$Y = b_0 + cX + \varepsilon \qquad (7)$$

where b_0 = constant, X = initial variable, c = regression effect of X on Y, ε = a disturbance term.

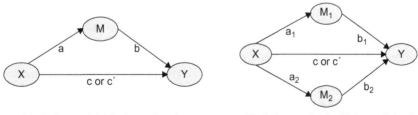

Mediation model (single mediator)   Mediation model (multiple mediators)

X = Independent variable, Y = Dependent variable, M = Mediating variable

Fig. 10. Mediating Model.

Step 2: The variations in levels of the initial variable should significantly account for variations in the presumed mediator. This step essentially involves treating the mediating variable as if it was an outcome variable.

$$M = b_0 + aX + \varepsilon \tag{8}$$

where b_0 = constant, M = mediating variable, a = regression effect of X on M, ε = a disturbance term.

Step 3: The variations in the mediating variable should significantly account for variations in the criterion variable.[14]

$$Y = b_0 + bM + \varepsilon \tag{9}$$

where b_0 = constant, M = mediating variable, b = regression effect of M on Y, ε=a disturbance term.

Step 4: In complete mediation, the relationship between the initial variable and criterion variable is no longer significant (in control of the mediating variable).

$$Y = b_0 + c'X + bM + \varepsilon \tag{10}$$

where b_0 = constant, X = initial variable, M = mediating variable, c'= regression effect of X on Y (in control for M), b = regression effect of M on Y, ε = a disturbance term.

The purpose of Steps 1–3 is to establish that zero-order relationships among the variables exist. If all the relationships explained in Steps 1–3 (Eqs. 7–9) are seen to be significant, researchers anticipate that the third variable M may act as a process variable which may explain the effects of the initial variable X on the criterion variable Y. The variable M is then called a mediating variable or process variable. Assuming there are significant relationships from Step 1 to Step 3, one proceeds to Step 4. In Step 4, some form of mediation is supported if the effect of M (path b) remains significant after controlling for X. If X is no longer significant when M is controlled, the finding supports full mediation. If X is still significant (i.e. X and M both significantly predict Y), the finding supports partial mediation.

If the mediation process involves only one mediating variable, it is termed simple mediation. More than one variable may perform a mediating role in a causal model. Thus, mediation processes involving more than one intervening variable, termed 'multiple mediation', may also be analysed through the above-mentioned procedure.

6.5.3.1. Mediating Role of ICT Integration. Table 35 and Fig. 11 illustrate that Model 1 shows a direct relationship between the initial variable *ICT use* and the criterion variable *SMEs' performance* ($c = 0.511$, $t = 9.94$); Model 2 shows a relationship between the initial variable *ICT use* and the mediating variable *ICT integration* ($a_1 = 0.640$, $t = 13.94$), while Model 3 shows that the mediating variable *ICT integration* has significant effects on the criterion variable *SMEs' performance* ($b_1 = 0.696$, $t = 16.21$). Since all of the above-mentioned relationships are significant, it may be assumed that *ICT integration* may perform a mediating role in explaining the relationship between *ICT use* and *SMEs' performance*. To further prove whether any mediating relationship exists and, if it exists, what type of mediation it is, the researcher should estimate the regression stated in Step 4. As shown in Table 35, Model 4 illustrates a significant effect of *ICT integration* on *SMEs' performance* ($b_1 = 0.625$, $t = 11.24$): the effects of *ICT use* on *SMEs' performance* is also significant ($c' = 0.111$, $t = 1.99$). It is important to note that, although the effects of *ICT use* on *SMEs' performance* are significant (in control of *ICT integration*), the magnitude of the effect is reduced in comparison to the direct relationship between *ICT use* and *SMEs' performance* ($c = 0.511$, $t = 9.94$). Thus, in applying the basic concept of mediation analysis (Baron & Kenny, 1986; Judd & Kenny, 1981), it is observed that *ICT integration* plays a partial moderating role in explaining the relationship between *ICT use* and *ICT integration* (see Fig. 11).

Table 35. Mediating Role of Integration in Explaining Performance.

	Model 1	Model 2	Model 3	Model 4	Comments
c or c'	0.511**			0.111*	Partial mediation
	(9.94)			(1.99)	
a_1		0.640**			
		(13.94)			
b_2			0.696**	0.625**	
			(16.21)	(11.24)	
R^2	0.261	0.410	484	0.491	

$**p < 0.01$, $*p < 0.05$.

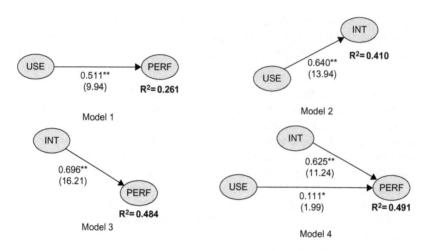

**p < 0.01, USE = ICT use, INT = Integration, PERF = Performance*

Fig. 11. Mediating Effects of Integration.

The significance of indirect effects is examined by the z statistic (Sobel, 1982). The z value is formally defined as follows:

$$z = \frac{a \times b}{\sqrt{b^2 \times s_a^2 + a^2 \times s_b^2 + s_a^2 \times s_b^2}} \tag{11}$$

$$z = \frac{0.640 \times 0.696}{\sqrt{(0.696)^2 \times (0.0459)^2 + (0.640)^2 \times (0.0429)^2 + (0.0459)^2 \times (0.0429)^2}} = 10.56$$

The results support the mediating effects of *ICT integration* which implies that it has an indirect influence on *SMEs' performance*. The variance accounted for (VAF) value is used to estimate the ratio of the indirect effects.

$$\text{VAF} = \frac{a \times b}{a \times b + c} = 87.17 \tag{12}$$

The VAF value indicates that 87.17% of the total effect of *ICT use* on *SMEs' performance* is explained by indirect effects through *ICT integration*.

6.5.3.2. Mediating Role of ICT Utilisation. The study contained another conceptualisation of ICT usage which was ICT utilisation, in examining SMEs' performance. *ICT use* is the measure of the assessment of using different levels of ICT applications while *ICT utilisation* is the measure of the assessment of the degree of ICT utilisation among different functional areas of the organisation. The study assumed that using only ICT usage may not adequately explain organisational performance in the absence of ICT utilisation throughout the organisation. As shown in Table 36, Model 1, Model 2, Model 3 and Model 4 illustrate the results that may be concluded about any mediating relationship among the three latent variables (see Fig. 12).

Model 1 shows the direct relationship between the initial variable *ICT usage* and the criterion variable *SMEs' performance* ($c = 0.511$, $t = 9.94$); Model 2 shows the relationship between the initial variable and the mediating variable *ICT utilisation* ($a_2 = 0.283$, $t = 9.22$) and Model 3 shows that the mediating variable *ICT utilisation* had significant effects on the criterion variable *SMEs' performance* ($b_2 = 0.530$, $t = 10.45$). Since all of the above-mentioned relationships are significant, it may be assumed that *ICT utilisation* may perform a mediating role in explaining the relationship between *ICT usage* and *SMEs' performance*. To further prove whether any mediating relationship exists and, if it exists, what type of mediation it is, the researcher should estimate the regression stated in Step 4 (as stated in Section 6.5.3). As shown in Table 36, Model 4 illustrates a significant effect of *ICT utilisation* on *SMEs' performance* ($b_2 = 0.369$, $t = 6.78$): the effects of *ICT use* on *SMEs' performance* is also significant ($c' = 0.333$, $t = 6.11$). It is important to note that although the effects of *ICT use* on *SMEs' performance* is significant (in control of *ICT utilisation*), the magnitude of the effect is largely reduced in comparison to the direct relationship between

Table 36.   Mediating Role of ICT Utilisation in Explaining Performance.

	Model 1	Model 2	Model 3	Model 4	Comments
c or c'	0.511**			0.333**	Partial mediation
	(9.94)			(6.11)	
a_2		0.283**			
		(9.221)			
b_2			0.530**	0.369**	
			(10.45)	(6.78)	
R^2	0.261	0.233	0.230	0.365	

**$p < 0.01$.

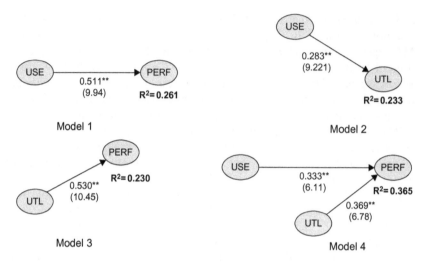

**p < 0.01, USE = ICT use, UTL = Utilisation, PERF = Performance*

Fig. 12. Mediating Effects of Utilisation.

ICT usage and *SMEs' performance* ($c = 0.511$, $t = 9.94$). Thus the results indicate a partial mediation of *ICT utilisation* in explaining the relationship between *ICT use* and *SMEs' performance* (Baron & Kenny, 1986; Judd & Kenny, 1981).

The significance of the indirect effects of *ICT use* on *SMEs' performance* through *ICT utilisation* (mediating variable) was examined by the z statistic (Sobel, 1982). The results supported the mediating effects of *ICT utilisation* ($z = 5.39$, VAF $= .238$) which implies that it has an indirect influence on *SMEs' performance*.

The VAF value indicated that 23.8% of the total effect of *ICT use* on *SMEs' performance* was explained by indirect effects through *ICT utilisation*.

Through understanding the above-mentioned characteristics and applying the steps from Baron and Kenny (1986), it has been assumed that ICT use influences the performance growth of SMEs through a process which comprises ICT integration and ICT utilisation as intervening variables. Baron and Kenny's (1986) steps also helped to detect whether there was any mediating relationship and also answered the question of whether the target variable was feasible for mediation analysis. The process produced reliable estimates of indirect effects and their power through multiple regression analysis. However, researchers face difficulties when more than one intervening variable is involved in a process in a causal model.

6.5.3.3. Mediating Roles of ICT Integration and ICT Utilisation. Different types of mediation occur in a causal set-up such as simple mediation and multiple mediation. Simple mediation involves the analysis of the effects of independent variables on a criterion variable by a single intervening variable. Multiple mediation involves the relatively complex analysis of the effects of independent variables on a criterion variable by multiple mediators or intervening variables.

Although the analysis of mediation has received the bulk of researchers' attention in behavioural studies, most of the previous initiatives have focused on simple mediation analysis, only a few authors have focused on the simultaneous testing of multiple indirect effects which is a worthwhile method for addressing the complex mediated relationship (e.g. Bollen, 1987, 1989; Brown, 1997; MacKinnon, 2000; West & Aiken, 1997).

In multiple mediation, the specific indirect effect of X on Y via mediator i (Brown, 1997) is defined as the product of the two unstandardised paths linking X to Y via those mediators. For example, the specific indirect effect of X on Y through M_1 is quantified as a_1b_1. If another variable M_2 is included in the model as a simultaneous mediator, the specific indirect effect of X on Y through M_2 is quantified as a_2b_2. The complex relationship in a simultaneous multiple mediator model is estimated by utilising the formulas as stated in Eqs. (13) and (14).

$$\text{The total indirect effect} = \sum_{i=1}^{j} a_i b_i \qquad (13)$$

$$\text{Total effect } c = c' + \sum_{i=1}^{j} a_i b_i \qquad (14)$$

Total indirect effects may also be calculated by $c - c'$.

The conceptual model of the study included the simultaneous multiple mediators *ICT integration* and *ICT utilisation* to address the impact of *ICT use* on *SMEs' performance*. The preceding subsections have addressed the effects of two mediators when applying Baron and Kenny's (1986) procedure by multiple regression separately with a single mediator.

The emergence of SEM created remarkable progress in mediation analysis. SEM, a second generation statistical tools, produces multiple mediators' direct and indirect effects in a causal framework. CBSEM has been widely used as an analytical tool for assessing mediating effects in a common and integrated platform. As SEM produces comprehensive results, Baron and Kenny's (1986) four-step procedure was not entirely required for the analysis.

With the emergence of sophisticated SEM software, mediation analysis has not only become popular, but new and easier ways have been provided for obtaining estimates to examine mediating effects. The new procedure considers three different models – no mediation, complete mediation and partial mediation – for mediation analysis. The values of different para-meter estimates and fit indices are the criteria for comparison to select the preferred model. In order to prove the mediating effects, this study's pre-viously estimated model was restructured by developing three different models to investigate the mediating roles of *ICT integration* and *ICT utili-sation* on *organisational performance*.

In the complete mediation model, ICT use was hypothesised to have only an indirect effect on SMEs' performance through ICT integration and ICT utilisation. The partial mediation model anticipated significant direct and indirect effects while the no-mediation model involved assessment of the predictor variables' impact only on the outcome variable.

In CBSEM, researchers estimate the model's extension as a no-mediation model, full mediation model and partial mediation model. The study thus estimated different fit indices to examine which model would produce acceptable and high fit indices. The strength of different fit indices was the basis for the preferred model selection which also justified the pattern of mediation. CAIC (comprehensive Akaike information criteria), chi-squared, comparative fit index (CFI), normed fit index (NFI), incre-mental fit index (IFI), root mean square error of approximation (RMSEA) and adjusted goodness-of-fit index (AGFI) statistics were estimated to select the preferred model. CBSEM can compute the fit indices and easily compare different models while component-based SEM only uses R^2 to anticipate the variations in the model. A different form of fit index, Goodness of fit (GoF), a global fit measure, is conducted for PLS path modelling. The GoF value is computed by the average communality and average R^2 for the endogenous constructs (Tenenhaus, Vinzi, Chatelin, & Lauro, 2005).

$$GoF = \sqrt{\overline{AVE} \times \overline{R}^2} \qquad (15)$$

The estimated GoF values may be used to assess the global validation of PLS models. The validation of the PLS model was examined by comparing the GoF values with different cut-off values set for the model with different explanatory power (Wetzels et al., 2009). The GoF values followed the basic three cut-off values as:

$$GoF_{small} = 0.1, \quad GoF_{medium} = 0.25, \quad GoF_{large} = 0.36.$$

The high GoF values suggested a satisfactory fit which may help to select the preferred model for assessing the form of mediation with adequate support to globally validate the PLS model.

As shown in Table 37 (see also Fig. 13), Model 1 (no-mediation model), Model 2 (complete mediation model) and Model 3 (partial mediation model) have GoF values of 0.405, 0.467 and 0.466, respectively. Thus, each of the models exceeded the cut-off value of 0.36 for large sizes of R^2 which, in turn, provided adequate supports for global validation of the PLS models.

Model 2 showed significant direct effects of ICT use on SMEs' performance ($c = 0.556$, $t = 15.18$, $R^2 = 0.309$). The complete mediation model showed significant effects of the initial variable on both the intervening variables. The initial variable *ICT use* had a significant effect on the mediator, *ICT integration* ($a_1 = 0.640$, $t = 17.65$, $R^2 = 0.41$), and also had a

Table 37. Mediating Roles of ICT Integration and Utilisation.

	Model 1 (No Mediation)	Model 2 (Full Mediation)	Model 3 (Partial Mediation)	Comments
c or c'	0.556**	na	0.074	Complete
	(15.18)		(1.13)	mediation
a_1	na	0.640**	0.640**	
		(17.65)	(20.80)	
b_1	na	0.589**	0.549**	
		(12.16)	(8.24)	
a_2	na	0.494**	0.491**	
		(12.06)	(11.86)	
b_2	na	0.182**	0.169**	
		(3.59)	(2.78)	
R^2	0.309	0.41 (M_1)	0.41 (M_2)	
		0.244 (M_2)	0.241 (M_2)	
		0.507 (Y)	0.509 (Y)	
GoF	**0.405**	**0.467**	**0.466**	

**$p < 0.01$.

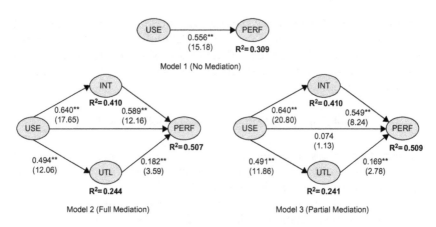

**p < 0.01, USE = ICT use, INT = Integration, UTL = Utilisation, PERF = Performance*

Fig. 13.   Mediating Effects of Integration and Utilisation.

significant effect on another mediator *ICT utilisation* ($a_2 = 0.494$, $t = 12.06$, $R^2 = 2.44$). The model again projected the significant effects of the mediators, *ICT integration* ($b_1 = 0.589$, $t = 12.16$) and *ICT utilisation* ($b_2 = 0.182$, $t = 3.59$) on the criterion variable *SMEs' performance*.

The partial mediation model also showed the significant effects of *ICT use* on the two mediators *ICT integration* and *ICT utilisation*. The result also indicated the significant influence of the two mediators (*ICT integration* and *ICT utilisation*) on *SMEs' performance* while the effect of *ICT use* on *SMEs' performance* was seen to be non-significant ($c' = 0.74$, $t = 1.13$, $R^2 = 0.509$). The combined model showed a reduced strength of c, which was also insignificant. Thus, the analyses posited a complete mediating process in assessing the effects of *ICT use* on *SMEs' performance* through two intervening variables, *ICT integration* and *ICT utilisation* (see Table 38).

Further indirect effects of *ICT use* on *SMEs' performance* through *ICT integration* ($a_1 \times b_1 = 0.377$) were higher than the effects through *ICT utilisation* ($a_2 \times b_2 = 0.09$). The total indirect effect was given by $\sum_{i=1}^{j} a_i b_i = 0.467$.

The hypotheses tests results for mediating effects of Integration and Utilisation on SME performance are summarised in Table 38.

The study results showed the significant effects of *ICT usage* on *SMEs' performance* in a complete mediational process which involved the multiple intervening variables, *ICT integration* and *ICT utilisation*. Interestingly, *ICT usage* significantly affected *SMEs' performance* in a single mediational

Table 38.   Summary of Hypotheses Tests for Mediating Effects of
Integration and Utilisation.

	Hypotheses	Comments
H_{11a}	Integration plays a significant mediation role in explaining the effects of ICT usage on SME performance.	Partial mediation
H_{11b}	Utilisation plays a significant mediation role in explaining the effects of ICT usage on SME performance	Partial mediation
H_{11c}	Integration and utilisation jointly play a significant mediation role in explaining the effects of ICT usage on SME performance	Complete mediation

process. That is, in the no-mediation model, the effect of *ICT usage* on *SMEs' performance* was observed to be significant. The effects of *ICT* usage were reduced in the single mediation process (either *ICT integration* or *ICT utilisation*) which vanished in the multiple mediation process in the presence of both *ICT integration* and *ICT utilisation* as mediators.

6.6. Summary

This section has presented the results of the quantitative analysis of a nation-wide survey conducted in Bangladesh to study the diffusion of ICT and its role in generating the performance of SMEs. The study employed PLS-SEM) with a data set of 282 SMEs in Bangladesh used for data analysis. The nature of the study (practical and exploratory), and the nature of the latent variables under study (reflective and formative) justified the use of the PLS technique as the main analytical tool. The procedures of data collection, data screening by investigating possible biases and data analysis were elaborated in detail.

The analysis of the data by PLS was performed in two stages (assessment of the measurement model and structural model estimation) which were reported separately. The measurement model was assessed by estimating the convergent validity and discriminant validity of the constructs. The convergent validity of the reflective indicators was examined by item loadings while weights of the items and absence of multicollinearity among them were the criteria for the formative indicators. CR and AVE were also computed to test convergent validity. The study used 0.5, 0.7 and 0.5 as threshold levels (cut-off values) for the item loadings, CR and AVE, respectively. The study examined the square root of AVE and inter-construct correlations for construct level discriminant validity, and the item cross-loading matrix for item level discriminant validity of the study constructs. The hypotheses of the study were tested by estimating the structural model. The magnitude and degree of the estimates were examined by path coefficient (γ) and critical ratio (t-statistic) while the nomological validity was examined by R^2. The structural model explained 58.5% of variance in *expectation* while 76.5% and 48.5% of variance were explained in *ICT use* and *organisational performance*, respectively. The estimates nullified five hypotheses while all other hypotheses developed in Section 5 were accepted. The implications of these results and outcomes are discussed in Section 7.

7. DISCUSSION AND INTERPRETATION

7.1. Introduction

This section presents the discussion of the results and interpretation of the quantitative data analysis. The premise of the data analysis was developed by anticipating the structural relationships between endogenous and exogenous variables. The estimated results, through applying PLS-SEM), showed the degree and magnitude of the relationships between the constructs under study. The discussion of the results and their interpretations was performed based on the anticipated hypotheses and statistical estimations. The hypotheses of the research and test results were shown in Sections 5 and 6, respectively. This section discusses and debates the results in light of the respective hypotheses.

7.2. Hypothesis Related to Cognitive Evaluation

7.2.1. Hypothesis H_1

The TRA (Fishbein & Ajzen, 1975) suggests that overall affective evaluation, that is, one's beliefs (cognitive) towards performing a behaviour and respective evaluations (affective) heavily influence the individual's intention of performing the behaviour. The evaluation is made based on one's cognitive evaluation of the consequences of that behaviour (Ajzen & Fishbein, 1980; Sheppard et al., 1988).

Based on the notion of the TRA and supported by previous studies, it was anticipated that *cognitive evaluation* would have a direct and positive influence on *expectation* (Mehta & Sivadas, 1995; Reynolds, 1974;

Schlosser et al., 1999). The findings of the study revealed that *cognitive evaluation* ($\gamma = 0.155$) was directly related to *expectation*. This finding was consistent with past studies (Liao & Cheung, 2001; Mehta & Sivadas, 1995; Reynolds, 1974; Schlosser et al., 1999) and also complied with the notion of the TRA and the TPB.

With a strong positive and significant influence on *expectation*, *cognitive evaluation* played an important role in ICT adoption by SMEs. The result indicated that highly positive evaluation, that is, firms' favourable perception about ICT created positive expectation regarding the use or implementation of the technology. From the model, it was observed that the construct *cognitive evaluation* was a compound higher-order latent variable constructed by the reflections of two perceptual beliefs, *perceived ease of use* and *perceived usefulness*. These two factors were internal and developed through the adopter's own knowledge and perceptions about ICT.

This result has some implications for existing and potential users of ICT as well as for policy makers. Policy makers may be interested to know how *cognitive evaluation* could be developed in a positive way to boost the general level of ICT usage by SMEs in Bangladesh.

7.3. Hypotheses Related to Owner Innovativeness

Applying the notion of the DOI theory (Rogers, 1983, 1995, 2003), it has been argued that the first adopters of an innovation are innovators themselves who usually try a new idea, concept or product first and take the associated risks. Their good or bad experiences are transmitted to other potential adopters through the communication channels in an innovation diffusion process. The innovator's first experience of an innovation works as a reference which attracts different potential adopters and an innovation finally gains popularity. In support of the past literature, the field study justified three different hypotheses related to owner innovativeness.

7.3.1. Hypothesis H_{2a}
The estimates showed a significant positive association between *owner innovativeness* ($\gamma = 0.163$) and *cognitive evaluation*. Traditionally, the literature has suggested a positive link between adopter innovativeness and intention and/or actual use. This hypothesis was developed through the field study analysis. The finding of the structural model estimation was in line with the field study and was also consistent with the basic assumption of the DOI theory (Rogers, 2003).

The result indicated that innovative owners or CEOs favourably evaluate the usefulness and operational ease of ICT. An innovative owner or CEO usually generates new ideas or concepts for the development or sustainability of the organisation and has the ability to bear any risk associated with implementing those ideas or concepts. Thus, although in general, SME owners anticipate various constraints in accepting ICT, by their nature, innovative owners positively evaluate the outcome of the innovation and proceed to have actual experience. This result has some implications for the Bangladeshi government, policy makers and concerned organisations who are involved in promoting ICT usage among SMEs. Innovative SME owners may play a significant role, as a reference group, in fostering the adoption rate of ICT by SMEs in Bangladesh.

7.3.2. Hypothesis H_{2b}

It was anticipated that *owner innovativeness* would have direct and significant effects on *expectation*. The estimation rejected the hypothesis by revealing a non-significant association between *owner innovativeness* ($\gamma = -0.067$) and *expectation*. Surprisingly, the result was not consistent with the field study nor with past studies (Thong, 1999; Thong & Yap, 1995). The result indicated that owner or CEO innovativeness had no impact on expectation. In general, the innovative owner or CEO, by their nature, initiates things differently; thus, they are not hesitant to try an innovation. The innovators bear the risks associated with the adoption of an innovation and use the innovation at the first stage (Rogers, 2003) which implies that innovative owners highly intend to use an innovation. This result may have happened because the research model included *expectation* as an immediate antecedent of *actual usage* which was explained as a state of rational intention. Unlike intention, *expectation* is an expressed state of willingness which is formed by evaluating many internal, external and environmental factors. Thus, although previous studies had found that *owner innovativeness* had a strong and significant effect on *intention* (Thong, 1999; Thong & Yap, 1995), this study, logically, did not find a significant relationship between them. The adoption of ICT was highly associated with the resources and operational skills (Venkatesh et al., 2003, 2008) of the organisation as well as the compatibility (Rogers, 2003) of the ICT with existing systems and procedures. Thus, innovative owners, although holding new ideas and positive evaluations about the technology, consider their ability in terms of resources and operational skills as well as compatibility which may produce a realistic expectation whereas innovativeness has no significant impact.

7.3.3. Hypothesis H_{2c}

The estimation revealed a non-significant association between *owner innovativeness* ($\gamma = -0.038$) and *SMEs' actual usage of ICT*. Contrary to the field study outcome and previous studies, this finding indicated that owner innovativeness had no impact on the usage of ICT (Thong & Yap, 1995). It may be argued that, unlike innovations which are non-technical in nature that may be adopted and used by the will or preference of an entrepreneur, technological innovations particularly ICT require competent human resources, technology resources and a compatible working environment. As the technology involves operation of the Internet, the use, that is, the level of ICT application and depth of use, is related to its compatibility with customers, suppliers, regulatory authorities, partners and other stakeholders. This study investigated SMEs in Bangladesh where small enterprises face many problems regarding their resources and are mostly operated in an informal manner. The Bangladeshi government, although aiming to develop a digital-based economy by 2021, runs with a manual and traditional working environment in different departments and functional areas. Thus, SMEs, having the required facilities and resources, are also less inclined to use technology.

Furthermore, the SMEs that are involved in international operations are compelled to use ICT as their foreign counterparts require their ICT competency, particularly their online participation, and in this situation it is not important whether the entrepreneurs are innovative.

7.4. Hypotheses Related to Environmental Pressure

7.4.1. Hypothesis H_{3a}

It was anticipated that *environmental pressure* would have a significant influence on *expectation*. The structural model estimation showed a direct significant association between *environmental pressure* ($\gamma = 0.405$) and *expectation* which was consistent with previous studies (Ajzen, 1985; Kuan & Chau, 2001; Teo et al., 2003). *Environmental pressure* was measured as a composite of *coercive pressure* (DiMaggio & Powell, 1983; Quaddus & Hofmeyer, 2007); *mimetic pressure* (Premkumar & Ramamurthy, 1995; Teo et al., 2003); *normative pressure* (Teo et al., 2003; Venkatesh et al., 2003) and *global pressure* (field study); thus, this finding indicated the overall impact of *environmental pressure* on *expectation*. It was argued that firms that received positive experience about the use of ICT from their suppliers, partners or other stakeholders were highly inclined to adopt the same technology in their organisation to reap the advantages of using ICT. The results also suggested that customers' expectations and competitors' ICT usage's trends and patterns influence SMEs' ICT usage expectation. This study reported a unique environmental influence which may arise from ongoing technological development and globalisation.

7.4.2. Hypothesis H₃b

Following the notion of the TOE framework (Tornatzky & Fleischer, 1990), it was anticipated that *environmental pressure* would have a significant influence on *SMEs' actual use of IT*. The results of the structural model revealed a positive and significant effect of *environmental pressure* ($\gamma = 0.191$) on *actual usage* behaviour which was consistent with the TOE framework and other past studies (Teo et al., 2003; Tornatzky & Fleischer, 1990; Zhu & Kraemer, 2005). As with Hypothesis H_{3a}, the overall impact of *environmental pressure* was anticipated by Hypothesis H_{3b}. The result indicated that *SMEs' actual use of ICT* was largely influenced by *environmental pressure* arising from competitors (*mimetic pressure*); partners/customers (*normative pressure*); demands from the regulatory authority or dominant customers/suppliers (*coercive pressure*); or technological development/globalisation (*global pressure*). The results suggested that firms that have had good experiences using ICT with their close stakeholders, partner organisation and suppliers and whose customers expected to see them using technology would use ICT. The trend, status and success of competitors' ICT use also influenced SMEs' level of ICT use. Most importantly, SMEs used ICT due to pressure from their dominant customer organisations or suppliers. This was very common in the RMG industry. Most of the customers or suppliers of Bangladeshi RMG organisations are large internationally reputable companies. They are completely ICT-based. They communicate, interact and transact with all parties online. Without ICT competency and online participation, it is not possible to interact with them. Thus, the RMG organisations had no choice but to use ICT to become compatible with their customers or suppliers and also to match the competition.

Globalisation has created new opportunities for business organisations. SMEs have become more international to gain the competitive advantage from being active in international business. ICT, particularly the Internet, offers easy access to the international arena and ensures effectiveness and reliability in communication, negotiations and transactions.

7.5. Hypotheses Related to Facilitating Condition

7.5.1. Hypothesis H_{4a}

The estimation showed a significant correlation between *facilitating condition* ($\gamma = 0.294$) and *expectation* which was consistent with past research studies (Ajzen, 1985; Taylor & Todd, 1995c; Thompson et al., 1991; Venkatesh et al., 2008) and the field study. The operationalisation of the construct *facilitating condition* emphasised external resources such as organisational, technological and human resources. *Facilitating condition* referred to the degree to which an individual believed that an organisational and technical infrastructure existed to support the use of the system. The result indicated that the SMEs with the necessary technical and organisational resources (e.g. hardware and Internet connectivity, ICT-competent employees, compatible procedures, etc.) had high expectation of using ICT.

7.5.2. Hypothesis H_{4b}

In accordance with the UTAUT model (Venkatesh et al., 2003), it was anticipated that *facilitating condition* would have a significant influence on SMEs' *actual use of ICT*. The estimation showed a significant association between *facilitating condition* ($\gamma = 0.70$) and *actual ICT usage* behaviour. The results indicated that firms with adequate hardware and network connectivity, competent employees and compatible working environments were likely to use ICT. The results also indicated that firms lacking some technical and organisational infrastructure were logically less inclined to use ICT. This result supported the findings of past researchers (Gupta et al., 2008; Venkatesh et al., 2003).

7.6. Hypotheses Related to Country Readiness

In reference to Rogers (1983), Tornatzky and Fleischer (1990), Caselli and Coleman (2001) and Zhu and Kraemer (2005), it was anticipated that *country readiness* would have a significant influence on *SMEs' expectation* (Hypothesis H_{5a}) and *actual usage* (Hypothesis H_{5b}) *of ICT*.

7.6.1. Hypothesis H_{5a}

The structural model estimation showed a significant association between *country readiness* ($\gamma = -0.135$) and *SMEs' expectation* to use ICT. The result indicated that overall *country readiness* was an important predictor of *expectation* which was consistent with the findings of previous studies

(Marques et al., 2011; Molla & Licker, 2005). *Country readiness*, an aggregated variable, explained the overall effects of contextual factors as the construct was a higher-order composite of *technology infrastructure, human infrastructure, legal infrastructure, financial infrastructure,* and *government policy and supports.* The overall effect of *country readiness* was negative which meant that the overall infrastructure of the country was not favourable for the adoption of ICT particularly from the SMEs' perspective. This result may be debated as Bangladesh is now in its infancy in the implementation of ICT in different sectors. Although the government of the country is dedicated to establishing a digital-based society by 2021 by applying the ICT potential in economic development and governance, the responses from different parties have not been very satisfactory.

For example, Internet penetration of Bangladesh on June 2012 was calculated as 0.5% which was very low in comparison to many developed and developing countries.[15] The Bangladeshi government is trying hard to overcome these challenges by providing subsidies and grants, initiating favourable ICT policy and tax rebates, and also providing computer hardware at a lower price. However, ICT users are facing several constraints, such as coverage of the Internet network, Internet speed, power supply, legislative supports in different kinds of online disputes and lack of online banking facilities which restrict them from using ICT and establishing ICT-dependent working environments.

7.6.2. Hypothesis H_{5b}

The structural model estimation did not find any significant association between *country readiness* ($\gamma = -0.005$) and *SMEs' actual ICT usage* behaviour. The result was inconsistent with previous studies (Dewan & Kraemer, 2000; Zhu, Dong, et al., 2006; Zhu & Kraemer, 2005). Surprisingly, the aggregated impact of the contextual factors was not found to be significantly related to *SMEs' ICT use* while it had significant negative effects on *expectation*. It is argued that this result occurred because the Bangladeshi infrastructure, namely, *technology infrastructure, human infrastructure, legal infrastructure, financial infrastructure* or *government policy and supports* negatively affected *SMEs' expectation of using ICT*. That is, the SMEs that were willing to adopt ICT were afraid about the outcome of the investment when evaluating the overall infrastructural supports required for ICT operation. Their negative perception of the infrastructure as Internet speed was, in general, very slow, frequent power outages occurred, banking and legal supports were incompatible, and the absence of online consumer protection law all adversely affected their expectation.

Despite inadequate and incompatible infrastructural supports, some organisations were compelled to use ICT due to their interactions with international companies (many of whom were large multinational enterprises) as a collaborator, supplier or customer.

Organisations in foreign countries were completely computer-based working in automated environments. They demanded that their foreign collaborators were compliant with their systems. Thus, SMEs in underdeveloped countries, although facing several constraints and having had no expectation of adopting such technology, were using ICT to comply with their foreign customers and collaborators and to match the competition. In this context, although *country readiness* had strong negative effects on *expectation*, there was no relationship with *actual usage* behaviour.

7.7. Hypotheses Related to Culture

Culture, as an important aspect of the external environment, affected organisational *ICT usage* behaviour. Based on the field study outcomes and past studies (Bertolotti, 1984; Burn, 1995; Erez & Early, 1993; Gefen & Straub, 1997; Hill et al., 1998; Ho et al., 1989), it was anticipated that *culture* would have a significant influence on *cognitive evaluation* (Hypothesis H_{6a}) and *expectation* (Hypothesis H_{6b}).

7.7.1. Hypothesis H_{6a}
The results of the structural equation model estimation showed a significant negative association between *culture* ($\gamma = -0.333$) and *cognitive evaluation*. This result was consistent with the field study and prior studies (Dolecheck & Dolecheck, 1987; Lu, Rose, & Blodgett, 1999; Ralston, Giacalone, & Terpstra, 1994). Culture is composed of values, norms and beliefs which individuals of a collective acquire through their long-term interactions with their fellow community members, society and the environment. Individuals' preferences and behaviours are largely influenced by their own culture. The result suggested that the culture of Bangladesh was not supportive to the operation and implementation of computer-driven communication systems or working environments among SMEs.

Bangladesh is a developing country which is characterised by a culture with high power distance and high in-group collectivism. Small businesses are mostly operated in an informal manner. Individuals in this society usually interact through face-to-face communication, maintaining close social ties and mostly use the Bengali language as their medium of communication. Nepotism, political influence and interference have become a part of the country's culture. The overall culture of the country is now polluted through exercising bribery and unethical ways of conducting business in different sectors.

Utilisation of computers in the working environment requires the establishment of structured and formal working procedures, technology resources and skilled human resources. Entrepreneurs of SMEs are usually confused when considering the usefulness of ICT as it is not compatible with the overall culture of the country. They may also not perceive the technology as being easy to use as the basic interfaces of computer-driven programs are English language-based.

This study has measured *culture* by applying higher-order hierarchical modelling where culture was conceptualised as a second-order composite of *power distance, in-group collectivism, uncertainty avoidance, ethical culture* and *Bengali values*. The estimation revealed a gross summated effect of *culture* on *cognitive evaluation* which was negative.

7.7.2. Hypothesis H_{6b}

The statistical estimation did not reveal any significant association between *culture* ($\gamma = -0.048$) and *expectation*, which thus rejected Hypothesis H_{6b}. Prior studies have supported the view that *culture* influences *organisational ICT use* (Bertolotti, 1984; Burn, 1995; Erez & Early, 1993; Gefen & Straub, 1997; Harris & Davison, 1999; Hill et al., 1998; Ho et al., 1989; Straub, 1994). The field interviews explored the view that *culture* was associated with *expectation* and *cognitive evaluation*. Although interview participants supported the link between *culture* and *expectation*, statistical analysis of the national survey data indicated that this prediction, based as it was on a small sample, could not be applied to a larger population.

The assumption, justified through the qualitative field study, may be rejected by a quantitative survey. This is a common problem of mixed-method research as some ideas primarily considered through the field study which comprises a small sample size may be rejected through the responses from a comparatively large sample used in the quantitative survey (Jackson, 2008; Quaddus, Islam, & Stanton, 2006). However, this result may be argued against, according to England (1975), who stated that culture was a key determinant in determining individual beliefs, values and attitudes. *Cognitive evaluation* represented individuals' favourable or unfavourable feelings towards an innovation which was completely internal and projected as attitude, thus a significant association between *culture* and *cognitive evaluation* was justified. This result is consistent with the findings of numerous past studies (Dolecheck & Dolecheck, 1987; Lu et al., 1999; Ralston et al., 1994).

Surprisingly, *culture* was not found to have a significant effect on *expectation*. One possible explanation of this result was that the comprehensive research model included *cognitive evaluation* as a predictor of *expectation* with *culture*. Cognitive evaluation was more highly influenced by culture than expectation as culture is a determinant of individuals' values, beliefs and attitudes (England, 1975). Cognitive evaluation, as the relatively expressed state of individuals' favourableness or unfavourableness toward an innovation, produced a strong and significant effect on expectation while culture did not provide any significant effect on expectation but significantly explained cognitive evaluation. As an individual's favourableness or unfavourableness towards an innovation formed their intention or expectation, cognitive evaluation was found to have a strong significant effect on expectation.

Importantly, *culture*, although it was not found in this study to have a positive effect on *expectation*, was indirectly related to *expectation* through its strong and significant influence on *cognitive evaluation*.

7.8. Hypothesis Related to Expectation

7.8.1. Hypothesis H₇

Applying the notion of the TRA (Fishbein & Ajzen, 1975), TPB (Ajzen, 1985) and TAM (Davis, 1989) with the outcome of a recent study (Venkatesh et al., 2008), *expectation* was predicted to have a significant positive influence on *actual usage* behaviour (Hypothesis H_7). Finally, the structural model estimation depicted *expectation* ($\beta = 0.697$) as a strong and significant determinant of actual behaviour when referring to *actual use* of ICT among SMEs in Bangladesh. The finding supported previous theories and empirical studies (Ajzen & Fishbein, 1980; Azam & Quaddus, 2009b; Chang, 1998; Fishbein & Ajzen, 1975; Mathieson, 1991; Taylor & Todd, 1995a, 1995b; Venkatesh & Davis, 2000; Venkatesh & Morris, 2000; Venkatesh et al., 2003, 2008). Consistent with the theoretical framework, this result indicated that a positive and strong expectation, that is, the willingness to adopt would foster the use of ICT at firm level.

7.9. Hypotheses Related to ICT Use

7.9.1. Hypothesis H_{8a}

Based on the field study findings, *ICT use* was anticipated to have a significant influence on *ICT integration* (Hypothesis H_{8a}). The structural model
estimation revealed a strong significant positive association between *ICT
use* ($\gamma = 0.643$) and *integration*. This result was consistent with the field
study. This study measured *ICT use* as a summated subjective assessment
of different levels of ICT applications, namely, use of the Internet and
homepage (capable of product cataloguing); use of interactive homepage
(capable of receiving online orders); use of interactive homepage for transactions (capable of online transactions) and use of ERP. Consistent with
the field study outcome, this result indicated that the higher levels of ICT
application would speed up the process of ICT integration between different functional areas within the organisation as well as with other organisations at industry level.

7.9.2. Hypothesis H_{8b}

As with Hypothesis H_{8a}, based on the field study findings, it was proposed
that *ICT use* would have a direct significant influence on *degree of utilisation* (Hypothesis H_{8b}). The structural model estimation revealed a strong
significant positive association between *ICT use* ($\gamma = 0.488$) and *degree of
utilisation*. This result was consistent with the field study. *Degree of utilisation* was measured through a summated subjective assessment of how
appropriately ICT was utilised in different functional areas in the firm,
namely, production, administration and accounts, and marketing and sales.
Consistent with the field study outcome, this result indicated that the higher
level of ICT applications would ensure proper utilisation of ICT in various
functional areas of the firm.

7.9.3. Hypothesis H_{8c}

Applying the notion of the RBV of the firm (Barney, 1991) and its application to ICT at the firm level (Bharadwaj, 2000; Powell & Dent-Micallef,
1997), it was anticipated that *ICT use* would have direct positive effects on
firm *performance* (Hypothesis H_{8c}). Surprisingly, the structural model estimation did not find any significant association between *ICT use* ($\gamma = 0.077$)
and *performance*. This result was also not consistent with previous studies
(Bharadwaj, 2000; Powell & Dent-Micallef, 1997; Zhu, Dong, et al., 2006;
Zhu & Kraemer, 2005). This result also was contrary to the outcome of the
field study.

However, the result apparently was similar to the productivity paradox of IT. This was argued according to the RBV (Barney, 1991) which explains that valuable, rare, imperfectly imitable and imperfectly substitutable resources could generate sustainable competitive advantage for the firm with the prerequisite of heterogeneity and imperfectly mobile resources among competing firms. The constructs, *ICT integration* and *degree of utilisation*, combine ICT resources with different functionalities of a firm and utilise them properly which produces unique capabilities that are intangible and unable to be imitated. Thus, ICT use alone, without integrated and properly utilised applications, may not have any significant impact on firm performance.

7.10. Hypothesis Related to ICT Integration

7.10.1. Hypothesis H_9
ICT integration was anticipated to have a significant influence on *organisational performance* (Hypothesis H_9). The structural model estimation revealed a strong significant association between *ICT integration* ($\gamma = 0.541$) and *firm performance*. This result was consistent with the field study outcome and past studies (Zhu & Kraemer, 2002, 2005). *Firm performance* was measured by applying higher-order hierarchical modelling where *competitive performance*, *internal operation productivity* and *financial performance* were the manifest variables. However, this result indicated that overall *firm performance* largely depended on how ICT was integrated between different functional areas. This result was logical as organisations would not receive the benefit if they introduced computer-based operation only in one particular department while other departments operated through manual procedures. Furthermore, organisations would not receive productive output even in the case where computer-based operations were introduced in many departments if they were not integrated.

7.11. Hypothesis Related to Degree of Utilisation

7.11.1. Hypothesis H_{10}
Based mainly on the field study findings, it was anticipated that *degree of utilisation* would have a significant effect on *firm performance* (Hypothesis H_{10}). The structural model estimation accepted the hypothesis portraying *degree of utilisation* ($\gamma = 0.180$) as having a significant association with *firm*

performance. This result was consistent with the findings of past studies (Forster & Cornford, 1992; Ordedra et al., 1993). This result indicated that organisations benefit from ICT use if the degree of utilisation is satisfactory; that is, the technology is utilised properly. It is important to note that ICT usage indicates the frequency or rate of usage of various ICT applications while degree of utilisation explains the extent to which the proper and actual use of technology is ensured.

The logical interpretation of this finding is that most of the functions in Bangladesh, from household day-to-day operations to business and social formalities as well as government services are performed through manual processes. Thus, numerous functions of ICT, although implemented, are un-utilised or under-utilised which causes adverse effects on the productivity of ICT and finally on firm performance.

Furthermore, ICT, particularly the Internet, although not new in Bangladesh, is still at an introductory level as most people are reluctant and/or incapable of utilising it in communications, services and businesses. As the Bangladeshi government has declared that it is seeking to achieve a digital Bangladesh by 2021 and has set the country the target of establishing e-governance by 2014, the people are being motivated and pushed towards the adoption of technology. Unfortunately, this is confined to the operation of entertainment-related ancillary functions, such as audio, video, games, video streaming and chat rooms.

The application of ICT, although promoted in various sectors across the country, unfortunately is not reasonably involved in accomplishing economic or business functions. As a consequence, the productivity impact of ICT at firm level has become questionable. Organisations invest and introduce ICT with a view to performing some specified organisational functions. Proper accomplishment of those tasks results in productivity of the investment. Consistent with this notion, this study has revealed that organisations that fail to accomplish the tasks properly would suffer from adverse effects on firm performance.

7.12. *Hypothesis Related to Mediating Effects of ICT Integration and Degree of Utilisation*

Based on the field study outcome, it was anticipated that *ICT integration* and *degree of utilisation* would play mediation roles in explaining the effects of ICT use on firm performance. The structural model estimation depicted a mediational process explaining the effects of *ICT use* on *organisational performance* which involved two intervening variables, *ICT integration* and *degree of utilisation*. The mediational relationship was examined by applying the procedure of Baron and Kenny (1986).

It was revealed that the variation in ICT use alone would significantly account for a variance in SMEs' performance, the effects becoming reduced in the presence of a single mediator (*integration* or *utilisation*) which would finally disappear in a multiple mediation environment (with the presence of *ICT integration* and *degree of utilisation* together). The results indicated that the effect of *ICT use* on *firm performance* was completely mediated through *ICT integration* and *degree of utilisation*.

It is argued that this result occurred because, due to the lack of infrastructural supports and the lower level of ICT and Internet penetration, organisations did not apply ICT intensively to accomplish all major organisational or business functions. Moreover, although organisations used ICT, their inability to integrate major business functionalities would impact adversely on organisational performance. Likewise, organisations did not attain performance growth if ICT was not utilised properly.

7.13. Summary

This section has provided a discussion of the SEM estimates presented in Section 6. The interpretations of the findings have been carried out to support the hypotheses. This section has discussed the effects of the antecedent factors of ICT adoption and diffusion by SMEs. In analysing the impact of ICT on firm performance, it was found that ICT use may not generally create enhanced firm performance. Integration and proper utilisation of ICT were important indicators of firm performance. The discussion in this section has indicated that firms generally experience performance growth if ICT is integrated and properly utilised. The final section comprises the conclusion and presents future research directions.

8. CONCLUSIONS AND FUTURE RESEARCH DIRECTIONS

8.1. Introduction

This section presents the conclusions of the current research. In order to state the contribution of the research to the body of knowledge, a summary of the entire research process and outcomes is provided in Section 8.2. Section 8.3 then discusses the theoretical and practical contributions of the research. The final section states the limitations of this study and outlines directions for future research.

8.2. Research Summary

This research project was initiated to study the impact of the diffusion of ICT on SMEs' performance with special attention given to the mediating effects of ICT integration and utilisation. Previous studies have reported a clear differentiation in the level of usage of ICT between rich and poor countries, as well as between developed and developing countries. The introduction of the usage of ICT, particularly Internet-dependent technology, by individuals and organisations involves changes to the systems, procedures and processes of relevant services and also affects the way through which customers, suppliers, regulatory bodies and other external parties deal with business organisations. The rapid and exponential growth of ICT usage has attracted the bulk of researchers' attention in looking at the phenomena of the adoption and diffusion of the technology. Although numerous research initiatives have focused on the adoption intention (Gefen & Straub, 2000; Kendall et al., 2001; Lal, 1999; Pavlov & Chai, 2002) and actual usage (Anandarajan et al., 2002; Johnson & Hignite, 2000; Thatcher et al., 2006; Venkatesh et al., 2008) of the technology, the question of whether ICT usage impacts on firm performance in SMEs has not been clearly answered (see Jean, 2007). Furthermore, previous studies on innovation diffusion have focused on the developed country perspective and, mostly, on the American perspective (Zhu & Kraemer, 2005). Due to the infrastructural, environmental and cultural differences, and a wide digital divide between developed and developing countries, the theories constructed from a developed country perspective may logically suffer from their lack of generalisability and applicability in the developing country context. It has been assumed that the theoretical framework constructed in a developed country perspective would also fit the developing country environment. However, it is not unlikely that the theoretical framework would vary in different contexts. To examine the effects of the diffusion of ICT on SMEs' performance, this study firstly developed a comprehensive theoretical model and then examined the research model from a developing country perspective with survey data collected from various SMEs in Bangladesh.

The theoretical framework of the research (described in Section 2) was developed by combining the technology adoption-diffusion theories, namely the TRA (Fishbein & Ajzen, 1975); Rogers' DOI theory (Rogers, 1983); the TPB (Ajzen, 1985); the TAM (Davis, 1986); UTAUT (Venkatesh et al., 2003) and the TOE framework (Tornatzky & Fleischer, 1990) with institutional theory (DiMaggio & Powell, 1983) and resource-based theory/view (Barney, 1991). The initial research model was refined and contextualised by the field study and a comprehensive research model was developed. The hypotheses for the research were formulated from the comprehensive model.

As previously discussed in the methodological section (described in Section 3), this study has employed a mixed-method research approach, combining qualitative and quantitative methods of data collection and analysis to attain the research objectives. The qualitative phase of the study extended and contextualised the initial model. It is not unlikely that due to contextual differences the subject of this study may have a manifestation which differs from and may be beyond the scope of the existing literature. Furthermore, the new model developed through synpapering different models needed to be contextualised. A field study was conducted by interviewing 11 SMEs in Bangladesh (as described in Section 4). Content analysis (by NVivo 10) was performed to analyse the data. The findings, in general, supported the initial model. However, some adjustments were also applied to the initial model to build a comprehensive and integrated research model (Fig. 3). Importantly, the field study suggested reducing the number of related latent variables in order to construct a higher-order latent variable combining related first-order variables. *Cognitive evaluation, culture, environmental pressure, country readiness* and *performance* were developed as second-order constructs through this process. Finally, the comprehensive model comprised *owner innovativeness, cognitive evaluation, facilitating condition, environmental pressure, culture* and *country readiness* as antecedents of the adoption and use of ICT by SMEs while organisational performance was predicted through the influence of *ICT use, integration* and *degree of utilisation*. Based on the comprehensive research model, 21 hypotheses were formulated under 11 groups (as described in Section 5).

The second phase of the research employed a quantitative approach to test these hypotheses. Since this study stands under the positivist research paradigm, the main and most voluminous work was associated with this phase (the quantitative research) of the study. The quantitative research study involved the development of the survey instrument, questionnaire pre-testing, survey design, data collection, data coding, recording and manipulation, outlier checking and model estimation (as described in Section 6). The questionnaire was finalised after pre-testing. Next, a pilot study was conducted on 60 respondents. Based on the feedback, some modifications were made and the final questionnaires were distributed to SMEs in Bangladesh seeking their responses. In total, 282 responses were gathered. A PLS-SEM) technique was employed to analyse the quantitative data with this performed through PLS-Graph Version 3.

The analysis revealed that the adoption and diffusion of ICT by SMEs in Bangladesh were largely influenced by *cognitive evaluation, facilitating condition, environmental pressure* and *country readiness* with *owner innovativeness* and *culture* indirectly affected through *cognitive evaluation*. Organisations were interested in implementing ICT for better organisational performance. Surprisingly, ICT use was not found to have any significant effect on overall organisational performance. However, the structural model depicted a unique inter-relationship between *ICT use, integration, degree of utilisation* and *organisational performance*. The analysis revealed that ICT use, although not directly related to organisational performance, was indirectly related through *integration* and the *degree of utilisation*. This result suggests that organisations may not attain better performance by implementing ICT in their firm if it is not integrated with different functional areas and utilised properly.

8.3. Contributions of the Research

This study successfully employed a mixed-method research approach which has provided some unique results to address the main research questions. As opposed to most studies in the adoption area which commonly engage in a mono-method approach, this research applied a mixed method that combined qualitative and quantitative approaches in the data collection process. For the qualitative method, a field study was employed while the quantitative method used a survey as the data collection process. The overall design of the study and its implementation were challenging on several counts as the study examined the innovation diffusion phenomena from a developing country perspective while most diffusion theories have been constructed from a developed country perspective and, particularly, an American perspective (Zhu & Kraemer, 2005). The mixed-method research approach was appropriate and has made significant contributions which included building a comprehensive research model (contextualised and fine-tuned); exploring a few new constructs, variables and their measurement items; exploring the causal links between the study variables; testing of hypotheses and drawing inferences by reliable and valid research outcomes. The main contributions of the study, both the theoretical and practical contribution, are reported in the following section.

8.3.1. Theoretical Contribution

This study was initiated to examine SMEs' ICT usage behaviour and firm performance. This study extended its exploration from simply addressing the innovation adoption-diffusion phenomena to analyse the effects of ICT diffusion on organisational performance. In examining the ICT diffusion process in SMEs, its antecedents and consequences from the viewpoint of generating organisational performance growth, this study has reviewed existing innovation diffusion theories and has combined those theories with institutional theory and the RBV.

In summary, this study has reviewed the TRA (Fishbein & Ajzen, 1975); DOI theory (Rogers, 1983); TPB (Ajzen, 1985); TAM (Davis, 1986); UTAUT (Venkatesh et al., 2003) and the TOE framework (Tornatzky & Fleischer, 1990) combined with institutional theory (DiMaggio & Powell, 1983) and resource-based theory/view (Barney, 1991). The results of this synpaper have helped to construct a comprehensive model which has focused on the process of the diffusion of ICT and its impact on organisational performance. The existing theories have mostly addressed the ICT diffusion phenomena from a developed country perspective while their applicability in addressing similar phenomena from a developing country perspective is questionable. The initial theoretical model developed through reviewing the existing literature underwent a screening process using a qualitative field study to fine-tune and contextualise the research model.

The field study interviews suggested some adjustments that were needed to the model which had been primarily developed from theory. These adjustments involved changes in the interrelationships between some constructs, omission of some variables and also inclusion of some new variables and measurement items. This screening process yielded an integrated research model which enabled the study of the ICT diffusion process and the post-adoption phenomena (i.e. the effects of ICT usage on firm performance) in the context of SMEs in Bangladesh.

The comprehensive theoretical model includes various factors from different levels which involve individual, organisational, cultural, environmental and country-specific factors. The model also uses three different levels of ICT use: *ICT use*, *integration* and *degree of utilisation* to address the depth, breadth and appropriateness of ICT use, respectively. The theoretical model predicts that the effects of ICT use on organisational performance are mediated through integration and utilisation. This prediction was validated through analysis of the survey data. By including ICT integration and utilisation and their mediational roles, the theoretical model is comprehensive and unique in addressing ICT diffusion and organisational performance. This presents a major theoretical contribution.

The model measures organisational performance (SME performance) as a higher-order construct comprising three different performance-related manifest variables: *competitiveness, internal operation productivity* and *financial performance*. The model also explains *cognitive evaluation* as a higher-order construct which comprises two internal manifest variables: *perceived usefulness* and *perceived ease of use*.

The model includes three different aspects of external *environmental pressure*, namely, pressure arising from cultural aspects, pressure arising from the industrial environment and pressure arising from the macro-country environment. Each of the environment-related factors is addressed by applying a higher-order modelling procedure. *Culture* is formed by the effects of *power distance, in-group collectivism, uncertainty avoidance, ethical culture* and *Bengali values; environmental pressure* is composed of *coercive pressure, mimetic pressure, normative pressure* and *global pressure;* while *country readiness* comprises *technology infrastructure, human infrastructure, legal infrastructure, financial infrastructure* and *government policy and supports*. Although most of the variables being studied were borrowed from previous literature, a number of the variables explored in the field study were very much context-specific and were the first of their kind to examine technology innovation diffusion phenomena from a developing country perspective. For example, *Bengali values, ethical culture* and *degree of utilisation* of ICT, as well as the measurement procedure of *cognitive evaluation* and country-specific variables, were new thus adding to the significance of this study.

The theoretical framework is innovative and provides a holistic approach for looking at the antecedents of ICT diffusion and its consequences for organisational performance. More clearly, the theoretical framework offers an opportunity to examine the whole process of innovation diffusion and its effect on organisational performance from a single platform. The robustness of analysis, furthermore, suggests the suitability of the comprehensive model for analysing the diffusion of ICT by SMEs and its effects on organisational performance. This framework is potentially suitable for testing similar phenomena in the large organisation environment from both a developing and developed country perspective.

8.3.2. Practical Contribution

This study has provided a clear picture of how internal and external factors affect ICT usage by SMEs (in a developing country) and the consequential effects of this usage on organisational performance mediated through integration and utilisation. By categorising SMEs by their different levels of ICT use, it was revealed that SMEs that have positive cognitive evaluation towards ICT and adequate technological resources, and that receive positive pressure from their institutional environment are more likely to use ICT while the overall culture and country infrastructure were not supportive of the use of ICT.

Previous studies investigating adoption or usage of ICT have assumed that the use of ICT would generate performance growth. Interestingly, this study has found that ICT use did not immediately increase performance growth in SMEs. Organisations needed to acquire integration and proper utilisation of the technology in order to achieve performance growth. This was consistent with the notion of the RBV of ICT which emphasises that combining ICT into different organisational functionalities (i.e. integration with front-end functionalities or back-end integration) can create IT capabilities that are rare, unable to be imitated, valuable and sustainable, thereby contributing to value generation. Managers, interested stakeholders and policy makers may follow these findings and focus on ICT integration and the degree of utilisation with the view of attaining superior firm performance.

This study may also suggest some changes and modifications in Bangladesh's existing policies and strategies for promoting ICT adoption and ICT use by SMEs in order to achieve economic development.

Bangladesh is a developing country in which SMEs play a significant role in its development processes. The Bangladeshi government is dedicated to the utilisation of the potential of ICT in its economic development and to the establishment of a digitally based society by 2021. In light of the country's *Vision 2021*, the government has already revised the ICT policy and has made provision for various supports to promote ICT use in different sectors of the country. For example, the government has withdrawn all taxes from computer hardware, provides interest-free loans for ICT (software) businesses, and launches pro-ICT policies, grants, subsidies and motivational programs.

Government offices are gradually developing and becoming equipped with ICT devices to introduce e-governance systems. The last few years have witnessed significant physical and infrastructural development in terms of the installation of a large number of computer devices in different government offices, business enterprises and households. Frustratingly, most of these technological facilities are either un-utilised or under-utilised. For example, the majority of ICT users only access audio-visual entertainment programs, such as using their MP3 players, listening to audio or video music and playing online games. In recent years, computer users have increasingly participated in online social networks, audio and video chat rooms and other forms of communication. The patterns of ICT usage by individuals, households and organisations are similar. Thus, although a good number of SMEs use ICT, the productivity of the technology is questionable.

Entrepreneurs are apprehensive about a reduction in productivity as a result of the installation of computers in the workplace. They fearfully anticipate the risk that employees will participate in entertainment programs, games or personal communication during business hours using the technologies which have been installed to increase firm performance.

Furthermore, organisations, in general, use ICT to conduct some of their tasks while a number of functions are still carried out by the traditional means which, in many cases, are not compatible with the computerised online environment. The lack of implementation of completely computerised operations (i.e. the installation of computers to accomplish the tasks of all functional areas) prevents the attainment of the full benefits of ICT usage. This study's findings may provide a lesson for entrepreneurs who are confused about the possible outcome of computer device installation at their workplace as the findings suggest that partial implementation of ICT in the workplace may not result in organisational productivity. The costs of computerisation, that is, operational, maintenance and installation costs, are substantial. Only very high performance growth can make it worthwhile to invest in computerisation. In reality, partial use of the computerised operation, although producing some enhanced performance, is not enough to cover the significant costs associated with ICT-based operations. However, organisation-wide usage of the technology, although seeming to involve very high costs, may regain the reduction in productivity lost through these costs.

Organisation-wide complete ICT-based operations are not possible until and unless other closely associated organisations and important stakeholders use the same system. For example, organisations cannot gain benefits from ICT-based operations if their suppliers or customers are not ICT-based. In these circumstances, organisations, although they have highly sophisticated ICT devices, will need to use manual operations to interact or communicate with their stakeholders as ICT will not provide any help. The introduction of ICT-dependent communication and exchanges between organisations and external parties, for example, customers, suppliers, government regulatory authorities, partners and trade bodies, may help to develop this difficult situation.

Although some organisations perform some financial functions through ICT, most are confined to managing employees' salaries and account-keeping tasks. Organisations generally employ one or a few computer operators to perform computer-related tasks which means that a large number of functions remain external to their computers. It is not unlikely that some offices have computer hardware which is not used for operations but simply for social prestige as a showpiece. Moreover, the reality is that organisations, although using ICT, generally fail to ensure its proper utilisation and integrated use. Thus, the productivity of ICT usage has become questionable. In this situation, the Bangladeshi government may take the initiative to develop an integrated plan to promote the proper and integrated use of ICT which may include motivational programs, training and supports. This new initiative may help to develop the productivity of ICT usage and economic growth of the country.

The study thus calls for the initiation of a new ICT research direction exploring the status of ICT integration and ICT utilisation by SMEs and finding a way for ICT to contribute positively to organisational performance.

This study has also explored the patterns of ICT use by SMEs and has forecast the degree and magnitude of the effects of various individual, organisational and environmental factors on the adoption and usage of different levels of ICT applications. Cognitive evaluation emerged as a strong predictor of the expectation of SMEs' ICT use. The study revealed that organisations with adequate knowledge and a favourable perception of the usefulness and operational ease of the technology were more likely to use a higher level of ICT. Organisations that held a higher level of what was termed facilitating condition were also more likely to implement technological innovations than those who were lacking in this attribute. The facilitating condition comprised adequate resources, such as technological resources, human resources or systems compatible with computerised operations which facilitated the use of ICT in an organisation.

Entrepreneurs or the government may utilise this notion to develop policies or strategies to foster the growth of ICT use by SMEs. Providing useful information about the applicability of ICT to performing various organisational functions, to operational know-how and to technological facilities will potentially attract SMEs to using ICT for organisational competitiveness. The government and policy makers should undertake mass promotional programs to disseminate information about the various uses of computers and their contribution in developing better organisational performance. Organising specialised training programs for SMEs' capacity building may succeed in attaining SMEs' motivation to use ICT. Ensuring easy access to the technology by providing loans, grants and subsidies is also important.

The comprehensive model also forecast significant environmental pressure on SMEs' use of ICT. It suggested that organisations were highly influenced by various institutional stakeholders such as peer groups, competitors, dominant suppliers, customers or regulatory authorities, and by the changing environment arising from the globalisation process. Surprisingly, SMEs used ICT mainly to comply with the demands of their significant suppliers or dominant customers' requirements. Most of the SMEs, particularly in the RMG sector, have implemented ICT-based operations as their suppliers and dominant customers allow only online communications and exchanges. Thus, they have installed computers and ICT devices in their organisation in accordance with their customers' requirements in order to maintain their business deals while all other internal functions and domestic communications are performed through traditional means of operations. In reality, the technology is only used to accomplish a part of their organisational functionalities. Although the technology ensures the success of the most important task of the business being the carrying out of its orders and deals, this is still not considered productive in terms of the costs and investment associated with the technology installation and operation.

This study urges business enterprises' management and the government to look at the environmental and cultural factors with the view of achieving ICT usage success which may foster the country's economic development.

Initiating strategic adjustments to improve organisational practices by eliminating the traditional power distance inside the organisation as well as introducing formal working procedures by implementing necessary rules and regulations may result in productive use of technology. Furthermore, the application of a Bengali user interface may help to ensure the productivity of ICT use by SMEs in Bangladesh.

Finally, the government, various stakeholders and regulatory authorities should rationally adapt their policy and strategies focusing on the integrated and appropriate use of technology rather than only promoting the use of technology. However, the question may be asked regarding how a rational strategy to move towards appropriate and integrated utilisation of

ICT could be implemented before its promotion for mass usage. My argument is that the government and many financial and non-government agencies have already made significant efforts and provided enormous support promoting the usage of ICT at the government and non-government organisational level including in SMEs. Unfortunately, most of these organisations are using the computer as a typewriter or, in some cases, as an alternative to postal mail or telephone. The situation of most small businesses is similar. The quantitative analysis indicated that organisations with high ratings with regard to the ease or usefulness of the technology were more likely to use ICT. However, the field study and subsequent survey have suggested that numerous SMEs, although currently ICT users, were not able to accomplish the expected tasks by using the technology. The practical implication of this study is that the integration and proper utilisation of ICT should be implemented for superior organisational performance.

Interestingly, the study has explained SMEs' ICT usage phenomena by employing both organisational and consumer behaviour theories. However, the growth and economic potential of SMEs demand the development of a theoretical branch which will address the adoption and usage behaviour of SMEs.

8.4. Limitations of the Study

Despite this study's substantial contribution by studying SMEs' ICT usage (from a developing country perspective) and its analysis of the effects of a range of variables on the adoption and diffusion of ICT and its consequences for organisational performance, it has some limitations. By its nature, this study has analysed the aggregated effects of macro-environmental variables on ICT use and has explored how this affects aggregated firm performance. The results have implications for industry as well as for Bangladesh. However, as the study does not clearly answer how the first-order or manifest variables (the variables which construct a higher-order hybrid variable) affect ICT use and organisational performance, this may be considered a limitation of the study.

Secondly, this study focuses on the manufacturing industry sector in Bangladesh. As the RMG industry is the major contributor to the country's economy (contributing 75% of export earnings), the ICT diffusion phenomena have been analysed mainly from this industry's perspective. The study has also included responses from the leather industry which is an emerging industry in the manufacturing industry sector in terms of its export contribution. The number of responses from the leather industry was proportionate to the RMG industry responses, determined through the respective industry's contributions in export earnings. The proportion of export earnings by the RMG industry and leather industry in Bangladesh is roughly 80:20. The application of a proportionate stratified random sampling (in fact, given the disproportion between the respective industries, a disproportionate stratified random sampling) technique for data collection was therefore methodologically sound. Moreover, in its design, the services industry was beyond the study's scope which may be considered to be a limitation in drawing general implications for SMEs. For example, the IT industry, software and telecommunications industries, media and education industries, financial institutions, and tourism industry have high potential and make a significant contribution to the national economy.

Finally, this study utilised cross-sectional data which was collected at a single point in time. Thus, assessing the impact of the antecedent factors on the diffusion of ICT and its role in explaining SMEs' performance at different points in time was not possible.

This study has estimated the ICT adoption and diffusion phenomena by introducing a new conceptualisation of ICT use which was constructed by a composite measure of various levels of ICT applications. Although dealing with the aggregated use of ICT by SMEs is an innovative measure and has great importance in developing policy strategies at entrepreneur, industry and government level, this may be considered as a limitation as there is significant variation in the diffusion of different levels of ICT applications, such as ERP, e-commerce and e-business.

8.5. Future Research Directions

The limitations of this study may provide direction for new research investigating the adoption-diffusion of ICT by SMEs in Bangladesh. Analysis of the direct effects of the various dimensions of a higher-order composite, with these used as manifest variables or first-order variables, may provide clearer understanding of the phenomena. The effects of various dimensions of culture and the institutional environment as well as country-specific factors may help in developing policy and strategies to foster SMEs' ICT usage. Future research could compare the aggregated results with the specific outcomes of different dimensions of performance such as competitiveness, internal operation productivity and financial performance.

The changes in patterns of ICT usage and the effects of various antecedent factors could be examined by the analysis of longitudinal data collected from the same or similar panels of organisations at different points in time. The inclusion of diversified industries in the sample would enhance the validity of the predictions. Future studies could include the services industry as well as the manufacturing industry to produce representative results.

Finally, a comparison between the diffusion phenomena of specific ICT systems such as customer relationship management (CRM), e-commerce or ERP could provide a detailed picture of the adoption-diffusion patterns of specific systems. A future research initiative could validate this theoretical foundation by comparing the aggregated results with the adoption behaviour of various specific ICT systems. This could help in developing appropriate policies and strategies to foster the usage growth of various levels of ICT applications by SMEs in Bangladesh with the view of ensuring ICT's positive impact on organisational performance.

The final research model comprises numerous latent variables for studying SMEs' ICT usage behaviour and its impact on organisational performance. Due to the scope of the chapter, the influence of control variables, such as size and experience (age of the organisation) have not been examined. Future research could add various control variables to the existing model to examine variations in the effects of the study constructs in the presence of different control variables.

This study has explored some new constructs that arose from the field study, namely Bengali values, ethical culture, global pressure and degree of ICT utilisation. By using higher-order conceptualisation, the study has also introduced different measurement procedures for some latent variables such as cognitive evaluation, culture, environmental pressure, country readiness and organisational performance. Various indices explored through the field study have been employed to estimate the composite of the higher-order latent variables, with the exception of cognitive evaluation for which a well-recognised measurement scale is applicable for measuring perceived usefulness and perceived ease of use. Development of a set of reliable measurement scales for these newly developed constructs could significantly contribute to future research initiatives thus providing a logical grounding for future research.

8.6. Conclusion

The modelling approach employed in this study was based on the premise that ICT usage by SMEs ensures improved organisational performance.

However, this study, in particular, has addressed these questions: (1) does ICT usage affect enhanced organisational performance; and (2) how does ICT usage by SMEs contribute to enhanced organisational performance? The short answers to these questions are that ICT usage by SMEs in Bangladesh does not immediately ensure firm performance. Integration and proper utilisation of the technology play the key role in ensuring enhanced performance. The study also forecast the strong and significant effects of *cognitive evaluation, facilitating condition, country readiness* and *environmental pressure* on SMEs' expectation of using ICT which is an antecedent of ICT use. In addition, the study forecast a strong and positive impact of *expectation* on *actual usage* behaviour. The impacts of *culture* and *owner innovativeness* were found to be very strong on *cognitive evaluation*.

This study has several implications for SME owners, the coordinating authorities or trade bodies, and the Bangladeshi government who are interested in enhancing the pace of computerisation and the implementation of various ICT applications in SMEs with the view that new technology implementation will enhance organisational performance. One methodologically oriented finding was that the structural model estimations clearly indicated that integration and utilisation of ICT are more important than simply deciding on the use of ICT. Integration and utilisation, although sounding very normal in general terms, are not easy to ensure in the ICT-based working environment within SMEs. Integration and proper utilisation of ICT are heavily dependent on the firm's resources, technical capability and operational skill, and compatible intra- and inter-organisational systems, availability of hardware and connectivity. The government, regulatory authorities and concerned organisations need to show their support by providing competent infrastructure, resources and policy guidelines to ensure proper utilisation and integrated use of ICT in SMEs.

Expectation has been revealed as an important construct which has a very strong and significant impact on ICT usage. The findings also indicated that those SME owners who had favourably evaluated the technology and who had the resources and skills were more receptive, that is, they had a higher expectation to use ICT. *Culture* provided a negative impact on expectation. Interestingly, *country readiness* provided a positive impact on expectation while providing a negative impact on ICT usage. The finding implied that when SMEs are in the process of deciding to use ICT, they assume that various supports and concerns related to the expected use and outcome exist; therefore, they favourably evaluate the country's overall development, infrastructure and supports. However, during the implementation phase, that is, actual use, they experience different services and supports. It is the reality that Bangladesh, as is the case in many developing countries, has a lack of technological, legal and financial infrastructure. Thus, the SMEs that use ICT-based applications suffer from various constraints which include lack of Internet speed; connectivity; availability of experts and resources; a compatible legal and financial environment, institutional supports, etc. Interestingly, although use of ICT depends on the choice made by the SME owner or manager, in reality, ICT use is seriously affected by the government and regulatory authorities. The government could build capable technology, legal and financial infrastructure and formulate policies and supports to motivate various concerned authorities and SME owners to ensure an integrated and properly utilised ICT operational environment.

NOTES

1. Particular ICT advantages include: service accuracy (quality service); immediacy (real-time capability); service ubiquity (i.e. services are conducted 'anywhere'); efficiency (low-cost service capability); privacy (services conducted are personal and private); and service customisation (person-specific services). Important emerging ICT applications include: communications (email, web browsing, social networks); management (accounts management, human resource management, production management); business (homepage, product cataloguing, order processing); transactions (interactive homepage, online payment processing); finance (e-banking); services (entertainment, information, tourism and facilitation of services in relation to gas, water, electricity supply, etc.) and governance (government–citizen, government–business and government–government communication, interaction and transactions).

2. According to the International Telecommunication Union (ITU, 2013), in 2013, over 2.7 billion people are using the Internet which corresponds to 39% of the world's population. In the developing world, 31% of the population is online, compared with 77% in the developed world. The Internet penetration in developed and developing countries is significantly different with developed countries in an advantageous position in various ICT applications. However, at 30 June 2012, the Internet penetration of North America, Europe, Australia, Africa and Asia stood at 78.6%, 63.2%, 67.6%, 15.6% and 27.5% while the growth of Internet usage between 2000 and 2012 was estimated as 153.3%, 393.4%, 218.7%, 3,606.7% and 841.9%, respectively (Internet World Stats, 2012). The high Internet usage growth in African and Asian countries spells out the potential of ICT usage in developing and LDCs.

3. The parsimonious research model attracts researchers seeking accuracy in outcomes and ease of estimations. For instance, the TAM has been found to be the most frequently used model across multidisciplinary fields of study around the world due to the parsimony of the conceptual framework.

4. Inclusion of additional relevant variables can improve the explanatory power of the model and also cause changing patterns of the explanatory variables. A parsimonious model (such as TAM), although it ensures robustness in the analysis, may not be able to adequately explain the phenomena due to not including all relevant variables in the model. Thus the recent adoption-diffusion studies have employed a relatively large number of diversified variables for comprehensive and reliable results (viz., Tornatzky & Fleischer, 1990; Venkatesh et al., 2003, 2008; Zhu & Kraemer, 2005; Zhu et al., 2004, 2006).

5. Information source: Internet World Stats (http://www.internetworldstats.com/stats.htm, accessed on 18 July 2013).

6. Dhaka is the capital city of the People's Republic of Bangladesh.

7. Recently, a significant development has occurred through the participation of the mobile service provider in providing Internet connectivity to remote areas. However, urban inhabitants are still gaining more benefits on several counts than rural inhabitants.

8. SEA-ME-WE means South East Asia, Middle East and West Europe.

9. The DOI theory, widely used in the past few decades to study the adoption of an innovation, is popularly known as Rogers' (1983) model. The theory was mostly cited from the book 'Diffusion of Innovations' by E. M. Rogers published by the Free Press, New York in 1983. The publisher released two more editions of the same book in 1995 and 2003 which analyse the theory in relation to contemporary issues. However, the basic model (Rogers, 1983) appears unchanged in the three editions of the book. Although much of the contemporary literature refers to the model as Rogers (1995) or Rogers (2003), this study refers to this theoretical framework as Rogers' (1983) model to indicate its origin and applicability at different points of time.

10. A detailed review of some important literature has been provided in Table 3. The reviews take a tabular form to clearly address various aspects of research in detail. The literature are organised according to their contribution and relevance with the current study. Sections 2.5 and 2.6 also deal with literature review for the construction of a primary research model.

11. Orlikowski and Baroudi's (1991) classification of research paradigm is not too dissimilar from Guba and Lincoln's (1994) suggestion: positivist, post-positivist, constructivist and critical paradigm. Critical analysis is an emerging stream of research in IS which usually focuses upon the opposites, conflicts and contradictions (Myers, 1997). However, positivist research paradigm is still a dominant paradigm which guides 75% researches in IS while 17% and 5% researches apply interpretive and critical research, respectively (Mingers, 2003).

12. See a Global Corruption Perceptions Index at http://www.transparency.org/research/cpi/

13. Hair et al. (1998) suggest 200 sample units to estimate any multivariate analysis which was widely executed when using CBSEM. However, researchers have followed different suggestions for sample size determination for the PLS-SEM estimation. According to Gefen et al. (2000), the sample size should be at least 10 times the number of items within the most complex, formative construct of the model. Barclay et al. (1995) and Chin (1998a) stated that the sample size must be 10 times the indicators within the most complex formative construct.

14. Although 'zero' level regression is logically required to test the influence of the mediation variable on the criterion variable as in Eq. (9), Baron and Kenny (1986) suggested that the same equation be used to ascertain the relationship stated in Step 3 and Step 4 by multiple regression as modelled in Eq. (6.8). Thus, the influence of mediating variables on the outcome variable (in control of the initial variable) is also assessed through Eq. (10).

15. Internet penetration is higher in Australia (88.8%), USA (78.1%), the UK (83.6%), Egypt (35.6%), South Africa (17.4), Malaysia (60.7%), China (40.1%) and India (11.4%) in comparison to Bangladesh (Internet World Stats, 2013).

ACKNOWLEDGEMENT

Every reasonable effort has been made to acknowledge the owners of the copyright materials. I would be pleased to hear from any copyright owner who has been omitted or incorrectly acknowledged.

REFERENCES

Aaker, D. A., Kumar, V., & Day, G. S. (2004). *Marketing research* (8th ed.). New York, NY: Wiley.

Agarwal, R., & Prashad, J. (1997). The role of innovation characteristics and perceived voluntariness in the acceptance of information technologies. *Decision Science, 28*(3), 557–582.

Agarwal, R., & Prashad, J. (1998). The antecedents and consequences of user perceptions in information technology adoption. *Decision Support Systems, 22*(1), 557–582.

Agarwal, R., & Prashad, J. (1999). Are individual differences Germane to the acceptance of new information technologies? *Decision Sciences, 30*(2), 361–391.

Ajzen, I. (1985). From intentions to actions: A theory of planned behavior. In J. Kuhl & J. Beckman (Eds.), *Action-control: From cognition to behavior* (pp. 11–39). Heidelberg: Springer.

Ajzen, I. (1991). The theory of planned behavior. *Organizational Behavior and Human Decision Processes, 50*, 179–211.

Ajzen, I., & Fishbein, M. (1980). *Understanding attitudes and predicting social behavior.* Englewood Cliffs, NJ: Prentice Hall.

Ajzen, I., & Madden, T. J. (1986). Prediction of goal-directed behavior: Attitudes, intentions, and perceived behavioral control. *Journal of Experimental Social Psychology, 22*, 453–474.

Akter, S., D'Ambra, J., & Ray, P. (2010). Service quality of mHealth platforms: Development and validation of a hierarchical model using PLS. *Electron Markets, 20*, 209–227.

Akter, S., D'Ambra, J., & Ray, P. (2011). Trustworthiness in mHealth information services: An assessment of a hierarchical model with mediating and moderating effects using

Partial Least Squares (PLS). *Journal of the American Society for Information Science and Technology*, *62*(1), 100–116.

Alreck, P. L., & Settle, R. B. (1995). *The survey research handbook* (2nd ed.). Burr Ridge, IL: Irwin.

Anandarajan, M., Igbaria, M., & Anakwe, U. P. (2002). IT acceptance in a less-developed country: A motivational factor perspective. *International Journal of Information Management*, *22*, 47–65.

Anderson, J. C., & Gerbing, D. W. (1988). Structural equation modeling in practice: A review and recommended two-step approach. *Psychological Bulletin*, *103*(3), 411–423.

Anderson, R. E. (1973). Consumer dissatisfaction: The effect of disconfirmed expectancy on perceived product performance. *Journal of Marketing Research*, *10*(1), 38–44.

Andreev, P., Maoz, T., Heart, T., & Pliskin, N. (2009). Validating formative Partial Least Square (PLS) models: Methodological review and empirical illustration. Paper presented at the International Conference on Information Systems.

Attewell, P. (1992). Technology diffusion and organizational learning – The case of business computing. *Organization Science*, *3*(1), 1–19.

Avgerou, C. (2008). State of the art information systems in developing countries: A critical research review. *Journal of Information Technology*, *2*(3), 133–146.

Azam, M. S. (2004, July 21–25). Factors influencing the adoption of Internet: An inquiry into the perceptions of university academics in Bangladesh. Paper presented at the 10th International Conference on Information Systems Analysis and Synpaper: ISAS 2004 and the International Conference on Cybernetics and Information Technologies, Systems and Applications, Orlando, FL, USA.

Azam, M. S. (2005, July 28–30). Adoption of personal computers in Bangladesh: The effects of perceived innovation characteristics. Paper presented at the 2nd International Conference of the Asian Academy of Applied Business (AAAB), Padang, Indonesia.

Azam, M. S. (2006a). *E-commerce in Bangladesh: Adoption intention and strategic options*. M. Phil Paper. Bangladesh: Institute of Bangladesh Studies (IBS), University of Rajshahi.

Azam, M. S. (2006b). E-commerce in Bangladesh: Understanding SMEs' intention and exploring barriers. *Journal of Business Studies*, *2*, 37–58.

Azam, M. S. (2006c). Implementation of B2C e-commerce in Bangladesh: The effects of buying culture and e-infrastructure. *Advances in Global Business Research*, *3*, 55–66.

Azam, M. S. (2007). Adoption and usage of internet in Bangladesh. *Japanese Journal of Administrative Science*, *20*(1), 43–54.

Azam, M. S. (2013). Towards digital communication and transaction: An inquiry into the individuals' Internet acceptance and usage behaviour in Bangladesh. *Journal of International Technology and Information Management*, *22*(1), 123–140.

Azam, M. S., & Lubna, N. (2008a). Concerns and constraints of e-commerce: An investigation into the service industry and manufacturing industry in Bangladesh. In D. S. Chundawat, K. Saxena, & S. S. Bhadu (Eds.), *Managing global competition: A holistic approach* (pp. 101–121). Delhi: Macmillan India Ltd.

Azam, M. S., & Lubna, N. (2008b). Implementation of e-commerce in Bangladesh: Does it benefit SMEs? In M. Z. Mamun & S. M. Jahan (Eds.), *Small medium enterprise in Bangladesh: Issues involving enterprise competitiveness* (pp. 79–100). Dhaka: Association of Management Development Institutions of Bangladesh (AMDIB).

Azam, M. S., & Quaddus, M. (2009a, April 11–12). Adoption of B2B e-commerce by the SMEs in Bangladesh: An empirical analysis. Paper presented at the Asian Business Research Conference, Dhaka, Bangladesh.

Azam, M. S., & Quaddus, M. (2009b, November 29–December 2). Adoption of B2B e-commerce by the SMEs in Bangladesh: The effects of innovation characteristics and perceived risk. Paper presented at the Proceedings of Australia New Zealand Marketing Academy Conference (ANZMAC), Melbourne, Australia.

Azam, M. S., & Quaddus, M. (2009c, December 2–6). How organizational characteristics explain the adoption of e-commerce by the SMEs in Bangladesh. Paper presented at the Australian Association for Information Systems (ACIS) Conference, Melbourne, Australia.

Azam, M. S., & Quaddus, M. (2009d, December 9–11). Internet usage behavior in Bangladesh: A test of the theory of planned behaviour through structural equation modeling. Paper presented at the Curtin International Business Conference (CIBS), Mirri, Malaysia.

Babbie, E. R. (2001). *The practice of social research* (9th ed.). Belmont, CA: Wadsworth Publishing Co.

Bagozzi, R. P. (1981). Attitudes, intentions and behaviour: A test of some key hypotheses. *Journal of Personality and Social Psychology, 41*, 607–627.

Bagozzi, R. P. (1982). A field investigation of causal relations among cognitions, affect, intention, and behaviour. *Journal of Marketing Research, 19*(4), 562–583.

Bagozzi, R. P., & Yi, Y. (1998). On the evaluation of structural equation models. *Journal of the Academy of Marketing Science, 16*(1), 74–94.

Baldwin, J. R., & Sabourin, D. (2001). *Impact of the adoption of advanced information and communication technologies on firm performance in the Canadian manufacturing sector.* Micro-Economic Analysis Division. Retrieved from http://www.statcan.gc.ca/pub/11f0019m/11f0019m2001174-eng.pdf. Accessed on September 10, 2009.

Bandura, A. (1986). *Social foundations of thought and action: A social cognitive theory.* Englewood Cliffs, NJ: Prentice Hall.

Bang, H., Ellinger, A. E., Hadjimarcou, J., & Traichal, P. A. (2000). Consumer concern, knowledge, belief, and attitude toward renewable energy: An application of the reasoned action theory. *Psychology & Marketing, 17*(6), 449–468.

Barclay, D., Higgins, C., & Thompson, R. (1995). The Partial Least Squares (PLS) approach to causal modeling: Personal computer adoption and uses as an illustration. *Technology Studies, 2*(2), 285–309.

Barney, J. B. (1986). Strategic factor markets: Expectations, luck and business strategy. *Management Science, 32*(10), 1231–1241.

Barney, J. B. (1991). Firm resources and sustained competitive advantage. *Journal of Management, 17*(1), 99–120.

Barney, J. B. (2001). Is the resource-based "view" a useful perspective for strategic management research? Yes. *Strategic Management Journal, 26*(1), 41–56.

Barney, J. B., Wright, M., & Ketchen, D. (2001). The resource-based view of the firm: Ten years after 1991. *Journal of Management, 27*(6), 625–641.

Baron, R. M., & Kenny, D. A. (1986). The moderator-mediator variable distinction in social psychological research: Conceptual, strategic, and statistical considerations. *Journal of Personality and Social Psychology, 51*(6), 1173–1182.

Bassellier, G., Benbasat, I., & Reich, B. H. (2003). The influence of business managers' IT competence on championing IT. *Information Systems Research*, *14*(4), 317−336.

Bayo-Morionesa, A., & Lera-López, B. F. (2007). A firm-level analysis of antecedents of ICT adoption in Spain. *Technovation*, *27*, 352−366.

Bazeley, P. (2002). The evolution of a project involving an integrated analysis of structured qualitative and quantitative data: From N3 to NVivo. *International Journal of Social Research Methodology*, *5*(3), 229−243.

Bazeley, P. (2007). *Qualitative data analysis with NVivo*. Thousand Oaks, CA: Sage.

Beard, T. R., Madden, G., & Azam, M. S. (2014). Blended traditional and virtual seller market entry and performance. In J. Alleman, Á. NíShúilleabháin, & P. Rappoport (Eds.), *Demand for communication services − Insights and perspectives: Essays in honor of Lester D. Taylor*. New York, NY: Springer-Verlag New York, Inc.

Beckett, H. (2003). Half of SMEs have no IT strategy. *Computer Weekly*, *1*, 34.

Berg, B. L. (2001). *Qualitative research methods for the social sciences* (4th ed.). Boston, MA: Allyn and Bacon.

Berg, B. L. (2004). *Qualitative research method for the social sciences* (5th ed.). Boston, MA: Pearson Education.

Bertolotti, D. S. (1984). *Culture and technology*. Bowling Green, OH: Bowling Green State University Press.

Bharadwaj, A. S. (2000). A resource-based perspective on information technology capability and firm performance: An empirical investigation. *MIS Quarterly*, *24*(1), 169−196.

Blalock, H. M. (1960). *Social statistics*. New York, NY: McGraw-Hill Book Company Inc.

Bock, G., Zmund, R. W., Kim, Y., & Lee, J. (2005). Behavioral intention formation in knowledge sharing: Examining the roles of extrinsic motivators, social-psychological forces, and organisational climate. *MIS Quarterly*, *29*(1), 87−111.

Boes, D. C., Graybill, F. A., & Mood, A. M. (1974). Introduction to the Theory of Statistics. *Series in probabili.*

Bollen, K. A. (1987). Total, direct, and indirect effects in structural equation models. In C. C. Clogg (Ed.), *Sociological methodology 1987* (pp. 37−69). Washington, DC: American Sociological Association.

Bollen, K. A. (1989). *Structural equations with latent variables*. New York, NY: Wiley.

Bollen, K. A., & Lennox, R. (1991). Conventional wisdom on measurement: A structural equation perspective. *Psychological Bulletin*, *110*, 305−314.

Brancheau, J. C., & Wetherbe, J. C. (1990). The adoption of spreadsheet software: Testing innovation diffusion theory in the context of end-user computing. *Information Systems Research*, *1*(2), 115−143.

Broderick, R., & Boudreau, J. (1992). Human resource management, information technology, and the competitive edge. *The Executive*, *7*(2), 7−17.

Brown, R. L. (1997). Assessing specific mediational effects in complex theoretical models. *Structural Equation Modeling*, *4*(2), 142−156.

Brynjolfsson, E. (1993). The productivity paradox of information technology. *Communication of the ACM*, *35*, 66−67.

Brynjolfsson, E., & Hitt, L. (1996). Paradox lost? Firm-level evidence on the returns to information systems spending. *Management Science*, *42*(4), 541−558.

Burn, J. M. (1995). The new cultural revolution: The impact of EDI on Asia. *Journal of Global Information Management*, *3*(4), 6−23.

Burns, A. C., & Bush, R. F. (2000). *Marketing research* (3rd ed.). Sydney, Australia: Prentice Hall.

Burt, R. S. (1982). *Toward a structural theory of action: Network models of social structure, perception, and action*. New York, NY: Academic Press.

Byrne, B. M. (2001). *Structural equation modeling with AMOS: Basic concepts, applications, and programming*. London: Lawrence Erlbaum Associates.

Carmines, E. G., & Zeller, R. A. (1979). Reliability and validity assessment. Sage University Paper Series on Quantitative Applications in the Social Sciences. No. 07-017. Beverly Hills, CA: Sage.

Carr, N. G. (2003). IT doesn't matter. *Harvard Business Review, 81*(5), 41−49.

Caselli, F., & Coleman, W. J. I. (2001). Cross-country technology diffusion: The case of computers. *The American Economic Review, 91*(2), 328−335.

Celuch, K., Taylor, S. A., & Goodwin, S. (2004). Understanding insurance salesperson internet information management intentions: A test of competing models. *Journal of Insurance Issues, 27*(1), 22−40.

Chang, M. K. (1998). Predicting unethical behaviour: A comparison of the theory of reasoned action and the theory of planned behaviour. *Journal of Business Ethics, 17*, 1825−1834.

Chatfield, A. T., & Bjørn-Anderson, N. (1997). The impact of IOS-enabled business process change on business outcomes: Transformation of the value chain of Japanese airlines. *Journal of Management Information System, 14*(1), 13−40.

Chau, P. Y. K. (1997). Reexamining a model for evaluating information center success using a structural equation modelling approach. *Decision Sciences, 28*(2), 309−334.

Chau, P. Y. K., & Hu, P. J. H. (2002). Investigating healthcare professionals' decisions to accept telemedicine technology: An empirical test of competing theories. *Information and Management, 39*(4), 197−311.

Cheung, M. W. L. (2007). Comparison of approaches to constructing confidence intervals for mediating effects using structural equation models. *Structural Equation Modeling: A Multidisciplinary Journal, 14*(2), 227−246.

Cheung, W., Chang, M. K., & Lai, V. S. (2000). Prediction of internet and world wide web usage at work: A test of an extended Triandis model. *Decision Support Systems, 30*(1), 83−101.

Chin, W. W. (1995). Partial least squares is to LISREL as principal components analysis is to common factor analysis. *Technology Studies, 2*, 315−319.

Chin, W. W. (1998a). Issues and opinion on structural equation modeling. *MIS Quarterly, 22*(1), vii−xvi.

Chin, W. W. (1998b). The partial least squares approach to structural equation modeling. In G. A. Marcoulides (Ed.), *Modern methods for business research* (pp. 295−336). Mahwah, NJ: Lawrence Erlbaum Associates, Publisher.

Chin, W. W. (2002). *PLS-Graph user's guide*. Retrieved from http://www.pubinfo.vcu.edu/carma/Documents/OCT1405/PLSGRAPH3.0Manual.hubona.pdf. Accessed on February 12, 2010.

Chin, W. W. (2010). How to write up and report PLS analyses. In V. E. Vinzi, W. W. Chin, J. Henseler, & H. Wang (Eds.), *Handbook of partial least squares: Concepts, methods and application* (pp. 645−689). Heidelberg: Springer.

Chin, W. W., & Gopal, A. (1995). Adoption intention in GSS: Importance of beliefs. *Data Base Advances, 26*, 42−64.

Chin, W. W., Marcolin, B. L., & Newsted, P. R. (2003). A partial least squares latent variable modeling approach for measuring interaction effects: Results from a Monte Carlo simulation study and an electronic-mail emotion/adoption study. *Information Systems Research, 14*(2), 21–41.

Chin, W. W., & Newsted, P. R. (1999). Structural equation modeling analysis with small samples using partial least squares. In R. Hoyle (Ed.), *Statistical strategies for small sample research* (pp. 307–341). Thousand Oaks, CA: Sage.

Cho, J. (2004). Likelihood to abort an online transaction: Influences from cognitive evaluations, attitudes, and behavioral variables. *Information & Management, 41*, 827–838.

Churchill, J. G. A. (1991). *Marketing research: Methodological foundation*. Chicago, IL: Dryden Press.

Churchill, J. G. A., & Iacobucci, D. (2002). *Marketing research: Methodological foundations*. Mason, OH: SouthWestern Cengage Learning.

Clemons, E., & Weber, B. (1990). London's big bang: A case study of information technology, competitive impact, and organizational change. *Journal of Management Information Systems, 6*(4), 41–60.

Clemons, E. K., & Row, M. C. (1991). Sustaining IT advantage: The role of structural differences. *MIS Quarterly, 15*(3), 275–292.

Cockburn, C., & Wilson, T. D. (1996). Business use of the world wide web. *International Journal of Information Management, 16*, 83–102.

Cohen, J. (1988). *Statistical power analysis for the behavioral sciences* (2nd ed.). Hillsdale, NJ: Lawrence Erlbaum Associates.

Coltman, T., Devinney, T. M., Midgley, D. F., & Venaik, S. (2008). Formative versus reflective measurement models: Two applications of formative measurement. *Journal of Business Research, 61*(12), 1250–1262.

Cool, A. L. (2000, January 28). A review of methods for dealing with missing data. Paper presented at the Annual Meeting of the Southwest Educational Research Association, Dallas, TX.

Cooper, R. B., & Zmund, R. W. (1990). Information technology implementation research: A technological diffusion approach. *Management Science, 36*(2), 123–139.

Cox, E. P. (1980). The optimal number of response alternatives for a scale: A review. *Journal of Marketing Research, 17*(November), 407–422.

Cragg, P., King, M., & Hussin, H. (2002). IT alignment and firm performance in small manufacturing firms. *Journal of Strategic Information Systems, 11*, 109–132.

Crawley, F. E. (1988). Antecedents of physical science teachers' intention to use investigative teaching methods: A test of the theory of reasoned action. Paper presented at the 61st Annual Meeting of the American Educational Research Association, New Orleans, LA (ERIC Document Reproduction Service No. Ed 243 672).

Crawley, F. E., & Coe, A. S. (1990). Antecedents of middle school students' intention to enroll in a high school science course: An application of the theory of reasoned action. *Journal of Research in Science Teaching, 27*(5), 461–476.

Creswell, J. W. (2003). *Research design: Qualitative, quantitative, and mixed methods approach*. Thousand Oaks, CA: Sage.

Dada, D. (2006). E-readiness for developing countries: Moving the focus from the environment to the users. *The Electronic Journal of Information Systems in Developing Countries, 27*(6), 1–14.

Daily Star. (2006). *The Daily Star* (Dhaka), A national English daily, May 21.

Davenport, T. (1994). Saving IT's soul: Human-centered information management. *Harvard Business Review, 72*(2), 119–131.

Davila, A., Gupta, M., & Palmer, R. J. (2002). Moving procurement systems to the Internet: The adoption and use of e-procurement technologies models. Stanford GSB Research Paper No. 1742.

Davis, D. (2000). *Business research for decision making* (5th ed.). Belmont: Duxbury Press.

Davis, F. D. (1986). *A technology acceptance model for empirically testing new end-user information systems: Theory and results.* PhD dissertation, Massachusetts Institute of Technology, USA.

Davis, F. D. (1989). Perceived usefulness, perceived ease of use, and user acceptance of information technology. *MIS Quarterly, 1*(3), 319–340.

Davis, F. D. (1993). User acceptance of information technology: Systems characteristics, user perception and behavioral impacts. *International Journal of Man-Machine Studies, 38*, 475–487.

Davis, F. D., Bagozzi, R. P., & Warshaw, P. R. (1989). User acceptance of computer technology: A comparison of two theoretical models. *Management Science, 35*(8), 982–1003.

Day, G. S. (1994). The capabilities of market-driven organizations. *Journal of Marketing, 58*(October), 37–52.

Deal, T. E., & Kennedy, A. A. (1982). *Corporate culture: The rights and rituals of corporate life.* Reading, MA: Addison-Wesley Publishing Company.

Denzin, N. K., & Lincoln, Y. S. (1994). Introduction: Entering the field of qualitative research. In N. K. Denzin & Y. S. Lincoln (Eds.), *Handbook of qualitative research* (pp. 1–17). Thousand Oaks, CA: Sage.

Denzin, N. K., & Lincoln, Y. S. (2005). *The sage handbook of qualitative research.* Thousand Oaks, CA: Sage.

Deshpande, R. (1983). Paradigms lost: On theory and method in research marketing. *Journal of Marketing, 47*(4), 101–110.

Dess, G. G., & Robinson, R. B., Jr. (1984). Measuring organizational performance in the absence of objective measures: The case of the privately held firm and conglomerate business unit. *Strategic Management Journal, 5*, 265–273.

Devaraj, S., & Kohli, R. (2003). Performance impact of information technology: Is actual usage the missing link? *Management Science, 49*(3), 273–289.

Dewan, S., & Kraemer, K. L. (2000). Information technology and productivity: Evidence from country-level data. *Management Science, 46*(4), 548–562.

Diamantopoulos, A., & Schlegelmilch, B. B. (1994). Linking manpower to export performance: A canonical regression analysis of European and US data. *Advances in International Marketing, 6*, 161–181.

Diamantopoulos, A., & Siguaw, J. A. (2006). Formative versus reflective indicators in organizational measure development: A comparison and empirical illustration. *British Journal of Management, 17*, 263–282.

Diamantopoulos, A., & Winklhofer, H. M. (2001). Index construct with formative indicators: An alternative to scale development. *Journal of Marketing Research, 38*(2), 269–277.

DiMaggio, P. J., & Powell, W. W. (1983). The iron cage revisited: Institutional isomorphism and collective rationality in organizational fields. *American Sociological Review, 48*(2), 147–160.

Dolecheck, M. M., & Dolecheck, C. C. (1987). Business ethics: A comparison of attitudes of managers in Hong Kong and the United States. *The Hong Kong Managers, 1*, 28–43.

Doolin, B., McLeod, L., McQueen, B., & Watton, M. (2003). Internet strategies for establishing retailers: Four New Zealand case studies. *Journal of Information Technology Cases and Applications, 5*(4), 3–19.

Doukidis, G. I., Lybereas, P., & Galliers, R. D. (1996). Information systems planning in small business: A stages of growth analysis. *The Journal of Systems and Software, 33*(2), 189–201.

Dvir, D., Segev, E., & Shenhar, A. (1993). Technology's varying impact on the success of strategic business units within the miles and snow typology. *Strategic Management Journal, 14*, 155–162.

Edwards, J. R. (2001). Multidimensional constructs in organizational behaviour research: An integrative analytical framework. *Organizational Research Methods, 4*(2), 144–192.

Edwards, J. R., & Bagozzi, R. P. (2000). On the nature and direction of relationships between constructs. *Psychological Methods, 5*(2), 155–174.

Eagly, A. H., & Chaiken, S. (1993). *The psychology of attitudes.* Orlando, FL: Harcourt Brace Jovanovich College Publishers.

Eisenhardt, K. M. (1989). Building theories from case study research. *The Academy of Management Review, 14*(4), 532–550.

England, G. (1975). *The manager and his values—An international perspective.* Cambridge, UK: Ballinger Publishing Co.

Erez, M., & Early, P. C. (1993). *Culture, self-identity and work.* New York, NY: Oxford University Press.

Erumban, A. A. A., & Jong, S. B. D. (2006). Cross country differences in ICT adoption: A consequence of culture? *Journal of World Business, 41*, 302–314.

Falk, R. F., & Miller, N. B. (1992). *A primer for soft modelling.* Akron, OH: University of Akron Press.

Fazio, R. H., & Zanna, M. P. (1978). Attitudinal qualities relating to the strength of the attitude-behavior relationship. *Journal of Experimental Social Psychology, 14*(4), 398–408.

Feeny, D., & Ives, B. (1990). In search of sustainability: Reaping long-term advantage from investments in information technology. *Journal of Management Information Systems, 7*(1), 27–46.

Fichman, R. G. (2000). The diffusion and assimilation of information technology innovations. In R. W. Zumond (Ed.), *Framing the domains of IT management: Projecting the future through the past* (pp. 105–127). Cleveland, OH: Pinnaflex Publishing.

Filstead, W. J. (1979). Qualitative methods: A needed perspective in evaluation research. In T. D. Cook & C. S. Reichardt (Eds.), *Qualitative and quantitative methods in evaluation research* (pp. 33–48). Beverly Hills, CA: Sage.

Fishbein, M., & Ajzen, I. (1975). *Beliefs, attitude, intention, and behavior: An introduction to theory and research.* Reading, MA: Addison-Wesley.

Fitzgerald, B., & Howcroft, D. (1998). Towards dissolution of the IS research debate: From polarisation to polarity. *Journal of Information Technology, 13*(4), 313–326.

Fornell, C., & Larcker, D. F. (1981). Evaluating structural equation models with unobservable variables and measurement error. *Journal of Marketing Research, 18*(1), 39–50.

Fornell, C., Lorange, P., & Roos, J. (1990). The cooperative venture formation process: A latent variable structural modeling approach. *Management Science, 36*, 1246–1255.

Forster, D., & Cornford, T. (1992). Evaluation of information systems: Issues, models and case studies. In S. Bhatnagare & M. Odedra (Eds.), *Social implications of computers in developing countries* (pp. 304–314). New Delhi: Tata McGraw Hill.

Galliano, D., & Roux, P. (2007). Organisational motives and spatial effects in internet adoption and intensity of use: Evidence from French industrial firms. *The Annals of Regional Science, 42*(2), 425–448.

Gefen, D., & Straub, D. (2000). The relative importance of perceived ease of use in IS adoption: A study of E-commerce adoption. *Journal of the Association for Information Systems, 1*(8), 1–28.

Gefen, D., Straub, D., & Boudreau, M. (2000). Structural equation modeling techniques and regression: Guidelines for research practice. *Communications of the Association for Information Systems, 7*(7), 1–78.

Gefen, D., & Straub, D. W. (1997). Gender differences in the perceptions and use of e-mail: An extension of the technology acceptance model. *MIS Quarterly, 21*(4), 389–400.

Gehrt, K., & Carter, K. (1992). An exploratory assessment of catalog shopping orientation: The existence of convenience and recreational segments. *Journal of Retailing, 6*(1), 29–39.

George, J. F. (2002). Influence on the intent to make internet purchases. *Internet Research: Electronic Networking Applications and Policy, 12*(2), 165–180.

George, J. F. (2004). The theory of planned behavior and Internet purchasing. *Internet Research, 14*(3), 198–212.

Gibbs, J. L., & Kraemer, K. L. (2004). A cross-country investigation of the Antecedents of scope of e-commerce use: An institutional approach. *Electronic Markets, 14*(2), 124–137.

Givon, M. M., & Shapira, Z. (1984). Response to rating scales: A theoretical model and its application to the number of categories problem. *Journal of Marketing Research, 21*(4), 410–419.

Goldsmith, R. E. (1990). The validity of scale to measure global innovativeness. *Journal of Applied Business Research, 7*(2), 89–97.

Government of Bangladesh (GOB). (1999). *The industrial policy 1999*. Dhaka: Ministry of Commerce and Industry of the People's Republic of Bangladesh.

Greene, J. C., Caracelli, V. J., & Graham, W. F. (1989). Toward a conceptual framework for mixed-method evaluation designs. *Educational Evaluation and Policy Analysis, 11*(3), 255–274.

Gretton, P., Gali, J., & Parham, D. (2004). The effects of ICTs and complementary innovations on Australian productivity growth. In OECD (Ed.), *The economic impact of ICT: Measurement, evidence and implications* (pp. 105–130). Paris: OECD.

Guba, E. G., & Lincoln, Y. S. (1994). Competing paradigms in qualitative research. In N. K. Denzin & Y. S. Lincoln (Eds.), *Handbook of qualitative research* (pp. 105–117). Thousand Oaks, CA: Sage.

Gupta, B., Dasgupta, S., & Gupta, A. (2008). Adoption of ICT in a government organization in a developing country: An empirical study. *Journal of Strategic Information Systems, 17*, 140–154.

Hair, J. F., Anderson, R. I., Tatham, R. L., & Black, W. C. (1998). *Multivariate data analysis* (5th ed.). Englewood Cliffs, NJ: Prentice Hall.

Hair, J. F., Ringle, C. M., & Sarstedt, M. (2011). PLS-SEM: Indeed a silver bullet. *Journal of Marketing Theory and Practice, 19*(2), 139–151.

Hanlon, D. (2001). Vision and support in new venture start-ups. Paper presented at the Frontiers of Entrepreneurship Research Conference, Jonkoping, Sweden.

Harris, R., & Davison, R. (1999). Anxiety and involvement: Cultural dimensions of attitudes toward computers in developing societies. *Journal of Global Information Management*, 7(1), 26–38.

Hill, C., Loch, K., Straub, D. W., & El-Sheshai, K. (1998). A qualitative assessment of Arab culture and information technology transfer. *Journal of Global Information Management*, 6(3), 29–38.

Hitt, L., & Brynjolfsson, E. (1996). Productivity, business profitability, and consumer surplus: Three different measures of information technology value. *MIS Quarterly*, 20(2), 121–142.

Ho, T. H., Raman, K. S., & Watson, R. T. (1989). Group decision support systems: The cultural factors. Paper presented at the Proceedings of the 10th Annual International Conference on Information Systems, Boston, MA.

Hoelter, J. W. (1983). The analysis of covariance structures: Goodness-of-fit indices. *Sociological Methods and Research*, 11, 325–344.

Hofstede, G. (1984). *Culture's consequences: International differences in work related values.* London: Sage.

Hofstede, G. (2001). *Culture's consequences comparing values, behaviours, institutions, and organizations across the nations* (2nd ed.). London: Sage.

Hohental, J. (2006). Integrating qualitative and quantitative methods in research on international entrepreneurship. *Journal of International Entrepreneurship*, 4(4), 175–190.

Holak, S. L., & Lehman, D. R. (1990). Purchase intentions and the dimensions of innovation: An exploratory model. *Journal of Product Innovation Management*, 7, 59–73.

Hong, W., Thong, J. Y. L., Wong, W. M., & Tam, K. Y. (1999). Antecedents of user acceptance of digital libraries: An empirical examination of individual differences and system characteristics. *Journal of Management Information System*, 16(2), 91–112.

Hong, W., & Zhu, K. (2006). Migrating to internet-based e-commerce: Factors affecting e-commerce adoption and migration at the firm level. *Information & Management*, 43, 204–221.

Hoppe, R., Newman, P., & Mugera, P. (2001, October 17). Factors affecting the adoption of internet banking in South Africa: A comparative study. Paper presented to the Department of Information Systems, University of Cape Town.

Horton, N. J., & Kleinman, K. (2007). Much ado about nothing: A comparison of missing data methods and software to fit incomplete data regression models. *The American Statistician: Statistical Software Review*, 61(1), 79–90.

Hossain, N. (2000). *E-commerce in Bangladesh: Status, potential and constraints.* Retrieved from http://www.iris.umd.edu/publications/detail.asp?ID=bd&number=6. Accessed on September 23, 2003.

House, R. J., Hanges, P. J., Javidan, M., Dorfman, P. W., & Gupta, V. (2004). *Culture, leadership, and organizations: The GLOBE study of 62 societies.* London: Sage.

Hudson, L. A., & Ozanne, J. L. (1988). Alternative ways of seeking knowledge in consumer research. *Journal of Consumer Research*, 14(4), 508–521.

Huisman, M., Krol, B., & Sonderen, E. V. (1998). Handling missing data by re-approaching non-respondents. *Quality and Quantity*, 32, 77–91.

Hulland, J. (1999). Use of Partial Least Squares (PLS) in strategic management research: A review of four recent studies. *Strategic Management Journal*, 20(2), 195–204.

Huy, L. V., & Filiatrault, P. (2006). The adoption of e-commerce in SMEs in Vietnam: A study of users and prospectors. *Proceedings of the 10th Asia-Pacific Conference on Information Systems* (pp. 1335–1344).

Hyman, H. H. (1955). *Survey design and analysis*. Glencoe, IL: Free Press.

Iacovou, C., Benbasat, I., & Dexter, A. (1995). Electronic data interchange and small organizations: Adoption and impact of technology. *MIS Quarterly, 19*(4), 465–485.

Igbaria, M., Guimaraes, T., & Davis, G. B. (1995). An assessment of structure and causation of IS usage. *The Database for Advances in Information Systems, 27*(2), 61–67.

Igbaria, M., Zinatelli, N., Cragg, P., & Cavaye, A. L. M. (1997). Personal computing acceptance factors in small firms: A structural equation model. *MIS Quarterly, 21*(3), 279–302.

Internet World Stat. (2012). *Internet world stats: Usage and population statistics*. Retrieved from http://www.internetworldstats.com/stats.htm. Accessed on December 29, 2012.

ITRC. (2000). E-commerce in Bangladesh: A readiness assessment. *ITRC Research Brief*. Retrieved from http://www.itrc.techbangla.org. Accessed on February 21, 2005.

ITU. (2010). *World telecommunication/ICT development report 2010: Monitoring the WSIS targets: A mid-term review*. Geneva: International Telecommunication Union.

ITU. (2013). *The world in 2013 − ICT facts and figures*. Geneva: International Telecommunication Union.

Jackson, E. L. (2008). *Behavioral antecedents of the adoption of forward contracts by Western Australia wool producers*. Perth: Curtin University of Technology.

Jarvis, C. B., MacKenzie, S. B., & Podsakoff, P. M. (2003). A critical review of construct indicators and measurement model misspecification in marketing, and consumer research. *Journal of Consumer Research, 30*, 199–218.

Jean, R. B. (2007). The ambiguous relationship of ICT and organizational performance: A literature review. *Critical Perspectives on International Business, 3*(4), 306–321.

Jehangir, M., & Downe, A. G. (2011). Technology resources and e-commerce impact on business performance. In V. Snasel, J. Platos, & E. El-Qawasmeh (Eds.), *ICDIPC 2011* (pp. 440–447). Berlin Heidelberg: Springer. Part II, CCIS 189, 440–447.

Jeon, B. N., Han, K. S., & Lee, M. J. (2006). Determining factors for the adoption of e-business: The case of SMEs in Korea. *Applied Economics, 13*(16), 1905–1916.

Jiang, J. J., Hus, M. K., Klien, G., & Lin, B. (2000). E-commerce user behavior model: An empirical study. *Human System Management, 19*(4), 265–276.

Johnson, R. A., & Hignite, M. A. (2000). Applying the technology acceptance model to the WWW. *Academy of Information and Management Sciences Journal, 3*(2), 130–142.

Jones, E., Sundaram, S., & Chin, W. (2002). Factors leading to sales force automation use: A longitudinal analysis. *Journal of Personal Selling & Sales Management, 22*(3), 145–157.

Judd, C. M., & Kenny, D. A. (1981). Process analysis: Estimating direction in evaluation research. *Evaluation Research, 9*, 602–618.

Kaplan, B., & Maxwell, J. A. (1994). Qualitative research methods for evaluating computer information systems. In J. G. Anderson, C. E. Aydin, & S. J. Jay (Eds.), *Evaluating health care information systems: Methods and applications* (pp. 45–68). Thousand Oaks, CA: Sage.

Kappos, A., & Rivard, S. (2008). A three-perspective model of culture, information systems, and their development and use. *MIS Quarterly, 32*(3), 601–634.

Karahanna, E., Straub, D. W., & Chervany, N. L. (1999). Information technology adoption across time: A cross-sectional comparison of pre-adoption and post-adoption beliefs. *MIS Quarterly, 23*(2), 183−213.

Kendall, J. D., Tung, L. L., Chua, K. H., Ng, C. H. D., & Tan, S. M. (2001). Receptivity of Singapore's SMEs to electronic commerce adoption. *Journal of Strategic Information Systems, 10*, 223−242.

Kettinger, W., Grover, V., Guha, S., & Segars, A. (1994). Strategic information systems revisited: A study in sustainability and performance. *MIS Quarterly, 18*(1), 31−58.

Kim, D., Cavusgil, S. T., & Calantone, R. J. (2006). Information system innovations and supply chain management: Channel relationships and firm performance. *Journal of the Academy of Marketing Science, 34*(1), 40−54.

King, G., Honaker, J., Joseph, A., & Scheve, K. (2001). Analyzing incomplete political science data: An alternative algorithm for multiple imputation. *American Political Science Review, 95*(1), 49−69.

Kleinbaum, D. G., Kupper, L., Muller, K. E., & Nizam, A. (1998). *Applied regression analysis and other multivariable methods* (3rd ed.). Pacific Grove, CA: Duxbury Press.

Kline, R. B. (2010). *Principles and practices of structural equation modelling* (3rd ed.). New York, NY: Guilford Press.

Konings, J., & Roodhooft, F. (2002). The effect of e-business on corporate performance: Firm level evidence from Belgium. *De Economist, 150*, 569−581.

Kraemer, K. L., & Dedrick, J. (1994). Payoffs from investment in information technology: Lessons from the Asia-Pacific region. *World Development, 22*(12), 1921−1931.

Kroeber, A. L., & Kluckhohn, C. (1952). *Culture: A critical review of concepts and definitions.* Papers of the Peabody Museum of Archaeology & Ethnology, Harvard University.

Kuan, K., & Chau, P. (2001). A perception-based model of EDI adoption in small businesses using a technology-organizational-environmental framework. *Information and Management, 38*(8), 507−521.

Kuhn, T. (1962). *The structure of scientific revolutions.* Chicago, IL: University of Chicago Press.

Kurnia, S., & Peng, F. (2010). Electronic commerce readiness in developing countries: The case of the Chinese grocery industry, E-commerce. In K. Kang (Ed.), *E-commerce* (pp. 203−227). Shanghai, China: Intech.

Lal, K. (1999). Antecedents of the adoption of information technology: A case study of electrical and electronic goods manufacturing firms in India. *Research Policy, 28*, 667−680.

Law, K. S., & Wong, C. (1999). Multidimensional constructs in structural equation analysis: An illustration using the job perception and job satisfaction constructs. *Journal of Management, 25*(2), 143−160.

Law, K. S., Wong, C., & Mobley, W. H. (1998). Towards taxonomy of multidimensional constructs. *Academy of Management Review, 23*(4), 741−755.

Lederer, A., Mirchadani, D. A., & Sims, K. (1997). The link between information strategy and EC. *Journal of Organizational Computing and Electronic Commerce, 7*(1), 17−34.

Lee, C., & Shim, J. (2007). An exploratory study of Radio Frequency Identification (RFID) adoption in the healthcare industry. *European Journal of Information Systems, 16*, 712−724.

Leinder, D. E., & Kayworth, T. (2006). Review: A review of culture in information systems research: Toward a theory of information technology culture conflict. *MIS Quarterly, 30*(2), 357−399.

Li, M., & Ye, L. R. (1999). Information technology and firm performance: Linking with environmental, strategic and managerial contexts. *Information & Management, 35*(1), 3–51.

Liao, Z., & Cheung, M. T. (2001). Internet-based e-shopping and consumer attitudes: An empirical study. *Information and Management, 38*, 299–306.

Lim, P., & Speece, M. W. (2002). *The effects of perceived characteristics of innovation on e-commerce adoption by SMEs in Thailand.* Retrieved from http://www.blake.montclair. edu/~cibconf/conference/DATA/Theme7/Thailand.pdf. Accessed on October 11, 2004.

Lincoln, Y. S., & Guba, E. G. (1985). *Naturalistic inquiry.* Beverly Hills, CA: Sage.

Lindley, P., & Walker, S. N. (1993). Theoretical and methodological differentiation of moderation and mediation. *Nursing Research, 42*(5), 276–279.

Lu, J., Yu, C. S., Liu, C., & Yao, J. E. (2003). Technology acceptance model for wireless Internet. *Internet Research, 13*(3), 206–222.

Lu, L. C., Rose, G. M., & Blodgett, J. G. (1999). The effects of cultural dimensions on ethical decision making in marketing: An exploratory study. *Journal of Business Ethics, 18*(1), 91–106.

MacCallum, R. C., & Browne, M. W. (1993). The use of causal indicators in covariance structure models: Some practical issues. *Psychological Bulletin, 114*(3), 533–541.

MacCorquodale, K., & Meehl, P. E. (1948). On a distinction between hypothetical constructs and intervening variables. *Psychological Review, 55*, 95–107.

MacKenzie, S. B., Podsakoff, P. M., & Jarvis, C. B. (2005). The problem of measurement model misspecification in behavioral and organizational research and some recommended solutions. *The Journal of Applied Psychology, 90*(4), 710–730.

MacKinnon, D. P. (2000). Contrasts in multiple mediator models. In J. S. Rose, L. Chassin, C. C. Presson, & S. J. Sherman (Eds.), *Multivariate applications in substance use research: New methods for new questions* (pp. 141–160). Mahwah, NJ: Erlbaum.

Madden, G., Azam, M. S., & Beard, T. R. (2013). Small firm performance in online markets. *Economics of Innovation and New Technology, 22*(1), 99–111.

Malhotra, N. K. (2002). *Basic marketing research—Applications to contemporary issues.* Upper Saddle River, NJ: Prentice Hall.

Malhotra, N. K. (2004). *Marketing research – An applied orientation* (4th ed.). Upper Saddle River, NJ: Prentice Hall.

Malhotra, N. K., Agarwal, J., & Peterson, M. (1996). Methodological issues in cross-cultural marketing research: A state-of-the-art review. *International Marketing Review, 13*, 7–43.

Mandal, T. (2007). *Small and medium enterprises in BIMSTEC synergies and emerging issues for cooperation.* CSIRD Discussion Paper #22. Centre for Studies in International Relations and Development, Kolkata.

Marin, G., & Marin, B. V. O. (1991). *Research with hispanic populations:* Applied social research series. Beverly Hills, CA: Sage.

Marques, A., Oliveira, T., Dias, S. S., & Martins, M. F. O. (2011). Medical records system adoption in European hospitals. *The Electronic Journal of Information Systems Evaluation, 14*(1), 89–99.

Marsden, D., & Littler, D. (1996). Evaluating alternative research paradigms: A market-oriented framework. *Journal of Marketing Management, 12*(7), 645–655.

Mata, F. J., Fuerst, W. L., & Barney, J. B. (1995). Information technology and sustained competitive advantage: A resource-based analysis. *MIS Quarterly, 19*(4), 487–505.

Mathieson, K. (1991). Predicting user intention: Comparing the technology acceptance model with the theory of planned behavior. *Information Systems Research, 2*(3), 173–191.

Mathieson, K., Peacock, E., & Chin, W. W. (2001). Extending the technology acceptance model: The influence of perceived user resources. *The Data Base for Advances in Information Systems, 32*(3), 86–112.

Matlay, H., & Addis, M. (2003). Adoption of ICT and e-commerce in small businesses: An HEI-based consultancy perspective. *Journal of Small Business and Enterprise Development, 10*(3), 321–335.

Maykut, P., & Morehouse, R. (1994). *Beginning qualitative research: A philosophical and a practical guide.* Washington, DC: Falmer Press.

McKnight, P. E., McKnight, K. M., Sidani, S., & Figueredo, A. J. (2007). *Missing data: A gentle introduction.* New York, NY: The Guilford Press.

Mehta, R., & Sivadas, E. (1995). Direct marketing on the internet: An empirical assessment of consumer attitudes. *Journal of Direct Marketing, 8*(3), 21–32.

Merriam, S. B. (1998). *Qualitative research and case study applications in education.* San Francisco, CA: Jossey-Bass.

Mingers, J. (2003). The paucity of multi-method research: A review of the information systems literature. *Information Systems Journal, 13*(3), 233–249.

Miniard, P., & Cohen, J. B. (1979). Isolating attitudinal and normative influences in behavioural intentions models. *Journal of Marketing Research, 16*, 102–110.

Miniard, P., & Cohen, J. B. (1981). An examination of Fishbein-Ajzen behavioral-intentions model's concepts and measures. *Journal of Experimental Social Psychology, 17*, 309–339.

Miniard, P., & Cohen, J. B. (1983). Modelling personal and normative influences on behaviour. *Journal of Consumer Research, 10*, 169–179.

Molla, A., & Licker, P. S. (2005). eCommerce adoption in developing countries: A model and instrument. *Information & Management, 42*, 877–899.

Moore, G. C., & Benbasat, I. (1991). Development of an instrument to measure perceptions of adopting an information technology innovation. *Information Systems Research, 2*(3), 192–222.

Mukhopadhyay, T. S., Kekre, S., & Kalathur, S. (1995). Business value of information technology: A study of electronic data interchange. *MIS Quarterly, 19*(2), 137–156.

Mustamil, N. M. (2010). *The influence of culture and ethical ideology on the ethical decision making process of Malaysian managers.* Perth, Australia: Doctor of Business Administration (DBA), Curtin University.

Myers, M. (1997). Qualitative research in information systems. *MIS Quarterly, 21*(2), 241–242.

Myers, M. D., & Klein, H. K. (2011). A set of principles for conducting critical research in information systems. *MIS Quarterly, 35*(1), 17–36.

Nejadirani, F., Behravesh, M., & Rasouli, R. (2011). Developing countries and electronic commerce: The case of SMEs. *World Applied Sciences Journal, 15*(5), 756–764.

Neuman, W. L. (2006). *Social research methods – Qualitative and quantitative approaches.* Boston, MA: Allyn and Bacon.

Nieswiadomy, R. M. (2011). *Foundations of nursing research* (6th ed.). New York, NY: Pearson Education.

Nunnally, J. C. (1994). *Psychometric theory* (3rd ed.). New York, NY: McGraw-Hill.

O'Donnell, A., Gilmore, A., Carson, D., & Cummins, D. (2002). Competitive advantage in small and medium-sized enterprises. *Journal of Strategic Marketing, 10*, 205–223.

Oliveira, T., & Martins, M. F. O. (2010). Firms' patterns of e-business adoption: Evidence for the European Union-27. *The Electronic Journal of Information Systems Evaluation, 13*(1), 47–56.

Ordedra, M., Lawrie, M., Bennett, M., & Goodman, S. (1993). Sub-Saharan Africa: A technological desert. *Communications of the ACM, 35*(2), 25–29.

Orlikowski, W. J., & Baroudi, J. J. (1991). Studying information technology in organizations: Research approaches and assumptions. *Information Systems Research, 2*(1), 1–28.

Oxley, J. E., & Yeung, B. (2001). E-commerce readiness: Institutional environment and international competitiveness. *Journal of International Business Studies, 32*(4), 705–723.

Parker, P. M., & Sarvary, M. (1996). *A cross cultural study of consumer innovativeness.* A working paper in the INSEAD working paper series. INSEAD, Fontainebleau, France.

Patton, M. Q. (1999). Enhancing the quality and credibility of qualitative analysis. *Health Services Research, 34*(5), 1189–1208.

Pavlov, P. A., & Chai, L. (2002). What drives electronic commerce across cultures? A cross-cultural empirical investigation of the theory of planned behavior. *Journal of Electronic Commerce Research, 3*(4), 240–253.

Perry, C. (1998). Processes of a case study methodology for postgraduate research in marketing. *European Journal of Marketing, 32*(9–10), 785–802.

Peteraf, M. A. (1993). The cornerstones of competitive advantage: A resource-based view. *Strategic Management Journal, 14*(3), 179–191.

Peteraf, M. A., & Barney, J. B. (2003). Unravelling the resource-based tangle. *Managerial and Decision Economics, 24*(4), 309–323.

Petter, S., Straub, D., & Rai, A. (2007). Specifying formative constructs in information systems research. *MIS Quarterly, 31*(4), 623–656.

Pham, L. T., & Jordan, E. (2007). Information technology capability, the effects on organizational performance. *Proceedings of the 13th Asia-Pacific Management Conference*, Melbourne, Australia (pp. 261–269).

Pilat, D., & Wyckoff, A. W. (2005). The impact of ICT on economic performance: An international comparison of three-level analysis. In W. H. Dutton, B. Kahin, R. O'Callaghan, & A. W. Wyckoff (Eds.), *Transforming enterprise, the economic and social implications of information technology* (pp. 77–108). Cambridge, MA: Massachusetts Institute of Technology.

Porter, M. E. (1985). *The competitive advantage.* New York, NY: The Free Press.

Porter, M. E. (1998). *The competitive advantage of the nation.* New York, NY: Palgrave.

Powell, T. C., & Dent-Micallef, A. (1997). Information technology as competitive advantage: The role of human, business, and technology resources. *Strategic Management Journal, 18*(5), 375–405.

Premkumar, G., & Potter, M. (1995). Adoption of Computer Aided Software Engineering (CASE) technology: An innovation adoption perspective. *ACM SIGMIS Database, 26*(2–3), 105–124.

Premkumar, G., & Ramamurthy, K. (1995). The role of interorganizational and organizational factors on the decision mode for adoption of interorganizational systems. *Decision Science, 26*(3), 303–336.

Premkumar, G., Ramamurthy, K., & Nilakanta, S. (1994). Implementation of electronic data interchange: An innovation diffusion perspective. *Journal of Management Information Systems, 11*(2), 157–179.

Prothom Alo. (2006). *The Prothom Alo (Dhaka)*, A Bengali national daily, June 16.

Quaddus, M., & Hofmeyer, G. (2007). An investigation into the factors influencing the adoption of B2B trading exchanges in small business. *European Journal of Information Systems, 16*(3), 202–215.

Quaddus, M., Islam, N., & Stanton, J. (2006, August 12–18). An investigation of significant factors influencing Western Australian wool producers to produce wool: A Structural Equation Modelling approach. In *Proceedings of The International Association of Agricultural Papers presented at the Economists Conference*, Gold Coast, Australia.

Quaddus, M., & Tung, L. L. (2002). Explaining cultural differences in decision conferencing. *Communications of the ACM, 45*(8), 93–98.

Raghunathan, T. E. (2004). What do we do with missing data? Some options for analysis of incomplete data. *Annual Review of Public Health, 25*, 99–117.

Rahim, M. A., Antonioni, D., & Psenicka, C. (2001). A structural equation model of leader power, subordinate styles of handling conflict, and job performance. *International Journal of Conflict Management, 12*(3), 191–211.

Rahman, M. L. (2002). E-commerce and concerns for e-commerce in Bangladesh. *Journal of the Institute of Bankers Bangladesh, 48*, 88–113.

Rahman, M. L. (2003). Global context of ICT development and Bangladesh. In *Proceedings of the National Conference of Inter-University IT Professionals in Bangladesh*, 30 September–1 October 2003, Dhaka, Bangladesh (pp. 1–22).

Rai, A., Patnayakuni, R., & Seth, N. (2006). Firm performance impacts of digitally enabled supply chain integration capabilities. *MIS Quarterly, 30*(2), 225–246.

Ralston, D. A., Giacalone, R. A., & Terpstra, R. H. (1994). Ethical perceptions of organizational politics: A comparative evaluation of American and Hong Kong managers. *Journal of Business Ethics, 13*(12), 918–999.

Ramayah, T., Ignatius, J., & Aafaqi, B. (2005). PC usage among students in a private institution of higher learning: The moderating role of prior experience. *Educators and Education Journal, 20*, 131–152.

Ramayah, T., Jamaludin, N., & Azam, M. S. (2007, May 21–25). Applying theory of planned behavior (TPB) in predicting intention to use Internet tax filing. In *Proceedings of the 7th International Conference of Asian Academy of Management*, Penang, Malaysia (pp. 102–109).

Ramayah, T., Jantan, M., Noor, N., Razak, R. C., & Ling, K. P. (2003). Receptiveness of Internet banking by Malaysian consumers. *Asian Academy of Management Journal, 8*(2), 1–29.

Ramayah, T., Noor, M. N. M., Nasurdin, A. M., & Sin, Q. B. (2004). The relationships between belief, attitude, subjective norm, intention, and behavior towards infant food formula selection: The views of the Malaysian mothers. *Gadjah Mada International Journal of Business, 6*(3), 405–418.

Ravichandran, T., & Lertwongsatien, C. (2005). Effect of information systems resources and capabilities on firm performance: A resource-based perspective. *Journal of Management Information Systems, 21*(4), 237–276.

Raymond, L., & Magnenat-Thalmann, N. (1982). Information systems in small business: Are they used in managerial decisions? *American Journal of Small Business, 6*(4), 20–23.

Regan, D. T., & Fazio, R. (1977). On the consistency between attitudes and behavior: Look to the method of attitude formation. *Journal of Experimental Social Psychology, 13*(1), 28–45.

Reynolds, F. D. (1974). An analysis of catalog buying behavior. *Journal of Marketing, 38,* 47–51.

Reynolds, F. D., & Neter, J. (1982). How many categories for respondent classification? *Journal of Market Research Society, 24*(4), 345–346.

Reynolds, N. L., Simintiras, A. C., & Diamantopoulos, A. (2003). Theoretical justification of sampling choices in international marketing research: Key issues and guidelines for researchers. *Journal of International Business Studies, 34*(1), 80–89.

Rhodes, R. E., & Courneya, K. S. (2003). Investigating multiple components of attitude, subjective norm, and perceived control: An examination of the theory of planned behaviour in the exercise domain. *The British Journal of Social Psychology, 42,* 129–146.

Rigdon, E. E., Ringle, C. M., & Sarstedt, M. (2010). Structural modeling of heterogeneous data with partial least squares. In N. K. Malhotra (Ed.), *Review of marketing research* (Vol. 7, pp. 255–296). Armonk, NY: M. E. Sharpe.

Rockart, J. F., Earl, M. J., & Ross, J. W. (1996). Eight imperatives for the new IT organization. *Sloan Management Review, 38*(1), 43–55.

Roessner, J. D. (1988). Innovation policy in the United States: An overview of the issues. In J. D. Roessner (Ed.), *Government innovation policy: Design, implementation, evaluation,* New York, NY: St. Martin's Press, Inc.

Rogers, E. M. (1983). *Diffusion of innovation* (3rd ed.). New York, NY: Free Press.

Rogers, E. M. (1995). *Diffusion of innovation* (4th ed.). New York, NY: Free Press.

Rogers, E. M. (2003). *Diffusion of innovation* (5th ed.). New York, NY: Free Press.

Rossiter, J. R. (2002). The C-OAR-SE procedure for scale development in marketing. *International Journal of Research in Marketing, 19,* 305–335.

Sager, M. (1988). Competitive information systems in Australian retail banking. *Information and Management, 15,* 59–67.

Saleh, M. A. (2006). *Antecedents of commitment to an import supplier.* PhD dissertation, Queensland University of Technology, Brisbane, Queensland, Australia.

Sandelowski, M. (1995). Sample size in qualitative research. *Research in Nursing & Health, 18*(2), 179–183.

Sanders, N. R., & Premus, R. (2005). Modeling the relationship between firm IT capability, collaboration, and performance. *Journal of Business Logistics, 26*(1), 1–23.

Santosa, P. I., Wei, K. K., & Chan, H. C. (2005). User involvement and user satisfaction with information-seeking activity. *European Journal of Information Systems, 14,* 361–370.

Sathye, M., & Beal, D. (2001). Adoption of electronic commerce by SMEs: Australian evidence. *Journal of E-Business, 1*(1), 1–11.

Schlosser, A. E., Shavitt, S., & Kanfer, A. (1999). Survey of internet users' attitudes toward Internet advertising. *Journal of Interactive Marketing, 13*(3), 34–54.

Schwarz, G. (1978). Estimating the dimensions of a model. *The Annals of Statistics, 6*(2), 461–464.

Schwarzer, B. (1995). Organizing global IS management to meet competitive challenges: Experiences from the pharmaceutical industry. *Journal of Global Information Management, 3,* 5–16.

Scupola, A. (2003a). Adoption of e-commerce in SMEs: Lessons from stage models. In *IFIP international federation for information processing* (pp. 291–308). Springer.

Scupola, A. (2003b). The adoption of internet commerce by SMEs in the south of Italy: An environmental, technological, and organizational perspective. *Journal of Global Information Technology Management*, 6(1), 52–71.

Segars, A. H., & Grover, V. (1998). Strategic information systems planning success: An investigation of the construct and its measurement. *MIS Quarterly*, 22(2), 139–163.

Sethi, V., & King, W. R. (1994). Development of measures to assess the extent to which an information technology application provides competitive advantage. *Management Science*, 40(12), 1601–1627.

Shamsuddoha, A. K. (2004). *Antecedents of firm export performance: The role of export promotion programs*. PhD dissertation, Queensland University of Technology, Brisbane, Queensland, Australia.

Sheppard, B. H., Hartwick, J., & Warshaw, P. R. (1988). The theory of reasoned action: A meta-analysis of past research with recommendations for modifications and future research. *Journal of Consumer Research*, 15(3), 325–343.

Shih, C., Dedrick, J., & Kraemer, K. L. (2005). Rule of law and the international diffusion of e-commerce. *Communications of the ACM*, 48(11), 57–62.

Shih, H. (2004). Extended technology acceptance model of internet utilisation behaviour. *Information & Management*, 41, 719–729.

Shih, Y., & Fang, K. (2004). The use of a decomposed theory of planned behavior to study internet banking in Taiwan. *Internet Research*, 1(3), 213–223.

Shih, Y., & Fang, K. (2006). Effects of network quality attributes on customer adoption intentions of Internet banking. *Total Quality Management & Business Excellence*, 17(1), 61–77.

Shimp, T., & Kavas, A. (1984). The theory of reasoned action applied to coupon usage. *Journal of Consumer Research*, 11, 795–809.

Siltaoja, M. E. (2006). Value priorities as combining core factors between CSR and reputation – A qualitative study. *Journal of Business Ethics*, 68(1), 91–111.

Sobel, M. (1982). Asymptotic confidence intervals for indirect effects on structural equation modeling. In S. Leinhardt (Ed.), *Sociological methodology* (pp. 290–312). New York, NY: Jossey-Bass.

Solomon, S. (1986). *Small business USA: The role of small enterprises in sparking America's economic transformation*. New York, NY: Crown.

Song, G., & Mueller-Falcke, D. (2006). The economic effects of ICT at firm-levels. In M. Torero & J. Braun (Eds.), *Information and communication technologies for development and poverty reduction: The potential of telecommunications* (pp. 166–184). Baltimore, MD: John Hopkins University Press.

Steinhoff, D., & Burgess, J. F. (1986). *Small business management fundamentals* (4th ed.). Singapore: McGraw-Hill.

Stewart, K. A., & Segars, A. H. (2002). An empirical examination of the concern for information privacy instrument. *Information Systems Research*, 13(1), 36–49.

Straub, D. (1989). Validating instruments in MIS research. *MIS Quarterly*, 13(2), 147–169.

Straub, D. W. (1994). The effects of culture on IT diffusion: E-mail and fax in Japan and the US. *Information Systems Research*, 5(1), 23–47.

Strauss, A., & Corbin, J. (1998). *Basics of qualitative research techniques and procedures for developing grounded theory*. London: Sage.

Subramanian, G. H. (1994). A replication of perceived usefulness and perceived ease of use measurement. *Decision Science*, 25(5–6), 863–874.

Suppe, F. (Ed.). (1977). *The structure of scientific theories* (2nd ed.). Urbana, IL: University of Illinois Press.

Szajna, B. (1996). Empirical evaluation of the revised technology acceptance model. *Management Science, 42*(1), 85–92.

Szymanski, D. M., Bharadwaj, S. G., & Varadarajan, P. R. (1993). An analysis of the market share profitability relationship. *Journal of Marketing, 57*(3), 1–18.

Tabachnick, B. G., & Fidell, L. S. (1996). *Using multivariate statistics*. New York, NY: Harper Collins College Publishers.

Tabachnick, B. G., & Fidell, L. S. (2001). *Using multivariate statistics* (4th ed.). Boston, MA: Allyn and Bacon.

Tan, M., & Teo, T. S. H. (2000). Factors influencing the adoption of internet banking. *Journal of the Association for Information Systems, 1*, Article 5, 1–42.

Tashakkori, A., & Teddlie, C. (1998). *Mixed methodology: Combining qualitative and quantitative approaches*. Thousand Oaks, CA: Sage.

Taylor, S., & Todd, P. A. (1995a). Assessing IT usage: The role of prior experience. *MIS Quarterly, 19*(2), 561–570.

Taylor, S., & Todd, P. A. (1995b). Understanding information technology usage: A test of competing models. *Information Systems Research, 6*(4), 144–176.

Taylor, S., & Todd, P. A. (1995c). Decomposition and crossover effects in the theory of planned behavior: A study of consumer adoption intentions. *International Journal of Research in Marketing, 12*, 137–155.

Tenenhaus, M., Vinzi, V. E., Chatelin, Y.-M., & Lauro, C. (2005). PLS path modeling. *Computational Statistics and Data Analysis, 48*(1), 159–205.

Teo, H. H., Wei, K. K., & Benbasat, I. (2003). Predicting intention to adopt interorganizational linkages: An institutional perspective. *MIS Quarterly, 27*(1), 19–49.

Teo, T. S. H., & Ranganathan, C. (2004). Adopters and non-adopters of business-to-business electronic commerce in Singapore. *Information and Management, 42*, 89–102.

Teo, T. S. H., Tan, M., & Buk, W. K. (1998). A contingency model of internet adoption in Singapore. *International Journal of Electronic Commerce, 2*(2), 89–102.

Thatcher, S. M. B., Foster, W., & Zhu, L. (2006). B2B e-commerce adoption decisions in Taiwan: The interaction of cultural and other institutional factors. *Electronic Commerce Research and Applications, 5*, 92–104.

The New Nation. (2008). *The New Nation*, A national English daily, January 2. Retrieved from http://povertynewsblog.blogspot.com/2008/01/bangladesh-bank-report-says-development.html. Accessed on June 3, 2008.

Thompson, R. L., Higgins, C. A., & Howell, J. M. (1991). Personal computing: Toward a conceptual model of utilization. *MIS Quarterly, 15*(1), 124–143.

Thong, J. Y. L. (1999). An integrated model of information systems adoption in small businesses. *Journal of Management Information Systems, 15*(4), 187–214.

Thong, J. Y. L., & Yap, C. S. (1995). CEO characteristics, organizational characteristics and information technology adoption in small businesses. *Omega: The International Journal of Management Science, 23*(4), 429–442.

Tippins, M. J., & Sohi, R. S. (2003). IT competency and firm performance: Is organizational learning a missing link? *Strategic Management Journal, 24*(8), 745–761.

Tolbert, P. S. (1985). Institutional environments and resource dependence: Sources of administrative structure in institutions of higher education. *Administrative Science Quarterly, 30*(1), 1–13.

Tornatzky, L. G., & Fleischer, M. (1990). *The process of technological innovation.* Lexington, MA: Lexington Books.

Triandis, H. C. (1979). Values, attitudes, and interpersonal behavior. In Nebraska Symposium on Motivation, Beliefs, attitudes, and values (pp. 195–259). Lincoln, NE: University of Nebraska Press.

Twati, J. M., & Gammack, J. G. (2006). The impact of organisational culture innovation on the adoption of IS/IT: The case of Libya. *Journal of Enterprise Information Management, 19*(2), 175–191.

United Nations Conference on Trade and Development (UNCTAD). (2006). *Using ICTs to achieve growth and development.* Background paper by the UNCTAD Secretariat. New York, NY: United Nations.

Venkatesh, V., Brown, S. A., Maruping, L. M., & Bala, H. (2008). Predicting different conceptualizations of system use: The competing roles of behavioral intention, facilitating conditions, and behavioral expectation. *MIS Quarterly, 32*(3), 483–502.

Venkatesh, V., & Davis, F. D. (2000). A theoretical extension of the technology acceptance model: Four longitudinal field studies. *Management Science, 46*(2), 186–204.

Venkatesh, V., & Morris, M. D. (2000). Why don't men ever stop to ask for directions? Gender, social influences and their role in technology acceptance and usage behaviour. *MIS Quarterly, 24*(1), 115–139.

Venkatesh, V., Morris, M. G., Davis, G. B., & Davis, F. D. (2003). User acceptance of information technology: Toward a unified view. *MIS Quarterly, 27*(3), 425–478.

Venkatesh, V., & Zhang, X. (2010). Unified theory of acceptance and use of technology: U.S. vs. China. *Journal of Global Information Technology Management, 13*(1), 5–27.

Venkatraman, N. (1990). Performance implications of strategic co-alignment: A methodological perspective. *Journal of Management Studies, 27*(2), 19–41.

Venkatraman, N., & Zaheer, A. (1990). Electronic integration and strategic advantage: A quasi-experimental study in the insurance industry. *Information Systems Research, 1*(4), 377–393.

Verbeek, M. (2000). *A guide to modern econometrics.* New York, NY: Wiley.

Vijayasarathy, L. R. (2004). Predicting consumer intentions to use on-line shopping: The case for an augmented technology acceptance model. *Information and Management, 41*(6), 747–762.

Voss, G. B., & Voss, Z. G. (2000). Strategic orientation and firm performance in an artistic environment. *Journal of Marketing, 64*(January), 67–83.

Wahab, E. (2010). *Perceived organizational support and organizational commitment in medium enterprises in Malaysia.* PhD dissertation, Curtin University, Perth, WA, Australia.

Wang, Y., Wang, Y., Lin, H., & Tang, T. (2003). Antecedents of user acceptance of Internet banking: An empirical study. *International Journal of Service Industry Management, 14*(5), 501–519.

Warner, T. N. (1987). Information technology as a competitive burden. *Sloan Management Review, 29*(1), 55–61.

Warshaw, P. R., & Davis, F. D. (1984). Self understanding and the accuracy of behavioural expectations. *Personality and Social Psychology Bulletin, 10*(1), 111–118.

Warshaw, P. R., & Davis, F. D. (1985). Disentangling behavioral intention and behavioral expectation. *Journal of Experimental Social Psychology, 21,* 213–228.

Watson, R. T., Kelly, G., Galliers, R. D., & Brancheau, J. C. (1997). Key issues in information systems management: An international perspective. *Journal of Information Management Systems, 13*(4), 91–115.

Weber, D. M., & Kauffman, R. J. (2011). What drives global ICT adoption? Analysis and research directions. *Electronic Commerce Research and Applications, 10,* 683–701.

West, S. G., & Aiken, L. S. (1997). Toward understanding individual effects in multicomponent prevention programs: Design and analysis strategies. In K. J. Bryant, M. Windle, & S. G. West (Eds.), *The science of prevention: Methodological advances from alcohol and substance abuse research* (pp. 167–209). Washington, DC: American Psychological Association.

Werner, O., & Campbell, D. T. (1970). Translating, working through interpreters, and the problem of decentering. In R. Naroll & R. Cohen (Eds.), *A handbook of method in cultural anthropology* (pp. 398–420). New York, NY: The Natural History Press.

Wetzels, M., Odekerken-Schröder, G., & van Oppen, C. (2009). Using PLS path modeling for assessing hierarchical construct models: Guidelines and empirical illustration. *MIS Quarterly, 33*(1), 177–195.

Woodworth, R. S. (1928). Dynamic psychology. In C. Murchison (Ed.), *Psychologies of 1925.* Worcester, MA: Clark University Press.

World Bank. (2010). *Country level Internet usage statistics.* Retrieved from http://data.worldbank.org/indicator/IT.NET.USER.P2?cid=GPD_44. Accessed on June 28, 2008.

Wright, S. (1921). Correlation and causation. *Journal of Agricultural Research, 20,* 557–585.

Wu, F., Yeniyurt, S., Kim, D., & Cavusgil, S. T. (2006). The impact of information technology on supply chain capabilities and firm performance: A resource-based view. *Industrial Marketing Management, 35*(4), 493–504.

Wymer, S., & Regan, E. (2005). Factors influencing e-commerce adoption and use by small and medium businesses. *Electronic Markets, 15*(4), 438–453.

Xu, J., & Quaddus, M. (2005). Adoption and diffusion of knowledge management systems: Field studies of factors and variables. *Knowledge-Based Systems, 18,* 107–115.

Xu, S., Zhu, K., & Gibbs, J. (2004). Global technology, local adoption: A cross-country investigation of internet adoption by companies in the United States and China. *Globalization and Electronic Commerce, 14*(1), 13–24.

Yap, C. S., Soh, C. P. P., & Raman, K. S. (1992). Information systems success factors in small business. *OMEGA — International Journal of Management Science, 20*(5–6), 597–609.

Yoon, C. (2009). The effects on national cultural values on consumer acceptance of e-commerce: Online shoppers in China. *Information & Management, 46,* 294–301.

Zhang, C., Cui, L., Huang, L., & Zhang, C. (2007). Exploring the role of government in information technology diffusion: An empirical study of IT usage in Shanghai firms. In T. McMaster, D. Wastell, E. Femeley, & J. DeGross (Eds.), *Organizational dynamics of technology-based innovation: Diversifying the research agenda* (Vol. 235, pp. 393–407). Boston, MA: Springer.

Zhu, K. (2004). The complementarity of information technology infrastructure and e-commerce capability: A resource-based assessment of their value. *Journal of Management Information Systems, 21*(1), 167–202.

Zhu, K., Dong, S., Xu, S. X., & Kraemer, K. L. (2006). Innovation diffusion in global contexts: Antecedents of post-adoption digital transformation of European companies. *European Journal of Information Systems, 15*(6), 601–616.

Zhu, K., & Kraemer, K. L. (2002). E-commerce matrics for net-enhanced organisations: Assessing the value of e-commerce to firm performance in the manufacturing sector. *Information Systems Research, 13*(3), 275–295.

Zhu, K., & Kraemer, K. L. (2005). Post-adoption variations in usage and value of e-business by organizations: Cross-country evidence from the retail industry. *Information Systems Research, 16*(1), 61–84.

Zhu, K., Kraemer, K. L., & Xu, S. (2003). Electronic business adoption by European firms: A cross-country assessment of the facilitators and inhibitors. *European Journal of Information Systems, 12*, 251–268.

Zhu, K., Kraemer, K. L., & Xu, S. (2006). The process of innovation assimilation by firms in different countries: A technology diffusion perspective on e-business. *Management Science, 52*(10), 1157–1576.

Zhu, K., Kraemer, K. L., Xu, S., & Dedrick, J. (2004). Information technology payoff in e-business environments: An international perspective on value creation of e-business in the financial services industry. *Journal of Management Information Systems, 21*(1), 17–54.

Zikmund, W. G. (2000). *Business research methods*. Orlando, FL: The Dryden Press.

Zikmund, W. G. (2003). *Business research methods*. Cincinnati, OH: Thomson/South-Western.

Zmud, R. W. (1984). An examination of 'push-pull' theory applied to process innovation in knowledge work. *Management Science, 30*(6), 727–738.

APPENDIX A

Sample Design
(Stratified random sampling)

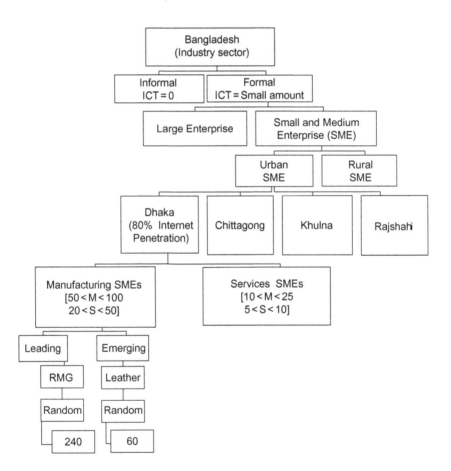

APPENDIX B

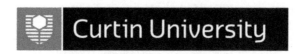

Graduate School of Business

Interview Guide

Participant Information Sheet   .

My name is Md. Shah Azam. I am currently conducting a research entitled 'Diffusion of ICT and SMEs Performance: The Mediating Effects of Integration and Utilisation' under Doctor of Philosophy Programme, Graduate School of Business (GSB), Curtin University of Technology, Australia.

Purpose of Research

I am investigating how diffusion of ICT links with organisational performance. The study focuses Small and Medium-Sized Enterprises (SMEs) in Bangladesh. Exploring the effects of different factors the study looks for the strategies that may help develop the SMEs in Bangladesh.

Your Role

I am interested in finding out the factors that influence your company's ICT use, related decision and performance.

I would like to talk about your status of ICT use, your internal desire, attitude towards ICT improvements, exchanges with the internal peoples and external parties. The issues related to ICT resources, capabilities, national infrastructure, as well as national culture will further be discussed as to explore how they may link with organisational ICT decision. I would also like to discuss about any indicators you use to determine ICT performance as well as overall organisational performance. I will use a set of semi-structured questions to organise a formal and fluent discussion with you which brings in required information for the study.

The interview process will take approximately 60 minutes.

Consent to Participate

Your involvement in the research is entirely voluntary. You have the right to withdraw at any stage without it affecting your rights or my responsibilities. When you have signed the consent form I will assume that you are agreed to participate and allow me to use your data in this research.

Confidentiality

The information you provide will be kept separate from your personal details, and only I will have access to this. The interview transcript will not have your name or any other identifying information on it and in adherence to university policy, the interview tapes and transcribed information will be kept in a locked cabinet for five years, before it is destroyed.

Further Information

This study has been approved by the Curtin University Human Research Ethics Committee. If needed, verification of approval can be obtained by either writing to the Curtin University Human Research Ethics Committee, c/- Office of Research & Development, Curtin University of Technology, GPO Box U1987, Perth 6845, or telephone +618-92662784. If you would like further information about the study, please feel free to contact me on +610432224840 or by email: ashantonu@yahoo.co.uk. Alternatively, you can contact my supervisor Professor Mohammed Quaddus on +618-92662862 or by email: mohammed.quaddus@gsb.curtin.edu.au

Thank you very much for your involvement in this research, your participation is highly appreciated.

Interview Guide

Diffusion of ICT and SMEs Performance: The Mediating Effects of Integration and Utilisation

PhD Programme,
Curtin University of Technology, Australia

This interview guide will help explore theoretical constructs and their inter-relationship; and fine-tune proposed model for the study entitled 'Diffusion of ICT and SMEs Performance: The Mediating Effects of Integration and Utilisation' under PhD programme, Graduate School of Business, Curtin University of Technology, Australia.

GENERAL

Q.1.1. Do you use any type of ICT applications in your organisation at present?

Q.1.2. What ICT system do you use in your organisation? Please describe the level of use of the system (High, Medium or low, etc.).

OWNER AND CEO CHARACTERISTICS

Q.2.1. How would you describe the characteristics of the owner/CEO of the enterprise that may influence organisational ICT use?

Q.2.2. Please describe the owners'/CEOs roles in ICT adoption and other ICT-related decision.

BELIEFS AND EVALUATIONS

Q.3.1. How would you describe your beliefs and evaluations about ICT which may influence you to use or not use ICT in your organisation?

Q.3.2. Describe how your belief or evaluation about ICT would relate with the firms' overall ICT use or ICT-related decision? Please give example.

ENVIRONMENTAL PRESSURE

Q.4.1. Please describe the ICT status of your different stake holders (such as supplier, distributor, competitor, customer and govt. agencies). Please state if you have received any encouragement or constraints from them to use or not use or enhance the current mode of ICT use in your organisation? Please give examples.

Q.4.2. Please describe how above-mentioned issues would link with the firms' ICT-related decisions?

BEHAVIOURAL INTENTION

Q.5.1. If you have all the resources (and no constraint at all) to implement ICT, how would you express your intention in next few months?

Q.5.2. How does your above-mentioned intention (internal desire) relate with ICT use at firm level? Please give example.

BEHAVIOURAL EXPECTATION

Q.6.1. Considering external environment, infrastructure, law and culture can your intention be put into practice?

Q.6.2. Please describe how expectation would relate with firms' ICT use or associated decisions.

MACRO AND MICRO FACILITATING CONDITION

Q.7.1. What are the resources and skills essential to implement ICT in an organisation like you? Please state the strengths and weaknesses of your organisation to implement ICT. Please detail as much as possible.

Q.7.2. How would you describe the resources and facilities at national level that may encourage you to implement or not implement ICT in your organisation. Please detail it as much as possible.

Q.7.3. How would you describe the way the above-mentioned facilities or condition link with your firms' ICT use or related decisions.

NATIONAL CULTURE

Q.9.1. How would you describe the cultural issues and its impact on organisational technology usage behaviour?

Q.9.2. How would you describe other national cultural issues (as you see it) in addition to the above dimensions.

Q.9.3. Please describe how the national cultural issues are linked with ICT use or ICT-related decisions.

ICT USE, INTEGRATION AND DEGREE OF UTILISATION

Q.10.1. What types of organisational ICT supports do you have in place currently (ICT resources, its application, etc.)?

Q.10.2. How long have you been using ICT system in your organisation.

Q.10.3. How do you describe the way ICT use and its level of use relate with firms' overall performance?

ORGANISATIONAL PERFORMANCE

Q.11. Would you kindly let me know how could you evaluate the overall performance of your organisation? Give examples.

DEMOGRAPHIC PROFILE OF THE INTERVIEWEE

Q.12.1. Please mention your demographic information:

a. Name: ....

b. Position: ....

c. Age:

(i) below 25 Years	(ii) 25–34 Years	(iii) 35–44 Years
(iv) 45–60 Years	(v) 60 < Years	

d. Gender:

(i) Male	(ii) Female

e. Education:

(i) PhD	(ii) Post graduate	(iii) Graduation	(iv) HSC
(v) SSC	(vi) Primary school	(vii) Literate	(viii) Others

f. Monthly income:

(i) <10,000 Tk.	(ii) 10,000–20,000 Tk.	(iii) 20,000–30,000 Tk.
(iv) 30,000–50,000 Tk.	(v) 50,000–80,000 Tk.	(vi) above 80,000 Tk.

g. ICT experience: ....

h. How long you been in this organisation: ....

i. Your field of Specialisation: ....

j. How long you are working in this position: ....

Q.12.2. Please brief about your organisation (Business type, nature etc.).

a. Type of industry: ....

b. Nature of business (Manufacturing industry, Whole sale, retail etc.)
....

....

Q.12.3. Please let me know the numbers of worker employed in the organisation.

Full time: ....

Part-time/casual: ....

Q.12.4. Please state about your market position in terms of the completion:

very bad	1	2	3	4	5	6	7	very good

Q.12.5. Please state about your revenue in last year:

substantially decreased	1	2	3	4	5	6	7	substantially increased

Q.12.6. Please state about your sales in last year:

substantially decreased	1	2	3	4	5	6	7	substantially increased

Q.12.7. Please state about your profit in last year:

substantially decreased	1	2	3	4	5	6	7	substantially increased

Q.12.8. Please state about your expenditure in last year:

substantially decreased	1	2	3	4	5	6	7	substantially increased

Q.13.1. Have you received any kind of privilege or benefits for your organisation as SMEs?

(i) Yes	(ii) No

Q.13.2. Have you received any grants or subsidies for ICT development in your organisation?

(i) Yes	(ii) No

Q.14. Does your organisation have 9001 or 14001 certification? Please describe about acquiring the certification (9001:14001 Certificate) and its usefulness (Please mention whether you have been refused or have any desire to get 9001:14001 certification in the case of no certification).

APPENDIX C

Questionnaire code

Surveyor code

Survey Questionnaire

Participation information sheet

Dear survey participant,

This survey is part of an academic research project. In response to the Government's recent move towards establishing digital Bangladesh, this study is being undertaken to discover the level of small and medium-sized enterprises' preparations and willingness to adopt ICT in their organisation and the resultant outcomes in terms of organisational performance. The outcome of the survey will provide the basis for a chapter towards my PhD degree in the Graduate School of Business, Curtin University, Western Australia.

Your role in this survey is to answer the questions to the best of your knowledge. There is no right or wrong answer. We are only interested in your opinions on the issues.

Your responses will be kept strictly confidential and in no cases will your personal or organisational identity be disclosed. The outcome of the study will be used solely for academic purposes. However, your participation in this study is completely voluntary. You can participate or you can with-draw yourself anytime from the research.

It is important to be noted here that the study has been approved by the Curtin University Human Research Ethics Committee. If needed, verifica-tion of approval can be obtained by either writing to the Curtin University Human Research Ethics Committee, Office of Research and Development; Curtin University, GPO Box U1987, Perth, WA 6000, Australia, or con-tacting to +61-8-92662784.

My contact details are provided below if you would like further information about the study. Alternatively, you can contact my supervisor, Professor Mohammed Quaddus at +61-8-92662862, or +61-8-92667147, or mohammed.quaddus@cbs.curtin.edu.au.

It is my pleasure to receive the completed questionnaire directly or via post, email or fax at the address below.

Thank you for your co-operation and valuable response. Your participation is highly appreciated.

Kind regards,
Md Shah Azam
PhD Candidate
Graduate School of Business,
Curtin University
78 Murray Street, Perth 6000, Western Australia
Phone: +61-8-92881171 or +61-0432224840
Fax: +61-8-92663368
Email: mdshah.azam@postgrad.curtin.edu.au

Questionnaire

Name of the respondent: ....

Name of the organisation:...

Nature of Business (wholesaler, retailer etc.)..................................

Industry category:...

Address: ....
....

Phone: .... *email:* ....

[**Kindly put tick (✓) marks in the appropriate check boxes**]

Please specify the category of your business:

☐ Small business   ☐ Medium Business

☐ Other (please specify)...

Are you currently using any kind of ICT?

☐ No   ☐ Yes

	Please indicate the level of ICT you are currently using in your organisation:
☐	Basic Computer operation
☐	Internet with own static home page
☐	Interactive homepage which supports product cataloguing and order processing (Online order receiving and processing)

☐	Interactive home page which supports online transaction and account management (E-business)
☐	Complete digital communication and exchanges within and outside the organisation (ERP or digitisation)

Please indicate which types of software you are currently using:	
☐ **Basic computing software packages**	☐ **Human resource management**
☐ **Finance/accounting software**	☐ **Supply chain management**
☐ **Inventory management**	☐ **E-commerce**
☐ **Customer relations management**	☐ **Resource planning**

[*Please circle the number that best matches your views on the statements*]

Section A: Please indicate your perceptions about the use of ICT in your organisation (where 1 = Strongly disagree, 2 = Disagree, 3 = Neither agree nor disagree, 4 = Agree and 5 = Strongly agree)

	Perceived usefulness					
a.	I find ICT useful in our organisation	1	2	3	4	5
b.	Using the technology enables us to accomplish tasks more quickly	1	2	3	4	5
c.	Using the technology increases our productivity	1	2	3	4	5
d.	I feel that using the technology will increase our chances of growing or developing the organisation	1	2	3	4	5
	Perceived ease of use					
a.	I think our interaction with the technology is clear and understandable	1	2	3	4	5
b.	It is easy for us to become skilful at using the technology	1	2	3	4	5
c.	We find the technology easy to use	1	2	3	4	5
d.	Learning to operate the technology is easy for us	1	2	3	4	5

Section B: Please state your opinion about the characteristics of the owner or CEO of this organisation (where 1 = Strongly disagree, 2 = Disagree, 3 = Neither agree nor disagree, 4 = Agree and 5 = Strongly agree)

	Owner characteristics					
a.	He often bears risk in doing things differently	1	2	3	4	5
b.	He has original ideas	1	2	3	4	5

Section C: Please indicate your estimates of various pressures you face from the external environment that influence your interest or rate of, ICT adoption in your organisation (where 1 = strongly disagree, 2 = Disagree, 3 = Neither agree nor disagree, 4 = Agree and 5 = Strongly agree)

	Coercive pressure					
a.	Our parent company directs us to use ICT	1	2	3	4	5
b.	Our major customers demand we use ICT	1	2	3	4	5
c.	Our major suppliers demand we use ICT	1	2	3	4	5
	Competitive pressure					
a.	All of our competitors have already adopted ICT	1	2	3	4	5
b.	Our main competitors that have adopted ICT have benefitted a great deal	1	2	3	4	5
	Normative pressure	(where 1 = None has adopted, and 5 = All have adopted)				
a.	What is the current extent of ICT adoption by your firm's customers?	1	2	3	4	5
b.	What is the current extent of ICT adoption by your suppliers?	1	2	3	4	5
c.	What is the current extent of ICT adoption by your important business partners?	1	2	3	4	5
d.	What is the extent of ICT adoption by your regulatory bodies?	1	2	3	4	5

	Global pressure					
a.	We are encouraged to adopt ICT in accessing the opportunities arising from globalisation	1	2	3	4	5
c.	It has become necessary to embrace ICT for sustainability	1	2	3	4	5

Section D: Please indicate your estimates of the facilitating condition of your organisation (where 1 = Strongly disagree, 2 = Disagree, 3 = Neither agree nor disagree, 4 = Agree 5 = Strongly agree)

	Facilitating condition					
a.	ICT is compatible with other existing systems we use	1	2	3	4	5
b.	Our employees have the skill and competency necessary to handle the technology	1	2	3	4	5
c.	We have the resources necessary to use the technology	1	2	3	4	5

Section E: Please indicate your estimation on the status of the following infrastructural supports and their ability to motivate you or your organisation in adopting ICT (where 1 = Highly dissatisfactory, 2 = Dissatisfactory, 3 = Neither dissatisfactory nor satisfactory, 4 = Satisfactory and 5 = Highly satisfactory)

	Technology Infrastructure					
a.	Availability and coverage of Internet service in the country	1	2	3	4	5
b.	Speed and sophistication of the Internet	1	2	3	4	5
c.	Availability of necessary hardware and accessories	1	2	3	4	5
d.	Availability and continuity of power supply	1	2	3	4	5
	Human Infrastructure					
a.	Peoples knowledge and skill on IT and Internet-based business	1	2	3	4	5
b.	IT and Internet-based business operational knowledge and skill at institutional level	1	2	3	4	5
c.	Institutional support for computer education	1	2	3	4	5

	Legal Infrastructure					
a.	Legal support for digital communication and E-business	1	2	3	4	5
b.	Law relating to online consumer protection	1	2	3	4	5
	Financial Infrastructure					
c.	Online banking facility	1	2	3	4	5
d.	Credit and debit card usage trend in the country	1	2	3	4	5
	Government Policy and Supports					
a.	Government tax and customs policy	1	2	3	4	5
b.	Government's motivational programme	1	2	3	4	5
c.	Government grants	1	2	3	4	5
d.	Governments subsidies	1	2	3	4	5

Section F: Please indicate your estimate on the following statements about the cultural issues (where 1 = Strongly disagree, 2 = Disagree, 3 = Neither agree nor disagree, 4 = Agree, 5 = Strongly agree)

	Power distance					
a.	In this society employees are expected to obey and follow their leader without question	1	2	3	4	5
b.	Power is concentrated at the top management	1	2	3	4	5
c.	Employees should obey their leaders without questions	1	2	3	4	5
d.	Employees don't question any of the decisions taken by their leaders	1	2	3	4	5
	Uncertainty avoidance					
a.	In this society organisations have orderliness and consistency to face any future uncertain events	1	2	3	4	5
b.	Rules and regulations are important because they inform what the organisation expects	1	2	3	4	5
	In-group collectivism					
a.	In this society, group members take pride in the individual accomplishments of their group managers	1	2	3	4	5

		1	2	3	4	5
b.	Group managers take pride in the individual accomplishments of their group members	1	2	3	4	5
c.	Managers encourage group loyalty even if individual goals suffer	1	2	3	4	5
	Bengali value					
a.	In this society, face-to-face communication is vital among the employees in day-to-day operation	1	2	3	4	5
b.	Employees are comfortable and like to interact through Bengali language	1	2	3	4	5
c.	Employees have an intimate and tight social bond with other fellow members.	1	2	3	4	5
	Ethical culture					
a.	Bribes and corruption are seen as common phenomena in the main institutions of the society	1	2	3	4	5
b.	Politicisation and Nepotism are seen as common phenomena in the main institutions of the society	1	2	3	4	5

Section G: Please indicate your expectation or plans for ICT use in your organisation (where 1 = Current user, 2 = Going to use by 1 year, 3 = Within 1-2 years, 4 = Within 2-3 years, 5 = We are not going to use ICT in near future)

	Behavioural Expectation					
a.	Basic computer operation	1	2	3	4	5
b.	Internet with own static home page	1	2	3	4	5
c.	Interactive homepage which supports product cataloguing and order processing (Online order receiving and processing)	1	2	3	4	5
d.	Interactive home page which supports online transaction and account management (E-business)	1	2	3	4	5
e.	Complete digital communication and exchanges within and outside the organisation (ERP or digitisation)	1	2	3	4	5

Section H: Please indicate how often you use the following ICT technology (where 1 = Not use at all, and 5 = Use quite often)

	ICT Use					
a.	Basic computer operation	1	2	3	4	5
b.	Internet with own static home page	1	2	3	4	5
c.	Interactive homepage which supports product cataloguing and order processing (Online order receiving and processing)	1	2	3	4	5
d.	Interactive home page which supports online transaction and account management (E-business)	1	2	3	4	5
e.	Complete digital communication and exchanges within and outside the organisation (ERP or digitisation)	1	2	3	4	5

Section I: Please indicate your evaluation about ICT utilisation in your organisation (where 1 = ICT not at all utilised; 2 = utilised to conduct 20% of functions; 3 = utilised to conduct 20–50% of functions; 4 = utilised to conduct 50–80% of functions and 5 = utilised to conduct more than 80% of functions)

	Degree of utilisation					
a.	ICT is properly utilised in production and service-related functions	1	2	3	4	5
b.	ICT is properly utilised in admin and accounts-related functions	1	2	3	4	5
c.	ICT is properly utilised sales and marketing-related functions	1	2	3	4	5

Section J: Please indicate your estimates of the level of ICT integration in your organisation (where 1 = Strongly disagree, 2 = Disagree, 3 = Neither agree nor disagree, 4 = Agree and 5 = Strongly agree)

	Level of Integration					
a.	ICT is used in the entire working areas in the organisation	1	2	3	4	5
b.	All departments and functional areas of this organisation are integrated through a single ICT system	1	2	3	4	5

c.	Our website is well developed for front-end functionality which supports information, product catalogue, customer customisation and account management	1	2	3	4	5
d.	Our web applications are electronically integrated with back-office systems and data bases	1	2	3	4	5
e.	Company's data bases are electronically integrated with suppliers and partners	1	2	3	4	5

Section K: Please indicate your estimate about the performance of your organisation on the following counts since starting the technology (ICT) use (where 1 = Strongly disagree, 2 = Disagree, 3 = Neither agree nor disagree, 4 = Agree and 5 = Strongly agree)

	Competitiveness					
a.	Our sales area has been widened	1	2	3	4	5
b	Interaction with customers has been increased	1	2	3	4	5
c.	Competitive position has been improved	1	2	3	4	5
	Internal operation productivity					
a.	Internal operation of the organisation became transparent	1	2	3	4	5
b.	Internal operation of the organisation became structured	1	2	3	4	5
c.	Productivity of the employees has been improved	1	2	3	4	5
	Financial performance					
a.	Overall performance is increased	1	2	3	4	5
b.	Profitability of the company has increased	1	2	3	4	5
c.	Sales of the company have increased	1	2	3	4	5

Demographic questions

1. Please indicate your role in the organisation:

   ☐ Owner ☐ Owner-manager ☐ Manager ☐ Employee

   ☐ Other (please specify) ....

2. Your age group?

   ☐ Under 25 Years, ☐ 25–34 Years,

   ☐ 35–44 Years, ☐ 45–60 Years,

   ☐ Over 60 Years

3. Your gender? ☐ Male ☐ Female

4. Please indicate the level of your educational attainment:

   ☐ Postgraduate, ☐ Graduate, ☐ HSC, ☐ SSC,

   ☐ Primary school, ☐ Literate,

   ☐ Others (please specify)....................................

5. Your monthly income:

   ☐ Less than10,000 Tk. ☐ 10,000–20.000 Tk.

   ☐ 20,000–30,000 Tk. ☐ 30,000–50,000 Tk.

   ☐ 50,000–80,000 Tk. ☐ above 80,000 Tk.

6. Do you have any prior experience in using ICT?

☐ No   ☐ Yes

7. Number of employees engaged in your firm?

Full time: ——————————————————————————.

Part-time/casual——————————————————————

8. Number of computer literate employees engaged in your firm?

Computer specialist: ————————————————
(System analyst/programmer, etc.)

Computer operator: ————————————————————

General employees having computing skills:———————————

9. Percentage of employees who are involved with ICT use in your organisation? ——————————————————————————————

10. Please indicate the types of internet connectivity in your organisation:

☐ Dial-up/DSL   ☐ Broadband cable

☐ Mobile broadband ☐ Other (please specify).................

11. How long have you been connected to the internet?

———————————————————————————— Years.

12. Kindly state the monthly average expenditure on internet and online communications in your organisation:

Expenditure for Internet:————————————————————

Expenditure for homepage:———————————————————

Others (please specify):...

13. Do you employ any specialised employees for ICT operation and homepage management in your organisation?

☐ No   ☐ Yes   [if no go to question 15]

14. Please state the average monthly expenditure that you are incurring for salaries and other benefits to the specialised employees (Please give your best estimate)?

Salary————————————————————————————————————

Other benefit—————————————————————————————————

15. Please provide the total ICT investment/expenditure in your organisation (Please give your best estimates)?

ICT investment/expenditure in last year:———————————— Tk

ICT investment/expenditure in last three years:———————— Tk.

16. How many offices/sales centres/stores does your organisation have?

——————————————————————————————

17. Is your entire business setup located in the same region?

☐ No   ☐ Yes

18. Are your customers geographically dispersed?

☐ No   ☐ Yes

19. Is your company involved in international business operations?

☐ No   ☐ Yes

20. When did you start ICT operations in your organisation?

Year: ....

21. When was your company established?

Year: ....

22. Have you received any kind of privilege or benefits for your organisation as an SME?

☐ No   ☐ Yes

23. Have you received any grants or subsidies for ICT development in your organisation from any source?

☐ No   ☐ Yes

24. Does your organisation have 9001 or 14001 certification?

☐ No   ☐ Yes

25. Would you kindly state your annual turnover in the Year 2010−2011?

☐ Up to 200,000 Tk.   ☐ 200,001−500,000 Tk

☐ 500,001−1,000,000 Tk.

☐ 1,000,001−2,000,000 Tk.

☐ 2,000,001−5,000,000 Tk   ☐ 5,000,001−10,000,000 Tk.

☐ 10,000,000 Tk.

26. Are you operating online banking?

☐ No   ☐ Yes

27. Are you communicating with your regulatory authorities online?

☐ No   ☐ Yes

28. Are you communicating with your major customers online?

☐ No   ☐ Yes

29. Are you communicating with your major suppliers online?

☐ No   ☐ Yes

Questionnaire code

APPENDIX D

Surveyor code

গবেষণা প্রশ্নপত্র

সুপ্রিয় উত্তরদাতা,

এই জরীপ-কাজটি একটি একাডেমিক গবেষণা প্রকল্পের অংশ। সর্বস্তরে আই.সি.টি'র ব্যাপক প্রসারের লক্ষ্যে বাংলাদেশ সরকারের সাম্প্রতিক উদ্যোগের প্রেক্ষিতে দেশের ক্ষুদ্র ও মাঝারি শিল্পসমূহে আই.সি.টি ব্যবহারের প্রস্তুতি ও আকাংখ্যা এবং এর ফলাফল স্বরূপ সংস্থার সার্বিক পারফরমেন্স মূল্যায়নের জন্য এই গবেষণাটি প্রণীত হয়েছে। এই গবেষণার ফলাফল কার্টিন ইউনিভার্সিটি, অস্ট্রেলিয়া'র গ্রাজুয়েট স্কুল অব বিজনেস হ'তে পি-এইচ.ডি ডিগ্রীর জন্য রচিত থিসিসের ভিত রচনা করবে।

এই জরীপকাজে আপনার ভূমিকা একজন উত্তরদাতা হিসাবেসর্বোচ্চ আন্তরিকতা ও ধারনানুযায়ী প্রশ্নসমূহের উত্তর প্রদান করা। এখানে ভুল বা সঠিক উত্তর বলে কিছু নেই। সংশ্লিষ্ট ইস্যুতে আমরা শুধুমাত্র আপনার মতামত জানতে আগ্রহী।

আপনার উত্তর সমূহের কঠোর গোপনীয়তা রক্ষা করা হবে এবং কোনো অবস্থাতেই আপনার কিংবা আপনার সংগঠনের পরিচয় প্রকাশ করা হবে না। এই জরীপের ফলাফল সম্পূর্ণ একাডেমিক উদ্দেশ্যে ব্যবহৃত হবে। যাহোক,এই জরীপকাজে আপনার অংশগ্রহণ সম্পূর্ণই আপনার ইচ্ছাধীন। আপনি ইচ্ছে করলে এই গবেষণায় অংশ নিতে পারেন আবার যেকোনো সময় নিজেকে আলোচ্য গবেষণা থেকে সরিয়ে নিতে পারেন।

আপনার সুচিন্তিত মতামতসহ পূরণকৃত প্রশ্নপত্র সরাসরি, ডাকযোগে, ই-মেইল অথবা ফ্যাক্সের মাধ্যমে নিম্নঠিকানায়প্রেরণ করলে বাধিত হবো।

আপনার সহযোগিতা ও মূল্যবান মতামতের জন্য ধন্যবাদ।

বিনীত,
মোঃ শাহ্ আজম
ঠিকানা:

Md Shah Azam, PhD Candidate
Graduate School of Business, Curtin University
78 Murray Street, Perth 6000, Western Australia
Phone: +61-8-92881171 or +61-0432224840
Fax: +61-8-92663368
E-mail: mdshah.azam@postgrad.curtin.edu.au

গবেষণা প্রশ্নপত্র

উত্তরদাতার নাম: ....

সংস্থার নাম:..

ব্যবসার ধরন: (উৎপাদনকারি, সেবাদানকারি, পাইকার, খুচরা করবারী ইত্যাদি)

....

ব্যবসায় সেক্টর (গার্মেন্টস, লেদার, ট্যুরিজম, আই.সি.টি ইত্যাদি):.................................

ঠিকানা: ....

....

ফোন: .... ই–মেইল: ....

[অনুগ্রহকরে সঠিক ঘরে টিক √ চিহ্ন দিন]

- অনুগ্রহকরে সরকারি নথি বা রেজিস্ট্রেশন অনুযায়ী আপনার ব্যবসার আকার উল্লেখ করুন:

  ☐ ক্ষুদ্র ব্যবসা   ☐ মাঝারি ব্যবসা

  ☐ অন্যান্য (অনুগ্রহকরে বিস্তারিত উল্লেখ করুন).....................................

- বর্তমানে আপনারা কোনো ধরনের আই.সি.টি ব্যবহার করছেন কি?

  ☐ না   ☐ হ্যাঁ

বর্তমানে আপনার সংস্থায় নিম্নের কোন্ ধরনের আই.সি.টি ব্যবহার করছেন অনুগ্রহকরে তা নির্দেশ করুন:

☐ বেসিক কম্পিউটার অপারেশন

☐ ইন্টারনেট ও ই-মেইল

☐ হোম-পেজ (সাধারণ হোম-পেজ)

☐ ইন্টারেকটিভ হোম পেজ যা পণ্য ক্যাটালগিং ও অনলাইন অর্ডার প্রসেসিং-এ সক্ষম

☐ ইন্টারেকটিভ হোম-পেজ যা অনলাইন লেনদেন ও একাউন্ট ম্যানেজমেন্টে সক্ষম (ই-বিজনেস)

☐ সংগঠনের বাইরে ও ভিতরে সম্পূর্ণ ইলেকট্রনিক যোগাযাগ ও বিনিময় ব্যবস্থার
প্রবর্তন(ই.আর.পি/ডিজিটাইজেশন).

বর্তমানে আপনার সংস্থায় নিম্নের কোন্ ধরনের সফটওয়ার ব্যবহার করছেন অনুগ্রহ করে তা নির্দেশ করুন:

☐ বেসিক কম্পিউটিং সফটওয়্যার	☐ হিউম্যান রিসোর্স ম্যানেজমেন্ট
☐ ফাইন্যান্স/একাউন্টিংসফটওয়্যার	☐ সাপ্লাই চেইন ম্যানজমেন্ট
☐ ইনভেন্টরি ম্যানেজমেন্ট	☐ ই-কমার্স
☐ কাস্টমার রিলেশনস	☐ ম্যানেজমেন্টরিসোর্স প্ল্যানিং

অনুগ্রহ করে নিম্নোক্ত অভিব্যক্তিগুলো অনুধাবনকরে আপনার দৃষ্টিতে সঠিক সংখ্যাটি বৃত্তাকারে চিহ্নিত করুন

(বিঃদ্রঃ এই গবেষণাতে আই.সি.টি বলতে কম্পিউটার, কম্পিউটার নেটওয়ার্ক বা ইন্টারনেট ভিত্তিক টেকনোলজীকে বোঝানো হয়েছে)

Section A: আই.সি.টি সংক্রান্ত আপনার ধারনা (প্রত্যক্ষণ) নির্দেশকরুন
(যেখানে ১= সম্পূর্ণ ভিন্নমত পোষণ করি, ২= জোরালোভাবে ভিন্নমত পোষণ করি, ৩=ভিন্নমত পোষণ করি, ৪=ভিন্নমত বা একমত কোনোটাই নয়, ৫=একমতপোষণ করি, ৬=জোরালোভাবে একমত পোষণ করি, ৭=সম্পূর্ণএকমত পোষণ করি)

Perceived usefulness

ক.	আই.সি.টি'র ব্যবহার আমাদের প্রতিষ্ঠানের সার্বিক কার্যক্রমের জন্য জন্য খুবইকার্যকর	১	২	৩	8	৫
খ.	আই.সি.টির ব্যবহার আমাদের প্রতিষ্ঠানের সমুদয় কার্যক্রম দ্রুততার সাথে সম্পাদন করতে সক্ষম করেছে	১	২	৩	8	৫
গ.	আই.সি.টির ব্যবহার আমাদের প্রতিষ্ঠানের সার্বিক উৎপাদনশীলতা বৃদ্ধি করেছে	১	২	৩	8	৫
ঘ.	আই.সি.টি'র ব্যবহার আমাদের সংগঠনের উন্নয়নের বিভিন্নমুখী সুযোগ সৃষ্টি করেছে	১	২	৩	8	৫

Perceived ease of use

ক.	প্রতিষ্ঠানে আই.সি.টি'র বিভিন্ন ব্যবহার শেখা আমাদের জন্য খুবইসহজ	১	২	৩	8	৫
খ.	সংগঠনে আই.সি.টি'র প্রয়োগে যা যা করণীয় সে বিষয়ে আমাদের পূর্ণাঙ্গ ও স্বচ্ছ ধারনা আছে	১	২	৩	8	৫
গ.	আমরা খুব সহজেই সংগঠনের বিভিন্ন কার্যক্রমে আই.সি.টি'র ব্যবহারে দক্ষ হয়ে উঠেছি	১	২	৩	8	৫
ঘ.	প্রতিষ্ঠানে আই.সি.টি'র ব্যবহার খুবই সহজ বলে আমরা মনে করি	১	২	৩	8	৫

Section B: আপনার সংগঠনে আই.সি.টি'র ব্যবহার বা প্রয়োগেবাহ্যিক বিভিন্ন উপাদানের প্রভাব সম্পর্কে আপনার মূল্যায়ন নির্দেশ করুন
(যেখানে ১= সম্পূর্ণভাবে ভিন্নমত পোষণ করি, ২= ভিন্নমত পোষণ করি, ৩=ভিন্নমত বা একমত কোনোটাই নয়, ৪=একমতপোষণ করি, ৫=সম্পূর্ণ একমতপোষণ করি)

	Coercive pressure					
ক.	প্যারেন্ট কোম্পানির নির্দেশে আমরা আই.সি.টি'র ব্যবহার করছি	১	২	৩	৪	৫
খ.	প্রধান ক্রতাদের চাহিদা ও প্রয়োজনীয়তার প্রেক্ষিতে আমাদের আই.সি.টি'র ব্যবহার ছাড়া গত্যান্তর নেই	১	২	৩	৪	৫
গ.	প্রধান সরবরাহকারিদের চাহিদা ও প্রয়োজনীয়তারপ্রেক্ষিতে আমাদেরআই.সি.টি'র ব্যবহার ছাড়া গত্যান্তর নেই	১	২	৩	৪	৫
	Competitive pressure					
ক.	আমাদের সকল প্রতিযোগী প্রতিষ্ঠান ইতিধ্যেই আই.সি.টি'র ব্যবহার শুরু করেছে	১	২	৩	৪	৫
খ.	যেসমস্ত প্রতিযোগী প্রতিষ্ঠান আমাদের আগেআই.সি.টি'র ব্যবহার শুরু করেছে তারা নানাদিক থেকে আমাদের চেয়ে বেশীসুযোগ-সুবিধা ভোগ করছে	১	২	৩	৪	৫
	Normative pressure					
ক.	আমাদের ক্রেতারা আমাদের প্রতিষ্ঠানের সার্বিক কর্মকাণ্ডে আই.সি.টি'র প্রয়োগ করা উচিৎবলে মনে করে	১	২	৩	৪	৫
খ.	সরবরাহকারিরা আমাদেরপ্রতিষ্ঠানেরসার্বিক কর্মকাণ্ডেআই.সি.টি'র ব্যবহার প্রত্যাশা করে	১	২	৩	৪	৫
গ.	আমাদের ব্যবসায়িক পার্টনাররা আমাদের আই.সি.টি নির্ভরসার্বিক কর্মকাও প্রত্যাশা করে	১	২	৩	৪	৫
ঘ.	সংশ্লিষ্ট সরকারি নিয়ন্ত্রণকারি বা রেগুলেটরি সংস্হাসমূহ প্রত্যাশা করে আমাদের প্রতিষ্ঠানের সার্বিকআই.সি.টি নির্ভর কর্মকাও	১	২	৩	৪	৫

Global pressure

ক.	গ্লোবালাইজেশনের ফলে উদ্ভূত সুযোগসমূহ কাজে লাগাতে আমরা আই.সি.টি'র ব্যবহার শুরু করেছি	১	২	৩	৪	৫
খ.	বর্তমান সময়ে আই.সি.টি'র ব্যবহার ছাড়া কোনো প্রতিষ্ঠানের পক্ষেই টিকে থাকা সম্ভব নয় বলে মনে করি, বিধায় এর ব্যবহার শুরু করেছি	১	২	৩	৪	৫

Section C: আই.সি.টি'র ব্যবহারে প্রভাব বিস্তারকারি সংগঠনের নিম্নলিখিতউপাদানগুলো সম্পর্কে আপনার মূল্যায়ন নির্দেশ করুন
(যেখানে ১= সম্পূর্ণভাবে ভিন্নমত পোষণ করি, ২= ভিন্নমত পোষণ করি, ৩=ভিন্নমত বা একমত কোনোটাই নয়, ৪=একমতপোষণ করি, ৫=সম্পূর্ণ একমত পোষণ করি)

Facilitating condition

ক.	আমাদের সংগঠনের বিদ্যমান বিভিন্ন সিস্টেম ও কার্য প্রক্রিয়ার সাথে আই.সি.টি সামঞ্জস্যপূর্ণ (compatible)	১	২	৩	৪	৫
খ.	আই.সি.টি ব্যবহারে আমাদের কর্মীরা দক্ষ এবং উপযুক্ত	১	২	৩	৪	৫
গ.	এই টেকনোলজী ব্যবহারের জন্য প্রয়োজনীয় সকল সম্পদ (resource) আমাদের সংগঠনে বিদ্যমান	১	২	৩	৪	৫

Section D: সংগঠনের মালিক বা প্রধানের বৈশিষ্ট সম্পর্কে আপনার মতামত দিন
(যেখানে১= সম্পূর্ণভাবে ভিন্নমত পোষণ করি, ২= ভিন্নমত পোষণ করি, ৩=ভিন্নমত বা একমত কোনোটাই নয়, ৪=একমতপোষণ করি, ৫=সম্পূর্ণ একমত পোষণ করি)

Owner characteristics

ক.	একটা কাজ নতুনভাবে করতে তিনি প্রায়শই বড় ধরনের ঝুঁকি গ্রহন করেন	১	২	৩	৪	৫
খ.	সংগঠনের যেকোনো কাজের মূল ধারণা তাঁর মাথা থেকেই আসে	১	২	৩	৪	৫

Section E: রাষ্ট্র ও অন্যান্য সহযোগী শিল্পসমূহের অবকাঠামো সংক্রান্ত নিম্নলিখিত অভিব্যক্তিগুলো সম্পর্কে আপনার মূল্যায়ন নির্দেশ করুন

(যেখানে ১= সম্পূর্ণভাবে ভিন্নমত পোষণ করি, ২= ভিন্নমত পোষণ করি, ৩=ভিন্নমত বা একমত কোনোটাই নয়, ৪=একমতপোষণ করি, ৫=সম্পূর্ণ একমত পোষণ করি)

	Technology infrastructure					
ক.	ইন্টারনেট সেবা সহজলভ্য ও দেশব্যাপী সুবিস্তৃত	১	২	৩	৪	৫
খ.	দেশের ইন্টারনেট সার্ভিস উচ্চ-গতি সম্পন্ন ও সুলভ (high-speed and affordable)	১	২	৩	৪	৫
গ.	দেশে প্রয়োজনীয় হার্ডওয়ার ও এক্সেসরীজ সহজলভ্য ও সুলভ (available and affordable)	১	২	৩	৪	৫
ঘ.	বিদ্যুৎ সরবরাহ সহজলভ্য ও পর্যাপ্ত (available and adequate)	১	২	৩	৪	৫
	Human infrastructure					
ক.	দেশের সর্বস্তরে ব্যক্তি পর্যায়ে কম্পিউটার ব্যবহার ও ইন্টারনেট ভিত্তিক ব্যবসায় সংক্রান্ত জ্ঞান ও দক্ষতা সন্তোষজনক বলে মনে করি	১	২	৩	৪	৫
খ.	দেশের সর্বস্তরে প্রতিষ্ঠানিক পর্যায়ে কম্পিউটার ব্যবহার ও ইন্টারনেট ভিত্তিক ব্যবসায় সংক্রান্ত জ্ঞান ও দক্ষতা সন্তোষজনক বলে মনে করি	১	২	৩	৪	৫
ঙ.	দেশের সর্বস্তরে আই.সি.টি শিক্ষা বিস্তারে কম্পিউটার বিষয়ক শিক্ষা প্রতিষ্ঠানের সার্ভিস সহজলভ্য ও সুলভ (available and affordable)	১	২	৩	৪	৫
	Legal infrastructure					
ক.	আমাদের দেশের আইনগত পরিবেশ ডিজিটাল কমিউনিকেশন এবং ই-বিজনেসের জন্য সহায়ক বলে মনে করি	১	২	৩	৪	৫
খ.	আমাদের দেশের প্রচলিত আইন অনলাইন কনজুমার প্রটেকশনের জন্য কার্যকর বলে মনে করি	১	২	৩	৪	৫

Financial infrastructure

ক.	দেশের বিদ্যমান অনলাইন ব্যংকিং সুযোগ সুবিধা সমূহ আই.সি.টি নির্ভর ব্যবসায় পরিবেশ গঠনের জন্য পর্যাপ্ত বলে মনে করি	১	২	৩	৪	৫
খ.	দেশের সর্বস্তরে ক্রেডিট কিংবা ডেবিট কার্ড ব্যবহারের প্রবণতা (রেট) আই.সি.টি নির্ভর ব্যবসায় পরিবেশের জন্য পর্যাপ্ত বলে মনে করি	১	২	৩	৪	৫

Government policy and supports

ক.	সরকারের কর ও শুল্ক নীতিমালা দেশের ব্যবসায় পরিমন্ডলে আই.সি.টি'র বিস্তারে অত্যন্ত কার্যকর ভূমিকা রাখছে বলে মনে করি	১	২	৩	৪	৫
খ.	সরকারী প্রণোদনামূলক কর্মসূচিসমূহ (motivational programmes) ব্যবসায় পরিমন্ডলে আই.সি.টি'র বিস্তারে অত্যন্ত কার্যকর ভূমিকা রাখছে বলে মনে করি	১	২	৩	৪	৫
গ.	সরকারি অনুদান আমাদের সংগঠন এবং আমাদের মত ক্ষুদ্র ও মাঝারি ব্যবসায় প্রতিষ্ঠানসমূহে আই.সি.টি'র প্রয়োগ বা বিস্তারে বিশেষ কার্যকর ভূমিকা রেখেছে	১	২	৩	৪	৫
ঘ.	সরকারী ভর্তুকি আমাদের সংগঠন এবং আমাদের মত ক্ষুদ্র ও মাঝারি ব্যবসায় প্রতিষ্ঠানসমূহে আই.সি.টি'র প্রয়োগ বা বিস্তারে বিশেষ কার্যকর ভূমিকা রেখেছে	১	২	৩	৪	৫

Section F: সংস্কৃতি সংক্রান্ত নিম্নলিখিত অভিব্যক্তিগুলো সম্পর্কে আপনার মূল্যায়ন নির্দেশ করুন (যেখানে ১= সম্পূর্ণভাবে ভিন্নমত পোষণ করি, ২= ভিন্নমত পোষণ করি, ৩=ভিন্নমত বা একমত কোনোটাই নয়, ৪=একমত পোষণ করি, ৫=সম্পূর্ণ একমত পোষণ করি)

Power distance

ক.	কর্মীরা তাঁদের নেতাদের মান্য করে এবং বিনাবাক্য ব্যয়ে তাঁদের কার্যদেশ মেনে চলে	১	২	৩	৪	৫
খ.	উচ্চতর ব্যবস্থাপনা স্তরেই সকল ক্ষমতা কেন্দ্রীভূত	১	২	৩	৪	৫
গ.	কর্মীরা তাঁদের নেতাদের মান্য করবে এবং বিনা বাক্যব্যয়ে তাঁদের কার্যাদেশ মেনে চলবে, সেটাই প্রত্যাশিত হওয়া উচিৎ	১	২	৩	৪	৫
ঘ.	ব্যবস্থাপকের যেকোনো সিদ্ধান্তে অধঃস্তন কর্মীরা কোনো প্রকার প্রশ্ন করে না	১	২	৩	৪	৫

	Uncertainty avoidance					
ক.	ভবিষ্যত যেকোনো অনিশ্চিত পরিস্থিতির মোকাবেলার জন্য সংগঠনসমূহে নিয়মানুবর্তিতা ও সামঞ্জস্যপূর্ণ বিধিবিধান বিদ্যমান	১	২	৩	৪	৫
খ.	সংগঠন সমূহে চাকুরী সংক্রান্ত নির্দেশনা ও করনীয় বিশদভাবে প্রকাশিত হয় যার ফলে কর্মিরা তাদের করনীয় সম্পর্কে পরিপূর্ণভাবে অবগত হতে পারে	১	২	৩	৪	৫
	In group collectivism					
ক.	এই সমাজে, দলের সদস্যরা তাদের ম্যানেজারের ব্যক্তিগত অর্জনে গর্ববোধ করে	১	২	৩	৪	৫
খ.	দলের সদস্যদের ব্যক্তিগত অর্জনে ম্যানেজারেরা গর্ববোধ করে	১	২	৩	৪	৫
গ.	ব্যক্তিগত লক্ষ্যার্জন বাধাগ্রস্ত হলেও ম্যানেজারেরা দলীয় আনুগত্যকে উৎসাহিত করে	১	২	৩	৪	৫
	Bengali value					
ক.	এই সমাজে, মুখোমুখি যোগাযোগই (face to face)কর্মিদের দৈনন্দিন কার্যপ্রক্রিয়ার প্রধানতম যোগাযোগ পদ্ধতি	১	২	৩	৪	৫
খ.	যোগাযোগ এবং অনুভুতি প্রকাশের বাহন হিসাবে বাংলা ভাষায় যোগাযোগে কর্মিরা সাবলীল ও সাচ্ছন্দ বোধ করে	১	২	৩	৪	৫
গ.	কর্মিরা খুব ঘনিষ্ট এবং মজবুত সামাজিক সম্পর্ক বজায় রাখে	১	২	৩	৪	৫
	Ethical culture					
ক.	আমাদের সংগঠন এবং আমাদের মত আন্যান্য ক্ষুদ্র ও মাঝারি প্রতিষ্ঠানের বিভিন্ন কার্যক্রমে ঘুষএবংদুর্নীতি (bribe and corruption) বিদ্যমান বলে মনে করি	১	২	৩	৪	৫
খ.	আমাদের সংগঠন এবং আমাদের মতঅন্যান্য ক্ষুদ্র ও মাঝারি প্রতিষ্ঠানের বিভিন্ন কার্যক্রমে অনিয়ম, রাজনীতিকরণবা আত্মীয়করণ (politicisation or nepotism) বিদ্যমান	১	২	৩	৪	৫

Section G: প্রতিষ্ঠানে আই.সি.টি ব্যবহারসম্পর্কিত আপনাদের সুপ্ত আকাংখ্যা পূর্বেই উল্লেখ করেছেন, যা হতে পারে একান্তই কল্পনা প্রসূত। পারিপার্শ্বিক সামাজিক-সাংস্কৃতিক অবস্থা, দেশের অর্থনৈতিক ও আইনগত অবস্থা, এবং আপনার নিজস্ব ব্যক্তিগত ও প্রাতিষ্ঠানিক সক্ষমতা বিচার করে উক্ত আকাংখ্যা বাস্তব সম্মত নাও হতে পারে। অর্থনৈতিক, সামাজিক ও অন্যান্য পরিবেশগত বিষয়াদি বিবেচনা করেআই.সি.টি'র মাধ্যমে নিম্নলিখিত সাংগঠনিক কার্যক্রম সমূহসম্পাদনে উক্তসুপ্ত আকাংখ্যার বাস্তব রুপদান সংক্রান্ত আপনার ধারনা নির্দেশ করুন

(যেথানে ১= বর্তমান ব্যবহারকারি,২= ১ বৎসরের মধ্যে ব্যবহার করবো,৩=১-২ বৎসরের মধ্যে ব্যবহার করবো, ৪=২-৩ বৎসরের মধ্যে ব্যবহার করবো, ৫=অদুর ভবিষ্যতে ব্যবহার করা সম্ভব হবে না)

	Behavioural Expectation					
ক.	সাধারণ ব্যবহারকারি (কম্পিউটার ও ইন্টারনেট)	১	২	৩	৪	৫
খ.	ইন্টারনেট ও সাধারণ হোমপেজ (webpage) পরিচালনা	১	২	৩	৪	৫
গ.	ইন্টারনেট এবং অর্ডার-গ্রহন ও প্রসেসিং-এ সক্ষম হোমপেজ পরিচালনা	১	২	৩	৪	৫
ঘ.	ইন্টারনেট ও অনলাইন লেনদেন বা ই-কমার্স-এ সক্ষম হোমপেজ পরিচালনা	১	২	৩	৪	৫
ঙ.	আভ্যন্তরীন ও প্রতিষ্ঠানের বাইরের সকল কার্যক্রম ও যোগাযোগ কম্পিউটার প্রযুক্তির মাধ্যমে পরিচালনা (ই.আর.পি.)	১	২	৩	৪	৫

Section H: নিম্নলিখিত কার্যক্রম সমূহ সম্পাদনে আপনাদের প্রতিষ্ঠানে আই.সি.টিব্যবহারের ধরন নির্দেশ করুন

(যেথানে ১=কখনোই ব্যবহার করি না, ২= মাঝে মধ্যে ব্যবহার করি, ৩= প্রায়শঃই ব্যবহার করি, ৪=ঘন ঘন ব্যবহার করি এবং ৫=খুবই ঘন ঘন ব্যবহার করি)

	ICT Use					
ক.	সাধারণ ব্যবহারকারি (কম্পিউটার ও ইন্টারনেট)	১	২	৩	৪	৫
খ.	ইন্টারনেট ও সাধারণ হোমপেজ (webpage) পরিচালনা	১	২	৩	৪	৫
গ.	ইন্টারনেট এবং অর্ডার-গ্রহন ও প্রসেসিং-এ সক্ষম হোমপেজ পরিচালনা	১	২	৩	৪	৫
ঘ.	ইন্টারনেট ও অনলাইন লেনদেন বা ই-কমার্স-এ সক্ষম হোমপেজ পরিচালনা	১	২	৩	৪	৫
ঙ.	আভ্যন্তরীন ও প্রতিষ্ঠানের বাইরের সকল কার্যক্রম ও যোগাযোগ কম্পিউটার প্রযুক্তির মাধ্যমে পরিচালনা (ই.আর.পি.)	১	২	৩	৪	৫

Section I: আপনার প্রতিষ্ঠানে আই.সি.টি ইন্টিগ্রেশনের স্তর সম্পর্কে মূল্যায়ন করুন
(যেখানে ১= সম্পূর্ণ ভিন্নমত পোষণ করি, ২= জোরালোভাবে ভিন্নমত পোষণ করি, ৩=ভিন্নমত পোষণ করি, ৪=ভিন্নমত বা একমত কোনোটাই নয়, ৫=একমতপোষণ করি, ৬=জোরালোভাবে একমত পোষণ করি, ৫=সম্পূর্ণ একমত পোষণ করি)

	Level of Integration					
ক.	আমরা সংগঠনের সকল কার্যক্রমে আই.সি.টি'র ব্যবহার করছি	১	২	৩	৪	৫
খ.	সংগঠনের সকল বিভাগ এবং কার্যক্রম একটি সিস্টেমের অধীনে ইন্টিগ্রেটেড	১	২	৩	৪	৫
গ.	ক্রেতা সেবা এবং অন্যান্য সম্মুখ-অফিস কার্যক্রম পরিচালনার জন্য আমাদের ওয়েবসাইটটি তৈরী করা হয়েছে যা তথ্য সেবা দিতে সক্ষম	১	২	৩	৪	৫
ঘ.	আমাদের ওয়েব এপ্লিকেশনসমূহ ব্যাক অফিস এবং ডাটাবেজের সাথে ইন্টিগ্রেটেড	১	২	৩	৪	৫
ঙ.	প্রতিষ্ঠানের ডাটাবেজসমূহ সাপ্লাইয়ার এবং পার্টনারদের ডাটাবেজের সাথে ইলেক্ট্রনিক্যালি ইন্টিগ্রেটেড	১	২	৩	৪	৫

Section J: আপনার প্রতিষ্ঠানে নিম্নলিখিত ক্ষেত্রে কার্যকরভাবে আই.সি.টি প্রয়োগের স্তর নির্দেশ করুন
(যেখানে ১= আই.সি.টি'র কোনোরূপ প্রয়োগ নাই, ২= ২০% কার্যক্রম আই.সি.টি নির্ভর,৩= ২০%-৫০% কার্যক্রম আই.সি.টি নির্ভর, ৪=৫০%- ৮০% কার্যক্রম আই.সি.টি নির্ভর, ৫= ৮০% এর অধিক কার্যক্রম আই.সি.টি'র মাধ্যমে সম্পাদন করা হয়)

	Degree of utilisation					
ক.	উৎপাদন ও সেবা সংক্রান্ত কার্যক্রম	১	২	৩	৪	৫
খ.	প্রশাসন ও হিসাব সংক্রান্ত কার্যক্রম	১	২	৩	৪	৫
গ.	বিক্রয় ও মার্কেটিং সংক্রান্ত কার্যক্রম	১	২	৩	৪	৫

Section K: আই.সি.টি ব্যবহারের ফলে নিম্নলিখিত প্রেক্ষিত সমূহে আপনার প্রতিষ্ঠানের পারফরমেন্স সম্পর্কে আপনার মূল্যায়ন নির্দেশ করুন
(যেখানে ১=১০% এর অধিক কমেছে, ২= ৫%-১০% কমেছে, ৩=২%-৫% কমেছে, ৪= মোটামুটি স্থিতিশীল (±২%), ৫= ২%-৫% বেড়েছে, ৬= ৫%-১০% বেড়েছে,৭= ১০% এর অধিক বেড়েছে)

	Competitiveness					
ক.	সার্বিক বিক্রয় এলাকা	১	২	৩	৪	৫
খ.	ক্রেতা-সম্পর্ক ও ক্রেতা সেবা	১	২	৩	৪	৫
গ.	প্রতিযোগিতামূলক অবস্থান	১	২	৩	৪	৫
	Internal operation					
ক.	কর্ম প্রক্রিয়ায় স্বচ্ছতা (transparency in process)	১	২	৩	৪	৫
খ.	কর্ম প্রক্রিয়ায় শৃংখলা ও পদ্ধতিগত উৎকর্ষতা	১	২	৩	৪	৫
গ.	কর্মীদের উৎপাদনশীলতা	১	২	৩	৪	৫
	Financial performance					
ক.	সার্বিক কার্যক্রম (overall performance)	১	২	৩	৪	৫
খ.	লাভ (profit)	১	২	৩	৪	৫
গ.	বিক্রয় (sales)	১	২	৩	৪	৫

ডেমোগ্রাফিক প্রশ্ন

১.অনুগ্রহ করে আপনার প্রাতিষ্ঠানিক ভূমিকা নির্দেশ করুন:

☐ মালিক   ☐ ব্যবস্থাপক(ICT)   ☐ ব্যবস্থাপক(general)   ☐ কর্মচারী (ICT)

☐ কর্মচারী(general)   ☐ অন্যান্য(অনুগ্রহ করে উল্লেখ করুন) ....

২.আপনার বয়স গ্রুপ?

☐ ২৫ বৎসরের কম, ☐ ২৫-৩৪বৎসর, ☐৩৫-৪৪বৎসর,

☐ ৪৫-৬০বৎসর,   ☐ ৬০বৎসরের অধিক

৩.আপনার জেন্ডার? ☐পুরুষ   ☐ মহিলা

৪.অনুগ্রহ করে আপনার শিক্ষাগত অর্জন নির্দেশ করুন:

☐ স্নাতেকাত্তর,   ☐ স্নাতক,   ☐এইচ.এস.সি,   ☐এস.সি,

☐ প্রাইমারি,   ☐ সাক্ষর জ্ঞান,   ☐ অন্যান্য(অনুগ্রহ করে উল্লেখ করুন).................

৫.আপনার মাসিক আয়:

☐ ২০,০০০ টাকার কম   ☐২০,০০০-৩০,০০০ টাকা   ☐৩০,০০০-৫০,০০০ টাকা

☐ ৫০,০০০-৭০,০০০ টাকা,   ☐৭০,০০০-১,০০,০০০ টাকা   ☐১,০০,০০০ টাকার অধিক

৬.আই.সি.টি'র ব্যবহার সংক্রান্ত আপনার কোনোরুপ পূর্ব অভিজ্ঞতা আছে কি?

☐ না   ☐হ্যাঁ

৭.আপনার প্রতিষ্ঠানে নিয়োজিত শ্রমিক কর্মীর সংখ্য?

ফুল টাইম: -------------------------.

পার্ট টাইম/ক্যাসুয়াল:------------------------------

৮.আপনার প্রতিষ্ঠানে কম্পিউটার লিটারেট কর্মীর সংখ্যা?

কম্পিউটার বিশেষজ্ঞ: --

(সিস্টেম এনালিস্ট/কম্পিউটার প্রোগ্রামার ইত্যাদি)

কম্পিউটার অপারেটর: --

সাধারণ কর্মচারী কিন্তু কম্পিউটার জ্ঞান আছে এমন কর্মির সংখ্যা:--------------------

৯. আপনার প্রতিষ্ঠানের কত পারসেন্ট কর্মী আই.সি.টি ব্যবহারের সাথে সম্পৃক্ত?

----

১০. অনুগ্রহ করে আপনার প্রতিষ্ঠানের ইন্টারনেট সংযোগের ধরন নির্দেশ করুন:

☐ ডায়াল-আপ/ ডি.এস.এল   ☐ ব্রডব্যান্ড (ক্যাবল)   ☐ মোবাইল ব্রডব্যান্ড

☐ অন্যান্য (অনুগ্রহ করে উল্লেখ করুন)..............

১১. আপনি ব্যক্তিগতভাবে কতদিন ইন্টারনেট ব্যবহার করছেন?

....বৎসর

১২.অনুগ্রহকরে আপনার প্রতিষ্ঠানের ইন্টারনেট বা আনলাইন যোগাযোগেরমাসিক গড় খরচ উল্লেখ করুন:

ইন্টারনেট বাবদ গড়ে খরচ:..

হোম-পেজ বাবদ খরচ:--------------------------------------

অন্যান্য (অনুগ্রহ করে উল্লেখ করুন):..

১৩.আপনার প্রতিষ্ঠানের আই.সি.টি কিংবা হোম-পেজ পরিচালনার জন্য কোনো বিশেষজ্ঞ কর্মী নিয়োগ করেছেন কি?

☐ না   ☐ হ্যাঁ

[উত্তর না হলে ১৫ নং প্রশ্নে গমন করুন]

১৪.উক্ত বিশেষজ্ঞ কর্মীদের বেতন বা অন্যান্য ভাতা বাবদ মাসেক কত টাকা খরচ করছেন অনুগ্রহ করে তা উল্লেখ করুন

বেতন ও অন্যান্য ভাতা বাবদ:--

১৫. অনুগ্রহ করে আপনার প্রতিষ্ঠানের মোট বিনিয়োগ/খরচ উল্লেখ করুন (আপনার ধারনা থেকেই উত্তর করুন)?

আই.সি.টি বিনিয়োগ/খরচ (গত বৎসর):..টাকা

আই.সি.টি বিনিয়োগ/খরচ (গত ৩ বৎসর):.. টাকা

১৬. আপনার প্রতিষ্ঠানের অফিস/বিক্রয়কেন্দ্র/স্টোরের সংখ্যা?

----

১৭. আপনার সার্বিক ব্যবসায় একই অঞ্চলে আবস্থিত কি?

☐ না   ☐ হ্যাঁ

১৮. আপনাদের ক্রেতাগণ আঞ্চলিকভাবে আপনাদের থেকে বিচ্ছিন্ন কি?

☐ না   ☐ হ্যাঁ

১৯. আপনার প্রতিষ্ঠান আন্তর্জাতিক ব্যবসায়ের সাথে জড়িত কি?

☐ না   ☐ হ্যাঁ

২০. আপনার প্রতিষ্ঠানে কবে আই.সি.টি'র ব্যবহার শুরু করেছেন?

বছর: ....

২১. আপনার প্রতিষ্ঠান কবে প্রতিষ্ঠিত হয়েছে?

বছর: ....

২২. ক্ষুদ্র ও মাঝারী শিল্প (এস.এম.ই) হিসাবে আপনার প্রতিষ্ঠানের জন্য কোনো ধরনের অগ্রাধিকার বা বেনিফিট গ্রহণ করেছেন কি?

☐ না   ☐ হ্যাঁ

২৩. আপনার প্রতিষ্ঠানের আই.সি.টি'র উন্নয়নের জন্য কোনোপ্রকার অনুদান বা ভর্তুকি গ্রহন করেছেন কি?

☐ না   ☐ হ্যাঁ

২৪. আপনার প্রতিষ্ঠান ৯০০০ বা ১৪০০১ সার্টিফাইড সংস্থা কি?

☐ না   ☐ হ্যাঁ

২৫.অনুগ্রহকরে আপনার প্রতিষ্ঠানের২০১০-২০১১ (গত অর্থ বছর) অর্থ বছরের আয় নির্দেশ করুন:

☐ ২০ লক্ষ টাকার কম   ☐ ২০-৫০ লক্ষ টাকা   ☐ ৫০ লক্ষ-১ কোটি টাকা

☐ ১-৫ কোটি টাকা   ☐ ৫-১০ কোটি টাকা   ☐ ১০-২০ কোটি টাকা

☐ ২০ কোটি টাকার বেশী

২৬. আপনারা অনলাইন ব্যাংকিং অপারেশন করছেন কি?

☐ না   ☐ হ্যাঁ

২৭. আপনারা সংশ্লিষ্ট রেগুলেটরী অথরিটির সাথে অনলাইনে যোগাযোগ করেন কি?

☐ না   ☐ হ্যাঁ

২৮. আপনার প্রতিষ্ঠানের প্রধান ক্রেতাদের সাথে অনলাইনে যোগাযোগ করেন কি?

☐ না   ☐ হ্যাঁ

২৯.আপনার প্রতিষ্ঠানের প্রধান সাপ্লাইয়ারদের সাথে অনলাইনে যোগাযোগ করেন কি?
☐ না   ☐ হ্যাঁ

APPENDIX E

Table E1.   Decision Rules for Formative or Reflective Measurements.

	Formative Model	Reflective Model
1. Direction of causality from construct to measure implied by the conceptual definition	Direction of causality is from items to construct	Direction of causality is from construct to items
Are the indicators (items) (a) defining characteristics or (b) manifestations of the construct?	Indicators are defining characteristics of the construct	Indicators are manifestations of the construct
Would changes in the indicators/items cause changes in the construct or not?	Changes in the indicators should cause changes in the construct	Changes in the indicator should not cause changes in the construct
Would changes in the construct cause changes in the indicators?	Changes in the construct do not cause changes in the indicators	Changes in the construct do cause changes in the indicators
2. Interchangeability of the indicators/items	Indicators need not be interchangeable	Indicators should be interchangeable
Should the indicators have the same or similar content?	Indicators need not have the same or similar content	Indicators should have the same or similar content theme
Do the indicators share a common theme?	Indicators need not share a common theme	Indicators should share a common theme
Would dropping one of the construct indicators alter the conceptual domain of the construct?	Dropping an indicator may alter the conceptual domain of the construct	Dropping an indicator should not alter the conceptual domain of theconstruct
3. Covariation among the indicators	Not necessary for indicators to covary with each other	Indicators are expected to covary with each other
Should a change in one of the indicators be associated with changes in the other indicators?	Not necessarily	Yes
4. Nomological net of the construct indicators	Nomological net for the indicators may differ	Nomological net for the indicators should not differ
Are the indicators/items expected to have the same antecedents and consequences?	Indicators are not required to have the same antecedents and consequences	Indicators are required to have the same antecedents and consequences

Source: Jarvis et al. (2003).

ACRONYMS

AGFI	Adjusted goodness-of-fit index
AVE	Average variance extracted
B2B	Business to business
BBS	Bangladesh Bureau of Statistics
BDT	Bangladeshi Taka
BGMEA	Bangladesh Garment Manufacturers and Exporters Association
BKMEA	Bangladesh Knitwear Manufacturers and Exporters Association
CAIC	Comprehensive Akaike information criteria
CATI	Computer-aided telephone interview
CBIS	Computer-based information systems
CBSEM	Covariance-based structural equation modelling
CEO	Chief Executive Officer
CFI	Comparative fit index
CIS	Commonwealth of Independent States
C-TAM-TPB	Combined TAM and TPB
DOI	Diffusion of innovation
DSS	Decision support system
DTPB	Decomposed theory of planned behaviour
EB	Electronic business
ECaTT	Electronic Commerce and Telework Trends
EDI	Electronic data interchange
ERP	Enterprise resource planning
GDP	Gross domestic product
GLOBE	Global Leadership and Organisational Behaviour Effectiveness
GoF	Goodness of fit
GSS	Group support system
HOTE	Human, organisation, technology and environment
HOT-fit	Human, organisation and technology fit
ICT	Information and communications technology
IFI	Incremental fit index
IS	Information systems
IT	Information technology
ITRC	Information Technology Research Cell
ITU	International Telecommunication Union
LDCs	Least developed countries
LLMEB	Leather and Footwear Manufacturers and Exporters Association of Bangladesh
MDG	Millennium Development Goals
ML	Maximum likelihood
MM	Motivational model
MPCU	Model of PC utilisation
NFI	Normed fit index
PLS	Partial least squares
PLS-SEM	Partial least squares-based structural equation modelling
RBV	Resource-based view
RMG	Ready-made garments

RMSEA	Root mean square error of approximation
SCCS	Supply chain communication systems
SCT	Social cognitive theory
SEA-ME-WE	South East Asia, Middle East and West Europe
SEM	Structural equation modelling
SME	Small and medium-sized enterprise
SPSS	Statistical package for the social sciences
TAM	Technology acceptance model
TOE	Technology, organisation and environment
TPB	Theory of planned behaviour
TRA	Theory of reasoned action
UK	United Kingdom
UNCTAD	United Nations Conference on Trade and Development
USA	United States of America
UTAUT	Unified theory of acceptance and use of technology
VAF	Variance accounted for
VIF	Variance inflation factor
WB	World Bank
WSIS	World Summit on the Information Society

TOWARD A COMPREHENSIVE CONCEPTUALIZATION OF DIGITAL DIVIDE AND ITS IMPACT ON E-GOVERNMENT SYSTEM SUCCESS

Arief Rahman

ABSTRACT

Citizens are substantial stakeholders in every e-government system, thus their willingness to use and ability to access the system are critical. Unequal access and information and communication technology usage, which is known as digital divide, however has been identified as one of the major obstacles to the implementation of e-government system. As digital divide inhibits citizen's acceptance to e-government, it should be overcome despite the lack of deep theoretical understanding on this issue. This research aimed to investigate the digital divide and its direct impact on e-government system success of local governments in Indonesia as well as indirect impact through the mediation role of trust. In order to get a comprehensive understanding of digital

E-Services Adoption: Processes by Firms in Developing Nations
Advances in Business Marketing & Purchasing, Volume 23A, 291–488
ISSN: 1069-0964/doi:10.1108/S1069-096420150000023003

divide, this study introduced a new type of digital divide, the innovativeness divide.

The research problems were approached by applying two-stage sequential mixed method research approach comprising of both qualitative and quantitative studies. In the first phase, an initial research model was proposed based on a literature review. Semi-structured interview with 12 users of e-government systems was then conducted to explore and enhance this initial research model. Data collected in this phase were analyzed with a two-stage content analysis approach and the initial model was then amended based on the findings. As a result, a comprehensive research model with 16 hypotheses was proposed for examination in the second phase.

In the second phase, quantitative method was applied. A questionnaire was developed based on findings in the first phase. A pilot study was conducted to refine the questionnaire, which was then distributed in a national survey resulting in 237 useable responses. Data collected in this phase were analyzed using Partial Least Square based Structural Equation Modeling.

The results of quantitative analysis confirmed 13 hypotheses. All direct influences of the variables of digital divide on e-government system success were supported. The mediating effects of trust in e-government in the relationship between capability divide and e-government system success as well as in the relationship between innovativeness divide and e-government system success were supported, but was rejected in the relationship between access divide and e-government system success. Furthermore, the results supported the moderating effects of demographic variables of age, residential place, and education.

This research has both theoretical and practical contributions. The study contributes to the developments of literature on digital divide and e-government by providing a more comprehensive framework, and also to the implementation of e-government by local governments and the improvement of e-government Readiness Index of Indonesia.

Keywords: Digital divide; e-government; mixed methods; local government; Indonesia

1. INTRODUCTION

1.1. Overview

E-government refers to the use of information and communication technology (ICT) which enhances access to and delivery of all facets of government services and operations for the benefit of citizens, business, employees, and other stakeholders (Srivastava & Teo, 2007). Most countries in the world have implemented e-government, but its success rate in developing/transitional countries is only 15% (Heeks, 2008b). The critical factor determining the success of e-government is users' acceptance (Evans & Yen, 2005).

However, economic and social disparity in the world today is leading to what is known as the digital divide, or digital inequality. The digital divide refers to the gap between individuals, households, businesses, and geographic areas at different socioeconomic levels, with regard to the opportunities to access ICT and the opportunity to use them in a wide variety of activities (OECD, 2001). Despite the lack of empirical evidence (Pascual, 2003; UN, 2005), the digital divide is acknowledged to be one of the main obstacles to the success of the e-government system.

This research examines the impact of the digital divide on the success of e-government systems in the local government at Indonesia. In doing so, this study applies two-stage mixed methods research, where a field study is conducted in the first stage and data are collected from interviews. The data are then analyzed and compared with the available literature to build a comprehensive research model. This model is then examined using the Partial Least Square (PLS) approach to Structural Equation Modeling (SEM) in the second stage, where data are collected via survey.

This study begins with an introduction to the issues under study and the research objectives. It is followed by an extensive literature review and a detailed outline of research methodologies. The data collected in the field study are analyzed and the results presented along with the development of the hypotheses and instruments used for the survey. The results of the quantitative data analysis on 237 respondents participating in the survey are presented, followed by interpretation and discussion. The study concludes with a summary of the study and its limitations, along with suggestions for future research.

1.2. Research Background

The phenomenon of the digital divide has been one of the most popular topics for many researchers and policy makers since the late 1990s, as all countries worldwide have experienced the divide to some extent. Even in well-developed countries as the United States, the problem of the digital divide, or digital inequality, is still evident (Hsieh, Rai, & Keil, 2008; Mossberger, Tolbert, & McNeal, 2008; Venkatesh & Morris, 2000). Considering the importance of ICT in today's world, attempts have been made to understand and explain this phenomenon. Initially, the digital divide was defined as the inequality between those who have access to ICT and those who do not (De Haan, 2004; DiMaggio, Hargittai, Neuman, & Robinson, 2001). Policy makers in many countries then used this definition as a basis for increasing public access to computers and basic ICTs in schools and public places. In the United States, former President Bill Clinton proposed a tax incentive to businesses to donate computers to poor schools and communities (Lacey, 2000). Some worldwide corporations also initiated a home-computer benefit for their employees who did not have computers (Atewell, 2001).

Despite the policies and efforts to close the access gap, the UN has indicated that the digital divide has not diminished; in fact it is growing wider (UN, 2010). Some scholars have argued that the understanding of the digital divide at that time was not comprehensive enough, and it led to insufficient policies. In light of this, Dewan and Riggins (2005) suggested that there are two orders of digital divide; the first order refers to the access divide, while the second order refers to the ability divide, which is an inequality in ability to use ICT among those who already have access. Furthermore, Wei, Teo, Chan, and Tan (2011) asserted that there is a third order of digital divide, the outcome divide, which is an inequality of the outcomes of exploiting ICT resulting from the first and second order digital divides. Regardless of the differences around defining the digital divide, it is clear that a comprehensive understanding of the issue is needed.

1.3. E-Government in Indonesia

The Government of Indonesia comprises a central government and 497 local governments (regencies and municipalities). Since 1999, Indonesia has entered a decentralization era, in which regencies and municipalities have become the key administrative units responsible for the provision of most government services (Amri, 2000). Laws 22/1999 and 25/1999 provide regulatory frameworks for decentralization. In accordance with these laws, local government plays a significant role in Indonesia's public administration.

E-government in Indonesia has been established since 2001 through Presidential Directive No. 6/2001 (Harijadi & Satriya, 2000; Haryono & Widiwardono, 2010). The objectives of e-government in Indonesia are to improve democratic process, enhance accountability and transparency, and enable the transformation toward an information society (Furuholt & Wahid, 2008). Currently, there are approximately 450 websites managed by local governments throughout Indonesia (Wahid, 2008). Local government in Indonesia has implemented some forms of e-government systems, most of which are in the form of the electronic systems used for its internal processes (G2G – Government to Government). Moreover, many local governments, departments, and government agencies have produced websites in order to interact with their stakeholders (G2C – Government to Citizens and G2B – Government to Businesses).

Another form of e-government commonly found in Indonesia is the one-stop service, also known to some organizations as the "one-roof service." One-Stop Service is an integrated service provided by an umbrella organization, which operates on top of functional government agencies in order to improve the convenience and satisfaction of users (Ho, 2002). One-Stop Service is a gateway for the government to provide information and services to citizens and businesses. It coordinates with functional departments and government agencies to deliver public services. Since 2003, some local governments have established One-Stop Service centers, although the range of services delivered varies from one local government to another. The driver in the One-Stop Service is basically the simplification of the bureaucratic process by providing for the various needs of citizens and other stakeholders (Ho, 2002). According to the survey of e-government readiness by the United Nations, Indonesia's ranks and e-government indices reflect an unsuccessful implementation of e-government in the country in comparison to other countries (illustrated in Table 1). It is evident that Indonesia requires a strategic policy in order to improve the quality of e-government, and underlying this must be a readiness to implement e-government.

The implementation of e-government in Indonesia is facing some challenges (Harijadi, 2004), which include: lack of financial resources, low quality of human resources, low ICT penetration, and lack of regulation and culture. Furthermore, a study by Hwang and Syamsuddin revealed some other main obstacles to the development of e-government in Indonesia, particularly at the local government level, where there exists

Table 1. United Nations Survey on E-Government Readiness (Selected Countries and Region).

Countries	2005[a]		2008[b]		2010[c]		2012[d]	
	Rank	Index	Rank	Index	Rank	Index	Rank	Index
Indonesia	96	0.382	106	0.411	109	0.403	97	0.495
Australia	6	0.868	8	0.811	8	0.786	12	0.839
USA	1	0.906	4	0.864	2	0.851	5	0.869
Malaysia	43	0.571	34	0.606	32	0.610	40	0.670
Thailand	46	0.552	64	0.503	76	0.465	92	0.509
Vietnam	105	0.364	91	0.456	90	0.445	83	0.522
South Eastern Asia average		0.439		0.429		0.425		0.479
World average		0.427		0.451		0.441		0.488

[a]UN (2005).
[b]UN (2008).
[c]UN (2010).
[d]UN (2012).

technical difficulties, the digital divide, and the absence of willingness to use e-government systems by citizens and government employees alike (Hwang & Syamsuddin, 2008).

1.4. Focus of the Research

Norris (2001) believes that the digital divide reflects social inequality. Therefore, to understand the digital divide, the issue requires contextualizing. In developing countries, where most social and cultural aspects are unequal, the perspective taken on the digital divide requires expansion. In order to obtain a comprehensive understanding of the issue, this research categorizes the digital divide into five types, being: *access divide* (disparity of access to ICT), *economic divide* (disparity in access to ICT associated with economic conditions), *demographic divide* (differences in individual characteristics of the population such as age and place of residence – which affects access to ICT), *capability divide* (inequality of ability to use ICT), and *innovativeness divide* (disparities between individual willingness to change and try out new information technology).

DeLone and McLean had developed a model to examine information system (IS) success (DeLone & McLean, 1992), which was later updated (DeLone & McLean, 2003). This model has been validated in the area of e-commerce, where it was originally developed (Gelderman, 1998; Lee & Chung, 2009) and in the area of e-government (Teo, Srivastava, & Jiang, 2009; Wang & Liao, 2008). Based on the study by Ruttan (1996), the model is robust and outperformed the other IS success model. Therefore this study adopts this model to measure IS success (especially, e-government system success).

The updated model indicates that IS success depends on IS quality (Information Quality, System Quality, and Service Quality), which influences system usage and user satisfaction, and in turn benefits the user. Thus, the framework by DeLone and McLean basically consists of two parts, one is the quality of the product (System Quality, Information Quality, and Service Quality) and the other is the effectiveness or influence of the product (use, user satisfaction, and impact or net benefit) (Mason, 1978). Moreover, DeLone and McLean state that "use," "user satisfaction," and "benefit" are the important indicators of system success; some researchers have previously used them individually to measure system success (DeLone & McLean, 1992).

Previous researchers have also modified the DeLone and McLean model to accord with the focus of their research. Lee and Chung (2009) have modified the model to incorporate trust in their research. Floropoulos, Spathis, Halvatzis, and Tsipouridou (2010) have also modified the model in order to include Perceived Usefulness. The research undertaken here applies the DeLone and McLean framework with an emphasis on the effectiveness or influence of the system, as system success cannot be claimed if the system doesn't influence its users despite its good quality. Hence, this research modifies the original model by focusing on usage, user satisfaction, and benefit as indicators of system success, excluding the quality of the system itself, as it is beyond the control of the user.

In the area of ICT, the quality or attribute of trust is seen as an important factor in ICT use (McKnight & Chervany, 2002; Teo et al., 2009; Vance, Elie-Dit-Cosaque, & Straub, 2008). The cognitive process in the formation of trust has been shown to positively influence an individual's intention to use e-commerce (Gefen, Karahanna, & Straub, 2003; McKnight & Chervany, 2002). With the e-government system in particular, the trust of a citizen is believed to be important in the use of e-government, especially when use of the system is voluntary (Teo et al., 2009; Warkentin, Gefen, Pavlou, & Rose, 2002). In the context of the e-government system, trust in e-government refers to the "belief that the e-government system can be used to get the desired outcome satisfactorily" (Teo et al., 2009). Teo et al. (2009) found that trust in e-government influences e-government quality (information, system, and service) significantly.

This study examines the impact of the digital divide on the success of e-government both directly and indirectly, through the mediating role of trust in e-government. In doing so, the focus of this research is examining interactive and voluntary G2C and G2B systems provided by local government in Indonesia. The reasons for using trust in e-government as a mediating variable are threefold: first, from a sociological perspective, trust is an important factor on which various sets of expectations converge in order to reduce social complexity (Gefen, 2000; Lewis & Weigert, 1985). Second, trust has been recognized as acting as a mediating variable in many disciplines, including behavioral intention in management (Cropanzano & Mitchell, 2005; Vlachos, Tsamakos, Vrechopoulos, & Avramidis, 2009), and marketing and consumer loyalty (Morgan & Hunt, 1994; Sirdeshmukh, Singh, & Sabol, 2002). Third, a citizen's trust in e-government system is an important contributing factor in the success of e-government (Teo et al., 2009). In a voluntary e-government system, the building of citizen trust is often considered as a key success factor (Warkentin et al., 2002).

1.5. Research Questions and Objectives

Empirical evidence on the impact of the digital divide on the success of e-government systems is currently lacking. Despite of its popularity among researchers, the issue of the digital divide itself is not yet understood comprehensively, as evidenced by the limitations and gaps in the literature on the digital divide. Apart from the digital divide, the mediating role of trust in e-government success has been identified, although, as yet it has not been validated. Hence, this chapter aims to answer two main research questions. What is the impact of the digital divide on e-government system success in Indonesian local government? Does trust in e-government mediate in the relationship between the digital divide and e-government system success in Indonesian local government?

Based on the research questions above, the objectives of this research include the following actions: to examine the impact of the digital divide on e-government system success in Indonesian local government; to investigate the relationships between the digital divide constructs; to investigate the mediating role of trust in e-government in the impact of the digital divide on e-government system success in Indonesian local government; and to assess the moderating impact of the demographic and economic divide on e-government system success in Indonesian local government.

1.6. Significance of the Research

The development of e-government is one of the biggest trends in public sector management (McKinnon, 2005); however, extensive research on this issue has not been conducted. This research aims to provide empirical evidence and hence contributes significantly to the understanding of e-government and the role of the digital divide in e-government. In doing so, the study will: First, provide evidence of the impact of the digital divide on e-government system success in developing countries, particularly Indonesia. Since empirical evidence on the influence of digital divide on e-government system success is currently lacking, the results of this research will contribute to IS research. For practical implications, this study provides basis for policy formulation to improve e-government readiness.

Second, on the theoretical side, this study will categorize five types of the digital divide in order to understand and conceptualize it in a more comprehensive manner. By understanding the issue of digital divide more comprehensively, the policy makers will be able to develop and implement comprehensive strategies to resolve it. The model on digital divide in this study extends the previous model by Dewan and Riggins (2005) and Wei et al. (2011), which also aims to contribute to the theoretical understanding of this issue.

Third, the study will bring in "trust in e-government" as a mediating variable affecting the impact of the digital divide on e-government system success. In terms of the contributions to research development, this study is significant since the concept of trust has been discussed within many disciplines, including psychology, sociology, economics, and organization theory. This has resulted in a body of research that is widely divergent and at times contradictory (Goldfinch, 2007; Kelton, Fleischmann, & Wallace, 2007). In the area of ISs, trust has also been discussed, resulting in disagreements among researchers as to whether discussing trust is either necessary or appropriate (Gefen, Benbasat, & Pavlou, 2008). By examining the mediating role of trust in e-government in the influence of digital divide on e-government system success, this study aims to provide an insight for research in ISs. The findings aim to enrich the theoretical understanding of trust in e-government in particular and in the information technology (IT) area in general. The comprehensive understanding of the concept of the

digital divide and the role of "trust in e-government" contributed by this
research is expected to assist in the formulation of strategies and policies to
close the digital divide. For local governments in developing countries in
particular, the outcome of this research should prove significant in the formulation of strategic policies for the successful implementation of
e-government.

1.7. Organization of the Study

The study is organized and presented in eight sections, as described in
Table 2. Following Section 1; the introductory section, Section 2 presents a

Table 2. Organization of the Study.

Structure	Description	Aim
Section 1	*Introduction* Defines the research problems	To provide research questions and objectives
Section 2	*Literature Review* Provides the theoretical background, reviews previous research, and identifies gaps in the literature	To propose a tentative research model
Section 3	*Research Design* Provides a detailed research design	To describe and justify the chosen research design
Section 4	*Field Study and Comprehensive Research Model* Presents the process and results of the field study	To propose a comprehensive research model
Section 5	*Hypotheses and Questionnaire Development* Presents the hypotheses of the comprehensive research model and the questionnaire design	To provide the hypotheses of the research and questionnaire development
Section 6	*Data Analysis Using PLS-based SEM* Provides a detailed survey method followed by data analysis using PLS Graph	To analyze the findings to confirm the model and hypotheses
Section 7	*Discussion and Implications* Presents an in-depth discussion based on data analysis	To provide interpretation of the findings and the implications for the literature as well as the actual practice
Section 8	*Conclusion and Future Directions* Overview of the research	To present the summary of the research, its limitations, and contributions of the research

literature review as the underlying foundation of this research. The litera-ture review provides a theoretical framework for the research, reviews rele-vant research associated with this study, identifies the gaps in the existing literature, and, finally, proposes a tentative research model. A range of books, journal articles, proceedings, websites, and newspaper articles are reviewed in Section.

The research paradigm and method are discussed in detail in Section 3. The stages of the research and the methods applied in each stage are cov-ered in this section. Furthermore, Section 3 describes how qualitative as well as quantitative methods were used in data collection and how content analysis was applied in the exploratory qualitative stage and illustrates SEM in the confirmatory quantitative stage. Rationales for the choice of methods are given.

Section 4 describes in detail the field study that was conducted to exam-ine the tentative research model. This field study involved interviews with e-government users in Indonesia. The description of the process of the field study is then followed by data analysis with content analysis, using both inductive and deductive approaches. A comprehensive research model is developed based on the result, which is then examined using the quantita-tive method in Section 5.

Following the development of the comprehensive research model in Section 4, relationships among constructs are hypothesized in Section 5. Section 5 describes the development of the hypotheses and discusses the justification for each hypothesis; whether that be from previous research and literature or the findings from the field studies. The hypotheses were used to develop a questionnaire (tested for reliability and validity) for the quantitative stage.

Section 6 provides a detailed description of the quantitative stage, with information being gathered via a survey of Indonesian local government. The PLS approach, based on SEM, was used to analyze the survey data. Included in Section 6 are details of the data examination, model assess-ment, and hypothesis testing.

Section 7 basically explains the research findings from the survey data analysis based on theoretical and practical perspectives. The findings are discussed and comments given about the implications of the findings for theory development and practice.

Finally, Section 8 highlights the summary of the research and its signifi-cant contributions. Research limitations and future research direction are also presented in Section 8. A list of references and appendices used as sup-porting evidence are provided at the end of the study.

1.8. Summary

Section 1 provides the background of the relevant issues in order to clarify and underline the importance of the current research. Based on the existing literature, the section addresses the research gap in the studies of digital divide and e-government. Since the research is undertaken in Indonesia, a brief overview of e-government implementation in Indonesia was described. The overview was then followed by the description of the research focus and research questions and objectives, as well as the significance of this research. Finally, the last section presents the organization of the study in order to provide a structured picture of this study.

2. LITERATURE REVIEW

Today, many people could not imagine daily life without the use of increasingly sophisticated information and communication technologies (ICTs), from television and radio to the mobile telephone and the Internet. Yet for millions of people in the world's poorest countries, there remains a digital divide excluding them from the benefits of ICTs (Annan, 2004).

2.1. Introduction

ICT is acknowledged to be one of the key factors for economic and social development and cohesion. A research by James and Ziebell (2003), for instance, found that a project in Central Western Victoria, Australia, was substantially transforming the community. The project, which established what so called Community Enterprise Centers (CEC), aims to revitalize the community through education and improvement of business profile using ICT network. The results were impressive in the sense that it strengthens communication and cohesion within the community, which in turn improve the economic level and learning culture of the community. Similar results were found by Jaggi (2003), Lehr, Osorio, Gillett, and Sirbu (2005), Pigg (2011), and Moshiri and Nikpoor (2011), who investigated the impact of broadband and ICT in general on economic development.

In broader context, ICT is also considered as catalysts for the social, economic, and cultural transformation of communities. Some studies show that ICT contributes to the community as well as individual capacity building. Shearman (2003) argues that ICTs are "... enabling individuals and groups within local communities to engage with and benefit from the information or knowledge economy, but also in developing their capacity ..." (p. 13). As an example, ICT has significant roles in poverty eradication strategy in Kenya (Ndeta, 2003). ICT through Learning and Development Kenya (LDK) was utilized to improve education, agriculture, and microcredit. Apart from that, ICT was also used to help the youths from the slum area to access information so that they can stay in touch with the other groups of society. By an organization named SIDAREC (Slums Information Development and Resource Centers), ICT was very useful to support their programs in community service, such as counseling against HIV/AIDS, drug abuse, and prostitution. Furthermore, Warschauer (2003b) and UN (2005) argued that ICT contributes to social equality and inclusion of those who are marginalized. ICT helps to solve problems caused by lack of mobility, physical disabilities, or social discrimination.

For private and public organizations, ICT and internet in particular trigger a revolution in ways to operate business and manage organizations. The revolution introduced efficiency in operations, many opportunities in delivering service and flexibilities in responding the market (Gurstein, 2003; UNCTAD, 2010). As a result, dramatic changes can be seen in customer relationship systems and supply chain systems. New services, such as e-commerce, e-banking, and e-government, have been generated by ICT.

ICT also plays crucial roles in reinventing government and improving the quality of democracy. Some projects have been implemented, such as in Sweden (Ranerup, 1999), South Africa (Benjamin, 1999), United States of America (Brown, 1999; Wolfe, 1999), Ecuador (Salazar, 1999), Jamaica (Brown & Thompson, 2011), and other countries across the world. Although some projects may not be as successful as expected because of their complexities, but the researchers found that to some extent ICTs elevate the quality of communication between governments and their citizens, improve the accountability, and help the improvement of public administration. Those are the basic reasons for some international organizations, such as UN and Organization of Economic Cooperation and Development (OECD) strongly suggest the implementation of e-government systems to their members.

As the relationships between ICT and development studies gain more and more attention, research on this theme also has emerged since late of 1990s (Heeks, 2008a, 2009). This field is known as Development Informatics, Community Informatics or ICT4D (ICT for Development), which will be discussed in the following section.

2.2. Development Informatics, Community Informatics, and ICT4D

Although some scholars made distinctions between "development informatics," "community informatics," and "ICT4D" (and some other scholars
also mentioned "social informatics"), the difference between them is not
always clear (Johanson, 2011a). The only difference is in the subject of the
informatics. A research on the impact of the uses of internet by a certain
community would be an example of "community informatics"; an examination of the social values of internet would be an example of "social informatics"; and a study that investigates the benefits of ICT for marginalized
people would fit into the category of "development informatics." All of
them actually refer to the relationships between ICT and development studies (Heeks, 2007).

The increase use of ICT, particularly internet, and the introduction of
the Millennium Development Goals (MDGs) by United Nations resulted
in the emergence of research in development informatics and ICT4D
(Heeks, 2008a). Development informatics or community informatics is the
application of ICT to empower and develop community process (Gurstein,
2007). Furthermore, Gurstein (2007) argues that it is an emerging framework for approaching ISs from the perspective of community in the development of strategies to manage their community use and applications.

Fig. 1 describes that the development of ICT is only the first step of
informatics lifecycle. The development must be followed by ICT adoption
and use; and finally the impact could be enjoyed by its users. ICT adoption
and use thus attract concern of researchers in the field of ISs. Many theories and competing models in ICT adoption have been yielded.

2.3. ICT Adoption

Among theories and models in ICT adoption, there are at least four promi-
nent models. They are: the Theory of Reasoned Action (TRA), the
Technology Acceptance Model (TAM), the Theory of Planned Behavior
(TPB), and the Innovation Diffusion Theory. The following sections discuss each of the theory.

Fig. 1.   Informatics Lifecycle Stage of Applicability. *Source*: Heeks (2007, p. 2).

2.3.1. Theory of Reasoned Action

This theory is one of the most influential theories of human behavior and has been used to predict a wide range of behavior, including in ICTs adoption. Drawn from social psychology, this theory assumes that individuals are rational and use the information available to them (Ajzen & Fishbein, 1980). TRA argues that intention of individual determines actual behavior, because basically people usually do what they intend to do. The intention itself is a function of two determinants; they are personal in nature and social influence. The personal variable is termed *attitude toward behavior*, refers to the individual's judgment that performing a certain behavior is good or bad. On the other hand, social influence or *subjective norm* is the individual's perception of the social pressures put on him/her to perform or not perform the behavior.

As illustrated in Fig. 2, *attitudes toward behavior* and *subjective norm* are determined by beliefs. Attitudes are a function of *beliefs and evaluations*. An individual who believes that conducting a certain behavior will lead to mostly positive outcome will hold a favorable attitude conducting the behavior, and vice versa. However, subjective norm is determined by other kind of beliefs, which are *normative beliefs*. An individual who believes that most referents with whom he/she is motivated to comply think he/she should conduct the behavior will receive social pressure to do so.

TRA has been used as a fundamental theory to develop other models, such as TAM and TPB. TRA has also been validated by many researchers in predicting general behavior as well as in ICT adoption in particular. Among those are: Sheppard, Hartwick, and Warshaw (1988, 1980), Thompson, Higgins, and Howell (1991), Peace, Galletta, and Thong (2003), and Quaddus and Hofmeyer (2007).

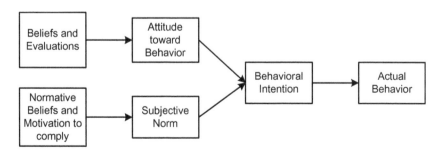

Fig. 2. Theory of Reasoned Action.

However, some researchers have criticized TRA model and suggested improvements. Bagozzi, Baumgartner, and Yi (1992) conducted a study about moderating variables of the TRA and noted that the model does not take into account the concept of favorable attitudes and "subjective norms" leading to intentions to act. Bagozzi (1992) also engaged a research which found that "attitudes" and "subjective norms" are not strong determinant for "intention" and the "intention" is not adequate determinant for "actual action." Similarly, a study by Shimp and Kavas (1984) examined eight behavioral models and found that the TRA model is only able to predict part of the actual adoption of behavior, despite that TRA resulted in the best goodness-of-fit among other models. Another study by Charng, Piliavin, and Callero (1988) found a flaw in the TRA. Although the model has been validated to test wide variety of behaviors, there is little evidence to show that TRA is useful to predict repeating behaviors, such as repeat behavior of blood donors or continuation of smoking. In terms of the robustness of the TRA, Thompson and Thompson (1996) and Bagozzi (1992) found that substantial factors have been omitted from the TRA. They noted that TRA does not take into account situations where behavior is not completely under the individual's control.

2.3.2. Technology Acceptance Model
Based on TRA and literatures in psychology, Davis et al. introduced TAM (Davis, Bagozzi, & Warshaw, 1989, 1992). TAM aims to explain the determinants of computer acceptance, by tracing the influence of external variables on internal beliefs, attitudes, and intentions (Fig. 3). Davis argues that two particular beliefs, *Perceived Usefulness* and *Perceived Ease of Use*, are of substantial relevance for ICTs acceptance behaviors (Davis, 1989).

Both TRA and TAM models postulate that ICT usage is determined by behavioral intention. However, TAM views behavioral intention is jointly determined by the individual's attitude toward using the ICTs and Perceived Usefulness. TAM excludes subjective norm as a determinant of

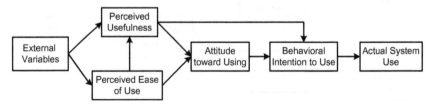

Fig. 3. Technology Acceptance Model.

behavioral intention. Indeed, the external variables are the bridge between all of the variables represented in TAM and the various individual differences and constraints (Davis et al., 1989).

TAM is a robust model, which has been modified and tested by some researchers. Venkatesh and Davis (2000) proposed an extension of TAM and called the model as TAM2. Other researchers, such as Straub, Limayem, and Karahanna-Evaristo (1995), Chau (1996), Hu, Chau, sheng, and Tam (1999), Cheng (2011), and Escobar-Rodriguez, Monge-Lozano, and Romero-Alonso (2012) validated and extended TAM.

In his research, Mathieson (1991) discusses some flaws of TAM. There could be some other factors besides ease of use and usefulness that determine intention, such as accessibility, which is not part of the model. Furthermore, TAM does not explicitly include any social factors in the model, although they are important in the behavioral research. Unlike Ajzen (1991) who differentiates between internal control factors (refers to characteristics of the individual) and external factors (include time, opportunity, and cooperation of others), TAM does not considered external control explicitly.

2.3.3. Theory of Planned Behavior

TPB is an extension of TRA. This theory was introduced by Ajzen (1991). As also posits by TRA, a focus variable in the TPB is the person's intention to perform certain behavior. The intentions indicate the willing to try and represent how much effort persons are willing to exert in performing the behavior. Similar to TRA, TPB also argues that *attitudes toward behavior* and *subjective norm* as the determinants of intention.

However, as depicted by Fig. 4, TPB adds a factor of "perceived behavioral control" as a determinant of behavioral intention. Ajzen (1991, p. 183) defines "perceived behavioral control" as "people's perception of the ease or difficulty of performing the behavior of interest." "Perceived behavioral control" is similar to the Bandura's concept of "perceived self-efficacy" (Bandura, 1977). TPB states that person's behavior is influenced by his/her confidence in their ability to perform it (i.e., by perceived behavioral control). Furthermore, the TPB considers the variable of self-efficacy or perceived behavioral control within a more general framework of the relations among other variables, beliefs, attitudes, intentions, and behavior.

Ajzen (1991) argues that although the perceived behavioral control is a key point in the TPB, it is only achievable if the behavior is under volitional control or when the individual has freedom to choose whether or not to perform the behavior. In fact, performance of most behaviors involves

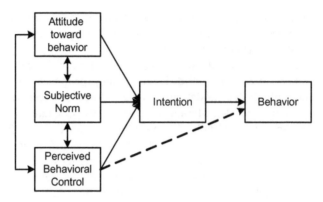

Fig. 4. Theory of Planned Behavior.

some elements of non-motivational factors, thus "perceived behavioral control" and "actual control" are not the same.

TPB has been widely used to investigate behavior in many areas. In the behavior of ICT adoption, TPB has been used by researchers such as: Taylor and Todd (1995a), Mathieson (1991), de Guinea and Markus (2009), Bulguru, Cavusoglu, and Benbasat (2010), and Lee and Rao (2012). TPB has also been decomposed and extended by Taylor and Todd (1995b) and Pavlou and Fygenson (2006).

Criticisms of the TPB come from many researchers. Ajzen (1991), the author itself, admits that at the time of publication, the strength of correlation between the constructs was not as strong as desired in terms of global measures. Beedell and Rehman (2000) and Bagozzi and Kimmel (1995) pointed out that "perceived behavioral control" fails to predict both "intention" and "behavior," and the "subjective norms" does not contribute to "intention." Those researchers concluded that the model is incomplete for predicting behavior. Therefore some researchers have added some constructs in the model, such as habit, moral obligation, and self-identity (Burton, 2004); constructs related to past behaviors (Bagozzi & Kimmel, 1995; East, 1993).

2.3.4. Diffusion of Innovation (DI)

Rogers (2003, p. 5) defines diffusion as *"the process in which an innovation is communicated through certain channels over time among the members of a social system."* The process, which a person (or an organization) passes through from obtaining initial knowledge of an innovation to confirmation

Fig. 5. Diffusion of Innovation Model.

of the decision, is described in Fig. 5. The process involves series of choices and actions over time. The behavior also involves uncertainty that is inherent in determining about a new choice to an idea previously in existence. Compared to other types of decision making, this innovation diffusion is distinct in the sense that it includes perceived newness of an innovation and the uncertainty associated with the newness.

The model consists of five stages, started with "knowledge," when a person is exposed to an existence of innovation and its functions. It is then followed by "persuasion," when the person determines a favorable or an unfavorable attitude toward the innovation. "Decision" or activities that lead to a choice to adopt or reject the innovation would be made by the person. After deciding, the person then "implements" or puts a new idea into use. The process is ended by a "confirmation," when the person seeks reinforcement of the decision that already made. If the person exposed to conflicting message about the innovation, he/she may reverse this previous decision.

In the DIs process, communication is substantial, as posited by Rogers (1995) that "communication is a process in which participants create and share information with one another in order to reach a mutual understanding" (pp. 5−6). There is a great deal of literature which highlighted the importance of communication or information networks to support DI. Wilkening (1950) noted the role of mass media as conduits for information diffusion. Chiffoleau (2005), on the other hand, suggests that the most important means to transfer the information is peer relationships.

DI has been criticized in terms of the variation found in the speed of adoption of technologies (Fisher, Norvell, Sonka, & Nelson, 2000), its application in developing countries (Ruttan, 1996), and its different application to individuals and firms (Hausman, 2005; Jensen, 2001). However, the model has been applied by many researchers in broad variety of innovations (Abdulai & Huffman, 2005; Forte-Gardner, Young, Dillman, & Carroll, 2004; Hategekimana & Trant, 2002; Quaddus & Xu, 2005).

2.3.5. Unified Theory of Acceptance and Use of Technology
Based on review of the eight previous models in ICT acceptance, Venkatesh, Morris, Davis, and Davis (2003) formulate a unified model,

which integrates factors across the previous models. The unified model, known as Unified Theory of Acceptance and Use of Technology (UTAUT), includes four determinants of intention and usage and four moderators of key relationships, as depicted in Fig. 6. The variables used in the UTAUT are similar to variables in the previous models, although different labels. *Performance expectancy* is comparable to variable of Perceived Usefulness, while *effort expectancy* is similar to Perceived Ease of Use in TAM. *Social influence* has a same definition as subjective norm in TPB and TRA. *Facilitating conditions* captures concepts of perceived behavioral control in TPB.

The purpose of UTAUT is to understand system usage as a dependent variable (Venkatesh et al., 2003). Venkatesh et al. (2003) admitted that the measures for UTAUT are still in the preliminary stage and should be developed and validated through research in the future. The model has been criticized to be more focusing on intention to use than on actual use (van Dijk, Peters, & Ebbers, 2008). Datta (2010, p. 5) also pointed out that the "*reference frame of UTAUT has been captive to individuals and organizations in the developing world.*"

Despite some criticism on the model, the results showed that UTAUT did better in explaining the variance in usage intention (adjusted R^2 of

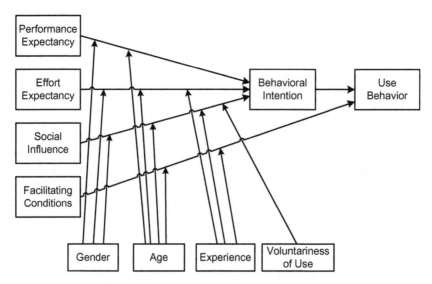

Fig. 6.   Unified Theory of Acceptance and Use of Technology.

70%) compared to all of the individual models which were used in developing this model (Venkatesh et al., 2003). The comprehensiveness, validity, and reliability of the UTAUT model have encouraged researchers to extend and validate it in the context of e-government service adoption (e.g., Carter, Shaupp, Hobbs, & Campbell, 2011; van Dijk et al., 2008; Wang & Shih, 2009) as well as e-commerce adoption (e.g., AbuShanab & Pearson, 2007; Datta, 2010; Keong, Ramayah, Kurnia, & Chiun, 2012; Venkatesh, Thong, & Xu, 2012).

The theories and models reviewed above show that ICT adoption is one of the most important topics in ISs research. As mentioned before that the ICT adoption is the first step of informatics lifecycle stage of applicability and will lead to the impact that could be enjoyed by its users (Fig. 1). However, many observers in international government and non-government organizations, including the various agencies of the United Nations, World Bank, OECD, and UNCTAD (United Nations Conference on Trade and Development), among other organizations, have recognized through their research reports that the ICT has not been evenly adopted globally. This issue has been known as digital divide or digital inequality. It has been one of the most fruitful topics for many researchers and policy makers since the late 1990s.

2.4. Digital Divide

Digital divide occurs at two levels, international level and national level. At the international level, the gap is obvious. A composite telecommunication index released by United Nations illustrates the gap (Table 3), particularly in terms of telecommunication infrastructure. The indicators are internet users/100 inhabitants, personal computer/100 inhabitants, telephone cellular subscribers/100 inhabitants, main telephone lines/100 inhabitants, and fixed broadband users/100 inhabitants. To compare telecommunication infrastructure, some countries have been selected and presented in the table. The countries presented in Table 3 represent developed countries, developing countries, as well as least developed countries (LDCs). All of the indicators convince us that there is a wide divide among countries. In 2012, 95% citizens of Iceland have access to internet, while in Liberia, only 0.07% of its citizens connected to internet (UN, 2012). Moreover, there are still 15 countries without fixed broadband connection at all; most of them are African countries. Africa seems struggle in providing ICTs infrastructure, while Europe is the most connected region in contrast. The

Table 3. Telecommunication Infrastructure of Selected Countries, Regional Groups, and Economic Groups.

Country	Internet/100 Persons			PCs/100 Persons			Cellular Subscribers/100 Persons			Main Tel Lines/100 Persons			Broadband/100 Persons		
	2008	2010	2012	2008	2010	2012	2008	2010	2012	2008	2010	2012	2008	2010	2012
Australia	75.12	71.89	76.00	76.61	60.29	n/a	97.02	104.96	101.04	48.81	44.46	38.89	19.15	24.39	23.19
USA	69.10	74.00	79.00	76.22	78.67	n/a	77.40	86.79	89.86	57.15	51.33	48.70	19.31	25.35	26.34
United Kingdom	56.03	79.62	85.00	76.52	80.23	n/a	116.39	123.41	130.25	56.16	54.24	53.71	21.71	28.21	31.38
Saudi Arabia	18.66	30.55	41.00	12.82	68.25	n/a	78.05	142.85	187.86	15.68	16.27	15.18	0.87	4.16	5.45
Ecuador	11.54	9.71	24.00	6.55	12.95	n/a	63.23	86.01	102.18	13.07	14.17	14.42	0.20	0.26	1.36
Indonesia	7.18	11.13	9.10	1.47	2.03	n/a	28.30	61.83	91.72	6.57	13.36	15.83	0.05	0.13	0.79
India	5.44	6.95	7.50	1.54	3.18	n/a	14.83	29.36	61.42	3.64	3.21	2.87	0.21	0.45	0.90
Bangladesh	0.31	0.32	3.70	2.42	2.25	n/a	13.25	27.90	46.17	0.79	0.84	0.61	0.00	0.03	0.04
Liberia	0.03	0.55	0.07	n/a	n/a	n/a	4.87	19.30	39.34	0.21	0.06	0.15	0.00	0.00	0.00
Ethiopia	0.21	0.45	0.75	0.39	0.68	n/a	1.09	3.93	7.86	0.91	1.13	1.10	0.00	0.00	0.00
Somalia	1.11	1.12	1.16	0.91	0.90	n/a	6.08	6.87	6.95	1.22	1.15	1.07	0.00	0.00	0.00
Regional groups															
Africa	n/a	6.57	9.85	n/a	3.44	n/a	n/a	38.02	56.45	n/a	3.86	3.93	n/a	0.58	0.66
America	n/a	30.78	36.63	n/a	15.04	n/a	n/a	86.86	107.53	n/a	21.83	21.26	n/a	6.94	9.08
Asia	n/a	21.59	29.33	n/a	14.99	n/a	n/a	70.75	91.64	n/a	15.62	15.06	n/a	5.15	5.41
Europe	n/a	53.15	66.01	n/a	38.90	n/a	n/a	113.24	119.52	n/a	42.31	40.40	n/a	18.86	23.63
Oceania	n/a	20.28	21.26	n/a	15.21	n/a	n/a	38.32	59.06	n/a	16.29	17.22	n/a	5.24	4.41
Economic groups															
Developed countries	n/a	57.99	67.45	n/a	46.14	n/a	n/a	112.04	117.24	n/a	43.75	40.69	n/a	21.08	23.92
Developing countries other than LDCs	n/a	22.84	28.62	n/a	12.08	n/a	n/a	77.74	98.11	n/a	17.43	16.11	n/a	4.29	5.24
Least developed countries	n/a	4.47	5.75	n/a	2.45	n/a	n/a	25.70	40.04	n/a	2.35	2.13	n/a	0.44	0.23

Source: UN (2008, 2010, 2012).

figures based on economic groups underline the wide gap between those of developed countries and those of LDCs. There are as much as 97.55% people in LDCs live without any PC at home (UN, 2010). Indeed, research by Dewan, Ganley, and Kraemer (2005) and Billon, Marco, and Lera-Lopez (2009) also found the inequalities across countries of ICT use as the impact of inequalities in terms of economic, demographic, and in terms of ICT infrastructures.

At the national level, some studies revealed the digital divide in most countries across the world. Even within the developed countries, such as United States or United Kingdom, the problem of digital divide or digital inequality is inevitable. Mossberger, Tolbert, and Gilbert (2006), Hargittai (2006), Venkatesh and Morris (2000), and Mossberger et al. (2008) investigated the inequality of ICT use in United States and found that some demographic factors, such as gender, race, and residential place determining the ICT use. In the United Kingdom, a study by Kuk (2003) revealed gap between regions of high and low household internet access. In developing country, Warschauer (2003a), for example, examined the digital divide in Egypt and concluded that the gap is the result of educational problems.

2.4.1. Definition of Digital Divide

The definition of digital divide has been evolved as the reflection of the attempts to understand this issue more comprehensively. Initially, digital divide was defined as the "inequality between those who had access to ICT and those who had not" (De Haan, 2004; DiMaggio, Hargittai, Neuman, et al., 2001), particularly in terms of ICT infrastructure. National Telecommunications and Information Administration (NTIA) of the US Department of Commerce for instance, in its first report of digital divide noted that telephone penetration was the most common indicator of the nation's success in achieving universal service (NTIA, 1995).

Table 4 lists previous research on digital divide. The list shows that most of the researchers use access to ICT as the main variable. Although the definition of access varies from one researcher to another, the main indicator is still ICT infrastructure. As the awareness on the complexity of the issue of digital divide rises, several researchers (e.g., Bertot, 2003; Kauffman & Techatassanasoontorn, 2005; Warschauer, 2003b) suggest that the typical definition of digital divide that is commonly used – which points to ICT access gaps – is too narrow. As a consequence, there are some recognition that broader definitions and approaches that may be used to look into these issues from a number of different

Table 4. Previous Research on Digital Divide.

Research	Variables	Location	Key Findings
Kuk (2003)	Internet access	United Kingdom	Quality of local government websites in regions of low household internet access is poorer that in regions of high internet access.
van Dijk and Hacker (2003)	Age; gender; education; ethnic group	The Netherlands	Age and gender determine PC possession.
Quibra, Ahmed, Tschang, and Reyes-Macasaquit (2003)	Income; population size; education; ICT infrastructures	Asian countries	Income, education, and infrastructures are determinants of ICT adoption.
Oyelaran-Oyeyinka and Lal (2005)	GDP per capita; ICT infrastructures; human capital	Sub-Saharan countries	High correlation between ICT infrastructure and GDP per capita. ICT infrastructures significantly influence internet diffusion.
Mariscal (2005)	GDP per capita; urban population; privatization; autonomous regulator; IT penetration	Latin-American countries	All of the independent variables are significantly impacting IT penetration.
Dewan et al. (2005)	Economic; demographic; environmental; IT penetration	Cross country	National income is positively associated with IT penetration. There are differences of demographic and economic effects.
Hargittai (2006)	Age; education; income; internet experience	USA	Education is significantly influencing one's likelihood to make mistakes.
Mossberger et al. (2006)	Income; education; race; place of residence	USA	Disparities among ethnic groups are due to place effects rather than race. Concentrated poverty is important for computer and internet access.
Stern, Adams, and Elsasser (2009)	Access divide; proficiency divide; demographic	USA	There is access divide based on county type. Proficiency is influenced by type of connection.
Billon et al. (2009)	ICT infrastructures; GDP per capita; population	Cross country	In developed countries, GDP and education are the important factors influencing ICT adoption, while age and urban population are influencing ICT adoption in developing countries.

Reference	Country	Variables	Findings
Agarwal, Animesh, and Prasad (2009)	USA	Gender; age; education; race; housing density	All of the independent variables influence internet use. By controlling individual and regional characteristics, peer effects have stronger influence.
Dewan, Ganley, and Kraemer (2009)	Cross country	ICT infrastructures	Co-diffusion effects between PC and internet are complementary. Impacts of PCs on internet diffusion are stronger in developing countries than developed countries.
Hsieh et al. (2008), Hsieh, Rai, and Keil (2011)	USA	Household income; education level; age; gender; ethnic group	Internet PC ownership and personal network exposure in social-economically advantaged group are more significantly influencing continued use intention.
Belanger and Carter (2009)	USA	Access; computer and internet skill; gender	Income, education, age, internet usage, and online information search are significant predictors of e-government use.
Schleife (2010)	Germany	County type; age; gender; education; occupational status; income	Education, age, income, and county type are the most important determinants of internet use.
Wei et al. (2011)	Singapore	Digital access divide; digital capability divide; digital outcome divide	Digital access divide impacts computer self-efficacy. Gender also significantly influencing computer self-efficacy.
Sipior, Ward, and Connoly (2011)	USA	Age; education level; employment status; household income; internet experience	Education, employment and income, and Perceived Ease of Use are the most significant factors for e-government use.

perspectives might be more appropriate to extend our understanding beyond the idea of an access gap.

Bertot (2003) argues that the digital divide, especially on the Internet, should be considered along some dimensions, including the breadth and quality of access to ICT, the availability of effective telecommunication infrastructures, the presence of parallel economic growth, and information literacy. Similarly, DiMaggio and Hargittai (2001) suggest that research should move on from the dichotomous measure of the digital divide as "haves" and "have-nots" to study differences among people with access to ICT.

As the implication of narrow understanding on the issue of digital divide, policy makers in many countries have been using it as the basis of their policy. Governments in many countries increase public access to computers and basic ICTs in schools and other public places. In the United States, former President Bill Clinton proposed a US$2.3 billion tax incentive for businesses, which donate computers to poor schools and communities, sponsor the establishment of technology centers in poor neighborhood, and provide internet training (Lacey, 2000). Some corporations worldwide also initiated a home-computer benefit for their employees who did not own computers (Atewell, 2001). As part of the attempts to narrow the digital divide, Bill and Melinda Gates Foundation supports the access to computer and internet service in the United States and some developing countries (Foundation, 2012).

Table 3 shows that gaps exist from time to time, even in term of ICT infrastructures. The United Nations indicates that the digital divide is not diminishing rather it is growing wider (UN, 2010). Some scholars argue that this was a result of incomprehensive understanding of digital divide which led to insufficient policy. The World Bank, the United Nations, and other international organizations endorsed the development of a set of indicators to measure the extent of the digital divide across countries over time (Kauffman and Techatassanasoontorn, 2005).

Warschauer's note on a competition of an "Information Age Town" in Ireland provides us a good example of the insufficient policy (Warschauer, 2003b, pp. 2–4). In 1997, there was a competition held by Ireland's national telecommunication company. In order to narrow the gap of ICT use, the company would provide US$22 million fund to implement a proposal of what an Information Age Town should be in a competition basis. Ennis, a small town, came out as a winner and gave an internet-ready PC to every family in town. The town also provided ISDN line, website, and other sophisticated technologies to all businesses. Unfortunately, many people didn't know how to operate the equipment, some other didn't want to use internet as they see that internet deprived them to socializing. As a result, many computers reportedly sold on the black market and the aims of the program couldn't be achieved (Warschauer, 2003b).

Despite calls from several researchers to recognize the broader definition of the digital divide beyond the "haves" and "have-nots" dichotomy, much of the existing research examines the issue through the simplistic perspective of technology access. This is helpful for a first-cut understanding of the digital divide associated with a particular technology, but further studies are needed to provide deeper understanding. Scholars believe that this will occur through the application of multidimensional definitions of the digital divide. Norris (2001), for example, argues that understanding on the issue of digital divide should be put on the social inequality context.

Dewan and Riggins (2005) advance the understanding of digital divide by suggesting two orders of digital divide. As new ICT innovations are publicly launched, individuals would adopt them at varying rates. This leads to inequality in the level of access. Furthermore, there is variation among the adopters in the ability to use the innovations effectively. Accordingly, there are two types of inequality, one in access to ICTs and the other in the ability to use the ICTs. Those inequalities are corresponding to the first order and second order digital divides, respectively, as shown in Fig. 7. The second order divide starts to become more important, as the majority of the participants in some social system have obtained access to a technology (Dewan & Riggins, 2005).

Wei et al. (2011) introduce a third order of digital divide, by extending the framework of Dewan and Riggins (2005), the outcome divide. It refers to inequality of outcomes of exploiting ICT, resulted from the first and second order of digital divide (Fig. 8). Wei et al. (2011) argue that the access to and use of ICT at homes and at schools (or so called digital access divide) impact computer self-efficacy (CSE), the central factor pertaining to the digital capability divide for individuals. In turn, CSE affects learning outcomes of individuals, which represent digital outcome divide. Further, this framework could be examined at the level of individual, organization, as well as global.

This research explored and investigated digital divide beyond access and demographic factors. In this research, digital divide was defined as an "inequality between individuals, households, businesses and geographic areas at different socio-economic levels with regard to both their opportunities to access information and communication technologies (ICTs) and

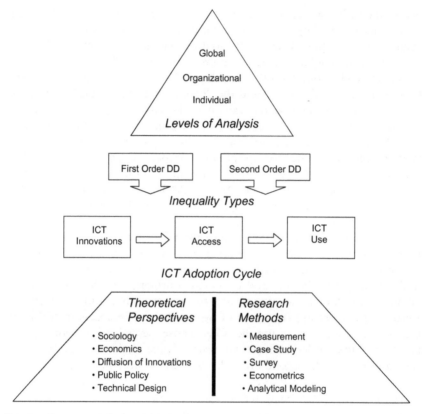

Fig. 7. Conceptual Framework for Research in Digital Divide.
Source: Dewan and Riggins (2005, p. 302).

IT adoption stages				
Individual	Digital access divide	Digital capability divide	Digital outcome divide
Organization			
Global			

Fig. 8. Three Levels Digital Divide Framework. *Source*: Wei et al. (2011, p. 3).

their use for a wide variety of activities" (OECD, 2001, p. 5). It is a comprehensive definition covering all important elements of digital divide, which are demographic factors, socioeconomic levels, access to ICTs, and the use of ICTs. Based on the definition and a consideration that previous research in digital divide predominantly focused on inequality of access (Table 4), this research will attempt to fill the gap in digital divide studies. This research proposes a more comprehensive investigation of digital divide by categorizing it into five levels, namely demographic divide, economic divide, access divide, capability divide, and innovativeness divide.

2.4.2. Demographic Divide

Demographic factors have been recognized by previous research as important factors determining ICT adoption or usage. Residential place has been investigated by Mossberger et al. (2006) who found that it is one of the important factors in Internet use. Research by Mariscal (2005), Kuk (2003), and Stern et al. (2009) also confirm the importance of residential place. Venkatesh and Morris (2000) examined the role of gender in the technology adoption, and found the significant difference between men and women. Wei et al. (2011), Agarwal et al. (2009), and Schleife (2010) have also studied the role of gender in Internet use. Agarwal et al. (2009), Hargittai (2006), and Schleife (2010) investigated the impact of age in Internet use in Germany and concluded that age is one of the influencing factors. On the other hand, the role of education in technology adoption have been examined by Jung, Qiu, and Kim (2001) and Mossberger et al. (2006).

2.4.3. Economic Divide

Socioeconomic factors are believed as internal and external resources that together shape experiences, opportunities, and even ways in which the world is viewed (Williams, 1990). Socioeconomic factors also substantially bring about a synergy of social and economic forces to individuals and resources contained in their surrounding environments (Hsieh et al., 2008). Hence, socioeconomic factors have been associated with behavioral patterns in many fields, including psychology and ISs. In the field of ISs, prior researchers found that socioeconomic circumstances influenced the ICT use (Agarwal et al., 2009; Mossberger et al., 2006; Schleife, 2010) and that economic condition was the most important factor to widen the opportunity for accessing the ICTs (Dewan et al., 2005; Quibra et al., 2003).

2.4.4. Access Divide

Access divide represents the physical access to ICT (Quibra et al., 2003). As mentioned earlier, most of the researches in digital divide focused on access divide as the dependent variable to ICT use (Table 3). Those who have examined access divide and its influence on ICT use suggested that the access to ICT was a key factor of ICT use. According to the framework provided by Dewan and Riggins (2005), access divide is considered as the first order of digital divide, because access to ICT is the primary requirement to ICT use. Dewan and Riggins (2005) and Wei et al. (2011) also found that access divide had significantly influenced capability in utilizing ICT.

2.4.5. Capability Divide Based on Social Cognitive Theory

Digital capability divide is derived from Social Cognitive Theory (Bandura, 1977), which argues that individual possesses a self-belief system. Furthermore, Bandura (1977, 2001) argues that the system allows each individual to control his/her cognitive processes, feelings, motivation and behavior, with self-efficacy being the core of the system. Self-efficacy refers to an individual's belief in his or her capability to perform a specific task, which may not necessarily reflect actual competence.

Although Bandura originally developed the self-efficacy theory for treating severe phobic, researchers in other areas including ISs have used the concept widely. In the area of ISs, CSE has been examined by previous research (Compeau, Higgins, & Huff, 1999; Marakas, Yi, & Johnson, 1998; Wei et al., 2011). The results suggested that self-efficacy was a strong predictor of behavior and attitudes. Based on Dewan and Riggins' framework and Social Cognitive Theory, Wei et al. (2011) developed a more comprehensive model for digital divide to include capability divide. Capability divide is then considered as the second order of digital divide (Dewan & Riggins, 2005; Wei et al., 2011).

2.4.6. Innovativeness Divide Based on Personal Innovativeness

With regards to attitude toward new technology, van Dijk and Hacker (2003) admitted that information *want-not* was a more important problem than information *have-not*. As new technological innovation is introduced, potential users will consider perceived benefits as well as perceived risks or costs. Technological innovations will be adopted if the benefits earned by its users exceed the risks or costs (Ellen, Bearden, & Sharma, 1991). Rogers

(1995) believes that innovators and early adopters were individuals who were able to cope with high level of risks and uncertainty. On the other hand, Hofstede (1983, 2009) found that in Indonesia as well as in most Asian countries, levels of "uncertainty avoidance" index, the society's tolerance for uncertainty and ambiguity, were generally high. Consequently, majority of Indonesians did not easily accept any changes and innovations.

The innovativeness divide refers to the willingness to change and try out any new information technology (Agarwal & Prasad, 1998; Hurt, Joseph, & Cook, 1977). Innovation, by its nature, is associated with greater risks and uncertainty (Kirton, 1976). In this research, Personal Innovativeness was used to explain the influence of innovativeness divide on IT usage. Rogers (1995) argued that individuals were categorized as "innovative," if they were early to adopt an innovation and "non-innovative" if they adopted later. Based on the research by Midgley and Dowling (1978) and Flynn and Goldsmith (1993), Agarwal and Prasad (1998) suggested that Personal Innovativeness was an important construct in the acceptance of information technology innovations.

To summarize the types of digital divide, which are examined in the current research, Table 5 presents the criteria for each type of digital divide.

This research intends to explore the phenomenon of digital divide in e-government context, based on two reasons: *first*, digital divide is one of the serious problems in implementing e-government systems (Harijadi, 2004; Hwang & Syamsuddin, 2008; UN, 2010). Unlike e-commerce, where the businesses are allowed to choose customers, e-government systems are developed to serve the entire population (Carter & Belanger, 2005). Therefore, the existence of digital divide is a big challenge for e-government. *Second*, understanding of this issue is important for government in order to develop "citizen-centered" e-government systems and improve citizens' readiness for e-government.

Table 5. Criteria for Each Type of Digital Divide.

Digital Divide	Criteria
Demographic divide	Gender, age, place of residence, and education
Economic divide	Socioeconomic circumstances
Access divide	Physical access to ICT
Capability divide	Individual's belief in his or her capability to utilize ICT
Innovativeness divide	Willingness to change and try out any new information technology

2.5. E-Government Systems

Table 6 presents e-government Readiness Index of Indonesia in comparison with some Asian countries (UN, 2005, 2008, 2010). The indices and ranks of Indonesia do not show a significant progress, which indicate that Indonesia's e-government systems face substantial problems.

The Readiness Index is a composite measurement of the capacity and willingness of countries to use e-government for ICT-led development. Along with an assessment of the website development patterns in a country, the e-government Readiness Index incorporates the infrastructure and educational levels, to reflect how a country is using information technologies to promote access and inclusion of its citizens. In 2010, the index is extended by incorporating e-participation to reflect the emphasis on interactive and transactional services (UN, 2010). Although the index does not measure the usage of e-government systems by the citizens, the e-participation index indicates how useful the services in e-government are for the citizens. Thus the poor Readiness Index reflects unsuccessful (use and benefit) e-government.

E-government refers to the use of ICTs to enhance the access to and delivery of all facets of government services and operations for the benefit of citizens, business, employees, and other stakeholders (Srivastava & Teo, 2007). E-government system is an important tool for human development and for the achievement of development goals, such as MDGs (UN, 2010). Therefore, all countries are encouraged to implement e-government system.

2.5.1. Reinventing Government Paradigm

The e-government initiative can be traced back to the paradigm of New Public Management or Reinventing Government. The paradigm, which started in the late 1980s, is an effort to reorient the focus of government

Table 6. UN E-Government Readiness Index of Some Asian Countries.

Countries/Region	2005		2008		2010	
	Rank	Index	Rank	Index	Rank	Index
Republic of Korea	5	0.873	6	0.832	1	0.879
Singapore	7	0.850	23	0.701	11	0.748
Malaysia	43	0.571	34	0.606	32	0.610
Vietnam	105	0.364	91	0.456	90	0.445
Indonesia	96	0.382	106	0.411	109	0.403

operations from an inward-looking approach to an outward-looking one by emphasizing the concerns and needs of end users. The new paradigm is a critics to the previous paradigm which also known as Weberian paradigm.

Weberian model of organization focuses on internal and managerial concerns and emphasizes departmentalization, specialization, and standardization of the production process (Schachter, 1995; Weber, 1947). Officials who perform similar functions are grouped and organized into the same administrative unit or department. Each unit is responsible for understanding its clients, assessing the demand for its services, delivering those services, and setting administrative goals for planning and evaluation purposes. To ensure that departmental plans are consistent with each other and fiscally feasible, the budget office, city manager's or mayor's office, and the city council are responsible for centralized control and coordination. However, the Weberian bureaucracy is often criticized for its rigidity, inefficiency, and incapability to serve "human clients," who have preferences and feelings (Bozeman, 2000). A simple example of these drawbacks is the fact that a newcomer to a city may have to fill out many forms for different departments, even though the forms ask for similar information, such as name, address, and household characteristics.

In the Reinventing Government or New Public Management paradigm, Osborne and Gaebler (1992) proposed that citizens should be regarded and treated as customers, suggesting that the delivery of government services should be redesigned with a customer focus. Mintzberg (1996) even argues that citizens have rights that go far beyond those of customers or even clients, although citizens have obligations in the same time. The paradigm also emphasizes the principles of "catalytic government" and "community-ownership." Public officials are challenged to think about how to empower citizens to take ownership of community problems. The approach urges officials to partner with citizen groups and nonprofit organizations to identify solutions and deliver public services effectively.

2.5.2. Role of ICT in Reinventing Government

A major obstacle to the Reinventing Government reform is the burden of transaction costs imposed on public officials and citizens. Government officials may find citizen engagement time consuming and costly. Given the time pressure they already face in the daily operation of government, networking with citizens and proactively soliciting public input seem an unnecessary and unwanted burden. Citizens also may be reluctant to participate in the decision-making process of the government. Attending meetings, writing formal feedback, and responding to surveys about public services may require a time commitment that many citizens are not willing to give regularly.

In addressing those challenges, ICT has played an increasingly important role in public administration (Heeks, 1999). Before the Internet emerged in the late 1980s, some governments were already actively pursuing information technology to improve operating efficiency and to enhance internal communication (Brown, 1999; King, 1982; Norris & Kraemer, 1996). However, the focus of e-government in this era was primarily internal and managerial. The introduction of the Internet and the World Wide Web marked a new stage in information technology usage by shifting the focus of governance to its external relationship with citizens (Seneviratne, 1999). Technology certainly plays an important role in fostering the change.

Early adopters of Internet technology applications in public organizations tended to automate existing business processes, with little redesign or innovation. It didn't attempt to integrate and redesign the business as a whole in order to make it truly web-centric. Burn and Robins (2003, p. 26) state, "e-government is not just about putting forms and services online. It provides the opportunity to rethink how the government provides services and how it links them in a way that is tailored to the users' needs." The failure of many dot.coms should alert governments to the risk that e-government initiatives may also go wrong. Consequently, "government must develop a far more sophisticated view of the people it is there to serve and devolve real power to regions and localities as an integral part of its approach to e-government and provide more freedom of information" (Burn & Robins, 2003, p. 26). If the governments can achieve this new conception of their role, then there is the potential for e-government to transform fundamental relationship between government and citizen. There are many opportunities for e-government applications, whether they involve the provision of information, handling complaints and queries electronically, processing applications for permits/licenses electronically, paying taxes, duties, and fees electronically.

2.5.3. Benefits of E-Government
An e-government system offers some benefits. La Porte, Demchak, and Jong (2002) and Vigoda (2000) argue that e-government facilitates citizens access to government and policy information individually and contact responsible officials. The access promotes better accountability of public officials to citizens and in turn restores public confidence in government

(Thomas, 1998). More information delivered in a more timely fashion to citizens is expected to increase transparency of government, empowering citizens to more closely monitor government performance. Enhanced interactivity is also expected to improve government accountability as it makes government more responsive to the needs and demands of individual citizens (Wong & Welch, 2004).

Srivastava and Teo (2007) found that e-government implementation in 99 countries has significant impact on efficiency, national performance, and national business competitiveness. Similar findings are also concluded by previous research about the impact of e-government in helping improve service delivery (Al-Kibsi, Boer, Mourshed, & Rea, 2001; Haldenwang, 2004; West, 2004), in reducing corruption (Cho & Choi, 2004; Haldenwang, 2004; Wong & Welch, 2004), in improving national performance (Barua, Kriebel, & Mukhopadhayay, 1995), and in the long run also contributing in the process of democratization (Evans-Cowley & Conroy, 2004; Haldenwang, 2004; West, 2004). Hence, considering its benefits, e-government is seen as no longer an option but a necessity for all countries aiming for better governance (Gupta & Jana, 2003).

Despite the positive impacts of e-government, e-government initiatives actually have mostly fallen short of their potential. This issue is even more visible in the context of developing countries, where only about 15% of all e-government initiatives have been successful in attaining their major goals without any significant undesirable outcomes (Heeks, 2008b). Stakeholders and leadership play the primary role in making e-government a success (Luk, 2009). Technology plays a supportive role, but important, although it cannot work in isolation. Section 2.5.6 will discuss about the challenges for e-government further.

2.5.4. Stages of E-Government Development

Layne and Lee (2001) posit four stages of e-government development model (as illustrated in Fig. 9). In stage one of cataloguing, government focuses on the efforts to develop a website, which its content most limited to online presentations of government information. Government starts to focus on integrating the internal systems to online interfaces and allowing its citizens to transact with government through online systems in the stage two. This stage is known as "transaction-based" e-government, and at this stage, e-government efforts consists of putting live database links to online interfaces, so that, for example, citizens may renew their licenses and pay fines online.

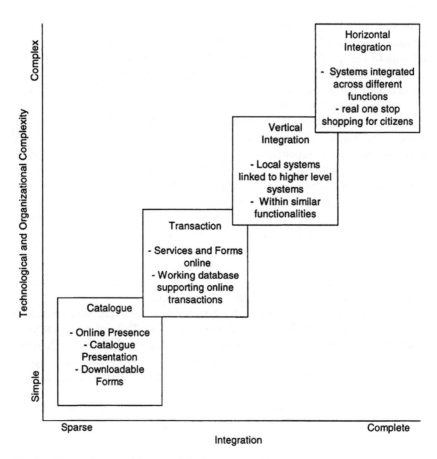

Fig. 9. Dimensions and Stages of E-Government Development.
Source: Layne and Lee (2001, p. 124).

By having similar agencies across different levels of governments and by having different agencies with different functionality connect to each other, citizens will see the government as an integrated information base. Citizen can contact one point of government and complete any level of governmental transaction. From the viewpoint of all levels of government, this could eliminate redundancies and inconsistencies in their information bases for citizens. This integration may happen in two ways: vertical and horizontal. Vertical integration refers to local, provincial, or states and national or federal governments connected for different functions or services of government. In an ideal situation where systems are vertically integrated, once a citizen filed for a business license at the city government, this information would be propagated to the state's business licensing system and to the central government to obtain an employer identification number. In contrast, horizontal integration is defined as integration across different functions and services at the same level of government.

E-government services are basically categorized into four types, namely Government to Citizens (G2C), Government to Business (G2B), and Government to Government (G2G) (Evans & Yen, 2005). G2C service focuses on the ability of the government and citizen to communicate information to each other in an efficient and electronic manner. The citizen greatly benefits from these government communications. The G2B systems allow the government and business practice to communicate each other. The goal of this service is to make available online regulations for agencies and increasing electronic tax capabilities for business. Another goal is to consolidate trade information for export and import data. This service also helps the government obtain data necessary in decision making. The G2G service strives to improve the efficiency of delivery when transacting information within itself or with other governments. This allows the government to communicate efficiently by eliminating redundancy and duplication. This also has benefits in terms of crime detection and homeland security.

The emergence of the internet also facilitates the growth of a "One-Stop Service center" model because a government website can itself serve as a convenient and cost-effective platform for centralized service provision (Ho, 2002). Businesses, residents, visitors, and intergovernmental liaisons easily can access public information and services related to their specific needs simply by clicking on different web links in the city website. They can also contact government officials directly through email or online request forms to give feedback about specific issues. A One-Stop Service center is an umbrella organization that operates on top of existing functional departments and is intended to maximize the convenience and satisfaction of users through service integration. As the gateway for specific client groups such as businesses, residents, or visitors, the center collects information about user demand for inquiries and service assistance and processes the information centrally. It then coordinates with functional departments.

2.5.5. Trust in E-Government

Website is much more than an IT interface. Different types of risks and uncertainties prevail in online transactions (Teo & Liu, 2006). Hence, trust is a substantial key for retaining website users through the establishment and improvement of an interactive, multisession, online relationship (Gefen et al., 2003). Prior studies identify trust to be one of the enablers of e-commerce transactions (Gefen et al., 2008; Pavlou & Gefen, 2004; Pennington, Wilcox, & Grover, 2003) and e-loyalty (Cyr, 2008). In the context of e-government, the role of trust for usage of websites is even more important as citizens using e-government Websites are unlikely to find alternative websites serving the same purpose. In the absence of sufficient trust in e-government systems, users may be motivated to revert to the traditional offline means of interaction with the government. Therefore, building citizen trust is often considered as a key factor for the successful implementation of e-government websites (Teo et al., 2009; Warkentin et al., 2002).

The early psychology and sociology studies on trust defined it as a set of beliefs that other people would fulfill their expected favorable commitments (Gefen, Straub, & Boudreau, 2000). Recent business research has taken a comparable stand, defining trust as the expectation that other individuals or companies will behave ethically (Hosmer, 1995), dependably (Kumar, 1996), and will fulfill their expected commitments (Rotter, 1971; Schurr & Ozanne, 1985). Trust in e-government in this study is defined as belief that the e-government system can be used to get the desired outcome satisfactorily (Teo et al., 2009).

2.5.6. Challenges for E-Government Implementation

Applying e-government system is not simply transferring the system from one country to another-mostly from developed to developing country as additional efforts are needed in implementing e-government system in a developing country (Schuppan, 2009). It is suggested that the cause of the unsuccessful implementation of e-government is associated with practices and cultures (Marche & McNiven, 2003), as well as the inherent difficulties associated with integrating operational procedures and ISs, which may not be computer-based, among individual government agencies, departments, and bureau. Specific barriers associated with the e-government initialization process are many, including issues of citizen privacy and security, inadequately skilled citizens and government employees, and the tendency for e-government to replicate traditional government (Marche & McNiven, 2003). Finally there is the issue digital divide in society is still a huge one, although the empirical evidence on its impact on e-government systems success is currently lacking. As the primary stakeholder in e-government systems, citizens play a substantial role in e-government success (Davison, Wagner, & Ma, 2005). Citizens' usage of e-government is vital for e-government success. Table 7 presents previous studies about the success factors for e-government initiatives. The list reflects the complexity of e-government implementation.

Table 7 also reveals that most of the studies are technologies focused. Others have examined manager's attitude and behavior, organizational diversity, multiple goals, resistance to change, turf and conflict, autonomy of agencies, laws and regulations, intergovernmental relationships, and political pressures. There is a lack of studies that examine citizen's perceptions on and use of e-government or the "demand side" (Gauld, Goldfinch, & Horsburgh, 2010). Much of the research on e-government seems forgetting that individuals do not simply adopt technology as it becomes available, but may resist its use or undermine its purported benefits (Fountain, 2001). Hence, this research will attempt to fill the gap in e-government research and integrate all five digital divide constructs and trust construct into one framework.

In some cases, e-government projects experience user failure because the citizens as the main users do not use the systems, in spite of the systems are successful in terms of technological and project development (Goldfinch, 2007). Therefore, their perception on e-government is substantial and is going to be used as the indicator of e-government system success in this research.

2.6. Information System Success

IS success and its determinants have been considered critical to the field of ISs (Ahmad, Amer, Qutaifan, & Alhilali, 2013; DeLone & McLean, 1992, 2003; Hategekimana & Trant, 2002; Ruttan, 1996; Willis, 2007). Researchers have been measuring IS success at different levels, including the technical level, the semantic level, and the effectiveness level (Carter et al., 2011). Furthermore, Carter et al. (2011) define the technical level as the accuracy and efficiency of the system which produces the information, the semantic level as the success of the information in conveying the intended meaning, and the effectiveness level as the effect of the information on the receiver. By adapting communication theory, Mason (1978) labels the effectiveness level as influence level. The IS creates information which is communicated to the recipient who is then influenced by the information. In this sense, information flows through a series of stages from its production through its use or consumption to its influence on individual and/or organizational performance. Furthermore, Mason (1978) suggests that there may need to be separate success measures for each of the levels of information.

Table 7. Previous Research on E-Government Success Factors.

Category	Factors	Authors
Information and data	Information and data quality	Dawes (1996), Redman (1998), Ballou and Tayi (1999), Burbridge (2002), Prybutok, Zhang, and Ryan (2008)
	Dynamic information needs	Brown and Brudney (2003)
	Usability	Davis (1989), Mahler and Regan (2002)
	Security issues	Moon (2002), Holden, Norris, and Fletcher (2003), Roy (2003)
	Technological incompatibility	Dawes (1996), Chengalur-Smith and Duchessi (1999), Brown (2001), Burbridge (2002), Holden et al. (2003)
	Technology complexity	Chengalur-Smith and Duchessi (1999), West and Berman (2001)
	Technical skills and experience	Brown (2001), Ho (2002), Moon (2002), Holden et al. (2003)
	Technology newness	Ho (2002), Roy (2003)
	Project size	McFarlan (1981), Barki, Rivard, and Talbot (1993)
Organizational and management	Manager's attitudes and behavior	Heintze and Bretschneider (2000), Gagnon (2001), Prybutok et al. (2008), Luk (2009)
	Users or organizational diversity	McFarlan (1981), Brown and Brudney (2003), Roy (2003)
	Multiple or conflicting goals	Brown (2003), Kim and Kim (2003)
	Resistance to change	Burbridge (2002), Ho (2002), Edmiston (2003)
	Turf and conflicts	Barki et al. (1993), Dawes (1996), Burbridge (2002), Edmiston (2003), Roy (2003)
	Autonomy of agencies	Dawes (1996), Landsbergen Jr. and Wolken Jr. (2001)
Legal and regulatory	Restrictive laws and regulations	Chengalur-Smith and Duchessi (1999), Mahler and Regan (2002)
	Intergovernmental relationships	Landsbergen Jr. and Wolken Jr. (2001), Burbridge (2002), Rocheleau (2000), Luk (2009)
	Policy and political pressures	Heintze and Bretschneider (2000), Mahler and Regan (2002), Brown and Brudney (2003), Roy (2003)
Institutional and environmental	Privacy concerns	Moon (2002), Edmiston (2003), Holden et al. (2003)
	Environmental context (social, economic, demographic)	La Porte et al. (2002), Warkentin et al. (2002), Vathanopas, Krittayaphongphun, and Klomsiri (2008), Gauld et al. (2010)

Source: Adapted and expanded from Gil-Garcia and Pardo (2005).

Based on prior studies on IS success, DeLone and McLean (1992) developed a model, which is known as DeLone and McLean IS Success (D&M Model). As depicted by Fig. 10, System Quality and Information Quality individually as well as jointly influence both use and user satisfaction. Furthermore, the amount of use will influence the degree of user satisfaction, as well as the reverse. Use and user satisfaction are the antecedents of Individual Impact, which finally affects the Organizational Impact.

The model has been validated and examined by hundreds of research. Based on critics and suggestions, DeLone and McLean then updated the model in 2003 in order to develop a more parsimonious model. The updated model is illustrated in Fig. 11. Unlike in the previous model, in the updated model, quality has three dimensions, which are Information Quality, System Quality, and Service Quality. Furthermore, the updated model distinguishes between intention to use as an attitude and use as a behavior. However, DeLone and McLean (2003) admit that many researchers may choose to stay with use, since the links between attitude and behavior are difficult to measure. As also argued in the previous model, use and user satisfaction are closely interrelated, positive experience with use will lead to greater user satisfaction in a causal sense. Finally, as a result of this use and user satisfaction, certain net benefits will occur.

D&M IS Success Model is not the only model to measure the IS success. Hategekimana and Trant (2002), for example, proposed a well-known respecifications of the D&M IS Model. However, based on the comparison between D&M Model and Seddon's Model by Ruttan (1996), The D&M

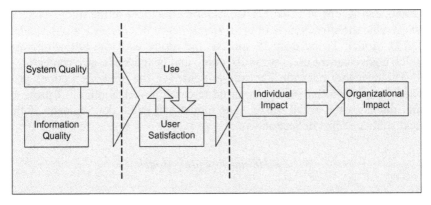

Fig. 10. D&M IS Success Model. *Source*: DeLone and McLean (1992, p. 87).

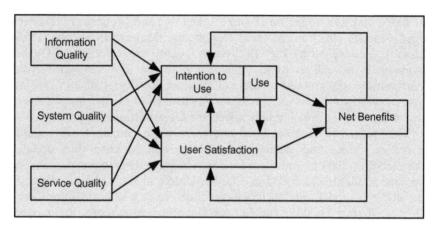

Fig. 11. Updated D&M IS Success Model. *Source*: DeLone and McLean (2003, p. 24).

Model stood up reasonably well and outperformed the Seddon Model. Therefore, this study adopts the D&M Model.

The D&M Model has also been modified and expanded by some studies in accordance with the focus of their research. Lee and Chung (2009) modified the model by incorporated trust in the model. Similarly, Floropoulos et al. (2010) included Perceived Usefulness to measure the IS success. In order to incorporate Intensity to IT investment, and four separate dimensions of IT impact, Venkatesh et al. (2012) have modified the D&M Model as well. Other studies have also been expanding and modifying the D&M Model, such as AbuShanab and Pearson (2007), Loo, Yeow, and Chong (2009), and Keong et al. (2012). Considering the focus of the study, which is to examine the effectiveness of the systems, hence this research also modified D&M Model. To measure IS success, this study used the following variables: e-government use, user satisfaction, and benefits of e-government.

The review of relevant literature presented in the previous sections provides foundation to develop an initial research model. Section 2.7 presents and discusses the initial model. The model will guide development of the field study detailed in Section 4.

2.7. Initial Research Model

This study is conducted with the objectives of examining the impact of digital divide on e-government system success (Section 1.5). Hence, by reviewing previous theories and empirical studies, this current research proposes five types of digital divide, namely demographic divide, economic divide, access divide, capability divide, and innovativeness divide on e-government system success, which is represented by e-government use, user satisfaction, and benefits of e-government. Fig. 12 describes the initial research model for the current research.

As shown in the model, the e-government system success is directly influenced by four variables digital divide – *economic divide* (Agarwal et al., 2009; Mossberger et al., 2006; Schleife, 2010), *access divide* (Dewan et al., 2005; Wei et al., 2011), capability divide (Compeau et al., 1999; Marakas et al., 1998; Wei et al., 2011), and innovativeness divide (Agarwal & Prasad, 1998; Flynn & Goldsmith, 1993; Midgley & Dowling, 1978). The research also investigates the moderating effect of demographic divide, which is represented by residential place (Kuk, 2003; Mariscal, 2005; Mossberger et al., 2006; Stern et al., 2009); gender (Agarwal et al., 2009; Schleife, 2010; Venkatesh & Morris, 2000; Wei et al., 2011); age (Agarwal et al., 2009; Hargittai, 2006; Schleife, 2010); and education (Jung et al., 2001; Mossberger et al., 2006).

In addition, the research investigates the relationships among the variables of digital divide in such way that *economic divide* influences *access divide* (Dewan et al., 2005; Quibra et al., 2003), *access divide* influences

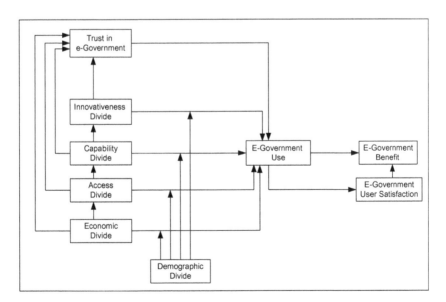

Fig. 12. Initial Research Model.

capability divide (Dewan & Riggins, 2005; Wei et al., 2011), and finally *capability divide* influences *innovativeness divide* (Burkhardt & Brass, 1990; Ellen et al., 1991).

Considering the importance of trust in e-government in e-government system success, and also the role of trust in reducing social complexity (Gefen, 2000; Lewis & Weigert, 1985), this study expects the mediating role of *trust in e-government* in the impact of *digital divide* on *e-government system success*. Previous studies found that *trust in e-government* is an important factor for *e-government use* (Teo et al., 2009; Warkentin et al., 2002). On the other hand, other research also concluded that trust in technologies is influenced by socioeconomic factors, personality variables, and self-efficacy (Cole, 1973).

Compared to previous models in digital divide research whereby most of the models and studies focus on access divide, demographic divide, and economic divide, this current study has extended the analysis. Five levels of digital divide and trust in e-government as well as the e-government systems success are examined simultaneously in order to understand the issue of digital divide more comprehensively and its impact on e-government system success. The initial model is hence insightful in such theory building framework to explain the phenomenon of digital divide.

2.8. Summary

This section has provided a comprehensive review of relevant literature as underlying theoretical foundation for the current research. The main literatures are discussed to provide justification of selected constructs. In summary, this section has covered the theories in development informatics explaining the benefits of ICT for humans, especially for marginalized people. This was followed by a discussion of theories in ICT adoption. The existence of several theories in ICT adoption reflects the importance and hence, big concern from researchers. However, the ICT adoption is facing a significant issue, which is known as digital divide.

The issue of digital divide is getting more attention from researchers, international organizations, and policy makers. The understanding on the issue itself is also evolving as the awareness in the complexity of digital divide rises. This research is proposing more comprehensive factors of digital divide in order to understand it better. Each of the factors has been discussed. The discussion on digital divide was then followed by a literature review on e-government. The review was started from a discussion on the history of e-government initiatives, the benefits of e-government, the stages of e-government implementation, challenges for e-government initiatives, and the importance of trust in e-government.

In the final part, the initial research model that describes the relationship of all factors is presented. In conclusion, the model presents a more comprehensive understanding of digital divide and its impact on e-government system success. The initial model will be explored and examined further in this research.

3. RESEARCH DESIGN

3.1. Introduction

This section describes the design of this research. In doing so, researcher used a framework by Crotty (1998) as illustrated in Fig. 13. Crotty suggests that there are four major elements in developing a research design. At the highest level is the issue of philosophical assumptions or a paradigm, which mainly explains the epistemology and ontology behind the research. The

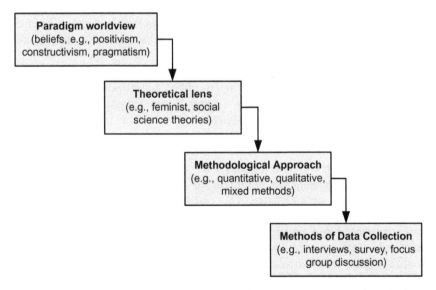

Fig. 13. Levels for Developing a Research Study. *Source*: Adapted from Crotty (1998, p. 4).

philosophical assumptions then relate to the use of theoretical lens that the researcher use. This theoretical lens, in turn, determines the methodology used. Finally, the methodology incorporates the methods, which refer to the procedures used to obtain, analyze and interpret the data.

This section is divided into five sections, in following manner: introduction; research paradigm, which discusses the epistemology behind the study; methodological approach or a research design; research methods, which describe the phases of this study and the steps of data collection and analyses; and finally, conclusion of this section. Since the theoretical lens was already explained in Section 2 in terms of various theoretical models and concepts, this section would not present it again.

3.2. Research Paradigm

A paradigm (also known as "worldview") is a set of generalizations, beliefs, and values of a community of specialists (Kuhn, 1970). Guba and Lincoln (1994) define paradigm as "... *the basic belief system or worldview that guides the investigator, not only in choices of method but in ontologically and epistemologically fundamental ways*" (p. 105). While Morgan (2007) referred to paradigm as "*systems of beliefs and practices that influence how researchers select both the questions they study and methods that they use to study them*" (p. 49). Thus, a paradigm reflects research questions, design, and data collection in research.

In the world of research, there are many paradigms although the major paradigms are positivism (which then modified as postpositivism) and constructivism. There have been long debates between those two major paradigms, especially in social and behavioral science (Onwuegbuzie & Leech, 2005; Sechrest & Sidani, 1995). The differences between both paradigms are actually from the ontological level until the rhetorical level (Creswell & Clark, 2011) as presented in Table 8.

In order to determine the paradigm for this research, the research objectives and context were revisited. This research is investigating the behavior of individuals; therefore it is very subjective issue. Each individual has their own experience and perspective. Moreover, the issue of digital divide is relatively a new problem (Atewell, 2001) and this study is going to conceptualize it more comprehensively. It is very challenging to conduct a research to understand a behavior of individuals and at the same time, attempt to generalize the findings. Researcher needs to carefully explore and capture this complex phenomenon and provides meaningful explanations.

Table 8.   Differences between Positivism and Constructivism.

Paradigm Elements	Postpositivism	Constructivism
Ontology	Singular reality (e.g., researchers reject or fail to reject hypotheses)	Multiple realities (e.g., researchers provide quotes to illustrate different perspectives)
Epistemology	Distance and impartiality (e.g., researchers objectively collect data on instruments)	Closeness (e.g., researchers visit participants at their sites to collect data)
Axiology	Unbiased (e.g., researchers use checks to eliminate bias)	Biased (e.g., researchers actively talk about their biases and interpretations)
Methodology	Deductive (e.g., researchers test an a priori theory)	Inductive (e.g., researchers start with participants' views and build "up" to patterns, theories, and generalizations)
Rhetoric	Formal style (e.g., researchers use agreed-on definitions of variables)	Informal style (e.g., researchers write in a literary, informal style)

Source: Creswell and Clark (2011, p. 42).

Based on the above reasons, this research applied positivism paradigms where researchers are independent of the object of research (Krauss, 2005). Researchers should be emotionally detached and uninvolved with the object of research and should be eliminated their biases. Positivists believe that social research should be objective and time and context-free generalization, and the cause of social scientific outcomes can be determined validly and reliably (Johnson & Onwuegbuzie, 2004). Positivism is closely linked to empirical science and its proponents have always great lovers of science, because scientific knowledge is accurate and certain (Crotty, 1998).

Although this paradigm is generally associated with the use of quantitative methodology, the current study will also collect and analyze qualitative data to explore and enhance the understanding of the object of the research. The qualitative method is based on the constructivism interpretive paradigm because the informants' perspective is given importance (Willis, 2007). The use of both quantitative and qualitative data collection in a single study is known as a mixed method research, which will be discussed more comprehensively in the next section.

3.3. Research Methodology

One of the basic considerations in choosing positivism paradigm is the methodology that was going to be applied in this research. Following the long debate on the level of paradigm, there have been long debates on methodological level: quantitative on one side and qualitative on the other side. From the paradigm wars, three perspectives have evolved. They are purists, situationalists, and pragmatists (Onwuegbuzie & Leech, 2005; Rossman & Wilson, 1985).

Positivism dominates the ISs field (Mingers, 2001; Trauth & Jessup, 2000; Wu, 2012). Orlikowski and Baroudi (1991) investigated 155 articles published in top ranked ISs journals between 1985 and 1989 and concluded that 96.8% research applied quantitative methodology, and left only 3.2% applied qualitative methodology. Similar research was conducted by Chen and Hirschheim (2004), and found that 81% of research in ISs were empirical positivistic studies.

Despite of its dominance, applying only a quantitative study using close-ended questionnaire raise the problem of effectiveness. Although that methodology provides advantages in collecting large numbers of data and easiness in recording and statistical analyses, it increases the likelihood of researcher bias (Converse & Presser, 1986b). It may limit respondents' freedom in answering the questionnaire, trap them into responding based on answers provided, and omit the real perspectives or actions. As a result, those studies have found that self-reported use intention might not lead to actual use (Manfredo & Shelby, 1988). Some scholars even blame on the continual use of statistical significance testing for the slow progress of social sciences (Meehl, 1978).

However, using a qualitative methodology alone would not be free of problem. There is always a question about generalization of data, because limited number of people involved in interviews or focus group discussion or other qualitative methods. Furthermore, users such as policy makers, practitioners, and others demand forms of what so called "sophisticated" evidence, which are difficult to fulfill by those methods (Creswell & Clark, 2011). In the same time, we understand that qualitative approach provides detail understanding of an issue, because it arises out of researching few individuals and exploring their views in great depth. Thus, each method actually offers advantages and in the same time also has its limitations.

In light of the above-mentioned issues, this research applied mixed methods. Mixed methods research has been known as the third methodological movement or the third research community (Teddlie & Tashakkori, 2009) as an alternative to the dichotomy of qualitative and quantitative methodologies. The history of mixed methods research actually started with researchers who believe that both quantitative and qualitative methods are useful as they address the research questions. Mixed methods researchers believe that combining both methods would compensate their weaknesses and would provide cohesive and comprehensive outcomes (Greene, Caracelli, & Graham, 1989; Hohenthal, 2006). However, in the field of ISs in particular, mixed method is still under-utilized (Wu, 2012). Thus, applying a mixed methods research would be a contribution for research in ISs.

In its early development, this method was used largely by cultural anthropologists and sociologists (Johnson, Onwuegbuzie, & Turner, 2007). This method then known as "multiple operationalism" or "mixed methods." In implementing the mixed methods, this study uses the definition by Tashakkori and Teddlie (2003), "*type of research design in which quantitative and qualitative approaches are used in type of questions, research methods, data collection, and analysis procedures, or in inferences.*"

Creswell and Clark (2011) explained six major mixed methods research designs. They are convergent parallel design, explanatory sequential design, exploratory sequential design, embedded design, transformative design, and multiphase design. The decision of the most appropriate design for this research was again based on the research questions and objectives. As stated earlier in Section 1 that this research is exploring the impacts of digital divide on e-government system success in Indonesian local governments. Based on the discussion on theoretical framework in Section 2, researcher proposed an initial research model (Fig. 10). In order to test the applicability of the initial model, a qualitative approach based on field study of semi-structured interview was conducted. The field study was important to explore and refine the initial model, which then examined through quantitative approach based on survey (detail of research methods will be discussed in the next section). Based on the brief description of the methods and research objective, this research employed *exploratory sequential design* with the quantitative approach (*instrument-development variant*) as the major method. Fig. 14 describes the design of this research. This design is best suited to explore a phenomenon in depth (Creswell, 2003; Morgan, 1998).

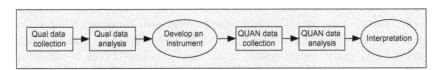

Fig. 14. Diagram of Exploratory Design. *Source*: Creswell and Clark (2011, p. 124).

3.4. Research Methods

Fig. 15 describes the methods of this research. It began with extensive literature review to identify the issues and gaps in the phenomenon of digital divide. Researcher identified potential key variables and developed an initial research model. The initial research model then was explored and enhanced using qualitative method. Qualitative method is suitable in exploring and capturing reality in detail, especially when the experiences of the actors are important (Chan & Ngai, 2007). A field study by conducting one-on-one, face-to-face semi-structured interview was carried out. The objectives of the interview were: (1) to explore concepts and procedures that might not be recognized in the existing literature yet; and (2) to evaluate the worthiness of the concepts identified in the literature review. After being transcribed and translated into English, the results then analyzed using content analysis. As a result, researcher refined the model and developed a comprehensive research model.

Based on the comprehensive research model, hypotheses were proposed to justify the relationships among constructs. Items for each construct were also identified and a questionnaire was designed. To ensure the applicability and understandability of the questionnaire, researcher carried out pilot study. And finally, national survey was conducted involving 237 respondents in Indonesia. Data of the survey were analyzed using SEM based on PLS. Therefore, this research basically employed three basic steps of data collection, which are field study, pilot study, and national survey. Detail of each step is explained in the following sections.

3.4.1. Qualitative Field Study
3.4.1.1. Sample Selection. This research was conducted in Sleman regency and Tulungagung regency in Indonesia (see Appendix F to be aware of where those two regencies are located). Two sampling strategies were applied; stratified random sampling in Sleman regency and snowball sampling in Tulungagung regency. Stratified random sampling was prioritized to ensure that the demographic characteristics (gender and residential place) were represented. In Sleman regency, researcher acquired e-government users' data list from the government. Based on the list, the users were divided into subgroups by the demographic characteristics (gender and place of residence), and then members of each subgroup were contacted randomly by phone to participate in an interview. Unfortunately, researchers could not get a list of e-government users due to technical difficulties in Tulungagung regency. Instead, the One-Stop Service

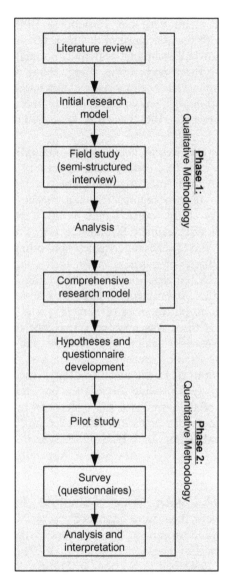

Fig. 15. Research Methods.

Bureau (Badan Pelayanan Perijinan Terpadu — BPPT) gave one user's identity, and then with the assistance of this user, researcher contacted four other users. This snowball sampling strategy is popular among researchers when it is difficult-to-reach populations (Berg, 2004). Most of the cases in which snowball sampling has been used are characterized by less than optimal research conditions, as researcher found in this study, where other methodologies are not applicable (Cohen & Arieli, 2011).

3.4.1.2. Data Collection. Researchers applied qualitative method by conducting one-to-one and face-to-face semi-structured interviews with 12 informants who previously used e-government systems in Indonesia. The research took place in two regions (Sleman regency and Tulungagung regency). Preliminary study revealed that by 2011 there were four local governments in Indonesia, namely Sleman regency, Tulungagung regency, Pemalang regency, and Tangerang regency, providing interactive online service directly to citizens or business within their voluntary e-government systems, which enable citizens and business to log in and make some transactions with the government online. However, the interactive e-government systems in the regencies of Pemalang and Tangerang had just started in 2011, thus there was no user yet. Hence this research is conducted in two regencies, which are Sleman and Tulungagung. E-government systems in those regencies are similar and in the stage of "transaction" according to Layne and Lee (2001). In those two regencies, the e-government systems provide services for business as well as citizens registrations. Most of the users used the systems to register permission to build or renovate homes. Prior to the data collection, researcher obtained an ethical approval from the Human Research Ethics Committee (Protocol Approval GSB 01-11 attached in Appendix B) as required by Curtin University.

3.4.1.3. Data Analysis. After being transcribed and translated into English, the interview data were managed using NVivo8. Researchers applied modus operandi approach, which refers to the analysis the same factors from multiple instances (Chan & Ngai, 2007) (further explanation on the approach is described in Section 4). During developing all of the variables, this research followed both theoretical replication as well as literal replication (Chan & Ngai, 2007). Theoretical replication refers to the selection of cases because they produce contrasting results for predictable reasons, while literal replication refers to the selection of cases based on their similarities and they support the theoretical explanation.

The findings then were compared to the initial research model to be refined as a comprehensive research model (see Section 4 for details).

3.4.2. Hypotheses and Questionnaire Development

A questionnaire was designed based on the comprehensive research model to test the relationship among constructs. The dimensions in the questionnaire were based on the previous research and the Likert scale was used to measure all of them. In order to avoid central tendency error of the respondents, this research adopted six-point scale as suggested by Matell and Jacoby (1972). Central tendency error is observed when respondent answer a middle answer "neutral" or "neither agree or disagree" without really meaning it. Section 5 explains further about the questionnaire development.

3.4.3. Pilot Study

For the pilot study, the questionnaires were distributed to two groups of sample, researchers (three persons are PhD student and researchers in Islamic University of Indonesia) and potential respondents (five persons) by adopting convenient sampling method. The reason for involving researchers was to get comments and suggestions in terms of research perspective. The potential respondents were obtained from the list of e-government users provided by government of Sleman regency. From the potential respondents, researcher expected valuable response in terms of the applicability and understandability of the terms used. They were asked for their review and suggestions. This procedure was conducted continuously until agreements were made.

Data analysis in the pilot study was done using descriptive statistics. It allows evaluation for the main survey. Based on the feedback from the respondents, there was no modification needed to the questionnaire. The analysis is presented in Section 6.

3.4.4. Quantitative Survey

3.4.4.1. Sample Selection. For the survey, the unit analysis is individual. The samples are citizens who have experience in using e-government systems or the users. Considering the research objectives, the researcher set the criteria for the e-government systems used in this study, which are, *first*, G2C (Government to Citizens) systems or G2B (Government to Business) systems provided by local governments in Indonesia. *Second*, the systems are interactive, which means the systems enable the citizens to access the systems through online or internet. Referring to the stages of e-government development by Layne and Lee (2001), the e-government systems required in this research are at least in the stage of "Transaction." *Third*, the systems should be voluntary as well, or in other words citizens have other alternative than accessing the systems via internet (e.g., traditional offline). Because this study is investigating variable of trust in e-government and citizen's willingness to try out the systems, thus voluntary system is required. In the absence of sufficient trust in e-government and willingness, users may be motivated to revert to the traditional offline means of interaction with the government (Teo et al., 2009). As mentioned before in the qualitative survey, only two e-government systems fulfill the above criteria. They are e-government systems in Tulungagung regency and Sleman regency. Therefore this study took place in those two regencies.

3.4.4.2. Data Collection. Samples should be sufficient and representative (Cavana, Sekaran, & Delahaye, 2001; Tashakkori & Teddlie, 1998). By using sufficient and representative samples, results are more likely to be valid, externally as well as internally. In quantitative research, the issue of external validity is not limited to generalizability to the population, but also includes generalizability to situations other than the one that has been researched (Tashakkori & Teddlie, 1998). On the other hand, internal validity refers to the confidence that changes in the dependent variable can be attributed to the independent variables rather than to other potential causal variables (Tashakkori & Teddlie, 1998).

Prior to the survey, researcher was granted an ethical approval by Human Research Ethic Committee through Protocol Approval GSB 11-11 (Appendix C) as required. For this study, data of users were obtained from both local governments, Tulungagung regency and Sleman regency. Following formal inquiry and procedure in both regencies, researcher could obtain data of users within year of 2010 until the mid of 2012 in Sleman regency, while in Tulungagung regency the data were the users within year of 2011 until midyear of 2012. Based on the lists provided by both regencies, the total e-government users are 668 persons. Considering the number of population, hence researcher conducted personally administered survey in the data collection. Personally administered survey refers to face-to-face survey with the respondents (Frazer & Lawley, 2000). However, not all of the users provide telephone number. Based on the telephone number provided by the users, researcher and some research assistants contacted them and ask them to participate in the survey. For those who were willing to participate in the survey, then research assistants brought the questionnaire to them and ask them to complete the questionnaire by themselves. As suggested by Frazer and Lawley (2000), this survey method offers a very high response rate compare to other methods. As a result, 354 copies of questionnaires were distributed, of which 251 were retrieved. A review then was undertaken to seek out errors in the form of invalid data, including missing values or incomplete responses and finally 237 responses were usable in this research. Therefore the effective response rate in this study is 35.5%.

3.4.4.3. Data Analysis. In this research, the analysis is divided into three parts. *First,* the analyses of the influence of the digital divide on the e-government systems success as well as the relationships among variables of digital divide. *Second,* the multi-group analysis examining the moderating effect based on demographic and economic factors. *Third,* the mediating roles of trust in e-government between the influences of digital divide on e-government systems success. The analysis was conducted using the PLS-SEM, based on the consideration of small sample size in this research and the research design applied in this current study, which is exploratory research (Hair, Sarstedt, Ringle, & Mena, 2012). SEM itself is "... *a method for representing, estimating, and testing a theoretical network of mostly linear relations between variables ...*" (Rigdon, 1998).

Two-stage procedures were undertaken in the PLS analysis; measurement model assessment and structural model assessment. Details of the analysis are explained in Section 6. As a summary, Table 9 presents the analyses using PLS technique, as suggested by Barclay, Higgins, and Thompson (1995).

In the first stage, the focus was to assess the relationships between the observed variables and the constructs (Igbaria, Guimaraes, & Davis, 1995), to ensure that the items, which represent the observed variables, measure

Table 9. Two-Stage Approach of PLS Analyses.

Stage	Data Examination	Analyses
1	Measurement model assessment	a. Item reliability b. Internal consistency c. Discriminant validity
2	Structural model assessment	a. Amount of variance explained (R^2) b. Path coefficient (β) c. Statistical significance of t-values

the constructs. The assessment in the first stage involved the calculations of loadings that indicate the strength of the measures. Table 10 describes the procedures undertaken in the first stage of the measurement model assessment.

In assessing the convergent validity, the first step is to examine the item reliability. Item reliability refers to an analysis of estimating the amount of variance in each individual item's measure that is due to the construct (Barclay et al., 1995). Item reliability tests how strong each item related to their respective construct, which is frequently referred to as simple correlations. The calculated correlation leads to an item loading, which provides an indication of the item's strength. Since all of the items in this research are reflective items, hence item reliability can be assessed by evaluating the loading score in PLS.

Although researchers have different opinion in regard with the acceptable value of the item loading, but the rule of thumb is that the higher the item loading, the better it would represent the construct. Most researchers suggest that most of the loadings should at least 0.6 and ideally 0.7 or above (Chin, 1998). Some scholars believe that the items with extremely low loadings should be carefully reviewed, especially if the items have been taken from strong theoretical foundation (Nunnally & Bernstein, 1994). In such circumstances, some errors such as incorrect wording in the questionnaire, misunderstanding by the respondents, or using inappropriate items to measure constructs might be the causes (Hulland, 1999).

Table 10. Measurement Model Assessment Procedure and Requirements.

Measurement	Acceptable Value
1. Convergent validity	
a. Item reliability	Item loading ≥ 0.7
b. Internal consistency	
i. Composite reliability (CR)	Calculated value ≥ 0.7
ii. Average Variance Extracted (AVE)	Calculated value ≥ 0.5
2. Discriminant validity	
a. Construct level	Square root of AVE of construct > correlation between the construct and other construct
b. Item level	Item loadings of construct > all other cross-item loadings of the construct

Beside item reliability, it is also important to examine internal consistency in order to assess convergent validity. Internal consistency refers to the measure of reliability of the constructs (Fornell & Larcker, 1981). Although many quantitative researchers have been using Cronbach's alpha as an indicator for internal consistency, Chin and Gopal (1995) argue that Cronbach's alpha represents a lower-bound indicator of internal consistency because of its parallel measures. Thus, they suggest using composite reliability (CR) formula by Werts, Linn, and Joreskog (1974). CR is considered to be more general and more superior than Cronbach's alpha, because it is not influenced by the number of items in the scale. The value of the CR can be calculated using the following formula (Barclay et al., 1995; Chin, 1998):

$$\rho_c = \frac{\left(\sum \lambda_i\right)^2}{\left(\sum \lambda_i\right)^2 + \sum \text{Var}(\varepsilon_i)}$$

where

λ_i = component loading to an indicator; and $\text{Var}(\varepsilon_i) = 1 - \lambda_i^2$, the unique/error variance.

As suggested by Nunnally and Bernstein (1994) and Barclay et al. (1995), the threshold of 0.7 is considered as the minimum value for CR to establish a convergent validity of the measurement model.

In addition to CR, Average Variance Extracted (AVE) is also common indicator to assess internal consistency for reflective constructs (Fornell & Larcker, 1981). AVE represents the Average Variance Extracted of a construct by its corresponding items and assesses the amount of variance that is captured by an underlying factor in relation to the amount of variance due to measurement error. AVE indicates the variance shared between a construct and its measures. The formula for obtaining AVE is as follows (Chin, 1998):

$$\text{AVE} = \frac{\sum \lambda_i^2}{\sum \lambda_i^2 + \sum \text{Var}(\varepsilon_i)}$$

where

λ_i = factor component loading to an indicator; and $\text{Var}(\varepsilon_i) = 1 - \lambda_i^2$.

In term of the minimum value, scholars suggest that a construct should achieve a value greater than equal to 0.5 for AVE to achieve adequate reliability (Fornell & Larcker, 1981; Nunnally & Bernstein, 1994).

To assess the discriminant validity of the measurement model, the square root of AVE is compared to the inter-construct correlations. The discriminant validity itself refers to the degree to which constructs differ with each other within the same model (Hulland, 1999). Discriminant validity at the construct level is considered adequate when the AVE for one's construct is greater than their shared variance (Chin, 1998; Fornell & Larcker, 1981).

In the item level, discriminant validity was assessed by examining cross loading for each item and comparing across all constructs, and is presented in a form of cross-loading matrix. The cross-loading analysis measures the correlation of an item with respect to all of the constructs within the model (Chin, 1998). An item has strong discriminant validity when it has higher loading value on the construct it intends to measure, than on other constructs. To produce the analysis, researcher has to manually calculate the output produced by the PLS Graph software using other statistical software package, namely SPSS.

The second stage concerned with the relationships that exist between the paths in the model (Igbaria et al., 1995). By using the software of PLS Graph, researcher calculated the estimated path coefficient for each path in the model. The results indicate the strength and direction of the theoretical relationship. The assessment process covers examining the explanatory power of the independent variables (R^2), the path coefficient, and the value of t-statistics (Barclay et al., 1995).

The R^2 values were examined to assess the predictive power of the proposed research model (Barclay et al., 1995). It represents the extent of the independent constructs that explain the dependent constructs. The interpretation of it is similar to regression model (Fornell & Larcker, 1981). The R^2 indicates the amount of variance in the construct which is explained by its corresponding independent constructs. It is produced by the bootstrap process and the values of 0.75, 0.50, or 0.25 for endogenous latent variables (LVs) in the structural model can be described as substantial, moderate, or weak, respectively (Hair, Ringle, & Sarstedt, 2011).

To evaluate the relationship of the construct as hypothesized in this research, examinations of path coefficient (β) and the t-value were undertaken. Those β and t-statistics were obtained from the bootstrapping process. Bootstrapping itself represents nonparametric test for estimating the precision of the PLS estimates (Chin, 1998). Through bootstrap procedure, N samples sets are created in order to obtain N estimates for each parameter in the PLS model.

Finally, whether the impact of a particular independent LV on a dependent LV has substantive impact or not can be explored by examining the f^2 (Chin, 1998). The f^2 value of 0.02, 0.15, or 0.35 is considered has a small, medium, or large effect at the structural level, respectively (Cohen, 1988). The value of f^2 can be calculated by the following formula (Chin, 1998):

$$f^2 = \frac{R^2_{\text{included}} - R^2_{\text{excluded}}}{1 - R^2_{\text{included}}}$$

where $R^2_{\text{included}} = R^2$ provided on the dependent LV when the independent LV is used and $R^2_{\text{excluded}} = R^2$ provided on the dependent LV when the dependent LV is omitted

Fig. 16 summarizes the research methods that have been undertaken in this study. Researcher conducted literature review, which was presented in Section 2, as the starting step in order to provide theoretical background of this research. The literature review also aimed to identify the research gaps in the previous research and existing literature, from which the researcher developed research questions, objectives, and initial research model. Furthermore, in order to explore and enhance the initial research model, a field study has been undertaken. From the semi-structured interviews, researcher analyzed the data using content analysis. Based on the findings, comparisons with the initial model have been made and comprehensive research model was proposed. Section 4 described the process and findings in detail.

In the next step, researcher developed hypotheses to examine the relationships among variables. For the measurement tool, a questionnaire was developed based on previous research and the findings in the field study. In order to test the questionnaire, a pilot study was undertaken by distributing the questionnaire to the researchers and potential respondents. As a result, questionnaire was finalized and ready to be distributed to the respondents. Section 5 presented those processes.

As the main research, quantitative data were collected through survey by mail and directly to the respondents. The data were then analyzed using PLS-based SEM. All of these processes were detailed in Section 6. Finally, the findings based on the quantitative data analysis were interpreted and researcher discussed the implications of the findings for theoretical development and for practice, as described in Section 7.

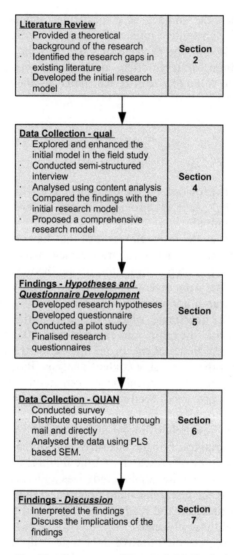

Fig. 16. Summary of Research Methods.

3.5. *Summary*

The discussion on the paradigm started this section and followed by under-lying justifications in using positivism paradigm for this research. However, mixed methods with the exploratory sequential design were chosen as the platform in conducting this research. The design started with a qualitative study by conducting semi-structured interview and followed by quantitative research as the major method by using PLS-based SEM.

4. FIELD STUDY AND COMPREHENSIVE RESEARCH MODEL[1]

4.1. Introduction

As discussed in Section 3, the mixed method approach was adopted in this research. In this stage, a qualitative research analysis was conducted through a field study. This section presents the analyses of the data generated from the field study. The qualitative approach was primarily performed to fine-tune the tentative research model proposed earlier (Fig. 12). The field study was also required in order to ensure the validity and relevance of the model, since the research was conducted in Indonesia and most related theories are written from a Western perspective. The field study also aimed to explore the dimensions of each construct in the research. The qualitative approach was conducted through semi-structured interviews with 12 users of e-government in Indonesia.

The findings of the field study were analyzed using content analysis. Based on the analysis, a field study model was developed and comparisons made with the initial proposed research model. As a result, a comprehensive research model was developed and presented in the final part of this section.

4.2. Interview Questionnaire Development

In order to cover the three main topics in this research, the interview questionnaire was designed using seven questions (a full set of interview guides can be found in Appendix A). The first topic investigates the success of the e-government system. To this end, three questions were prepared (Table 11). Question 1 asks whether the interviewees are the users of the e-government system and if so why. It also asks about the influence of informant's economic conditions on the use of e-government system. Question 2 explores the satisfaction of the interviewees with the

Table 11.   Questions in Field Study.

Topics	Question Number	Brief Description of Questions
E-government system success	1	• Users' experience in using e-government system • Reasons of using e-government system • The influence of economic condition on the use of e-government system
	2	• Users' satisfaction of e-government system
	3	• Benefits of e-government system
Influence of digital divide on e-government system success	4	• Dimensions of access divide • The influence of access divide on capability divide • The influence of economic divide on access divide • The influence of access divide on trust in e-government system • The influence of access divide on the use of e-government system
	5	• Dimensions of capability divide • The influence of capability divide on innovativeness divide • The influence of capability divide on trust in e-government system • The influence of capability divide on the use of e-government system
	6	• Dimensions of innovativeness divide • The influence of innovativeness divide on trust in e-government system • The influence of innovativeness divide on the use of e-government system
Mediating effect of trust in e-government system	7	• Dimensions of trust in e-government system • The influence of trust in e-government system on the use of e-government system • The influence of economic divide on the trust in e-government system

e-government system. Question 3 relates to the benefits of the e-government system to interviewees.

The second topic in the research covers the impact of the digital divide on the success of e-government. There are three questions, which examine this topic. In each question, there are two kinds of probe-questions, probes for exploring the dimensionality of the particular digital divide and probes for understanding the influence of the digital divide on the success of the e-government system. Questions 4, 5, and 6 investigate the access divide, the capability divide, and the innovativeness divide, respectively. To enhance the dimensionality of each construct, the informants were asked whether they had any other comments to make regarding each particular construct.

The third topic inquired into the mediating effect of trust on the success of the e-government system. To examine this, a question (Question 7) was posed about the influence of trust in the e-government system with regard to its success. This question consisted of probes of dimensionality of trust in the e-government system and probes relating to the relationship of trust in the e-government system and other constructs.

It was a requirement of Curtin University that the Human Research Ethics Committee examined and approved the interview guide prior to use. The Committee granted approval on the guide through Protocol Approval number GSB 01-11, attached in Appendix B.

Prior to the field study, to test the comprehensibility and applicability of the questions to the participants and to estimate the duration of the interviews, two participants were engaged in a review. One interviewee was a potential participant in the field study and the other was a researcher at a local university. Based on their feedback, all of the questions were deemed comprehensible, with the exception of a probe in question 6, which was: "*Do you think that the One-Stop Service is sincere and genuine?*" This probe was removed in order to avoid any misunderstanding and/or unexpected responses from the informants. No other issues were raised and the estimated duration of a single interview was between 45 and 60 minutes.

The pilot study found to be a valuable experience. The researcher felt that the sequence of the questions should not follow the interview guidance. Rather, questions should be asked about the dimensions of the constructs and this would be followed by questions about the relationships between the constructs. The reasoning was due to the fact that the informants might not clearly understand the concept of the constructs. By asking questions about dimensions of the constructs, it would be easier for informants to understand each construct. The informants might then respond more easily to questions about the relationships between constructs. The final interviews were conducted with 12 users of the Indonesian e-government system.

Since the interviews take place in Indonesia and the interviewees are Indonesian, the interviews are conducted in Bahasa Indonesia. The questions are translated into Bahasa Indonesia by the researcher prior to the period of data collection. Back translation approach is used in translating

the questionnaire, when translators interpret a document previously translated into English backs to the original language (Indonesian) and compared. Plain language is used and any jargon or difficult word is avoided.

4.3. Sample Selection and Data Collection

A preliminary study has revealed that up until 2011 there were four local
governments in Indonesia, which provide online services directly to citizens
in their e-government systems. In other words, their e-government systems
enable citizens to log into the systems and perform some transactions with
the government through the online system. The local governments under
study were to be the governments of the Sleman regency, the Tulungagung
regency, the Tangerang regency, and the Pemalang regency. Upon further
investigation, it seemed that the interactive e-government systems in the
Tangerang regency and the Pemalang regency had only been set up as
recently as 2011, limiting access to users. The field study had therefore to
limit itself to the Sleman regency and the Tulungagung regency.

The field study applied two methods of sample selection. In the Sleman
regency, the researcher applied a stratified random sampling method, as
suggested by Berg (2004). This method was chosen due to the need to
ensure that the sample represented the demographic characteristics (gender
and residential place) of the location. In the Sleman regency, data regarding
e-government users were obtained from the government by requesting the
data through a formal procedure. From the data, the users were divided
into subgroups (strata), being the demographic groups. Each group was
then approached randomly via telephone to request their participation in
the interview. Seven users in the Sleman regency were interviewed.

In the Tulungagung regency, due to technical difficulties, data on
e-government users were unavailable. The officer in the One-Stop Service
Bureau (BPPT) was able to give only one name of an e-government user.
With the assistance of this user, four other users were found, in line with
the Snowball Sampling method. As suggested by Berg (2004), this method
is popular among researchers seeking difficult-to-reach populations. Once
interview permission was granted, date, time, and venue of the interview
was arranged, with regard to the most suitable conditions for the interviewees. Those who accepted were also given an outline of the course the
interview would take.

Prior to the interview, an information sheet was shown to the participants as part of the ice-breaking procedure to dispel any hesitancy and

make the participants more comfortable for the interview. The participants were also asked permission to be recorded during interviews. Notes were taken throughout the interviews. After the interviews, the recordings were transcribed verbatim immediately. As the interviews were in Indonesian, the transcripts were then translated into English. In order to maintain accuracy, other researchers were asked to recheck the transcripts and translations and some corrections on the translations were made.

4.4. Data Analysis

A two-step content analysis, namely deductive and inductive, was carried out to analyze the data of the semi-structured interviews (Berg, 2004; Siltaoja, 2006). The process of the data analysis is presented in Fig. 17. Content analysis is a useful and the most appropriate way to learn the relationship among the concept (Flick, 2007), the interview data, and the theoretical framework in order to fulfill the objectives of the field study. The field study researcher utilized the NVivo 9 software program to help manage the data. NVivo is able to record, search, and explore patterns of data and ideas (Richards, 1999).

At the inductive stage, themes, sub-themes, and concepts explaining variables, factors, and measurement scales are explored. This is followed by induction of the explored factors and variables into a single framework, which is then compared to the initial research model (Fig. 10 presented in Section 2). In comparing the models, theoretical replication as well as literal replication (Chan & Ngai, 2007) is carried out. Theoretical replication is conducted by contrasting the differences in cases between the informants; while literal replication shows where the similarities in cases exist.

In the data coding, using NVivo, the data were reviewed and examined on an individual informant basis. Based on the findings, individual research models were then developed (Appendix D). These research models are fundamental to the contextualization of the individual findings. The models were then compared to one other and a further model was developed to represent the overall findings of the field study.

Following inductive analysis, the initial research model and the model of field study were compared and reviewed. This step was undertaken to examine the significant constructs and their dimensionalities. The findings in the field study were then revisited to determine the most significant constructs that represent antecedent factors along with the relationships

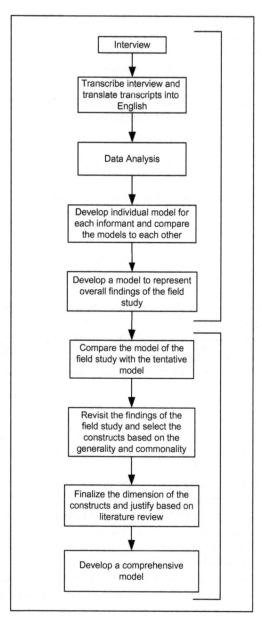

Fig. 17.   Data Analysis Process.

between variables. Based on the literature review and the field study, the dimensions of the constructs were then finalized and justified.

The following sections explain the findings of the process.

4.5. Inductive Analysis: Findings of Antecedents Factors

4.5.1. Influence of the Economic Divide on E-Government Use

Most of the informants (12 of 14) stated that economic conditions do not influence e-government users (see Table 12). Participants in the field study mostly believe that an Internet connection nowadays is not problematic in terms of accessibility. For example, informant 5 and informant 8 made the following statements, "I think people at all levels of income might access the online service provided by the government. In fact, with the online system, I don't have to pay transportation costs. I mean the government actually provides a cheaper service via the online system. People just don't understand the benefits of the online system" (Inf. 5). "I don't think that personal economic circumstances influence the usage of the e-government online system, as nowadays we can easily find Internet facilities in shopping centers, restaurants, and other public areas. We can access the Internet for free. Although I frequently find people just access the Internet to check their email, chat, and social network, I think the government should promote its online facilities, like e-government, to broader society. Once people know that they are able to process their registration or license via the internet, I believe they will choose this kind of facility instead of the traditional system" (Inf. 8).

However, three participants (Inf. 7, Inf. 8, and Inf. 12) suggested that e-government use is influenced by economic conditions to some degree. Informant 7 felt that economic conditions had a weak influence on e-government use, as described in his statement, "Yes obviously it costs to access the e-government online system, well maybe there is a correlation

Table 12. Link between the Economic Divide and E-Government Use.

Variable	Informant												Frequency
	1	2	3	4	5	6	7	8	9	10	11	12	
ED → EU	✗	✗	✗	✗	✗	✗	✓	✓	✗	✗	✗	✓	3

Note: ED = economic divide; EU = e-government use; ✓ = agree; ✗ = disagree.

with one's personal economic circumstances but I don't think that is really significant" (Inf. 7).

While informant 8 and informant 12 stated, "As we have an adequate income, we are able to have all the facilities including the Internet. I believe if more people have an Internet connection, they will use the e-government system, because it makes everyone's business easier and simpler" (Inf. 8). "I believe that some people feel that an Internet connection is still expensive and that they have a lot of basic needs to be fulfilled first. They might not even think about an internet connection and e-government" (Inf. 12).

Based on the content analysis of the influence of the economic divide on e-government use, Table 12 shows the response of each informant to the link. The findings from the field study do not support the relationship between those variables.

4.5.2. Influence of the Access Divide on E-Government Use

With regard to the influence of the access divide on e-government use, all of the informants ($N = 12$) agreed that access is a vital factor. According to the informants, access is the prerequisite for citizens to use the e-government system. Informant 9 and informant 3 emphasized this, "Yes I believe that Internet access is important for e-government use. How can you use the system if you cannot access it? I believe that many citizens are actually keen to use the OSSOS (One-Stop Service Online System), because it is easier, cheaper and simpler ..." (Inf. 9). "I find the online system very useful, with it I don't have to go to out and visit various agencies. I don't like bureaucracy because it's difficult. Therefore I will use the online system whenever it's possible and available. To do that I need to be able to access to the system" (Inf. 3).

Table 13 provides the responses from each individual participant based on content analysis. The responses confirm that the access divide is one of the key determinants in e-government use. Hence, a relationship between those variable can be expected.

Table 13.   Link between Access Divide and E-Government Use.

Variable	Informant												Frequency
	1	2	3	4	5	6	7	8	9	10	11	12	
AD → EU	✓	✓	✓	✓	✓	✓	✓	✓	✓	✓	✓	✓	12

Note: AD = access divide; EU = e-government use; ✓ = agree; ✗ = disagree.

In term of dimensions of access divide, there are three dimensions used to describe the access divide. All of the informants agreed with the first dimension (easiness) and the third (comfort), although only half of the informants (six informants) agreed regarding the second dimension (place). Table 14 demonstrates the responses of each informant toward each dimension of the access divide.

With regard to the dimension of "easiness," informant 6 and informant 7 were of following opinion, "Actually it is quite easy: in terms of finding the website, it's easy, in terms of operating the online system, that's easy too. You just go to the web, then click and follow the menus" (Inf. 6); "When I used it for the first time, I didn't find any problems. I could access the system easily. I was even able to do the registration at night (after office hours), and basically I can use the system any time I want. Overall I think the system is easy for me to use. It's just like using other websites" (Inf. 7).

Regarding the dimension of "comfort," informants 2 and 3 suggested that the online system was more comfortable "... compared to manual system." Furthermore, six informants agreed that "place of residence limits access to online system." Informant 2, who lives in a remote area, stated "... it is more difficult in mountainous area, like my area." Informant 11 also found the same issue, "It is difficult to access the OSSOS in my village as it is a 'black spot', but when I go to the neighbouring area, the Internet kiosks are like mushrooms, they're just everywhere."

The other six informants, however, believed that place of residence is not an issue nowadays. They believe that Internet connections are fairly easily accessible in some public areas. Informant 9 and informant 10 argued, "... In term of internet access, I can access the internet from my house. Now it's easy to get Internet access. In the shopping centers, in the restaurants, it's possible for us to connect to the Internet through the WiFi system. Even at my restaurant, I was able to install a WiFi service. I tell

Table 14. Dimensionality of Access Divide.

Dimensionality	Informant												Frequency
	1	2	3	4	5	6	7	8	9	10	11	12	
Easiness	✓	✓	✓	✓	✓	✓	✓	✓	✓	✓	✓	✓	12
Place	✗	✓	✓	✓	✗	✗	✓	✓	✗	✗	✗	✓	6
Comfort in Access	✓	✓	✓	✓	✓	✓	✓	✓	✓	✓	✓	✓	12

Note: ✓ = agree; ✗ = disagree.

you; nowadays people prefer to go to a restaurant with a WiFi service than one which does not have it ..." (Inf. 9).

> ... Internet kiosks are everywhere now. Even in some remote areas, we can find Internet kiosks. In the restaurants and shopping centres we are able to access the Internet for free. (Inf. 10)

4.6. Influence of the Capability Divide on E-Government Use

Content analysis of the semi-structured interviews shows that all of the informants consider capability as the key determinant in e-government use. Table 15 represents individual agreement on this aspect. Informants believe that a comprehensive ability to operate an online system is required for e-government use. Informant 1 strongly suggests, "Capability is a must. Without it, citizen cannot use e-government." While informant 11 stated, "I think technology literate is the most important factor." Thus, the relationship between the capability divide and e-government use, as proposed by the initial model, was supported by the findings in the field study.

The responses to the dimensions of the capability divide also describe strong agreement on each dimension. All informants agreed on the first, third, and fourth dimensions, whereas none of the informants found any difficulty with operating an online system or with IT in general (dimension 2). Table 16 represents each response regarding the dimensions of the capability divide.

The informants in the field study appeared to be familiar with ICT. They reported feeling confident and comfortable with using ICTs, although some of the informants only use ICTs insofar as they need to in order to support their business. Informant 3, for example, is a lecturer in the field of ISs. He mentioned, "I'm a lecturer at the college (college of ISs). I use ICT in my everyday life basically. Computer, Internet, telephone, software, I use them every day. Capability in using these is a must for me. I don't find

Table 15. Link between Capability Divide and E-Government Use.

Variable	Informant												Frequency
	1	2	3	4	5	6	7	8	9	10	11	12	
CD → EU	✓	✓	✓	✓	✓	✓	✓	✓	✓	✓	✓	✓	12

Note: CD = capability divide; EU = e-government use; ✓ = agree; ✗ = disagree.

Table 16. Dimensionality of Capability Divide.

Dimensionality	Informant												Frequency
	1	2	3	4	5	6	7	8	9	10	11	12	
Confidence	✓	✓	✓	✓	✓	✓	✓	✓	✓	✓	✓	✓	12
Difficulty	✗	✗	✗	✗	✗	✗	✗	✗	✗	✗	✗	✗	0
Comfort in using	✓	✓	✓	✓	✓	✓	✓	✓	✓	✓	✓	✓	12
Ability	✓	✓	✓	✓	✓	✓	✓	✓	✓	✓	✓	✓	12

Note: ✓ = agree; ✗ = disagree.

any difficulty in using ICT. In fact, it helps me. I feel comfortable using the gadgets. Sometimes, if I leave one of my gadgets at home accidentally, I feel nervous. Something is missing, you know ..."

Informant 7 on the other hand, stated, "I run a business in computer maintenance and trade, although at first, computers were just a hobby. But now I always update the latest developments. I follow it all in the computer magazines, on the Internet, via my colleagues, etc. Every day, I find something new about computers and ICTs. That's why I like this business. But I need to learn more. Learning about things we like is exciting."

4.6.1. Influence of the Innovativeness Divide on E-Government Use
The initial model proposed a relationship between the innovativeness divide and e-government use (Fig. 10) and the findings of the field study offer some level of support of the potential relationship. Among the informants, 10 informants suggested a link between the innovativeness divide and e-government use. From Table 17, it can be seen that the innovativeness divide is considered by most of the informants as one important factor influencing e-government use. Informant 10 answered, "Yes, it can be one of the factors I believe, but I have seen many people capable of operating a computer and using websites, but they just utilise it all narrowly. Many people just use the Internet to check email and do social networking. Basically it's more just for fun. I suspect they are hesitant in utilising the computer further, say for online transactions, for example."

Informant 11 also stated, "As I mentioned before, I ended up using this service by accident. I mean, because I was curious, I just browsed the Internet and found that this online system was already available. Because I get to explore new websites and ICTs in general, I just feel confident in filling in forms and following the online procedures ..."

Table 17.   Link between Innovativeness Divide and E-Government Use.

Variable	Informant												Frequency
	1	2	3	4	5	6	7	8	9	10	11	12	
ID → EU	✓	✓	✓	✓	✗	✓	✓	✓	✓	✓	✓	✗	10

Note: ID = innovativeness divide; EU = e-government use; ✓= agree; ✗ = disagree.

Table 18.   Dimensionality of Innovativeness Divide.

Dimensionality	Informant												Frequency
	1	2	3	4	5	6	7	8	9	10	11	12	
Curiosity	✓	✓	✓	✓	✓	✓	✓	✓	✓	✓	✓	✓	12
First mover	✗	✗	✗	✗	✓	✗	✓	✗	✗	✓	✓	✗	4
Hesitancy	✓	✗	✗	✗	✗	✓	✓	✓	✗	✗	✗	✓	5
Experiment	✗	✓	✓	✗	✓	✓	✓	✓	✓	✓	✓	✓	10

Note: ✓= agree; ✗ = disagree.

Based on the content analysis, all of the informants ($N = 12$) appeared curious regarding new ICTs. They would seek a way to try new ICTs if they heard about them. Furthermore, the majority of the informants (10 informants) liked to experiment with new ICTs. Informant 11, for example, reported, "Because I'm a photographer, if I hear of new software or a gadget via the Internet or my colleagues, I always look for a way to try it. I like to go to exhibitions, because at the exhibitions I can try out a new gadget or some software. Then if I need it and I can afford it, then I'll buy it."

Most of the informants (seven informants) do not hesitate to try new ICTs. On the other hand, five informants are hesitant, citing fears of viruses, data theft, and hackers as articulated by Informant 12, "I am afraid someone steal or misuse my personal data." Informant 1 also expresses his concern, "I'm afraid of fake website." Furthermore, in term of "first mover"; most of the participants (eight participants) were reluctant to be first movers. Most of them heard about new ICT from their peers, as uttered by Informant 3, "Usually I try new ICT based on a recommendation, from an expert or my colleague." Table 18 presents the responses of each participant on the dimensionality of the innovativeness divide.

Table 19. Link between Trust in E-Government and E-Government Use.

Variable	Informant												Frequency
	1	2	3	4	5	6	7	8	9	10	11	12	
T → EU	✓	✓	✓	✓	✓	✓	✓	✓	✓	✓	✓	✓	12

Note: T = Trust in e-government; EU = e-government use; ✓ = agree; ✗ = disagree.

4.6.2. Influence of Trust in E-Government on E-Government Use

Based on the content analysis, all of the participants ($N = 12$) demonstrated that trust in e-government influences the usage of e-government. Table 19 describes the relationship between these variables, according to the informants. Trust in e-government appears to be a factor in determining e-government use. It influences the decision to use e-government. Therefore, the relationship between these variables can be expected, as proposed in the initial model. Informant 10 stated, "I trust the website, because the web address lets me know that the site is a government website. I won't use any website if I don't trust it, especially if it requires my personal data."

Similarly, informants 7 and 9 stated, "I can say that because we trust the online system we are ok to use the system, just like when trust a product in general. Once you trust it, you use it" (Inf. 7).

> ... I think trust is important factor in using online services, such as e-commerce and e-government. Without any trust, people wouldn't use an online system. They'd be afraid that the website's fake; you know nowadays the websites of some banks are counterfeited and if we enter our PIN or password our money could be stolen. (Inf. 9)

In term of dimensionality, content analysis of the data demonstrates five dimensions to describe "trust in e-government." Table 20 presents the findings of these dimensions. All dimensions were confirmed by most of the informants. For dimension "care" in particular, 11 informants agreed that e-government cares for its citizens' needs. Participant 12 confirmed, "I can say that the e-government online system accommodates the public need. Citizens need a simple, cheap and quick process ..." However, for the dimension of "competent and effective," only one informant disagreed with it. This particular informant (Inf. 6) stated, "The e-government system was created on the basis of the assumption that everyone has an IMB (Ijin Mendirikan Bangunan/Registration to Build). The question is, is it true? The system is too complicated for me and it's not effective."

Table 20.   Dimensionality of Trust in E-Government.

Dimensionality	Informant												Frequency
	1	2	3	4	5	6	7	8	9	10	11	12	
Truthful and honest	✓	✗	✓	✓	✓	✗	✓	✓	✓	✓	✓	✗	9
Competent and Effective	✓	✓	✓	✓	✓	✗	✓	✓	✓	✓	✓	✓	11
Care	✓	✓	✓	✓	✓	✗	✓	✓	✓	✓	✓	✓	11
Stable and predictable	✓	✗	✓	✓	✓	✗	✓	✓	✓	✓	✗	✓	9
Committed	✓	✗	✓	✓	✓	✗	✓	✓	✓	✓	✗	✗	8

Note: ✓ = agree; ✗ = disagree.

On the other hand, the other 11 informants agreed that the system is effective and competent. Informant 3, for example, mentioned, "I believe the system is effective in serving citizens' needs. And because it is provided by the Office of the One-Stop Service by the government of Sleman, I also believe that it is competent."

With regard to the stability and predictability of the e-government system, there were three participants who did not agree. They felt that they could not find any information with regard to the time and costs needed to finish the registration. They commented that the system was unpredictable and unstable. Informant 2 complained, "It's difficult to predict time and money used. I keep wondering about the money that I might have to come up with. We may be asked to pay again and again, who knows?"

However the other nine informants confirmed confidence in the stability and predictability of the e-government system. They found the information regarding the requirements of the process, and based on their experience there was not a great deal of deviation from the information. Therefore they might predict the process of registrations.

4.6.3. Relationships among the Variables in the Digital Divide

The initial model in this chapter proposed that the economic divide influences the access divide, while the access divide influences the capability divide, and ultimately, the innovativeness divide is influenced by the capability divide (Fig. 10). Based on the content analysis, links between the access divide, capability divide, and innovativeness divide appear to be supported by the participants. However, the influence of the economic divide on the access divide appears to be supported by only half of the informants

Table 21. Link of Variables in Digital Divide.

Variable	Informant												Frequency
	1	2	3	4	5	6	7	8	9	10	11	12	
ED → AD	✗	✗	✗	✗	✗	✓	✓	✓	✓	✓	✗	✓	6
AC → CD	✓	✓	✓	✓	✓	✓	✓	✓	✓	✓	✓	✓	12
CD → ID	✓	✓	✓	✓	✓	✓	✓	✓	✓	✓	✓	✓	12

Note: ED = economic divide; AD = access divide; CD = capability divide; ID = innovativeness divide; ✓ = agree; ✗ = disagree.

($N = 6$). Table 21 shows the relationships between variables in the digital divide as perceived by each informant.

For the relationship between the economic divide and access in particular, six informants confirmed that the economic divide influences the access divide. Most of them believed that many people are still struggling with basic needs, regardless of the fact that the cost of accessing ICT is getting cheaper nowadays. Accessing ICT is not a priority for those people. Informant 3 states, "The cost of accessing the Internet is much cheaper now. Despite this I will only access the Internet more when my personal economic circumstances improve." Similarly, informant 9 believed, "... when their personal economic circumstances improve, there will be more people who will access the online system more. It costs to connect to the Internet, for sure. For people with low levels of income, they first must fulfill their basic needs, that's what's most important to them. It is for me too. I'll access the internet more when my income level increases."

The other six informants suggested that the economic divide does not have a link with access divide. The differences were based on the argument that the cost of accessing the Internet is getting cheaper, and they believe that it is not a significant issue anymore. Informant 5 for example, states that: "... *Anyone at any level of income can access the internet, and the e-government system. I don't see any connection with one's financial situation.*" Participant 12 similarly comments: "*It's possible to find free Internet access in public spaces. I don't think income-level is an issue.*"

Furthermore, the participants suggested that there is a link between the access divide and the capability divide. They believe that the more intensely they access ICT, the more they become familiar with ICT and their capability in using ICT will increase. Participant 7 states: "*I learnt the computer and how to use the Internet by myself. I just browse the Internet and I also try out software. The more frequently I use the gadgets and the software, the more capable I become.*" Participant 4 also argues: "*I believe so. How can we capable of using ICT if we don't have access to it?*"

In terms of the link between capability divide and innovativeness divide, all of the informants ($N = 12$) demonstrated support for such a link. Most of the participants believed that in trying new ICTs, they needed to have some ability. Participant 11 stated: "*I need at least basic capability when I try a new gadget or software. Otherwise, I won't try them,*" while informant 1 said: "*I usually find out about new software before I try it. I read a book about it or find something on the Internet.*" Based on the content analysis, the relationship among the variables of the digital divide is as expected in the initial model.

4.6.4. Influence of the Digital Divide on Trust in E-Government
The initial proposed model pointed to links between the digital divide and trust in e-government (Fig. 12). However, the field study found that a link between the economic divide and trust in e-government might be weak. Alternatively, a possible links between the capability divide and trust in e-government, and between the innovativeness divide and trust in e-government were uncovered by all of the informants ($N = 12$). Eleven of the 12 informants also suggested that there might be a link between the access divide and trust in e-government. Table 22 summarizes the findings of the field study.

With regard to the possible link between the economic divide and trust in e-government, most of the participants appeared to be unclear about such a link. Informant 5 stated: "*I don't understand the link between the two. As for me, my trust is not based on my economic circumstances.*" However informants 7 and 12 believed that one's personal economic

Table 22. Link of Digital Divide and Trust in E-Government.

Variable	Informant												Frequency
	1	2	3	4	5	6	7	8	9	10	11	12	
ED → T	✗	✗	✗	✗	✗	✗	✓	✗	✗	✗	✗	✓	2
AC → T	✓	✓	✓	✓	✗	✓	✓	✓	✓	✓	✓	✓	11
CD → T	✓	✓	✓	✓	✓	✓	✓	✓	✓	✓	✓	✓	12
ID → T	✓	✓	✓	✓	✓	✓	✓	✓	✓	✓	✓	✓	12

Note: ED = economic divide; AD = access divide; CD = capability divide; ID = innovativeness divide; T = trust in e-government; ✓ = agree; ✗ = disagree.

circumstances affect one's belief to trust in any kind of technology. Informant 12 is of the opinion:

> I believe that those who are at lower levels of the economic spectrum tend to have a lower level of trust in government, and that includes e-government. Although I can't see a direct relationship, I believe somehow they are related. In e-government and e-commerce in particular, I think people don't want to use them because they don't trust them. They tend to prefer the traditional system, where they can meet with the customer service officer personally.

As presented in Table 22, 11 participants suggested the influence of access divide is important to trust in e-government. Participant 9 commented: "*I will trust a system that is easy and comfortable to access.*" While participant 12 argued:

> I believe that every system is developed to make our business easier. When I feel comfortable in using a system, I put more trust more in it. On the other hand, when a system is difficult and too complex for me, I'm hesitant to use it. I think complexity might be a cause of corruption.

In terms of the influence of the capability divide and the innovativeness divide on trust in e-government, all of the informants demonstrated that this link is likely important. Most informants argued that in trusting a system, they need to understand and to be capable of using it. Informant 10 stated: "*... I trust in a system that I'm capable of using. Without any understanding and capability, I'd feel anxious.*"

Based on the content analysis, all of the informants demonstrated a proclivity to believe that innovativeness divide is linked to trust in e-government. Informants believe that a willingness to try new ICT is one of the important factors in trust in e-government. Informant 5, for example, answered:

> I like to try new gadgets and software. And I like to browse the Internet. On the Internet we can find anything, through Google or other search engines. By browsing and constantly trying new things, I can maybe understand and distinguish between trustworthy and untrustworthy websites. (Inf. 5)

Similarly, informant 12 stated:

> Based on my experience in trying and exploring ICTs, I now have a better understanding and awareness of new ICTs. So I should be able to tell if information about new ICTs is honest. (Inf. 12)

It is evident from the field study that there is general agreement and synergy with the proposed initial model (Fig. 12). Only the link between the economic divide and trust in e-government demonstrated some lack of confirmation.

4.6.5. E-Government System Success

The variables of "e-government system success" as proposed in the initial
model are "e-government use," "e-government user satisfaction," and "benefit of e-government" (Fig. 10). These variables are derived from an established model (DeLone & McLean, 2003). Hence the objectives of the field
study are to investigate the dimensionalities of each variable. The dimensions of each variable and the responses of each individual informant on
each dimension are described in Table 23.

Table 24 shows the amount of times each individual informant has used
the e-government system. Eight of the informants were first-time users,
while the other four had used the system more than once. Among the informants, there were five informants whose registrations were not finished
yet.[2] For one informant (Inf. 6), there was a possibility of ineligibility for
registration, due to his failure to provide the requested documents.

Most of the informants ($N = 9$) appeared satisfied with the system, and
eight informants stated that the systems met their expectations. Most of the
participants expected a simpler process from the new system as compared
with the traditional system, and more efficiency in term of costs and time.
Informant 9 said:

> ... it is simpler in term of process, and costs less. You know, when we have business
> with the government, we expect it to be a difficult process. Bureaucratic processes, you
> know ... (expression of dislike). However I found this service very easy and simple.

Table 23. Dimensionality of E-Government System Success.

Variable	Dimensionality	Informant												Frequency
		1	2	3	4	5	6	7	8	9	10	11	12	
E-government use	Use	✓	✓	✓	✓	✓	✓	✓	✓	✓	✓	✓	✓	12
User satisfaction	Satisfaction	✓	✗	✗	✓	✓	✓	✓	✓	✓	✓	✓	✓	10
	Expectation	✓	✗	✗	✓	✓	✗	✓	✓	✓	✓	✓	✓	9
Benefit	Cost efficient	✓	✓	✓	✓	✓	✓	✓	✓	✓	✓	✓	✓	12
	Time efficient	✗	✓	✓	✓	✗	✓	✓	✓	✓	✓	✓	✓	10
	Simpler process	✓	✗	✗	✓	✓	✗	✓	✓	✓	✓	✓	✓	9

Note: ✓ = agree; ✗ = disagree.

Table 24. E-Government Usage by Each Informant.

Informant	Region	Number of Use
Inf. 1	Sleman regency	1
Inf. 2		1
Inf. 3		1
Inf. 4		2
Inf. 5		1
Inf. 6		1
Inf. 7		2
Inf. 8	Tulungagung regency	10
Inf. 9		1
Inf. 10		1
Inf. 11		1
Inf. 12		3

However, participants 2 and 3 did not complete the use of the system due to their experiences of technical failures where they have to repeat the process manually. Interestingly, although participant 6 was satisfied with the system, he felt that the system does not serve customers as expected. For example, he expects simplicity in term of the ability of the system to receive scanned documents, which was not available.

With regard to the benefits of the e-government system, all of the informants ($N = 12$) suggested that the online system saved them money. Informant 4 commented: "*Yes, I don't have to pay for transport.*" Informant 6 also argued:

Actually the costs will not be any problem for businessmen like me, as long as the costs are reasonable and predictable. And I think the costs of the e-government system in Sleman are reasonable and as stated on their website. Business needs certainty you know, to calculate cost and profit.

Most of the informants also found the system saves time. Informant 8 stated: "*I can do the registrations whenever I want to do. Even in the middle of the night.*" Furthermore, informant 5 stated:

Because it's a One-Stop Service, it accommodates our need to process registrations through one office. In the traditional service, we had to go to various departments. The one-stop service saves time. Moreover, it's an online system and it's much better than the traditional system.

The e-government system also benefits its users by providing a simpler process. In the Sleman regency, users must fill in the form through the online system and submit the required documents to the Office of the One-Stop

Service. In the Tulungagung regency, after filling in the form, the users must prepare the required documents. An officer from the Office of the One-Stop Service collects the required documents from the users. As mentioned previously, informant 6 expected the system to accept the required documents by scanning and uploading them to the system. However, the system at that time was not accepting documents in that format. Informants 2 and 3 had to repeat the process all over again due to a technical failure. This caused some frustration and these informants felt that the system was too complicated.

Beside the three benefits of cost efficiency, time efficiency, and simplicity of process, six informants (Inf. 4, Inf. 5, Inf. 8, Inf. 9, Inf. 10, Inf. 12) mentioned *"transparency"* as one of the benefits they received from the e-government system. They felt that they would be able to find information about costs, time, and steps in the process of registration on the government's website. Hence, they found the system more transparent.

4.6.6. Influence of Gender, Residential Place, and Age on E-Government Use
In the initial model, the "demographic divide" was proposed as the moderating variable between the digital divide and e-government system success. Demographic factors such as residential place, gender, and age will be investigated in the second stage of this research (quantitative research). In the field study, residential place, gender, and age were not included as variables in the list of interview questions. However, in determining the informants in the field study, efforts were made to accommodate a range of demographic groups. Table 25 describes the characteristics of informants based on their demographic groups.

According to the informants resident in the city area, access to the Internet and e-government online system was not a problem; they felt that they could easily access the Internet. However, for the informants who lived in remote areas, finding an Internet connection was more difficult. Informant 11 was resident in a mountainous area and his village was located in a "black" or "blank spot," where telephone signals had not yet reached the area due to lack of infrastructure development. Informant 11 had to go to another location or to his office in the city area to find an Internet connection. On the other hand, informant 6 who also lived in a remote area did not experience any difficulties in finding an Internet connection. This informant also felt that residential place did not limit his access to the One-Stop Service Online System.

Table 25. Characteristics of Informants Based on Demographic Groups.

Informant	Region	Residential Place	Age Group	Gender
Inf. 1	Sleman regency	City area	40–50	Male
Inf. 2		Remote area	30–40	Female
Inf. 3		Remote area	30–40	Male
Inf. 4		City area	40–50	Male
Inf. 5		City area	30–40	Male
Inf. 6		Remote area	30–40	Male
Inf. 7		City area	20–30	Male
Inf. 8	Tulungagung regency	City area	30–40	Male
Inf. 9		City area	30–40	Male
Inf. 10		City area	20–30	Male
Inf. 11		Remote area	30–40	Male
Inf. 12		City area	40–50	Male

In terms of age groups, it was observed that most of the informants ($N = 7$) were in the range of 30–40 years old. Informants 1 and 12 revealed that their children assisted them in using the e-government system. All of the informants in the age group of 40–50 reported no difficulties in term of access, capability, and innovativeness.

One of the interesting findings in the field study was the influence of gender on e-government use. Although efforts were made to find female informants for the field study, only one informant participated. Five female potential informants were contacted; however four of them declined to participate in the field study. They stated that although the registrations for e-government were under their name, it was actually their husbands used the system. This finding reveals that gender is one of the influential factors in e-government use.

4.6.7. Findings Regarding Other Relevant Factors
As mentioned earlier, the main objective of this field study is to fine-tune the initial model. In addition, the applicability of the model was also assessed. Other related variables and dimensions in the research came up unexpectedly but only served to enhance the explanatory power of the research model. Based on the content analysis, some interesting findings were discovered via the informants.

Informants 5 and 7 commented on the variable "*Perceived Ease of Use,*" although from differing viewpoints. Informant 5 mentioned "*Perceived*

Ease of Use" as the mediating variable between the "*capability divide*" and "*e-government use.*" He stated:

> Increasing my capability in using a particular system, I believe, will increase my under-
> standing of it. And if I think that the system is easy to use, then I might use it.

On the other hand, Informant 7 mentioned "*Perceived Ease of Use*" as the moderating variable between the "access divide" and "e-government use." He argued: "*If my access to IT gets easier, my preference to use the e-government system will also increase, as long as I believe that I am able to use it.*"

Another noteworthy variable for informants was "*Perceived Usefulness.*" Informant 1 mentioned "*Perceived Usefulness*" as the moderating variable between the "*access divide*" and "*e-government use.*" Informant 1 commented:

> An increase in my access to IT will in turn influence my usage of the e-government,
> that's what I believe. However, if the system or IT is not useful to me, I won't use it
> even if I have better access.

Since each of the two informants mentioned the variables "*Perceived Ease of Use*" and "*Perceived Usefulness*" and they commented on them in different ways; it was decided to omit these variables (as per Flick, 2007) to remove any uncertainty.

4.7. The Field Study Model

Based on the content analysis, individual models were developed to illustrate the findings that come from each informant in the field study. There were 12 models produced, and these can be found in Appendix E. Comparison among the models was made in order to develop the field study model. Fig. 18 was developed as a result of the comparisons and combinations.

4.8. Deductive Analysis: Review of the Findings of the Field Study

In this phase, three steps were undertaken to review the initial model and the findings of the field study. The first step involved a comparison between the initial model and the field study model. As a result of the first step, the influence of antecedent factors and the moderating factors of the

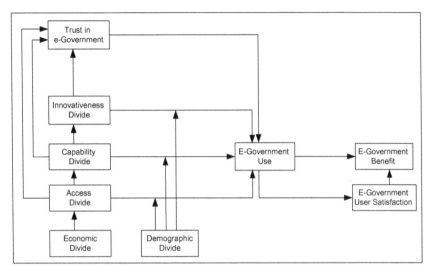

Fig. 18. Field Study Model.

demographic divide could be verified. In addition, the possible links between the variables of the digital divide were also discussed.

Findings from the field study were then revisited and reviewed in the second step. In comparing the initial model and the field study model, the focus was centered on the differences between the two models. Therefore, the analysis focused on the least significant antecedent constructs, and the additional construct, which was mentioned by participants.

Based on the data in the field study, the links between the "*economic divide*" and "*e-government use*" and between the "*economic divide*" and "*trust in e-government*" were questioned by most of the informants in terms of influence. As shown in Table 12 and Table 22, only three informants perceived any level of influence between "*economic divide*" and "*e-government use*," and two informants perceived any level of influence between "*economic divide*" and "*trust in e-government*." Hence, these two variables appear to have the least importance in the research model according to the field study.

The constructs and dimensions resulting from the second step were then reviewed with regard to the existing literature in the third step. This step was undertaken to ensure that the selected constructs were adequate and competent, based on the existing theory along with empirical research.

4.8.1. Findings Regarding the Economic Divide, E-Government Use, and Trust in E-Government

Referring to the findings from the inductive analysis, links between *"economic divide"* and *"e-government use"* and *"trust in e-government"* were perceived by most of the informants. Therefore those particular links have a basis for inclusion in the model following the existing literature and the findings of the field study. Alternatively, Table 26 shows the response of each individual informant on the perception of the links between *"economic divide"* and *"e-government use"* and *"trust in e-government."*

Since the two links above were generally not perceived by most of the informants, literature and previous research was then revisited (see the following section). Despite the fact that most of the variables and links in the initial research model were supported by literature, as discussed in Section 2, the literature and previous research produced mixed results. Therefore the links may be changed based on the findings in the field study and literature.

4.8.2. Relationships among Variables – the Economic Divide, E-Government Use, and Trust in E-Government

In terms of the link between *"economic divide"* and *"e-government use,"* there has been a large body of research into this, although the results are mixed. Socioeconomic factors have been associated with behavioral patterns in many fields, including those in the area of ISs. Previous research has found that socioeconomic conditions influence acceptance of technology (Agarwal et al., 2009; Hsieh et al., 2008; Schleife, 2010). Furthermore, Norris (2001) and Mossberger et al. (2006, 2008) have examined the impact

Table 26. Link of Economic Divide, E-Government Use, and Trust in E-Government.

Variable	Informant												Frequency
	1	2	3	4	5	6	7	8	9	10	11	12	
EC → EU	✗	✗	✗	✗	✗	✗	✓	✓	✗	✗	✗	✓	3
ED → T	✗	✗	✗	✗	✗	✗	✓	✗	✗	✗	✗	✓	2

Note: ED = economic divide; EU = e-government use; T = Trust in e-government; ✓= agree; ✗ = disagree.

of the economic divide on internet use in particular. Norris (2001), who investigated the Internet use in certain countries in terms of unit analysis, concluded that Internet penetration had a strong correlation to economic development. In addition, Mossberger et al. (2006) found that in the United States, personal economic circumstances are one of the significant factors influencing internet use.

Moreover, the variable, "economic condition" has also been put to use in different roles. Some researchers use it as an antecedent factor (e.g., Agarwal et al., 2009; Mossberger et al., 2006; Norris, 2001; Quibra et al., 2003; Schleife, 2010), while others have used it as a moderator variable (e.g., Hsieh et al., 2008, 2011; Jung et al., 2001).

On the other hand, ideas around the link between the "*economic divide*" and "*trust in e-government*" have been initially developed based on the sociological approach (Lewis & Weigert, 1985). Moreover, Lewis and Weigert (1985) argue that trust is essential in a society in order to reduce complexity. Trust plays a significant role as generalized expectancy in a heterogeneous society. Despite the lack of literature and of empirical research in the area of ISs exploring the relationship between economic circumstances and trust, Cole (1973) revealed that socioeconomic factors significantly influence political trust. Furthermore, Gefen et al. (2003) argue that levels of trust may be assessed by economic analysis and shaped by rational and calculative assessment, such as cost/benefit. Therefore, the economic circumstances of the "trusting" individual are important in this view.

Despite the arguments above, empirical research has produced inconsistent findings on the relationship between economic circumstances and trust. Research by Cole (1973) found that economic circumstances do not influence an individual's trust in government. This finding concurs with research by Campbell (1962, p. 14) which concludes that "trust depends on something other than simple socioeconomic status."

Having considered the lack of literature justifying the direct impact of economic circumstances on trust in e-government, along with the disagreement of most of the informants in the field study carried out, the role of the economic divide in this research was altered. The economic divide, represented by household income, was adjusted to perform the role of a moderator variable on the impact of the digital divide on the success of the e-government system. Previous studies (e.g., Hsieh et al., 2008, 2011) similarly examined household income as moderator variable.

4.9. The Comprehensive Research Model

Based on the literature and the field study, the section presented here proposes a comprehensive research model, illustrated in Fig. 19.

The comprehensive model argues that the digital divide (this research examined the access divide, the capability divide and the innovativeness divide as independent variables and the demographic divide and the economic divide as moderating variables) has a significant impact on the success of the e-government system. The dependent variable is represented by e-government use, user satisfaction and ultimately, the benefits of e-government (DeLone & McLean, 2003). In addition, this study also investigated the relationships between variables in the digital divide from the point of view that access to ICT influences the ability to utilize ICT and in turn, ability has a significant impact on willingness to try new ICT.

Furthermore, this research proposed that trust in e-government has a mediating role to play in the impact of the digital divide on the success of the e-government system. In the other words, trust is an important factor in improving e-government success in an unequal or divided society.

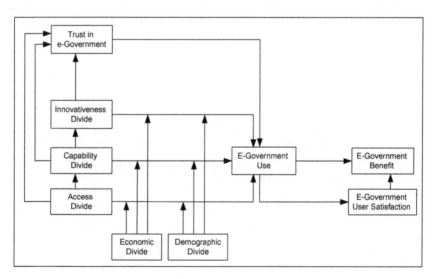

Fig. 19. Comprehensive Research Model.

4.10. Summary

This section presented the findings of the field study and proposed a research model. Qualitative data were generated from 12 interviews with e-government system users. The main objective of this field study was to test the applicability of the initial research model proposed earlier along with exploring the dimensionality of related constructs.

The content analysis technique, consisting of inductive and deductive stages, was undertaken to analyze the data. Moreover, theoretical and lateral replications were employed in the deductive stage. Factors, variables, some measures and the links among variables were explored based on the literature. Based on the analysis, a combined model, which integrated all the variables from each interview, was developed. The model was then compared to the initial model, which was derived from the literature review, to propose the comprehensive research model. In Section 5, hypotheses are developed from this comprehensive research model, and these are then examined with the quantitative approach in Section 6.

5. HYPOTHESES AND QUESTIONNAIRE DEVELOPMENT

5.1. Introduction

Section 4 discusses the field study which was conducted to fine-tune the initial research model and develop it into a comprehensive research model in the context of Indonesia. As shown in the model (Fig. 19), a more comprehensive framework on the digital divide is offered by this study. As highlighted before, this research investigates the influence of the digital divide on the success of e-government systems. The current study also examines the mediating role of trust in e-government.

Referring to the research model below (Fig. 20), this section discusses the development of hypotheses, which are justified by the relevant literature. The hypotheses describe the relationships among the constructs as proposed in the model.

The development of the questionnaire as the survey instrument in order to test the hypotheses is also presented following the hypotheses development. Structure and format of the questionnaire is explained in this section.

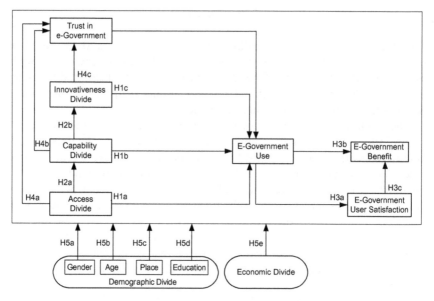

Fig. 20. The Hypotheses Research Model.

The measurement items are supported by previous studies as well as the results from the field study. The questionnaire appears as Appendix D.

5.2. Hypotheses Development

5.2.1. Hypotheses Related to the Digital Divide

In this research, the digital divide is defined as an inequality between individuals, households, businesses, and geographic areas at different socioeconomic levels with regard to both their opportunities to access ICTs and their use for a wide variety of activities (OECD, 2001). Based on the definition, a more comprehensive understanding of the digital divide is proposed by three categories: namely the access divide, the capability divide, and the innovativeness divide.

5.2.1.1. Access Divide. As previously discussed in Section 2, most of the previous research into the digital divide focused on the access divide as the dependent variable in ICT use (Rahman & Quaddus, 2012), although operational definitions of "access" vary from study to study. Some researchers refer to "access" as an individual possessing the means to connect to the internet (e.g., Atewell, 2001; Corrocher & Ordanini, 2002; Ferro, Helbig, & Gil-Garcia, 2011; James, 2004, 2007; Wei et al., 2011). Other researchers use the term "access" as a synonym for use, drivers of access and choice whether an individual had the means to connect to the Internet or not (e.g., Mossberger et al., 2006, 2008; Norris, 2001).

However, those who have examined the access divide and its influence on ICT use suggest that access to ICT was a key factor in ICT use. This current research refers the access divide to physical access to ICT.

5.2.1.2. Capability Divide. Section 2 was discussed the capability divide and Social Cognitive Theory. However this section is discussing them more detail and in relation with variables in the research model.

Based on Dewan and Riggins' framework and Social Cognitive Theory, Wei et al. (2011) developed a more comprehensive model for the digital divide to include the capability divide. The capability divide is then considered as the second order of the digital divide (Dewan & Riggins, 2005; Wei et al., 2011). The digital capability divide itself is resulted from Social Cognitive Theory (Bandura, 1977), which argues that an individual possesses a self-belief system. This system allows each individual to control his/her cognitive processes, feelings, motivation, and behavior (Bandura, 1977), with self-efficacy being the key to the system. Self-efficacy may not necessarily reflect their actual competence.

In the area of ISs, CSE has been examined in previous research (Compeau et al., 1999; Marakas et al., 1998; Warschauer, 2003b; Wei et al., 2011), which suggested that self-efficacy has a significant influence on behavior and attitudes.

The literature is confirmed by the findings in the field study. All of the informants agreed in the relationship between the two variables, as articulated by informant 11, "I think technology literacy is the most important factor."

5.2.1.3. Innovativeness Divide. As mentioned in Section 2, the innovativeness divide refers to the willingness to change and try out any new information technology (Agarwal & Prasad, 1998; Hurt et al., 1977). Innovation is closely related to greater risks and uncertainty (Kirton, 1976). As new technological innovations are introduced, potential users will consider perceived benefits as well as perceived risks or costs. Technological innovations will be adopted if the benefits earned by its users exceed the risks or costs (Ellen et al., 1991). Similarly, Rogers (1995) believed that innovators and early adopters were individuals who were able to cope with high levels of risk and uncertainty. With regard to attitudes toward new technology, van Dijk and Hacker (2003) admitted that information *want-not* was a more important problem than information *have-not*. Hofstede (1983, 2009) found that in Indonesia as well as in most Asian countries, levels of the "uncertainty avoidance" index, a society's tolerance for uncertainty and ambiguity, were generally high. Consequently, Indonesians and Asians in general did not easily accept any changes and innovations.

Personal Innovativeness was utilized to explain the influence of the innovativeness divide on IT usage. Research by Midgley and Dowling (1978), Flynn and Goldsmith (1993), and Agarwal and Prasad (1998) concluded that Personal Innovativeness is a significant predictor of the acceptance of information technology innovations. Similar findings also generated by a study by Yi, Fiedler, and Park (2006). The influence of the innovativeness divide on e-government use is also supported by the informants (10 out of 12 informants) in the field study.

Referring to the findings of the literature and the field study, the hypotheses that describe the interrelationship between the variables have been developed as follows: H1a: access divide positively influences e-government use; H1b: capability divide positively influences e-government use; H1c: innovativeness divide positively influences e-government use.

In addition, CSE is influenced by access to ICT. Wei et al. (2011) assert that the availability of IT resources provides the foundation from which individuals acquire CSE. Previous studies also show that access to ICT is a determinant of CSE (Bertot, 2003; Gripenberg, 2011; Wei et al., 2011). Gripenberg (2011) suggests that the availability of computer access may increase the learning and development of IT skills, especially when the support persons are also available. Similarly, Wei et al. (2011) concluded that access divide among students is significantly influencing CSE of students.

The participants in the field study also confirmed the positive influence of the access divide on the capability divide. They believe that the more intensively they access ICT, the more familiar they will become with ICT and therefore their capability in using ICT will increase. H2a is hence proposed. H2 (a): access divide positively influences capability divide.

Self-efficacy is based on self-judgment of an individual's own performance capability in specific settings. This subjective evaluation of ability to perform the required tasks is determined by the individual's interactions with and feedback from the environment (Bandura, 1977). Even when a given alternative is acknowledged as better, feelings of low self-efficacy often lead individuals to choose the alternatives they can handle rather than the one that is "better" or "best" (Seltzer, 1983). In other words, individuals attempt to avoid or minimize discomfort. Thus, when faced with a change, which the person feels less capable of handling, s/he may resist due to feelings of incapability or discomfort, which may arise from the anticipated change.

Previous studies which have examined the influence of self-efficacy on willingness to change or try new IT include Burkhardt and Brass (1990) who found that self-efficacy is closely related to willingness to early adopt new technology. Ellen et al. (1991) also suggest that greater self-efficacy would be associated with less resistance to the technological innovations. In line with those studies, all of the participants in the field study believed that in trying new ICTs, they needed to be capable of them. Informant 1 says, "I usually find out about new software before I try it. I read a book or find it on Internet."

Based on above discussion, H2b is proposed. H2b: capability divide positively influences innovativeness divide.

5.2.2. Hypotheses Related to E-Government Systems Success

DeLone and McLean develop a model to examine IS success (1992), which was then updated (2003). The model has been validated in the area of e-commerce where it was originally developed (e.g., Gelderman, 1998; Lee & Chung, 2009) as well as in the area of e-government (e.g., Teo et al., 2009; Wang & Liao, 2008). The updated model indicates that IS success depends on IS quality (Information Quality, System Quality, and Service Quality). These qualities influence system usage and user satisfaction, and in turn benefit users.

The framework by DeLone and McLean basically consists of two parts, one is the quality of the product (System Quality, Information Quality, and Service Quality) and the other is the effectiveness or influence of the product (use, user satisfaction, and impact or net benefit) (Mason, 1978). This research will use this framework with an emphasis on the effectiveness or influence of the system, as system success cannot be claimed if the system doesn't influence its user despite its good quality. DeLone and McLean also admitted that "use," "user satisfaction," and "benefit" are the important indicators of system success, and these indicators have previously been used on an individual basis by some researchers to measure system success (DeLone & McLean, 1992).

This research will focus on usage, user satisfaction, and benefit as indicators of system success, excluding the quality of the system as it is beyond the control of the users. Previous researchers have also modified the

DeLone and McLean Model in accordance with the focus of the research (Floropoulos et al., 2010; Lee & Chung, 2009).

The use of ISs has often been the measure of MIS success (DeLone & McLean, 2003; Zmud, 1979). The broad concept of use can be measured from many perspectives. However, many scholars (e.g., Kim & Lee, 1986; Lucas, 1978; Wang & Liao, 2008) suggest that in a voluntary system, "actual use" is the most appropriate to measure IS success. Furthermore, DeLone and McLean (2003) "use" and "user satisfaction" are interrelated. In a process sense "user satisfaction" must be preceded by "use," while in a causal sense positive experience with "use" will lead to greater "user satisfaction." As a result of the "use" and "user satisfaction," "net benefit" will occur (DeLone & McLean, 2003). A research by Wang and Liao (2008) on e-government system success concluded that citizens perceive benefit of the system because they have used the system and satisfied with it.

Due to DeLone and McLean's framework and the findings from the previous studies, the sequential process of e-government systems success is expected as follows:

H3(a): E-government use positively influences user satisfaction; H3b: E-government use positively influences benefits of e-government; H3(c): User satisfaction positively influences benefits of e-government.

5.2.3. Hypotheses Related to Trust in E-Government

Trust is basically a social and psychological phenomenon (Kelton et al., 2007). In the area of ICT, trust is believed to be an important factor in ICT use (McKnight & Chervany, 2002; Teo et al., 2009; Vance et al., 2008). The cognitive process of trust formation has been shown to positively influence an individual's intention to use e-commerce (e.g., Gefen et al., 2003; McKnight & Chervany, 2002) and e-government (e.g., Teo et al., 2009; Warkentin et al., 2002).

Many scholars define "trust" with a particular emphasis on the psychological aspect. Some argue that "trust" is "willingness to depend" (Gefen et al., 2000, 2003). In the context of the e-government system, trust in e-government refers to the "belief that the e-government system can be used to get the desired outcome satisfactorily" (Teo et al., 2009).

An e-government system is a surrogate or a proxy for the government that provides public services to citizens and businesses through traditional channels (Teo et al., 2009). Therefore, if a government shows sincere care for its citizens and is able to effectively conduct its services, citizens are more likely to believe that the e-government systems developed and maintained by the government will be able to serve their needs. In countries such as Indonesia where the trust in government fluctuates (LSI, 2010), it is interesting to examine the influence of "trust in e-government" on "e-government system success." Moreover, the findings in the field study also support the link between trust in e-government and e-government use, as articulated by Informant 9, for example, "… I think trust is important factor in using online services, such as e-commerce and e-government. Without any trust, people wouldn't use the online system …"

On the other hand, trust is constructed by cognitive processes, emotional bonds, and behavioral enactment. These three basic modes of human social experience are interpenetrating and work together in constructing trust (Lewis & Weigert, 1985). Previous studies in political science suggest that trust is influenced by socioeconomic factors, personality variables, and self-efficacy (Cole, 1973).

This research will investigate the mediating role of "trust in e-government" in the relationship between the digital divide and e-government system success. A construct may be said to function as a mediator to the extent that it accounts for the relation between the independent and dependent variables (Baron & Kenny, 1986). The reasons are: first, trust is a substantial sociological factor on which converge various sets of expectations in order to reduce social differences (Lewis & Weigert, 1985). Second, trust in the e-government system from the citizen is a vital factor for the success of e-government system (Pavlou, 2003; Teo et al., 2009; Warkentin et al., 2002). And third, trust has been recognized as a mediating variable in many areas, including behavioral intention in management (Cropanzano & Mitchell, 2005; Vlachos et al., 2009), marketing and consumer loyalty (Bontis, Booker, & Serenko, 2007; Morgan & Hunt, 1994; Sirdeshmukh et al., 2002).

In their study, Vlachos et al. (2009) report that trust fully mediates the relationship between stakeholder-driven attribution and recommendation and partially mediates the relationship between stakeholder-driven attribution and patronage intentions. Morgan and Hunt (1994) also concluded that trust is a key mediating construct in the successful relationship marketing.

Based on the discussion above, the following hypotheses are posited. H4a: Trust in e-government has a mediating effect on the relationship between the access divide and e-government use. H4b: Trust in e-government has a mediating effect on the relationship between the capability divide and e-government use. H4c: Trust in e-government has a mediating effect on the relationship between the innovativeness divide and e-government use.

5.2.4. Hypotheses Related to Demographic Divide and Economic Divide
Differential behavioral patterns in fields such as sociology, marketing, and
psychology have been associated with socioeconomic inequality.
Socioeconomic characteristics instigate a synergy of social and economic
forces from infrastructure to individuals and resources in the surrounding
environment (Borstein & Bradley, 2003). Furthermore, Borstein and
Bradley (2003) state that education background, income, and other life factors also tend to correlate and be distributed unequally across the socioeconomic continuum in a such pattern that proves unfavorable to the
socioeconomically disadvantaged. As a consequence, these inequalities
have been interpreted as internal and external resources, or constraints,
that together, shape experiences and opportunities, living and working conditions, place in society, and even ways in which the world is viewed
(Williams, 1990).

In the field of ISs, the influence of socioeconomic inequality on system
acceptance has also been explored and investigated. As a matter of fact,
research into the digital divide has been dominated by studies on socioeconomic inequalities, such as gender (e.g., Agarwal et al., 2009; Schleife,
2010; Venkatesh & Morris, 2000; Wei et al., 2011); age (e.g., Agarwal et al.,
2009; Hargittai, 2006; Morris & Venkatesh, 2000; Schleife, 2010); residential place (e.g., Kuk, 2003; Mariscal, 2005; Mossberger et al., 2006; Stern
et al., 2009); and income and educational attainment (e.g., Hsieh et al.,
2008, 2011). In this research, demographics and the economic divide will be
used as moderating variables as suggested by previous research. The moderating effect of gender, age, place of residence, education, and income are
discussed in each of the following section.

5.2.4.1. Gender. Gender is potentially critical to our understanding of user
acceptance because it plays an important role in determining how users
make decisions about using new technology (Venkatesh & Morris, 2000).
From a psychological stand point, Bem and Allen (1974) found that gender
difference influences decision-making processes through the differences in
schematic processing by men and women. Bem (1981) argues that men and
women encode and process information using different socially constructed
cognitive structures, which in turn, help determine and direct an individual's perception. As a result, individuals tend to make decisions, which
reflect biases inherent in the individual's perceptions.

In the studies on technology adoption, it has been found that women
typically show a higher level of computer anxiety (Igbaria & Chakrabarti,
1990; Rosen & Maguire, 1990) and lower computer aptitude (Fetler, 1985).

As a consequence, gender difference plays significant role as a moderating variable in Internet use. Agarwal et al. (2009) examined the moderating role of gender and concluded that men are somewhat less likely to use Internet. Similarly, Venkatesh and Morris (2000) found in their longitudinal study that men and women are different with respect to technology adoption both in the long and short term. While in term of CSE, Fetler (1985) who studied the difference between sixth and twelfth grade boys and girls, concluded that boys outperformed girls in every area of computer literacy. In addition, Fetler also found that the girls have less opportunity to interact with computer than the boys. Similar results are also found by Wei et al. (2011).

5.2.4.2. Age. A large body of research examines socio-cognitive changes among individuals based on age. In the area of psychology, a great deal of research focuses on understanding the differences in abilities, traits, or performance outcomes (e.g., Czaja & Sharit, 1993; Myers & Conner, 1992; Rhodes, 1983; Sharit & Czaja, 1994). Age affects influencing attitudes caused by a number of factors, including social role (psychosocial) changes and biological changes (Rhodes, 1983). Furthermore, Rhodes (1983, p. 329) explains that psychosocial aging consists of "systematic changes in personality, needs, expectations, and behaviour as well as performance in a sequence of socially prescribed roles and accumulation of experiences." Biological ageing is characterized by changes in anatomical as well as psychological states that naturally occur with age, such as changes in sensorimotor performance, visual acuity, reaction time, and so on.

Confirming the studies in psychology, a study by Czaja and Sharit (1993) shows that age has an impact on the performance of computer-based tasks. Similar research was also conducted by Morris and Venkatesh (2000). By examining the effect of age on the use of technology in the workplace directly and indirectly as a moderator variable, the results indicated that in the short term, age acts as a moderating role instead of acting as an independent variable. Bucy (2000) suggests that age, together with income, education, and family structure are important determinants of internet use. His research indicated that older respondents are disadvantaged in terms of internet use. Similar results were also reported by Hindman (2000), Loges and Jung (2001), Mills and Whitacre (2003), van Dijk and Hacker (2003).

5.2.4.3. Place of Residence. Disparity in access to and use of computers and the Internet is based on geographical factors as well. Studies by Newburger (2001) and Mills and Whitacre (2003) concluded that an access and use gap existed in the United States between metropolitan and non-metropolitan areas. Similar research into the differences in internet use in rural and urban areas were conducted by Hindman (2000), Nicholas (2003), and Schleife (2010). The rural geographical disadvantage has not yet been eliminated by the existence of the Internet. Nicholas (2003) and Schleife (2010) concluded that the patterns of development exacerbated rural disadvantage. However, Hindman (2000) and Mills and Whitacre (2003) found different results where the place of residence appears to be less of a constraint than other factors, such as income, age, and education.

Despite inconsistent conclusions on the significance of place of residence regarding internet and computer use, unlike the residents in cities or metropolitan areas, residents in rural or non-metropolitan regions do not have the same variety of learning and observation possibilities (e.g., free public internet access and internet cafés). Rural areas also have lower income levels and less financial resources compared to cities due to higher rural unemployment rates. This further decreases the possibilities of adopting the internet for people living in these regions (Schleife, 2010).

5.2.4.4. Education and Income. Norris (2001) suggests that the digital divide relates to entrenched societal inequalities. Acknowledging the existence of various forms of social inequalities, DiMaggio, Hargittai, Celeste, and Shafer (2001) underlined the need for a theoretical understanding of the behavioral differences between people in different socioeconomic circumstances and, more importantly, whether these differences diminish if every individual has easy and autonomous access to technology. This emphasis is reasonable, as income and education have been found to play an important role in explaining the use and non-use of ICT (e.g., Hsieh et al., 2008, 2011; Jung et al., 2001; Mossberger et al., 2006).

As mentioned previously, an individual's socioeconomic status is associated with both the internal capacities and external resources that jointly shape behavior. Unfortunately, educational achievement together with other life factors, such as, income level, employment status, and feelings of self-control and self-esteem, correlate with one another and tend to be lower for the socioeconomically disadvantaged (Williams, 1990). Furthermore, the inequalities in internal and external capitals between the socioeconomically advantaged and the socioeconomically disadvantaged impact upon life opportunities, living and working conditions, social ranking, and even world views (Williams, 1990). In the meantime, the capital or resources required to use digital technology seems to be unequally distributed between these two groups (De Haan, 2004; Kvasny & Keil, 2006).

Consumer research suggests that individuals with different backgrounds may have distinct dispositions toward and expectations of a technology and may actually use it differently (Tsikriktsis, 2004). Individuals tend to perceive a resource as having a higher value if that resource matches their distinctive needs and background (Sirgy, Efraty, Siegel, & Lee, 2001). In fact, people with different backgrounds and needs perceive differential values to be derived from their use of similar information technologies (Au, Ngai, & Cheng, 2008).

Research has shown that lower income and education groups have significantly lower online access. Even among individuals with material access to online resources, computer skills differ (van Dijk, 2006). In the case of skill access as well, some socioeconomic factors are predictors of the digital divide. For example, age, education level, and time spent online are predictors of users' skills. Mossberger et al. (2006) also found that respondents residing in poorer areas, with lower household income and educational attainment, are statistically less likely to use the Internet.

In examining the impacts of education and income, some studies used both of them as one single factor (e.g., Hsieh et al., 2008, 2011) but most of the research examined them separately (Mossberger et al., 2006; Schleife, 2010; van Dijk, 2006). Thus the current research examines the impact of education and income as two separate variables. A respondent's education is representative of the demographic divide together with gender, age group, and place of residence, while household income represents the economic divide.

Following the discussion on demographics (gender, age, residential place, and education) as well as economic circumstances (income), the following hypotheses have been developed. H5a: Gender has a moderating effect on the relationship between the digital divide and e-government system success. H5b: Age group has a moderating effect on the relationship between the digital divide and e-government system success. H5c: Place of residence has a moderating effect on the relationship between the digital divide and e-government system success. H5d: Education has a moderating effect on the relationship between the digital divide and e-government system success. H5e: Income has a moderating effect on the relationship between the digital divide and e-government system success.

5.3. Summary of Hypotheses Development

Overall there are five hypotheses describing 16 relationships based on the comprehensive research model proposed earlier. Table 27 presents all

Table 27. Summary of Hypotheses Statements.

Construct	Link	H#	Hypotheses Statement
Digital divide	AD → EU	H1a	Access divide positively influences e-government use
	CD → EU	H1b	Capability divide positively influences e-government use
	ID → EU	H1c	Innovativeness divide positively influences e-government use
	AD → CD	H2a	Access divide positively influences capability divide
	CD → ID	H2b	Capability divide positively influences innovativeness divide
E-government systems success	EU → US	H3a	E-government use positively influences user satisfaction
	EU → BE	H3b	E-government use positively influences benefits of e-government
	US → BE	H3c	User satisfaction positively influences benefits of e-government
Trust in e-government	AD → T → EU	H4a	Trust in e-government has a mediating effect on the relationship between access divide and e-government use
	CD → T → EU	H4b	Trust in e-government has a mediating effect on the relationship between capability divide and e-government use
	ID → T → EU	H4c	Trust in e-government has a mediating effect on the relationship between innovativeness divide and e-government use
Demographic divide and economic divide	Gender × DD → ESS	H5a	Gender has a moderating effect on the relationship between digital divide and e-government system success
	Age × DD → ESS	H5b	Age group has a moderating effect on the relationship between digital divide and e-government system success
	Place × DD → ESS	H5c	Place of residence has a moderating effect on the relationship between digital divide and e-government system success
	Education × DD → ESS	H5d	Education has a moderating effect on the relationship between digital divide and e-government system success
	Income × DD → ESS	H5e	Income has a moderating effect on the relationship between digital divide and e-government system success

hypotheses. Supplementing Table 27, Fig. 20 illustrates the hypotheses in the comprehensive research model.

5.4. Questionnaire Development

5.4.1. Overview of the Questionnaire
A questionnaire was developed based on previous research and the relevant literature in order to conduct the survey for this study (see Appendix C). Its structure was designed in a format, which the respondents found easy to understand and answer, and to avoid response bias. As suggested by Polgar and Thomas (2008) and Rattray and Jones (2007), the questionnaire contained the following components.

5.4.1.1. Introduction. The statement in the introduction described the topic of the research briefly, the objectives of the research and information for the respondents. The information included the approximate time it should take to complete the questionnaire, a statement that the participation was voluntary, and that the information was confidential and anonymous. The researcher in attendance also provided general instructions on how to answer the questions, followed by brief definitions of some key terms.

5.4.1.2. Demographic Information. The demographic information was positioned at the beginning, in the initial questions, as these questions were thought to be the easiest to answer and that they would serve as a warm-up to the questions that followed.

5.4.1.3. Factual Questions. Following the demographic questions were the factual questions or the questions, which required direct answers, for example, "Do you have computer at home?" These questions were thought to be easier to answer than the perception or opinion questions. This type of question was positioned early in the questionnaire to serve as an additional warm-up for respondents.

5.4.1.4. Perception Questions. This part was the main part of the questionnaire and required the views or opinions of the respondents on the statements provided.

5.4.1.5. Closing Statements. The closing statements in the questionnaire thanked the respondents for their participation and it contained a statement that the questionnaire had been approved by Curtin University Human Research Ethics Committee. Their contact number, email, and postal address were provided for the respondents who required verification of the approval.

The questions in the questionnaire were formatted as closed-response questions, which refer to the type of questions followed by the provision of a predetermined list of response choices (Polgar & Thomas, 2008). This format of questions is easily encoded, and more meaningful for comparison purposes as the answers tend to be less variable and take less time to collect responses, although it is noted that the choices may serve to "lead" the respondents (Frazer & Lawley, 2000). The questions provided options for answers and required the respondent to tick the box, which corresponded to the most appropriate response in the "*demographic questions*" and "*factual questions.*"

In the "perception questions," the response format was a six point "forced" choice. The respondent was required to indicate the extent to which he/she agreed or disagreed by circling a number on a scale of 1 (strongly disagree) to 6 (strongly agree). This format forced the respondent to give either a negative response or a positive response. In other words, the format did not allow an "undecided" response. The reason underlying the choice of this format is to avoid a central tendency error. The central tendency error refers to the tendency of the respondent to answer using a neutral response or "neither agree or disagree." This error commonly occurs when conducting research in Asian countries, including Indonesia (Trompenaars & Hampden-Turner, 2012).

The questionnaire, consisting of 37 questions, was designed to test the hypotheses discussed earlier in this section. It was divided into seven sections according to the focus of the research. The first section aimed to collect information about the demographic characteristics of the respondents, with their economic background as the moderating variable. The second section focused on measuring the dependent variables; e-government systems success factors, by asking questions about the variables of "*e-government use,*" "*user satisfaction,*" and "*benefits of e-government*" of the respondents. Furthermore, measuring the main independent factors, the digital divide was the focus of the third, fourth, and fifth sections. "*Access divide*" as the third section measured the access of respondents to ICT in general. In the "*capability divide*" section, the researcher's aim was to measure the respondents' capability in using ICT. The section, "innovativeness *divide*" focused on measuring the respondents' willingness to try out any new ICT. Finally, the last section measured respondents "*trust in e-government system*" as the mediating variable.

In developing the questionnaire, the research considered the issue of common method bias. Common method bias occurs particularly in behavioral research when relations among constructs are measured by the same method (Spector, 1987). Podsakoff, MacKenzie, Lee, and Podsakoff (2003) identified potential sources of common method bias. Some of the potential causes that should be avoided by researchers are: "acquiescence" and "intermixing" or "grouping." Acquiescence refers to the tendency to agree with questionnaire statements regardless of content (Winkler, Kanouse, & Ware, 1982). This particular bias occurs when the items are ambiguous or when the questionnaire is poorly developed (Cronbach, 1950). Thus in dealing with acquiescence, Winkler et al. (1982) suggest that design, especially in terms of wording, should administer the instrument carefully. Intermixing or grouping is a bias caused by grouping together items from different constructs (Podsakoff et al., 2003). To cope with such bias, the structure is developed in sections, based on examining the constructs separately.

5.4.2. Measurement Instrument Development

5.4.2.1. Moderating Variables – Demographic and Economic Background. In this section, the research had two objectives; first, to obtain demographic information about the respondents involved in the research. Demographic information in the research covers "*gender*," "*age group*," "*level of education*," and "*place of residence*." Second, the research intended to measure the wealth of the respondents by questioning their monthly income. Table 28 presents all of the items in this section and the related references. All items in this section used a nominal scale. In order to reflect the research context, some modifications (e.g., education and monthly income) to the original instrument were made.

5.4.2.2. Dependant Variables – E-Government System Success. As discussed in Section 2, and earlier in this section, the dependant variables in this study are originally from the framework of DeLone and McLean (2003). Most of the measurement items are also obtained from that particular research, aside from other relevant studies. Table 29 shows the details of the items and references to justify the measurements.

The questions in this section measured the constructs of "*e-government use*," "*e-government user satisfaction*," and "*benefits of e-government*." In terms of the construct of "*e-government use*," two items are measured using a nominal scale (USE1 and USE2) while one item is presented in interval scale (USE3). Moreover, all measurement items related to the constructs "*e-government user satisfaction*" and "*benefit of e-government*" are in

Table 28. Measurement Items Related to Demographic and Economic Background.

Dimensions	Item	Statements	Reference	Measurement
Gender	DD1	Gender	Hsieh et al. (2011), Agarwal et al. (2009), Mossberger et al. (2006)	Dichotomous scale: Male and female
Age group	DD2	Age group	Hsieh et al. (2011), Agarwal et al. (2009), Mossberger et al. (2006)	Categorical: Under 20; 21−30; 31−40; 41−50; and over 50
Place of residence	DD3	How far is your home from the city center?	Mossberger et al. (2006), field study	Categorical: Under 5 km; 5−10 km; 10−15 km; 15−20 km; more than 20 km
Level of education	DD4	What is your highest level of education?	Hsieh et al. (2011), Agarwal et al. (2009), Mossberger et al. (2006)	Categorical: High school; diploma; undergraduate; Master's degree; and Doctoral degree
Monthly income	ED1	Approximately, the total monthly income before taxes and other deductions of my immediate family − including my own job income, income from other sources, and the income of my spouse − is	Mossberger et al. (2006), Hsieh et al. (2011)	Categorical: Under Rp. 2.5 million; Rp. 2.5−5 million; Rp. 5−7.5 million; Rp. 7.5−10 million; Rp. 1−12.5 million; more than Rp. 12.5 million

interval scale. For the measurement items for the construct of *"benefit of e-government"* in particular, participants in the field study emphasized three benefits of e-government systems, which were cost, time efficiency, and that the systems made respondents' business easier. Therefore those three benefits were used to measure the construct.

5.4.2.3. Independent Variable − Access Divide. As proposed in the research model, measuring the influence of the digital divide on e-government

Table 29. Measurement Items Related to E-Government Systems Success.

Dimensions	Item	Statements	Reference	Measurement
Number of uses	USE1	How many times have you used One-Stop Service Online System so far?	DeLone and McLean (2003)	Categorical: Once; 2–3 times; 3–5 times; more than 5 times
Number of transactions completed	USE2	Among your total usages of One-Stop Service Online System, how many times have you completed your transactions?	DeLone and McLean (2003)	Categorical: Once; 2–3 times; 3–5 times; more than 5 times
Using e-government system is a good idea	USE3	Using the One-Stop Service Online System is a good idea.	Taylor and Todd (1995b)	Likert scale from 1–6, where 1 = strongly disagree and 6 = strongly agree
Satisfied with the system	SAT1	I am satisfied with the One-Stop Service Online System	Lee and Chung (2009), Kohli, Devaraj, and Mahmood (2004)	Likert scale from 1–6, where 1 = strongly disagree and 6 = strongly agree
System has met user expectation	SAT2	The One-Stop Service Online system has met my expectations	Wang and Liao (2008)	Likert scale from 1–6, where 1 = strongly disagree and 6 = strongly agree
Recommend the system to others	SAT3	I strongly recommend the One-Stop Service Online System to others	Lee and Chung (2009), Kohli et al. (2004)	Likert scale from 1–6, where 1 = strongly disagree and 6 = strongly agree
Made correct decision to use the system	SAT4	I think that I made a correct decision to use the One-Stop Service Online System	Lee and Chung (2009)	Likert scale from 1–6, where 1 = strongly disagree and 6 = strongly agree
The system makes business easier	BEN1	The One-Stop Service Online System makes my business easier	Wang and Liao (2008), field study	Likert scale from 1–6, where 1 = strongly disagree and 6 = strongly agree
The system saves the time	BEN2	The One-Stop Service Online System saves my time	DeLone and McLean (2003), Wang and Liao (2008), field study	Likert scale from 1–6, where 1 = strongly disagree and 6 = strongly agree
The system costs less	BEN3	The One-Stop Service Online System costs less than manual system	DeLone and McLean (2003), field study	Likert scale from 1–6, where 1 = strongly disagree and 6 = strongly agree

system success is the focus of this research. The digital divide, as the independent variable, covers three constructs in the current study, which are the "*access divide*," "*capability divide*," and "*innovativeness divide*."

The access divide has been the most common indicator of the digital divide and has been investigated and measured in previous studies. The focus of measurement for the access divide was the respondents' perceptions regarding their access to ICTs in general, and the availability of both a computer and an internet connection in the home, as the basic requirements for accessing the e-government system. In this research, four dimensions were used to measure the variable of the access divide. These dimensions are referred to in previous studies, as shown in Table 30.

5.4.2.4. Independent Variable — Capability Divide. Table 31 presents five dimensions for the construct of the capability divide. These dimensions are derived from previous research, mainly research by Wei et al. (2011) and Hsieh et al. (2011). Adjusting the research context of Indonesia, this study does not adopt all of the measurement items in the references. The questions measure the perception of respondents on their capability in using not just e-government systems, but ICTs in general.

5.4.2.5. Independent Variable — Innovativeness Divide. As discussed earlier, the variable of the "*innovativeness divide*" is derived from Personal

Table 30. Measurement Items Related to Access Divide.

Dimensions	Item	Statements	Reference	Measurement
Computer availability at home	AD1	Do you have computer at home?	Wei et al. (2011)	Dichotomous: Yes or No
Internet connection at home	AD2	Do you have internet connection at home	Agarwal et al. (2009)	Dichotomous: Yes or No
Easiness to access ICT	AD3	I can access ICT easily	Ynalvez and Shrum (2006)	Likert scale from 1–6, where 1 = strongly disagree and 6 = strongly agree
Comfortable to access ICT	AD4	I feel comfortable in getting access to ICT	Ynalvez and Shrum (2006)	Likert scale from 1–6, where 1 = strongly disagree and 6 = strongly agree

Table 31. Measurement Items Related to Capability Divide.

Dimensions	Item	Statements	Reference	Measurement
Confidence in using ICT	CD1	I am confident in using ICT	Wei et al. (2011), Hsieh et al. (2011)	Likert scale from 1–6, where 1 = strongly disagree and 6 = strongly agree
Difficulty in using ICT	CD2	I do not have any difficulty in using ICT	Wei et al. (2011)	Likert scale from 1–6, where 1 = strongly disagree and 6 = strongly agree
Comfortable in using ICT	CD3	I feel comfortable in using ICT	Wei et al. (2011), Hsieh et al. (2011)	Likert scale from 1–6, where 1 = strongly disagree and 6 = strongly agree
Sure be able to use ICT	CD4	I am sure I can use ICT	Wei et al. (2011)	Likert scale from 1–6, where 1 = strongly disagree and 6 = strongly agree
Able to operate, even if no one tells	CD5	I can operate ICT, even if no one tells me how to do it	Wei et al. (2011), Hsieh et al. (2011)	Likert scale from 1–6, where 1 = strongly disagree and 6 = strongly agree

Innovativeness regarding information technology, which is a variable already used in previous research. Research by Agarwal and Prasad (1998) and Yi et al. (2006) are the main references to measure this variable, as shown in Table 32. This construct is rooted in the DI (Rogers, 1976), and is used in the area of marketing. In the early stages of the conception of innovativeness, it is measured by the time taken for an individual to adopt an innovation and ownership of new products. Midgley and Dowling (1978) noted that among studies of innovativeness, 48% used the indicator of "relative time of adoption," 39% the cross-section technique, while 13% utilized purchase intention.

To develop a more valid and reliable measurement, Goldsmith and Hofacker (1991) introduced self-reporting for the "innovation scale" which was then validated by Flynn and Goldsmith (1993). Furthermore, in the area of ISs, Leonard-Barton and Deschamps (1988) developed a scale to measure innovativeness. Based on the previous scales by Goldsmith and Hofacker (1991) and Leonard-Barton and Deschamps (1988), Agarwal and Prasad (1998) developed measurement items, which is used in the current research. However, not all of the items are utilized in this research, only those appropriate to the context of e-government systems and Indonesia are used.

Table 32.   Measurement Items Related to Innovativeness Divide.

Dimensions	Item	Statements	Reference	Measurement
Look for ways to try new ICT	ID1	If I hear about new ICT, I would look for ways to try it	Agarwal and Prasad (1998), Yi et al. (2006)	Likert scale from 1–6, where 1 = strongly disagree and 6 = strongly agree
First to try out new ICT	ID2	Among my peers, I am the first to try out new ICT	Agarwal and Prasad (1998), Yi et al. (2006)	Likert scale from 1–6, where 1 = strongly disagree and 6 = strongly agree
Hesitant to try out new ICT	ID3	I am hesitant to try out new ICT	Agarwal and Prasad (1998)	Likert scale from 1–6, where 1 = strongly disagree and 6 = strongly agree
Like to experiment with new ICT	ID4	I like to experiment with new ICT	Agarwal and Prasad (1998), Yi et al. (2006)	Likert scale from 1–6, where 1 = strongly disagree and 6 = strongly agree

5.4.2.6. Mediating Variable – Trust in E-Government. This section measures the construct of *"trust in e-government"* as a mediating variable between the constructs of the digital divide and the success of the e-government system. To measure the construct, this research utilized five items drawn from Hsieh et al. (2011), Gefen et al. (2003), McKnight and Chervany (2002), Teo et al. (2009), and Pavlou (2003), as described in Table 33. However, most of the previous studies investigated "trust in e-commerce" and "trust in government," thus this research has modified the measurement items. A pretest was conducted in order to ensure that the items were understandable to the respondents. Three local researchers were involved in the pretest. They were required to compare the modified and original items. The analysis shows that the modified items were understandable although some improvements in terms of wording were made, based on their suggestions.

5.4.3. Empirical Pilot Study
A pilot study was conducted to test the validity of the questionnaire and also to check any other problem with questionnaire and measurement items. The questionnaires were distributed to two groups of respondents: researchers and potential respondents. Ten questionnaires were distributed to a group of researchers from multi-disciplines (accounting, ISs, marketing, and economics). The main objective of involving these researchers was

Table 33. Measurement Items Related to Trust in E-Government.

Dimensions	Item	Statements	Reference	Measurement
Truthful and honest	TE1	I think the information in One-Stop Service Online System seems to be truthful and honest	Gefen et al. (2003), Hsieh et al. (2011), Teo et al. (2009)	Likert scale from 1–6, where 1 = strongly disagree and 6 = strongly agree
Competent and effective	TE2	I think the One-Stop Service Online System is effective in facilitating my needs	McKnight and Chervany (2002)	Likert scale from 1–6, where 1 = strongly disagree and 6 = strongly agree
Cares about its users	TE3	I think the One-Stop Service Online System is designed to accommodate the needs of its users	Gefen et al. (2003), Hsieh et al. (2011), Teo et al. (2009)	Likert scale from 1–6, where 1 = strongly disagree and 6 = strongly agree
Predictability of output	TE4	I can predict the output of One-Stop Service Online System (in terms of time, costs, and process)	Field study, Gefen et al. (2003); Hsieh et al. (2011)	Likert scale from 1–6, where 1 = strongly disagree and 6 = strongly agree
Keep its commitment	TE5	I think the One-Stop Service Online System provides appropriate outcomes for its users	Pavlou (2003)	Likert scale from 1–6, where 1 = strongly disagree and 6 = strongly agree

to ensure that the questionnaire met the research objectives. Meanwhile, 25 questionnaires were distributed to potential respondents (apart from the main study) to ensure that the questions were applicable and understandable.

The pilot test was not intended as detailed analysis but rather as a test the content validity and appropriateness of the questions by using a simple frequency. The pilot test was also conducted to find out the length of time it would take to complete the questionnaire. In general, the findings from the pilot study showed that all of the items in the questionnaire were understandable and appropriate in the research context. The test also indicated on average, the respondents required 30–40 minutes to answer all of the items in the questionnaire.

5.5. Summary

This section presented the development of the hypotheses together with the rationale and justification derived from the comprehensive research model previously developed in Section 4. There are 16 hypotheses in total to describe the relationships among the variables, as proposed in the model (Fig. 20). This section also described the development of the questionnaire and measurement items. To test the developed hypotheses, the questionnaire was developed based on prior literature along with findings in the field study. The questionnaire contained 37 items in total. In order to test the validity of the questionnaire, a pilot study was conducted. The final questionnaire was then distributed for a national survey, and this is discussed in the next section.

6. DATA ANALYSIS USING PARTIAL LEAST SQUARE BASED STRUCTURAL EQUATION MODELING[3]

6.1. Introduction

In this section, an analysis of the data collected from 237 respondents is undertaken in order to test the reliability and validity of the model as well as the hypotheses. The analysis was conducted using the PLS approach to SEM. PLS is a powerful tool of analysis due to minimum reliance on measurement scales, sample size, and residual distributions (Wold, 2006).

There are three parts to the quantitative analysis detailed in this section. Part one examines the influence of the digital divide on e-government systems success. Part two analyses the mediating role of trust in e-government in the relationship between the digital divide and the success of e-government systems. Finally, the last part assesses the moderating effect of demographics and the economic divide using multi-group analysis. In each stage, measurement model and structural model are examined.

The structure of this section starts with an overview of the survey that was conducted. It is followed by a descriptive analysis of the respondents participating in the survey. The results, based on the three parts of analysis, are then presented. The section closes with the summary.

6.2. Overview of the Survey

6.2.1. Response Rate

Although a low response rate has been acknowledged as one of the major problems in research surveys, there are many techniques to overcome this problem. The techniques include using nontechnical general statements and avoiding technical jargon in the questionnaire (Converse & Presser, 1986a). With this in mind, the current questionnaire was examined through the pilot test not only by other researchers but also by potential respondents to ensure that the questionnaire was understood. The respondents of the survey were also offered a complimentary souvenir gift. This research adopted the personally administered survey format (Frazer & Lawley, 2000), which allowed the researcher to deliver the questionnaires directly to the respondents. However, to maintain the independency and secrecy, the questionnaire was completed by the respondent. This kind of survey offers a high response rate, quick data collection, and gives the respondents the opportunity to ask direct questions about the research and questionnaire. However, this type of survey is costly. The researcher worked in tandem with research assistants who were final year undergraduate students, with qualifications in research method subjects. The assistants were trained by the researcher prior to distribution of the questionnaires on how to contact the potential respondents and handle the questionnaires. The importance of respondents' independency and secrecy were also emphasized.

In order to secure the confidence of the respondents, it was ensured, and they were assured, that their identities could not be traced thus protecting their privacy and keeping their anonymity. Therefore the research did not include any codes, which also made it impossible for the researcher to link the survey to respondents' identity, to find the responses from a certain criteria and compare the responses. This was intentional for the purposes of increasing test reliability and thus the response rate.

The minimum requirement for the sample size for PLS research is 10 times the number of items in the most complex formative construct or the largest number of antecedent constructs leading to an endogenous construct in the research model (Barclay et al., 1995; Gefen et al., 2000). Since the most complex constructs in this research are the "capability divide" and "trust in e-government," which have five items each, the minimum sample size for this study was 50.

As presented in Table 34, the survey received 251 total responses. A review was then undertaken to seek out errors in the form of invalid data, including missing values or incomplete responses. This step was conducted to produce clean data for research analysis. As a result, 14 questionnaires were found to be incomplete. Therefore, those incomplete questionnaires were excluded to avoid fallacious results. Finally, 237 responses were found to be useable in this research, indicating the effective response rate of 35.5% from the total e-government users of 668. Compared to other studies in the stream (e.g., Hsieh et al., 2008; Morris & Venkatesh, 2000), the level of response rate is considered acceptable.

Based on the useable questionnaires, pre-analysis tests were undertaken using PLS to get an overview of the applicability of the data in this study. The pre-analysis tests covered assessment of the measurement and the structural model. The results revealed that the minimum R^2 was 0.288 (user satisfaction), and R^2 of the ultimate dependent variable, which is benefits of e-government, is 0.481. As suggested by Hair et al. (2011), the R^2 values of 0.481 for endogenous LV in the structural model is considered moderate to strong structural model. Therefore, the results indicate the applicability of the data and the increment of the explanatory power of the model. A full analysis was then conducted and this is explained in a later section.

Table 34.   Result of Response Review.

Response	Number
Total responses	251
Incomplete responses	14
Usable responses	237

6.2.2. Non-Response Bias

In order to examine whether the responses from the survey represent the larger population, a non-response-bias test is undertaken. The test checks whether there is any difference in opinion between the respondents and non-respondents, who could have participated in the survey. The rationale for the test is that the late respondents were likely to have a similar characteristics to non-respondents, as suggested by Thong (1999).

As mentioned in Section 3, the survey was conducted in 2011 until the midyear of 2012. The responses were split into early (within 2011) and late (beginning until mid of 2012) respondents. As a result, the number of early respondents was 153 and the late was 84. Independent sample Mann-Whitney U test was undertaken to test the differences between demographic and selected items (Table 35). The minimum acceptable value of significance in the test is 0.05 that detect the non-response bias.

The test was performed in terms of gender, age groups, place of residence, household income, and one e-government use-related, one access divide-related, and one capability divide-related items. The results of Mann-Whitney U test demonstrated that there is no significant difference between the two groups. Therefore, it would be reasonable to conclude that this study does not have the issue of non-response bias.

6.2.3. Common Method Bias

One of the threats to construct validity is common methods bias (Doty & Glick, 1998), which occurs when there is divergence between observed and true relationships among constructs. The divergence might be the result of the respondents' misperception, since the measurement of the constructs based on the responses of a single respondent with no additional assessment from other individuals. However, the factor analysis using Harman's single factor test (Podsakoff & Organ, 1986) presented in Table 36 shows

Table 35.   Mann-Whitney U Test to Test Non-Response Bias.

Item	z-Value	Significance
Gender	−0.37	0.71
Age	−1.01	0.31
Place	−1.20	0.23
Income	−1.19	0.24
I can access ICT easily	−0.12	0.90
I am confident in using ICT	−0.39	0.70

Table 36.   Harman's Single Factor to Test Common Method Bias.

Component	Initial Eigenvalues			Extraction Sums of Squared Loadings		
	Total	% of Var	Cum %	Total	% of Var	Cum %
1	10.683	35.611	35.611	10.683	35.611	35.611
2	6.469	19.562	55.173	6.469	19.562	55.173
3	1.905	8.351	63.524	1.905	8.351	63.524
4	1.502	5.006	68.530	1.502	5.006	68.530
5	1.277	4.256	72.785	1.277	4.256	72.785
6	1.191	3.971	76.757	1.191	3.971	76.757
7	0.922	3.075	79.831			
8	0.760	2.533	82.364			
9	0.687	2.291	84.656			
10	0.605	2.018	86.674			
11	0.547	1.822	88.496			
12	0.502	1.673	90.169			
13	0.415	1.385	91.554			
14	0.359	1.198	92.752			
15	0.291	0.968	93.720			
16	0.279	0.930	94.650			
17	0.229	0.763	95.413			
18	0.207	0.691	96.104			
19	0.184	0.615	96.719			
20	0.166	0.552	97.271			
21	0.152	0.508	97.779			
22	0.129	0.430	98.209			
23	0.114	0.381	98.591			
24	0.104	0.345	98.936			
25	0.088	0.293	99.229			
26	0.069	0.229	99.458			
27	0.061	0.202	99.660			
28	0.048	0.159	99.819			
29	0.039	0.131	99.950			
30	0.015	0.050	100.000			

that a single factor solution does not emerge. Hence, there is unlike to be any common method bias in this research.

6.3. Descriptive Analysis of the Sample

Based on the final data, a descriptive analysis using PLS was undertaken to understand the respondents' demographic characteristics in this research. Tables 37–41 present the results.

Table 37. Respondents by Gender.

Gender	Frequency	Percentage
Male	184	77.6
Female	53	22.4
Total	237	100.0

Table 38. Respondents by Age Group.

Age Group	Frequency	Percentage
Under 20	2	0.8
21–30	63	26.6
31–40	104	43.9
41–50	58	24.5
Over 50	10	4.2
Total	237	100.0

Table 39. Respondents by Residential Place.

Residential Place	Frequency	Percentage
Under 5 km	75	31.6
5–10 km	93	39.2
10–15 km	30	12.7
15–20 km	24	10.1
More than 20 km	15	6.3
Total	237	100.0

Table 40. Respondents by Education.

Residential Place	Frequency	Percentage
High school	6	2.5
Diploma	49	20.7
Undergraduate	148	62.4
Master's degree	28	11.8
Doctoral degree	6	2.5
Total	237	100.0

6.3.1. Gender

As presented in Table 37, 184 respondents were males (78%) and 53 respondents were females. A male majority was to be expected due to the results of the field study.

Table 41. Two-Step PLS Examination.

Phase	Examination	Analysis
1	Measurement model assessment	Item reliability Internal consistency Discriminant validity
2	Structural model assessment	Path coefficient (β) t-Values R^2 f^2

Source: Chin (1998).

6.3.2. Age Group
Table 38 shows that most of the respondents (44%) were in the age groups "31–40," followed by the group of "21–30" (27%) and group of "41–50" (26%). The remainder is in group "under 20" and "over 50" (5%).

6.3.3. Residential Place
Based on Table 39, most of the respondents lived within a radius of 10 km or less from the center of the city (total of 71%). The results show that most of the respondents lived in the city area, and only 29% lived in remote areas.

6.3.4. Education
As shown in Table 40, the majority of the respondents (77%) had received higher education (to undergraduate level and/or above), while only 23% or 55 respondents have attended less than undergraduate degree (high school and diploma).

6.4. Data Examination

6.4.1. PLS Examination
The PLS-SEM approach was used for data analysis, since the nature of this research is exploratory and an extension of an existing theory (Hair et al., 2011). Chin (1998) suggests that the advantages of PLS include fewer restrictions on measurement scales, sample size, data distribution, and normality.

Table 39 presents two stages of the application of the PLS technique, namely the assessment of the measurement model and the assessment of the structural model. The objective of the first stage assessment is to examine the validity and reliability of the measurements of the constructs. In doing so, this research tested item reliability, internal consistency, and discriminant validity. The second stage focused on examining the relationships that existed between the paths in the model (Igbaria et al., 1995). The examinations in the second stage involved the value of β or path coefficient, t-values or the statistical significance, the examination of R^2 or the amount of variance explained, and f^2 or effect size. To obtain the path coefficient and t-values, a bootstrap procedure was undertaken by using a resample size of 500. Bootstrap is a general resampling procedure for estimating the distributions of statistics based on independent observations (Chin, 1998).

6.4.2. Analysis Details

Consistent with the research objectives, this research undertook data analysis in four stages. Table 42 outlines those three stages.

The objectives of the first stage were to examine the impact of the digital divide on the success of the e-government system and to investigate the

Table 42. Overview of the Analyses.

Stage	Objective of the Analysis	Constructs
1	To examine the impact of digital divide on e-government system success in Indonesian local governments	Access divide Capability divide Innovativeness divide E-government use E-government user satisfaction Benefits of e-government
	To investigate the relationship among the digital divide constructs	Access divide Capability divide Innovativeness divide
2	To investigate the mediating role of trust in e-government in the impact of digital divide on e-government system success in Indonesian local governments	Trust in e-government
3	To assess the moderating impacts of demographic divide and economic divide on the relationship between digital divide and e-government system success in Indonesian local governments	Demographic divide Economic divide

relationships between the digital divide constructs. In doing so, the related constructs were examined. Although the first stage had two objectives, the PLS analyses were completed simultaneously.

In the second stage, an analysis was undertaken to investigate the mediating effect of trust in e-government on the impact of the digital divide on the success of the e-government system. In the third stage, the moderating impact of the demographic divide and the economic divide on the relationship between the digital divide and e-government system success was the focus of the assessment.

6.5. Analysis Stage 1: Impact of Digital Divide on E-Government System Success

6.5.1. Assessment of the Measurement Model – Stage 1

In total, there were 23 items in measuring the total of six constructs: *access divide* (ACCE_1 – ACCE_4), *capability divide* (CAPA_1 – CAPA_5), *innovativeness divide* (INNO_1 – INNO_4), *e-government use* (USE_1 – USE_3), *user satisfaction* (USAT_1 – USAT_4), and *benefits of e-government* (BENE_1 – BENE_3). In order to assess the measurement model, examinations of reliability, internal consistency, and discriminant validity were undertaken (Barclay et al., 1995). The focus of the assessments was to examine the relationships between the observed variables and the constructs, to ensure that the items which represent the observed variables could measure the constructs (Igbaria et al., 1995).

6.5.1.1. Item Reliability – Stage 1. As suggested by Hair et al. (2011), a minimum value of PLS loading is 0.7. Table 43 shows that all items in all constructs achieved the required minimum value in the first run, therefore all items can be used. This result indicates that all items are able to represent their respective constructs.

6.5.1.2. Internal Consistency – Stage 1. Table 44 presents the measures of internal consistency and AVE of each construct. The values met the acceptable criterion for internal consistency as suggested by Hair et al. (2011), which was a minimum of 0.7. The *capability divide* and *benefits of e-government* shared the same value of internal consistency, 0.966, which was the highest. The lowest value, belonging to *e-government use* was 0.877.

In terms of the values of AVE, Hair et al. (2011) and Fornell and Larcker (1981) consider 0.50 as the acceptable minimum value. AVE

Table 43. Item Loading.

Construct	Item	PLS Loading
Access divide	ACCE_1	0.763
	ACCE_2	0.829
	ACCE_3	0.901
	ACCE_4	0.925
Capability divide	CAPA_1	0.883
	CAPA_2	0.934
	CAPA_3	0.925
	CAPA_4	0.940
	CAPA_5	0.932
Innovativeness divide	INNO_1	0.911
	INNO_2	0.758
	INNO_3	0.904
	INNO_4	0.906
E-government use	USE_1	0.912
	USE_2	0.808
	USE_3	0.794
User satisfaction	USAT_1	0.963
	USAT_2	0.942
	USAT_3	0.946
	USAT_4	0.755
Benefits of e-government	BENE_1	0.957
	BENE_2	0.959
	BENE_3	0.938

measures the amount of variance that a LV captures from its items relative to the amount due to measurement error. The AVE value of each construct exceeded the requirement; therefore the convergent analysis for these constructs was satisfied. The lowest AVE value was *e-government use* (0.705), and the highest value was achieved by *benefits of e-government* (0.906). The results could be interpreted such that at the highest point, 90.6% variance of indicators accounted for the construct of *benefits of e-government*.

6.5.1.3. Discriminant Validity — Stage 1. To examine the discriminant validity at the construct level, the square root of AVE was compared to the correlation of the LV. In order to meet the requirements, each construct should have a greater value of square root of AVE than the variance shared between a construct and other constructs in the model (Barclay et al., 1995). Table 45 presents the square root of AVE (diagonal elements in parent study), and the correlations between constructs

Table 44. Measures of Internal Consistency and AVE.

Construct	Internal Consistency	AVE
Access divide	0.916	0.734
Capability divide	0.966	0.852
Innovativeness divide	0.927	0.761
E-government use	0.877	0.705
User satisfaction	0.947	0.820
Benefits of e-government	0.966	0.906

Table 45. Correlation of Latent Variables and Square Root of AVE.

	ACCE	CAPA	INNO	USE	USAT	BENE
ACCE	**0.857**					
CAPA	0.849	**0.923**				
INNO	0.791	0.804	**0.872**			
USE	0.662	0.677	0.664	**0.840**		
USAT	0.348	0.405	0.477	0.536	**0.906**	
BENE	0.466	0.601	0.562	0.625	0.590	**0.952**

(off-diagonal elements). The results demonstrate that the values met the requirements and they confirm the establishment of the discriminant validity at the construct level.

At the items level, assessment of discriminant validity is undertaken by calculating the loading and cross-loading values for each item and construct. The matrix of loading and cross loading is presented in Table 46 with the matrix showing the correlations of the items with the constructs. The results indicate that all items met the requirements, which were higher than cross-loadings in other constructs. Thus it is confirmed that the measurement model has strong discriminant validity at the items level.

Based on the results as presented in Tables 43–46, the assessment of the measurement model provided satisfactory support for the reliability, consistency, and validity requirements. Having adequate and sufficient results for the measurement model, the next stage of PLS analysis was undertaken: the assessment of the structural model. The analysis is described in the next section.

6.5.2. Assessment of the Structural Model – Stage 1
6.5.2.1. Path Coefficient (β) and Statistical Significance of t-Value. Table 47 shows the evaluation of each hypothesis. Based on the path coefficient (β)

Table 46. Loading and Cross-Loading Matrix.

	ACCE	CAPA	INNO	USE	USAT	BENE
ACCE_1	**0.763**	0.525	0.515	0.218	0.064	0.079
ACCE_2	**0.829**	0.641	0.622	0.326	0.090	0.097
ACCE_3	**0.901**	0.814	0.769	0.753	0.429	0.616
ACCE_4	**0.925**	0.845	0.746	0.765	0.452	0.581
CAPA_1	0.732	**0.883**	0.671	0.537	0.338	0.530
CAPA_2	0.799	**0.929**	0.763	0.616	0.339	0.510
CAPA_3	0.698	**0.922**	0.718	0.621	0.399	0.628
CAPA_4	0.841	**0.937**	0.749	0.651	0.370	0.549
CAPA_5	0.831	**0.933**	0.809	0.654	0.382	0.556
INNO_1	0.718	0.766	**0.911**	0.677	0.544	0.578
INNO_2	0.565	0.544	**0.758**	0.432	0.204	0.292
INNO_3	0.762	0.749	**0.904**	0.600	0.454	0.521
INNO_4	0.696	0.716	**0.906**	0.574	0.406	0.525
USE_1	0.619	0.610	0.593	**0.912**	0.468	0.560
USE_2	0.469	0.487	0.440	**0.808**	0.488	0.538
USE_3	0.575	0.604	0.635	**0.794**	0.395	0.474
USAT_1	0.331	0.396	0.472	0.555	**0.963**	0.572
USAT_2	0.347	0.419	0.485	0.593	**0.942**	0.590
USAT_3	0.286	0.326	0.428	0.433	**0.946**	0.502
USAT_4	0.292	0.309	0.315	0.302	**0.755**	0.454
BENE_1	0.465	0.613	0.575	0.587	0.584	**0.957**
BENE_2	0.452	0.584	0.502	0.603	0.567	**0.959**
BENE_3	0.411	0.516	0.529	0.594	0.531	**0.938**

and t-value, all of the hypotheses are supported. In Fig. 21, the path coefficient value and t-value are shown near to each link among the constructs.

The results indicate that all factors of the digital divide, namely the: access divide, capability divide, and innovativeness divide are important factors influencing e-government system success, and at the same time the results also provide evidence of the relationships between the variables of the digital divide. The significant influence of the access divide on e-government use was proven by the path coefficient of 0.208 and t-value of 1.367. The path coefficient and t-value for the influence of capability divide on e-government use were 0.279 and 2.135, respectively. On the other hand, the influence of the innovativeness divide on e-government use had a path coefficient of 0.275 and the t-value of 2.668. In other words, the influence of the innovativeness divide on e-government use was the strongest among other factors of the digital divide. The results are further discussed in Section 7.

Table 47. Evaluation of the Research Hypotheses.

Hypothesis	Link	Path Coefficient (β)	t-Value	Result
H1a	AD→ EU (+)	0.208	1.367*	Supported
H1b	CD → EU (+)	0.279	2.135**	Supported
H1c	ID → EU (+)	0.275	2.668***	Supported
H2a	AD → CD (+)	0.849	32.985****	Supported
H2b	CD → ID (+)	0.804	20.748****	Supported
H3a	EU → US (+)	0.536	12.470****	Supported
H3b	EU → BE (+)	0.433	9.722****	Supported
H3c	US → BE (+)	0.357	8.140****	Supported

Significant *$p < 0.1$; **$p < 0.05$; ***$p < 0.005$; ****$p < 0.0005$.

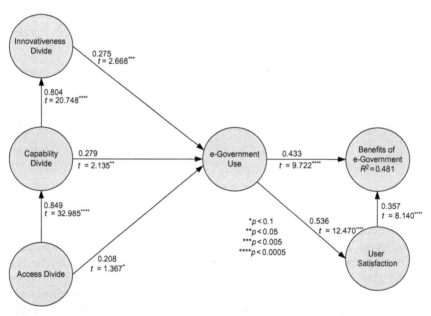

Fig. 21. Assessment of Path Coefficient and Statistical Significance in Stage 1.

In terms of the variance explained, the ultimate endogenous variable which was *benefits of e-government* had the R^2 value of 0.481 (Table 48). This means that the model explained 48.1% of the variance in the *e-government systems success*. Hair et al. (2011) and Teo, Wei, and Benbasat (2003) argue that the value is considered moderate and satisfies the minimum threshold of 0.10.

Table 48. Evaluation of R^2 and Effect Size (f^2).

Construct	R^2	f^2
ACCE	–	0.029
CAPA	0.727	0.029
INNO	0.646	0.047
USE	0.513	0.258
USAT	0.288	0.175
BENE	0.481	–

In order to explore whether the impact of a particular independent LV on a dependent LV is substantive or not, the calculation of f^2 was undertaken. With a formula that has been explained in Section 3, Table 48 shows the results of the f^2. As per the recommendation of Chin (1998), all of the constructs fulfilled the requirement of a minimum value (0.02). The results indicate that *e-government use* is the most substantive construct with the f^2 value of 0.258.

6.6. Analysis Stage 2: The Mediating Role of Trust in E-Government

6.6.1. Assessment of the Measurement Model – Stage 2
There are 21 items to measure five constructs, namely the *access divide* (ACCE_1 – ACCE_4), *capability divide* (CAPA_1 – CAPA_5), *innovativeness divide* (INNO_1 – INNO_4), *e-government use* (USE_1 – USE_3), and *trust in e-government* (TRUS_1 – TRUS_5). In assessing the measurement model, analyses of item reliability, internal consistency, and discriminant validity were undertaken, as in the previous stage.

6.6.1.1. Item Reliability – Stage 2.
All items in all constructs achieved the requirement minimum value of 0.7 as suggested by Hair et al. (2011) in the first run (see Table 49). The smallest value of item loading was 0.736 (TRUS_3), which is still above the threshold. Therefore we can conclude that all items were sufficient to represent their respective constructs and no item needs to be deleted.

6.6.1.2. Internal Consistency – Stage 2.
CR analysis was conducted to verify convergent validity and discriminant validity. Values greater than 0.70 in CR imply that the construct retains both its internal consistency and

Table 49. Item Loading.

Construct	Item	PLS Loading
Access divide	ACCE_1	0.733
	ACCE_2	0.804
	ACCE_3	0.918
	ACCE_4	0.937
Capability divide	CAPA_1	0.882
	CAPA_2	0.933
	CAPA_3	0.927
	CAPA_4	0.940
	CAPA_5	0.931
Innovativeness divide	INNO_1	0.910
	INNO_2	0.754
	INNO_3	0.905
	INNO_4	0.909
E-government use	USE_1	0.912
	USE_2	0.780
	USE_3	0.819
Trust in e-government	TRUS_1	0.915
	TRUS_2	0.850
	TRUS_3	0.736
	TRUS_4	0.849
	TRUS_5	0.904

convergent validity (Hair et al., 2011). The factor loading and AVE were also examined to determine the convergent validity. The criteria for the acceptable level of convergent validity is an individual factor loading greater than 0.60 and an AVE greater than 0.50 (Gefen et al., 2000). Table 50 summarizes the CR and AVE of the constructs. All factor loading, CR, and AVE in this measurement model were deemed acceptable.

6.6.1.3. Discriminant Validity − Stage 2. Table 51 outlines the square root of AVE and the correlations between constructs. The results show that the values meet the minimum requirements and thus are adequate for the establishment of the discriminant validity at the construct level.

At the item level, Fornell and Larcker (1981) argue that a construct should share greater variance with its respective indicators rather than with another construct in the structural model. In other words, the indicator's loading with its associated construct should be greater than its loadings with all of the remaining constructs (Table 52). All of the items here satisfied the requirements.

Table 50. Measures of Internal Consistency and AVE.

Construct	Internal Consistency	AVE
Access divide	0.913	0.726
Capability divide	0.966	0.852
Innovativeness divide	0.927	0.760
E-government use	0.876	0.703
Trust in e-government	0.930	0.728

Table 51. Correlation of Latent Variables and Square Root of AVE.

	ACCE	CAPA	INNO	USE	TRUS
ACCE	**0.852**				
CAPA	0.856	**0.923**			
INNO	0.796	0.804	**0.872**		
USE	0.690	0.681	0.671	**0.838**	
TRUS	0.639	0.701	0.719	0.610	**0.853**

Table 52. Loading and Cross-Loading Matrix.

	ACCE	CAPA	INNO	USE	TRUS
ACCE_1	**0.734**	0.522	0.515	0.222	0.365
ACCE_2	**0.804**	0.639	0.622	0.337	0.450
ACCE_3	**0.918**	0.814	0.770	0.754	0.643
ACCE_4	**0.937**	0.845	0.746	0.766	0.620
CAPA_1	0.737	**0.882**	0.669	0.539	0.618
CAPA_2	0.808	**0.933**	0.756	0.634	0.641
CAPA_3	0.716	**0.927**	0.716	0.641	0.626
CAPA_4	0.845	**0.940**	0.751	0.660	0.656
CAPA_5	0.836	**0.931**	0.809	0.662	0.691
INNO_1	0.730	0.767	**0.910**	0.682	0.657
INNO_2	0.561	0.543	**0.754**	0.447	0.448
INNO_3	0.764	0.748	**0.905**	0.602	0.680
INNO_4	0.701	0.716	**0.909**	0.583	0.687
USE_1	0.641	0.610	0.592	**0.912**	0.550
USE_2	0.492	0.487	0.440	**0.780**	0.480
USE_3	0.589	0.604	0.635	**0.819**	0.501
TRUS_1	0.535	0.596	0.694	0.556	**0.915**
TRUS_2	0.725	0.762	0.674	0.560	**0.850**
TRUS_3	0.462	0.451	0.389	0.391	**0.736**
TRUS_4	0.449	0.544	0.579	0.501	**0.849**
TRUS_5	0.513	0.582	0.662	0.558	**0.904**

6.6.2. Assessment of the Structural Model – Stage 2
In this stage, the objective is to investigate the mediation role of *trust in e-government* in the relationships between the *digital divide* and *e-government systems success*. In doing so, the mediation hypotheses were tested using a statistical technique suggested by Baron and Kenny (1986). They suggested that a given variable might function as a mediator (M), if the following conditions held: (1) a significant relationship existed between the independent variable (X) and the dependent variable (Y); (2) a significant relationship existed between X and M; and (3) in the presence of a significant relationship between M and Y, the previous relationship between X and Y was no longer significant, or the strength of the relationship was significantly decreased.

Fig. 22 describes the results of the data analysis when the link from the mediator variable (trust in e-government) to the dependent variable (e-government use) was excluded. The links among variables were significant, except the link which showed the positive influence of the *access divide* on *trust in e-government*. The results in Fig. 22 were then compared to the results in Fig. 23.

When the mediator variable is included in the data analysis, the results (Fig. 23) show that the positive influence of the capability divide and the innovativeness divide on e-government use turns out to be insignificant. The *t*-values were decreased to 0.815 and 1.519 for the links between the capability divide and e-government use and between the innovativeness divide and e-government use, respectively. On the other hand, the positive influence of trust in e-government on e-government use was confirmed with *t*-value of 2.940.

The results of the assessment of the mediating effect of trust in e-government on the relationship between the digital divide and e-government systems success (Table 53) indicate that the access divide does not have a mediation effect. The influence of the access divide on trust in e-government is not significant (*t*-value = 0.463), and therefore it does not meet the conditions as outlined by Baron and Kenny (1986). In other words, we can conclude that the trust in e-government does not have a mediation role. However, since the inclusion of a mediator variable decreases the *t*-value significantly, the results imply that trust in e-government is a complete and valid mediator in the relationship between the capability divide and e-government use, as well as between the innovativeness divide and e-government use. The assessment was then followed by the calculation of the *z*-value using the Sobel test (Sobel, 1982).

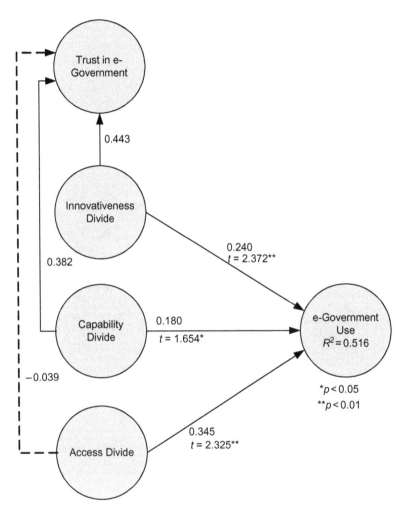

Fig. 22. Data Analysis Results of a Model Excluding the Mediator.

The assessment of the significance of the reduction of the relationship between the independent and dependent variables cannot be assessed from the coefficient. Rather it has to be mathematically proven. The Sobel test (Sobel, 1982) has long been a traditional method for testing the significance of mediation effects. The Sobel test was used in this research, as it has been

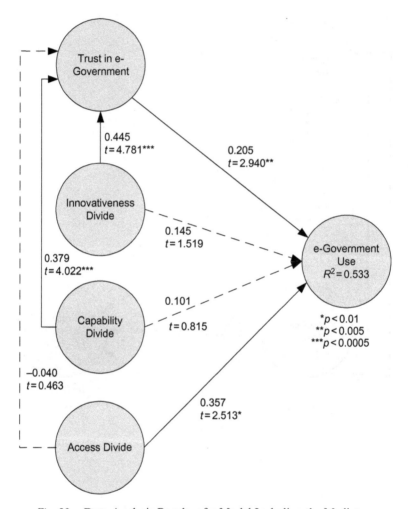

Fig. 23. Data Analysis Results of a Model Including the Mediator.

the most widely utilized (Bontis et al., 2007; Preacher & Hayes, 2008). The significance was measured using the following formula:

$$z\text{-value} = a*b/\text{SQRT}\left(b^2*s_a + a^2*s_b^2\right)$$

The formula required the use of the non-standardized regression coefficient (a) and the standard error (s_a) of the relationship between the

Table 53. Assessment of Mediation Effect.

	t-Value				Mediation Effect
	$X \to Y$		$M \to Y$	$X \to M$	
	Without *M*	With *M*			
Access divide	2.372*	2.513**	2.94**	0.463	No mediation
Capability divide	1.654*	0.815		4.022***	Fully mediation
Innovativeness divide	2.325*	1.519		4.781***	Fully mediation

*$p < 0.05$; **$p < 0.005$; ***$p < 0.0005$.

Table 54. Calculation of Sobel Test.

	$X \to M$		$M \to Y$		z-Value
	a	s_a	*b*	s_b	
Capability divide − trust − e-government use	0.379	0.110	0.205	0.0863	1.966*
Innovativeness divide − trust − e-government use	0.445	0.118			2.010*

*$p < 0.05$.

independent variable and the mediating variable, and the non-standardized regression coefficient (*b*) and standard error (s_b) of the path from the mediating to the dependent variable. Table 54 below summarizes the data and the results of the Sobel test. The results show that both the capability divide and the innovativeness divide have a significant *z*-value.

6.7. Analysis Stage 3: The Moderating Role of the Demographic Divide and the Economic Divide

The last stage of analysis in this research aimed to examine the moderating effect of the *demographic divide* and the *economic divide* on the relationship between the *digital divide* and *e-government system success*. Variables of gender, age group, place of residence, and education were tested, representing the *demographic divide*, while household income represents the *economic divide*. In examining the moderating effect, multi-group analysis was undertaken (Baron & Kenny, 1986; Moores & Chang, 2006). The procedure and results of the analyses are explained in the following sections.

However, before proceeding with the analyses, the characteristics of the respondents were examined, as shown in Table 55. This describes the

Table 55. Summary of Demographic and Economic Characteristics of
Respondents.

Characteristics	Total	Percentage
Gender		
Male	184	78
Female	53	22
Age		
Younger (40 years old and below)	169	71
Older (above 41 years old)	68	29
Place of residence		
City area (10 km and lesser from city center)	168	71
Remote are (further than 10 km from city center)	69	29
Level of education		
Lower (diploma and below)	55	23
Higher (undergraduate and above)	182	77
Household income		
Lower (7.5 million per month and lower)	130	55
Higher (above 7.5 million)	107	45

characteristics of the respondents based on gender, age group, place of residence, education, and household income. As shown in the table, the majority of the respondents were males ($N = 184$), belonging to the age group "40 years old and below" ($N = 169$), living in the city area or living within a radius of 10 km or less from the city center ($N = 168$), attending higher education or possessing an undergraduate degree or above ($N = 182$), and earning an income of 7.5 million per month or less ($N = 130$).

6.7.1. Assessment of the Measurement Model – Stage 3

Assessment of the measurement model was carried out to ensure the reliability and validity of the measurements. The assessment covered three parts, being (1) item reliability, (2) internal consistency, and (3) discriminant validity. In this stage, the assessment was conducted for two categories: the whole sample ($N = 237$), and groups of the sample based on the subgroups of gender, age, place of residence, level of education, and household income.

Table 56 presents the measurement analysis for the whole sample ($N = 237$). Item reliability was examined based on the item's loading along with its respective construct. As suggested by Gefen et al. (2000), the minimum value for the item loading was 0.7. Hence, all items satisfied the requirements. In terms of internal consistency, all constructs exceed 0.60, hence

Table 56. Measurement Model Analysis (All Samples = 237).

Construct	Item	Item Loading	Internal Consistency	AVE
Access divide	ACCE_1	0.763	0.916	0.734
	ACCE_2	0.829		
	ACCE_3	0.901		
	ACCE_4	0.925		
Capability divide	CAPA_1	0.883	0.966	0.852
	CAPA_2	0.934		
	CAPA_3	0.925		
	CAPA_4	0.940		
	CAPA_5	0.932		
Innovativeness divide	INNO_1	0.911	0.927	0.761
	INNO_2	0.758		
	INNO_3	0.904		
	INNO_4	0.906		
E-government use	USE_1	0.912	0.877	0.705
	USE_2	0.806		
	USE_3	0.794		
User satisfaction	USAT_1	0.963	0.947	0.820
	USAT_2	0.942		
	USAT_3	0.946		
	USAT_4	0.755		
Benefits of e-government	BENE_1	0.957	0.966	0.906
	BENE_2	0.959		
	BENE_3	0.938		

they were sufficient, as suggested by Bagozzi and Yi (1988). The values of AVE from the constructs were also above the threshold, which was 0.50 (Fornell & Larcker, 1981). The results demonstrate that the measurement model for all respondents ($N = 237$) was sufficient.

The assessments of the measurement model for each group sample, namely gender, age, place of residence, educational attainment, and household income are shown in Tables 57 and 58. The results also demonstrate that all measurements were valid and reliable in terms of the level of item and the construct. Having achieved effective results, the next stage undertaken was the analysis of the structural model to examine the moderating effect of the *demographic divide* and *economic divide*.

6.7.2. Assessment of the Structural Model – Stage 3
One of the main objectives of this study is assessing the moderating impact of the Demographic and economic divide on e-government system success

Table 57.   Item Loading Based on Each Variable.

Item	Gender		Age Group		Residence		Education		Income	
	Male	Female	Younger	Older	City	Remote	Higher	Lower	Higher	Lower
ACCE_1	0.713	0.817	0.779	0.809	0.765	0.839	0.755	0.876	0.814	0.763
ACCE_2	0.819	0.865	0.779	0.912	0.744	0.918	0.779	0.921	0.863	0.767
ACCE_3	0.874	0.895	0.888	0.942	0.937	0.947	0.896	0.927	0.900	0.905
ACCE_4	0.885	0.946	0.911	0.955	0.941	0.959	0.915	0.953	0.935	0.917
CAPA_1	0.759	0.914	0.835	0.924	0.818	0.935	0.867	0.914	0.929	0.831
CAPA_2	0.884	0.940	0.904	0.953	0.968	0.970	0.919	0.952	0.943	0.925
CAPA_3	0.867	0.909	0.918	0.933	0.924	0.943	0.924	0.931	0.922	0.932
CAPA_4	0.885	0.958	0.919	0.956	0.891	0.971	0.925	0.960	0.954	0.920
CAPA_5	0.863	0.945	0.905	0.951	0.877	0.969	0.911	0.956	0.957	0.902
INNO_1	0.831	0.921	0.895	0.927	0.916	0.930	0.902	0.937	0.901	0.932
INNO_2	0.779	0.850	0.745	0.928	0.794	0.925	0.774	0.896	0.825	0.766
INNO_3	0.838	0.914	0.877	0.915	0.871	0.944	0.882	0.950	0.933	0.871
INNO_4	0.837	0.897	0.904	0.901	0.857	0.948	0.882	0.944	0.907	0.905
USE_1	0.885	0.928	0.907	0.912	0.914	0.923	0.900	0.935	0.879	0.933
USE_2	0.849	0.796	0.822	0.713	0.814	0.837	0.808	0.747	0.756	0.834
USE_3	0.789	0.859	0.777	0.830	0.756	0.835	0.797	0.737	0.810	0.794
USAT_1	0.947	0.984	0.964	0.958	0.962	0.979	0.967	0.944	0.920	0.985
USAT_2	0.926	0.955	0.947	0.926	0.945	0.943	0.946	0.922	0.908	0.960
USAT_3	0.922	0.956	0.940	0.951	0.945	0.938	0.945	0.952	0.911	0.962
USAT_4	0.794	0.763	0.783	0.741	0.726	0.819	0.764	0.729	0.740	0.820
BENE_1	0.959	0.940	0.971	0.926	0.955	0.965	0.962	0.938	0.968	0.951
BENE_2	0.958	0.941	0.971	0.933	0.966	0.954	0.960	0.967	0.957	0.964
BENE_3	0.943	0.896	0.968	0.843	0.945	0.928	0.936	0.944	0.950	0.936

in Indonesian local government. E-government system success is represented by three variables, which are use, benefit, and user satisfaction. Thus multi-group analysis is applied in this study to assess the moderating variables.

In the structural model, the data were divided into two categories, which were full sample and multi-group based on gender, age, place of residence, education, and income. PLS analysis using the bootstrap procedure was employed to obtain the path coefficients, standard errors, and t-values to determine the statistical significance.

Fig. 21 presents the results of the assessment of the structural model for the full sample of respondents ($N = 237$). The results confirm that the three variables of digital divide took the form of a sequential process. The results demonstrate the strong influence of the access divide on the capability divide (t-value of 32.985) and of the capability divide on the innovativeness divide (t-value of 20.748). The influence of the digital divide on e-government

Table 58. Internal Consistency and AVE Based on Each Variable.

Construct	Gender				Age Group				Residence			
	Male		Female		Younger		Older		City		Remote	
	IC	AVE	IC	AVE	IC	AVE	IC	AVE	IC	AVE	IC	AVE
ACCE	0.895	0.681	0.933	0.778	0.872	0.635	0.948	0.822	0.712	0.741	0.955	0.841
CAPA	0.930	0.727	0.971	0.871	0.953	0.804	0.976	0.890	0.943	0.768	0.982	0.917
INNO	0.858	0.607	0.942	0.802	0.888	0.672	0.955	0.842	0.874	0.644	0.966	0.877
USE	0.852	0.659	0.818	0.715	0.875	0.700	0.861	0.676	0.869	0.690	0.900	0.750
USAT	0.944	0.809	0.931	0.778	0.951	0.831	0.930	0.773	0.944	0.809	0.957	0.850
BENE	0.968	0.909	0.947	0.856	0.979	0.940	0.928	0.813	0.969	0.913	0.965	0.901

Construct	Education				Income			
	Higher		Lower		Higher		Lower	
	IC	AVE	IC	AVE	IC	AVE	IC	AVE
ACCE	0.854	0.602	0.956	0.846	0.931	0.773	0.890	0.672
CAPA	0.960	0.827	0.976	0.889	0.975	0.885	0.957	0.815
INNO	0.905	0.706	0.964	0.869	0.940	0.797	0.911	0.723
USE	0.874	0.699	0.851	0.659	0.857	0.666	0.891	0.732
USAT	0.650	0.827	0.939	0.795	0.913	0.728	0.965	0.872
BENE	0.967	0.908	0.965	0.901	0.971	0.918	0.966	0.903

system success was also significant for the innovativeness divide, the capability divide, and the access divide, with the t-values of 2.668, 2.135, and 1.367, respectively. The relationships between the variables of e-government systems success were also confirmed. The R^2 of the ultimate dependent variable (benefits of e-government) gave the value of 0.481, which represents a medium strength of explanation (Hair et al., 2011).

The assessment of the structural model based on the groups of gender, age, residential place, educational attainment, and income was conducted, as shown in Figs. 24(a)–(i). The assessment of the groups of subsamples was compared to the structural model for the full sample, as shown in Fig. 21.

Figs. 24(a) and (b) compare the results between a group of male and female respondents. The results in the group of male respondents demonstrate similar results to those of the total respondents (Fig. 21). However, groups of male and female respondents produced different results; especially the influence of the *access divide* and capability divide on e-government use in the female group, which were statistically insignificant. The relationships among the variables of the digital divide appeared to be stronger in the group of female respondents than in the male group. The influence of the access divide on the capability divide in the male group was $\beta = 0.805$, $t = 10.053$, while in the female group it was $\beta = 0.874$, $t = 71.592$. The influence of the capability divide on the innovativeness divide in males was $\beta = 0.693$, $t = 5.867$ and in females $\beta = 0.755$, $t = 25.942$.

In terms of the structural models based on age, the results for both groups (younger and older respondents) were found to be similar to the structural model of the full sample. The relationships among variables in the digital divide in both groups were significant. However the influence of the *digital divide* on *e-government systems success* in the group of older respondents appeared to produce a different result than that which was expected, especially regarding the influence of the *access divide* on *e-government use* which was not significant ($\beta = -0.041$, $t = 0.355$), while in the group of younger respondents the relationship was significant ($\beta = 0.400$, $t = 2.203$).

With regard to the structural models for the groups of respondents who lived in the city and remote areas, inconsistencies were also found. Compared to the full sample, the influence of the *capability divide* on *e-government use* was found to be insignificant for the city residents ($\beta = -1.106$, $t = 1.271$), as shown in Fig. 24(e). Other than that, all relationships were significant: *access divide* to *e-government use* ($\beta = 0.844$, $t = 14.140$); *innovativeness divide* to *e-government use* ($\beta = 0.093$, $t = 1.680$); *access divide* to *capability divide* ($\beta = 0.758$, $t = 16.636$); *capability divide* to *innovativeness divide* ($\beta = 0.654$, $t = 12.376$).

Different results were also found in the structural models for the respondents who had a lower and higher educational background. In the group of respondents who had received higher degree education, the *capability divide* was not a significant factor for *e-government use* ($\beta = 0.111$, $t = 1.048$). However, the other relationships were significant in both groups.

Finally, the assessment for the moderating effect of the economic divide, which is represented by household income, shows that the results differ for both groups (higher and lower income), as shown in Figs. 24(i) and (j). In the lower income group, the influence of the *capability divide* on *e-government use* was not significant ($\beta = 0.170$, $t = 1.133$), while the other relationships were significant. On the other hand, the influence of the *access divide* on *e-government use* was not significant in the high-income group ($\beta = 0.139$, $t = 1.259$).

In addition to the assessment of the models for each group of respondents, this research also employed the Smith-Satterwait test to examine the moderating effect. The Smith-Satterwait test was chosen because the

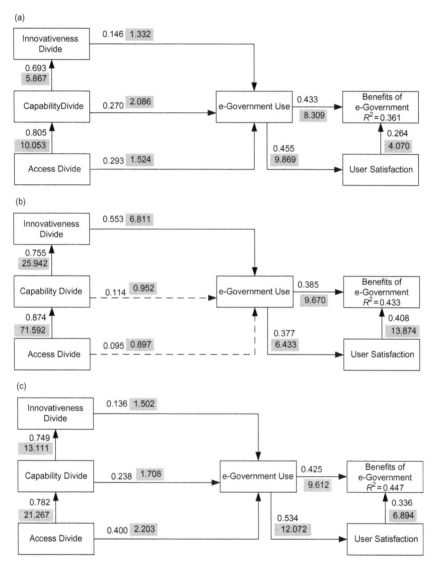

Fig. 24. The structural model of each group (a) The structural model of male group. (b) The structural model of female group. (c). The structural model of younger group. (d) The structural model of older group. (e) The structural model of city area group. (f) The structural model of remote area group. (g) The structural model of lower education group. (h) The structural model of higher education group. (i) The structural model of lower income group. (j) The structural model of higher income group.

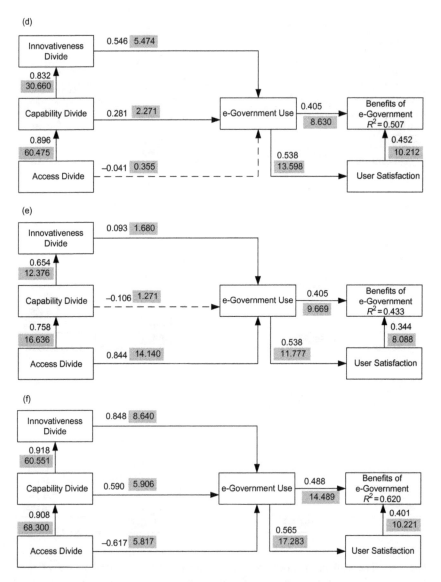

Fig. 24. (*Continued*)

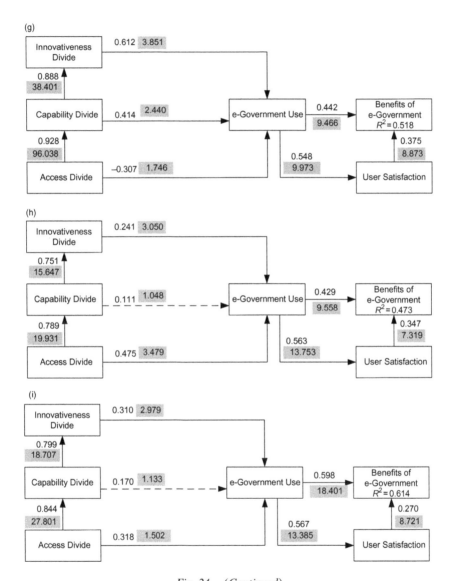

Fig. 24. (*Continued*)

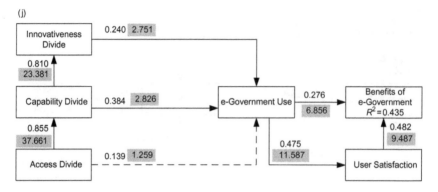

Fig. 24. (*Continued*)

samples are not normally distributed and the variances of the group are not equal (Hsieh et al., 2008; Moores & Chang, 2006).

Table 59 presents the results of the *t*-statistics to determine the significant effects of gender, age, residential place, education, and income. If more than four relationships have significant results, the moderating effect is supported. Whereas, if less than four relationships are significant, the hypothesis is partially supported. However, the hypothesis is not supported if there is no significant result for any relationship.

To recap, five hypotheses − H4a−H4e − were proposed to describe the moderating effect. As shown in Table 59, the findings demonstrate only two significant differences (significant *t*-values are shadowed in Table 59) in the impact of the *digital divide* on *e-government systems success* and *user satisfaction* on *benefits of e-government* for males and females. The significant moderating effect of gender on the influence of the *innovativeness divide* on *e-government use* implies that males and females differed in terms of their willingness to try e-government systems. However, the overall results indicate that the impact on male and female users is similar, and thus H5a is *partially supported*.

With regard to the moderating of age, the results show four links with significant differences between younger and older groups of respondents. The links are: *access divide* to *e-government use* ($t = 2.049$), *innovativeness divide* to *e-government use* (3.043), *access divide* to *capability divide* ($t = 2.874$), *user satisfaction* to *benefits of e-government* ($t = 1.762$). The results indicate that access was a most important factor for younger users (younger $\beta = 0.400$, older $\beta = -0.041$), whereas willingness to try the systems

Table 59. Results of Pooled Error Term t-Test by Subgroup.

Path Relation	Male		Female		t-Value	Younger		Older		t-Value	City		Remote		t-Value
	β	SE	β	SE		β	SE	β	SE		β	SE	β	SE	
ACCE–USE	0.293	0.192	0.095	0.106	0.903	0.400	0.182	−0.041	0.116	2.049	0.844	0.0597	−0.617	0.106	12.001
CAPA–USE	0.270	0.130	0.114	0.120	0.884	0.238	0.139	0.281	0.124	0.231	−0.106	0.0834	0.590	0.100	5.348
INNO–USE	0.146	0.110	0.553	0.081	2.984	0.136	0.091	0.546	0.100	3.043	0.093	0.0554	0.848	0.098	6.701
ACCE–CAPA	0.805	0.080	0.874	0.012	0.852	0.782	0.037	0.896	0.015	2.874	0.758	0.0456	0.908	0.013	3.158
CAPA–INNO	0.693	0.118	0.755	0.029	0.510	0.749	0.057	0.832	0.027	1.313	0.654	0.0528	0.918	0.015	4.805
USE–USAT	0.455	0.046	0.377	0.059	1.046	0.534	0.044	0.508	0.037	0.449	0.538	0.0457	0.565	0.033	0.480
USE–BENE	0.433	0.052	0.385	0.040	0.732	0.425	0.044	0.366	0.042	0.963	0.405	0.0419	0.488	0.034	1.544
USAT–BENE	0.264	0.065	0.408	0.029	2.021	0.336	0.049	0.452	0.044	1.762	0.344	0.0425	0.401	0.039	0.986

Path Relation	High Education		Low Education		t-Value	High Income		Low Income		t-Value
	β	SE	β	SE		β	SE	β	SE	
ACCE–USE	0.475	0.137	−0.307	0.176	3.513	0.139	0.110	0.318	0.2117	0.703
CAPA–USE	0.111	0.106	0.414	0.170	1.515	0.384	0.136	0.170	0.1500	0.927
INNO–USE	0.241	0.079	0.612	0.159	2.091	0.240	0.087	0.310	0.0104	0.644
ACCE–CAPA	0.789	0.040	0.928	0.010	3.377	0.855	0.023	0.844	0.0304	0.264
CAPA–INNO	0.751	0.048	0.888	0.023	2.572	0.810	0.035	0.799	0.0427	0.181
USE–USAT	0.563	0.041	0.548	0.055	0.219	0.475	0.041	0.567	0.0424	1.410
USE–BENE	0.429	0.449	0.442	0.047	0.029	0.276	0.040	0.598	0.0325	5.311
USAT–BENE	0.347	0.047	0.375	0.042	0.441	0.482	0.051	0.270	0.0310	2.961

or innovativeness was the most important factor for older users (younger $\beta = 0.136$, older $\beta = 0.546$) in the use of e-government systems. Furthermore, access to ICT was seen as an important factor for increasing user capability, especially for older users. Despite this, some links were insignificantly different, and based on the overall results; we can conclude that age has a *significant moderating effect* on the impact of the *digital divide* on *e-government systems success*, as proposed in H5b.

In terms of the moderating effect of residential location, the results support five links, namely *access divide* to *e-government use* ($t = 12.001$), *capability divide* to *e-government use* ($t = 5.348$), *innovativeness divide* to *e-government use* ($t = 6.701$), *access divide* to *capability divide* ($t = 3.158$), and *capability divide* to *innovativeness divide* ($t = 4.805$). Therefore H5c or the moderating effect of age on the impact of the *digital divide* on *e-government systems success* is *supported*.

The assessment of the moderating effect of education reveals that the links *access divide* to *e-government use*, *innovativeness divide* to *e-government use*, *access divide* to *capability divide*, and *capability divide* to *innovativeness divide* are confirmed. Table 59 illustrates that for the users who attended higher education, access to ICT was more significant than for those who possessed lower educational levels. On the other hand, CSE and willingness to try new technologies were more important for less educated users. The

Table 60. Hypotheses Evaluation of Analyses (Antecedent Factors).

Construct	Link		Hypothesis Statement	Outcome
Digital divide	AD → EU	H1a	Access divide positively influences e-government use	Supported
	CD → EU	H1b	Capability divide positively influences e-government use	Supported
	ID → EU	H1c	Innovativeness divide positively influences e-government use	Supported
	AD → CD	H2a	Access divide Positively Influences capability divide	Supported
	CD → ID	H2b	Capability divide positively influences innovativeness divide	Supported
E-government systems success	EU → US	H3a	E-government use positively influences user satisfaction	Supported
	EU → BE	H3b	E-government use positively influences benefits of e-government	Supported
	US → BE	H3c	User satisfaction positively influences benefits of e-government	Supported

Table 61. Hypotheses Evaluation of Analyses (Mediating Effect).

Construct	Link		Hypothesis statement	Outcome
Trust in e-government	AD → T → EU	H4a	Trust in e-government has a mediating effect on the relationship between access divide and e-government systems success	Not supported
	CD → T → EU	H4b	Trust in e-government has a mediating effect on the relationship between capability divide and e-government systems success	Supported
	ID → T → EU	H4c	Trust in e-government has a mediating effect on the relationship between innovativeness divide and e-government systems success	Supported

Table 62. Hypotheses Evaluation of Analyses (Moderating Effect).

Construct	Link		Hypothesis statement	Outcome
Demographic divide and economic divide	Gender × DD → ESS	H5a	Gender has a moderating effect on the relationship between digital divide and e-government systems success	Partially supported
	Age × DD → ESS	H5b	Age has a moderating effect on the relationship between digital divide and e-government systems success	Supported
	Place × DD → ESS	H5c	Residential place has a moderating effect on the relationship between digital divide and e-government systems success	Supported
	Education × DD → ESS	H5d	Education has a moderating effect on the relationship between digital divide and e-government systems success	Supported
	Income × DD → ESS	H5e	Income has a moderating effect on the relationship between digital divide and e-government systems success	Partially supported

relationships among the variables of the digital divide also appear stronger in users who had attained lower educational levels. Based on the assessment, H5d is *supported*; age has a moderating effect on the influence of the digital divide on the success of e-government systems.

As shown in Table 59, the differences between the low-income and high-income groups are only evidenced by the links of *e-government use* to *benefits of e-government* ($t = 5.311$) and *user satisfaction* to *benefits of e-government* ($t = 2.961$). Other than these links, the assessment did not show significant differences between the two groups. Therefore, based on the overall results, the links and assessment *partially support* H5e.

6.8. Summary of the Hypotheses Evaluation

As presented in a Section 5, 16 hypotheses were developed to explain the relationships among the constructs in the comprehensive research model. In order to test these hypotheses, analyses based on the PLS were undertaken to examine the data that were gathered from the survey.

Previous sections explained three stage analyses, consistent with the research objectives. Hence to provide the overall results based on the analyses, Tables 60–62 summarize the evaluation of the research hypotheses. The discussion of the results is presented in the Section 7.

6.9. Summary

This section described research findings based on the analyses of the research data that was undertaken by using PLS analysis. In Section 6.2, the overview of the survey was presented to explain the research process that was conducted. It was followed by a section describing the characteristics of the respondents in terms of demographic factors, such as gender, age, residential place, and education, and in terms of economic factors, represented by household income. This research involved 237 respondents who were users of e-government systems provided by local governments in Indonesia.

Furthermore, full analyses using PLS were explained in Sections 6.5–6.7, following the sequence of research objectives. The first stage of the PLS analyses examined the influence of antecedent factors (*digital divide*), including the *access divide*, *capability divide*, and the *innovativeness divide* on *e-government systems success*, represented by the constructs of *e-government use, user satisfaction* and *benefits of e-government*. At the same time, the analysis also tested the relationships among variables in the *digital divide*. The second stage investigated the mediating effect of *trust in e-government* on the influence of the *digital divide* on *e-government systems success*. In the final stage, the analysis focused on the assessment of the moderating effect of the *demographic divide* and *economic divide* on the impact of the *digital divide* on *e-government systems success*.

At every stage, two major procedures of assessment were undertaken, namely the assessment of the measurement model and the assessment of the structural model. Nevertheless, the analysis was extended in stage two by using the Baron and Kenny (1986) test and the Sobel (1982) test in order to investigate the mediating effect. The extension of the analysis was also conducted in stage three using multi-group analysis. Based on the findings of the analyses, the research hypotheses were evaluated. Overall, of the 16 hypotheses proposed in this research, 13 hypotheses were supported, with the other 3 hypotheses being rejected. Thus in the next section, the discussion and implication of the findings are discussed, based on theoretical development and practical significance.

7. DISCUSSION AND IMPLICATIONS

7.1. Introduction

The previous section discussed the results of the hypotheses testing whereby 13 of the 16 hypotheses were supported. In this section, the findings related to the hypotheses are discussed in detail, along with the implications of each finding. Any significant relationships found are then linked to practical propositions, and it is hoped that these may serve as guidelines toward the implementation of effective measures to increase the use of e-government systems. The theoretical implications of the results and their impact on current research gaps are also deliberated. Possible explanations for the rejected hypotheses are also discussed.

7.2. Interpretation and Discussion of Data Analysis Results

As presented in Fig. 25, the results reveal that the explanatory power of all the endogenous constructs in the model exceeds the minimum R^2, which is 0.25, as suggested by Hair et al. (2011). The overall model explains 48.1%

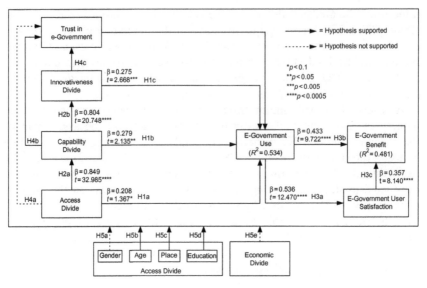

Fig. 25.   Results of Hypotheses Testing.

of the variance of citizens' actual use of e-government systems, (figures provided by local governments). The results of the hypotheses testing, as depicted in Fig. 25, found 13 relationships to be statistically significant.

7.2.1. Hypotheses Related to the Digital Divide

The literature review and field study identified three variables that could potentially influence the success of e-government systems. The influence of each variable was explored through hypotheses H1a, H1b, and H1c. The results of the hypotheses testing are discussed in detail in the following sections.

7.2.1.1. H1a.

This research argues through H1a, that access to information and communications technology (ICT, also referred to as the access divide) has a positive influence on e-government use. The results of the hypothesis testing indicate that there is significant statistical evidence to support the fact that the access divide influences e-government use in that inequalities of access result in limiting people's ability to use the system. This finding is consistent with previous research on ICT adoption (e.g., Atewell, 2001; Corrocher & Ordanini, 2002; Ferro et al., 2011; James, 2007), which found that access to ICT significantly influences ICT adoption. As Rahman and Quaddus (2012) argue, most of the research into the digital divide that examines the role access to ICT plays with regard to ICT adoption has reached similar conclusions.

The results are also in accordance with the studies by the United Nations (2010, 2012) which include access to ICT infrastructures as one of key indicators of e-government readiness. The results are also congruent with field study findings where all of the informants agreed upon the substantial role that access to ICT played in increasing e-government use. Hence, this study confirms that the access divide is an important factor, which influences e-government use.

The practical implications of this finding are that policy makers in Indonesia, especially local governments, in attempting to increase the use of e-government, should improve the availability of ICT infrastructures to their citizens, especially the provision of Internet connections. As mentioned by some informants, free Internet access in public spaces, such as offices, shopping centers, parks, airports, and other places would help citizens have access to the Internet. Ease of access to the Internet would more easily encourage citizens to use the e-government system.

Evidence of success regarding e-government may be found in the United Kingdom, where in 2005, the government spent 1.14% of its GDP on ICT investments, making the United Kingdom the biggest spender on public sector IT in Europe (Irani, Elliman, & Jackson, 2007). The ICT investments were made in e-government and back office infrastructures. By implementing e-government, the UK government will make savings in terms of significant improvements to efficiency of service delivery. Prattipati (2003) argues that provision of public Internet access is found to be the most important factor affecting the use of e-government services. The experience of Singapore in developing its e-government shows that the Indonesian government would be wise to undertake measures to make the Internet accessible to every citizen. To help citizens on the disadvantaged side of the digital divide, the Singapore government partnered with private industry to implement the PC Reuse Scheme to distribute second hand PCs to needy parties (Ke & Wei, 2004).

7.2.1.2. H1b. Statistical evidence indicates the significant positive impact of the capability divide on e-government use ($\beta = 0.279$; $t = 2.135$). The findings confirm previous studies (Dewan & Riggins, 2005; Warschauer, 2003b; Wei et al., 2011) that suggest the significant influence of CSE on ICT use. Compared to the influence of the access divide, the statistical results suggest that the capability divide has a stronger influence on e-government use. Therefore, as hypothesized in the study, the capability divide has a substantial effect in increasing e-government use.

The practical implications are that the government, as the provider of the e-government system, should play a greater role in improving the capability of its citizens in using ICT in general and the e-government system in particular. Warschauer (2003b, pp. 1−2) recounts that in 2000, the government of New Delhi, India, provided computer access in slum areas for the city's street children. The project, known as Hole-in-the-Wall, allowed the street children to have 24-hour access to computers and the Internet. Besides the Internet connection being made through dial up access, the computers were also equipped with some essential programs, such as Microsoft Office and Paint. Without any instruction whatsoever, the children were able to access computers and the Internet at their own pace and speed, in the hope that learning would take place.

The results indicated that the access to Internet was negligible, with the majority of the children using a computer to draw with Paint programs or to play games. The failure of the project was caused by the fact that no specific computer education was made available to the children. Some parents expressed their concern that the absence of instruction took away from the project's value. Some others even raised negative feelings about the project, complaining that the computers distracted their children from their homework and schoolwork.

The story above represents the nature of incomplete policies by many governments to overcome the digital divide where they perceive the main problem to be merely inequality of access (especially physical access) to ICT. Although access to ICT is an important factor, capability in using ICT is essential.

7.2.1.3. H1c. Rogers (1995, 2003), through the DIs Theory, argues that innovators are individuals who are able to cope with high levels of risk and uncertainty. With regard to attitude toward e-government initiatives, this research attempts to examine the influence of the innovativeness divide on the willingness to change and try new ICT. Through H1c, this research proposed that the innovativeness divide positively influence e-government use.

Based on the PLS analysis, the results confirm the significant positive influence of the innovativeness divide on e-government use ($\beta = 0.275$, $t = 2.668$). The results show that the effect of the innovativeness divide is the strongest, when compared to the access divide and the capability divide. This finding supports the findings of previous studies by Agarwal and

Prasad (1998, 1997), and Yi et al. (2006). Moreover, the findings are also in congruence with the results in the field study, in which 10 informants (out of 12) confirmed the importance of the innovativeness divide on e-government use.

The results imply that on top of access to ICT and the capability to use ICT, the willingness to change and try new ICT is vital for e-government use. van Dijk and Hacker (2003) assert that there are four type of access, namely: (1) "Motivational access" or lack of elementary digital experience because of lack of interest, computer anxiety, or unattractiveness of the new ICT; (2) "Material access" or lack of ownership of (or access to) computers and network connections; (3) "Skills access" or lack of digital skills caused by insufficient user-friendliness and/or inadequate education; and (4) "Usage access" or significant usage opportunities. Furthermore, the access problems may be shifted or translated from the first two types of access to the last two types. As illustrated in Fig. 26, when the problems of mental and material access are solved, wholly or partially, the problems of skill and use become more operative (van Dijk, 2006). Van Dijk and Hacker (2003) underline the problem of information *want-not* that is more important than information *have-not*.

The implications of the findings suggest that government should increase awareness and create a positive attitude in its citizens toward the implementation of e-government systems. Referring to van Dijk and Hacker (2003), some reasons for not using the innovations could be: *"do not need it," "can't handle it,"* or *"don't want it."* By more actively socializing the

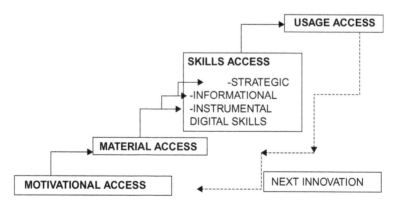

Fig. 26. Cumulative and Recursive Model of Successive Types of Access to Digital Technologies. *Source:* van Dijk (2006, p. 224)

existence and benefits of e-government, citizens' lack of interest, anxiety, and lack of attraction to the technology could be removed. Another significant factor in the improvement of innovativeness is the development of user-friendly e-government systems.

In addition, this study also advances the theoretical account of the digital divide by going beyond previous studies and introducing a new type of digital divide, which is the innovativeness divide. The results provide a theoretical and more comprehensive understanding of the digital divide. This framework can be applied and examined in a variety of contexts to test the boundaries of its applicability.

7.2.2. Hypotheses Related to the Relationships among Variables in the Digital Divide

7.2.2.1. H2a. According to Dewan and Riggins (2005), individuals acquire CSE through the availability of ICT resources. The digital access divide refers to the first level of the digital divide, while the digital capability divide refers to the second level (Dewan & Riggins, 2005). In order to examine the positive influence of the access divide on the capability divide, this research proposed H2a. The results indicate that the relationships are significantly positive, as illustrated in Fig. 25 ($\beta = 0.849$, $t = 32.985$). The findings confirm previous research by Seltzer (1983), Selwyn (1998), Bertot (2003), Wei et al. (2011), and Gripenberg (2011). All of the participants in the field study also agreed on the influence of the access divide on the capability divide.

Based on Social Cognitive Theory, Wei et al. (2011) posit that access to ICT partly influences the individuals experience of mastering mastery CSE. Bertot (2003) argues that access to ICT would assist in individuals becoming more information-literate. Once they have access, they need to know how: to (1) use the technology; (2) to find and retrieve the information needed; (3) to evaluate and assess the relevance of the information; and (4) to synthesize the information in order to solve their particular problem.

The findings highlight the importance of the provision of access to ICT. The availability of the ICT infrastructure is a prerequisite for improving an individual's capability in using ICT. The same reason leads local governments in many countries to expand the availability of computers and Internet connections, with a particular emphasis on public schools, libraries, higher education institutions, and the broader community. In the United States, for example, former President Bill Clinton proposed a tax incentive for businesses to donate computers to poor schools and communities (Lacey, 2000). The government of Texas also established the telecommunication Infrastructure Fund (TIF) to address the ICT infrastructure in Texas, specifically with regard to educational institutions and health care facilities (Bertot, 2003). By focusing on the educational institutions, the computers and Internet connection could be used for daily teaching and learning processes, and these processes in turn would contribute to improving the ability of the next generation to utilize ICT.

7.2.2.2. H2b. Organizations, including those in the public sector, are continually reminded that technological innovation, both within the organization and for its customers, is key to success and technological innovations are vital to survival in a highly competitive environment (Blackler & Brown, 1985). While the purported benefits to the organization may be attractive, researchers have found that the end users often have a less than enthusiastic response to the many technological innovations introduced by organizations (Blackler & Brown, 1985; O'Connor, Parsons, Liden, & Herold, 1990). This study therefore proposed H2b in order to investigate the influence of the capability divide on the innovativeness divide.

The findings in this study shows that there is a significantly positive influence of the capability divide on the innovativeness divide ($\beta = 0.804$, $t = 20.748$). The results support previous research by Frantzich (1979), Burkhardt and Brass (1990), and Ellen et al. (1991). The results are in congruence with the findings in the field study, where all of the informants confirmed the influence of the capability divide on the innovativeness divide.

Numerous factors influence an individual to change from a pre-existing product/service or pattern of behavior. These include the effects of environmental factors (Gatignon & Robertson, 1989), the degree of tolerance for risks and switching costs (Gatignon & Robertson, 1989; Watson, 1971), and the loss of autonomy (Coch & French Jr., 1948; Nadler, 1981). At an individual level, Frantzich (1979, p. 968) posit that "technological innovation requires knowledge of one's needs and goals, awareness of optional ways of reaching the goals, the willingness and ability to take risk and access to the skills necessary for putting the innovation to use." Moreover, studies by Cody, Dunn, Hoppin, and Wendt (1999) suggest that the provision of adequate training, to improve one's capability in utilizing the Internet, may increase one's willingness to use the internet.

Studies in Personal Innovativeness or individual willingness to change have been dominated by market research. This research contributes to the theoretical understanding of Personal Innovativeness in the area of ISs. The results provide an underlying foundation for the theoretical understanding of the influence of CSE on an individual's willingness to change and try new ICT.

Practically, the findings provide a basis for policy makers to formulate strategies to encourage change. Once any inhibiting factors have been identified, a variety of strategic approaches could be formulated. Where low self-efficacy exists, modification of the innovation may be necessary. However, since self-efficacy is often based on self-perception rather than reality, changes in the promotion of the innovation (i.e., training programs, availability of support services, toll-free help lines) may be effective in changing perceptions of self-efficacy (Blackler & Brown, 1985; O'Connor et al., 1990).

7.2.3. Hypotheses Relating to E-Government Systems Success

DeLone and McLean (2003) have updated their previous model (1992) based on several studies on IS success. Basically, the model consists of two levels of IS success, namely the *semantic level* and the *effectiveness level* (DeLone & McLean, 2003). The semantic level measures technical success including: Information Quality, System Quality, and Service Quality. The effectiveness level measures the effect of the information on the receiver or user and includes: system use, user satisfaction, and benefits of the system. The present study focuses on measuring the effectiveness of e-government systems. This study argues that key elements of e-government system success are: e-government use, user satisfaction, and benefits of e-government. The elements and sequential relationships between elements of e-government system success are adapted from DeLone and McLean (2003). Hypotheses H3a, H3b, and H3c represent the influence of e-government use on user satisfaction, the influence of e-government use on the benefits of e-government, and the influence of user satisfaction on the benefits of e-government, respectively.

7.2.3.1. Hypotheses H3a, H3b, and H3c. The findings in this research show the statistical significance of the influence of e-government use on user satisfaction (H3a), the influence of e-government use on the benefits of e-government (H3b), and the influence of user satisfaction on the benefits of e-government (H3c). The findings in the field study also confirm the results of the quantitative analysis.

The results are in line with evidence from the literature review, which validated the model of IS success. This model was initially developed in the context of e-commerce; however the model has been applied in wide variety of systems (Fisher et al., 2000; Gelderman, 1998; Lee & Chung, 2009;

Ruttan, 1996;) and in an e-government context in particular (Floropoulos et al., 2010; Wang & Liao, 2008).

The findings imply that by increasing e-government use and user satisfaction, the benefits will be tangible to the users. As discussed in Section 2, the e-government system is believed to be able to elevate the quality of communication between government and their citizens, and to improve the quality of public administration as well as accountability. The informants in the field study also confirmed the benefits that they received from using the e-government system, including more efficiency in terms of cost and time consumed, and this was in addition to transparency and accountability. Therefore the findings in this study suggest that government encourage its citizens to increase their use of e-government systems.

7.2.4. Hypotheses Relating to Trust in E-Government
The current study argued that trust in e-government has a mediating effect on the influence of the digital divide on the success of e-government systems. Based on the literature, trust in e-government mediates the influence of the access divide (H4a), the capability divide (H4b), and the innovativeness divide (H4c) on the success of e-government systems. The following section discusses the results, including the implications.

7.2.4.1. Hypotheses H4a, H4b, and H4c.
The results show that the direct influence of the access divide on e-government system success was not affected by the inclusion of the mediator variable. Hence, H4a, positing the mediating effect of trust in e-government on the influence of the access divide on e-government system success is not supported by the results. On the other hand, the quantitative analyses demonstrate that H4b and H4c are supported. In the other words, the influence of the capability divide and the innovativeness divide on e-government system success is fully mediated by trust in e-government.

This study has implications for IS research on trust in e-government systems. This is due to disagreement among researchers as to whether or not the study of trust, in the context of information science, is necessary or appropriate. Some researchers argue that trust does not play an important role in a user's obtaining of information through the internet (Coch & French Jr., 1948; Nadler, 1981). Other researchers assert that trust is a construct that is only applied to people, not to computers or systems (Frantzich, 1979; Melitski & Holzer, 2007). However, some studies have acknowledged trust as an important factor for ICT use in general (Gatignon & Robertson, 1989; Kelton et al., 2007; McKnight & Chervany,

2002; Pavlou & Gefen, 2004), and in an e-government context in particular (e.g., Teo et al., 2009; Warkentin et al., 2002). Hence, this study confirms the applicability of the concept of trust in information sources such as websites and e-government systems.

Furthermore, one of the key insights in this study is in the findings on the role of trust in e-government. Previous research predominantly examined the direct influence of trust on the adoption of technology. The present study, on the other hand, found that trust in e-government plays an important role as a mediator in the success of e-government systems. Trust has previously been acknowledged as a mediating variable in many other disciplines, such as marketing (Morgan & Hunt, 1994; Sirdeshmukh et al., 2002) and behavioral intention in management (Cropanzano & Mitchell, 2005; Vlachos et al., 2009). The PLS analyses show that by introducing trust in e-government into the model, the direct influence of the capability divide, and the innovativeness divide on e-government system success become insignificant (see Section 6, Figs. 22 and 23). In other words, trust in e-government fully mediates the influence of the capability divide and Innovativeness on e-government.

As to the practical implications of the findings, it is imperative to build citizens' trust in e-government if the scheme is to succeed. In order to mitigate user uncertainty, the government could provide informative content and describe their services and benefits in terms of costs, required time, and step-by-step processes. The government might also make efforts to establish citizens' trust in e-government by promoting its commitment through effective and transparent leadership, which the public would be made aware of.

7.2.5. Hypotheses Relating to the Demographic Divide and Economic Divide
Williams (1990) asserts that inequalities in socioeconomic circumstances are found in the internal and external resources, or constraints, that together shape experience and opportunities, and in turn influence behavioral patterns. Based on this notion, the moderating effect of socioeconomic characteristics on the relationships between the digital divide and e-government system success is expected. To test the notion, H5a, H5b, H5c, H5d, and H5e were proposed to test the moderating effects of gender, age group, place of residence, education, and income, respectively.

7.2.5.1. H5a: Gender. In terms of gender, contrary to expectations, the findings of the multi-group PLS analysis partially support this variable as having a moderating effect, since only two significant differences were found between men and women regarding the influence of the digital divide on e-government system success (i.e., INNO-USE and USAT-BENE).

Despite the above findings, it is noteworthy that earlier studies presented some contradictory results on the effects of gender on e-government use. Research by Venkatesh, Thong, Chan, Hu, and Brown (2011) found that in the United Kingdom, e-government service users were predominantly male. Some studies, however, did not find gender differences in the use of, and attitudes toward, e-government systems (Abdulai & Huffman, 2005; Belanger & Carter, 2009; Colesca & Dobrica, 2008; van Dijk et al., 2008; Wang & Shih, 2009).

The research conducted in this chapter produced results that may bear re-examination. On the other hand, the users of e-government systems were predominantly male (see Table 35). Since this research only examined actual "hands-on" users of e-government systems, men and women in general might possibly share the same views once they had become users of e-government systems. Therefore, different results might be found by including both users and non-users in further research.

7.2.5.2. H5b: Age Group. Rhodes (1983, p. 329) states that psychologically, ageing can be defined as "systematic changes in personality, needs, expectations, and behaviour as well as performance in a sequence of socially prescribed roles and accumulation of experiences." Moreover, Rhodes further explains that biological ageing includes changes in anatomy and psychology, such as changes in sensorimotor performance and in visual acuity. In line with studies in psychology, previous research in ISs found similar results. Hindman (2000) and Loges and Jung (2001), for example, found different patterns in internet use between age groups in the United States.

Referring to the multi-group analysis, the results of this study indicate that younger and older age groups have different behavioral patterns. Morris and Venkatesh (2000) argue that those in younger age groups are much more likely to have been exposed to ICT at a relatively early age. In contrast, older individuals are much less likely to have ICT experience due to the completion of their education prior to the introduction of the personal computer. Hence, opportunities for older people to interact with ICT have been very limited. Younger people in general have more experience in making judgements about technology. As a consequence, older people tend to be less confident in their ability to utilize ICT and show less willingness to try new ICT. Similar conclusions were also drawn by Czaja and Sharit (1993) and Forte-Gardner et al. (2004).

One interesting result found among variables in the digital divide was that the access divide was the most important factor in e-government use for the younger age group. The influence was not significant for older age groups. A possible explanation of this phenomenon is that older age groups do not find access to ICT to be an important factor in e-government use, as, unlike the younger age group, they have more stable economic circumstances. Therefore, they are more capable of investing in home computers and Internet connections, and may have computer and Internet access in their offices.

7.2.5.3. H5c: Place of Residence. This study posited through H5c that place of residence moderates the influence of the digital divide on e-government system success. As discussed in Section 5, the hypothesis was proposed based on previous research that found differences in ICT use in rural and urban areas. The inequalities were found in developing countries (Akca, Sayili, & Esengun, 2007; Mariscal, 2005) and developed countries (Hindman, 2000; Mossberger et al., 2006; Schleife, 2010). This situation was related to the issues of "market efficiency gaps" and the "access gap" as suggested by the World Bank (Mariscal, 2005). The market efficiency gap refers to the differences between the levels of ICT infrastructure and service penetration that is reachable under current conditions, and the level one would expect under optimal market conditions. Furthermore, the access gap refers to situations where a gap between urban and rural areas continues to exist, even under efficient market conditions, where a proportion of the population cannot afford to pay market prices. Since rural areas tend to lag economically behind urban areas due to industrial and labor markets being concentrated in urban areas (Jensen, 2001), people in rural areas tend to lag behind in term of access to ICT.

The overall findings in the multi-group analysis demonstrate the fact that there is a moderating effect by residential place on the influence of the digital divide on e-government system success. The findings are consistent with prior research into the digital divide (Abdulai & Huffman, 2005; Hampton, 2010, 2003; Hausman, 2005; Schleife, 2010; Stern et al., 2009) indicating significant differences in ICT use based on place of residence.

7.2.5.4. H5d: Education. The present study proposed the moderating role of education on the influence of the digital divide on e-government system success. Based on the multi-group analysis, H5d receives support. Hence, the results of the analysis provided additional support for previous research which suggest that education is a powerful predictor of the use of and attitudes toward e-government services (Abdulai & Huffman, 2005;

Colesca & Dobrica, 2008; Hindman, 2000; van Dijk et al., 2008). These studies concluded that people with an advanced education tend to use more e-government online services than people with lower levels of education.

Education is crucial to ICT use as it provides the skills required for utilizing such technologies. Although it is possible for those who are near-literate to take advantage of certain technology applications, education becomes increasingly important as the technology becomes more complex (DiMaggio, Hargittai, Celeste, et al., 2001). Stern et al. (2009) argue that higher education plays an important in the adoption of ICT. They found that where computers and the Internet were first introduced into academic and research institutions, highly educated people adapted to these new technologies earlier than others. The important role of universities in the process of internet diffusion was also analyzed by Goldfarb (2006), who suggested the spillover effect of higher education into technology development and diffusion. Similar conclusions were also drawn by Tengtrakul and Peha (2013) and Agyapong and Ferreira (2009). Those studies found the spillover effect of ICT in schools on ICT utilization by adults who lived with students, and this was not just a case of Internet adoption in the home.

7.2.5.5. H5e: Income. It is expected that household income has a moderating effect on the influence of the digital divide on e-government system success. Therefore, a difference in such influences between higher income level users and lower income level users was proposed. Referring to the findings, although a significant difference was detected, it was limited to the link e-government use to benefits of e-government and user satisfaction to benefits to e-government.

Overall findings however, failed to support a moderating effect of income level on the influence of the digital divide on e-government system success. This outcome suggests that when it comes to e-government use, no differences between individuals with high or low economic circumstances can be derived. Therefore, H5e was partially supported. This result contradicts previous studies (DiMaggio, Hargittai, Celeste, et al., 2001; Mills & Whitacre, 2003; Nicholas, 2003; Peter & Valkenburg, 2006) demonstrating that people with higher levels of income tend to use the internet more than those on a lower income. Nevertheless, the finding provides additional support to previous studies, which found that income is unrelated to Internet usage (Abdulai & Huffman, 2005; Colesca & Dobrica, 2008; Shih & Venkatesh, 2004).

The findings in the field study were also consistent with the result of the quantitative analysis, where only 3 out of 12 informants agreed that there was a relationship between the economic divide and e-government use, with the majority of the informants not acknowledging a relationship. Informant 8, for example, said:

> I don't think that personal economic circumstances influence the usage of the e-government online system, as nowadays we can easily find Internet facilities in shopping centres, restaurants and other public areas. We can access the internet for free ...

Hence, the possible explanation on insignificant moderating effect of economic divide refers to the argument of one of the informants as presented earlier. Local government in cooperation with the private companies have provided free Internet access in public areas, such as parks, shopping centers, restaurants, and airports.

7.2.5.6. Implications of the Moderating Effect of the Demographic Divide and Economic Divide. The results of the multi-group analysis and the demographic and economic characteristics of e-government system users (Table 55), as well as the results in the field study, imply that gaps exist. E-government users in Indonesia are dominated by males, young people, city dwellers, those with a high-level education and those coming from middle to upper level economic backgrounds. The characteristics of users are in line with findings from previous research into ICT users. Studies across the globe on the digital divide have long been documenting the gaps in developing countries (Akca et al., 2007; Hwang & Syamsuddin, 2008; Schuppan, 2009; Warschauer, 2003a) and developed countries (Mossberger et al., 2006; Ono, 2006; Schleife, 2010; Stern et al., 2009), with similar results. Even in the United States, one of the most developed countries in the world, NTIA (2000, 2011) reported that groups of rural poor, ethnic minorities, and female head-of-households are the most disadvantaged groups in terms of ICT access.

Scholars in ICT4D (Information and Communication Technology for Development) such as Heeks (2009), Steyn (2011), and Johanson (2011b) posit that ICTs nowadays have become more and more important as economic, social, and political life becomes increasingly digital. Hence, the issue of the digital divide requires further understanding and ultimate resolution. Otherwise, those who are in disadvantaged groups living without ICTs will be increasingly excluded. Warren (2007) argues that non ICT users will suffer many disadvantages when offline services from government, corporations, and individuals are reduced as a result of increasing dependence on the internet. The use of online services is increasing rapidly as service providers take advantage of lowering costs and strive to improve the quality of their services (making them quicker, more interactive, and more flexible). Social gaps lead to a digital divide, which lead to deeper inequalities, and create a vicious digital cycle (Warren, 2007).

With the implications of the findings on the moderating effects of the demographic and economic divide, the current research suggests that in resolving the digital divide, policy makers must understand the complexity and dynamics of the issue, and incorporate the behavioral patterns of different demographic and economic groups (Hsieh et al., 2008), rather than implementing single generic policies that treat every individual as the same. Additional funds could be spent on the group alignment approach in order to understand the behavioral patterns of each group. This approach is believed by some to lead to a more effective outcome (Hsieh et al., 2011). Policies such as tax exemption for projects by corporations that bring ICT to low-income people through their Corporate Social Responsibility (CSR) and "E-rates" to subsidize Internet use and ICT for public schools and libraries might be implemented by Indonesia. These strategies have effectively boosted the connectivity rate in the United States (DiMaggio, Hargittai, Celeste, et al., 2001). Free Internet access in public places, which has been provided by some local governments in Indonesia, is a proven strategy in assisting disadvantaged people to access the Internet. In addition to access to ICT, the government might increase the awareness of the existence, and moreover the benefits of e-government services for disadvantaged groups.

Furthermore, the findings highlight the moderating role of place of residence in the influence of the digital divide on e-government system success. In this research, place of residence was proven to have the strongest moderating effect. Therefore, rural residents might be prioritized with regard to access to ICT and e-government services. As mentioned earlier, providing free public access to the Internet especially in rural areas is one of the keys to resolving the problem. In addition, the government could provide services that bring benefits to rural residents (Prattipati, 2003; Ramirez, 2001). In G2C (Government to Citizens) and G2B (Government to Business) e-government systems, the needs of citizens are paramount and need to be the focus in system planning and development. Citizens may lose their enthusiasm if there is no useable service and there are no tangible benefits.

7.3. Summary

This section presents the interpretation of the results of hypotheses tests undertaken. The results were discussed and compared with existing literature and field study analysis. The practical implications of the findings provide suggestions on effective measures that could be undertaken toward improving e-government system success, particularly in Indonesia. Theoretical implications were also underlined. Furthermore, plausible explanations for the statistically insignificant hypotheses were considered. The final section summarizes the research and draw attention to the theoretical and practical contributions of the research. The research limitations are discussed and suggestions made for future research.

8. CONCLUSION AND FUTURE DIRECTIONS

8.1. Introduction

This section presents the conclusions reached in the current research. A summary of the research is given in the next section and provides a brief description of the research objectives, methodology, analyses, results, and interpretation of the findings. This section also highlights the contributions of this research toward the advancement of relevant theories and practices. Furthermore, the implications of the findings on the development of e-government in Indonesia are also presented, followed by the limitations of the study. In the final section, suggestions for the future research are made in order to identify potential areas that could be valuable.

8.2. Summary of Research

Based on the extensive literature review and previous studies, this research explored the digital divide at an individual level. In order to understand the digital divide more comprehensively, the research examined five types of digital divide, namely the demographic divide, economic divide, access divide, capability divide, and innovativeness divide. Furthermore, the current study examined the impact of the digital divide on e-government systems success, directly as well as indirectly, through the mediating effect of trust in e-government.

In conducting the research, the mixed methods approach was utilized. This method combined qualitative and quantitative data in a two-stage data collection process. The qualitative research conducted in the first stage aimed to test the applicability of the initial model. The first stage was also useful for exploring the dimensionality of each construct. The field study was conducted by interviewing 12 users of e-government systems and using semi-structured interviews. To analyze the data, content analysis was performed. Overall, the findings support the initial model. Nevertheless, some adjustments were made to accommodate the findings from the field study. Most of the informants did not agree on the influence of the economic divide on trust in e-government, and the influence of the economic divide on e-government use. Due to the field study findings, the role of the economic divide was changed to that of a moderator variable in the influence of the digital divide on e-government systems success (Fig. 19). Consequently, the hypotheses within the model were developed and presented in Section 5. Overall, 16 hypotheses were proposed.

In the second stage, the quantitative approach was used by conducting a survey involving 251 respondents in the second stage in order to test the hypotheses. However, after the data screening process, only 237 questionnaires were used in the data analysis. Analyses using the PLS technique were carried out, in line with the research questions. Overall, the findings confirmed the impact of the digital divide on e-government systems success. The results also underline the relationships among the variables of the digital divide. Furthermore, with the exception of the access divide, the findings demonstrate the mediating role of trust in e-government in the influence of digital divide on e-government systems success. In terms of the moderating effect of the demographic divide and the economic divide, the results confirmed the role of age, residential place, and education as the moderating variables on the impact of the digital divide on e-government systems success.

8.3. Contributions of the Research

8.3.1. Theoretical Contributions
This research pioneers an advance in the theoretical account of the digital divide. As mentioned before, the previous studies on digital divide focused on the access divide. The study thus goes beyond previous research by more comprehensively describing the influence of three orders of digital divide on e-government use as well as how the access divide influences the capability divide, which in turn impacts upon the innovativeness divide. This finding contributes to the more advanced explanations of the digital divide as a socioeconomic phenomenon. Overall, this research makes four contributions to theory.

First, Dewan and Riggins (2005) and Wei et al. (2011) has expressed the need to extend our understanding of digital divide beyond access divide. In addition, they suggested the urgency to examine the capability divide. On the other hand, van Dijk and Hacker (2003) also admitted that the willingness of targeted users was a more important problem than the problem of access. Therefore, the current research extends the model into five types of digital divide framework. This framework can be applied and tested in wide variety of contexts to establish the boundaries of its applicability.

Second, the results provide explanations on how factors in the digital divide affect one another, as proposed in the research model. The findings highlight the relationships between the access divide and the capability divide as well as relationships between the capability divide and the innovativeness divide. Based on these results, a more comprehensive policy to close the digital divide is needed.

Third, this study introduces a new order of digital divide, namely the innovativeness divide. The results are in agreement with a previous study by van Dijk and Hacker (2003), which suggested that motivational problem existed in using new technology. Such cognitive/behavioral issues such as anxiety and hesitancy are also experienced in Indonesia and Asia in general, where culturally people tend to avoid taking risks (Hofstede, 2009). Thus, the barriers to trying any technological innovations, particularly Internet based technology, need to be lowered. Improving CSE is one of the significant ways to improve motivation or willingness to try technological innovations.

Fourth, this research finds that trust in e-government has a mediating effect, although previous studies were dominated by investigations of its direct influence to technology adoption (e.g., Gefen et al., 2003; Pennington et al., 2003; Sharma, 2008). There has been a disagreement among scholars on the role of trust in e-government system (Kelton et al., 2007), thus this current research confirms its applicability.

As presented in Fig. 1, scholars of ICT4D argue that development of a system, including e-government system, is just the first step toward the next steps, which are adoption, use, and impact. In order to be adopted and used, the development of e-government system should consider the need of the users. Those at the bottom of the pyramid or disadvantaged people should not be ignored. They need to be able to access government services transparently and at low cost. The findings of this research highlight the informatics lifecycle stage of applicability, and this is the fifth contribution.

8.3.2. Practical Contributions

The results of this research have important practical implications, particularly in relation to improving e-government use or e-government readiness. Lack of use and access to e-government systems can have a flow-on effect, causing wider inequalities in society (Jorgansen & Cable, 2002; Warren, 2007). The e-government Readiness Survey shows that the development of e-government systems in Indonesia has not been progressing. Indonesia needs strategic and integrative policies to improve their e-government systems. This research provides a more comprehensive understanding of the issue of the digital divide as the basis for a new integrative policy for the Indonesian government to close the gap.

The demographic characteristics of those who actually used the e-government system in this study were: male, aged 30–40, residing in the city area, well-educated, and mostly from a middle-income economic background. Most of the previous research into the digital divide found similar demographic characteristics for the Internet users. However, in order to expand the numbers of e-government users, the government could improve its customer base by paying more attention to other groups of people. By considering such factors as gender, socioeconomic status, and place of residence, it should be possible to increase the number of e-government users.

The results of multi-group analysis by using PLS show that place of residence has the strongest moderating effect, compared to other demographic and economic measures. Hence, special policies are needed to narrow the digital divide between rural and urban residents. Learning from the experiences of other countries, local governments in Indonesia should provide free public Internet and ICT access in rural areas. In addition, the government should develop the e-government services based on the needs of its citizens, including those disadvantage groups of citizens (those of lower socio-economic status, older age, with less education, female gender, and reside in rural areas). A comprehensive analysis of needs assessment is thus needed before planning and developing e-government systems.

The results of this study indicate that due to the low cost of an Internet connection nowadays, personal economic circumstances were not perceived as significant to e-government use. However, according to Badan Pusat Statistik (BPS) or Statistics Indonesia (2011), in 2011, there were 11.05 million and 18.97 million people living below the poverty line in rural and urban areas, respectively. This amounts to 9.23% and 15.72% of people in rural and urban area in Indonesia who live below the poverty line. These people are still struggling with basic needs and therefore may not consider investment in ICT, as their circumstances would not permit it.

The participants in this study emphasized the importance of the access divide, the capability divide, and the innovativeness divide on e-government use. This finding might be used by the government of the day to go beyond the fact that the digital divide is not only evidence of the inequality between those who have access and those who do not; providing access is one policy that will assist in closing the digital divide. However, in addition to access provision, the government might investigate the options for educating its citizens in the utilization of ICT, along with popularizing the existence and benefits of e-government in order to minimize its citizens' hesitancy.

This research underlines the importance of trust in e-government; trust plays a significant role as a mediator. It is imperative to build all citizens' trust in e-government if it is to succeed, particularly when inequalities and gaps are so wide. From this study, the government may now choose to upgrade its system by providing informative content, and by clearly describing their services and tariffs through their websites. The websites should be constructed in such a way that they are able to mitigate uncertainty and inspire trust.

8.4. Research Limitations

The first limitation of this study is in focus on the economic, social, and cultural environment that is distinctive and unique to Indonesia. This may restrict the generalization of the results to other cultures (Teo et al., 2003). Nevertheless, this restriction may not be as severe as it first appears, as in the context of culture, Asian countries and other countries share many similar cultural traits, as suggested by Hofstede (2009) and Hofstede, Jonker, Meijer, and Verwaart (2006). In terms of socioeconomic environment, other developing countries may also have a similar environment to that of Indonesia. Notwithstanding possible cultural limitations, this research makes an overall contribution to IS research by validating and assessing the applicability of the research in the context of both Asian countries and developing countries.

The second limitation in the research is regarding the actual use of the e-government system. The sample of users was limited to users of G2C (Government to Citizens) e-government systems provided by local governments. Users of other types of e-government systems as well as those of central government may have different views on e-government usage and the digital divide. Therefore, there is still a need to investigate and compare the perceptions of users of other e-government systems.

The third limitation is that evidence in the qualitative approach (field study) was collected using interviews, which were then interpreted by the researchers. The subjectivity of the researchers may possibly have influenced the data analysis (Chan & Ngai, 2007). Nevertheless the findings in the quantitative approach following the field study confirm the field study results.

Finally, since the quantitative data in this research were collected using self-reporting surveys, the data are potentially vulnerable to the common method bias (Podsakoff et al., 2003). For example, respondents may have attempted to guess the researchers' intentions, and responded accordingly, or each respondent may have perceived the strength of each Likert scale measurement in a different manner.

8.5. Future Research Directions

The above-mentioned limitations in this study imply the need for further research. The lack of ability to generalize, due to the socioeconomic and cultural environment in Indonesia, points to the need for cross-country studies. Cross-country research could widen the applicability of the conceptual model when used under different circumstances.

This study collected data from the users of e-government systems provided by local governments. Although the justification for the choice of these particular users is valid, future research might interview and survey other significant respondents. In addition, the use of multiple respondents would widen applicability.

Finally, in addition to researching the impact of the digital divide on e-government system success, the core of this model is applicable in other contexts, especially those that are influenced by the digital divide. Beyond the scope of e-government systems, the conceptual model could be applied to other systems such as e-commerce. Notwithstanding this, the model may require some extension and further construct operationalization for different types of services and contexts.

8.6. Summary

E-government has been acknowledged to be an essential system for delivering government services nowadays. It offers many benefits to the government internally, along with benefits for citizens and business.

However, e-government initiatives face some challenges in their implementation. The digital divide is known as one of these challenges, as empirical evidence is still lacking. Moreover, the understanding of the issue of digital divide requires further work. This study aims to fill the research gap.

A qualitative field study combined with a national survey and quantitative data analysis determined the influence of the digital divide on e-government system success. The access divide, capability divide, and innovativeness divide were proven to be substantial for e-government system success. Furthermore, this research confirmed the relationships among variables in the digital divide. The research also offered a theoretical contribution through the finding of the mediating effect of trust in e-government in the influence of the digital divide on e-government system success. The moderating effects of residential place, age, and education were proven.

Based on the findings, this research contributes significantly to theoretical developments in the literature on the digital divide and e-government, and to the ISs field by providing a more comprehensive framework for understanding the issue of the digital divide. Practically, this research should be valuable to governments as it provides evidence of the impact of the digital divide on e-government use.

NOTES

1. Part of this section has been presented at the following conferences: Rahman and Quaddus (2012), Rahman, Quaddus, and Galbreath (2012), and Rahman (2012).

2. Most informants used the e-government systems to register home renovation/ building. Before they build or renovate their home, they must get permission from the local government. Those five informants were applying the permission but the processes were not done yet.

3. Part of this section has been presented at the: Rahman (2013).

REFERENCES

Abdulai, A., & Huffman, W. E. (2005). The diffusion of new agricultural technologies: The case of crossbred-cow technology in Tanzania. *American Journal of Agricultural Economics*, 87(3), 645–660.

AbuShanab, E., & Pearson, J. M. (2007). Internet banking in Jordan: The Unified Theory of Acceptance and Use Technology (UTAUT) perspective. *Journal of System and Information Technology*, 9(1), 78–97.

Agarwal, R., Animesh, A., & Prasad, K. (2009). Social interactions and the digital divide: Explaining variations in internet use. *Information Systems Research, 20*(2), 277–294.

Agarwal, R., & Prasad, J. (1997). The role of innovation characteristics and perceived voluntariness in the acceptance of information technologies. *Decision Sciences, 28*(3), 557–582.

Agarwal, R., & Prasad, J. (1998). A conceptual and operational definition of personal innovativeness in the domain of information technology. *Information Systems Research, 9*(2), 204–215.

Agyapong, P., & Ferreira, P. (2009). *37th telecommunications policy research conference, spillover effects from wiring schools with broadband: Implications for universal service policy.* Arlington, VA. Retrieved from http://papers.ssrn.com/sol3/papers.cfm?abstract_id= 2004029. Accessed on June 21, 2013.

Ahmad, N., Amer, N. T., Qutaifan, F., & Alhilali, A. (2013). Technology adoption model and a road map to successful implementation of ITIL. *Journal of Enterprise Information Management, 26*(5), 553–576.

Ajzen, I. (1991). The theory of planned behavior. *Organizational Behavior and Human Decision Processes, 50*(2), 179–211.

Ajzen, I., & Fishbein, M. (1980). *Understanding attitudes and predicting social behavior.* Upper Saddle River, NJ: Prentice-Hall, Inc.

Akca, H., Sayili, M., & Esengun, K. (2007). Challenge of rural people to reduce digital divide in the globalized world: Theory and practice. *Government Information Quarterly, 24*(2), 404–413.

Al-Kibsi, G., Boer, K. d., Mourshed, M., & Rea, N. P. (2001). Putting citizens online, not in line. *The McKinsey Quarterly Special Edition,* (2), 65–73.

Amri, P. (2000). *Dampak Ekonomi dan Politik UU No. 22 dan 25 Tahun 1999 Tentang Otonomi Daerah.* Jakarta: CSIS.

Annan, K. (2004). *Secretary general, marking world telecommunication day, says affordable technologies can be effective engines of social, material change.* Retrieved from http://www.un.org/News/Press/docs/2004/sgsm9294.doc.htm

Atewell, P. (2001). The first and second digital divides. *Sociology and Education, 74*(3), 252–259.

Au, N., Ngai, E. W. T., & Cheng, T. C. E. (2008). Extending the understanding of end user information systems satisfaction formation: An equitable needs fulfillment model approach. *MIS Quarterly, 32*(1), 43–66.

Bagozzi, R. P. (1992). The self-regulation of attitudes, intentions, and behavior. *Social Psychology Quarterly, 55*(2), 178–204.

Bagozzi, R. P., Baumgartner, H., & Yi, Y. (1992). State versus action orientation and the theory of reasoned action: An application to coupon usage. *Journal of Consumer Research, 18*(4), 505–518.

Bagozzi, R. P., & Kimmel, S. K. (1995). A comparison of leading theories for the prediction of goal-directed behaviours. *British Journal of Social Psychology, 34*(4), 437–461.

Bagozzi, R. P., & Yi, Y. (1988). On the evaluation of structural equation models. *Journal of the Academy of Marketing Science, 16*(1), 74–94.

Ballou, D. P., & Tayi, G. K. (1999). Enhancing data quality in data warehouse environments. *Communications of the ACM, 42*(1), 73–79.

Bandura, A. (1977). Self-efficacy: Toward a unifying theory of behavioral change. *Psychological Review, 84*(2), 191–215.

Bandura, A. (2001). Social cognitive theory: An agentic perspective. *Annual Review of Psychology, 52*(1), 1−26.

Barclay, D., Higgins, C., & Thompson, R. (1995). Partial least squares approach to causal modelling: Personal computer adoption and use as an illustration. *Technology Studies, 2*(2), 285−324.

Barki, H., Rivard, S., & Talbot, J. (1993). Toward an assessment of software development risk. *Journal of Management Information Systems, 10*(2), 203−225.

Baron, R. M., & Kenny, D. A. (1986). The moderator-mediator variable distinction in social psychological research: Conceptual, strategic, and statistical considerations. *Journal of Personality and Social Psychology, 51*(6), 1173−1182.

Barua, A., Kriebel, C. H., & Mukhopadhayay, T. (1995). Information technologies and business value: An analytic and empirical investigation. *Information Systems Research, 6*(1), 3−23.

Beedell, J., & Rehman, T. (2000). Using social-psychology models to understand farmers' conservation behaviour. *Journal of Rural Studies, 16*(1), 117−127.

Belanger, F., & Carter, L. (2009). The impact of the digital divide on e-government use. *Communications of the ACM, 52*(4), 132−135.

Bem, D. J., & Allen, A. (1974). On predicting some of the people some of the time: The search for cross-situational consistencies in behavior. *Psychological Review, 81*(6), 506−520.

Bem, S. L. (1981). The BSRI and gender schema theory: A reply to Spence and Helmreich. *Psychological Review, 88*(4), 369−371.

Benjamin, P. (1999). Community development and democratisation through information technology: Building the new South Africa. In R. Heeks (Ed.), *Reinventing government in the information age: International practice in IT-enabled public sector reform*. New York, NY: Routledge.

Berg, B. L. (2004). *Qualitative research method for the social science* (5th ed.). Boston, MA: Pearson Education Inc.

Bertot, J. C. (2003). The multiple dimensions of the digital divide: More than the technology 'haves' and 'have nots'. *Government Information Quarterly, 20*(2), 185−191.

Billon, M., Marco, R., & Lera-Lopez, F. (2009). Disparities in ICT adoption: A multidimensional approach to study the cross-country digital divide. *Telecommunications Policy, 33*(10−11), 596−610.

Blackler, F., & Brown, C. (1985). Evaluation and the impact of information technologies on people in organizations. *Human Relations, 38*(3), 213−231.

Bontis, N., Booker, L. D., & Serenko, A. (2007). The mediating effect of organizational reputation on customer loyalty and service recommendation in the banking industry. *Management Decision, 45*(9), 1426−1445.

Borstein, M. H., & Bradley, R. H. (2003). *Socioeconomic status, parenting, and child development*. Mahwah, NJ: Lawrence Erlbaum Associates.

Bozeman, B. (2000). *Bureaucracy and red tape*. Upper Saddle River, NJ: Prentice Hall.

Brown, D. H., & Thompson, S. (2011). Priorities, policies and practice of e-government in a developing country context: ICT infrastructure and diffusion in Jamaica. *European Journal of Information Systems, 20*(3), 329−342.

Brown, D. M. (1999). Information systems for improved performance management: Development approaches in US public agencies. In R. Heeks (Ed.), *Reinventing government in the information age: International practice in IT-enabled public sector reform*. New York, NY: Routledge.

Brown, M. M. (2001). The benefits and costs of information technology innovations: An empirical assessment of a local government agency. *Public Performance and Management Review*, 24(4), 351–366.

Brown, M. M. (2003). Technology diffusion and the "knowledge barrier": The dilemma of stakeholder participation. *Public Performance and Management Review*, 26(4), 345–359.

Brown, M. M., & Brudney, J. L. (2003). Learning organizations in the public sector? A study of police agencies employing information and technology to advance knowledge. *Public Administration Review*, 63(1), 30–43.

Bucy, E. P. (2000). Social access to the internet. *The Harvard International Journal of Press/Politics*, 5(1), 50–61.

Bulguru, B., Cavusoglu, H., & Benbasat, I. (2010). Information security policy compliance: An empirical study of rationality-based beliefs and information security awareness. *MIS Quarterly*, 34(3), 523–548.

Burbridge, L. (2002). Accountability and MIS. *Public Performance and Management Review*, 25(4), 421–423.

Burkhardt, M. E., & Brass, D. J. (1990). Changing patterns or patterns of change: The effect of a change in technology on social network structure and power. *Administrative Science Quarterly*, 35(1), 104–127.

Burn, J., & Robins, G. (2003). Moving towards e-government: A case study of organizational change processes. *Logistics Information Management*, 16(1), 25–35.

Burton, R. J. F. (2004). Reconceptualising the 'behavioural approach' in agricultural studies: A socio-psychological perspective. *Journal of Rural Studies*, 20(3), 359–371.

Campbell, A. (1962). The passive citizen. *Acta Sociologica*, 6(1/2), 9–21.

Carter, L., & Belanger, F. (2005). The utilization of e-government services: Citizen trust, innovation and acceptance factors. *Information Systems Journal*, 15(1), 5–25.

Carter, L., Shaupp, L. C., Hobbs, J., & Campbell, R. (2011). The role of security and trust in the adoption of online tax filing. *Transforming Government People, Process and Policy*, 5(4), 303–318.

Cavana, R., Sekaran, U., & Delahaye, B. L. (2001). *Applied business research: Qualitative and quantitative methods*. Milton, Queensland: Wiley.

Chan, S. C., & Ngai, E. W. (2007). A qualitative study of information technology adoption: How ten organizations adopted web-based training. *Information Systems Journal*, 17(3), 289–315.

Charng, H.-W., Piliavin, J. A., & Callero, P. L. (1988). Role identity and reasoned action in the prediction of repeated behavior. *Social Psychology Quarterly*, 51(4), 303–317.

Chau, P. Y. K. (1996). An empirical assessment of a modified technology acceptance model. *Journal of Management Information Systems*, 13(2), 185–204.

Chen, W. S., & Hirschheim, R. (2004). A paradigmatic and methodological examination of information systems research from 1991 to 2001. *Information Systems Journal*, 14(3), 197–235.

Cheng, Y.-M. (2011). Antecedents and consequences of e-learning acceptance. *Information Systems Journal*, 21(3), 269–299.

Chengalur-Smith, I., & Duchessi, P. (1999). The initiation and adoption of client-server technology in organizations. *Information & Management*, 35(2), 77–88.

Chiffoleau, Y. (2005). Learning about innovation through networks: The development of environment-friendly viticulture. *Technovation*, 25(10), 1193–1204.

Chin, W. W. (1998). The partial least squares approach to structural equation modeling. In G. A. Marcoulides (Ed.), *Modern methods for business research* (pp. 295–336). Mahwah, NJ: Lawrence Erlbaum Associates.

Chin, W. W., & Gopal, A. (1995). Adoption intention in GSS: Relative importance beliefs. *Data Base Advances, 26*(2–3), 42–64.

Cho, Y. H., & Choi, B.-D. (2004). E-government to combat corruption: The case of Seoul metropolitan government. *International Journal of Public Administration, 27*(10), 719–735.

Coch, L., & French, J. R. P., Jr. (1948). Overcoming resistance to change. *Human Relations, 1*(4), 512–532.

Cody, M. J., Dunn, D., Hoppin, S., & Wendt, P. (1999). Silver surfers: Training and evaluating Internet use among older adult learners. *Communication Education, 48*(4), 269–286.

Cohen, J. (1988). *Statistical power analysis for the behavioral sciences* (2nd ed.). Hillsdale, NJ: Lawrence Erlbaum Associates.

Cohen, N., & Arieli, T. (2011). Field research in conflict environments: Methodological challenges and snowball sampling. *Journal of Peace Research, 48*(4), 423–435.

Cole, R. L. (1973). Toward as model of political trust: A causal analysis. *American Journal of Political Science, 17*(4), 809–817.

Colesca, S. E., & Dobrica, L. (2008). Adoption and use of e-government services: The case of Romania. *Journal of Applied Research and Technology, 6*(3), 204–217.

Compeau, D., Higgins, C. A., & Huff, S. (1999). Social cognitive theory and individual reactions to computing technology: A longitudinal study. *MIS Quarterly, 23*(2), 145–158.

Converse, J. M., & Presser, S. (1986a). Survey questions: Handcrafting the standardized questionnaire. In J. L. Sullivan & R. G. Niemi (Eds.), *Quantitative applications in the social science.* Beverly Hills, CA: SAGE.

Converse, J. M., & Presser, S. (1986b). *Survey questions: Handcrafting the standardized questionnaire.* Thousand Oaks, CA: SAGE.

Corrocher, N., & Ordanini, A. (2002). Measuring the digital divide: A framework for the analysis of cross-country differences. *Journal of Information Technology, 17*(1), 9–19.

Creswell, J. W. (2003). *Research design: Qualitative, quantitative, and mixed methods approaches.* Thousand Oaks, CA: SAGE.

Creswell, J. W., & Clark, V. L. P. (2011). *Designing and conducting mixed methods research* (2nd ed.). Thousand Oaks, CA: SAGE.

Cronbach, L. J. (1950). Further evidence on response sets and test design. *Educational and Psychological Measurement, 10*(3), 3–31.

Cropanzano, R., & Mitchell, M. S. (2005). Social exchange theory: An interdisciplinary review. *Journal of Management, 31*(6), 874–900.

Crotty, M. (1998). *The foundations of social research: Meaning and perspective in the research process.* Crows Nest: Allen & Unwin.

Cyr, D. (2008). Modelling web site design across cultures; Relationships to trust, satisfaction, and e-loyalty. *Journal of Management Information Systems, 24*(4), 47–72.

Czaja, S. J., & Sharit, J. (1993). Age differences in the performance of computer-based work. *Psychology and Aging, 8*(1), 59–67.

Datta, P. (2010). A preliminary study of ecommerce adoption in developing countries. *Information Systems Journal, 21*(1), 3–32.

Davis, F. D. (1989). Perceived usefulness, perceived ease of use, and user acceptance of information technology. *MIS Quarterly, 13*(3), 319–340.

Davis, F. D., Bagozzi, R. P., & Warshaw, P. R. (1989). User acceptance of computer technology: A comparison of two theoretical models. *Management Science, 35*(8), 982−1003.

Davis, F. D., Bagozzi, R. P., & Warshaw, P. R. (1992). Extrinsic and intrinsic motivation to use computers in the workplace. *Journal of Applied Social Psychology, 22*(14), 1111−1132.

Davison, R. M., Wagner, C., & Ma, L. C. (2005). From government to e-government: A transition model. *Information, Technology and People, 18*(3), 280−299.

Dawes, S. S. (1996). Interagency information sharing: Expected benefits, manageable risks. *Journal of Policy Analysis and Management, 15*(3), 377−394.

de Guinea, A. O., & Markus, M. L. (2009). Why break the habit of a lifetime? Rethinking the roles of intention, habit, and emotion in continuing information technology use. *MIS Quarterly, 33*(3), 433−444.

De Haan, J. (2004). A multifaced dynamic model of the digital divide. *IT Society, 1*(7), 66−88.

DeLone, W. H., & McLean, E. R. (1992). Information systems success: The quest for the dependent variable. *Information Systems Research, 3*(1), 60−95.

DeLone, W. H., & McLean, E. R. (2003). The DeLone and McLean model of information systems success: A ten-year update. *Journal of Management Information Systems, 19*(4), 9−30.

Dewan, S., Ganley, D., & Kraemer, K. L. (2005). Across the digital divide: A cross-country multi-technology analysis of the determinants of IT penetration. *Journal of the Association for Information Systems, 6*(12), 409−432.

Dewan, S., Ganley, D., & Kraemer, K. L. (2009). Complementarities in the diffusion of personal computers and the internet: Implications for the global digital divide. *Information Systems Research* (Article in Advance), 1−17.

Dewan, S., & Riggins, F. J. (2005). The digital divide: Current and future research directions. *Journal of the Association for Information Systems, 6*(12), 298−337.

DiMaggio, P., & Hargittai, E. (2001). *From the 'digital divide' to 'digital inequality': Studying internet use as penetration increases.* Princeton, NJ: Princeton University Center for Arts and Cultural Policy Studies.

DiMaggio, P., Hargittai, E., Celeste, C., & Shafer, S. (2001). *From unequal access to differentiated use: A literature review and agenda for research on digital inequality.* New York, NY: Russel Sage Foundation.

DiMaggio, P., Hargittai, E., Neuman, W., & Robinson, J. (2001). Social implication of the internet. *Annual Review of Sociology, 27*(1), 307−336.

Doty, D. H., & Glick, W. H. (1998). Common methods bias: Does common methods variance really bias results? *Organizational Research Methods, 1*(4), 374−406.

East, R. (1993). Investment decisions and the theory of planned behaviour. *Journal of Economic Psychology, 14*(2), 337−375.

Edmiston, K. D. (2003). State and local e-government: Prospects and challenges. *The American Review of Public Administration, 33*(1), 20−45.

Ellen, P. S., Bearden, W. O., & Sharma, S. (1991). Resistance to technological innovations: An examination of the role of self-efficacy and performance satisfaction. *Journal of the Academy of Marketing Science, 19*(4), 297−307.

Escobar-Rodriguez, T., Monge-Lozano, P., & Romero-Alonso, M. M. (2012). Acceptance of e-prescriptions and automated medication-management systems in hospitals: An extension of the technology acceptance model. *Journal of Information Systems, 26*(1), 77−96.

Evans, D., & Yen, D. C. (2005). E-government: An analysis for implementation: Framework for understanding cultural and social impact. *Government Information Quarterly, 22*(3), 354—373.

Evans-Cowley, J., & Conroy, M. M. (2004, May). What is e-governance? Planning Advisory Service Report 525, pp. 1—25.

Ferro, E., Helbig, N. C., & Gil-Garcia, J. R. (2011). The role of IT literacy in defining digital divide policy needs. *Government Information Quarterly, 28*(1), 3—10.

Fetler, M. (1985). Sex differences on the California statewide assessment of computer literacy. *Sex Roles, 13*(3—4), 181—191.

Fisher, D. K., Norvell, J., Sonka, S., & Nelson, M. J. (2000). Understanding technology adoption through system dynamics modelling: Implications for agribusiness management. *International Food and Agribusiness Management Review, 3*(3), 281—296.

Flick, U. (2007). *Designing qualitative research*. Los Angeles, CA: SAGE.

Floropoulos, J., Spathis, C., Halvatzis, D., & Tsipouridou, M. (2010). Measuring the success of the Greek taxation information system. *International Journal of Information Management, 30*(1), 47—56.

Flynn, L. R., & Goldsmith, R. E. (1993). A validation of the Goldsmith and Hofacker innovativeness scale. *Educational and Psychological Measurement, 53*(4), 1105—1116.

Fornell, C., & Larcker, D. F. (1981). Evaluating structural equation models with unobservable variables and measurement error. *Journal of Marketing Research, 18*(1), 39—50.

Forte-Gardner, O., Young, F. L., Dillman, D. A., & Carroll, M. S. (2004). Increasing the effectiveness of technology transfer for conservation cropping systems through research and field design. *Renewable Agriculture and Food Systems, 19*(4), 93—114.

Foundation, B. M. G. (2012). *Libraries*. Retrieved from http://www.gatesfoundation.org/libraries/Pages/default.aspx. Accessed on October 8.

Fountain, J. (2001). *Building the virtual state: Information technology and institutional change*. Washington, DC: Brookings Institution Press.

Frantzich, S. E. (1979). Technological innovation among congressmen. *Social Forces, 57*(3), 968—974.

Frazer, L., & Lawley, M. (2000). *Questionnaire design & administration*. Brisbane, Australia: John Wiley & Sons Australia, Ltd.

Furuholt, B., & Wahid, F. (2008). *41st Hawaii international conference on system sciences e-government challenges and the role of political leadership in Indonesia: The Case of Sragen*. Hawaii: IEEE.

Gagnon, Y. C. (2001). The behavior of public managers in adopting new technologies. *Public Performance and Management Review, 24*(4), 337—350.

Gatignon, H., & Robertson, T. S. (1989). Technology diffusion: An empirical test of competitive effects. *Journal of Marketing, 53*(1), 35—49.

Gauld, R., Goldfinch, S., & Horsburgh, S. (2010). Do they want it? Do they use it? The 'demand-side' of e-government in Australia and New Zealand. *Government Information Quarterly, 27*(3), 177—186.

Gefen, D. (2000). E-commerce: The role of familiarity and trust. *Omega, 28*(6), 725—737.

Gefen, D., Benbasat, I., & Pavlou, P. A. (2008). A research agenda for trust in online environments. *Journal of Management Information Systems, 24*(4), 275—286.

Gefen, D., Karahanna, E., & Straub, D. W. (2003). Trust and TAM in online shopping: An integrated model. *MIS Quarterly, 27*(1), 51—90.

Gefen, D., Straub, D. W., & Boudreau, M.-C. (2000). Structural equation modeling and regression: Guidelines for research practice. *Communications of the Association for Information Systems, 4*(7), 1−77.

Gelderman, M. (1998). The relationship between user satisfaction, usage of information system and performance. *Information and Management, 34*(1), 11−18.

Gil-Garcia, J. R., & Pardo, T. A. (2005). E-government success factors: Mapping practical tools to theoretical foundations. *Government Information Quarterly, 22*(2), 187−216.

Goldfarb, A. (2006). The (teaching) role of universities in the diffusion of the internet. *International Journal of Industrial Organization, 24*(2), 203−225.

Goldfinch, S. (2007). Pessimism, computer failure, and information systems development in the public sector. *Public Administration Review, 67*(5), 917−929.

Goldsmith, R. E., & Hofacker, C. F. (1991). Measuring consumer innovativeness. *Journal of the Academy of Marketing Science, 19*(3), 209−221.

Greene, J. C., Caracelli, V. J., & Graham, W. F. (1989). Toward a conceptual framework for mixed-method evaluation designs. *Educational Evaluation and Policy Analysis, 11*(3), 255−274.

Gripenberg, P. (2011). Computer self-efficacy in the information society: Design of learning strategies, mechanisms and skill areas. *Information Technology & People, 24*(3), 301−331.

Guba, E. G., & Lincoln, Y. S. (1994). Competing paradigms in qualitative research. In N. K. Denzin & Y. S. Lincoln (Eds.), *Handbook of qualitative research* (pp. 105−117). Thousand Oaks, CA: SAGE.

Gupta, M. P., & Jana, D. (2003). E-government evaluation: A framework and case study. *Government Information Quarterly, 20*(4), 365−387.

Gurstein, M. (2003). Perspectives on urban and rural community informatics: Theory and performance, community informatics and strategies for flexible networking. In S. Marshall, W. Taylor, & X. Yu (Eds.), *Closing the digital divide: Transforming regional economies and communities with information technology* (pp. 1−12). Westport, CT: Praeger Publishers.

Gurstein, M. (2007). *What is community informatics (and why does it matter)?* (Vol. 2). Milan: Polimetrica.

Hair, J. F., Ringle, C. M., & Sarstedt, M. (2011). PLS-SEM: Indeed a silver bullet. *Journal of Marketing Theory and Practice, 19*(2), 139−151.

Hair, J. F., Sarstedt, M., Ringle, C. M., & Mena, J. A. (2012). An assessment of the use of partial least squares structural equation modeling in marketing research. *Journal of the Academy of Marketing Science, 40*(4), 414−433.

Haldenwang, C. V. (2004). Electronic government (e-government) and development. *The European Journal of Development Research, 16*(2), 417−432.

Hampton, K. N. (2003). Grieving for a lost network: Collective action in a wired suburb. *The Information Society, 19*(5), 417−428.

Hampton, K. N. (2010). Internet use and the concentration of disadvantage: Glocalization and the urban underclass. *American Behavioral Scientist, 53*(8), 1111−1132.

Hargittai, E. (2006). Hurdles to information seeking: Spelling and typographical mistakes during users' online behavior. *Journal of the Association for Information Systems, 7*(1), 52−67.

Harijadi, D. A. (2004). Developing e-government: The case of Indonesia. In *29th meeting APEC telecommunication and information working group*. Hong Kong, China. UNPAN.

Harijadi, D. A., & Satriya, E. (2000). Indonesia's roadmap to e-government: Opportunities and challenges. In *APEC high-level symposium on e-government*. Seoul, Korea. UN APCICT-ESCAP.

Haryono, T., & Widiwardono, Y. K. (2010). *Current status and issues of e-government in Indonesia*. Retrieved from http://www.aseansec.org/13757.htm. Accessed on September 7, 2010.

Hategekimana, B., & Trant, M. (2002). Adoption and diffusion of new technology in agriculture: Genetically modified corn and soybeans. *Canadian Journal of Agricultural Economics, 50*(4), 357–371.

Hausman, A. (2005). Innovativeness among small businesses: Theory and propositions for future research. *Industrial Marketing Management, 34*(8), 773–782.

Heeks, R. (1999). Reinventing government in the information age. In R. Heeks (Ed.), *Reinventing government in the information age. International practice in IT-enabled public sector reform* (pp. 9–21). London: Routledge.

Heeks, R. (2007). Theorizing ICT4D research. *Information Technologies and International Development, 3*(3), 1–4.

Heeks, R. (2008a). *ICT4D 2.0: The next phase of applying ICT for international development. IEEE Computer Society*.

Heeks, R. (2008b). *Success and failure in e-government projects*. Retrieved from http://www.egov4dev.org/success/sfrates.shtml#survey. Accessed on June 5, 2010.

Heeks, R. (2009). The ICT4D 2.0 Manifesto: Where Next for ICTs and International Development. *Development informatics*. Working Paper Series. Manchester, UK. Development Informatics Group, Institute for Development Policy and Management.

Heintze, T., & Bretschneider, S. (2000). Information technology and restructuring in public organizations: Does adoption of information technology affect organizational structures, communications, and decision making? *Journal of Public Administration Research and Theory, 10*(4), 801–830.

Hindman, D. B. (2000). The rural-urban digital divide. *Journalism and Mass Communication Quarterly, 77*(3), 549–560.

Ho, A. T.-K. (2002). Reinventing local governments and the e-government initiative. *Public Administration Review, 62*(4), 424–444.

Hofstede, G. (1983). Cultural dimensions in management and planning. *Asia Pacific Journal of Management, 1*(2), 81–99.

Hofstede, G. (2009). *Cultural dimensions*. Retrieved from http://www.geert-hofstede.com/. Accessed on August 10, 2010.

Hofstede, G. J., Jonker, C. M., Meijer, S., & Verwaart, T. (2006). Modelling trade and trust across cultures. In K. Stolen (Ed.), *Trust management* (pp. 120–134). Berlin: Springer.

Hohenthal, J. (2006). Integrating qualitative and quantitative methods in research on international entrepreneurship. *Journal of International Entrepreneur, 4*(2), 175–190.

Holden, S. H., Norris, D. F., & Fletcher, P. D. (2003). Electronic government at the local level: Progress to date and future issues. *Public Performance and Management Review, 26*(4), 325–344.

Hosmer, L. T. (1995). Trust: The connecting link between organizational theory and philosophical ethics. *The Academy of Management Review, 20*(2), 379–403.

Hsieh, J. P.-A., Rai, A., & Keil, M. (2008). Understanding digital inequality: Comparing continued use behavioral models of socio-economically advantage and disadvantage. *MIS Quarterly, 32*(1), 97–126.

Hsieh, J. P.-A., Rai, A., & Keil, M. (2011). Addressing digital inequality for the socioeconomically disadvantaged through government initiatives: Forms of capital that affect ICT utilization. *Information Systems Research, 22*(2), 233–253.

Hu, P. J., Chau, P. Y. K., Sheng, O. R. l., & Tam, K. Y. (1999). Examining the technology acceptance model using physician acceptance of telemedicine technology. *Journal of Management Information Systems, 16*(2), 91–112.

Hulland, J. (1999). Use of Partial Least Squares (PLS) in strategic management research: A review of four studies. *Strategic Management Journal, 20*(2), 195–204.

Hurt, H. T., Joseph, K., & Cook, C. D. (1977). Scales of the measurement of innovativeness. *Human Communication Research, 4*(1), 58–65.

Hwang, J., & Syamsuddin, I. (2008). Failure of e-government implementation: A case study of South Sulawesi. *3rd international conference on Convergence and Hybrid Information Technology.* IEEE Computer Society.

Igbaria, M., & Chakrabarti, A. (1990). Computer anxiety and attitudes towards microcomputer use. *Behaviour & Information Technology, 9*(3), 229–241.

Igbaria, M., Guimaraes, T., & Davis, G. B. (1995). Testing the determinants of microcomputer usage via a structural equation model. *Journal of Management Information Systems, 11*(4), 87–114.

Indonesia, S. (2011, November). *Trends of the selected socio-economic indicators of Indonesia.* Jakarta: Badan Pusat Statistik Indonesia.

Irani, Z., Elliman, T., & Jackson, P. (2007). Electronic transformation of government in the UK: A research agenda. *European Journal of Information Systems, 16*(4), 327–335.

Jaggi, A. (2003). Transforming regional economies and communities with ICT developing countries: An Indian perspective. In S. Marshall, W. Taylor, & X. Yu (Eds.), *Closing the digital divide: Transforming regional economies and communities with information technology* (pp. 181–194). Westport, CT: Praeger Publishers.

James, D. W., & Ziebell, P. (2003). Community capacity building through ICT networking. In S. Marshall, W. Taylor, & X. Yu (Eds.), *Closing the digital divide: Transforming regional economies and communities with information technology* (pp. 45–62). Westport, CT: Praeger Publishers.

James, J. (2004). Reconstructing the digital divide from the perspective of a large, poor, developing country. *Journal of Information Technology, 19*(3), 172–177.

James, J. (2007). From origins to implications: Key aspects in the debate over the digital divide. *Journal of Information Technology, 22*(3), 284–295.

Jensen, R. A. (2001). Strategic intrafirm innovation adoption and diffusion. *Southern Economic Journal, 68*(1), 120–132.

Johanson, G. (2011a). Delineating the meaning and value of development informatics. In J. Steyn & G. Johanson (Eds.), *ICTs and sustainable solutions for the digital divide: Theory and perspectives.* Hershey, PA: IGI Global.

Johanson, G. (2011b). Delineating the meaning and value of development informatics. In J. Steyn & G. Johanson (Eds.), *ICTs and sustainable solutions for the digital divide* (pp. 1–18). Hershey, PA: IGI Global.

Johnson, R. B., & Onwuegbuzie, A. J. (2004). Mixed methods research: A research paradigm whose time has come. *Educational Researcher, 33*(7), 14–26.

Johnson, R. B., Onwuegbuzie, A. J., & Turner, L. A. (2007). Toward a definition of mixed methods research. *Journal of Mixed Methods Research, 1*(2), 112–133.

Jorgansen, D. J., & Cable, S. (2002). Facing the challenges of e-government: A case study of the city of Corpus Christi, Texas. *Advanced Management Journal, 67*(3), 1−7.

Jung, J.-Y., Qiu, J. L., & Kim, Y.-C. (2001). Internet connectedness and inequality: Beyond the "divide". *Communication Research, 28*(4), 507−525.

Kauffman, R. J., & Techatassanasoontorn, A. A. (2005). Is there a global digital divide for digital wireless phone technologies? *Journal of the Association for Information Systems, 6*(12), 338−382.

Ke, W., & Wei, K. K. (2004). Successful e-government in Singapore. *Communications of the ACM, 47*(6), 95−99.

Kelton, K., Fleischmann, K. R., & Wallace, W. A. (2007). Trust in digital information. *Journal of the American Society for Information Science and Technology, 59*(3), 363−374.

Keong, M. L., Ramayah, T., Kurnia, S., & Chiun, L. M. (2012). Explaining intention to use an enterprise resource planning (ERP) system: An extension of the UTAUT model. *Business Strategy Series, 13*(4), 173−180.

Kim, E., & Lee, J. (1986). An exploratory contingency model of user participation and MIS use. *Information & Management, 11*(2), 87−97.

Kim, S., & Kim, D. (2003). South Korean public officials' perceptions of values, failure, and consequences of failure in e-government leadership. *Public Performance and Management Review, 26*(4), 360−375.

King, J. L. (1982). Local government use of information technology: The next decade. *Public Administration Review, 42*(1), 25−36.

Kirton, M. (1976). Adaptors and innovators: A description and measure. *Journal of Applied Psychology, 61*(5), 622−629.

Kohli, R., Devaraj, S., & Mahmood, M. A. (2004). Understanding determinants of online consumer satisfaction: A decision process perspective. *Journal of Management Information Systems, 21*(1), 115−135.

Krauss, S. E. (2005). Research paradigms and meaning making: A primer. *The Qualitative Report, 10*(4), 758−770.

Kuhn, T. S. (1970). *The structure of scientific revolutions* (2nd ed.). Chicago, IL: The University of Chicago Press.

Kuk, G. (2003). The digital divide and the quality of electronic service delivery in local government in the United Kingdom. *Government Information Quarterly, 20*(4), 353−363.

Kumar, N. (1996). The power of trust in manufacturer-retailer relationships. *Harvard Business Review, 74*(2), 92−106.

Kvasny, L., & Keil, M. (2006). The challenges of redressing the digital divide: A tale of two US cities. *Information Systems Journal, 16*(1), 23−53.

La Porte, T. M., Demchak, C. C., & de Jong, M. (2002). Democracy and bureaucracy in the age of the web. *Administration & Society, 34*(4), 411−446.

Lacey, M. (2000). Clinton enlists top-grade help for plan to increase computer use. *The New York Times*. New York.

Landsbergen, D. Jr., & Wolken, G. Jr. (2001). Realizing the promise: Government information systems and the fourth generation of information technology. *Public Administration Review, 61*(2), 206−220.

Layne, K., & Lee, J. (2001). Developing fully functional e-government: A four stage model. *Government Information Quarterly, 18*(2), 122−136.

Lee, J. K., & Rao, H. R. (2012). Service source and channel choice in G2C service environ-ments; A model comparison the anti/counter-terrorism domain. *Information Systems Journal, 22*(4), 313–341.

Lee, K. C., & Chung, N. (2009). Understanding factors affecting trust in and satisfaction with mobile banking in Korea: A modified DeLone and McLean's model perspective. *Interacting with Computers, 21*(5–6), 385–392.

Lehr, W H., C A. Osorio, S E. Gillett, & M A. Sirbu. (2005). Measuring broadband's eco-nomic impact. In *33rd research conference on communication, information*, and Internet Policy (TPRC) September 23–25, Arlington, VA.

Leonard-Barton, D., & Deschamps, I. (1988). Managerial influence in the implementation of new technology. *Management Science, 34*(10), 1252–1265.

Lewis, D. J., & Weigert, A. (1985). Trust as a social reality. *Social Forces, 63*(4), 967–985.

Loges, W. E., & Jung, J.-Y. (2001). Exploring the digital divide: Internet connectedness and age. *Communication Research, 28*(4), 536–562.

Loo, W. H., Yeow, P. H. P., & Chong, S. C. (2009). User acceptance of Malaysian government multipurpose smartcard applications. *Government Information Quarterly, 26*(2), 358–367.

LSI. (2010). *Akuntabilitas Politik: Evaluasi Publik Atas Pemerintahan SBY-Boediono*. Jakarta: Lembaga Survei Indonesia.

Lucas, H. C. (1978). Empirical evidence for a descriptive model of implementation. *MIS Quarterly, 2*(2), 27–42.

Luk, S. C. Y. (2009). The Impact of leadership and stakeholders on the success/failure of e-government service: Using the case study of e-stamping service in Hong Kong. *Government Information Quarterly, 26*(4), 594–604.

Mahler, J., & Regan, P. M. (2002). Learning to govern online: Federal agency internet use. *The American Review of Public Administration, 32*(3), 326–349.

Manfredo, M. J., & Shelby, B. (1988). The effect of using self-report measures in tests of attitude-behavior relationships. *The Journal of Social Psychology, 128*(6), 731–743.

Marakas, G. M., Yi, M. Y., & Johnson, R. D. (1998). The multilevel and multifaceted charac-ter of computer self-efficacy: Toward clarification of the construct and an integrative framework for research. *Information Systems Research, 9*(2), 126–163.

Marche, S., & McNiven, J. D. (2003). E-government and e-governance: The future isn't what it used to be. *Canadian Journal of Administrative Sciences, 20*(1), 74–86.

Mariscal, J. (2005). Digital divide in a developing country. *Telecommunications Policy, 29*(5–6), 409–428.

Mason, R. O. (1978). Measuring information output: A communication systems approach. *Information and Management, 1*(2), 219–234.

Matell, M. S., & Jacoby, J. (1972). Is there an optimal number of alternatives for Likert-scale items?: Effects of testing time and scale properties. *Journal of Applied Psychology, 56*(6), 506–509.

Mathieson, K. (1991). Predicting user intentions: Comparing the technology acceptance model with the theory of planned behavior. *Information Systems Research, 2*(3), 173–191.

McFarlan, F. W. (1981). Portfolio approach to information systems. *Harvard Business Review, 59*(2), 142–150.

McKinnon, C. (2005). Challenges facing the public sector. *KM World, 14*(6), 53–54.

McKnight, D. H., & Chervany, N. L. (2002). What trust means in e-commerce customer relationships: An interdisciplinary conceptual typology. *International Journal of Electronic Commerce*, *6*(2), 35–59.

Meehl, P. E. (1978). Theoretical risks and tabular asterisks: Sir Karl, Sir Ronald, and the slow progress of soft psychology. *Journal of Consulting and Clinical Psychology*, *46*(4), 806–834.

Melitski, J., & Holzer, M. (2007). Assessing digital government at the local level worldwide: An analysis of municipal web sites throughout the world. In D. Norris (Ed.), *Current issues and trends in e-government research* (pp. 1–21). Hershey, PA: IGI Global.

Midgley, D. F., & Dowling, G. R. (1978). Innovativeness: The concept and its measurement. *Journal of Consumer Research*, *4*(4), 229–242.

Mills, B. F., & Whitacre, B. E. (2003). Understanding the non-metropolitan-metropolitan digital divide. *Growth and Change*, *34*(2), 219–243.

Mingers, J. (2001). Combining IS research methods: Towards a pluralist methodology. *Information Systems Research*, *12*(3), 240–259.

Mintzberg, H. (1996). Managing government, governing management. *Harvard Business Review*, *74*(3), 75–83.

Moon, M. J. (2002). The evolution of e-government among municipalities: Rhetoric or reality? *Public Administration Review*, *62*(4), 424–433.

Moores, T. T., & Chang, J. C.-J. (2006). Ethical decision making in software piracy: Initial development and test of a four-component model. *MIS Quarterly*, *30*(1), 167–180.

Morgan, D. L. (1998). Practical strategies for combining qualitative and quantitative methods: Applications to health research. *Qualitative Health Research*, *8*(3), 362–376.

Morgan, D. L. (2007). Paradigms lost and pragmatism regained: Methodological implications of combining qualitative and quantitative methods. *Journal of Mixed Methods Research*, *1*(1), 48–76.

Morgan, R. M., & Hunt, S. D. (1994). The Commitment-Trust Theory of relationship marketing. *Journal of Marketing*, *58*(3), 20–38.

Morris, M. G., & Venkatesh, V. (2000). Age differences in technology adoption decisions: Implications for a changing work force. *Personnel Psychology*, *53*(2), 375–403.

Moshiri, S., & Nikpoor, S. (2011). International ICT spillover. In J. Steyn & G. Johanson (Eds.), *ICTs and sustainable solutions for the digital divide: Theory and perspectives*. Hershey, PA: IGI Global.

Mossberger, K., Tolbert, C. J., & Gilbert, M. (2006). Race, place and information technology. *Urban Affairs Review*, *41*(5), 583–620.

Mossberger, K., Tolbert, C. J., & McNeal, R. (2008). *Digital citizenship: The internet, society, and participation*. Cambridge, MA: The MIT Press.

Myers, C., & Conner, M. (1992). Age differences in skill acquisition and transfer in an implicit learning paradigm. *Applied Cognitive Psychology*, *6*(5), 429–442.

Nadler, D. A. (1981). Managing organizational change: An integrative perspective. *The Journal of Applied Behavioral Science*, *17*(2), 191–221.

Ndeta, P. (2003). ICT integration in social and economic development: Kenya's perspective. In S. Marshall, W. Taylor, & X. Yu (Eds.), *Closing the digital divide: Transforming regional economies and communities with information technology* (pp. 93–100). Westport, CT: Praeger Publishers.

Newburger, E. C. (2001). *Home computers and internet use in the United States: August 2000*. Washington, DC: U.S. Census Bureau.

Nicholas, K. (2003). Geo-policy barriers and rural internet access: The regulatory role in constructing the digital divide. *The Information Society, 19*(4), 287–295.

Norris, D. F., & Kraemer, K. L. (1996). Mainframe and PC computing in American cities: Myths and realities. *Public Administration Review, 56*(6), 568–576.

Norris, P. (2001). *Digital divide: Civic engagement, information poverty, and the internet worldwide.* Cambridge: Cambridge University Press.

NTIA. (1995). *Falling through the net: A survey of the "have nots" in Rural and Urban America.* Washington, DC: US Department of Commerce.

NTIA. (2000). *Falling through the net: Toward digital inclusion.* Washington, DC: National Telecommunications and Information Administration.

NTIA. (2011). *Exploring the digital nation: Computer and internet use at home.* Washington, DC: Economics and Statistics Administration and National Telecommunications and Information Administration.

Nunnally, J. C., & Bernstein, I. H. (1994). *Psychometric theory* (3rd ed.). New York, NY: McGraw-Hill.

O'Connor, E. J., Parsons, C. K., Liden, R. C., & Herold, D. M. (1990). Implementing new technology: Management issues and opportunities. *The Journal of High Technology Management Research, 1*(1), 69–89.

OECD. (2001). *Understanding the digital divide.* Paris: OECD.

Ono, H. (2006). Digital inequality in East Asia: Evidence from Japan, South Korea, and Singapore. *Asian Economic Panel*, Keio University, Tokyo, Japan. The Earth Institute at Columbia University and the Massachusetts Institute of Technology.

Onwuegbuzie, A. J., & Leech, N. L. (2005). On becoming a pragmatic researcher: The importance of combining quantitative and qualitative research methodologies. *International Journal of Social Research Methodology, 8*(5), 375–387.

Orlikowski, W. J., & Baroudi, J. J. (1991). Studying information technology in organizations: Research approaches and assumptions. *Information Systems Research, 2*(1), 1–28.

Osborne, D., & Gaebler, T. (1992). *Reinventing government: How the entrepreneurial spirit is transforming the public sector.* Reading, MA: Addison-Wesley Pub. Co.

Oyelaran-Oyeyinka, B., & Lal, K. (2005). Internet diffusion in Sub-Saharan Africa: A cross-country analysis. *Telecommunications Policy, 29*, 507–527.

Pascual, P. J. (2003). *E-government.* Manila: e-ASEAN Task Force & UNDP-APDIP.

Pavlou, P. A. (2003). Consumer acceptance of electronic commerce: Integrating trust and risk with the technology acceptance model. *International Journal of Electronic Commerce, 7*(3), 101–134.

Pavlou, P. A., & Fygenson, M. (2006). Understanding and predicting electronic commerce adoption: An extension of the theory of planned behavior. *MIS Quarterly, 30*(1), 115–143.

Pavlou, P. A., & Gefen, D. (2004). Building effective online marketplaces with institution-based trust. *Information Systems Research, 15*(1), 37–59.

Peace, A. G., Galletta, D. F., & Thong, J. Y. L. (2003). Software piracy in the workplace: A model and empirical test. *Journal of Management Information Systems, 20*(1), 153–177.

Pennington, R., Wilcox, H. D., & Grover, V. (2003). The role of system trust in business-to-consumer transactions. *Journal of Management Information Systems, 20*(3), 197–226.

Peter, J., & Valkenburg, P. M. (2006). Adolescents' internet use: Testing the "disappearing digital divide" versus the "emerging digital differentiation" approach. *Poetics, 34*, 293–305.

Pigg, K. (2011). Information communication technology and its impact on rural community economic development. In J. Steyn & G. Johanson (Eds.), *ICTs and sustainable solutions for the digital divide: Theory and perspectives.* Hershey, PA: IGI Global.

Podsakoff, P. M., MacKenzie, S. B., Lee, J.-Y., & Podsakoff, N. P. (2003). Common method biases in behavioral research: A critical review of the literature and recommended remedies. *Journal of Applied Psychology, 88*(5), 879–903.

Podsakoff, P. M., & Organ, D. W. (1986). Self-reports in organizational research: Problems and prospects. *Journal of Management, 12*(4), 531–544.

Polgar, S., & Thomas, S. A. (2008). *Introduction to research in the health sciences* (5th ed.). New York, NY: Churchill Livingstone Elsevier.

Prattipati, S. N. (2003). Adoption of e-governance: Differences between countries in the use of online government services. *Journal of American Academy of Business, Cambridge, 3*(1–2), 386–391.

Preacher, K. J., & Hayes, A. F. (2008). Asymptotic and resampling strategies for assessing and comparing indirect effects in multiple mediator models. *Behavior Research Methods, 40*(3), 879–891.

Prybutok, V. R., Zhang, X., & Ryan, S. D. (2008). Evaluating leadership, IT quality, and net benefits in an e-government environment. *Information & Management, 45*(2), 143–152.

Quaddus, M., & Hofmeyer, G. (2007). An investigation into the factors influencing the adoption of B2B trading exchanges in small business. *European Journal of Information Systems, 16*(3), 202–215.

Quaddus, M., & Xu, J. (2005). Adoption and diffusion of knowledge management systems: Field studies of factors and variables. *Knowledge-Based Systems, 18*(2–3), 107–115.

Quibra, M., Ahmed, S. N., Tschang, T., & Reyes-Macasaquit, M.-L. (2003). Digital divide: Determinants and policies with special reference to Asia. *Journal of Asian Economics, 13*, 811–825.

Rahman, A. (2012). "Enhancing the social cognitive model in digital divide." *The Curtin Business School Doctoral Colloquium*, Perth, Australia, August 28–29 (peer reviewed).

Rahman, A. (2013). Rethinking the digital divide: mediation role of computer self-efficacy. *The Curtin Graduate School of Business*, Perth, Australia, May 20–21 (peer reviewed).

Rahman, A., & Quaddus, M. (2012). *Australasian conference on information systems, qualitative investigation of digital divide in Indonesia: Toward a comprehensive framework.* Geelong, Victoria, Australia: Deakin University. Retrieved from http://dro.deakin.edu.au/eserv/DU:30049100/rahman-qualitativeinvestigation-2012.pdf. Accessed on June 2, 2015.

Rahman, A., Quaddus, M., & Galbreath, J., (2012). The impacts of digital divide on e-government usage: A qualitative research. *CONF-IRM 2012, Vienna, Austria, 21–23 May 2012, Proceedings.* Paper 75. Retrieved from http://aisel.aisnet.org/confirm2012/75

Ramirez, R. (2001). A model for rural and remote information and communication technologies: A Canadian exploration. *Telecommunications Policy, 25*, 315–330.

Ranerup, A. (1999). Internet-enabled applications for local government democratisation: Contradictions of the Swedish experience. In R. Heeks (Ed.), *Reinventing government in the information age: International practice in IT-enabled public sector reform.* London: Routledge.

Rattray, J., & Jones, M. C. (2007). Issues in clinical nursing: Essential elements of question-naire design and development. *Journal of Clinical Nursing, 16*(2), 234–243.

Redman, T. C. (1998). The impact of poor data quality on the typical enterprise. *Communications of the ACM, 41*(2), 79–82.

Rhodes, S. R. (1983). Age-related differences in work attitudes and behavior: A review and conceptual analysis. *Psychological Bulletin, 93*(2), 328–367.

Richards, L. (1999). *Using NVivo in qualitative research.* Melbourne: Qualitative Solutions and Research.

Rigdon, E. E. (1998). Structural equation modeling. In G. A. Marcoulides (Ed.), *Modern methods for business research* (pp. 251–294). Mahwah, NJ: Lawrence Erlbaum Associates.

Rocheleau, B. (2000). Prescriptions for public-sector information management: A review, ana-lysis, and critique. *The American review of public administration, 30*(4), 414–435.

Rogers, E. M. (1976). New product adoption and diffusion. *Journal of Consumer Research, 2*(4), 290–301.

Rogers, E. M. (1995). *Diffusion of innovations* (4th ed.). New York, NY: The Free Press.

Rogers, E. M. (2003). *Diffusion of innovations* (5th ed.). New York, NY: Free Press.

Rosen, L. D., & Maguire, P. (1990). Myths and realities of computerphobia: A meta-analysis. *Anxiety Research: An International Journal, 3*(3), 175–191.

Rossman, G. B., & Wilson, B. L. (1985). Numbers and words: Combining quantitative and qualitative methods in a single large-scale evaluation study. *Evaluation Review, 9*(5), 627–643.

Rotter, J. B. (1971). Generalized expectancies for interpersonal trust. *American Psychologist, 26*(5), 443–452.

Roy, J. (2003). The relational dynamics of e-governance: A case study of the City of Ottawa. *Public Performance and Management Review, 26*(4), 391–403.

Ruttan, V. W. (1996). What happened to technology adoption-diffusion research? *Sociologia Ruralis, 36*(1), 51–73.

Salazar, A. (1999). Evaluating information systems for decentralisation: Health management reform in Ecuador. In R. Heeks (Ed.), *Reinventing government in the information age: International practice in IT-enabled public sector reform.* London: Routledge.

Schachter, H. L. (1995). Reinventing government or reinventing ourselves: Two models for improving government performance. *Public Administration Review, 55*(6), 530–537.

Schleife, K. (2010). What really matters: Regional versus individual determinants of the digital divide in Germany. *Research Policy, 39*(1), 173–185.

Schuppan, T. (2009). E-government in developing countries: Experiences from sub-Saharan Africa. *Government Information Quarterly, 26*(1), 118–127.

Schurr, P. H., & Ozanne, J. L. (1985). Influences on exchange processes: Buyers' preconcep-tions of a seller's trustworthiness and bargaining toughness. *Journal of Consumer Research, 11*(4), 939–953.

Sechrest, L., & Sidani, S. (1995). Quantitative and qualitative methods: Is there an alternative? *Evaluation and Program Planning, 18*(1), 77–87.

Seltzer, L. F. (1983). Influencing the "shape" of resistance: An experimental exploration of paradoxical directives and psychological reactance. *Basic and Applied Social Psychology, 4*(1), 47–71.

Selwyn, N. (1998). The effect of using a home computer on students' educational use of IT. *Computer Education, 31*, 211–227.

Seneviratne, S. J. (1999). Information technology and organizational change in the public sector. In G. D. Garson (Ed.), *Information technology and computer applications in public administration: Issues and trends* (pp. 41–61). Hershey, PA: Idea Group Publishing.

Sharit, J., & Czaja, S. J. (1994). Ageing, computer-based task performance, and stress: Issues and challenges. *Ergonomics, 37*(4), 559–577.

Sharma, L. (2008). Implementation of e-governance: Some technical issues and challenges. In H. Rahman (Ed.), *Developing successful ICT strategies: Competitive advantages in a global knowledge-driven society* (pp. 226–239). Hershey, PA: IGI Global.

Shearman, C. (2003). Strategies for reconnecting communities: Creative uses of ICTs for social and economic transformation. In S. Marshall, W. Taylor, & X. Yu (Eds.), *Closing the digital divide: Transforming regional economies and communities with information technology* (pp. 13–26). Westport, CT: Praeger Publishers.

Sheppard, B. H., Hartwick, J., & Warshaw, P. R. (1988). The theory of reasoned action: A meta-analysis of past research with recommendations for modifications and future research. *Journal of Consumer Research, 15*(3), 325–343.

Shih, C.-F., & Venkatesh, A. (2004). Beyond adoption: Development and application of a use-diffusion model. *Journal of Marketing, 68*(1), 59–72.

Shimp, T. A., & Kavas, A. (1984). The Theory of Reasoned Action applied to coupon usage. *Journal of Consumer Research, 11*(3), 795–809.

Siltaoja, M. E. (2006). Value priorities as combining core factors between CSR and reputation: A qualitative study. *Journal of Business Ethics, 68*(1), 91–111.

Sipior, J. C., Ward, B. T., & Connoly, R. (2011). The digital divide and t-government in the United States: Using the technology acceptance model to understand usage. *European Journal of Information Systems, 20,* 308–328.

Sirdeshmukh, D., Singh, J., & Sabol, B. (2002). Consumer trust, value, and loyalty in relational exchanges. *Journal of Marketing, 66*(1), 15–37.

Sirgy, M. J., Efraty, D., Siegel, P., & Lee, D.-J. (2001). A new measure of quality of work life (QWL) based on need satisfaction and spillover theories. *Social Indicators Research, 55*(3), 241–302.

Sobel, M. E. (1982). Asymptotic confidence intervals for indirect effects in structural equation models. *Sociological Methodology, 13,* 290–312.

Spector, P. E. (1987). Method variance as an artifact in self-reported affect and perceptions at work: Myth or significant problem? *Journal of Applied Psychology, 72*(3), 438–443.

Srivastava, S. C., & Teo, T. T. (2007). E-government payoffs: Evidence from cross country data. *Journal of Global Information Management, 15*(4), 20–40.

Stern, M. J., Adams, A. E., & Elsasser, S. (2009). Digital inequality and place: The effects of technological diffusion on internet proficiency and usage across rural, suburban and urban counties. *Sociological Inquiry, 79*(4), 391–417.

Steyn, J. (2011). Paradigm shift required for ICT4D. In J. Steyn & G. Johanson (Eds.), *ICTs and sustainable solutions for the digital divide* (pp. 19–44). Hershey, PA: IGI Global.

Straub, D., Limayem, M., & Karahanna-Evaristo, E. (1995). Measuring system usage: Implications for IS theory testing. *Management Science, 41*(8), 1328–1342.

Tashakkori, A., & Teddlie, C. (1998). *Mixed methodology: Combining qualitative and quantitative approaches* (Vol. 46). In L. Bickman and D. J. Rog (Eds., 48 vols.). Applied Social Research Methods Series. Thousand Oaks, CA: SAGE.

Tashakkori, A., & Teddlie, C. (2003). *Handbook of mixed methods in social and behavioral research*. Thousand Oaks, CA: SAGE.

Taylor, S., & Todd, P. (1995a). Assessing IT usage: The role of prior experience. *MIS Quarterly*, *19*(4), 561–570.

Taylor, S., & Todd, P. A. (1995b). Understanding information technology usage: A test of competing models. *Information Systems Research*, *6*(2), 144–176.

Teddlie, C., & Tashakkori, A. (2009). *Foundations of mixed methods research: Integrating quantitative and qualitative approaches in the social and behavioral science*. Thousand Oaks, CA: SAGE.

Tengtrakul, P., & Peha, J. M. (2013). Does ICT in schools affect residential adoption and adult utilization outside schools? *Telecommunications Policy*, *37*(6–7), 540–562.

Teo, H. H., Wei, K. K., & Benbasat, I. (2003). Predicting intention to adopt interorganizational linkages: An institutional perspective. *MIS Quarterly*, *27*(1), 19–49.

Teo, T. S., Srivastava, S. C., & Jiang, L. (2009). Trust and electronic government success: An empirical study. *Journal of Management Information Systems*, *25*(3), 99–131.

Teo, T. S. H., & Liu, J. (2006). Consumer trust in electronic commerce in the United States, Singapore and China. *Omega*, *35*(1), 22–38.

Thomas, C. W. (1998). Maintaining and restoring public trust in government agencies and their employees. *Administration & Society*, *30*(2), 166–193.

Thompson, N. J., & Thompson, K. E. (1996). Reasoned action theory: An application to alcohol-free beer. *Journal of Marketing Practice*, *2*(2), 35–48.

Thompson, R. L., Higgins, C. A., & Howell, J. M. (1991). Personal computing: Toward a conceptual model of utilization. *MIS Quarterly*, *15*(1), 124–143.

Thong, J. Y. L. (1999). An integrated model of information systems adoption in small business. *Journal of Management Information Systems*, *15*(4), 187–214.

Trauth, E. M., & Jessup, L. M. (2000). Understanding computer-mediated discussions: Positivist and interpretive analyses of group support system use. *MIS Quarterly*, *24*(1), 43–79.

Trompenaars, F., & Hampden-Turner, C. (2012). *Riding the waves of culture: Understanding diversity in global business* (3rd ed.). New York, NY: McGraw-Hill.

Tsikriktsis, N. (2004). A technology readiness-based taxonomy of customers: A replication and extension. *Journal of Service Research*, *7*(1), 42–52.

UN. (2005). *Global e-government readiness report 2005: From e-government to e-inclusion*. New York, NY: United Nations.

UN. (2008). *E-government survey 2008: From e-government to connected government*. New York, NY: United Nations.

UN. (2010). *E-government Survey 2010: Leveraging e-government at a time of financial and economic crisis*. New York, NY: United Nations.

UN. (2012). *E-government Survey 2012: E-government for the People*. New York, NY: United Nations.

UNCTAD. (2010). *Information economy report 2010: ICTs, enterprises and poverty alleviation*. Geneva: United Nations Conference on Trade and Development.

van Dijk, J., & Hacker, K. (2003). The digital divide as a complex and dynamic phenomenon. *The Information Society*, *19*(4), 315–326.

van Dijk, J. A. G. M. (2006). Digital divide research, achievements and shortcomings. *Poetics*, *34*(4–5), 221–235.

van Dijk, J. A. G. M., Peters, O., & Ebbers, W. (2008). Explaining the acceptance and use of government Internet services: A multivariate analysis of 2006 survey data in the Netherlands. *Government Information Quarterly*, *25*(3), 379–399.

Vance, A., Elie-Dit-Cosaque, C., & Straub, D. W. (2008). Examining trust in information technology artifacts: The effects of system quality and culture. *Journal of Management Information Systems*, *24*(4), 73–100.

Vathanopas, V., Krittayaphongphun, N., & Klomsiri, C. (2008). Technology acceptance toward e-government initiative in Royal Thai Navy. *Transforming Government: People, Process and Policy*, *2*(4), 256–282.

Venkatesh, V., & Davis, F. D. (2000). A theoretical extension of the technology acceptance model: Four longitudinal field studies. *Management Science*, *46*(2), 186–204.

Venkatesh, V., & Morris, M. G. (2000). Why don't men ever stop ask for direction? Gender, social influence and their role in technology acceptance and usage behavior. *MIS Quarterly*, *24*(1), 115–139.

Venkatesh, V., Morris, M. G., Davis, G. B., & Davis, F. D. (2003). User acceptance of information technology: Toward a unified view. *MIS Quarterly*, *27*(3), 425–478.

Venkatesh, V., Thong, J. Y. L., Chan, F. K. Y., Hu, P. J.-H., & Brown, S. A. (2011). Extending the two-stage information systems continuance model: Incorporating UTAUT predictors and the role of context. *Information Systems Journal*, *21*(6), 527–555.

Venkatesh, V., Thong, J. Y. L., & Xu, X. (2012). Consumer acceptance and use of information technology: Extending the unified theory of acceptance and use of technology. *MIS Quarterly*, *36*(1), 157–178.

Vigoda, E. (2000). Are you being served? The responsiveness of public administration to citizens' demands: An empirical examination in Israel. *Public Administration*, *78*(1), 165–191.

Vlachos, P. A., Tsamakos, A., Vrechopoulos, A. P., & Avramidis, P. K. (2009). Corporate social responsibility: Attributions, loyalty, and the mediating role of trust. *Journal of the Academy Marketing Science*, *37*(2), 170–180.

Wahid, F. (2008). Evaluating focus and quality of Indonesian e-government Websites. In *Seminar Nasional Aplikasi Teknologi Informasi*. Yogyakarta: Islamic University of Indonesia.

Wang, Y.-S., & Liao, Y.-W. (2008). Assessing e-government systems success: A validation of the DeLone and McLean Model of information systems success. *Government Information Quarterly*, *25*(4), 717–733.

Wang, Y.-S., & Shih, Y.-W. (2009). Why do people use information kiosks? A validation of the unified theory of acceptance and use of technology. *Government Information Quarterly*, *26*(1), 158–165.

Warkentin, M., Gefen, D., Pavlou, P. A., & Rose, G. M. (2002). Encouraging citizen adoption of e-government by building trust. *Electronic Markets*, *12*(3), 157–162.

Warren, M. (2007). The digital vicious cycle: Links between social disadvantage and digital exclusion in rural areas. *Telecommunications Policy*, *31*(6–7), 374–388.

Warschauer, M. (2003a). Dissecting the "digital divide": A case study in Egypt. *The Information Society*, *19*(4), 297–304.

Warschauer, M. (2003b). *Technology and social inclusion: Rethinking the digital divide*. Cambridge, MA: The MIT Press.

Warshaw, P. R. (1980). A new model for predicting behavioral intentions: An alternative to Fishbein. *Journal of Marketing Research, 17*(2), 153−172.

Watson, G. (1971). Resistance to change. *The American Behavioral Scientist, 14*(5), 745−766.

Weber, M. (1947). *The Theory of Social and Economic Organization.* Alexandria, VA: Alexander Street Press.

Wei, K.-K., Teo, H.-H., Chan, H. C., & Tan, B. C. (2011). Conceptualizing and testing a Social Cognitive Model of the digital divide. *Information Systems Research, 22*(1), 170−187.

Werts, C. E., Linn, R. L., & Joreskog, K. G. (1974). Intraclass reliability estimates: Testing structural assumptions. *Educational and Psychological Measurement, 34*(1), 25−33.

West, D. M. (2004). E-government and the transformation of service delivery and citizen attitudes. *Public Administration Review, 64*(1), 15−27.

West, J. P., & Berman, E. M. (2001). The impact of revitalized management practices on the adoption of information technology: A national survey of local governments. *Public Performance and Management Review, 24*(3), 233−253.

Wilkening, E. A. (1950). Sources of information for improved farm practices. *Rural Sociology, 15*(1), 19−30.

Williams, D. R. (1990). Socioeconomic differentials in health: A review and redirection. *Social Psychology Quarterly, 53*(2), 81−99.

Willis, J. W. (2007). *Foundations of qualitative research: Interpretive and critical theory approaches.* Thousand Oaks, CA: SAGE.

Winkler, J. D., Kanouse, D. E., & Ware, J. E. (1982). Controlling for acquiescence response set in scale development. *Journal of Applied Psychology, 67*(5), 555−561.

Wold, H. (2006). Partial least squares. In S. Kotz (Ed.), *Encyclopedia of statistical sciences.* Hoboken, NJ: Wiley.

Wolfe, L. (1999). Transforming accountability for government information technology projects: The impacts of new US legislation. In R. Heeks (Ed.), Reinventing government in the information age: International practice in IT-enabled public *sector* reform. London: Routledge.

Wong, W., & Welch, E. (2004). Does e-government promote accountability? A comparative analysis of website openness and government accountability. *Governance: An International Journal of Policy, Administration, and Institutions, 17*(2), 275−297.

Wu, P. F. (2012). A mixed methods approach to technology acceptance research. *Journal of the Association for Information Systems, 13*(3), 172−187.

Yi, M. Y., Fiedler, K. D., & Park, J. S. (2006). Understanding the role of individual innovativeness in the acceptance of IT-based innovations: Comparative analyses of models and measures. *Decision Sciences, 37*(3), 393−426.

Ynalvez, M., & Shrum, W. (2006). International training and the digital divide: Computer and email use in the Philippines. *Perspectives on Global Development and Technology, 5*(4), 277−302.

Zmud, R. W. (1979). Individual differences and MIS success: A review of the empirical literature. *Management Science, 25*(10), 966−979.

APPENDIX A: INTERVIEW GUIDELINE

Interview Guideline

The main objective of this research is to examine the influence of digital divide and trust on e-government system success in Indonesian local governments. This interview aims to supplement the initial research model based on the users' experiences. This leads to the following interview questions:

About e-government system success:

Q1. Are you a user of e-government system (One-Stop Service) provided by local government?

> *Probe*:
> o How many times do you use the One-Stop Service?
> o How often do you use the One-Stop Service?
> o Which service have you used?
> o Why have you shifted from traditional system to One-Stop Service?
> o Do you think an increase of economic condition will increase your usage of the One-Stop Service?

Q2. How satisfied are you with e-government system (One-Stop Service)?

> *Probe:*
> o Are you satisfied with this One-Stop Service?
> o Do you think the One-Stop Service has met your expectations?

Q3. What benefits do you get from e-Government system (One-Stop Service)?

> *Probe*:
> o Do you think that the One-Stop Service makes your business easier?
> o Do you think that One-Stop Service saves your time?
> o Do you think that One-Stop Service cost you less?
> o Is there any other benefit from One-Stop Service?

About the influence of digital divide on e-government system success

Q4. What do you think of your accessibility of e-government system (One-Stop Service)?

Probe:
- Can you access to the One-Stop Service easily?
- Does your place of residence limit your accessibility of One-Stop Service?
- Do you feel comfortable in accessing this One-Stop Service?
- Do you think an increase of accessibility of ICT will increase your capability in using ICT?
- Do you think an increase of economic condition will increase your access to the One-Stop Service?
- Do you think an increase of accessibility of One-Stop Service will increase your trust in the One-Stop Service?
- Do you think an increase of accessibility of One-Stop Service will increase your usage of the One-Stop Service?
- Do you have any other comments on accessing One-Stop Service?

Q5. Are you confident in working with information technology?

Probe:
- Do you have any difficulties in using information technology?
- Do you feel comfortable working with information technology?
- Are you sure you can work with information technology?
- Do you think an increase of capability in using ICT will increase your willingness to try out any new ICT?
- Do you think an increase of capability in using ICT will increase your trust in the One-Stop Service?
- Do you think an increase of capability in using ICT will increase your usage the One-Stop Service?
- Do you have any other comments on your capability in using information technology?

Q6. What is your perception of new information technology?

Probe:
- If you hear about a new IT, would you look for ways to experiment with it?

o Among your peers, are you usually the first to try out new IT?
o In general, are you hesitant to try out new IT?
o Do you like to experiment with new IT?
o Do you think an increase of the willingness to try out any new ICT will increase your trust in the One-Stop Service?
o Do you think an increase of the willingness to try out any new ICT will increase your usage of the One-Stop Service?
o Do you have any other comments on your perception of new information technology?

About the influence of trust in e-government on e-government system success

Q7. Do you trust e-government system (One-Stop Service)?

Probe:
o Do you think that the One-Stop Service seems to be truthful and honest to you?
o Do you think that the One-Stop Service is competent and effective in facilitating your needs?
o Do you think that the One-Stop Service cares about its users?
o Do you think that the One-Stop Service is stable and predictable?
o Do you think that the One-Stop Service is sincere and genuine?
o Do you think that the One-Stop Service would keep its commitments?
o Do you think an increase of your trust in One-Stop Service will increase your usage of the One-Stop Service?
o Do you think an increase of economic condition will increase your trust in the One-Stop Service?
o Do you have any other comments on the trust in e-government?

APPENDIX B: ETHICS APPROVAL FOR QUALITATIVE INTERVIEW

Memorandum

To	Arief Rahman, Curtin Graduate School of Business
From	
Subject	Protocol Approval GSB 01-11
Date	9 February 2011
Copy	Mohammed Quaddus, Curtin Graduate School of Business

Office of Research and Development

Human Research Ethics Committee

Telephone: 9266 2784
Facsimile: 9266 3793
Email
hrec@curtin.edu.au

Thank you for your "Form C Application for Approval of Research with Low Risk (Ethical Requirements)" for the project titled *"Toward a comprehensive conceptualization of the digital divide and its impact on e-government system success: Evidence from local governments in Indonesia".* On behalf of the Human Research Ethics Committee, I am authorised to inform you that the project is approved.

Approval of this project is for a period of twelve months **09/02/2011** to **09/02/2012**.

The approval number for your project is **GSB 01-11**. *Please quote this number in any future correspondence.* If at any time during the twelve months changes/amendments occur, or if a serious or unexpected adverse event occurs, please advise me immediately.

Debra Jordan
Project Officer | Curtin Graduate School of Business

Curtin University
Tel | +61 8 9266 9083
Fax | +61 8 9266 3368

Hours | **Tues, Wed & Thurs**

Email | debra.jordan@gsb.curtin.edu.au
Web | gsb.curtin.edu.au

Please Note: The following standard statement must be included in the information sheet to participants:
This study has been approved by the Curtin University Human Research Ethics Committee (Approval Number
»Approval_Number»). If needed, verification of approval can be obtained either by writing to the Curtin University Human Research Ethics Committee, c/- Office of Research and Development, Curtin University of Technology, GPO Box U1987, Perth, 6845 or by telephoning 9266 2784 or hrec@curtin.edu.au

APPENDIX C : ETHICS APPROVAL FOR QUANTITATIVE SURVEY

Memorandum

To	Arief Rahman, CGSB
From	Debbie Jordan
Subject	Protocol Approval **GSB 11-11**
Date	21 July 2011
Copy	Mohammed Quaddus

Office of Research and Development

Human Research Ethics Committee

Telephone   9266 2784
Facsimile   9266 3793
Email   hrec@curtin.edu.au

Thank you for your "Form C Application for Approval of Research with Low Risk (Ethical Requirements)" for the project titled *"Toward A Comprehensive Conceptualization of the Digital Divide and Its Impact on e-Government System Success: Evidence from Local Governments in Indonesia "*. On behalf of the Human Research Ethics Committee, I am authorised to inform you that the project is approved.

Approval of this project is for a period of twelve months **20/07/11** to **20/07/12**.

The approval number for your project is **GSB 11-11.** *Please quote this number in any future correspondence.* If at any time during the twelve months changes/amendments occur, or if a serious or unexpected adverse event occurs, please advise me immediately.

Debra Jordan
Project Officer | Curtin Graduate School of Business

Curtin University
Tel | +61 8 9266 9083
Fax | +61 8 9266 3368

Hours | **Tues, Wed & Thurs**

Email | debra.jordan@gsb.curtin.edu.au
Web | gsb.curtin.edu.au

Please Note: The following standard statement must be included in the information sheet to participants:
This study has been approved by the Curtin University Human Research Ethics Committee (Approval Number «Approval_Number»). If needed, verification of approval can be obtained either by writing to the Curtin University Human Research Ethics Committee, c/- Office of Research and Development, Curtin University of Technology, GPO Box U1987, Perth, 6845 or by telephoning 9266 2784 or hrec@curtin.edu.au

APPENDIX D: RESEARCH QUESTIONNAIRE

Research Questionnaire

Digital Divide and E-Government System Success
The willingness to use and ability to access of citizens are critical in e-government system. However, unequal access and ICT usage, which is known as digital divide, has been identified as one of the obstacles to the implementation of e-government system. Digital divide inhibits citizen's acceptance to e-government; therefore, these gaps should be closed despite the lack of deep theoretical understanding on this issue. This research is conducted as part of the Doctoral program in Curtin University and aims to investigate the digital divide and its direct impact on e-government system success of local governments in Indonesia as well as indirect impact through the mediation role of trust. As part of this research, questionnaires will be distributed to the e-government system users. The questionnaire will need approximately 15–20 minutes to complete.

Your participation in this study is voluntary and you are free to withdraw at any time. Individual participant will not be identified, and *all information will be kept confidential* and will only be used for research purposes. The result of the study will be made available to all participants.

General Instructions

1. Please answer the questions to the best of your knowledge. Most of the questions require your view or opinion measured on a six-point scale. There are no right and wrong answers on the questionnaire. It is only about your own opinion on a number of topics.
2. Responses to all questions will be kept strictly confidential. Your responses are combined with all other respondents and are completely non-traceable. Individual responses cannot be identified in anyway.
3. The survey is made up of several short parts. Please complete them all.

Thank you so much for your help. I really appreciate it.

Researcher

Arief Rahman

Definitions

The following definitions are used for this survey questionnaire:

1. *E-government*: the use of information and communication technology to enhance the access to and delivery of all facets of government services and operations for the benefit of citizens, business, employees, and other stakeholders. In this research, e-government refers to systems include those such as One-Stop Service Online System used by many local government agencies.

2. *Information and communication technology*: all technical means used to handle information and aid communication, including mobile phones, televisions and other broadcast media, all types of audio and video processing, computer, internet, hardware, as well as necessary software.

*Section 1: Demographic Information. Please answer the questions below by **ticking** in the box, which corresponds to the most appropriate response.*

1. Gender	Female............................... ❏
	Male .... ❏
2. Age group	Under 20............................. ❏
	21–30 .... ❏
	31–40 .... ❏
	41–50 .... ❏
	Over 50............................... ❏
3. What is your highest level of education?	High school .... ❏
	Diploma............................... ❏
	Undergraduate .... ❏
	Master's degree.................. ❏
	Doctoral degree.................. ❏
	Other (please specify)
	_____ ❏
4. Approximately, the total monthly income before taxes and other deductions of my immediate family – including my own job income, income from other sources and the income of my spouse – is	Under Rp. 2.500.000 .... ❏
	Rp. 2.500.000–Rp. 5.000.000............................. ❏
	Rp. 5.000.000–Rp. 7.500.000............................. ❏
	Rp. 7.500.000–Rp. 10.000.000........................... ❏
	Rp. 10.000.000–Rp. 12.500.000........................... ❏
	More than Rp. 12.500.000.. ❏
5. How far is your home from the city center?	Under 5 km .... ❏
	5–10 km.............................. ❏
	10–15 km .... ❏
	15–20 km .... ❏
	More than 20 km................. ❏

6. Do you have computer at home?	No .... ❑
	Yes... ❑
7. Do you have internet connection at home?	No .... ❑
	Yes... ❑
8. How many times have you used One-Stop Service Online System so far?	Once .... ❑
	Two–Three times .... ❑
	Three–Five times .... ❑
	More than five times........... ❑
9. Among your total usages of One-Stop Service Online System, how many times have you completed your transactions?	Once .... ❑
	Two–Three times .... ❑
	Three–Five times .... ❑
	More than five times........... ❑

Section 2: About E-Government Use, Satisfaction, and Benefits. The statements below seek your experience and opinion about e-government, especially the One-Stop Service Online System provided by your local government. Please read each statement carefully, and then indicate the extent to which you agree or disagree by circling the number on a scale of 1 (strongly disagree) to 6 (strongly agree).

Please Answer All Statements		Strongly Disagree				Strongly Agree	
10.	Using the One-Stop Service Online System is a good idea	1	2	3	4	5	6
11.	I am satisfied with the One-Stop Service Online System	1	2	3	4	5	6
12.	The One-Stop Service Online system has met my expectations	1	2	3	4	5	6
13.	I strongly recommend the One-Stop Service Online System to others	1	2	3	4	5	6
14.	I think that I made a correct decision to use the One-Stop Service Online System	1	2	3	4	5	6
15.	The One-Stop Service Online System makes my business easier	1	2	3	4	5	6
16.	The One-Stop Service Online System saves my time	1	2	3	4	5	6
17.	The One-Stop Service Online System costs me less than manual system	1	2	3	4	5	6

Section 3: About Your Access to Information and Communication Technology. The statements below seek your opinion about your access to information and communication technology in general. Please read each statement carefully, and then indicate the extent to which you agree or disagree by circling the number on a scale of 1 (strongly disagree) to 6 (strongly agree).

Please Answer All Statements	Strongly Disagree				Strongly Agree	
18. I can access information and communication technology easily	1	2	3	4	5	6
19. I feel comfortable in getting access to information and communication technology	1	2	3	4	5	6

Section 4: About Your Capability in Using Information and Communication Technology. The statements below seek your opinion about your capability in using information and communication technology. Please read each statement carefully, and then indicate the extent to which you agree or disagree by circling the number on a scale of 1 (strongly disagree) to 6 (strongly agree).

Please Answer All Statements	Strongly Disagree				Strongly Agree	
20. I am confident in using information and communication technology	1	2	3	4	5	6
21. I do not have any difficulty in using information and communication technology	1	2	3	4	5	6
22. I feel comfortable in using information and communication technology	1	2	3	4	5	6
23. I am sure I can use information and communication technology	1	2	3	4	5	6
24. I can operate information and communication technology, even if no one tells me how to do it	1	2	3	4	5	6

Section 5: About Your Willingness to Try Out Any New Information and Communication Technology. The statements below seek your opinion about your willingness to try out any new information and communication technology. Please read each statement carefully, and then indicate the extent to

which you agree or disagree by circling the number on a scale of 1 (strongly disagree) to 6 (strongly agree).

Please Answer All Statements	Strongly Disagree			Strongly Agree		
25. If I hear about new information and communication technology, I would look for ways to try it	1	2	3	4	5	6
26. Among my peers, I am the first to try out new information and communication technology	1	2	3	4	5	6
27. I am hesitant to try out new information and communication technology	1	2	3	4	5	6
28. I like to experiment with new information and communication technology	1	2	3	4	5	6

Section 6: About Your Trust in E-Government. The statements below describe your opinion about your trust in e-government, especially One-Stop Service Online System provided by your local government. Please read each statement carefully, and then indicate the extent to which you agree or disagree by circling the number on a scale of 1 (strongly disagree) to 6 (strongly agree).

Please Answer All Statements	Strongly Disagree			Strongly Agree		
29. I think the information in One-Stop Service Online System seems to be truthful and honest	1	2	3	4	5	6
30. I think the One-Stop Service Online System is effective in facilitating my needs	1	2	3	4	5	6
31. I think the One-Stop Service Online System is designed to accommodate the needs of its users	1	2	3	4	5	6
32. I can predict the output of One-Stop Service Online System (in terms of time, costs, and process)	1	2	3	4	5	6
33. I think the One-Stop Service Online System provides appropriate outcomes for its users	1	2	3	4	5	6

Thank you very much for your time and cooperation!
I really appreciate it.

APPENDIX E: FIELD STUDY RESULTS: INDIVIDUAL MODEL

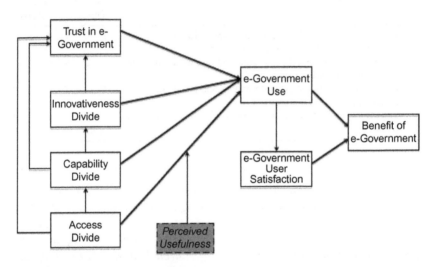

Fig. E1.   Model of the Field Study of Informant 1.

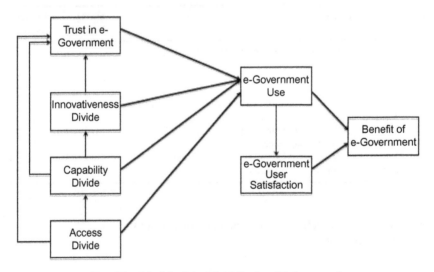

Fig. E2.   Model of the Field Study of Informant 2.

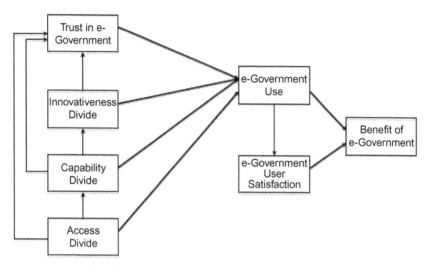

Fig. E3. Model of the Field Study of Informant 3.

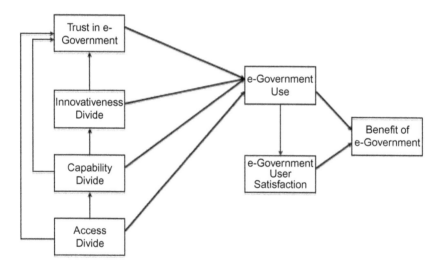

Fig. E4. Model of the Field Study of Informant 4.

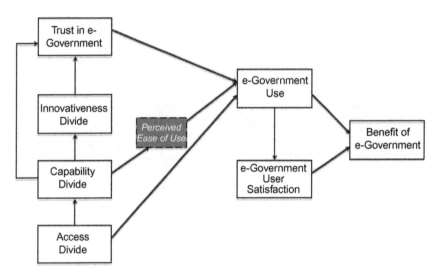

Fig. E5.   Model of the Field Study of Informant 5.

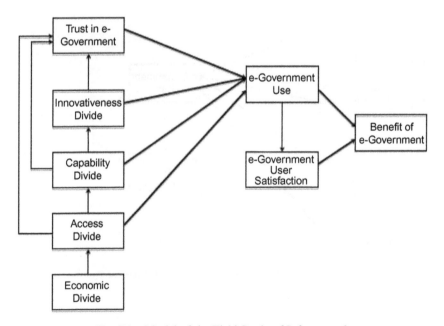

Fig. E6.   Model of the Field Study of Informant 6.

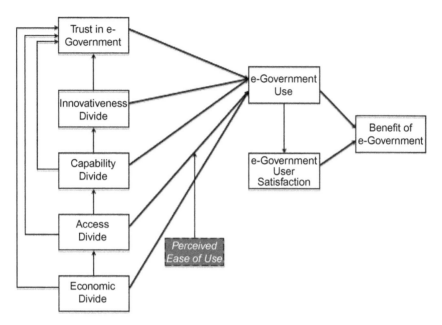

Fig. E7. Model of the Field Study of Informant 7.

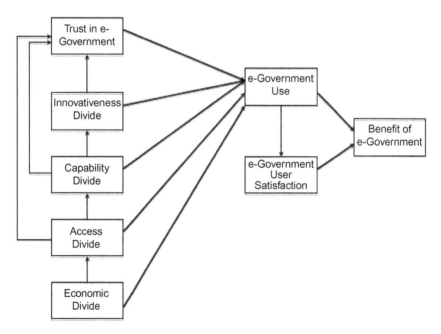

Fig. E8. Model of the Field Study of Informant 8.

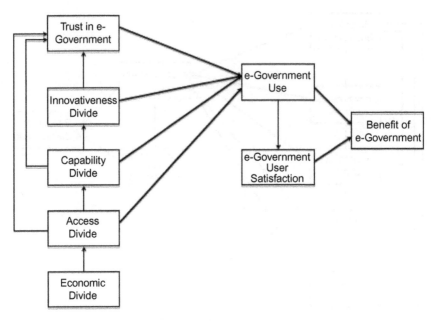

Fig. E9.   Model of the Field Study of Informant 9.

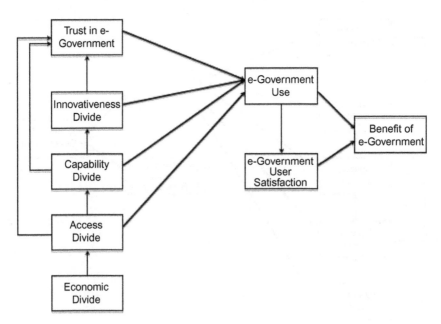

Fig. E10.   Model of the Field Study of Informant 10.

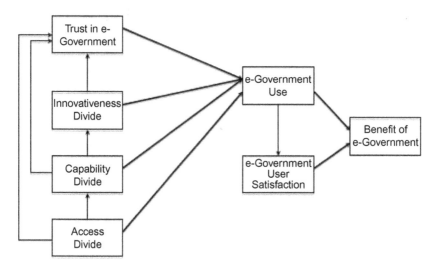

Fig. E11. Model of the Field Study of Informant 11.

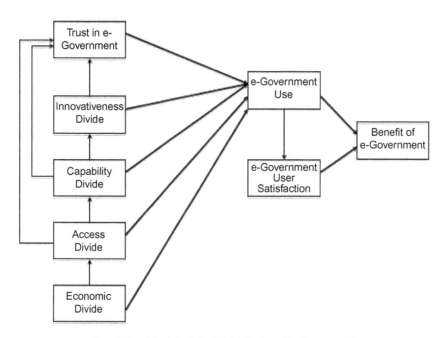

Fig. E12. Model of the Field Study of Informant 12.

APPENDIX F: MAP OF SLEMAN AND TULUNGAGUNG REGENCIES

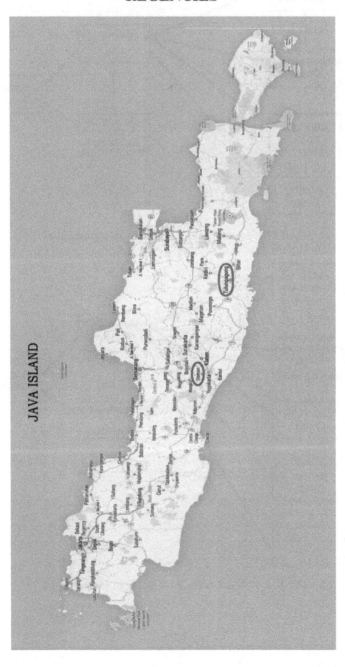